Library of
Davidson College

From Warsaw To Sofia

Henry Bogdan

From Warsaw To Sofia
A History of Eastern Europe

Edited by Istvan Fehervary

Pro Libertate Publishing

Santa Fe, New Mexico
USA

Originally published as *De Varsovie a Sofia: Histoire des Pays de l'Est*
© 1982 Dossiers d l'Histoire, Editions de l'Universite et
  de l'Enseignement Moderne

Pro Libertate Publishing Company, Santa Fe, New Mexico, 87501
© 1989 by Pro Libertate. All rights reserved.

Translations from the French by Jeanie P. Fleming
Maps by Cynthia Hobgood

Printed in the United States of America

Library of Congress Card Number: 88-063852
ISBN 0-9622049-0-0

Contents

List of Maps	ix
Foreward to the English Edition	xi
Note on Spelling and Statistical Information	xii
Introduction	xiii

Chapter 1. The Human Puzzle of Eastern Europe
Linguistic Diversity	1
Divided Nations and Ethnic Minorities	3
Dispersed and Uprooted Ethnic Groups	3
Religious Diversity	4
Demography	5

Chapter 2. A Land of Many Aspects
Geographic Diversity	8
Climatic Diversity	9
Economic Diversity	10
Diversity in the Exercise of Power	10

Part I. The Weight of the Past

Chapter 3. The Distribution of Peoples
Early History of Eastern Europe	15
Hellenization and Romanization of the Balkan and Danubian Countries	16
The First Wave of the Great Invasions, 2nd-5th Centuries	17
The Second Wave of Major Invasions, 6th-7th Centuries	19
The End of the Age of Invasions	22

Chapter 4. The Birth of Nation States 10th-13th Centuries

Formation of the First States in the 10th Century ... 25
> The Germanic Sphere of Influence / The Byzantine Sphere of Influence

Diverse Destinies in the 11th-13th Centuries ... 29
> The Consolidation of Westernized States: Bohemia, Poland and Hungary / The Balkans under Byzantium: the Serbs and the Bulgars / The Tartar Invasion and its Consequences

Chapter 5. The Age of Ruptures, 14th-16th Centuries

Humanism, Rebirth and Crisis in the Westernized Monarchies, 14th-15th Centuries ... 36
> Prosperity in Bohemia and Hungary in the 14th Century / Light and Shadow in Poland of the 14th Century / Crisis in Bohemia / Independent Hungary at its Height, 1458-1490

The Ottomans in Eastern Europe, 14th-15th Centuries ... 45
> The Beginnings of Ottoman Power / The Peak of Serbian Power / The Balkans in the Hands of the Turks / The Final Assault of the Turks

The Habsburgs against the Turks and the Reformation ... 49
> The Consequences of Mohacs / Reform and Counter-Reform in Central Europe / Conflict with the Turks

A Haven of Peace: Poland in the 15th and 16th Centuries ... 53
> Poland Under the First Jageillons, 1382-1572 / Poland's Golden Age / Successes of the Counter-Reformation

Chapter 6. Eastern Europe of the Habsburgs, the Turks and Russia

The Balkans under the Ottomans ... 58
> The Privileged Peoples / The Oppressed Peoples

Consolidation of the Habsburg Monarchy in the Danube Region ... 62
> Triumph of the Counter-Reformation in Bohemia / The Habsburgs, Hungary and the Turks

Decline and Demise of Poland ... 68

Part II. The Awakening of Nationalism

Chapter 7. Premonitory Signs of Nationalism

Origins of Nationalism ... 75
The Congress of Vienna and its Immediate Consequences ... 79

National Awakening of the Balkan People   81
The Tragic Fate of Poland   84
Nationalism in the Austrian Monarchy   88
> Nationalism Among the Slavs of the Empire / National Renewal in Hungary

Chapter 8. 1848—The Springtime of Nations: Success and Failure in Revolution

Apparent Calm in Poland   93
Rumanian Disturbances in the Ottoman Empire   94
Revolutions in the Habsburg Empire   95
> The First Revolutionary Wave (German and Czech Nationalism in Bohemia and Moravia) / Kossuth and the War of Independence, 1848-1849

Chapter 9. The Search for New Structures

The Powers and the Question of the Ottoman Empire   103
Napoleon III and the Balkan Question after The Treaty of Paris   105
> Polish Illusions / From Austria to Austria-Hungary

Chapter 10. The Austro-Hungarian Experiment 1867-1918

Contemporary Views on Austria-Hungary   113
The Ethnic Composition of Austria-Hungary   115
Operation of the System   119
Political Conflicts in the Dual Monarchy   121
> The Austrian Empire / The Kingdom of Hungary

Expectations for the Austro-Hungarian Monarchy Before the Outbreak of World War I   126

Chapter 11. The Awakening of the Polish Nation 1870-1914   128

Chapter 12. The Balkans Between the Great Powers 1878-1914

Beginnings of Austro-Russian Rivalry in the Balkans, 1870-78   131
Developments within the Balkan States up to the Crisis of 1908   136
> Rumania / Serbia and Montenegro / Independent Bulgaria

The Explosive Situation in the Balkans, 1908-1914   142
> The Macedonian Problem / 1908 Crisis in Bosnia / The Balkan Wars of 1912-1913

Chapter 13. Epilogue: The First World War   148

Part III. An Era of Confrontation
Chapter 14. Political Changes in Central and Eastern Europe After the First World War
The First Wave of Revolution in the Defeated Countries   159
The Bulgarian Revolution / The Austro-Hungarian Revolution
The Situation Among the Victors   164
Triumph for the Small Nations: Serbia and Rumania / The Birth of the Czechoslovakian State / Poland's Difficult Renaissance / Albania's Struggle for Freedom
Attempts to Bolshevize Eastern Europe   169
The Hungarian Soviet Republic and Its Failure, 1919 / The Failure of Bulgarian Bolshevism / The Russo-Polish War

Chapter 15. Eastern Europe in the Aftermath of the War
The Peace Settlements   174
The Treaties   177
The Fate of the Defeated Countries: Germany, Austria and Hungary, Bulgaria / The Beneficiaries of the Treaties: Poland, Czechoslovakia, Rumania, Yugoslavia

Chapter 16. Political Struggle and Internal Strife 1919-1939
Political Constraints   186
Diversity Between the Nations of Eastern Europe   187
Czechoslovakia: a "Westernized" Imitation of Democracy / Poland: From Parliamentary Democracy to Military Dictatorship / A Kingdom without a King: Hungary Under Admiral Horthy
The Balkan Dictatorships   197
From Tribalism to Royal Dictatorship: Albania / From the "Green" Dictatorship to the Royal Dictatorship: Bulgaria / From Corruption to Palace Revolts: Rumania / The Greater Serbian Dictatorship: Yugoslavia

Chapter 17. Interwar Economics: An Impossible Balance   208

Chapter 18. International Relations Between the Wars   214

Chapter 19. National Minorities: A Source of International Tension   220

Chapter 20. From Munich to Yalta, 1938-1945
The End of Czechoslovakia	229
The Fourth Partition of Poland	233
Changes in the Danubian and Balkan Area, 1939-1941	238
Hungarian Neutrality and Revisionism / The Fascistization of Rumania / Ambiguities in Bulgaria / The End of the Yugoslavian State	
The Eastern European Countries during the German-Soviet War, 1941-1945	244
Germany's Allies / The Defeated Countries	
1943—The Turning Point of the War	247
Rumania's Sudden Change of Allegiance / Bulgaria's Attempts to Negotiate / The Failure of Hungary's Diplomacy	
Resistance Movements during German Occupation	250
The End of the War in Central and Eastern Europe	255
Conclusion: Yalta	256

Part IV. In the Shadow of Moscow

Chapter 21. A Warning — 261

Chapter 22. The New Status of Eastern Europe
In Preparation for the Future Status of Eastern Europe	264
The New Territorial Framework of Eastern Europe	267
Sanctions against the Defeated Countries / Countries of the Victors	
National Minorities and Population Transfers	269
Conclusion	271

Chapter 23. The Birth of Popular Democracies
An Environment Favorable for the Communists	272
The Establishment of New Regimes	274
The Method of Expedience: Bulgaria, Albania and Yugoslavia; The Deception of Poland / The Progressive Method: Rumania, From Constitutional Monarchy to Popular Democracy; The Illusion of Democracy in Hungary; Czechoslovakia and the Communists; The Birth of the German Democratic Republic	

Chapter 24. The Age of Stalin, 1948-1953
Moscow and the Eastern European Countries	295
The Yugoslav Schism	

Evolution of the Popular Democracies During the Stalin Era   300
   Government Organization / Political Purges in the Eastern Bloc States / The Struggle Against the Church / Economic and Social Transformations

Chapter 25. Eastern Europe During Destalinization 1953-1968

Warning Storms Before 1956   311
   The First Explosion: Berlin 1953 / Destalinization in Hungary / The Moscow-Belgrade Reconciliation / Destalinization in the Other Eastern European Countries

The Crises of 1956   315
   The Illusion of Liberalization in Poland / The Hungarian Revolution of 1956

From Crisis to Crisis: Eastern Europe from 1956 to 1968   326
   New Directions in Eastern Bloc and Soviet Policy / A Note of Discord: Albania / The Evolution of Yugoslavia / "Kadarism" in Hungary / The "Neo-Stalinists" / The Prague Spring in 1968

Chapter 26. From the Prague Spring to Solidarity 1968-1981

General Trends of the 1970s   343
L'Enfants Terribles of the Adriatic: Albania and Yugoslavia   346
Poland in Crisis   351
   The Catholic Church / The End of Illusions

Chapter 27. The Age of Gorbachev

Gorbachev and the Reform Period   367
   The Continuing Economic Crisis in Eastern Europe / The Minority Problem in Eastern Europe: Hungarian Minorities; Minorities in the Balkan States

A Changing Eastern Europe   375
   Albania: Opening to the World / Yugoslavia: A Fragile Federation / Rumania: Legacies of the Ceausescu Dynasty / Bulgaria: The Good Satellite / Hungary: Window to the West / East Germany: COMECON's Wealthy Member / Czechoslovakia 1969-88: Husak's Solution / Poland: Solidarity's Resurrection

Conclusion   394

Appendix I—The Countries of Eastern Europe—1988   399
(Tables of Statistics)

Appendix II—Gallery of Faces	403
Names Index	408
Subject Index	422

List of Maps

Central-Eastern Europe at the end of the 4th Century	20
Migration of Rumanians (Vlachs), 10th-16th Centuries	23
Eastern Europe in 1025	26
Eastern Europe, circa 1265	33
French Dynasties in Central Europe, circa 1350	37
Progress and Defeats of Ottomans in Eastern Europe	59
Historical Poland in the 18th Century	68
The Habsburg Monarchy at the time of Dualism, 1867-1918	111
Nationalities of the Habsburg Monarchy	117
Eastern Europe in the 19th Century after the Congress of Berlin, 1878	134
Eastern Europe in 1913 (Ottoman Empire after the Balkan Wars)	147
Alliance Systems of 1914-18 and of 1921	151
The Dissolution of the Habsburg Monarchy	160
Poland, 1937-45	180
Czechoslovakia, 1919-38 and 1938-39	228
Expulsion of Germans from Eastern Europe, 1945-47 and Exodus of Germans from GDR to the FRG, 1945-60	269
Eastern Europe after the Second World War	276
Poland's New Frontiers, post-1945	352

Foreword to the English Edition

Sometime in 1978, while looking for source material for my books on Hungary, I discovered a dearth of serious, timely, comprehensive and objective books on the history of Eastern Europe. Millions of Americans have ancestors from the countries of Eastern Europe, yet the public, including the policy makers in Washington, D.C., show very little interest in what is happening behind the Iron Curtain. Only when some "event" has occurred—a strike, an anti-Soviet demonstration or the breaking out of revolution—do western officials and the mass media take notice.

Despite the fact that since 1945 Eastern Europe has played an important role in East-West relations, I have learned during my 20 years of involvement with an American college that, with a few exceptions, most college students know little or nothing about Eastern Europe and the Soviet occupation. They are not to blame; the interest to learn and to understand is there. The fault lies, rather, with an educational system in which history plays such a secondary role.

In 1982, my European friends called my attention to a new book written by Henry Bogdan, a professor of history in Paris. Published in France, the book was entitled *From Warsaw to Sofia, (De Varsovie a Sofia, Histoire des Pays de l'Est)* and covered the history of the entire Eastern European region from its origins to the present. I found the book very interesting, and a short time later met with Professor Bogdan. We agreed that the book should be published in English after being edited for the American public. Furthermore, we agreed that I would be responsible for bringing the book up to date, covering the historical events between the first publication in 1982 and the present, the Gorbachev era. Thus began our work on the English edition. The excellent translation from the French was made by Jean P. Fleming, and in editing and rewriting, I received indispensable help from my daughter, Krisztina Fehervary, whose studies at Brown University prepared her for the task. Here I would like to express my special thanks to her and to Jean. The maps were illustrated by Cynthia Hobgood.

Mr. Bogdan and I believe that this book will complete our goal of providing a comprehensive resource for those interested in history or politics, but also for anyone who would like to know more about the background of the peoples and nations of Eastern Europe.

Istvan Fehervary
Santa Fe, 1988

Note on Spelling and Statistical Information

Place names and the names of historical persons often have various spellings: the spelling of the original language in the original alphabet, and then the spellings given those places and persons by other nationalities. Often, place names change over time or with the shifting of borders and ethnic groups. In the French edition, Professor Bogdan used the French spelling for all names; here, in the English edition, we have attempted to use spellings which would be easily recognizable to an English speaker without completely anglicizing them. We have excluded the accents and diacritical markings, and hope that those readers familiar with the languages in question will not be jarred by their absence. Where place names were in transition or might cause confusion, we have tried to include both, for example: Fiume (Rijeka).

Throughout the book, miles have been substituted for kilometers where possible. We have kept to the use of hectares in delineating land area, with one hectare corresponding to 2.5 acres.

Introduction

In the first few years after World War II, Eastern Europe became an easily defined entity. "Eastern European countries" was the prevalent expression used to refer to the group of states directly or indirectly occupied by the Red Army during the last few months of the war. The states which subsequently became People's or Popular Democracies were defined by Andrei Zdanov—a Soviet politician later killed during the Stalinist purges—during a meeting of the Comintern as: "states where the power belonged to the people, where major industries, transportation, and the banks belonged to the state, and where the working class was the governing authority." Of course, Zdanov neglected to mention that the power held by the Communist parties was supported by the occupational Red Army. These states, which bordered the USSR, numbered eight and made up what was called the Soviet bloc or the Soviet satellite countries.

Defined and delimited this way, Eastern Europe essentially becomes a geopolitical concept: in Europe, but not belonging to the European community. The feeling that the West had little interest in liberating the peoples and nations of Eastern Europe became widespread. The Eastern European situation received publicity only when protests or revolutions broke out against the ruling Communist party or the occupying Soviet Army.

Eastern Europe, as we understand it throughout this work, bears little resemblance to what geographers traditionally call by that name. In fact, Eastern Europe is a political bloc which was created artificially by the superpowers at the Teheran and Yalta conferences. In his famous speech in Fulton in 1947, Winston Churchill was the first western statesman to call the boundary between the Western world and Eastern Europe the "Iron Curtain." Although the expression is officially considered inappropriate by

xiii

the governments of Western nations and has been banished from diplomatic language in the name of detente, the Iron Curtain still exists as a very real border with mine fields, watchtowers, guard dogs, and all the other paraphernalia of a police state. It covers over 1,000 miles, from East German Lubeck to Italian Trieste, from the Baltic to the Adriatic. It continues to divide two worlds in spite of increased trade and immigration—remaining a harsh reality which three million Berliners have the dubious privilege of observing every day.

Economically, Eastern Europe belongs to the Soviet organized and directed economic bloc, the Council for Mutual Economic Assistance (known as CMEA or COMECON). Founded in 1949 as a companion to the Red Army-led military bloc the Warsaw Pact, COMECON has since the 1960s encouraged national specialization in the production of industrial and agricultural products, and is a means of increasing Soviet leverage over its subject nations. The Warsaw Pact, in turn, places the Soviet Army in direct control of the national forces of the Eastern European nations, with the exceptions of Yugoslavia and Albania. Albania withdrew *de facto* in 1962 and *de jure* in 1968, following the severing of diplomatic ties with the Warsaw Pact nations.

In spite of appearances, the unity which characterized the countries of Eastern Europe for so many years seems more and more illusory. Differences and differing opinions abound in the Eastern Europe of today. Long hidden behind the veil of ideology, the ritual euphoria of official statements and the embarrassed silence of the media, national diversities and social and economic tensions are coming to light. Could they be merely coincidental phenomena isolated in time and space, or are they something more? We believe and will try to impress upon our readers that they are more a matter of long-term conditions linked to age-old problems that are resurfacing. In this case, we must seek the origins of the difficulties that the Eastern European governments are facing in the past as well as in the present.

If this hypothesis is correct, it means that after 40 years of socialist rule —during which political, economic, and social structures, ways of thinking, educational systems, and spiritual values have undergone radical transformations—the diverse nationalities and the cultural and religious traditions have remained intact, despite the dwindling numbers of those educated and raised before the Communist takeover in 1945-1948.

*****

More than 45 years have passed since the Soviet Red Army occupied Eastern Europe and despite growing tensions, it may be as long again before it is free from Soviet hegemony. During the four decades that have elapsed, Eastern Europe has merited the attention of the world press on numerous occasions: a partial list includes the worker's revolt in East Berlin of June, 1953, the Polish October and the Hungarian revolution of October, 1956, the Prague Spring of 1968 and the entry of Warsaw Pact troops into Czechoslovakia that followed, the Polish riots of 1970 and the Solidarity movement beginning in 1980. It comes as little surprise that the Hungarian Freedom fighters in 1956, Pope John Paul II in 1979, and Lech Walesa in 1980 were named Men of the Year. In October, 1978, the world witnessed the election of the Polish Cardinal Wojtyla as Pope John Paul II—a near-direct affront to the atheist Communist parties of the world. In June of 1979, the Pope publicly took a stand in favor of human rights and religious freedom, and followed his declaration with a triumphant visit to his native country.

The past eight years have witnessed the emergence of a new series of crises for the Eastern European regimes. May 1980 was marked by the death of Marshal Tito and the beginning of a difficult and complicated succession process in Yugoslavia. It is impossible to forget the beginning of a new social and political crisis in Poland in August, 1980; the official union evaporated and was replaced by the grassroots Solidarity Union, led by militant Catholic Lech Walesa. At the end of 1982, the Polish general Jaruzelski introduced martial law and outlawed Solidarity. The disturbances caused by the rapid changes of leadership in the Soviet Union itself hardly bear mentioning, as the policies of the State and Party leadership in the Eastern European nations are directly affected by decisions in Moscow.

Apart from sensationalist headlines, however, Eastern Europe is rarely examined in detail by the world press. We believe that this lack of interest is due not only to the overshadowing effect of events in Central America, Asia and the Middle East, considered to be more important to the United States, but also to a lack of knowledge of Eastern Europe's rich past and complex present. As Eastern Europe will be increasingly important both politically and economically in East-West relations, our intention in publishing this volume is to present a synthesis of Eastern European history incorporating precise documentation to the general public, journalists, teachers, students, and politicians. Our goal is to inform the reader about the real Eastern Europe—its inhabitants, their early and recent history, their similarities and their differences.

Any historical examination can only be partial and imperfect; the authors should accordingly be the first to deplore this fact and to present an apology to the reader. While accepting this, we wish to note that our study is inspired by a sincere desire to approach the truth, even if this entails assailing some of the myths surrounding Eastern European history.

Chapter 1

The Human Puzzle of Eastern Europe

More than 140 million inhabitants, eight states, at least a dozen languages, two alphabets in current use and six religions; these facts briefly illustrate the complexity of the human landscape in Eastern Europe at the end of its long history of invasions, civil and foreign wars, forced or voluntary population shifts, and territorial modifications and persecutions. Language is one of the principle criteria used to distinguish the peoples that inhabit the East European region, since in Eastern Europe, citizenship is an inadequate description of a population. In historical perspective, the existence of multinational states such as the Austro-Hungarian monarchy, as well as the partition of nations, has created a conflict between linguistic and state borders. The appearance and development of the concept of nationalism as a concept of international law in the 19th century did have an effect on the birth—or rebirth—of nation states, but the gap between ethnic and geographical borders still exists.

LINGUISTIC DIVERSITY

The great majority of peoples in Eastern Europe speak Indo-European languages. Among them, the Baltic languages of Latvian and Lithuanian and particularly the Slavic languages are the most prevalent. In 1987, 83 million East Europeans were estimated to be native speakers of a Slavic language, and it is also estimated that three East Europeans out of five are Slavic. There are also some 200 million Slavs from the Soviet Union in the immediate vicinity. While some Slavic peoples exist as scattered groups speaking dialects, the great majority of East European Slavs now live in coherent and homogenous groups. The Slavic peoples are divided into three major groups:

- —the western Slavic group, consisting of the Poles, the Czechs, the Moravians, and the Slovaks.
- —the eastern Slavic group, made up of the Ruthenian minority (directly related to the Ukrainians) who live in the Carpathian Ukraine.
- —the southern Slavic or Yugoslavian groups that include the Slovenes, the Croats, the Serbs, and the Bulgars. The latter were originally a tribe of Turanian stock who settled in the Balkans in the second half of the 7th century, and adopted the Slavic language of the more numerous indigenous population. Although the Bulgars were the conquerors, their severely diminished numbers encouraged the linguistic adoption.

Several other Indo-European languages are spoken in Eastern Europe. The most important linguistic group after Slav is Illyro-Balkan, represented by Albanian and Rumanian. Rumanian has been traditionally classed among the Romance languages because it contains a large number of vocabulary words of Latin derivation. Recent studies on the origins of the Rumanian language, however, reinforce an old theory that Rumanian was born in the Balkans. According to these studies, the language can be considered an Illyrian language formed symbiotically with Albanian—as witnessed by the undeniable relationship between the vocabularies of the two languages. Rumanian clearly has been enriched by Latin and Slavic borrowings. Today, Rumanian is spoken by a little over 19 million people, and Albanian by over three million.

The third linguistic group is Finno-Ugric, originating from the eastern Ural-Baikal region. Completely unrelated to the Germanic, Slavic, and Indo-European languages, Finno-Ugric languages were introduced into central Europe at the end of the 9th century as a result of the long pilgrimage that led the Hungarian people from the confines of the Urals to the plains of the middle Danube. The settling of the Hungarians in their present location also separated the northern Slavs from their southern relatives. Today, Hungarian is spoken by over 15 million persons, of which only 10.5 million live in Hungary as defined by its present boundaries. The other Finno-Ugric language spoken in Eastern Europe is Estonian, spoken by about one million persons in Estonia, today occupied by the Soviet Union. Finnish is the third member of the Finno-Ugric family.

Finally, German occupies a special place in the linguistic geography of Eastern Europe. German is of course spoken by the inhabitants of East Germany, but it is more or less understood and spoken by many other East Europeans by virtue of long periods of cohabitation with Germans over the course of the centuries. German has more or less tended to retain its status as the *lingua franca* of Eastern Europe, although since 1945 the study of Russian has been mandatory in the schools and universities of most Eastern European countries.

DIVIDED NATIONS AND ETHNIC MINORITIES

The changes brought by recent history and the territorial modifications that followed the two World Wars, have both more than occasionally resulted in political borders that separate members of the same ethnic group. The obvious example is the German nation, divided after World War II to form two sovereign states: the western-oriented Federal Republic of Germany and the Soviet bloc nation the German Democratic Republic. The most symbolic representation of this artificial dichotomy is the city of Berlin, divided in two on August 13, 1961 by the infamous Berlin Wall. This recent division, however, gives an incomplete picture of how the regionalistic Germans have been separated for centuries. In addition to Austrian and Swiss Germans, enclaves of German minorities still exist in several Eastern European countries, now considerably reduced in number as a result of the massive expulsions of 1945-1946. More than 10 million Germans were transferred from Poland, Czechoslovakia, Hungary, Rumania, and Yugoslavia to West Germany. In addition, thousands fled from Soviet occupied East Prussia and Poland to East Germany, and many continued from there to the West. Today, the number of Germans in Eastern Europe is not more than 0.5-0.1 percent of the population.

The Germans are hardly the only ethnic minority separated from their countrymen by the more or less arbitrary drawing of borders. As a result of the Treaty of Trianon in 1920, more than 30 percent of all Hungarians presently live in neighboring states outside the borders of Hungary. At present, concern for their welfare and treatment is an issue of national awareness in Hungary. At least 2.2 million live in Rumania, over 700,000 in Czechoslovakia, 450,000 in Yugoslavia, and nearly 200,000 in the Soviet Union. A great proportion of Albanians, about 1.7 million, live in Yugoslavian territory, and a limited number of Bulgars and Rumanians live in Yugoslavia. A minority Serbian population also exists in Rumania.

DISPERSED AND UPROOTED ETHNIC GROUPS

The relatively homogenous East European populations that have succeeded in gaining national representation share territory with the uprooted populations of once migrant peoples, who settled as foreigners in the regions their descendants now inhabit. These are the Armenians, the Gypsies, and the Jews.

During the Byzantine period, and later at the height of the Ottoman Empire, small groups of Armenian settlers came to the Balkans from Turkey. Their descendents still live in communities that are vital and aware of their Armenian origins. In Bulgaria, they number 55,000, and a smaller number is found in Rumania. Particularly in the 17th century, other communities of Armenians preferred to take refuge in the Austrian Empire, where some settled in Transylvania and were completely assimilated by the local Hungarian population.

Before World War I, the Gypsies were present in all parts of Eastern Europe, particularly in the Balkan countries. Their numbers were noticeably diminished by forced deportations between 1942 and 1944, and a sad fact of which very little note is made is the killing of 500,000 Gypsies in German concentration camps during the second World War. 200,000 Gypsies still live in Bulgaria and Rumania, and over 100,000 live in Yugoslavia and Hungary. Elsewhere they are far less numerous. The Gypsy population remains very unpopular in Eastern Europe for both traditionally racist and ideological reasons, despite governments' efforts to settle and to integrate them into the population; it is clear that these efforts have achieved very little success.

Before 1939, the Jews made up a substantial percentage of the urban population in the Central and East European countries. They were most numerous in Poland with a population of over three million, about 10 percent of the total population. Rumania possessed a Jewish population of about 700,000, and Hungary of about 500,000; Jewish communities in other Eastern European nations were much smaller. Nazi persecutions practically annihilated the Jewish communities in Poland, Rumania, and Czechoslovakia. The Hungarian Jews were spared until March, 1944, and as a result nearly 250,000 survived the war. Along with approximately 200,000 Jews in Rumania, today they make up the largest Jewish community in Eastern Europe. Since 1945, tens of thousands of Jews have emigrated to Israel and the United States, further reducing the Jewish element of the population.

RELIGIOUS DIVERSITY

Religion is a very important factor in differentiating Eastern European populations, partly because historically the various nationalities have been so intolerant of each other. Today, in spite of the official policy of atheism, religion is very much alive. Although current statistics on religious belief and participation in Eastern Europe simply do not exist as the entire religious question is rather pointedly ignored, it is apparent that the extent of belief at least parallels that found in the West. In Eastern Europe, all of the major monotheistic religions are represented. Catholicism is present in two forms. Roman Catholicism is the religion of nearly all Poles, Slovenes, and Croats;

85 percent of the Slovaks, 65 percent of the Hungarians, 60 percent of the Czechs, 10 percent of the Serbs, and 10 percent of East Germans are Roman Catholic. Greek Orthodox Catholicism (the Uniate Church) is actively practiced by the Ruthenian population in Slovakia, by several thousand Hungarians, and by about half the Rumanian population in Transylvania, despite an official ban by authorities in Bucharest in 1948.

Protestantism has attracted a majority in the German Democratic Republic in the form of Lutheranism. A minority in Czechoslovakia and Hungary adhere to Calvinism or Lutheranism, and in Rumania, a percentage of the German and Hungarian minorities in Transylvania are Protestant.

After four centuries of Turkish occupation, Islam took root among the Serbs of Bosnia-Herzegovina, and among the Bulgars of Rhodope (Pomoci). In Albania, it is the dominant belief with a percentage of 70 percent.

The attitude of the atheist and Marxist governments toward religion varies from one country to another, ranging from a tolerated freedom of religious teachings and practices in Poland to the total ban on all religious practices adopted by Albania in 1967. A variety of situations exists in between these two extremes. On the whole, the situation of Catholic and Protestant churches has improved from its precarious position in the 1950s. The Orthodox church in Rumania, Bulgaria, and Yugoslavia, for example, does not appear to be having any major difficulties in fulfilling its spiritual mission. And the election of the Bishop of Cracow, Karol Wojtyla, as Supreme Pontiff in 1978, followed by his triumphant tour of his native country during the following year, have had a considerable impact upon the population of Eastern Europe. Wojtyla's clear stance on matters of religious doctrine concerning human rights and religious freedom has also affected Eastern European believers and non-believers alike. The election of Wojtyla as Pope has also affected the national clergies, who have often been accused of being too willing to sacrifice the interest of their churches to their own personal comfort and safety.

DEMOGRAPHY

In terms of birth and mortality rates, Eastern European demography followed a relatively homogenous pattern before World War II, with the exception of Germany. Both birth and mortality rates were relatively high. Although discernable patterns have appeared between countries since 1945, some common characteristics remain: a fairly sharp decrease in fertility and a decline in mortality, especially infant mortality.

The following examples illustrate some national differences.

—Albania is a country with a strong natural growth rate due to a high birth rate, on the order of 30 per 1,000, and a low mortality rate, less

than 9 per 1,000. Accordingly, its population growth is the highest in east-central Europe.
—Poland, Rumania, and Yugoslavia have been able to sustain a natural annual growth rate of close to 10 per 1,000 despite a slow but regular decline in birth rate, because of noticeably lowered mortality rates and in particular, lowered infant mortality.
—The German Democratic Republic is a nation with a virtually nonexistent growth rate. The birth rate is around 14 per 1,000 while mortality is quite high, 13.9 per 1,000. This can best be explained by its aging population, linked to both the low birth rate and the consequences of massive emigrations of young people to the German Federal Republic between 1950 and 1961.
—In Bulgaria, Hungary, and Czechoslovakia, the natural growth rate is low, due to a relatively low birth rate and a fairly high mortality rate, again due to an aging population. Hungary has very recently experienced popular protests due to what is perceived as governmental policies leading to population decline; it is not unlikely that similar protests will eventually spread to the more authoritarian regimes practicing similar policies.

Eastern Europe has an average population density of almost 105 inhabitants per square kilometer; as a contrast, France has 98 inhabitants. The population densities of Bulgaria, Yugoslavia, Rumania, and Albania are lower than the average, as these are countries where mountainous terrain as well as a large agricultural population have discouraged highly concentrated living conditions. The four countries where the density is above average are those with plains and fertile interior basins, as well as the most highly developed industries. A considerable amount of variation also exists between regions within each country.

Similar variations exist in urban/rural population distribution. Urbanization has perceptibly progressed nearly everywhere in the course of the last thirty years, due to common policies of industrialization. As a result, urban populations now outnumber rural. The exceptions are bulgaria, where urban and rural populations are roughly equal, and Albania and Yugoslavia, where only 44 percent of the population live in cities. A difference that should be noted, however, is that some countries have a long tradition of urban living while for others urbanization is more recent. The best example of the former is the German Democratic Republic, where city-dwellers make up over three-fourths of the population. A new type of urban center, which can be termed the "socialist city" because Marxist ideology was an element of its creation, has developed alongside the traditional cities that functioned originally as administrative or commercial centers. These new urban centers have mushroomed on rural sites and in trading regions because of the focus on heavy industry. Examples are Leninvaros and Dunaujvaros in Hungary, Nowa-Huta in Poland, Eisenhuttedstadt in the German Democratic

Republic, and Hunedoara in Rumania. As an example, population density in Dunaujvaros is one of the highest in East or West Europe, despite its small size of under 65,000 inhabitants. Built in accordance with then-accepted Stalinist socialist principles, it was considered optimum to concentrate population in order to achieve the speedy creation of a "true" proletariat.

Chapter 2

A Land of Many Aspects

GEOGRAPHIC DIVERSITY

The countries of Eastern Europe differ geographically not only by three-dimensional relief, but by climate and landscape. In the north lies the central part of an immense plain that extends from the banks of the North Sea to the Urals. Known as the Germano-Polish plain by geographers, it is 250 to 300 miles wide and comprises most of the territory of the German Democratic Republic and of Poland.

In the center, extending from the German Democratic Republic to the White Russian border, rise a succession of forested, ancient and eroded mountainous masses alternating with fertile basins. These mountains, most of which contain ferrous and non-ferrous ores, reach elevations of 2,100 to 5,100 feet.

In the south—which includes over half of the Eastern European region—there are large systems of recently formed mountain chains, which are an extension of the Alpine chains to the east and the southeast. At their northernmost point, they form the Carpathian arc, rising to a maximum altitude of 7,800 feet. In the south, they form the Balkan and Rhodope mountains. These young mountains promoted the formation of large depositional basins: the Pannonian plain in the west, the Hungarian great plain—the Alfold—between the Danube and Tisza rivers, and the Vojvodine and Banat plains.

The ancient mountainous masses and the young mountains alike give rise to an abundant hydrographic network. One of the major north-south rivers is the Elbe, a natural waterway for Czechoslovakia and particularly for the German Democratic Republic. The Oder provides transportation northward for products from Silesia and from the industrial center of East Germany. The Neisse and the Oder have delineated the eastern border of Germany since 1945. Finally, the Vistula is a pre-eminently Polish river which crosses the country from north to south for a distance of 680 miles, and waters two capitals successively—Cracow, the capital of the past, and Warsaw, the present capital.

The Danube flows in the south, and more than 1,200 of its 1,600 mile length is in Eastern Europe. The Danube has always been a correcting link between Eastern and Western Europe, and will become even more so now that the Rhine-Maine-Danube canal is complete. But the Danube is above all an important commercial artery for the Eastern countries along its banks—Czechoslovakia, Hungary, Rumania, Yugoslavia, and Bulgaria. It is also vital for the U.S.S.R., which became a Danubian country with the annexation of Bessarabia in 1945.

CLIMATIC DIVERSITY

Eastern Europe differs also by climate, with several differing climatic zones. On the Germano-Polish plain, western winds often serve to mitigate the effects of the Siberian anticyclone in winter, and in summer they bring some cooling air. Their influence, however, decreases from west to east.

Mountainous regions have a distinct and more continental environment, with cold winters, hot summers, and abundant precipitation.

The continental climate is more evident in the countries along the Danube, as the western winds are checked by the Alps and the mid-German massif. On the plains in Hungary to the northeast of Yugoslavia, in Lower Rumania, and on the Bulgarian plains, the winters are harsh, ranging from an average of -2 Celcius in January in Budapest to -3.5 in Bucharest. The hot summers are sometimes influenced by the Mediterranean climate, especially in Rumania and Bulgaria, where the dryness is interspersed with heavy downpours. In general, however, the annual precipitation is low, averaging around 19 inches per year.

Finally, the shores of the Adriatic and Black Seas enjoy a Mediterranean climate, especially in the summer when it remains dry for at least three months. In winter, despite the predominantly mild and sunny weather, the cold winds from the interior—known as the Bora in Yugoslavia—can sometimes cause a sharp, though short-lived, drop in the thermometer.

Climate and landscape are mainly responsible for the uneven distribution of the population and the inequalities of economic development still evident in these regions, although of course it is impossible to separate these from the roles of circumstance and history.

ECONOMIC DIVERSITY

Clear economic differences exist between the countries of Eastern Europe. By 1938 the German Democratic Republic and Czechoslovakia had attained a level of economic development close to that of the great industrial powers of Western Europe. Others, such as the Balkan states and to a certain degree Poland, remained candidates for the term "developing country." Countries such as Rumania and Hungary fell somewhere in between, with a small industrial sector and fairly heavy reliance on agricultural products for export earnings.

After 1945, the economies of the Eastern European countries were faced with two series of problems: those linked to reconstruction and those resulting from changes in the political structure. In addition to the heavy damage received from bombings and military operations in the course of the bloodiest and most destructive war ever fought, the nations of Eastern Europe were also faced with the devastation caused by the looting and plundering committed by successive occupying forces. Concerning the second series of problems, changes in political structures included agrarian reforms, nationalizations, and the shift from a fairly liberal free-market economy to a socialist-communist one which gave priority to the development of heavy industry for ideological reasons. These nations were grouped in 1949 under the umbrella of the Council for Mutual Economic Assistance (CMEA or COMECON), an organization formed to counter the Marshall Plan offered to all European nations, both west and east. Politically dominated by the Soviet Union, the COMECON allows each country certain trading privileges *vis-a-vis* the others. The socialist division of work (specialization), set up in the early 1960s, has further strengthened cooperation and ties between the COMECON nations.

DIVERSITY IN THE EXERCISE OF POWER

Despite the oft-cited principles of ideological unity, universal membership in the socialist system, and identical principles guiding domestic and foreign politics, the reader should not forget that the Eastern European countries often display considerable differences in their political institutions and in the exercise of power.

A distinction can be made between the states whose political make-up allows a coalition of political parties grouped around the Communist party, and states in which the Communist party completely monopolizes political life. Sometimes the Communist party and even other political parties are grouped together into large popular assemblies whose names vary by country—the Bulgarian Front of the Fatherland, the Hungarian Patriotic Front, the Polish National Front, the Yugoslavian Socialist Alliance of

Working People, and so on. These groups take their place beside other mass organizations, such as unions, youth organizations, cultural associations, and carefully chosen representatives of the churches.

In all of the Eastern European countries, political power officially emanates from the people, who exercise it through their representatives elected by universal sufferage. The election procedure follows the principle of either direct or secret ballot, but with only a yes or no answer allowed. A single list of candidates prepared by the Communist party and the mass organizations is submitted for the approval of the voters. For several years, in countries such as Hungary and Poland, the lists have contained more names than there were offices to be filled, thus permitting the voters to cross out certain candidates. In 1985, for the first time since the Communist takeover in 1949, in Hungary the names of non-Communist candidates were also placed on the candidate list.

Part I

The Weight of the Past

Chapter 3

The Distribution of Peoples

EARLY HISTORY OF EASTERN EUROPE

The area known today as Eastern Europe was populated over a prolonged period of time, as a number of tribes migrated from the east to the Danubian plain and surrounding areas. Our knowledge of this subject is often imperfect, as until the beginning of the first millennium B.C., these regions were completely separated from the Mediterranean civilizations.

With the exception of the ancestors of present-day Finns and Estonians, who arrived in small groups and settled on the shores of the Baltic between the Niemen and Neva valleys throughout the first millennium B.C., the first known populations in Eastern Europe were the Indo-Europeans. In the third millennium B.C., the Indo-European tribes still lived in the steppes extending from the Carpathian mountains to the south of the Urals. While two tribes—the Cimmerians and the Scythians—stayed until the first centuries A.D., most of the Indo-European tribes had begun to disperse 3000 years before. Some groups, including the Hellenes, came into contact with the early Mediterranean cultures sometime during the second millennium B.C. Others, such as the Thraco-Illyrians, did not quite reach the warm seas. The Illyrians settled between the Sava and Danube rivers and the Adriatic Ocean; the Dacians were defined by the Tisza, the Danube, and the Black Sea; and the Thracians settled in the Balkans. Thus, they were all more or less in contact with Greek civilization. The great majority of Indo-Europeans, however, settled far away from the Mediterranean world.

Several tribes migrated to Scandinavia, where they merged with the ancestors of the Germans. The Early Balts—about whom we know very little—settled between the Oder and Neman (Memel) rivers. To the south they were in contact with the early Slavs, who were living north of the Carpathian mountains from the Vistula to the Dniester rivers. Beginning about the middle of the second millennium B.C., the heart of Europe was home to several civilizations started by the early Celts—civilizations about which we are well informed because of the abundant archeological material uncovered. From the third millennium forward, the Celts slowly extended their zone of influence to the south and southwest by assimilating the local Thraco-Illyrians. This gave birth to the mixed ethnic group, the Celto-Scythians in the eastern part of Europe, and the Celto-Thracians in the Balkans. By the end of the first millennium B.C., only present-day Hungary possessed a homogenous Celtic population.

THE HELLENIZATION AND ROMANIZATION OF THE BALKAN AND DANUBIAN COUNTRIES

From 1000 B.C. onward, the Greeks attempted to control the mountainous regions to the north of their country. In the 5th and 6th centuries B.C., they succeeded in doing so by establishing colonies in Epirus on the Adriatic coast, on the Thracian coast, and on the shores of the Black Sea as well. Through these colonies, Greek civilization slowly penetrated the Balkans. Rome replaced Greece in this region in the second century B.C., and with the creation of the province of Macedonia and the submission of Thrace, the destiny of the southern part of Eastern Europe became closely associated with that of Rome. Under the emperors Augustus and Tiberius, Rome subdued the territories located south of the Danube. The Danube became the northern frontier of the Empire. Also under the Romans, the provinces of Noricum (Austria), Pannonia (western Hungary) and Dalmatia (present-day Croatia) were created, and the protected state of Thrace became a province in 46 A.D. To the east, the countries south of the Danube became the provinces of Upper Messia (Serbia) and Lower Messia (Bulgaria). To the west, the Romans briefly occupied the banks of the Weser river, but in reality it was the Rhine and the Neckar that marked the limits of Roman penetration into the Germanic world. Along the Danube, the Romans came into violent contact with other Germanic peoples—the Quades of Moravia, the Marconans of Bohemia, and the Scythian peoples, the Lazyges and Sarmates. The latter two were living in the heart of the Hungarian plain between the Danube and the Tisza rivers along with the Dacians, who by the end of the first century A.D. had created an organized state under their king, Decebale. The Dacians made repeated forays into the Roman provinces of the Lower Danube, until the emperor, Trajan, overcame Dacia in two campaigns (101-102 and 106-107 A.D.), and made it a Roman province. A large portion of the Dacian population was massacred and the rest scattered around the Empire as slaves. Dacia was repopulated with colonists from all the provinces, particularly the Asian ones. Through its gold and silver mines, Dacia contributed to the prosperity of the Roman world.

By the beginning of the second century A.D., the part of eastern Europe conquered by the Roman Empire consisted of well-administered territories with prosperous cities where Roman officials and the more or less Romanized indigenous elite lived. It was from the cities that Roman culture reached out to the non-Roman peoples of the countryside where Romanization remained fairly superficial, although this varied by region. Even the indigenous peoples serving in the auxiliary Roman army remained proudly loyal to their ethnic origins, be they Dalmatians or Pannonians. The most lasting of the Roman presence, however, was the introduction of Christianity beginning in the 3rd century A.D. Christianity spread widely during the 4th and 5th centuries, principally in regions neighboring Greece along the Dalmatian coast, and in Pannonia.

THE FIRST WAVE OF THE GREAT INVASIONS
(2ND—5TH CENTURIES)

From the 3rd century on, the Roman Empire periodically suffered barbarian raids that devastated the provinces of the Rhine and the Danube. This marked the beginning of what historians have termed the "Great Invasions," but which are better described as migrations—the *Volkerwanderung* of German historians.

The first attacks began with the death of Marcus Aurelius in 180 A.D. The situation was temporarily contained by the first soldier-emperor, Septimius Severus, and his sons, but only with constant battles fought along the Rhine and Danube rivers. With the death of Alexander Severus in 235, the situation became critical again. The barbarians of central and eastern Europe were beginning a lengthy series of transformations. It was at this time that the long-isolated Germanic tribes began to form groups which eventually led to genuine federations of peoples: the Alamains, Burgones, and Francs in the West, the Angles and Jutes in present-day Denmark, and the Saxons and the Lombards between the mouths of the Weser and the Elbe. The Vandals were also coalescing in Galicia and in the northern Carpathian mountains, where they bordered the proto-Slavs, the Goths, and the Gepides between the Dniester and the Don. Taking advantage of difficulties in the Roman world, the Germans intensified their attacks between 235 and 270. The Goths were particularly aggressive in the Balkans and in Dacia. It was under these conditions that the emperor, Aurelian (270-275), decided to evacuate the province of Dacia. According to the Roman historian, Eutrope, the evacuation of Dacia was total:

> He made a desert of Dacia that Trajan had established beyond the Danube, because the devastation of all of Illyria and Messia robbed him of any hope he had of being able to keep it; having called back the Romans from the cities and country of Dacia, he settled them in central Messia (Eutrope, IX).

This text has been challenged by Rumanian historians seeking to demonstrate that the Rumanians of today are the descendents of the Dacians and the Romans who remained in Dacia after 270. Largely inspired by political motives, however, this theory lacks substance. In fact, after 270, Roman names for the cities, mountains, and rivers disappeared altogether, contrary to the case in other Romanized provinces conquered by the barbarians.

At the end of the 3rd century, the re-deployment of troops by Aurelian following the abandonment of Dacia succeeded in containing the barbarian advance. With Diocletian (285-305) and Constantine (306-337), a Roman Empire seemingly at peace drew up treaties with the barbarian chiefs, making them confederates with the duty of policing the Empire's borders.

Beginning in 370, however, the arrival of the Huns from Asia put an end to peace and cooperation. The first to suffer the Hun's assault were the Alains—an Indo-European people living north of the Caspian Sea. Then in 374-375, it was the Goth's turn—both the Ostrogoths living between the Volga and the Don, and the Visigoths living between the Don and the Dniester. Many Alains and Ostrogoths were massacred in the clash of 375, but a number did manage to escape toward the West. The remaining Ostrogoths joined the retreating Visigoths in seeking refuge in the Roman Empire. In the autumn of 376, most of them were settled in Thrace by the emperor, Valens II. After Valens' death, his successor, Theodosius I, encouraged the Goths to move westward. The Visigoths under Alaric moved into Italy, where they briefly occupied Rome before moving on to Gaul, and from there into Spain. After 378, the Ostrogoths settled in Pannonia.

After forcing the Visigoths and Ostrogoths west, the Huns became masters of the steppes and plains from Turkistan to the Carpathians. In order to keep them away from Constantinople, Theodosius encouraged them to settle in Pannonia, where they appeared around 390. The territory that is now Hungary slowly became the center of the Hunnish empire—the capital of Buda was named for Attila's son, while on the opposing bank of the Danube, Pest was named for the plague. In 434, Attila became master of the empire, which he governed jointly with his brother, Bleda, until 445, then alone until his death in 453. For nearly 30 years, the Huns carried out devastating raids from the plains of the Danube against the East Roman Empire. They pushed as far as Salonica in 447, and then from 449 on, turned toward the barbarian kingdoms of the West. There, the joint forces of the Roman and barbarian armies hurt them badly at the battle of Catalonie in 451, erroneously called the battle of Chalons by several historians. The defeat, however, did not prevent Attila from assaulting Rome the following year.

The death of Attila in 453 soon led to the breakup of his empire. The peoples conquered by the Huns—notably the Goths of Pannonia and the Romanized Pannonians—seized the opportunity to revolt. While most of the Huns withdrew toward Central Asia, some undoubtedly remained. A Hungarian legend documented by the 15th century humanist, Bonfini, asserts that the Sicules (Szekelys) of the eastern Carpathians are the descendents of Huns who remained in Europe. More likely, they are the descendents of Hungarians who accompanied the Huns on their initial migration toward the West.

With the crumbling of Attila's empire the first period of migrations into east-central Europe ended. Its end was accompanied by the fading of the Western Roman Empire, which officially disappeared in 476. The Eastern Empire was more successful in withstanding the barbarians. Its authority stopped at the Sava and Danube rivers to the north, while to the west its boundaries were more flexible, although theoretically the Illyric territories defined its western border. The former provinces of Pannonia and Dacia had been emptied of a large portion of their populations by successive waves of invasions. Beyond the Carpathians and the Bohemian mountains existed the still unstructured domain of the Slavs.

THE SECOND WAVE OF MAJOR INVASIONS (6TH—7TH CENTURIES)

At the end of the 5th century, the Lombards—a Germanic people of Scandinavian origin living in the low valley of the Elbe during the 3rd century—appeared first in Lower Austria and then in Pannonia. Under their king, Wacho (510-540), and his successor, Audoin, the Lombards created a state linked by treaty to the Roman Empire, reconstituted by Justinian. They participated in the Justinian reconquest of Ostrogothic Italy in 522 under this treaty. At the same time, new invaders appeared from the western steppes of Asia—the Avars. The Khan, Bayan, first collaborated with the Lombards to conquer the Gepides, who then controlled the region between the Tisza and the Black Sea. In 567, the defeated Gepides were integrated into the emerging Avar empire. Considering such close proximity to the Avars to be a risk to his people, the Lombard king, Alboin (561-572), left

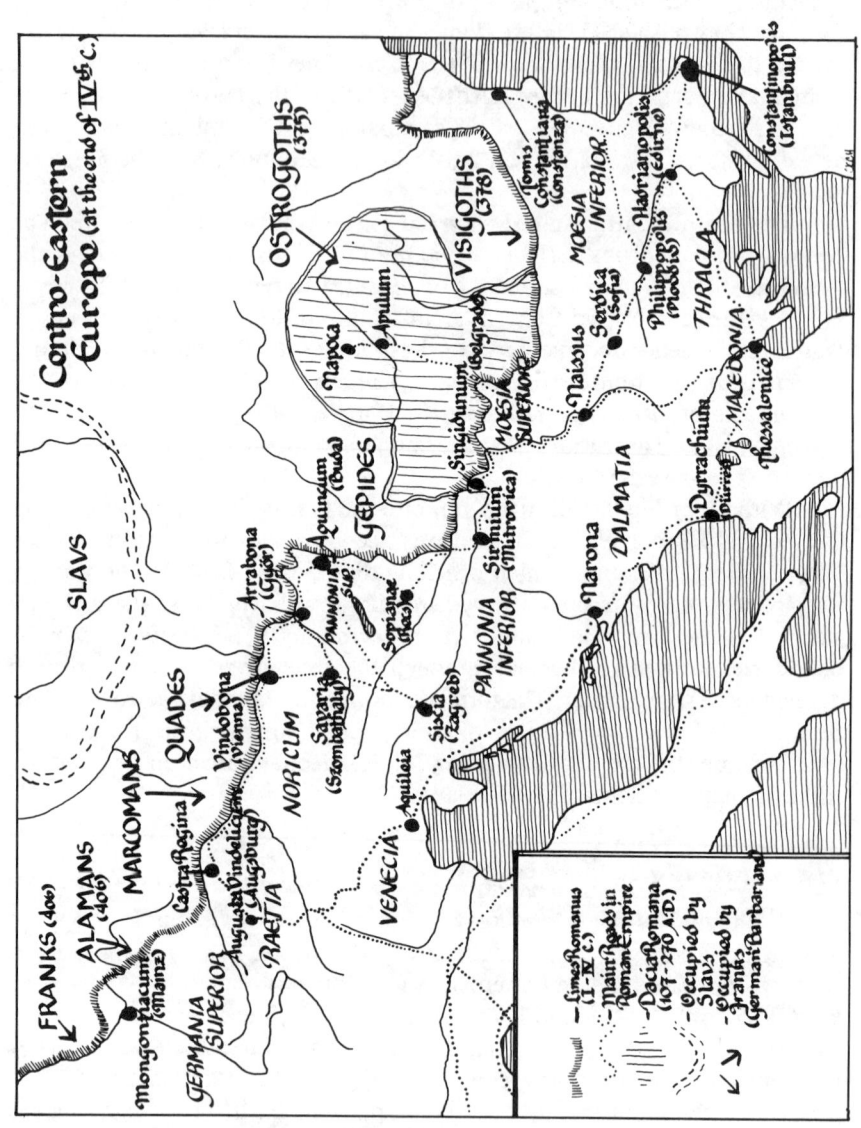

Pannonia in April of 568 to the conquest of Italy. From then on, the Avars dominated the middle valley of the Danube.

In many ways the Avars resembled the Huns. They were both nomadic horsemen who spoke an early Turkish language, and both were accompanied by a horde of peoples from the steppes. The Avar empire extended to the entire Carpathian zone and also to the lands of the Elbe and the Oder, while their border was delineated by the Sava and Danube. The capture of Sirmium in 582 marked their southernmost advance; the defeat of the Avars at Constantinople in 626 signaled the end of their conquering power.

The momentary lessening of Avar power gave the Slavs an opportunity to emerge. Until the 6th century, the Slavs had occupied an area between the Vistula and the middle course of the Don. By the time the Lombards and the Slavs came into conflict, the Slavs had already occupied present-day Bohemia and Moravia. In addition, several tribes had penetrated into Pannonia. From there, they broke apart, and one segment descended toward the Adriatic, where in 614 they destroyed the city of Salona, the administrative center of Byzantium in Dalmatia. At the beginning of the 7th century, Illyria and most of the Balkans were in the hands of the Slavs—the ancestors of the present Slovenes, Croats, and Serbs. The occupied areas began to adopt the Slavic ways.

The defeat of the Avars in 626 by Constantinople emancipated the Slavs of Bohemia and Moravia. The northern Slavs (from whom the Czechs and Moravians are descended) remained more or less autonomous, alternately subject to Germans or Avars, while the southern Slavs became increasingly established in the former Byzantine territories of Illyria and Messia, with the reluctant consent of the Eastern Empire.

The Avars who remained on the plains of the middle Danube were reinforced by new arrivals from Central Asia after 670. Among them were undoubtedly some proto-Hungarian tribes, as demonstrated by the Hungarian historian, G. Laszlo, in a comparative study of Hungarian and Avar gravesites. From the 7th century onwards, however, the Avars played only a minor role due in part to a series of successful campaigns led against them by the Carolingians from 791 to 796. After 822, no more was heard of them.

The 8th century witnessed the arrival of the Bulgars in Europe. In the 6th century, the Bulgars had possessed a vast empire in the northwest Caucasus mountains. Locked in a struggle with the Khazars, a segment of the Bulgars moved to the west, crossing the lower Danube in 679 and finally settling in Messia under the leadership of Khan Asparuk. Of Turkish origin, the Bulgars slowly adopted Slavic ways through contact with the populations of the Balkans; eventually, a Slavo-Bulgarian state emerged at the expense of Byzantium.

THE END OF THE AGE OF INVASIONS

The first Slavic principalities formed early in the 9th century, as the migratory peoples stabilized. Their organization varied by degree from one people to another. The least organized were the early Poles, who had remained close to their original Slavic habitat, occupying the Oder valley and the plains on both sides of the Vistula. On the other end of the scale, the Czechs and the Moravians were establishing the principality of Greater Moravia by the 9th century, which reached its apex under Swatopluk (874-884). The Slovenes were integrated into the Carolingian Empire by 788; the Croats, caught between the Carolingian world and Byzantium, managed to pry themselves free and set up a state under Tomislav. The Serbs were meanwhile split into two groups of tribes, one in Rascia and the other in Zeta.

During their migrations the Serbs remained pagan, as did the Bulgars. Byzantium and Rome zealously rivaled each other in Christianizing them. Through its intermediaries the Archbishop of Salzburg and the Patriarch of Aquilius, the Roman Church took in the Slovenes and the Croats during the 9th century. The Croatian prince, Tomislav, was even crowned by the Pope in 925. Byzantium, however, was more successful in the Balkans due to the actions of two monks, the Salonican brothers Cyril and Methodius. The brothers spoke Slavic and refined the Glagolithic alphabet for the purposes of converting the Slavic peoples they were journeying to visit. Cyril and Methodius went first to Moravia in 863, where they found several Christian communities created by missionaries from Salzburg: there was even a bishopric at Nitra. The hostility of the Germanic clergy soon closed the doors of Moravia and Pannonia to them. After 885, the disciples of Methodius were driven out of Moravia and took on the evangelization of the Balkans. The Greek missionaries were clearly successful with the Serbs and the Bulgars, whose prince, Boris, had been converted in 864. The Glagolithic alphabet was simplified, and in memory of Cyril was named the Cyrillic alphabet. Although Byzantium had lost most of its political influence in the east of Europe, the evangelizing actions of its missionaries succeeded in reestablishing a degree of influence. The bishopric of Ochrid, founded by Cyril and Methodius, became an important religious center, and is considered by some the home of Greco-Slavic culture.

At the very end of the 9th century, a new people, the Magyar, settled in east-central Europe. Known as the Hungarians, the Magyars were originally from the Urals, but had resided for centuries in Central Asia, where they had been part of both Attila's empire and that of the Avars. In the 9th century, they lived on the steppes of the southern Ukraine. Hard pressed by nomads from Central Asia, Hungarian tribes led by their chief, Arpad, crossed the Carpathians between 895 and 896. They settled on the vast plains of the middle Danube and in the valleys of Transylvania—sheltered by the Carpathian Arch that became the natural northern border of the Hungarian state for over 1,000 years. Due to their numbers (between 200,000 and 300,000 people), the Magyars overwhelmed the local populations, themselves

Migration of Rumanians (Vlachs) between Xth and XVIth C.

Main settlements of Rumanians (and their dates)
Main migrations

remnants of the different peoples who had either passed through or settled there. Those existing in greatest number prior to the arrival of the Magyars were the Romanized Celts, although the degree of their Romanization is subject to debate. The main force of the Magyars had been preceded by other Hungarians who had probably arrived with the Huns and certainly with the Avars. Examples of these early Hungarians are the Szekelys of Transylvania and Magyar Croats existing in scattered islands throughout Pannonia. The Hungarians shared valleys of the western Carpathians with relatively numerous, albeit unorganized, Slavs, who were distant ancestors of the present-day Slovaks.

Thus, at the beginning of the 10th century, the peoples whose descendents now populate Central and Eastern Europe were already in place, with the exception of the Rumanians. Under the name of the Vlachs, the Rumanians were still wandering with their herds in the Albano-Macedonian area, from which they were to descend onto the plains of the lower Danube.

Chapter 4

The Birth of Nation States
10th—13th Centuries

The settling of the Magyar tribes in central Europe put an end to the long series of migrations. With the inflow of new tribes at an end, the peoples of east-central Europe tried to organize themselves into structured nation-states. Most succeeded between the 10th and the 13th centuries.

FORMATION OF THE FIRST STATES IN THE 10TH CENTURY

The Germanic Sphere of Influence

As the 10th century dawned, the German kings still powerful in the 9th century had lost much of that power to feudal lords. The only coherent moral and political strength in east-central Europe belonged to the Church.

In the 8th and 9th centuries, bishoprics and archbishoprics were created in a number of German cities, as the Germanic zone of influence spread outward. They served as advance strongholds of Christianity against the still-pagan Slavs and Hungarians. From these bishoprics, missionaries departed for the east with the intention of converting the pagan peoples. It was generally by the conversion of the Magyar and northern Slavic chiefs, as well as some Czechs and Poles, that nation-states came about: Christianity proved to be a powerful force in fostering nationhood.

In the 10th century, the Duchy of Bohemia was established under the family of the Przemyslides. After initial contact with Christianity in the 9th century, the Duke of Wenceslas (915-929) was converted by missionaries from Ratisbonne. As shown by the assassination of Wenceslas by his brother, Boleslas, paganism retained deep roots. The unfortunate victim was canonized shortly afterward, and St. Wenceslas became the patron saint of

Eastern Europe in 1025

Bohemia. Boleslas I (929-961), named the Cruel, finally converted to Christianity himself and endeavored to maintain good relations with the king of Germany, Otto the Great. In 955, Boleslas fought beside Otto at the Battle of Lechfeld, a battle that put an end to Magyar invasions in the West. Boleslas then acknowledged himself a vassal of Otto, who became Emperor Otti I in 962. The Duchy of Bohemia thus became a fief of the Empire, and was granted a quasi-independent status with some feudal obligations, similar to the Empire's other fiefdoms. Under Boleslas II, the Pious (967-999), the Christian religion was firmly established. Boleslas founded the bishopric of Prague in 973. The first bishop of Prague, Vojtech, better known as Saint Adalbert, was a Czech by origin and had been active as a missionary among the Prussians, Poles, and Hungarians.

While the Przemyslides were beginning to organize Bohemia, Prince Mieszko of the Piast family, chief of one of the numerous Slav tribes living on the plains between the Oder and the Vistula, made Poznan the center of a confederation of tribes whose territory from that time on was known as Polska, meaning the plain. Mieszko ruled from 960 to 990 over the fledgling Polish state, and was influenced by German missionaries and by his Christian wife, sister of Boleslas I, Duke of Bohemia. Mieszko was baptized in 966 under the name of Mieszko I, and until his death encouraged the spread of Christianity in Poland. He founded a bishopric at Poznan in 968 under the jurisdiction of the archbishopric of Magdeburg. Here, as in Bohemia, the high German clergy guided the first steps of the Polish church. The son of Mieszko, Boleslaw the Valiant (992-1025), continued the unification of the Polish tribes. He extended his authority in Lusace, on the left bank of the Oder, and into Moravia. Poland in the year 1000 was a completely Christian Poland, and became independent of the German church with the foundation of the archbishopric of Gniezno—still the patriarchal seat of the Polish church today.

The conversion of the Hungarians proved more difficult. During the first half of the 10th century, the Hungarians used the plains of the middle Danube as a base of departure for devastating raids into the Germanic countries (907-913 A.D.) as well as in the direction of Byzantium in the years 927, 934, and 943. In 917-918, Hungarian horsemen pushed into Lorraine and Champagne, and in 924-925 they conducted an expedition that reached as far as Languedoc and Toulousain. In the years that followed, the expeditions became fewer until on August 10, 955, the Hungarians were dealt a crushing defeat at Lechfeld by the German king, Otto the Great. From then on, the influence of neighboring Slavs encouraged the Hungarians to settle down. Moreover, Christian missionaries sent by Bishop Pilgrim of Passau and by his colleague Vojtech in Prague accelerated the integration of the Hungarians into the western Christian community. Towards the end of the 10th century, the reigning prince, Geza, and his son, Vajk—descendents of the conqueror, Arpad—converted to Christianity. Vajk took the Christian name of Istvan (Stephen), and shortly thereafter married the daughter of the Duke of Bavaria, the princess Gisela. Under Istvan I (997-1035), Hungary became a Christian state organized in a manner similar to the western feudal monarchies. Istvan was sent the royal crown in the year 1000 by Pope Sylvester II. With his independence from the church in Rome recognized, Istvan proceeded to organize the Hungarian church around a national base, creating eight bishoprics and two archbishoprics with a patriarchate at Esztergom. To complete the evangelical task, he called in Benedictine monks who founded the Abbey of Pannonhalma—still an important cultural and spiritual center today. Istvan was canonized as Saint Istvan (St. Stephen) in 1081, and remains the patron saint of Hungary.

The Byzantine Sphere of Influence

In the 10th century, the Macedonian dynasty that had ruled Constantinople since 867 was experiencing increasing difficulties in Asia due to Arab expansion. The Balkan peoples, though still theoretically subject to Byzantium, took the opportunity to rebel.

Under Tomislav (910-928), the Croats had formed a kingdom that was independent from both the Francs and from Byzantium. This situation was solidified by Emperor Basil II at the end of the 10th century, who officially recognized Prince Drgislav (969-997) as king of Croatia and Dalmatia.

It was in fact the Bulgars who achieved the greatest success in attempting to form an independent state at Byzantium's expense. Converted to Christianity during the rule of Prince Boris (852-889), the Bulgars were, however, still living under Byzantine rule at the end of the 10th century. With the assistance of the southern Russian Petcheneges tribe, however, Boris' son, Symeon, initiated a rebellion. After his victory over the imperial armies in 896, Symeon proclaimed himself ruler of an independent Bulgaria to which Byzantium had to pay an annual tribute. Later, Symeon invaded the Empire and even appeared at the gates of Constantinople in 913. From 913 to 925, his armies laid waste to Thrace and Macedonia, and Symeon took the title of Tsar of the Bulgars in 925. Symeon's son, Peter, (927-969), continued to build a Bulgar empire, independent from Byzantium. He was also recognized as Tsar and tried to maintain good relations with the Empire. However, his close relations with Byzantium angered some Bulgars who turned away from traditional Christianity. Bulgaria was momentarily weakened, but with Prince Samuel (976-1014), the Bulgars rose again from their political and cultural center at Ochrid.

The Bulgarian patriarchate abolished in 971 was reestablished, and a Bulgarian empire was formed stretching from the Adriatic to the Black Sea.

Byzantine reaction under Emporer Basil II (976-1025), was brutal. After long and hard campaigns, Basil crushed the Bulgar army in July 1014. Thousands of Bulgar soldiers were blinded by order of the emperor and sent back to Tsar Samuel. The attempt to create an independent Bulgar empire in defiance of Byzantium had failed.

The Serbs called little attention to themselves in the 10th century. They were the fairly docile vassals of their most powerful neighbors of the moment—of the Bulgars under the Tsars Symeon and Samuel, and of Byzantium. The mountain tribes of the Albanian and Vlachs remained subjects of Byzantium; there were, however, slow but noticeable migrations of Vlach shepherds to the Bulgarian plains.

Thus, by around the year 1000 Byzantium had succeeded without undue effort in discouraging the formation of nation states within its area of influence.

The 10th century was a key period in the shaping of the future nations of central and eastern Europe. Wherever the Roman Church was successfully implanted among "barbarian" peoples, it fostered the creation of durable states independent of the German empire. By contrast, where Byzantine Christianity became dominant, the close association between the church and the empire hindered the formation of independent Slav states. Byzantium used the Greek Orthodox church—which willingly allowed itself to be used—as a means to political domination, just as later during the Ottoman period it would serve as the best agent of Turkish oppression over the Slavs of the Balkans.

DIVERSE DESTINIES IN THE 11TH—13TH CENTURIES

The contrast between the westernized states and the Byzantium-dominated Balkans continued and intensified over three centuries.

The Consolidation of Westernized States: Bohemia, Poland and Hungary

As a fief of the empire, the Duchy of Bohemia became increasingly organized. The duke, a vassal of the empire, was chosen by nobility from the Przemyslide family, but no prescribed order of succession existed. Consequently, upon the death of the sovereign, interior conflicts would arise and unfailingly require the intervention of the emperor. Upon election, the duke would pledge his homage to the emperor—an oath which implied duties on his part, but also granted him certain rights. The right to participate as elector-prince in the election of the emperor is an example of both his duties and rights as a vassal. The 12th century, however, saw the rise of hereditary dukedoms. Taking advantage of the difficulties plaguing the imperial power, in 1198 Premysl I made Bohemia a hereditary kingdom, a fact not confirmed until 1212.

The close ties that united Bohemia to the Empire fostered the growth of Germanic influences. From the 11th century on, German priests, monks and merchants mingled with the Czech peasantry in Bohemia. In order to increase revenues during the 12th century, the Czech nobility adopted a large-scale policy of clearing and settling land similar to that of the West. They invited German colonists to people the new territories, which were generally located in the mountainous regions. At the end of the 12th century, there was a massive influx of German merchants and artisans in Bohemian villages, of which many would organize into communities according to the Law of Magdeburg. The cities, however, maintained their Czech majorities even though the cultural and financial elite were often German. For an extended period of time, this duality of population presented no problems. Conflict between the two was absent even when Emperor Rudolph of Habsburg challenged the king, Premysl-Ottokar (1253-1278), at the end of the 13th century for the Babenberg heritage of Styria, Austria, and Carinthia, which the Bohemian kings had confiscated in 1246. After the defeat and death of Ottokar II on the battlefield at Durnkrut on August 26, 1278, during the minority of Wenceslas II (1278-1305), the regency of Otto of Brandenburg was imposed by the emperor—a regency bitterly resented by the Czechs. At his majority, Wenceslas II succeeded through several fortunate inheritances in briefly making his kingdom the center of an empire. He gathered the crowns of Poland and Hungary around Bohemia in 1300 and 1301, although only for a few years. In 1306, the assassination of Wenceslas' son put a violent end to this period of brilliance. With the death of Wenceslas III expired the masculine line of the national dynasty of the Przemyslides.

The beginnings of the feudal period in Poland were characterized by a constant tug of war between the dukes and the nobility. Surprisingly, the cities were increasingly a force on the side of the nobles. Since the 11th century, Cracow had claimed to be capital of the country, but the cities of Gdansk, Poznan, Wroclaw, and Gniezno were also developing functions as both strongholds and commercial centers. As in Bohemia, the arrival of German colonists in the 12th century modified the ethnic composition of the villages, and sparked growth in skilled crafts and trade. Here also, the communal movement arose in the 13th century, and the Law of Magdeburg was adopted. The more cultivated Germans became the elite of the cities and also served in the clergy. German ecclesiastics introduced the Cistercian reform, while 12 abbeys were founded between 1143 and 1260. The Germans also played an important role in the development of mineral resources; it was at this time that the salt mines of Widliczka, the copper and iron mines of Kielce, and the argentiferous lead mines of Olkusz and Chenciny were opened. In the 13th century, Gdansk, a member of the Hanseatic League, well located at the mouth of the Vistula, became the port through which Polish grain, lumber and ore destined for the West departed, and through which arrived Flemish textiles and Mediterranean products.

During this period the northern plains of Poland were constantly threatened by both the Prussian populations who remained pagan and the Teutonic knights who, under the pretext of converting the heathen, were quick to view the region as an area to be colonized. At the end of the 13th century, the Polish state claimed independence, but its structure was far less stable than that of Bohemia. In 1300, the German bourgeoisie of Cracow even went so far as to offer the crown to the Bohemian king, Wenceslas II.

After the death of St. Stephen, Hungary underwent nearly half a century of difficulties regarding succession: a situation which emperor Henry III tried to turn to his advantage. The problem was settled by Geza I and by his brother, Ladislas, who like St. Stephen, was canonized. St. Ladislas (1075-1095) completed the Christianization of the country. To counter the nobility who had taken advantage of the troubles to strengthen their hold on the government of the country, Ladislas looked to the cities. Already fairly numerous, Ladislas gained their support by often granting them the status of free royal cities. St. Ladislas also turned back attacks by the Cumans. Upon the death of his brother-in-law—the Croatian king, Zvonimir—Ladislas occupied Slavonia and part of Croatia between 1091 and 1095. The Croatian inheritance was definitively brought under the Hungarian crown by the nephew and successor to Ladislas, Coloman (1095-1116), who also occupied Dalmatia in 1105, giving Hungary access to the sea as well as direct contact with the Byzantine Empire. From then until 1918, the kingdom of Croatia-Slavonia was united with Hungary by a personal union. Croatia kept its institutions and privileges by authority of the Ban, a governor representing the king.

Byzantine influence in Hungary increased during the 12th century. Under Geza I, Emperor Michael VII Doukas had already attempted to win Hungarian friendship by offering the king a crown. Intended to be joined with the crown sent to St. Stephen by the Pope, the two were to create the Holy Crown, meant to symbolize the state's arrival at the Millennium. Under the successors of Coloman, notably under Stephen II (1162-1172), emperor Manual Comnenus openly intervened in Hungarian affairs and even occupied Dalmatia from 1163-1180. At the end of the 12th century, Hungary regained its strength and power under King Bela III (1172-1196), who, even though raised at the court of Constantinople, oriented Hungary toward the West. Bela III himself successively married two French princesses, Anne de Chatillon and then Marguerite, the daughter of King Louis VII. Like the rulers of Bohemia and Poland, he encouraged German colonists to immigrate, and settled them mainly in the eastern part of Transylvania. Vlach shepherds also infiltrated Transylvania at this time. Bela III took over St. Stephen's formula, according to which "a kingdom is weak and fragile if it has only one language and only one set of customs."

After the death of Bela III, royal power declined for a time while the nobility grew. Upon his return from the Crusades, King Andras II (1204-1235) was forced to concede the Golden Bull of 1222 to the rebellious nobles, granting them a measure of power over royal politics by means of an annual Diet that met at Szekesfehervar. The Golden Bull gave the nobles the right to dissent, but also guaranteed the rights of free men and of the royal cities. It is interesting to note that the Hungarian Golden Bull closely followed the signing of the Magna Carta by King John of England in 1215 to appease his rebellious English barons.

The Balkans Under Byzantium: The Serbs and the Bulgars

In the 11th century and through most of the 12th century, the Serbians, Bulgars, Albanians and the Vlachs were fairly docile subjects of Byzantium. Byzantine hegemony was both religious and political, and even those national princes that persisted found themselves vassals of the Byzantine Empire. However, upon the death of Manual Comnenus in 1180, those under the yoke of Byzantium seized the opportunity to free themselves during the struggles for succession.

The Serbs had lived divided into the two patriarchal principalities of Rascia and Zeta for a long time. In 1170, Stefan Nemanja, as great *Zupan* of Rascia since 1159, managed to extend his rule to the tribes of Zeta. When the Third Crusade led by Frederick Barbarossa passed through, Nemanja tried to gain the support of the Crusaders. He even held a meeting with Barbarossa at Nich in 1189, and the following year he obtained recognition of Serbian independence from the Byzantine Emperor, Isaac II Angelus. After abdicating in favor of his younger son, Stefan (1196-1227), Stefan Nemanja first withdrew to the Studenica monastery and then to Mount Athos, where he joined another of his sons, Rastko, better known as St. Sava. With some difficulty Stefan managed to keep Serbia independent, both from the Latin Empire set up in Constantinople after the Fourth Crusade and from the Byzantine Empire reorganized at Nicea.

Sava, as head of the autonomous Serbian church, led the coronation of his brother Stefan in 1219. It was in fact the second crowning, as Pope Honius III had already sent a royal crown to Stefan in 1217, hoping in vain to attract the Serbian church back to Rome. Crowned as Stefan I Prvovencani, Stefan was the true founder of the ruling house of Serbia known as the Nemanjic dynasty. After his death in 1227, Serbia completed its organization out of Rascia under Stefan's sons, Radoslav (1227-1233), Vladislav

Eastern Europe (circa 1265)

(1233-1243) and Uros I (1243-1276).

After the conquest by Basil II, the Bulgars were closely controlled by Byzantium and were integrated into the Empire. Even though the Bulgars were able to keep their religious autonomy through the independent archbishopric of Ochrid, Byzantine political and cultural hegmony was overwhelming. Demographically, the Bulgars were diluted in the cities by Greek, Jewish and Armenian newcomers, while Vlachs were slowly infiltrating Macedonia and the plains of the lower Danube, where they encountered another recently arrived tribe, the Cumans. The Vlachs and the Cumans played an important role during the Bulgar uprising staged from Macedonia by the brothers, Peter and Asen, in 1185-1186, with the assistance of Stefan Nemanja. In 1187, Isaac II Angelus left the area between the Danube and the Balkans to the Bulgars. This marked the beginning of the Second Bulgar Empire. In 1187, the Archbishop of Tirnovo solemnly crowned Emperor Asen I (1187-1196) in the church of St. Demetrios. Byzantium accepted this situation reluctantly, and Asen I was faced with constant struggle to defend his throne. In 1196 he was felled by the Boyar, Ivanko, who headed a rebellion incited by Byzantium. Asen's successor, Kalojan (1197-1207), restored the situation. As a result of the Fourth Crusade, Constantinople was in the hands of the Latins, and it was from Pope Innocent II that Kalojan received the imperial crown in 1204. This, however, did not prevent him from reconciling with the Greek Empire at Nicea. Under John Asen II (1218-1242), the Second Bulgar Empire reached its peak: other than Bulgaria, it extended over Thrace, Macedonia and part of Albania. But the Second Empire was as ephemeral as the first. After the death of Asen II, a period of decline began that coincided with the Tartar invasion of 1241, and led to the restoration of the Byzantine Empire 20 years later.

The Tartar Invasion and Its Consequences

In the early years of the 13th century, Genghis Khan consolidated under his command the Tartars of the Golden Horde. A Turkish-Mongolian people from Central Asia, the Tartars succeeded in conquering a vast territory reaching from China to the steppes of the Ukraine. In doing so the Tartars displaced certain nomadic peoples such as the Cumans; some settled on the plains of the Lower Danube, while others found asylum in Hungary. King Bela IV (1235-1270) settled many on the plains between the Danube and the Tisza.

Beginning in 1240, the Tartars launched a series of invasions toward the west. In 1241, under their leader, Orda, a party of Tartars devastated Galicia and Upper Silesia, but were not able to take Cracow. The main body of the Tartar force commanded by Genghis's son, Batu, moved toward Hungary, and on April 11 and 12, 1241, defeated the army of Bela IV at Mohi. The

Tartar army then moved north up the Hungarian plain in an orgy of plundering and devastation, in the process of which a good portion of the local population perished. After wintering in Hungary, the Tartars swept down into Slavonia and Croatia, and in May abruptly turned back toward the Ukraine. The cities and countryside of the Transylvanian valleys were not spared their attentions.

Having taken refuge in Dalmatia, Bela IV returned to find a country shattered by the Tartars. In order to repopulate the devastated areas, he invited foreign settlers—mainly Germans—to enter Hungary. Bela IV also welcomed Ruthenians, who settled on the southern slopes of the northern Carpathians, leaving the Galician plains to the Tartars. Bela also allowed increasing numbers of Vlach shepherds searching for new grazing grounds into Transylvania. Thus the Tartar invasion led to noticible changes in the ethnic composition of the kingdom. By the end of Bela IV's reign, over 15 percent of the Hungarian population was of foreign extraction. At the same time, in order to forestall any future attacks, Bela IV authorized the great lords to construct fortresses in their lands. Fortresses were accordingly built at Trencsen, Kesmark, and Beszterce. Bela himself saw to the fortification of the free royal cities of Buda, Visegrad, Pozsony, and Varasd. Another consequence of the Tartar invasion was the void left on the plains of the western banks of the Lower Danube. Numerous Vlachs seized the opportunity to settle there, and in 1247 the first attempt to establish a Vlacho-Rumanian state was made with the formation of the Principality of Vlacho-Wallachia.

Despite the difficulties encountered, as the 14th century dawned the westernized monarchies of Bohemia, Poland, and Hungary had become well structured political entities. The feudal system—modeled after that of western monarchies—was firmly in place. The dynasties that had originally formed these states, however, were in decline. In Hungary, the national dynasty founded by Arpad ended in 1301 with the death of his last descendent, Andras III (1293-1301). In Bohemia, the Przemyslide dynasty ended with the death of Wenceslas II, while in Poland, the Piast dynasty was experiencing an extremely difficult struggle for succession. The opportunity for foreign intervention was wide open, and the German Holy Roman Empire did not hesitate. The existence of these states as individual entities, however, was never questioned.

In the Balkans, while the Serbs and to a lesser degree the Bulgars had attained partial independence from Byzantium, this was due more to the weakness of the Eastern Empire rather than to any strength or unity on the Slavic peoples' part. The Balkan situation remained precarious for two reasons: their fragile political structures, and the arrival of a new menace—the Ottoman Turks.

Chapter 5

The Age of Ruptures
14th—16th Centuries

After 1300, the gaps that were already visible between the westernized monarchies and the Balkan principalities began to widen. The political, economic, and cultural development of the Latinized West no longer had much in common with the Balkan principalities, which had been dominated by Byzantium and the Orthodox Church since the schism of 1054. Also by 1300, the menace of the Ottomans was on the horizon, threatening to nearly all of Christian Europe.

HUMANISM, REBIRTH, AND CRISIS IN THE WESTERNIZED MONARCHIES (14TH—15TH CENTURIES)

Prosperity in Bohemia and Hungary in the 14th Century

The demise of the national dynasties that founded the states of Bohemia and Hungary was followed by the arrival of two French dynasties, who brought with them a new dynamism characterized by remarkable cultural flowering and economic growth. While the countries of western Europe were beset by the Hundred Years War and by economic and social problems in the wake of the Black Death of 1348-1349, Hungary and Bohemia were experiencing a veritable golden age.

After the grave crisis of succession that shook the country following the death of the last Przemyslide, Bohemia regained stability in 1310 with the ascension to the throne of John the Blind, son of Count Henry of Luxembourg. King John introduced French and Italian culture into a country where German influences had dominated. Under his reign, Bohemia became involved in the great controversies of the West. John sided with

French Dynasties in Central Europe (circa 1350)

Philip VI of Valois upon the outbreak of the Hundred Years War, and it was while fighting for this cause that he died on the battlefield at Crecy on August 26, 1346.

His son and successor, Charles IV (1346-1378), made Bohemia into a powerful state whose political and cultural influences reached into all of central Europe. Highly educated, Charles promoted the arts and letters and was a perfect example of an early humanist, summoning Italian scholars such as Cola di Rienzo to his court. Two years after his ascension to the throne, Charles IV founded the University of Prague, the first non-Germanic university in Central Europe. Charles preferred to accord it bylaws similar to those of the University of Paris. Under his reign the city of Prague expanded, particularly on the southern side of the Moldau with the beginning of construction on the New City *(Nove Mesto)*. The New City was dominated by the Powder Tower and was linked to the Old City *(Stare Mesto)* by a new bridge, named the Charles Bridge. Simultaneously, construction began on the Gothic cathedral of St. Guy, under the direction of the architect Matthew of Arras. Arras was aided by the Czech master-builder Peter Parlerj, who also worked on the Karlstein castle built to house the crown jewels. By the middle of the 14th century, Prague was already a city of 35,000 inhabitants, capital of a centralized state, and seat of an archbishopric. Accomplished in 1347, moving the archbishopric to Prague emancipated the Bohemian church from the rule of the high German clergy.

The state was organized around a framework consisting of a monarchy strongly supported by the aristocracy and the high clergy. The powers of the nobility, however, were clearly delimited by the *Majestas Carolina*, a code that defined the respective privileges of the Crown and the nobles.

Charles IV extended the northern borders of the kingdom toward Silesia, and toward Lusace in the south. Southern expansion was accomplished at the expense of Lower Austria. Elected emperor in 1355, he made Bohemia the heart of the German Holy Roman Empire, a move accomplished with no detriment to the Czechs, whose language remained the official language of Bohemia. The *Golden Bull of 1356* defined the rights of different political bodies within the Empire. Each of the seven prince electors—including the King of Bohemia—became ruler of his own territory, a shrewd move which also confirmed the sovereignty of the Bohemian kingdom, as the Emperor retained supreme judiciary powers.

Prosperity within Bohemia climbed steadily. The countryside possessed rich agricultural reserves, and Bohemia exported wheat and fish to all of southern Germany. Trade brought in considerable revenue to the landed aristocracy. Mines were excavated, producing copper, iron, tin, gold, and most particularly argentiferous lead. At Kutna Hora, standardized coins began to be minted, the first of which was the *gros* of Prague.

The golden age ended with the death of Charles IV, as his demise saw the beginnings of the serious political, economic, and religious crises that would weigh heavily on the future of the country.

In Hungary, the Anjous dynasty (1307-1382) produced the first renaissance. After six years of strife that followed the Arpadian dynasty, the Diet of 1307 offered the Hungarian crown to Charles-Robert of Anjou. Charles-Robert had been strongly supported by the Pope in his candidacy, and was a distant descendant of St. Louis. He was already ruler of Naples and Croatia. During his reign (1307-1342) order was brought to the country through the subduing of an over-bold nobility. Most notable among these was Matthias Csak, who had created a large principality north of the Danube. Charles-Robert also reorganized the army by creating *banderia* (banner regiments), in which the contingents furnished by the nobility were intermingled with the career army paid by the king. His son, Louis the Great (1342-1382), attempted to make the royal power even more efficient and structured. Alongside the Diet representing the nobility, Louis expanded the *King's Council* by inviting representatives of the clergy and the cities to take part.

Under the Anjous dynasty, Hungary became the most powerful country along the Danube. Its gold coin (the *florin*), of the same weight and purity of its namesake of Florence, was clear proof of the country's prosperity. Minting began in 1325, drawing on the vast mineral wealth of the northern Carpathian mountains in Transylvania. In the 14th century, a third of the gold produced in the known world and a fourth of the silver extracted in Europe came from the mines of Hungary. This abundance of precious metals provoked lively trade between Hungary and its neighbors. Italian, German, Czech, and Polish merchants flocked to Hungarian cities in great numbers. With more than three million inhabitants, Hungary was one of the most populous countries of Central Europe. It was part of the vast territory ruled by the House of Anjou, whose influence reached from the Mediterranean to the Baltic. Its power in Central Europe peaked in 1501, when the Polish Diet chose Louis the Great as King of Poland after the death of the last Piast, Casimir III.

The reign of the Anjou sovereigns in Hungary paralleled the appearance and development of a first Renaissance. Italians were numerous in most of the cities, and introduced their culture and techniques. Many Hungarians were also attending the universities of Bologna and Padua. In Hungary itself, religious colleges existed, attended by the growing bourgeoisie. King Louis created two national universities, one at Pecs in 1369, and the second at O-Buda in 1389. Hungarian artists enjoying princely patronage increased their production in all artistic mediums. Examples of civil architecture constructed during this period are the citadels of Zolyom and Pozsony, while

Gothic architecture peaked in Hungary with the construction of the church of Notre Dame in Buda. Sculpture also flourished, and was exemplified by the brothers George and Martin of Kolozsvar, who worked in Bohemia. Their major work was an equestrian statue of St. George at the Hradschin in Prague.

Light and Shadow in Poland of the 14th Century

Paradoxically, although its national Piast dynasty remained intact until 1382, Poland enjoyed a less brilliant history than did its two southern neighbors during the 14th century. Difficulties began in 1300, when the rebellion of the bourgeoisie in Cracow briefly deposed the national dynasty in favor of King Wenceslas II of Bohemia. Wenceslas' reign was short-lived, however, as the Piast Ladislas the Short led a victorious struggle against his Czech rival. Ladislas had himself crowned king in 1305, and in the years that followed attempted to restore unity to the country. Poland was marred by dynastic conflicts, however, conflicts that worked to the advantage of neighboring states by weakening Poland. King John of Bohemia gained a part of Silesia in exchange for the definitive renunciation of Bohemian claims to the Polish crown. A more serious threat came from the Margrave of Brandenburg, who seized several territories east of the Oder, while the Teutonic Knights established firm bases on the shores of the Baltic in Pomerania and at Gdansk. Poland began to recover under Casimir III (1333-1370). While he was forced to leave all of Silesia to Bohemia, Casimir III was able to extend his rule to Mazovia and Galicia. It was the beginning of a slow shift of the Polish center of gravity to the east.

Casimir III, who was the brother-in-law of Charles-Robert of Hungary, never managed to endow his country with the strength and brilliance that Bohemia and Hungary were enjoying. He did, however, improve the internal organization of his kingdom. Casimir consolidated the numerous Polish common laws into a single code, the *Statute of Sielicka* (1364), which among other duties, facilitated the function of judicial institutions. Under Casimir, the nobility was allowed to retain its privileged political and economic status. And like his predecessors, Casimir III encouraged foreign immigration. Germans and western Jews were among those who found asylum in Poland. Under his reign, the countryside was improved, new villages were founded, and the cities developed. A well-known proverb credits Casimir with finding a Poland of wood upon his ascension, and leaving a Poland of stone at his death. He died without a son, and the crown fell to his next of kin, his nephew Louis d'Anjou of Hungary, who ruled until 1382.

Crisis in Bohemia

In the last quarter of the 14th century, the kingdom of Bohemia entered a century-long period of turmoil, dominated by the Hussite controversy. Under Charles IV, Bohemia had already experienced a proliferation of heresies. They were disseminated mainly by individuals of German or Czech origin, who demanded the reform of an excessively wealthy church, and who preached a return to the principles espoused in the Bible. Beginning in 1360, a German priest named Conrad Waldhouser and a Czech prelate, Jean Milic, developed and polished these themes in their sermons. Others, many in contact with the Dutch *Devotio moderna* movement, soon amplified criticisms of the Church. The year 1378 marked the passing of Charles IV and the opening of the Great Schism, and its passing saw increasing demands for reform in a society beginning to feel the effects of a sagging economy. The Church was the sole organization that succeeded in retaining its wealth, and even attempted to augment the taxes received from its lands and the fees received for all new ecclesiastic appointments in order to compensate for the devaluation of the currency.

The economic crisis soon had political and cultural repercussions. While the high clergy and the great Lords looked to the new king Wenceslas IV (1378-1419) for support, others looked elsewhere. Ruined by the economic crisis, the petty nobility as well as the common people of the towns listened with growing interest to the words of the reformist preachers. It was in this context that Jan Hus (1370-1415) appeared. While a student at the University of Prague, Hus read the works of the reformers of the time, particularly those of Jan Wiclif. He also became conscious of the social contrast between the Germanized upper class and the mainly Czech petty bourgeois and commoners in the cities of Bohemia. As a priest and Master of the Faculty of Theology, Hus began to preach in Bethlehem Chapel in Prague in 1402. Speaking in the Czech language to a very mixed audience, Hus took a strong position against the wealth of the Church, and in particular against simony. Up until 1409, he believed it possible to reform the Church from above, should reform efforts be supported by the king and the Pope. But when the Archbishop of Prague excommunicated followers of Wiclif, Hus and his colleagues officially broke with the Church, along with the king and the segment of the nobility that had supported them from the beginning. The break increased the support Hus received from the common people.

From 1410 on, Hus wrote numerous works in Latin and in Czech, repeating his criticisms of the Church and emphasizing the necessity to return to the Holy Scriptures. In this spirit, he produced the first translation of the Bible in Czech. Summoned by the Council of Constance and equipped with a safe conduct from Emperor Sigismund, brother of Wenceslas IV, Hus went to Constance and vehemently defended his ideas against Church officers such as the Chancelor of the University of Paris, Jean Gerson, who criticized Hus's preachings for the social consequences they could produce.

The death of Jan Hus at the stake on July 6, 1415, followed by that of his disciple, Jerome of Prague, on May 30, 1416, instigated serious disturbances in Bohemia, peasant uprisings in the country, and revolts in the cities. Some of the nobles took advantage of the circumstances to seize church holdings, and followers of Hus—known as Hussites—organized a parallel "church," in which they practiced dual communion in order to demonstrate that despite the prohibition decreed by the Council in 1415, church priests and laymen were to be treated in the same way. The Bohemian rebellion reached its peak on July 30, 1419, when the most radical Hussites led by minister Jan Zeliv seized the city hall at *Nove Mesto* in Prague, and massacred ten magistrates who had remained faithful to the Roman Catholic church.

The unexpected death of Wenceslas IV on August 16, 1419, resulted in a break between the Hussites and the crown. The Bohemian Diet refused to recognize Emperor Sigismund as king, as on August 1, 1420, Pope Martin V called for a crusade against the followers of Wiclif and Hus. Supported by the common people of the towns and countryside and by a segment of the nobility, the Hussites attempted to organize a true "republic;" the high nobility and most of the Germans, however, sided with Sigismund. The religious crisis was compounded by social unrest, leading to open confrontation between the Germans and the Czechs. From 1420 to 1436, the Hussite Wars ravaged Bohemia and Moravia, not only pitting the Crusaders against the Hussites but also dividing the Hussites into moderates and radicals. Among the latter, John Zizka of Trocnov attempted an egalitarian republican experiment under the direction of reformers at Tabor from 1420 to 1424, based on Bible instruction. The Crusades failed one after the other, and by 1430 weariness began to overtake both sides. Finally, negotiations between King Sigismund and the Bohemian Diet resulted in the *Compacta*, the compromise of July 5, 1436. Catholicism was reestablished in Bohemia, but the *Utraquistes*—those who took dual communion—were recognized as "true and faithful children of the Church." At the same time, Sigismund ratified by royal decree all of the property conveyances that had been made at the expense of the Church. He also made Czech the only official language of the country. Religious peace was thus restored, and the moderate Hussites welcomed the reform of the Church as resolved by the Councils of Basil and Constance; the country, however, lay in ruins.

Hussite ideas were received with some interest outside of Bohemia and most notably in Hungary, where Sigismund had reigned since 1387. The Slovaks in the northwest of Hungary, related to the Czechs although separated from them since the 10th century, initiated several Hussite-inspired peasant uprisings. In 1437, Hungarian peasants and Transylvanian Vlachs revolted against the Church and their feudal lords. The cities were affected as well: in Pozsony, there were violent confrontations between the poor and the upper classes.

While the Hussite movement failed to accomplish its most radical intentions, it did succeed in shaking the foundations of the Catholic church in Bohemia. It also put an end to the peaceful coexistence of Germans and Czechs, and inspired a Czech patriotism associated with devotion to Jan Hus. Hus was accordingly elevated to the role of national hero. Confronted by the theoretically reconciled Catholics and Utraquistes, diehard Hussites reorganized in the form of the United Brotherhood, a movement that stressed the need for strict adherence to the letter of the laws in the scriptures, and for the equality and fraternity which they believed should unite all men. Peter of Chelcice (1390-1470) was the leader of the Brotherhood, which by 1460 was organized into a church combining faith and humanism.

After the death of Sigismund, the Catholics were briefly in command again under Albert of Habsburg (1437-1439) and his eldest son Ladislas (1440-1457). As was the case under Sigismund, Bohemia and Hungary were joined by a common sovereign. But in contrast to a Bohemia weakened and torn by religious conflicts, Hungary had remained loyal to the Roman church and represented a haven of peace in Central Europe.

Independent Hungary at Its Height (1458-1490)

After the death of Louis the Great, the Hungarian crown went to the deceased king's eldest daughter and Emperor Sigismund's wife, Marie. Under the reigns of Sigismund and his immediate successors, Hungary's destiny was intimately linked to that of the Empire and Bohemia. The frequent absence of a king concerned with crusades against the Turks and Hussites allowed the high nobility to strengthen its power at the expense of the cities and the peasants.

Upon the death of Ladislas V (also king of Bohemia under the title Ladislas I), the Hungarian Diet of January 1458 rejected the Habsburg candidate Emperor Frederick III in favor of a national king, Matyas Hunyadi. Born in 1443, Matyas came from a Transylvanian petty noble family that first made history when his father, Janos Hunyadi, stopped the Turks at Belgrade in 1456. Matyas is often referred to as Matthias Corvinus, a term originated by the Italian humanist, Bonfini. The name refers to the king's coat of arms; the coat of arms of the Hunyadi family contains a crow, *corvus* in Latin, which is an allusion to the family's origin in the village of Hollos, meaning "to crow" in Hungarian.

Matthias Corvinus was one of Europe's greatest sovereigns during the

15th century. Under his reign, Hungary became the heart of a vast empire centered around the Danube. Matthias' fidelity to Rome earned him a directive from the Pope to conduct a new crusade against the Bohemian Hussites, who were resurfacing. In 1458, the Bohemian Diet had elected as king a Czech lord, George of Podebrady, who had never attempted to disguise his sympathies for the Hussites. As King George of Podebrady (1458-1470), the monarch wished to reconcile the Catholics and the Utraquistes within a national Czech church free from Roman authority, and disentangled from the radical elements of the United Brotherhood. Pope Paul II excommunicated King George, and in 1466 gave Matthias Corvinus the responsibility for conducting the crusade. Beginning in 1468, the king of Hungary led several campaigns in Bohemia, having at his disposal the well-trained troops of the Black Army, who were well paid and supported by Czech Catholic lords of the Zelena Hora Union. During a Diet session held at Brno, Matthias was elected king of Bohemia and had himself crowned in 1470.

The death of King George of Podebrady in 1471 reopened the question. The Bohemian crown passed to the Polish prince, Vladislav Jagiello (1471-1516). Yet while under the peace terms of Olomouc, Matthias had to give up Bohemia, it was also understood that during his lifetime he would keep Moravia and Silesia. Matthias, however, did not discontinue his policies of expansion. He attacked his old rival, Emperor Frederick III, seizing Vienna in 1485 and the Duchy of Styria the following year. It seemed for a time that Matthias considered himself a candidate for the Imperial throne. Any such hopes were nourished by his reputation as the defender of Christianity against the forces of Islam, earned by his victories over the Turks in the Balkans.

Hungary under Matthias Corvinus was one of the great states of Europe, with a population of over 3,500,000 inhabitants of which 80 percent were Magyar. It was as populous as England at the time. While most of the inhabitants of the kingdom were either free peasants or serfs dependent upon the church and/or nobles, the cities continued to expand. The residence of the sovereign was Buda, which reached 20,000 inhabitants, while Pozsony, Kassa, and Kolozsvar came close to that number. Although the gold and silver mines were experiencing a period of stagnation, the copper mines of Besztercebanya produced a flourishing refining industry, promoted by the Polish financier and entrepreneur John Thuro.

Like the Italian princes of his time, Matthias Corvinus welcomed humanists at his court. Included were Hungarians such as his teachers Janos Vitez and John the Pannonian, or the financier Clement Ernuszt. Italians were also made welcome, and among those that were accepted were Bonfini, Galotti, Ugoletto, and Bartolome della Fonte. The influence of Italian culture began to increase and in 1476, King Matthias married the daughter of the king of Naples, Beatrice of Aragon. Education made great progress; a new university was created at Pozsony in 1467, and the old University of O-Buda was expanded and moved to Buda. This did not stop increasing numbers of Hungarian students from attending universities in Vienna, Cracow, Prague, Paris, Bologna, or Padua. In Buda, Matthias founded a royal library titled the Corvina, which housed nearly a thousand volumes including priceless Greek and Latin manuscripts. Adjoining the Corvina was a workshop where some thirty transcribers worked under the direction of the humanist Felix of Ragus. In 1471, at the invitation of the vice-chancellor Ladislas Kara, the German scholar Andreas Hess set up Buda's first printing press, which printed the *Chronica Hungarorum* by Thuroczy in 1473.

The spirit of humanism and the Renaissance was also expressed in art. In Buda, the king had a palace constructed and embellished with works of Italian masters such as Verrocchio and Botticelli. Unfortunately, like most buildings of that period, the Buda palace was destroyed by the Turks in the 16th century. Numerous retables and pieces of gold and silverware, however, still exist today as examples of the artistic expression of 15th century Hungary.

THE OTTOMANS IN EASTERN EUROPE (14TH—15TH CENTURIES)

The appearance of the Ottoman Turks in the early 14th century not only accentuated the striking contrasts between the westernized monarchies and the Balkans, but posed a permanent threat to all of centro-Danubian Europe.

The Beginnings of Ottoman Power

The decline of the Byzantine Empire began in 1204 with the conquest of Constantinople by the crusaders of the Fourth Crusade. It was not arrested by either the fall of the Roman Empire in 1261, nor the Byzantine restoration that followed. In Europe, the Bulgarian and Serbian subject peoples of Byzantium had succeeded in attaining their freedom, but the real danger to Byzantium as well as to the Slavic states of the Balkans came from Asia. Until the end of the 13th century, Asia Minor was in the hands of the Seljuk Turks. Around 1300, however, the Seljuks were deposed by a group of Turks from Central Asia, who took their name, Ottomans, from their leader, Osman (1288-1326). Osman and his son, Orkhan (1326-1360) set up a powerful Muslim state in Asia Minor, with an efficient army dominated by an elite corps called the Janissaries. The Ottomans soon relieved the Greeks of their last holdings in Asia with the seizure of Nicea in 1329, and of Nicomedia in 1337.

Confronted by the Ottomans, Byzantium followed a policy of cooperation with the newcomers rather than one of opposition. The usurper John VI, known as John of Cantacuzene, tried to flatter Sultan Orkhan by giving him his daughter in marriage in 1346, and by not hesitating to use the Ottomans against his rival, John V. John VI then paid the Ottomans homage by handing over the fortress of Gallipoli, which gave them a much-desired fortress in Europe.

As for the Slavic states of the Balkans, they were generally not powerful enough to successfully resist the Ottoman invasion. The Bulgars, in a period of decline since the end of the 13th century, were dealt another blow when Murat I (1359-1389) took part of Thrace and Macedonia, and established his capital at Andrinople in 1365. The newly-founded Vlach principalities north of the Danube—Wallachia in 1247 and Moldavia in 1352—were still too disorganized to counter the Turks. Only the Serbs possessed any degree of power at that time.

The Peak of Serbian Power

The disintegration of the Byzantine Empire and the eclipse of Bulgaria worked to the advantage of the Serbs in the Balkans. The Nemjanidic dynasty which founded the Serbian state in the early 13th century had succeeded in keeping Serbia out of the crises that affected the Balkans, and maintained the independence of their principality. Under Stephen VI Uros II (1282-1321) and Stephen VIII Uros III (1321-1331), Serbia extended its authority to include Macedonia and Bulgaria. But it was under Stephen IX Dusan (1333-1355) that Serbia reached its peak. Dusan ruled over an "empire" that included Rascia, Zeta, Macedonia, Albania, and Thessalia up to the Gulf of Corinth. Serbia was freed from the religious yoke of the Patriarch of Constantinople and in 1346, the Archbishop of Pec was raised to the rank of "Patriarch of all Serbs," and was elected solely by Serbian bishops. It was the same patriarch that crowned Uskub Stephen Dusan as Czar of the Serbs and Greeks.

Dusan improved the administration of the country and made the laws more just through the imposition of a king's code, the *zakonik*—a mixture of Serbian customs and Byzantine law. Serbia soon matured into a thoroughly organized feudal society. Enriched by royal donations, the lay nobility and the monasteries enjoyed full authority over the peasants, who tilled the hereditary plots in exchange for rent and services. The king invited "Saxon" colonists from Hungary to work the copper, gold and silver mines, which permitted the minting of Serbian coins. In spite of its power, however, the Serbian state was not strong enough to oppose the Ottomans.

The Balkans in the Hands of the Turks

From secure bases in Thrace, Murat I avoided attacking Byzantium directly, preferring to strike the first blows in the Balkan Slavic states. After 1370, Serbia underwent a period of difficulties culminating in the breakup of the country. The north was retained by Dusan's descendants, and the south remained torn by the internal bickering of the aristocracy. Murat I attacked the Serbs first, and southern Serbia fell without striking a blow; Sofia conceded in 1385 and Nich the following year. Northern Serbia resisted longer but on June 15, 1389, Murat crushed the army of the Serbian prince Lazar on the field of Kosovo. During the course of the battle, Murat was killed and Lazar was taken captive by the Turks and beheaded. Soon after, Bulgaria, which had remained weak during this period, yielded when Tirnovo fell on July 17, 1393. From there, the Turks moved toward the Danube. With the support of Hungarian reinforcements sent by King Sigismund, the Vlach prince, Mircea the Old, attempted to stop the Turkish army but was defeated. Mircea surrendered to the Turks and was required to pay them a tribute, although he was allowed to keep token political and religious autonomy of his principality.

The West was long in reacting. Only Emperor Sigismund took the initiative and mounted a crusade composed of German, Hungarian, and Vlach contingents, as well as a force of 10,000 men sent by the king of France under the command of John the Fearless, son of the Duke of Burgundy. The crusade ended in a bloody defeat at Nicopolis on September 28, 1396.

The new sultan, Bayezid, became master of the Balkans. The Ottoman danger, however, was temporarily delayed by a conflict between Bayezid and the Mongol prince Tamerlan Khan in 1402. Bayezid's grandson Murat II (1421-1451) reestablished Ottoman power, and the Serbs and Bulgars who had been briefly emancipated in the early 15th century yielded to the Ottoman regime again. The Turks, however, met fierce resistance from the Albanians, a people of shepherds isolated in their mountains, and who had been successively subjects of Byzantium, the Bulgars, the Serbs, and from the beginning of the 15th century, the Ottomans as well. Under the leadership of Skanderbeg, a nobleman and a Turkish government official, Albanian tribes rose and Skanderbeg proclaimed himself Prince of Albania and Epirus. The Albanian uprising coincided with a Hungarian intervention in Serbia under the leader of the Vajda of Transylvania, Janos Hunyadi. It was Hungary's response to the call for a crusade put forth by the Council of Florence in 1439. Hunyadi was successful at Nich in 1443, and pushed the Turks back as far as Sophia. During the battle, however, the king of Bohemia and Hungary, Vladislas I, was killed as was the papal delegate, Cesarini. Almost simultaneously, Skanderbeg was defeated at Kosovo.

Janos Hunyadi reinitiated the struggle in 1448. Defeated at first in

Serbia, between 1448 and 1452 he set up a system of fortresses along the Hungaro-Serbian borders which was dominated by the fortress of Belgrade, entrusted to Hunyadi by the Serbs. After Mohammed II took Constantinople on May 29, 1453—by which time the Turks were in firm control of the Balkans—the Turks launched a major offensive on the West. At the request of Pope Calixtus III and his legate John Capistrano, Hunyadi organized the defense of Belgrade. On August 6, 1456, he successfully withstood Turkish assaults, but both he and Capistrano were wounded. Both died a few days later, but Hungary had earned a reputation as the "Shield of Christianity." In honor of the victory at Belgrade, the Pope ordered that the bells of all Christian churches ring the midday *angelus*.

The Turks were on the defensive against Matthias Corvinus. Preoccupied as they were with absorbing their last conquest, the Byzantine Empire, the Turks neglected the Balkans. Corvinus briefly recaptured Bosnia in 1463, Moldavia and Wallachia in 1467, and Serbia in 1482, but he was not able to force the Turks out of the Balkans.

The Final Assault of the Turks

After the death of Matthias Corvinus, the regions that he had liberated were quickly recaptured by the Turks. In spite of resistance by the Vlach prince, Vlad the Impaler, Wallachia became a vassal state of the sultan, and was soon followed by Moldavia. In the early 16th century, the Turks continued their westward advance, reaching the plains of the Sava valley and circumventing the obstacle of the fortress of Belgrade, which they finally managed to take in 1521.

The Turks were in a fortunate position. They had as an ally the French king, Francis I, who was involved in a quarrel with Charles V. They also benefited from the weakening of Hungary under the successors of Matthias Corvinus, Vladislav II Jagiello (1490-1516) and his son Louis II (1516-1526), who were embroiled in a struggle with the aristocracy with the peasant revolt of George Dozsa. They were thus unable to resist the Turkish threat without assistance.

The two sovereigns also ruled Bohemia, but any assistance they might have wished for was limited by the permanent religious struggles in that country. Louis II appealed to western rulers for help several times, but in vain. The king of France was allied with the Turks, and Emperor Charles V was busy at war against France and also occupied by the religious crisis in Germany. Moreover, by the beginning of the 16th century the idea of a crusade had been dead for a long time. When the Turks invaded Hungary in 1525, Louis II could offer only weak resistance. The Vajda (viceroy) of Transylvania, John Zapolyai, did not even condescend to reply to his call for help. At the battle of Mohacs on August 29, 1526, the Hungarian army, including the majority of Magyar aristocracy, was crushed, and Louis II drowned in the Csele creek, pulled down by his armour. As well as its king, Hungary lost its independence that day. From then on, only the Habsburg monarchy, carefully reorganized by Charles V, could stop the Turks.

THE HABSBURGS AGAINST THE TURKS AND THE REFORMATION

Mohacs marked the definitive end of the age of national independent monarchies in Central Europe. Only the great powers of western Europe—France and the Holy Roman Empire—could defend Christianity from the threat posed by the Turkish advance. As France had become a Turkish ally under Francis I, the defense of the Christian world thus fell to the Holy Roman Empire under the reign of the Habsburgs. It was less a matter of reconquest than of salvaging what could still be saved; Hungary was considered lost.

The Consequences of Mohacs

The defeat of the Hungarian Army and the death of King Louis II on the battlefield at Mohacs had two serious consequences. First, Hungary was at the mercy of the Turkish armies. Fortunately, after pillaging and rampaging through the central and southern plains of the country, these armies returned to their bases in the Balkans. Secondly and more significantly, the thrones of Bohemia and Hungary were left vacant with the untimely passing of Louis II.

In a Bohemia divided again by religious strife kindled by Luther's ideas, the Diet announced its support for the brother-in-law of the deceased king, Archduke Ferdinand of Habsburg, also brother of Charles V. In Hungary, the succession was a more difficult matter. A diet dominated by the petty gentry designated the Vajda of Transylvania, John Zapolyai, as king, with hopes that this prince who had not participated in the struggle against the Turks would be able to forestall further attacks on the country. Another diet dominated by the high nobility held at Pozsony in 1526, however, decided against the "national" candidate in favor of the "German" one—Ferdinand, already king of Bohemia. While Zapolyai was Hungarian and not in the bad graces of the Turks, Ferdinand of Habsburg was not only related to the deceased king, giving him a certain legitimacy, but also offered greater security to the country. Ferdinand had behind him all the strength of both the Holy Roman Empire and the countries under the crown of Spain. Hungary thus had two kings, each with the support of a part of the country: Zapolyai in Transylvania, and Ferdinand in western and northern Hungary. Each tried energetically to oust his rival. Ferdinand I (1526-1560) took Buda on August 20, 1527, from Sultan Sulijman, who fled to Poland. Zapolyai (1526-1560) allied himself with the Turks, and with their help was able to establish himself in Transylvania, which he made the base of his power.

The breakup of the Hungarian kingdom after Mohacs altered the status of Transylvania. Until the 16th century, Transylvania had been an integral part of the Hungarian kingdom, with the same laws and institutions. The presence of a Vajda as representative of the king was explained by the geographical distance between Transylvania and Buda, the center of the state. With Zapolyai, Transylvania became an independent principality, with a diet at Gyulafehervar composed of delegates from the three privileged nationalities—Magyar, Saxon, and Szekely—whose role it was to elect the prince and to assist him through a council elected by the Diet. For two centuries, Transylvania would attempt to become a Hungarian state, yet one independent of the Habsburgs. It was to play the role of a third power between the Habsburgs and the Turks.

Reform and Counter-Reform in Central Europe

The Turkish advance into the Danubian region coincided with the breakup of Christian unity in Central Europe caused by the Protestant Reformation. Moral and religious unity had already been severely shaken in the 15th century by the heresies of Wiclif and Hus. In the Holy Roman Empire, the need for ecclesiastic reform was almost universally accepted, but the interpretations of the means to attain it differed. In Bohemia, Hussite ideas remained firmly entrenched among a large portion of the population, and the United Brotherhood continued to spread them.

In the early 16th century, the fragile religious peace in Bohemia was shattered by the preachings and writings of Luther and his disciples. Luther's ideas, set forth in his *Ninety-five Theses* posted in November 1517, called into question both church doctrine on salvation and the authority of the Pope and the church hierarchy. His ideas were very similar to those expressed by Hus over a century earlier. Condemned by Rome in 1520, Luther's ideas resounded throughout the Empire and launched a lively polemic. Many German princes took advantage of the situation to secularize the holdings of the Church, as the Czech lords had done a century earlier. In Bohemia and Hungary, Lutheran thought was well received at the court of Louis II, encouraged by Queen Maria. Lutheranism developed rapidly in Bohemia, uniting Germans and Czechs formerly divided by Hussite ideas. Some of the Utraquistes who had been reconciled with Rome after the agreement of 1436 came over to Luther's position, proclaiming the Scriptures to be the only source of faith. In spite of certain differences, Bohemian Lutherans and the United Brotherhood settled on a compromise in 1542. It appeared that the reformation had triumphed. Despite some difficulties, the United Brotherhood remained active, particularly in the cultural field. Their bishop Jan Blahoslav (1523-1571) was an active humanist. He founded a school and a printing press at Ivancine, where a Czech grammar book, the Bible of Kralice, and numerous works of religious music were published.

As a German in Hungary, Luther initially was not well received. Only the German communities in the cities paid any attention to his ideas. In Transylvania, the city of Brasso (Kronstadt), in which many Saxon colonists resided, was the first city to turn to Lutheranism largely through the efforts of John Honterus. The mining cities of Upper Hungary, also inhabited by German colonists, followed shortly thereafter. Finally, at the moment when the Turkish armies were about to descend on Hungary, the Reformation made its appearance among the Hungarian populations on the plains of the Tisza and the Transdanubia. The Reformation was even more successful after 1553 in its Calvinist form. In the part of Hungary that remained in the hands of the Habsburgs and particularly in the areas occupied by the Turks, Calvin's ideas spread rapidly. The Turks assisted their spread by weakening the Habsburgs. In the Middle of the 16th century, the city of Debrecen became the spiritual center of Hungarian Calvinism, under the direction of Martin Kalmancsehi, former canon of Gyulafehervar, who preached reform among the Hungarians of Transylvania. Protestants rapidly became a majority in Transylvania, where Church properties were quickly secularized. Side by side, Hungarian Calvinism and German Lutheranism opposed a Catholicism that was clearly diminished in size and influence, but that retained firm bases of support. In Transylvania, the Reformation proved to be tolerant, and the Diet of Torda proclaimed freedom of religion in 1558. In Hungary as in Bohemia, the Reformation showed intellectual leanings, favoring the vernacular language instead of Latin. In 1591, the humanist reformer Gaspar Heltai finished his translation of the Bible into Hungarian. Numerous Protestant colleges opened, some in Transylvania, others in Habsburg, Hungary, or in territory occupied by the Turks. The most famous were those at Sarospatak (still in use today), at Debrecen, and at Papa.

Rome did not stand idly by watching the fragmentation of western Christianity—particularly at a moment when Islam was gaining firm ground in the Danubian countries. In the Holy Roman Empire, the Peace of Augsburg concluded in 1555 formally recognized the Lutherans. The Habsburgs, however, in their role as traditional defenders of the Catholic faith, had not given up the desire of destroying Protestantism in their hereditary possessions—by force if necessary. Rome chose to act more by persuasion, countering the Protestant Reformation with the Counter-Reformation, which was essentially a Catholic Reformation. Elaborated at the Council of Trent (1545-1563) and entrusted to the Jesuits, the Counter-Reformation successfully won back a number of followers and positions that had been lost, notably in southern Germany, Austria, Bohemia, Hungary, and Poland.

The Counter-Reformation was most violent in Bohemia, because of the radical position adopted by the reformers and because under the pretext of religious reform, royal authority was called into question. At the beginning of the reign of Ferdinand I, religious peace ruled in Bohemia. Conflict broke out, however, when the king decided to raise an army without consent from the Diet in order to combat the German Protestants of the Smalkald League. Prague and most of the cities rose up declaring themselves for the League, and after defeating the German Protestants in 1547, King Ferdinand punished the rebellious cities harshly. He took away their hard-won privileges, installed Catholic administrators, and deprived them of their wealth by confiscating the land they owned in the flat country and giving it to the Catholic nobility. Taking advantage of his position, in 1554 Ferdinand successfully convinced the Diet to vote for the hereditary monarchy of the Habsburgs in Bohemia. Also concerned with reestablishing the position of the Catholic Church, the king abandoned the policy of tolerance he had practiced up until then. The United Brotherhood and the Utraquistes converted to Lutheranism were severely persecuted, as were their sympathizers. Taking over the business of restoration, in 1556 the Jesuits opened a university, the Clementium, in Prague. In Moravia they founded the colleges of Olomouc in 1566 and Brno in 1572. Jesuit colleges welcomed the sons of noble families, and these later became the zealous propagators of the Catholic Reformation.

The successors to Ferdinand, Maximilian II (1564-1576) and Rudolph II (1576-1612) carried on the efforts against heresy. However, in 1575 a Czech Confession modeled on the Peace of Augsburg of 1555 was accepted by the king, and established a climate of relative tolerance. In Hungary, on the other hand, tolerance dominated in all areas, and the Catholic Counter-Reformation moved more slowly and with a much more tolerant attitude, even when it gained the upper hand in the 17th century.

Conflict with the Turks

In early 1529, the Turks reappeared in Hungary and established firm bases on the South Hungarian plain. They benefited appreciably from the support of the national king, John Zapolyai. On August 18, 1529, "king" Zapolyai paid homage to Sultan Suliman II. His hostility to the Habsburg King Ferdinand led him to offer Hungary to the Turks, and it was in his name that the Turks made war on the country, "liberating" Buda on September 7. Only western Hungary and the mountainous regions of the north and northwest remained under the Habsburgs.

Nevertheless, despite the Hungarian captain Jurisich's victory over the Turks at Koszeg between August 10-29, 1532, Ferdinand I was forced to negotiate. Like his Transylvanian rival, he became a vassal of the sultan with jurisdiction over the part of Hungary that he controlled. He and Zapolyai quickly realized that their rivalry profited only the Turks, and in 1538 they concluded the Peace of Nagyvarad. The agreement stipulated that upon Zapolyai's death the crown would return to the Habsburgs, but that during his life Zapolyai would retain the title in Transylvania.

At the death of Ferdinand I, his successor, Maximilian (1564-1576) alone held the title of King of Hungary, while Zapolyai's son John-Sigmund became Prince of Transylvania. For the second half of the 16th century, the Habsburgs attempted to contain the advance of the Turks, with moderate success. At the close of the 16th century, the Habsburgs consolidated their position as defenders of Catholicism and champions of the struggle against Islam. They reigned uncontested over the parts of Bohemia and Hungary which were not controlled by the Turks. It was the beginning of a multinational empire possessing enough power from its Germanic possessions to seriously consider clearing the Turks out of the Danubian basin.

A HAVEN OF PEACE: POLAND IN THE 15TH AND 16TH CENTURIES

Poland Under the First Jagiellons (1382-1572)

Upon the death of Louis d'Anjou, Poland was again confronted with the problem of succession. The deceased king had promised his daughter, Hedwig, to the Grand Duke of Lithuania, Jagiellon. Hedwig was proclaimed queen at the age of 10 in 1384, and she brought to the throne her husband, who was baptized with the name of Ladislas II (Wladyslaw II).

Under Hedwig and Ladislas II (1386-1434), a union was affected between Poland and the Grand Duchy of Lithuania. The union fostered the spread of Christianity in Lithuania, where the bishopric of Wilno was founded. It also allowed the Lithuanians to escape the grasp of the Teutonic Knights, who attempted to intervene and were defeated at the battle of Tannenberg. The Polono-Lithuanian victory regained Lithuania an access to the Baltic Sea.

The Polono-Lithuanian union continued after the death of Ladislas II. His son, Ladislas III (1434-1444), who also reigned over Hungary after 1440, took part in the struggle against the Turks and died in the disastrous battle at Varna. He was succeeded by Ladislas II's other son Casimir IV Jagiellon (1444-1492), who battled the Teutonic Knights from 1454 to 1466. With the **Peace of Torun**, Casimir IV regained Pomerania between the Oder and the Vistula rivers. Poland also recovered an important maritime outlet, the port of Gdansk.

Under the first Jagiellons, Poland and Lithuania became an enormous state that reached from the Baltic to the steppes of the Ukraine. The cities, long populated by foreigners—mostly Germans—slowly became more Polish. The best example of this is the capital of Cracow, where by the end of the 15th century the Polish element had become a majority. Cracow was also the cultural capital of the country with a university founded in 1364. In the 15th century, Cracow's intellectuals distinguished themselves in theology, mathematics, and particularly in astronomy. Cracow's native son Nicolas Copernicus made the city famous in the early 16th century. By the mid-17th century, over 700 attended the University of Cracow.

The organization of the state was refined under Casimir Jagiellon. Along with the functions of the king and the high dignitaries of the kingdom—including the Archbishop Primate, entrusted with the continuity of the state in case of a power vacuum—Casimir Jagiellon established rules for the operation of the Diet. It was to be made up of two assemblies, the Senate and the Chamber of Deputies, both elected by the nobility. A principle was established requiring the unanimous consent of the senators and deputies for any new law, public or private. This provision was to cripple the operation of the Diet in years to come.

Poland's Golden Age

The military victories of the first Jagiellons gave Poland the strength to stand as an independent great power against the Holy Roman Empire and the Teutonic Knights in the west and in the north, and against the Tartars and the rising Muscovite state in the east. They also afforded the country an era of peace in the 16th century, which fostered the birth and development of a brilliant civilization. The absence of problems of succession and the advance toward a dynastic monarchy strengthened institutional stability. Although the first two successors to Casimir Jagiellon, Albert (1492-1501) and Alexander (1501-1506) reigned only briefly, Sigismund I (1506-1548) reigned long enough to prepare the way for a hereditary monarchy. Sigismund had only one son, and in 1530 had him recognized as King of Poland and Grand Duke of Lithuania. Sigismund Augustus (1548-1572) inherited both crowns without difficulty upon his father's death, and the union of Poland and Lithuania was consolidated. In fact, Sigismund Augustus had the Diet of 1569 adopt the Union of Lublin, a decision that made Poland and Lithuania a united and indivisible state. The consolidation was not complete as each of the two parts kept their own legal and judicial systems as well as their own armies, but a republic was formulated with a common sovereign elected by a *Sejm* (Diet) representing both nations. The resulting Great Poland encompassed more than 325,000 sq. miles of territory, contained nearly eight million inhabitants, and lasted for nearly two centuries. As was the Habsburg monarchy's formation at the same time,

Poland was a multinational state in which the Polish majority coexisted with urban-based Germans, as well as with Lithuanians and Ukrainians.

In the 16th century, Poland was profoundly affected by the Reformation. The Lutheran reform movement first reached the northern towns with their German populations. In 1525, the Grand Master of the Teutonic Order, Albert of Brandenberg, secularized the property of his order and took the title of Duke of Prussia, vassal of the Polish king. Within a few years, all of the towns on the Baltic coast had become Lutheran. At first, King Sigismund I was opposed to the Reformation. In 1526, he crushed a Lutheran sedition at Gdansk, but the development of the Reformation was so obvious that a climate of tolerance slowly took shape. German Poles and Polish intellectuals accepted nearly all of the principles of the Reformation. As in Hungary, the Germans followed Luther while Calvin's ideas found more of a following among the Poles. By the middle of the 16th century, Poland was a multi-religious state where, as in Transylvania, tolerance became official in 1572. Despite condemnation by the Catholic clergy, mixed marriages were frequent and accepted by the civil authorities. And when Henry of Valois was elected King of Poland in 1573, he took on the cause of preserving religious peace. Ironically, he was the brother of the French king Charles IX, who ordered the St. Bartholomew Day massacre. Before receiving the royal crown, however, Henry announced "I will see that peace reigns among those whom religion brings into discord."

As tolerance was the official policy, the Catholic Church attempted to recover lost territories through peaceful means. The Bishop of Varmy, Stanislas Hosius, was the main architect of the Polish Counter-Reformation. In 1551 he published the *Confession of Catholic Faith*, in which he advocated the principle doctrines of Catholicism. Hosius became a cardinal in 1560, participated in the Council of Trent, and subsequently moved to Rome. At his request, the Jesuits entered Poland in 1564 and reestablished the reputation of the University of Cracow. Colleges were founded throughout the country, notably at Wilno, Poznan, and Warsaw.

The Catholic reconquest was facilitated by the activities of a number of preachers, one of the most eloquent and active of which was the Jesuit P. Skarga (1536-1612). The Catholic Church tried to bring Poland's new subjects, the Orthodox Ukrainians, back into the fold of the Roman church. The resulting Compromise of Brest-Litovsk gave birth to the Uniate Church, which recognized the authority of the Pope while keeping the Greek rites.

The climate of tolerance favored the development of humanism and scientific advancement. King Sigismund, who had married an Italian princess, Bona Sforza, was a well educated patron of the arts and letters, as was his son Sigismund Augustus. The University of Cracow came into its hour of glory with the accomplishments of the School of Astronomy, exemplified by Copernicus. Nicolas Copernicus was born in Torun in 1473, and was considered the archetypal Renaissance man after having studied in Cracow, Prague, Padua, Bologna, and Ferrara. Copernicus held doctorates in canon law and in medicine, but is best known for his treatise *De Revolutionibus Oribium Celestium*, in which he put forth the idea of a helio-centric solar system as well as a modified view of orbital rotation. Copernicus was also interested in economics, and laid the groundwork for a study on monetary systems which foreshadowed the subsequent works of Gresham. The University of Cracow also was an active center in the field of ancient and eastern languages, and led the publication of works on history and geography.

The spiritual and intellectual wealth of Poland in the 16th century was matched by obvious economic prosperity. The Polish aristocracy continued with a policy pioneered in the 14th century of systematically clearing and developing land. As tax monies did not match the increase in prices, the nobility imposed a compulsory labor duty instead. In the 16th century, wealthy Polish businessmen moved into the area of grain, exporting Polish grain to Mediterranean Europe and in particular to the cities of northern and northwestern Europe. The port of Gdansk blossomed accordingly. Mining industries, on the other hand, underwent a prolonged period of economic stagnation.

Successes of the Counter-Reformation

The death of Sigismund Augustus, last of the Jagiellon family, put an end to the attempt to establish a hereditary monarchy in Poland. Led by John Zamoyski, the gentry won the right for all nobles of any rank to participate directly in the royal election. After eliminating a Habsburg prince, the Diet offered the throne to the brother of the king of France, Prince Henry of Valois, in 1573. King Henry spent little time in his kingdom, and even less after the death of his brother, when he returned to France to reign as Henry III. The crown was finally offered to Stefan Batory (1575-1587), who was able to bring his adversaries together in order to maintain the policy of tolerance. He did, however, give the Counter-Reformation his full support as well as increasing donations to the Jesuits. Many noble families who had accepted the Reformation at the beginning of the 16th century returned to the Catholic Church.

Through Stefan Batory, the Jesuits' educational efforts were very successful. The college at Wilno became a university run by the Jesuits, and was attended not only by Catholic students but by Protestants and Uniates as well.

Still, the success of the Counter-Reformation never brought on a persecution of the Protestants: they were allowed to keep their churches and schools. Protestant culture also experienced a period of brilliance toward the end of the century, due largely to the existence of a literary society grouped around the Italian humanist, Lelio Sozzino, a resident of Cracow since 1579. His disciples, known as the Polish Brethren, founded a center of protestant culture complete with schools and a printing press in the village of Rakow, near Sandomir. There, they developed original ideas on war and on the freedom of conscience—ideas which made them more humanists in the tradition of Erasmus than religious militants. By then, however, without persecutions or a war of religion, Poland had become a Catholic country.

At the close of the 16th century, what we call Eastern Europe was completely fragmented. The Balkans and part of Hungary were in the hands of the Turks, while the rest of Hungary and the kingdom of Bohemia had been integrated into the Habsburg monarchy—the single western Christian bulwark standing against the Turks. Only Poland had managed to remain independent and even thrive during the period. To the diversity of political experience was added the disintegration of a longstanding religious unity that had spiritually and morally united Bohemia, Hungary, and Poland. From then on, divisive forces seemed destined to overcome desire for reunification—probably the most decisive factor governing the fate of nations in this part of Europe.

Chapter 6

Eastern Europe of the Habsburgs, the Turks and Russia

With the arrival of the Turks in central and eastern Europe, the indigenous peoples lost control of their own destinies. Some became subjects of the Turks; others ended up, more or less voluntarily, under the protection of the Habsburgs, who through the strength of the Holy Roman Empire and from their hereditary properties, appeared to be the most effective bulwark against the Turks. Only the Poles managed to retain a kind of independence for a while, but their country was coveted by powerful neighbors ready to divide it among themselves.

THE BALKANS UNDER THE OTTOMANS

The peoples of the Balkans had fallen to Ottoman rule by the end of the 14th century. Ottoman hegemony was essentially political, though its application varied in manner and severity. Certain Balkan people enjoyed a relatively autonomous status—like the Albanians and the Rumanians. Others, such as the Serbs, were subjected to a rule of strict submission. But despite these diversities, certain characteristics of Turkish rule were common to all of the countries they subjected. All countries were assigned Turkish garrisons which were quartered in the towns and along strategic points. In spite of colonizing efforts in certain regions, the Turks were a minority everywhere in relation to the indigenous Christian populations. The Turks did not attempt to impose their Muslim religion on their Christian subjects.

The Privileged Peoples

Among the peoples ruled by the Turks, the Albanians and the inhabitants of Moldavia and Wallachia—ancestors of present-day Rumanians—enjoyed particularly favorable circumstances. After the death of the resistance leader, Skanderbeg, in 1469, the Albanians became loyal subjects of the Turks. Dissenters chose to emigrate to Calabria and Sicily where their present-day descendants still preserve the memory of their origins. But the great majority of Albanians stayed, accepted the Muslim religion and supplied the Turks with civil servants, officers and numerous soldiers.

In the principalities of the Lower Danube, the prince of Wallachia, Mircea the Great, and Stefan the Great of Moldavia, attempted to organize resistance, but by the end of the 15th century, both had become vassals of the Ottoman Empire. In fact, Turkish rule was far from heavy-handed there. It mainly consisted of collecting an annual tribute, the *pechkeche,* as well as fixed taxes and a monopoly on trade. In exchange, the Turks guaranteed the safety of the two principalities' borders against foreign intruders. Each principality retained a substantial measure of freedom in administrative and judiciary affairs. The local nobility, the Boyars, retained the right to elect the prince, but the Turks could veto their decision. Most of the time, the princes of Moldavia and Wallachia were content to remain loyal vassals of the sultan, maintaining luxurious courts in their respective capitals, Jassy in Moldavia and Bucharest in Wallachia. Taking advantage of Turkish tolerance, the Rumanian church flourished. It managed to break loose from the Patriarchate of Constantinople, and beginning in the 16th century, liturgical texts were translated into Rumanian. Numerous churches and monasteries were constructed in a style that illustrated the still-prevalent influence of Byzantine art.

During the 16th and 17th centuries, the Rumanian principalities experienced a noticeable cultural development. Prince Matei Basarab of Wallachia (1632-1654) and Prince Vasil Lupu of Moldavia (1634-1653) opened numerous schools and founded printing businesses at Jassy in 1646 and at Bucharest in 1652. The two capitals each had their own academy. This late-blooming renaissance was encouraged by the broad autonomy the two principalities enjoyed in the 17th century. But in the following century, severely tried by the reconquest of Hungary by the Habsburgs and very anxious about the growth of the Russian state, the Turks clamped down on the Danubian principalities. This policy instigated dissensions, and the Rumanians appealed to Czar Peter the Great. The Turks replied by replacing the local princes by the Pharnariots who were assigned as governors with power to rule in the name of the sultan. Through the Pharnariot middlemen, the Turks drew increased wealth from the Danubian principalities. The annual tribute was increased by five times during the course of the 18th century. Under such economic pressure from the Turks, many Rumanian peasants sought refuge in Transylvania. Others resorted to rebellion and were supported by Russia, who led a victorious war against the Turks (1768-1774). At the Peace of Kuciuk-Kainardji, the Turks pledged to respect the privileges of the Danubian principalities and granted the Czar the right to protect Orthodox Christians within the Ottoman Empire. From that time on, Russian "protection" was added to the Ottoman domination. At the same time, the Habsburgs, who had been supporting the Russians, forced the Turks to cede Bukovina.

The Oppressed Peoples

Bulgaria had a less desirable fate. After the failure of the crusade at Nicopolis in 1396, the Bulgar people fell under five centuries of Ottoman domination. The Bulgars mounted a much more obstinate resistance than the Rumanians, and were harshly treated. Since their territory was in the immediate vicinity of the center of the Turkish Empire, it was even more tightly controlled. Right after the conquest, the Bulgarian nobility was totally eliminated and its properties converted into military fiefs for Turkish officers and civil servants who simply continued the lordly rule of their predecessors. Bulgarian peasants underwent a change in masters, but continued to work feudal labor duty and to pay the head tax and the tithe to their new lords. And the Bulgar people, who had been decimated by massacres and slave markets dating back to the early days of Turkish occupation, were still periodically obliged to give up their sons when needed as recruits for the Janissaries.

In order to better control and exploit the country, the Turks dispersed the Bulgar peasants living on the coastal plains and in the Maritsa Valley, and replaced them with colonists from Asia Minor. Turks, Armenians, Greeks and Jews moved into the towns that quickly took on a cosmopolitan and oriental flavor with mosques and bazaars. The Orthodox religion was tolerated, but in order to keep it under control, the Turks entrusted Greek bishops with the task of watching over the Bulgarian clergy.

The fate of the Serbs was much closer to that of the Bulgars than that of the Albanians and Rumanians. Of course, the Serbs did manage to retain their independence and to form a solid bastion of Christianity surrounded by Turkish fortresses. Occasionally, these Montenegrins did not hesitate to attack the Turks, either alone or with the help of Austria and Venice which held the Dalmatian coast. But Montenegro could not be called a state. It was more a confederation of tribes under a chief, the *Vladika*. At the end of the 17th century, the Petrovic-Njegos dynasty took over the office of *Vladika* by passing it from uncle to nephew. As for the Serbs of Bosnia, among whom were many followers of the Bogomilian heresy, there were numerous conversions to Islam, which afforded them a relative tranquility reinforced by the mountainous nature of their country which discouraged Turks from entering in great numbers.

The Serbs of Serbia proper, who made up the great majority of the Serbian people, were subjected to a harsh military occupation. Their lands became the property of the sultan who converted them into hereditary or life-long military fiefs for Turkish civil servants. As in Bulgaria, the tribute of children was exacted of Serbian families to supply the ranks of future Janissaries.

The Serbian church was the center of the resistance. At the beginning of the Turkish occupation, tolerance prevailed, and the Serbian Patriarchate of Pec was even restored in 1557. But after the failure of the rebellion of 1688-1690, thousands of Serbs led by the Patriarch of Pec, Arsenije III, fled to Hungary where Emperor-King Leopold I granted them land and privileges. This was the origin of the Serbian population in the southern provinces of Hungary. In retaliation, the Turks abolished the Patriarchate of

Pec and the remaining Serbian clergy were put under the authority of the Greek church. Thus in Serbia, as in Bulgaria, the Greek clergy proved to be an effective agent of Turkish power.

CONSOLIDATION OF THE HABSBURG MONARCHY IN THE DANUBE REGION

At the beginning of the 17th century, the Habsburgs of Austria ruled over territories that reached from southern Germany to the Hungarian plain. Besides imperial functions, the Habsburgs added the crowns of Bohemia and Hungary to their possessions. Their empire constituted a solid bastion united around a Catholic dynasty from which the slow reconquest of regions under Turkish occupation would take place.

Triumph of the Counter-Reformation in Bohemia

Since the beginning of the 16th century, the countries of the Crown of St. Wenceslas (Bohemia, Moravia and Silesia), had been an integral part of the inheritance of the House of Austria. Religious dissent from the Hussite period and the spread of the Protestant Reformation continued to weigh on the life of the country for a long time. Emperor Rudolph II, hoping to put an end to the matter, granted Bohemia a Royal Decree in 1609 which allowed them freedom of religion and the right to open temples and schools. The Protestants were allowed to elect their own representatives, the Defenders of the Faith, to see that contents of the Royal Decree were respected. Religious peace seemed to have returned, and did last throughout the reign of Rudolph II and into the reign of his successor, Matthias (1612-1619). The Catholic Counter-Reformation was also active through the teachings and missionary efforts of the Jesuits.

From 1617, power was in the hands of the Archduke Ferdinand of Styria, who became King Ferdinand II two years later. Ferdinand II (1619-1637), a former student of the Jesuit college at Ingolstadt, wanted to restore religious unity in his states. Upon his ascendancy, he sought to curtail the privileges of the Protestants. The result was a full-scale war of religion, first in Bohemia and then throughout the Holy Roman Empire. This Thirty Years' War began in early 1618 with an incident involving the Bishop of Prague and Czech Protestants. The archbishop had closed a temple and forbidden the Protestant religion in a town under his authority. The Defenders of the Faith protested by calling together a Protestant assembly. On May 21, 1618, the lieutenant governors prohibited the meeting. A Protestant delegation led by a high Protestant noble of German origin, the Count of Thurn, went to the royal palace to plead before the lieutenant governors on May 23. It was a stormy conference, and the two lieutenant governors, as well as two Czech Catholic nobles, William of Slavata and Jaroslav of Martinic, and a secretary were thrown out of a window. The "defenestration of Prague" marked the beginning of the long conflict that raged for thirty years throughout central Europe. Meanwhile, Emperor Matthias died, and the Bohemian Diet refused to recognize the new sovereign, Ferdinand II. It also excluded the Habsburg family from the throne, then decided to expel the Jesuits from Bohemia and to confiscate their properties. Then in August 1619, the Diet chose a German Calvinist prince as king (the Palatin elector, Frederick I, head of the Evangelical Union). The "anti-king," Frederick I, had the support of most of the Protestant princes of the Empire, and that of the Prince of Transylvania, Gabriel Bethlen, who took advantage of it by declaring himself king of Hungary the following year. Ferdinand II pitted the Catholic League against the Protestant coalition. A Bavarian army under the command of the Count of Tilly entered Bohemia, and on November 8, 1620, soundly defeated the Protestant army of Frederick I near Prague. Frederick I was forced to flee Bohemia, and Prague yielded.

According to Czech historic tradition, reported by French historian Ernest Denis, the battle of the White Mountain marked the end of Czech independence. But in reality, it is better to regard it as the victory of the Catholic Counter-Reformation. The losers were severely punished, not because they were Czech, but because in setting up an "anti-king" in place of the legitimate king, they had committed treason. The repression was led by the governor, Prince Charles of Liechtenstein, a converted Protestant. A special tribunal condemned to death 27 leaders of the rebellion who were executed on June 21, 1621, on the square of the old city of Prague. Among the victims was the rector of the University of Prague, Jan Jensensky. A "Commission of Confiscation" proceeded to confiscate the rebels' properties from 1622 to 1629. Nearly three-quarters of Bohemian land changed hands, half of it in Moravia alone, but Silesia was not affected by the confiscations. Part of the confiscated lands were distributed to a new Catholic nobility, often of foreign origin, and another part was given to the Catholic Church. The reign of tolerance promised by the Royal Decree was abolished. Catholicism became the state religion; Protestantism and Utraquism were prohibited and all of their ministers expelled. Nobles and burghers who refused to abjure were forced into exile, leaving their wealth behind. During the ten years that followed the defeat of the White Mountain, nearly 15,000 persons were exiled. Among the famous exiles, a special place must be made for Jan-Amos Komensky, better known as Comenius (1592-1670), who was the last bishop of the United Brotherhood, a scholar, linguist and teacher—the Czech Descartes.

A subdued Bohemia received a new constitution from the king in 1627. According to this constitution, the crown became hereditary, passing through the masculine line of the Habsburg family. The king appointed all of the administrative officers and members of the superior courts. The Diet was maintained and kept the right to consent on taxes, but representation of the towns was diminished and the clergy was reintroduced. Finally, to emphasize that Bohemia belonged to the Empire, German became the official language.

The pacification of Bohemia did not put an end to the Thirty Years' War. To the contrary, the armies of Ferdinand II, led by General Wallenstein, a Czech Catholic adventurer, continued to war against the German Protestant princes and their Swedish allies. Under the new sovereign, Ferdinand III (1637-1657), a more liberal rule was slowly established. The Peace of Westphalia put an end to the Thirty Years' War in 1648. Imperial power came out of it weakened, and the principle of *Cujus Regio Ejus Religio* (to each region, its own religion) made each sovereign the master of his subjects' religion. The King of Bohemia was Catholic, and his subjects had to be also, or be exiled. But for Bohemia, as for the Empire, the wars had been ruinous. Bohemia had lost a fifth of its population and was partially repopulated with German Catholics driven from Protestant states.

After 1650, a pacified Bohemia began to rise from its ruins and was definitively integrated into the Habsburg monarchy. The economy began to recover its prosperity, which essentially rested on an agricultural base. The rule of the nobility was consolidated by extending the feudal labor tax to the reserves, which permitted the lords to sell excess harvests. In return, productivity of the mines which had been very active at the end of the Middle Ages declined due to exhaustion of resources. The population grew, and according to the census of 1754, the countries of the Crown of St. Wenceslas contained over three million inhabitants, only 50,000 of them in Prague since it had lost its role as home of the sovereign to Vienna.

By the end of the 17th century, through the efforts of the Jesuits, Bohemia and especially Moravia had returned to Catholicism. The Jesuits controlled higher education and had 175 colleges which trained the future elite. The Catholic Reformation did all that it could to garner the admiration of the lower classes, and stimulate their imagination. The introduction of baroque art with its sumptuously decorated churches and pompous, elaborate ceremonies was a valuable aid in the reconquest of hearts and minds. In 1729, the canonization of St. Jan Nepomucene, martyr of the secret of confession, gave Czech Catholics a spiritual rallying point that partially compensated for the impact of the Protestant Jan Hus. Despite its regained majority status, Catholicism in Bohemia would never have the same intensity nor the same fervor as in Poland. The memories of the religious wars were too strong and had too deeply affected the populace.

The Habsburgs, Hungary and the Turks

At the beginning of the 17th century, the Habsburgs in effect controlled the western and northwestern parts of the Hungarian kingdom. They were, at least in theory, masters of Transylvania—as the Transylvanian princes were their vassals as well as vassals of the Turks. Until 1660, the Habsburgs' policy as rulers of Hungary had been one of simply holding onto their gains. They adopted an essentially defensive attitude against the Turks, but the Thirty Years' War prevented them from acting effectively. To counter the many Protestants in the part of the kingdom they controlled, the Habsburgs staunchly supported the Catholic Reform movement led by Cardinal Peter Pazmany (1570-1637) and his successors. Pazmany was so successful in his preaching and persuasion in Hungary that Counter-Reformation did not produce the same tensions as in Bohemia. A university directed by the Jesuits was founded at Nagyszombat in 1635, numerous colleges were opened, and the education of the lower Catholic clergy was improved. Baroque religious art spread throughout western Hungary and, as in Bohemia, helped attract converts to the church. By the mid-17th century, the Counter-Reformation had triumphed in western Hungary without violence.

At the same time, Transylvania, a land of religious tolerance, maintained its autonomy and experienced a Golden Age under Gabriel Bethlen (1613-1648), and continued under his successors, George I (1630-1648) and George II Rakoczi (1648-1662). In spite of the ambitions of the princes, Transylvania remained in the sphere of influence of the Habsburgs while enjoying total autonomy.

Beginning in 1660, the Turks took up the offensive in Hungary. They first tried to intervene in Transylvania, where they opposed the new prince, Janos Kemeny (1660-1662). The Habsburgs, freed from conflicts in central Europe by the Peace of Westphalia, reacted under Emperor-King Leopold I (1657-1705). The struggle against the Turks was first led by a high noble from Western Hungary, Miklos Zrinyi, who harassed Turkish garrisons in central Hungary (1663-1664) and destroyed the bridge of Eszek, one of the traditional paths of invasion. The Turks tried to retaliate by sending the army of the Vizir Koprulu, but the joint forces of the emperor and Zrinyi defeated them at Szent-Gottard on August 1, 1664. The Treaty of Vasvar, which left the Turks the positions they held in Hungary, acutely displeased the Hungarian nobility. Certain nobles made contact with agents of Louis XIV who was then at war with Leopold I. One of the conspirators, Emeric Thokoly, took refuge in Transylvania where, beginning in 1672, he led a campaign against the Leopold supporters. Suddenly, Thokoly found himself on the side of the Turks, which alienated him from a number of his supporters. In order to aid Thokoly, to whom they granted the title "Prince of Hungary," the Turks launched a large expedition and laid siege to Vienna in July 1683. The intervention of the Polish king, Jan Sobieski and his victory at Kahlenberg on September 1, 1683, saved the city. It was then that an intensive counter-offensive began, leading to the liberation of Hungary. The Imperialists liberated Visegrad in 1684, then Buda on September 2, 1686, and finally Belgrade in 1688. After the victory of Prince Eugene of Savoy at Zenta on September 11, 1697, the sultan gave up Hungary and Transylvania to Leopold I by the Peace of Karlovici (January 26, 1699), but kept the Banat with Temesvar, which would be liberated later by the Peace of Passarovitz in 1718.

The prestige of the Habsburgs allowed them to consolidate their position in Hungary. At the Diet of October 1687, the Hungarian throne was proclaimed hereditary. In exchange, the sovereign recognized the nation's traditional rights, with the exception of the right to insurrection. In regard to Transylvania, Leopold I was also generous. *Diploma Leopoldianum* of 1691 recognized Transylvania as autonomous, with its diet and its freedoms, but the title of prince was inherited by the King of Hungary. Freedom of religion was solemnly reaffirmed everywhere. It was at this moment that part of the Rumanian Orthodox clergy of Transylvania reinstated the Rumanian Church to form the Uniate Church.

Hungary was exhausted by the civil and foreign wars that had waged in its territory since 1526. Its population had been severely reduced, numbering scarcely more than 2,500,000 inhabitants, including 900,000 foreigners. The Magyars were the most significantly affected element of the population, because the mountainous regions where the other ethnic groups lived were relatively spared by the wars.

Part of the nobility, most of them Protestant, accepted the Habsburgs' hereditary right to the crown only reluctantly and cherished thoughts of their former independence, particularly in Transylvania. The intrigues of Louis XIV and the Habsburgs' difficulties during the Spanish War of Succession induced Francis Rakoczi, who was related to the Zrinyi family and to Thokoly, to stage an insurrection. In May, 1703, Francis Rakoczi called on the Hungarians to revolt. As master of Upper Hungary with the support of the Hungarian, Slovak and Vlach peasants, he proclaimed himself Francis II, Prince of Transylvania. At the death of Leopold I, the rebels refused to recognize the new king, Joseph I (1705-1711), and announced the dethronement of the Habsburgs. But the country longed for peace. The Catholic Church was suspicious of the Protestant entourage of Francis II, and the nobility feared his projects for social reform. Finally, the support expected from Louis XIV turned out to be only symbolic. From 1708 on, the armies of Joseph I were victorious everywhere. The Peace of Szatmar on April 30, 1711, put an end to the insurrection. The rebels were granted amnesty and religious freedom, and constitutional guarantees were solemnly reaffirmed. After two centuries of war, Hungary was finally at peace again within its historic borders.

Integration of Hungary into the Habsburg monarchy allowed the country to rebuild its strength. The beneficial reigns of Charles III (1711-1740) and particularly of Maria-Theresa (1740-1780) made the difficulties and misfortunes of the preceding two centuries fade into memory. The sovereigns respected the constitution, and the Diet met regularly. During the time of Maria-Theresa, Hungary became a true center of the Empire. To cries of *Vitam et Sanguinem Pro Rego Nostro Maria Theresia*,* the Diet of 1741 voted to raise a 60,000-man army, permitting the sovereign to proceed with the war against Frederick II of Prussia, and it was a Hungarian general, Andras Hadik, who in October 1757 entered Berlin at the head of the imperial cavalry.

Despite Hungarian participation in all of the Empire's wars, the country experienced a period of prosperity in the 18th century. Under the enlightened influence of Chancellor Kaunitz, the Habsburg monarchy was endowed with an efficient administration and healthy financial management which benefited Hungary as well as Bohemia. Maria-Theresa was also interested in education, and in order to better educate the young nobles of the Empire, she founded the Theresianum in 1760 in Vienna, an elite school for future diplomats and administrators. French became the language of cultured society, and Latin remained the official language of Hungary. Latin had the advantage of putting all nationalities on an equal level, though it did risk weakening ethnic cultures and languages. But during Maria-Theresa's time, the benefits outweighed the disadvantages, especially because an influx of foreign peoples had been encouraged in order to repopulate the country after the wars of the preceding century. Foreign colonists, particularly Germans, had been invited, and refugees from regions still held by the Turks, especially Serbs and Rumanians, were welcomed.

Maria-Theresa intended to attain a unified empire while allowing Hungary to keep its privileges. Her son, Joseph II (1780-1790) was influenced by rationalist thought, and wanted to go even further with unification. As an enlightened despot, Joseph II abolished serfdom in 1785 and put an end to the rule of corporations and commercial monopolies. He incited the vehement protest of the Hungarian Diet, however, when he tried as a unifying measure to make German the official language of all the states. His death ended these attempts, but the unanimous reaction of the Diet indicated that in spite of loyalty to the dynasty, nationalist sentiment was rising again.

---

*"Our lives and our blood for our Queen Maria Theresa."

The Habsburg monarchy in Europe of the 18th century was still a viable structure however, being sufficiently centralized to be effective and at the same time flexible enough to avoid being oppressive. It had succeeded in driving the Turks out of the Middle Danube and in bringing together under the same political umbrella different nations united by a dynastic link and by certain common interests. The motto of the dynasty, A.E.I.O.U., *Austriae Est Imperare Orbi Universo,** seemed more than ever justified. But could this idea of a universal empire, inherited from the Christian Middle Ages and adapted to the modern world by the philosophy of Reason, be reconciled with the feelings of nationalism that were beginning to appear?

DECLINE AND DEMISE OF POLAND

Since the end of the 16th century, Poland had been an elective monarchy. With each vacancy on the throne, the election of a sovereign

---

*Austria has imperial influence over the world.

opened bargaining between the various groups in the Diet and between the candidates and the electors. Poland became an aristocratic republic in which the Diet held the real power. Little by little, a new principle of public law came into effect in the 17th century called the *liberum veto*, according to which all important decisions of the Diet had to be unanimous. The *liberum veto* led rapidly to the paralysis of the state and reinforced the power of the nobility. When a situation was deadlocked, the nobles, along with the king, called a "confederation," a kind of anti-Diet, in which the *liberum veto* did not apply. The need for many such confederations eventually led to a situation of civil war.

(Poland under Sigismund III Vasa (1587-1632) still gave the illusion of a powerful state, but at his death, the institutional weaknesses of the state along with the religious and ethnic diversity brought in by previous conquests became apparent in the face of mounting threats from the outside. By the 17th century, Poland's neighbors, Prussia, Sweden and Russia, had indeed become forces to be reckoned with. Problems came to light when King Jan Casimir (1648-1668) came to the throne. He was immediately confronted with the rebellion of the Cossaks in the Ukraine led by Bogdan Chmielnicki. After defeating the royal troops, the Cossaks placed themselves under the protection of Czar Alexis of Russia in 1654, and the resulting Russo-Polish war led to the division of the Ukraine between the contestants. The countries to the east of the Dnieper as well as the cities of Kiev and Smolensk were given to Russia. Simultaneously, Poland was drawn into the First War of the North; its territory was invaded by the Swedes whose king, Charles X, wanted to become King of Poland. By the Peace of Oliva in 1660, Poland ceded Livonia to Sweden and gave up its sovereignty over Prussia. With Jan Sobieski (1674-1696), Poland seemed to recover briefly. The king's victory over the Turks at Vienna in 1683 renewed the country's confidence, but quarrels among the various factions in the Diet prevented any reorganization of the state. Choice of a successor to Jan Sobieski opened up violent disagreements in which neighboring countries and France took part. The elector of Saxony, Augustus II the Strong (1697-1733), was supported by Austria and Russia. He was chosen king, but the agreement made with Peter the Great on this occasion brought Poland into the Second War of the North (1700-1721) on the side of Russia and against the Swedes and their Turkish allies. Charles XII of Sweden, victorious at Narva in November 1700, invaded Poland and had a new king, Stanislas Leczynski, elected in 1704. The defeat of Charles XII at Poltava in May 1709 allowed Augustus II to reclaim his throne, but he owed its restoration to the good will of Peter the Great whose troops had liberated Warsaw.

Poland was in ruins after a war in which it had once again served as a battlefield. The Peace Treaty of Nystadt in 1721 strengthened Russia's position. For Poland, Russia was soon to prove a dangerous neighbor as Peter the Great wished to establish direct contact with the West. Poland, however, as well as Sweden and Turkey, posed an obstacle to this contact. At the same time, the rise of the Prussian state, which became a kingdom in 1701, posed a danger to Poland because Polish lands bordering the Baltic blocked the formation of a contiguous Prussian state. Poland's independence was seriously threatened. This was obvious upon the death of Augustus II when in September, 1733, the Diet elected as king the national candidate, Stanislas Leczynski, father-in-law of the king of France, while Austria and Russia supported the son of the deceased king. Three weeks after the election of Stanislas, the Russian armies entered Warsaw and had Stanislas' rival, Augustus III, elected by a minority of nobles. The Polish succession opened a European war which ended with Stanislas Leczynski's renunciation of the throne. Poland then passed through a period of relative calm under Augustus III (1733-1763), but the *liberum veto* continued to paralyze the government internally. During this period, Poland slowly abandoned its policy of religious tolerance prevalent since the 16th century. Protestant and Orthodox dissidents were excluded from public office. This policy soon furnished neighboring countries with an excuse to intervene, Prussia to defend the Protestants, Russia to defend the Orthodox followers.

Poland's weakness was all too apparent upon the death of Augustus III. Catherine II of Russia and Frederick II of Prussia saw it as an excellent opportunity to act. Under the influence of the Czartoryski family, the Diet elected an old favorite of Catherine II, Stanislas-Augustus Poniatovski (1764-1795) as king, and Russian troops came immediately to reinforce the new sovereign's power. But the Czartoryskis were relying on the king to enact crucial reforms in order to save the country from anarchy. Among others, they hoped for the abolition of the *liberum veto* and for the creation of a standing army to defend the country. These attempts at reform alarmed Catherine II, who was becoming reconciled with Prussia. During the Diet of 1766, Russia and Prussia demanded by ultimatum the restoration of the *liberum veto* and the restitution of political rights to dissidents. To reinforce these demands the Russian ambassador, Repnin, called in Russian troops, and the Diet gave in to the demands of the two powers. Chancellor Zamoyski resigned and the Archbishop of Cracow—who had dared to protest the intervention by Russian troops—was arrested and deported to Smolensk. A few nobles retorted by organizing the Confederation of Bar "for faith and freedom" near the Austrian border in 1768. Russia reacted by instigating a rebellion of Orthodox peasants in the Ukraine and Podolia during which thousands of Poles were massacred. The confederates appealed to France; Foreign Minister Choiseul sent them a military envoy under the direction of General Dumouriez and pressured the Turks into declaring war on Russia.

The Turkish defeats of 1770 led Austria to reconcile with Prussia and Russia, as it did not want the Russians to occupy Turkey as they had already occupied Poland. The result was the Treaty of St. Petersburg on July 25, 1772, that led to the first partitioning of Poland "for fear of the total disintegration of the Polish state," as worded in the treaty. Austria received the county of Zips (Spisz) and Galicia. Prussia occupied the territory between eastern Pomerania and eastern Prussia, with the exception of Gdansk and Torun. As for Russia, it annexed all the territories to the north of the River Dvina as well as the lands of the Upper Dnieper.

The Polish Diet refused to ratify the treaty for a year, ceding only after the country was occupied by troops of the co-partitioning powers. The Diet also had to agree not to modify the constitution. Although Poland remained a state of 11,000,000 inhabitants, it was deprived of all freedom of action. King Stanislas-Augustus, stripped of all power, thus became a dependent sovereign.

The protectorate system worked fairly well until 1788. The Diet limited itself to passing a few economic reforms calculated to promote commerce and industry and to improve education. But beginning in 1788, the Diet, led by magnates of the Patriot Party, Ignace Potocki and Adam Czartoryski, took advantage of the reopening of the Russo-Turkish war in order to seriously address reforms. On May 3, 1791, King Stanislas-Augustus solemnly presented a new constitution that granted the House of Saxony the hereditary right to the throne. As the executive, the king was to govern along with the ministers, who were responsible to a diet which included the nobles as well as representatives of the cities. Certain magnates who opposed the reforms convoked a confederation at Targowica in May, 1792, and appealed to the Russians. Catherine II responded to their appeal. The Polish army under Prince Joseph Poniatovski and General Tadeusz Kosciuszko tried to risist, but on July 23, 1792, the king came over to the side of the confederates and withdrew the constitution while Russian troops occupied Warsaw. Prussia was disturbed by the spread of revolutionary ideas, and in January, 1793, sent in troops to prevent the Russians from deciding the Polish matter alone. Russia occupied all of Podolia, part of the Volhynia and all of White Russia with the city of Minsk, while Prussia annexed Gdansk and Torun, as well as Posnania.

Polish patriots wished to counter this show of force with a national insurrection, and they entrusted Kosciuszko with supreme powers. Kosciuszko appealed to the Polish nation from Cracow on March 24, 1794. A few days later, Warsaw rose up in arms, followed by Wilno. A month after Kosciuszko's call, Poland was liberated in a great burst of popular uprisings. The dictator tried to interest revolutionary France in the Polish cause, but to no avail. Austria had not acted up to that point, but then stepped in to reclaim its part of Poland, while the Prussians and Russians intervened militarily. On June 15, 1794, the Prussians took Cracow, and on November 5, the Russians under General Souvarov entered Warsaw. Kosciuszko and the leaders of the insurrection fell into the hands of the Russians. King Stanislas-Augustus, deposed in 1794, tried in vain to salvage the situation by placing Poland under the protection of Catherine II. He was forced to abdicate. On October 24, 1795, Russia, Prussia and Austria divided up what was left of Poland. During this Third Partition of Poland, Austria received Little Poland—with the cities of Lublin and Cracow—which enjoyed the status of an "independent republic" until 1846. Prussia retained all that had been gained in 1793 and secured Mazovia with Warsaw as well. Finally, Russia occupied all of Lithuania and the land east of the Niemen and the upper Bug with the city of Brest-Litovsk. Poland had ceased to exist.

Part II

The Awakening of Nationalism

Chapter 7

Premonitory Signs of Nationalism

In the last decade of the 18th century, central-eastern Europe was dominated by conflict between ethnic groups that were beginning to become aware of their own cultural individuality, and traditional states that had grown out of the political structures of the old order. The Europe of states begun in the 16th century and solemnly affirmed by the Congress of Vienna in 1815, became a Europe of nations.

ORIGINS OF NATIONALISM

By the end of the 18th century, eastern Europeans had accepted political structures that were for the most part foreign to them. Four powers shared responsibility for authority over central-eastern Europe. In the northwest, the kingdom of Prussia had just extended its authority to part of the Polish nation, while in the east, the Russian Empire ruled over another part of Poland and over all of the non-Slavic people along the Baltic: Estonians, Latvians, Lithuanians, and even Finns after 1809. In the Balkans, the Rumanians of Moldavia and Wallachia, the Bulgars, the Greeks and the Albanians had been subjects of the Ottoman Empire since the 14th century. Finally, along the Danube, Austria had amassed a vast multinational empire, constituted of the inhabitants of the Bohemian and Hungarian kingdoms, as well as all the refugees from Turkish-occupied zones. For this it was regarded as the stronghold of Christianity against Islam.

The relationship between the subjected peoples and Prussia, Russia and the Ottoman Empire was that of the conquered to the conquerors, of dominated peoples to the dominating. In contrast, the Austrian monarchy set up a relationship between the state and its subjects that rested on loyalty to the Habsburg dynasty and on an undeniable community of interests, even in the case of the small number of Poles brought into the Empire in 1795, who enjoyed the same treatment as other inhabitants of the Empire.

At the close of the 18th century, a new consciousness of nationality appeared, in subjected nations as well as associated nations. This new consciousness grew among the elite, the aristocracy, clergy and intellectuals, and was fostered by exterior influences. There was a birth, or an awakening, of nationalism everywhere at this time—a phenomenon not limited to eastern Europe. It was first seen in western Europe, especially in France under the influence of the *philosophes*. During the entire 18th century, French *philosophes* progressively developed new concepts of the relationships between the people and the state. These concepts, which were the work of Montesquieu, Voltaire, Diderot, D'Alembert and Rousseau, were set forth in the *Encyclopedie* whose influence reached far beyond the borders of France. The *philosophes* completely rejected the idea of a divine right monarchy solely dependent on the good will of the sovereign. They stressed the idea of national sovereignty and the notion that power came from the people. For some, the notion "people" was limited to an intellectual or wealthy elite; for others, it meant all of the people. Jean Jacques Rousseau held the latter point of view, and in *The Social Contract* he proclaimed that men were born free. For Rousseau, no one had the right to subject another against his will. These ideas inspired the English colonists in America when they rebelled against the authority of the government in London in 1776. It was not by chance that Kosciuszko, the head of the Polish insurrection of 1794, had fought beside George Washington with Lafayette and Rochambeau. The French Revolution and the Declaration of the Rights of Man greatly strengthened the development of nationalism and the concept of the right of peoples to govern themselves. The events in France in 1789 echoed resoundingly throughout Europe.

All of the European elite, including central and eastern Europeans, read and spoke French fluently. At the courts of Vienna and St. Petersburg, throughout the aristocracy, and in cultivated Hungarian, Polish and Czech circles, French was the common language. Private libraries overflowed with political and philosophic works published in France and French gazettes were read avidly. In Poland, Jean Jacques Rousseau's influence was considerable, and his ideas on education, as well as Condillac's, had a wide following during the time of King Stanislas-Augustus. Poniatovski himself acquired his political education in the Parisian salon of Madame Geoffrin. It was the same in Hungary, where the writer Alexander Kisfaludy was a fervent admirer of Rousseau, although there was an influential aristocrat in the Diet, Janos Fekete, who leaned more towards Voltaire. On the whole, the Hungarian aristocracy read *The Spirit of the Laws* with enthusiasm because they willingly identified themselves with the "corps intermediares" so dear to Montesquieu. When the French Revolution broke out, all those who hoped for reforms in Hungary, in Bohemia and in Poland were enthusiastic. The Hungarian Diet of 1793 even began a Hungarian Declaration of the Rights of Man. The distant Rumanian principalities of Moldavia and Wallachia were affected by the influence of French culture by the end of the 18th century through contact between their elite and the Frenchified Russian aristocracy.

France produced the idea of reform, and also the idea of nationalism. The concept that the people should have the right to choose their own destiny had been widely disseminated by the revolutionaries. This idea, viewed from eastern Europe, seemed to promise independence for subjected peoples— even if, in reality, it was often used to disguise imperialist aims. The idea was welcomed by the elite.

These French ideas arrived at a time when in all of central and eastern Europe the aristocracy and educated classes were slowly rediscovering their national past and relearning, with some difficulty, their national languages. Toward the end of the 18th century, the grammarian Kopczynski purified and codified the Polish language. At the same time in Hungary, the linguists Gyarmathi and Kazinczy standardized and enriched the national language which became the language of instruction in place of Latin in 1792. In Bohemia, there was also a resurrection of Czech language and literature with Abbot Joseph Dobrovsky who stressed the linguistic kinship of the Slavic people. This cultural renaissance combined with the enlightenment brought from France played a decisive role in the national awakening of centro-eastern Europe.

The first signs of this awakening occurred in Poland in 1794 with Kosciuszko's revolt. In spite of its failure and the extinction of the Polish state, Polish patriots paid careful attention to everything that came from France. Thus, Napoleon's first victories over the Russians and their Prussian allies in 1805-1806 caused great enthusiasm. Polish volunteers led by Dombrowski, a hero of 1794, rushed to enter the service of the emperor.

A provisional government was set up in Warsaw to welcome the French troops. In fact, when Napoleon's armies entered Polish territory, they were greeted as liberators. The sentimental liaison between Napoleon and the young Maria Walewska also decisively influenced the fate of Poland. The provisional government had the young woman plead her country's cause, and she was fairly successful. After the Peace of Tilsit, Napoleon created the Grand Duchy of Warsaw, with the king of Saxony as ruler and a constitutional statute establishing the freedom and equality of all citizens and abolishing serfdom. In 1809, the Grand Duchy of Warsaw was able to regain Austrian Poland, though the Russians kept the eastern provinces. The Poles took full advantage of their connection with the French and furnished innumerable troops to Napoleon. One Polish general, Joseph Poniatowski, was actually made Marshal of France and died on the battlefield at Leipzig on October 19, 1813.

In Hungary, the influence of the French revolution and its ideas on the right of the people to govern themselves was less warmly received than in Poland. Within the Habsburg monarchy, Hungary had been able to retain its autonomy and its institutions. Only the most radical elements of the intelligentsia were restless, and there were a few Hungarian Jacobins. The *Marseillaise* was translated into Hungarian, and on August 10, 1794, the young Jacobins led by Ignac Martinovics commemorated the seizure of the Tuilleries by singing the *ca ira* refrain of another revolutionary song. They were arrested and found guilty of conspiracy, and six of them, including their leader, were executed on May 20, 1795. This Jacobin movement, nipped in the bud, had very little influence. During the Napoleonic wars, the Hungarian diet supplied funds and soldiers, and Hungarians turned a deaf ear to Napoleon's call for revolt in his proclamation of May 15, 1809.

French influence reached the Slavs in the south of the monarchy through military conquest. Following the fifth coalition, the Peace of Vienna on October 14, 1809 made Istria and the greater part of Croatia into French territories. Until 1813, these Illyrian provinces benefited from reforms introduced by France: abolition of serfdom and civil equality. On the cultural level, Slovene became an official language like Italian and German, giving strength to efforts of the grammarian Kopitar in his battle for the Slovene language. Meanwhile, the Serbs in Hungary had been experiencing a cultural revival since the end of the 18th century. The first Serbian high school was founded in 1791 in Hungary—even though there was no high school in Serbia itself before 1855—and in 1791 the first newspaper in Serbian appeared in Vienna. Moreover, the cultural awakening of the southern Slavs living under the Habsburg monarchy sparked a similar movement among the Slavs in the Ottoman Empire, even though development there was slow. The awakening of nationalist feelings among Rumanians in Moldavia and Wallachia followed a similar course. French ideas had already begun to influence the Rumanian ruling classes by the end of the 18th century, but it was the better educated and culturally more independent Rumanians of Transylvania who truly aroused a national consciousness in the provinces of the Lower Danube. The Uniate bishop, Innocent Micu, was particularly responsible for originating the largely erroneous theory that the Rumanians were descendants of the Dacians. He coined the term "Rumanians" which we still use to designate people who were called Vlachs up until the 18th century.

Thus by the beginning of the 19th century, the nations of central and eastern Europe—or more specifically, the elite of these nations—were becoming conscious of their own national identities. They were rediscovering the individuality of their languages, their cultures, and their traditions in relation to others. Could they, or should they, let it go at that? Or would such cultural emancipation, accepted by the ruling powers, run the risk of encouraging claims for political independence? The debate was thus opened between those who wanted to maintain the traditional political structures and the supporters of nationalism, who believed that people who shared the same language, the same culture and the same traditions had a right to independence if they so desired, provided they occupied a clearly defined territory.

THE CONGRESS OF VIENNA AND ITS IMMEDIATE CONSEQUENCES

On September 22, 1814, a congress opened in Vienna attended by representatives of all the states of Europe. This congress, which convened after 20 years of nearly continuous warfare between revolutionary, then imperial France and the rest of Europe, was not intended for the sole purpose of deciding the fate of France. Its task was also to rebuild Europe, settling both political and territorial questions. Called together by Emperor Francis II of Austria and presided over by his chancellor, Metternich, the Congress of Vienna closed on June 26, 1815 with the signing of the *Final Act*, a document that reorganized Europe.

Throughout the duration of the congress, two groups of states clashed. One group, backed by Prussia and Russia, hoped to acquire the maximum territorial advantage, while others, backed by Austria and the United Kingdom, and supported behind the scenes by the French representative, Talleyrand, wished above all to establish a balance of power. All were in agreement, however, in opposing any revolutionary movement in any region. Their attitudes diverged once again on the matter of nationalistic movements then taking shape. Russia opposed nationalism in Poland, as did Prussia, but seemed ready to support it in the Ottoman Empire since the awakening of the Balkan people might serve a useful purpose in Russia's imperialistic designs on the Straits of Bosporous to the Mediterranean. Metternich was not necessarily opposed to nationalism, but he thought such aspirations could be channeled into creating not nation-states, but confederated states in which the leading citizens, the elite, the aristocracy, and the church would share the power, no matter what their ethnic group. Metternich was convinced that the Austrian example was the most able to guarantee a peaceful coexistence of ethnic groups without dividing them.

What was the final outcome of these various proposals for the peoples of eastern Europe? Poland was the object of long discussions. Its fate was closely linked to that of Saxony, whose king had been an ally of Napoleon and who had consequently been named sovereign of the Grand Duchy of Warsaw. In order to punish the King of Saxony for his treason toward the German nation, Prussia wanted purely and simply to annex Saxony. Russia agreed, on the condition that Prussia cede it the part of Poland it obtained in 1772 and 1791. That would have meant a partially restored Poland, but one ruled by Russia. Certain Polish magnates, including Prince Adam Czartoryski, a friend of Czar Alexander, opted for this solution. The other great powers opposed it, particularly Austria who feared an excessive encroachment of Russia on the west, and England who foresaw the disruption of future European balance in favor of Prussia and Russia. The secret treaty of January 3, 1815, between Austria, France and England led to the restoration of the Saxon lands to the King of Saxony in the name of legitimacy. Consequently, the Congress decided to maintain the division of Poland according to the former partitions, with only slight modifications. Austria kept Galicia, as well as a *de facto* sovereignty over the "free republic" of Cracow. Prussia kept Posnania, Danzig and the county of Thorn. Russia emerged advantageously; it kept all that it had acquired since 1772, in addition to the formerly annexed Grand Duchy of Warsaw, and created from this territory the Congress Kingdom. Czar Alexander of Russia thus became the king of Poland, but of a Poland stripped of its eastern provinces and of Lithuania which became part of the Russian Empire. Alexander gave his new kingdom a Charter in December, 1815. Poland had a diet made up of a senate of 30 members appointed by the king and a chamber of deputies elected by the nobles and representatives of the cities. This diet voted on taxes and laws, but the ministers were not responsible to the diet, only to the viceroy, the Grand Duke Constantine (who happened to be brother of the Czar) and to the imperial commissioner, Count Novosiltzov. In actual fact, the Polish aristocracy, who owned most of the land, administered the country under the supervision of Russia.

The Congress of Vienna did not change the status of the Balkans. In theory, the Ottoman Empire kept its entire territory, though in practice its authority had been severely weakened during the Napoleonic era following the wars between the Russians and the Turks from 1808 to 1812 and the resulting Russian occupation of Moldavia and Wallachia. The Peace of Bucharest in 1812 gave the Russians the Moldavian province of Bessarabia, between the River Prut and the Dniester. In addition Russia obtained a say in governing the Danubian provinces. As for the Serbs, in March 1804, they had attempted a rebellion under George Petrovitch, who was called Karageorge. The Serbs were moderately successful and were counting on

Russian aid, but after the Peace of Bucharest, the Russians cared little about a new war with the Turks, and abandoned the Serbian rebels. The insurrection was harshly repressed in 1812-1813, and Karageorge took refuge in Hungary. A new insurrection broke out in the spring of 1815 led by a rival of Karageorge, Miloch Obrenovitch, who was more skillful and more careful. He managed to get himself recognized as governor (*Knez*) of Serbia by the sultan, and two years later, the Turks recognized an autonomous Serbian principality. It was a vassal state, paid an annual tribute, and had Turkish troops stationed in the main cities. But as decided in Vienna, the Ottomans' authority over the Serbs, as well as over all the other Christian peoples in the Balkans, remained theoretically intact.

The hereditary borders of the Habsburg monarchy's possessions in the upper valley of the Danube were confirmed in 1792. Bohemia, like Hungary, remained an integral part of what had become the Austrian Empire in 1806, and, like the duchies and counties of traditional Austria, Bohemia was part of the German Confederation which replaced the Holy Roman Empire. Hungary did not take part in the Confederation because of its special constitutional status.

The Congress of Vienna was a triumph for the great powers who were able to impose their views on the smaller states. It was also a triumph for authority over liberalism, and of legitimacy over nationalism. On September 26, 1815, shortly after the Congress ended, the emperors of Austria, Russia and the king of Prussia signed a treaty setting up a Holy Alliance stating "the three monarchs will remain united by bonds of a true and indissoluble fraternity...and will grant each other assistance, aid and cooperation whenever and wherever requested." The treaty was open to all, and most of the European states, with the exception of the United Kingdom, supported it.

While the Holy Alliance had only a minor effect, the work of the Congress of Vienna was more lasting. Despite its imperfection, it provided Europe with almost a half-century of peace.

NATIONAL AWAKENING OF THE BALKAN PEOPLE

The Serb example and the *de facto* autonomy that they had managed to acquire for their struggles had a tremendous effect on the Balkans. Bulgars, Greeks, Serbs, Rumanians, and even Albanians were becoming more and more impatient with rule by an Ottoman Empire which was showing clear signs of weakness. Sultan Selim III had been forced to abdicate in 1808 by rebellious Janissaries, and his successor, Mohammad II (1808-1839) had been obliged to have those Janissaries massacred in order to regain authority, an act which considerably reduced his military force. Moreover, the Balkan

Christian people knew they had support on the outside. Russia, in fact, had demonstrated its interest in the Orthodox communities on several occasions since the 18th century. Since 1812, Russia had regarded the Rumanians of Moldavia and Wallachia as a *de facto* protectorate, and even though the Russians had left the Serbs to their fate in 1812-1813, they still followed developments in Serbia with great interest. In addition, numerous Serbian and Bulgarian refugees had settled in Bessarabia, which had become Russian. Nor was Austria indifferent to events taking place in the Balkans. Rumanian and Serbian populations living in Hungary maintained close contact with their Ottoman-dominated brothers. A plan to divide the Balkans between Austria and Russia had actually been devised in 1781 between Joseph II and Catherine II, but was never carried out. In any case, the Balkans were certainly an area of interest to both Austria and Russia.

Their interest heightened considerably, and the rest of Europe became concerned when Greece rose up against the Ottoman yoke in 1821. The revolt was instigated by the numerous patriotic societies that were formed in Greece in the early years of the 19th century, and whose influence was felt throughout Europe. A major role was played by one man, Alexander Ypsilanti. Though Greek, he had been an officer in the Russian army and an aide-de-camp of Czar Alexander. Ypsilanti had managed to obtain the cooperation of certain feudal lords, among them the Pascha of Jannina, the Albanian Ali Pascha Telepeleni. Russia, as expected, took the side of the Greek insurgents, but the British government in London, judging that it was better for the Turks instead of the Russians to control the Straits of Bosporus, tried to strike a compromise with the sultan. However, the declaration of independence of Greece at Epidaurus in January, 1822, and the massacre of Chios, during which several thousand Greeks were killed by the Turks, caused such strong feelings in western Europe that the great powers decided on a concerted intervention. The Ottoman Empire was forced to back down and give Greece its independence.

Other Balkan peoples also benefited from the Greek revolt. In Serbia, Miloch Obrenovitch, who had rid himself of his rival, Karageorge, by assassination in 1817 upon his return from exile in Austria, preferred to negotiate with the Turks rather than resort to combat. For this, the sultan granted him the title "Prince of the Serbs and Pashalik of Belgrade." During the Greek revolt, Serbia did not lift a hand, but benefited nonetheless from the intervention of the great powers, particularly Russia. After the convention at Akerman on October 7, 1826, which was ratified by the Peace of Adrianople on September 14, 1829, and then completed by a decree from the sultan on August 29, 1830, Serbia became an autonomous principality under a hereditary prince—in this case Miloch Obrenovitch—assisted by an assembly of leading citizens, the *Skupshtina*, to rule over a population numbering around 660,000. A locally recruited army was to guarantee order in the name of the sultan in this emerging Serbian state. The Turks retained the right to station troops in certain strongholds, but were not allowed to reside in other Serbian territory. Soon after, in 1832, the Serbian church was granted full independence. The archbishop (Metropolite) and the bishops would be elected from the ranks of the Serbian clergy and no longer appointed by the Patriarchate of Constantinople. Prince Miloch (1817-1839) was an authoritarian ruler, but had the support of the peasants. Opposing him were the intellectual elite of the country who supported the rival Karageorgevitch family. In 1838, Miloch retired, leaving the throne to his sons, Milan (1839-1839) and Michael (1839-1842). Michael was deposed by Alexander Karageorgevitch (1842-1859). But the *Skupshtina* later called back Miloch who reigned for one more year, and was then again succeeded by his son, Michael (1860-1868). Throughout their reign, both the Obrenovitch family and the Karageorgevitch family were interested in the idea of an eventual union of all the southern Slavs, an idea embraced by the Serbian and Croatian intellectuals. In general, Serbian sovereigns maintained excellent relationships with neighboring Montenegro whose rulers, Peter I (1784-1830) and Peter II (1830-1851) were openly supported by Czar Nicholas I of Russia.

The awakening of the Serbs in Serbia was not only political, but intellectual as well. Education had made obvious progress. In 1835, there were only 60 primary schools in Serbia and no secondary school at all. By 1859, the number of primary schools had reached 352, including 15 for girls. There was also a high school, opened in Belgrade in 1855. Still, in the area of education, the Serbs in Serbia were clearly behind their brothers living in the Austrian monarchy.

The Greek revolt also benefited the Rumanians. The secret society of *Hetaerie*, with Tudor Vladimirescu as leader, had tried to organize an uprising against the Phanariot government in 1820. When the Greeks rebelled, the Turks themselves removed the Phanariots from the government of the Rumanian principalities—because they were Greek—and named two Rumanian Boyars as "princes" or *hospodars* of Wallachia and Moldavia, Gregory Ghica (1822-1828) and Ioan Sturdza (1822-1828). When the Russians intervened on the side of the great powers in favor of the Greeks, their armies occupied Wallachia and Moldavia, and from 1828, Kissilev, a Russian general open to modern ideas, administered the principalities. Kissilev dismissed the two *hospodars* and convoked an assembly of leading citizens, nobles and leading merchants, who approved a kind of constitution, the *Reglement organique* in 1831. This ruling maintained the privileges of the Boyars and their authority over the peasants and gave the Boyar assembly in each principality the task of electing its own prince and voting on its laws.

In fact, when the Russians left the country in 1834, the czar and the sultan chose the *hospodars* themselves. They designated Micael Sturdza (1834-1849) as prince for Moldavia and Alexandru Ghica (1834-1848) followed by George Bibescu (1843-1848) as princes for Wallachia.

The 20 years between Kissilev's rise to power and the revolution of 1848 witnessed a resurrection of Rumania. Progressive numbers of Rumanian intellectuals and students attended French universities and then returned home with the liberal ideas in vogue in French intellectual circles. They demanded the freeing of the peasants and freedom of the press. Slowly, they adopted the idea of a united Rumania gathering together all Rumanians into one homeland.

The awakening of a national consciousness came later to the Bulgars. There, the new national sentiment originated in a cultural renaissance in the monasteries. Early impetus came from the monk, Paisi, who authored *A History of the Bulgarian People, Czars and Saints*. His disciples, especially Sofroni, refined and codified a Bulgar literary language. Through their work, the first book in literary Bulgar was printed in Bucharest. The cultural renewal also took place outside Bulgarian territory. Many Bulgars lived in Bucharest, Saloniki, Constantinople and even in Paris. But in Bulgaria itself, the small number of intellectuals were clearly separated and isolated from the people by a cultural barrier. This explains why the Bulgars, in comparison with their neighbors, were slow in developing a national consciousness. Here again, a national consciousness came from outside the country. The first Bulgarian revolutionary committee was founded in Bucharest by an exile, George Rakowski (1818-1868). Not until the last third of the 19th century did the Bulgars begin to seek independence.

THE TRAGIC FATE OF POLAND

The Congress of Vienna had ratified the dissolution of the Polish state because of the concerted and rival ambitions of its neighbors. Although the three parts of divided Poland went separate ways, the borders remained open to men and to ideas.

An unusual situation existed in the Polish territories annexed by Prussia where the populations were very mixed. The countryside of Posnania was mainly Polish, while the cities like Posnan (Posen), Bydogoszcz (Bromberg), and Gdansk (Danzig) were German. Until 1848, proper relations existed between Prussia and its Polish-speaking subjects. The Polish aristocracy "collaborated" with the German aristocracy. Prince Antoine Radziwill, who was married to a Hohenzollern princess, was entrusted with the provinces under the title of lieutenant governor. In 1823, an agrarian reform gave most Polish tenant-farmers ownership of the land they tilled in exchange for a moderate tax. Culturally, the state-financed village schools were taught in Polish and run by the clergy.

The situation in Austrian Poland was nearly the same, although their ethnic diversity arose from the coexistence of two Slavic populations, a Polish-Catholic population and an orthodox or uniate Ruthenian population. These ethnic contrasts were paralleled by social contrasts. The aristocracy and the urban population and clergy were Polish, while most of the peasants were Ruthenian. The Polish aristocracy and clergy fared well under Austrian rule, particularly since Austria tended to grant its Polish provinces a good deal of self-government. For all Poles, the University of Cracow was a place for the maintenance and the propagation of Polish culture.

Nothing of the sort happened in the Congress Kingdom. In the beginning, the Kingdom's ruler, Czar Alexander I, seemed to have a benevolent attitude toward Poland; he had an excellent relationship with several enlightened magnates like Prince Adam Czatoryski. In accordance with the Constitutional Statute of 1815, the country was administered by Poles, but the role of the diet was progressively reduced. The primary concern of the Czar and his representatives in Poland, was maintenance of law and order. Under Count Lubecki, who governed the country until 1821, there was some economic development. Lubecki set up the first Polish bank, strengthened public finances, and stabilized the currency. The country experienced a moderate prosperity along with an increase in agricultural production and the creation of the first cotton mills at Lodz. Economic progress did not distract Polish liberals and patriots from the facts that the Congress Kingdom was an incomplete territory without Lithuania and the eastern provinces and was in fact only an appendage of the Russian Empire. The University of Warsaw, founded in 1818 by Count Stanislas Potocki, Grand Master of the Freemasons and disciple of the Enlightenment, was shaken by patriotic student demonstrations which resulted in closing the university several times. Though closely watched by Russian authorities, the Polish army was also a hotbed of patriotism. In the early 1820s, relations between the Czar and his Polish subjects were becoming strained. The Diet repeatedly denounced the administration for abuses of power and received a harsh reprimand from the Czar, who then in 1825 forbade the Diet to publish the minutes of their meetings. This resulted in the formation of secret societies where students, burghers, writers, lawyers, military men and liberal nobles rubbed elbows as they worked out a framework for future projects. These secret societies were constantly harassed by the police, and the members, once discovered, were subjected to heavy prison sentences.

The abdication of Alexander I in December, 1825, was followed by a two-week interregnum in Russia. Prince Constantine, the Viceroy of Poland and eldest son of the ruler, should have succeeded his father, but he refused the crown. Finally, the youngest son took the throne under the name of Nicholas I (1825-1855). Certain liberal opponents, for the most part Russian officers, took advantage of the interregnum to try and seize the power from St. Petersburg, but the Decembrists' conspiracy failed. Nicholas I harshly put down the rebellion, and then came personally to Poland to be crowned king and to reinforce the constitution. In fact, Nicholas I practiced the same absolutist policy in Poland as he did in Russia. The Polish Diet no longer convened, and since the Poles involved in the Decembrist conspiracy had been acquitted by the Polish tribunals, the magistracy was purged, and judges' tenure for life, guaranteed by the Constitution of 1815, was abolished. In 1830, when Nicholas I decided to convene the Diet, the elections yielded a majority for the opponents. Polish politicians, elected by the nobility and the bourgeoisie, were divided into two groups. The Whites adopted a wait-and-see attitude, hoping reform would come from the Czar and trying to avoid all action that could lead to insurrection. The Reds, on the other hand, admired the French Revolution and made a cult-hero of Kosciuszko, the activist of the 1794 insurrection.

The successful revolutions in Paris and Brussels in July-August 1830, incited lively activity among the students in Warsaw. When news of the Czar's intent to send Polish troops against revolutionary Belgium in the name of the Holy Alliance was revealed, two young officers, Wysocki and Zaliwski, worked out a plan at the Cadet Academy in Warsaw to assassinate Viceroy Constantine and to launch a massive uprising against the Russian occupation on November 20. The plot was thwarted and the viceroy was able to leave the Polish capital in time. Throughout, the civilian population remained unmoved. In order to avoid a conflict, the White Party formed an administrative council and gave the command of Polish troops to General Chlopicki, who begged the viceroy to return to Warsaw. When he refused, the administrative council became a provisional government. General Chlopicki took the title of dictator—as Koskiuszko had done in 1794—and asked the Czar to recall Russian troops from Poland, to grant a general amnesty, to convoke the Diet, and to return former Polish territories under direct Russian administration to Poland. The Czar's answer was negative; in a manifesto dated December 27, 1830, Nicholas I demanded complete submission. The moderates of the White Party were uneasy about the development of events and resigned from the provisional government. In January, 1831, General Chlopicki left the dictatorship in order to devote himself fully to the organization of the Polish army, and in Warsaw the Reds took up the reins of government with support from the students, the petty bourgeoisie, and the Masonic lodges. The Polish government tried to interest France in the Polish cause, and a diplomatic mission was dispatched to Paris to negotiate the recognition and independence of Poland. The most concrete result of this mission was the formation of a Central Polish Committee in Paris which included generals Lafayette and Lamarque as well as the liberal minister Odilon Barrot. But the government of Louis-Philippe was still unsure of itself and refused to take part. Privately, however, many French officers left for Poland, bringing funds as well as arms. (The English government was similarly solicited by the Polish government, but made no move to involve itself.) Prussia, on the other hand, was nervous about the disturbances in Russian Poland. It closed its borders and gave its support to the Czar. Reduced to their own resources, the Poles were doomed, though in that spring of 1831, they were still full of hope. The Diet had just proclaimed Polish independence and its indissoluble union with Lithuania as well as the dethronement of the Romanov dynasty. While the Polish army did carry off several victories with generals Chlopicki and Skrznicki at the battles of Waver (February 19 and 21) and Grocho (February 25), it could not stand up to Marshal Paskievitch and his army of 120,000 men. By the end of July, 1831, Warsaw was nearly encircled, and Prussia was allowing Russian reinforcements to cross her territory. The most radical elements of the Polish insurrection under General Krukowizcki tried to continue the struggle, but on September 7, after a long artillery bombardment, Warsaw finally surrendered. The Diet broke up; many Poles fled to Austrian Galicia and from there emigrated to France. Paris became a refuge for numerous intellectuals like Adam Mickiewicz and Frederick Chopin who had been members of the secret republican societies.

Poland was harshly repressed. Marshal Paskievitch was named Governor of Poland and held the office throughout the reign of Nicholas I. A large Russian garrison was stationed in Warsaw to watch over the capital, and a stronghold was constructed to house it. The leaders of the insurrection who fell into Russian hands were hanged. Thousands of Poles were deported to Siberia. The properties of 286 emigrants who were condemned to death for contempt of court were confiscated and distributed to Russian generals and high officials. The Constitution of 1815 was abolished and replaced by the *Organic Statute* of February 26, 1832. The Diet and the Polish army were abolished. In principle, legislation and administration were to remain Polish, though little by little Russian officials progressively replaced local Polish authorities, and Russian was enforced as the official language.

The Russian regime set about breaking down the structures of the Polish nation. The University of Warsaw was closed as were most secondary schools, and Poles were forbidden to study in Cracow. The Catholic Church was tightly controlled by Russian administrators. In the eastern provinces, the Uniate Church, thought to be pro-Polish, was subordinated to the Orthodox Church. In 1945, the Soviet regime again adopted the same policy toward the Uniate Church in territories taken from Poland. Repression did not abate with time, instead intensifying so much that plots against the occupying forces were constantly being uncovered. In 1840, the Russian criminal code replaced the Polish code, then in 1844, Poland was divided into 10 provinces, each directed by a Russian general.

The Poles of Prussia and Austria were indirect victims of the failed revolution of 1830-1831. In Berlin and in Vienna, government officials were uneasy about the contagious liberal ideas from Warsaw, and hardened their attitudes toward their Polish subjects. Polish refugees living in Posnania tried to stage a new insurrection from the Republic of Free Cracow under the leadership of the writer Edward Dembrowski. During the night of February 21, 1846, Cracow rose in revolt. In order to counteract this revolt of the Poles, the Austrian authorities in Galicia incited the Ruthenian peasants to fight against them. The Austrians, however, reestablished order with moderation, unlike the Russians had in Poland. The Republic of Cracow lost only its "independence" and was absorbed by Galicia. To the Poles in Russia, the Prussian and Austrian Polish provinces were like privileged regions.

NATIONALISM IN THE AUSTRIAN MONARCHY

During the reigns of the Habsburg monarchs, Francis II (1792-1835) and Ferdinand (1835-1848), Chancellor Metternich directed the affairs of the government. In the eyes of the Western intelligentsia, Austria was an anachronistic and reactionary state. In reality, the system set up by Metternich afforded the different nations that made up the empire a kind of *Pax austriaca*. The system essentially rested on loyalties linking the national groups to the dynasty, on a large and efficient bureaucracy, and on the traditional administration of the Old Regime's aristocracy and Catholic church. But could this system cope with the rise of nationalism?

From the quiet rediscovery of national languages and cultures at the close of the 18th century, nationalism grew quickly, and by 1815, the cultural renaissance had spread into politics. The development of nationalism was encouraged by a population boom among the different national groups due primarily to high birth rates and decreasing death rates. Simultaneously, the industrial revolution fostered a noticeable development of urban and working classes who were more open to new ideas and quicker to question existing institutions. Nevertheless, it was the intellectuals and the liberals of the ruling classes who led the various national movements.

Nationalism Among the Slavs of the Empire

Within the Austrian Monarchy, there was a sizeable Slavic population.

All nationalities totaled, the Slavs made up about 40 percent of the entire population of the empire.

Among the northern Slavs, the Czech intellectuals in Bohemia played a leading role in awakening national feelings. Because of Father Dobrowski's work, Czech writers had a purified and structured literary language which they began to use widely in place of German. Joseph Jungmann (1773-1847), rector of the University of Prague and author of a Czech-German dictionary and a history of Czech literature, pursued research in comparative linguistics in Slavic languages. A Czech national consciousness was encouraged in the first half of the 19th century through the rediscovery of Czech history. The creation of the National Museum of Prague in 1818 and the regular publication of its bulletin in Czech were major contributions. Frantisek Palacky (1798-1876) stands out among those who furthered the study of history at this time. In his ten-volume *History of the Czech Nation*, Palacky wanted to teach his compatriots about their often glorious past, although he also emphasized—and sometimes exaggerated—the long-standing conflicts between Czechs and Germans. Political publications also appeared at this time, particularly the *Official Gazette of Prague*, begun in 1846 by Havlicek who used it to demand respect for the historical rights and the individuality of Bohemia. Still, the Czech national movement had no intention of destroying the Habsburg monarchy this early. Palacky demonstrated that clearly in his famous declaration of 1848. Like many of his compatriots, he hoped to alter the structures within a federal framework rather than through radical change.

About this time, there was a slow awakening of nationalism among the Slovak intellectuals. The Slovaks were few in number and isolated in the Carpathian mountains of north and northwestern Hungary, and had done little to merit attention. A population boom perceptibly increased the number of Slovaks in Hungary. The area inhabited by the Slovaks stretched out toward the Danubian plains, and Slovaks moved in increasing numbers to the cities, notably Pozsony (Bratislava) where the more educated among them came into contact with the reigning currents of thought. Certain intellectuals were conscious of Slovak qualities distinct from those of their Czech and Hungarian neighbors, and tried to create a literary language for themselves. One such intellectual was Louis Stur (1815-1856) who had the central Slovak dialect adopted as the written language. Others, such as Paul Safarik (1795-1861), once a librarian at the University of Prague, opted for a common course with the Czechs. Safarik was, however, a Protestant, and felt closer to the Czechs than to his Slovak compatriots who were primarily Catholic.

Among the southern Slavs, the national renewal served to diminish the divisions that separated the Orthodox Serbians from the Catholic Croats and

Slovenes. Three writers in particular began the cultural revival and tried to give the southern Slavs a common language. These were the Slovene Jernej Kopitar (1780-1844), the Serb Vuk Karadjitch (1787-1864) and the Croat Louis Gaj (1809-1872). All three developed the Serbo-Croatian literary language, although alongside it popular dialects remained strong and are still used today in the western provinces of Yugoslavia. Gaj, who played a major role, was the son of a doctor in Zagreb. He studied law in Graz and Vienna and became a close friend of the Czech poet Kollar. In all of his works, and especially in his newspaper, the *Illyrian National Gazette*, Gaj championed Illyrism—a sort of Yugoslavism before its time—or a union of all the southern Slavs into a single state within the Habsburg federation. Gaj's ideas were particularly well received in Croatia, a province state within Hungary that had a special status. Croatia had a diet and autonomous executive powers directed by the Ban, or viceroy. Because of Gaj's efforts, Croatian became the official language used in the Diet of Zagreb in 1847. The region's individualistic qualities remained strong, especially among the peasant masses, while German and Italian, which had been the languages of culture, lost ground to Serbo-Croatian.

National Renewal in Hungary

By 1815, the national renewal was well underway in Hungary. It expanded between 1815 and 1848 with an extraordinary production of literature, poetry in particular. Romanticism and patriotism culminated in the works of Mihaly Csokonai, Ferenc Kolcsey, author of the national anthem, Mihaly Vorosmarty and especially Sandor Petofi (1823-1849). Simultaneously, the composers Erkel and Liszt were introducing all of Europe to the treasures of Hungarian folk music.

This national renewal also had political ramifications. Metternich only reluctantly accepted the special status of Hungary with its own constitution and parliament and therefore, from 1812 to 1825, the parliament never met. As soon as it convened in 1825, however, the deputies demanded stronger constitutional guarantees. A politicized press appeared in the early 1840s. It was divided between two ideologies, one moderate, represented by Count Istvan Szechenyi's newspaper, *The Eastern People*, and the more radical, Lajos Kossuth's *Gazette of Pest*. The two voices echoed in programs for reform proposed to the parliament. Moderates like Count Szechenyi and the lawyer Deak wanted to transform Hungary into a constitutional monarchy like Great Britain without breaking the ties that linked Hungary to the rest of the Empire. Szechenyi (1791-1860) was aware of the economic interdependence that united the various peoples of the Danubian region, and especially emphasized the need to modernize Hungary by creating infrastructures. It was Szechenyi who instigated steamboat traffic on the Danube, and who in

1842 had the suspension bridge strung across the Danube to better link the twin cities of Buda, symbol of the past, and Pest, symbol of the future. It was also under his influence that the Commercial Bank of Pest, which financed construction of the first railway lines and factories, was founded in 1841. The other moderate leader, Ferenc Deak (1803-1876), was more politically oriented. According to Deak, "Hungary is a free country, independent, throughout its legislative and administrative system; she is subordinate to no country. We do not want to place the interest of our country counter to those of the monarchy's unity and of its security; ...for us, constitutional life is a treasure that we are not allowed to sacrifice to a foreign interest nor to greater military advantages. Our first duty is to preserve it and strengthen it...."

The most radical reformists were led by the lawyer Lajos Kossuth (1802-1894), who frequently served as deputy in the Hungarian Parliament, where he was the leader of the opposition during the 1847-1848 session. Kossuth founded the *Gazette of Pest* in which he demanded the full independence of Hungary with a government responsible to Parliament, an independent army, and separation from the rest of the Austrian Empire. Nevertheless, Kossuth did not question the monarchy as a form of government, nor the principle of a personal union with Austria. Kossuth made himself spokesman for a very uncompromising sort of Hungarian nationalism, and made his position clear to the Diet of 1844 when he ardently defended the law that made Hungarian the official language of the state. This language law, adopted in 1844, put Hungarian in a privileged position relative to the other languages spoken by nearly half the population. No language but Latin had enjoyed such a status.

The national awakening in Hungary thus led to the political movement of Nationalism, which came with a grave risk: that of creating an explosive situation at a time when the non-Hungarian populations of the kingdom were also becoming conscious of their unique cultural heritages, epitomized by their languages. In Transylvania, Hungarians demanded an end to the region's special status, but their request irritated the other nationalities who lived there and were also trying to assert themselves. The Germans, for example, had the Saxon Society formed by the Protestant minister, Roth, in 1840, and the Rumanians had published their own newspaper, *The Transylvanian Gazette* since 1838.

Thus, within the Austrian Empire, the new awareness of nationalism felt by all of the peoples created a volatile situation which could lead to the disintegration of a system that had been patiently refined over the centuries. In the 1840s the Austrian Empire was at a crossroads. Should it allow the current evolution to continue without reacting and risk confrontation among the various nationalities, or should it do as Metternich had always advised and maintain the monarchy as it was in order to guarantee peace in the Danubian region?

Chapter 8

1848—The Springtime of Nations
Success and Failure in Revolution

The Parisian revolution of February, 1848, which resulted in the abdication of Louis-Philippe and the proclamation of the Republic of France, had a considerable effect on the rest of Europe, inciting varying degrees of revolutionary fervor everywhere—with the exceptions of Great Britain and Russia. The revolutionary explosion in the spring of 1848, or the "Springtime of Nations," as it is often called, was the result of several converging factors. Beginning in 1845-1846, Europe had entered a period of economic difficulties and social tensions due to a series of bad harvests. Consumption of manufactured goods declined and investment came to a standstill. Misery stalked the countryside, and in the cities, prices and unemployment rose. These economic difficulties and their attendant social problems gave rise to widespread political dissent. As political discontent intensified, calls for nationalism grew more strident, although here too the intensity varied by country.

APPARENT CALM IN POLAND

The different parts of former Poland reacted differently to the general climate of agitation. The Poles of Prussia, like all other subjects of Frederick William IV, took part in demonstrations for freedom. Initially, the liberals were satisfied. The king of Prussia promised a constitution and announced to the Polish delegates in April, 1848, that Posnania would be granted special status. Polish delegates elected to the Constituent Assembly tried to assure that promises made would be kept, but in vain. The failure of the revolutionary movement in Berlin and the army's tight control of the country after December, 1848, put an end to liberal hopes. The constitution finally made public on January 31, 1830, by Prince Regent William made Prussia into a single state. It was a bitter disappointment for the Poles to be stripped of their political identity and absorbed by the Prussian state.

The Poles in Austria stayed out of the turmoil affecting the Empire for the most part. Still, a National Polish Council was organized in Leopol by Smolka, a lawyer. Smolka single-mindedly demanded the abolition of serfdom on the feudal estates, a measure immediately adopted by the Austrian government in order to cut short any unrest. To thwart Polish actions the Austrian authorities encouraged the creation of a National Ruthenian Council. On the whole, Polish territories under Austrian rule remained calm. Only a few Polish officers of the 1830-1831 revolution—Bem, Dobrowski, and Wysocki—who had taken refuge in Galicia, demonstrated their sympathy for the rebellious peoples. Galicia as a whole remained loyal, however, and in recompense Emperor Franz Joseph named a Polish aristocrat, Prince Goluchowski, as governor of the province in 1849.

Poland, under the close surveillance of the Russian occupying forces, appeared very calm in 1848. The Russian governor of Poland, Marshal Paskievitch, was even sent by Czar Nicholas I to restore order in Hungary in 1849 during the rebellion against Franz Joseph. Nevertheless, the Poles felt deep sympathy for all those who were fighting for their freedom.

RUMANIAN DISTURBANCES IN THE OTTOMAN EMPIRE

In the Ottoman Empire, 1848 was a relatively calm year. Neither the Serbs nor the Bulgars took part in the turmoil that most European countries were experiencing. Only the Rumanians in Moldavia and Wallachia demonstrated their interest in freedom. Intellectuals, students, and professors, as well as the progressive part of the nobility, were enthusiastic about the ideas from Paris.

In Moldavia, a revolutionary committee set up in Jassy on March 27, 1848, demanded that the Hospodar Sturdza respect the *Organic Ruling of 1831*, abolish censorship, and form a national guard. The Russians, who had troops stationed there, broke up the movement with the approval of Turkish authorities. The members of the Revolutionary Committee were arrested, and calm was quickly restored, mainly because the countryside had hardly been aware of the occurrances.

The revolutionary movement in Wallachia was of more consequence, however. As in Moldavia, the revolutionaries demanded certain reforms, but they also asked for a union of the two principalities. The *hospodar* of Wallachia, George Bibesco, appeared sympathetic to the request. Several years earlier, in 1846, he had abolished the customs border that separated his principality from Moldavia. Bibesco firmly opposed any restraint on his authority, however. Trouble began in April, and on June 11, 1848, the people of Bucharest revolted. Bibesco was forced to give in, and agreed to a constitution. Feudal rights and serfdom were abolished, the Jews were given equal rights, and a national guard established. The blue, yellow, and red flag—which is still the flag of the Rumanian Republic—was hoisted. Bibesco abdicated after having agreed to the liberals' demands, and a provisional government was formed under the direction of the archbishop and the principle leaders of the insurrection, including M. Balcescu and D. Bratianu. A split quickly developed between the moderates and radicals wishing to form a republic uniting all Rumanians, however. The radicals wished to include the Rumanians in Transylvania, who had been demonstrating since April, 1848, demanding independence from the Hungarian regime. Fearing further disturbances, the Russians and Turks together put down the Vlach Revolution, as it was called. In September, the Russians reinforced their troops in Moldavia and even occupied part of Wallachia, while the Turks set up a garrison in Bucharest. Then in May, 1849, through the Baltaliman Pact, the two powers agreed to designate two new *hospodars* to govern for seven years and restore order. Numerous exiles fled the country, mainly for Paris, where a number worked actively to interest the French government in the Rumanian cause. Reportedly, Napoleon III himself was receptive to their appeals.

REVOLUTIONS IN THE HABSBURG EMPIRE

The authoritarian character of the rule personified by Metternich and the rising tide of nationalism within the Empire set a course for an eventual explosion. The news from Paris, which had already set off revolutionary action in southern Germany, had a similar effect in the major cities of the Empire.

The First Revolutionary Wave

The first echo of the successful Parisian revolution resounded in Prague. On March 11, 1848, Bohemian liberals, Germans, and Czechs alike organized a public meeting on Wenceslas Square. The resulting Committee of St. Wenceslas worked out a program of demands to present to the government in Vienna: freedom of the press, equality of all nationalities and of all languages, and regular meetings of the Diet were foremost among them.

Since March 13, Viennese liberals and students had been noisily demonstrating in the streets, crying "Down with Metternich!" Faced with the gravity of the situation, Emperor Ferdinand and his entourage—*la camerilla*—demanded the aging chancellor's resignation. On March 15, the emperor gave in to all of the demands. He announced the abolition of censorship, the creation of a civil guard to guarantee order in place of the regular army, and the convocation of a constituent assembly.

The movement spread further. Lombardy and Venetia, the principle Habsburg possessions in northern Italy, revolted and between March 17 and March 22, drove out the Austrian garrisons. The Viennese government was forced to send reinforcements, since the Italian revolution seriously threatened the vital interests of Austria. This was in fact not only a liberal revolution; it was also a widespread national movement aimed at expelling the Austrians and unifying Italy.

From Prague and Vienna, the unrest spread to Hungary. Just as the revolution in Paris was claiming victory, the Hungarian Diet was in full session at Pozsony. On March 3, in the name of the liberal opposition, Lajos Kossuth had already demanded a Hungarian Ministry accountable for their actions, expansion of the right to vote, abolition of the political privileges accorded to Transylvania and Croatia, and the relocation of the Diet from Pozsony to Budapest. On March 5, a revolutionary mob invaded the assembly room and forced the deputies to vote for a message to the emperor containing Kossuth's demands. Soon after, a delegation was sent to "King" Ferdinand, not to the Emperor of Austria. This delegation arrived in Vienna on the day of Metternich's departure. The Emperor-King promised the Hungarians satisfaction, but in the meantime, the Diet proceeded to adopt a series of reforms known as the March Laws. The special privileges of the nobles and gentry were abolished, as was feudalism; all citizens were proclaimed equal, and freedom of the press was established. As Crane Brinton notes in his *A History of Civilization*,

> The March Laws instituted parliamentary government and substituted an elected legislature for the feudal Hungarian Diet. They abolished serfdom and ended the immunity of nobles and gentry from taxation.

In Pest, however, revolutionary spirit was riding high on the crest of events, and students far more radical than members of the Diet staged their own demonstration on March 15, even though the principle of the reforms had already been accepted. The students rallied around the poet Sandor Petofi and the writer Mor Jokai in front of the National Museum, and drew up a list of twelve demands. After the rally, the crowd proceeded to search the prisons for political prisoners and liberated all they found.

Fearing the spread of revolution, on April 7, King Ferdinand conceded to all the Hungarian demands. As *Palatin* (viceroy), he appointed his brother, Archduke Stephen, who was sworn in by the first elected Hungarian government. A liberal magnate, Count Lajos Batthyany, presided over the government, which included representatives of all political persuasions: moderates like Deak and Szechenyi, and radicals like Kossuth and Szemere. As King of Hungary, Ferdinand came in person on April 11 to close the parliamentary session and to swear to uphold the constitution. It was the last session of the Diet at Posony. From then on, Pest became the political center of the country.

The Hungarian and Austrian revolutions appeared to have succeeded, with Metternich's rule a feature of the past. Liberalism was the reigning ideology of all the new governments. In reality, the situation was far more complex. First, although the Austrian Empire was momentarily deprived of the armed forces sent to Italy, it still had several crucial advantages. Revolutionary fervor had touched only the cities, while the large majority of the population—that of the countryside—had hardly been affected. Second, the liberals in power were divided between moderates favoring an agreement based on loyalty to the throne, and radicals anxious to totally alter the political and social make-up of the Empire.

Demands for more freedom were soon joined by separatist demands from the various ethnic groups, while the contradictions inherent in such nationalist demands quickly made themselves apparent and led to violent internal struggles. Many German intellectuals in Austria hoped to integrate Austria into the Greater German confederation under consideration since 1815, and to this end sent deputies to the parliament in Frankfurt. But Czech liberals, who thought of themselves as Slavs and not Germans, rallied around Palacky to stand up for Bohemia's individual status. Kossuth's radicals wanted to transform Hungary into an independent national state, but in the process they both antagonized and intimidated the non-Hungarians within Hungary's borders. With the encouragement of conservative elements at court, different ethnic groups in Hungary quickly began to react. The Croats were the first to demonstrate their displeasure at the extremely pro-Magyar character of the revolution; the idea of total independence was beginning to make its way into Croatia. On March 25, the Diet at Zagreb named one of the leaders of the Illyrian movement, Colonel Jellachich, as *ban*. Fueled by nationalism and unhappy with the policies of the government at Pest, the Croatian deputies took matters into their own hands by declaring Croatia independent on June 5. The Magyar government refused to recognize an independent Croatia, however, and on August 16 Jellachich declared war on Hungary.

The Croats were not the only ones to rise up against the Magyars. On May 11, 1848, a group of prominent Slovak writers, teachers, and priests met at Lipto-Szent Miklos (today named Liptovsky Sv. Mikulas), and voted for a declaration of autonomy for the Slovak regions within Hungary. Simultaneously, representatives of the Hungarian Serbian minority were meeting at Karlovici, and on May 13, they assembled similar demands and sent a copy of their grievances to Vienna and Zagreb. Unrest was also fermenting among the Rumanians in Transylvania. In response to a call from the Uniate clergy, a large gathering at Balazsfalva (Blaj) voted to obtain special status. A minority agitated for the formation of a state incorporating Rumanians from both sides of the Carpathian mountains. The weight of all the ethnic groups' demands, however, only caused the Magyar government to harden its position. As all of the ethnic groups except the Slovaks had come as refugees to Hungary and had been warmly welcomed, their behavior seemed all the more outrageous. Their ingratitude was deemed incomprehensible, and Kossuth's allies blamed their behavior on imperialist intrigues.

> I am not German, or at least I am not consciously so... I am Czech, of Slavic origin, and the little that I am worth is entirely at the service of my country. This country is no doubt small, but from the moment of its birth onward, it has had a historic individuality. Its princes have joined with German princes, but its people have never thought of themselves as German... Moreover, you desire to weaken the existence of Austria as an independent state. But the maintenance of Austria's integrity and Austria's development are of the highest importance, not only for my people, but for all of Europe, for humanity, and for civilization itself...
>
> Excerpted from Frantisek Palacky's response to an invitation from the Vorparliament of Frankfurt, May, 1848.

> It would be a crime against all the rights of humanity if in Bohemia, Moravia, and Silesia they sacrificed a civilization built on German culture for a new attempt at political organization... Let us therefore rejoice in the victory that extinguished the Czech insurrection in Prague and look for ways to make this victory a lasting one...
>
> From a speech to the Parliament of Frankfurt by Karl Giskra, German deputy of Moravia, July 1, 1848.

The Imperial government was uncertain in its stance toward ethnic unrest, and its policies reflected its hesitancy. It saw advantages both in condemning the disturbances and in encouraging them in order to create trouble for the independent Hungarian government. This hesitation was also due to the fact that the Imperial government had more urgent problems to consider. Foremost was Italy, where nationalists led by King Charles Albert of Piedmont carried off several victories in May, 1848. The Piedmontese forces were finally defeated at Custoza on July 25 by the Imperial Army under Marshal Radetzky. Austria was also concerned with Bohemia, where the victorious liberal movement was quickly divided by quarrels between German nationalists and Czech patriots. The Pan-Slavic tendencies of the Czech intellectuals deeply worried the Bohemian Germans who, for their part, would have liked to see the province integrated into a united Greater Germany. The anti-German sentiment expressed by liberal Czechs emerged at the meeting of the Pan-Slav Congress on June 2, 1848, whose object was "to promote the solidarity of all Austrian Slavs and to resist incorporation of non-German peoples into the new German Empire." This declaration was an allusion to the Greater Germany idea favored by German nationalists in Bohemia and Austria. The Congress further declared that their intention was "to act together in the national interest, to find the means to organize Austria into a federated state, to send the rulers a document detailing the needs and desires of the Slavs." Not surprisingly, the declarations of the Congress infuriated German Bohemians, and the Imperial Army took advantage of the situation to step in, in order to "restore order." After bombarding Prague, General Windischgratz took the city on June 15 and dissolved the Congress. The other Bohemian cities and the countryside had not participated in the turmoil, and by the end of June all of Bohemia was back under Imperial authority.

The victories of the Imperial armies in Italy and Bohemia renewed confidence in Austrian rule. The court took note of this, and gave support to the Croats, who had just declared war on Hungary. Croatian troops, along with Serbian volunteers from southern Hungary, crossed the Drava and Danube rivers, and entered Hungarian territory. The Hungarians did not have a national army, and the Hungarian contingents of the Imperial Army were scattered in garrisons throughout the Empire. The undisciplined Serb forces engaged in massacre and pillage, most notably at Szeged, where hundreds of Magyars were slaughtered. In response to an appeal from Kossuth, Hungarian soldiers returned to serve their national government. The new Hungarian parliament, elected in July, 1848, had just declared a state of "national emergency," and decided to raise a national guard of 200,000 men, named the *Honved*. The first Croatian victories, as well as the quasi-official support given to Jellachich by the Imperial government, put Hungary in a delicate and potentially dangerous situation. The danger materialized with the emperor's repudiation of the Archduke Stephen, Palatin of Hungary. Stephen resigned on September 9, and his resignation was followed two days later by that of the Batthyany government.

The emperor decided that it was in his immediate interest to crush the Hungarian rebellion, and sent General Lemberg as Plenipotentiary Imperial

Commissioner to Pest with the task of reestablishing "order" in Hungary. The appointment of Lemberg and the threat of the advancing Croatian force galvanized the Magyar deputies into action. Kossuth was named president of the Committee for Defense on September 22, in the midst of a rapidly worsening situation. The Croats took Veszprem, only 60 kilometers from the capital, and the news incited mobs in Pest to riots which lasted for a week. On September 29, an incensed crowd lynched General Lemberg, and on the same day the *Honveds* defeated Jellachich's force at Pakozd. For the moment the country was saved, but in Parliament the moderates were alarmed at the violence of the extremists who appeared to be out of Kossuth's control. By October, 1848, the gap between Magyar moderates and radicals was complete, as was the separation between the Hungarian revolutionary government and the Imperial court.

Kossuth and the War of Independence (1848-1849)

By October, 1848, Kossuth was master of the country. His armies were led by such former Imperial Army generals as Arthur Gorgey and George Klapka, and by Polish officers such as General Bem, and succeeded in pushing the Croats westward toward the Austrian border. Count Latour, the Imperial government's Minister of War, wanted to send the Italian regiments stationed in Vienna against the Hungarians. The Italians, however, refused, and on October 6 pro-Hungarian Viennese workers and students began erecting barricades in the center of Vienna. During this second Viennese revolution, Minister Latour was killed, and a thoroughly intimidated Imperial court left Vienna for the safety of Olomouc in Bohemia.

The *Honveds* attempted to aid the Viennese revolutionaries, but were driven back at Schwechat on October 30 by the same Imperial Army that was laying siege to the Austrian capital. Vienna was finally stormed and taken after intense artillery bombardment on November 1. The Constituent Assembly was dissolved and most of the reforms of March, 1848, were abolished.

Shortly thereafter, a tired and ill Ferdinand abdicated and was succeeded by his 18-year-old nephew, Franz Joseph. Advised by the conservative factions of the court, Franz Joseph made it clear that he intended to restore order in his empire. Conscious of the problems that had arisen, however, he told a Viennese audience, "We are firmly resolved to preserve the unblemished magnificence of the crown, but are willing to share our prerogatives with representatives of the people, and we hope, with the aid of God, to reunite in one great state all the countries and all the races of the monarchy."

The accession of Franz Joseph and his words radicalized the Hungarian revolutionaries. Kossuth quickly made it known that Hungary would not recognize the new soveriegn's authority unless he pledged to uphold the Constitution. The Imperial government responded by launching a general military offensive against Hungary. On December 18, 1849, Imperial forces took Pozsony, and Buda and Pest fell on January 4. Kossuth's government and what remained of Parliament after the departure of the moderates took refuge in Debrecen. Seizing the opportunity, the Rumanians in Transylvania and the Serbs of the Banat and Bacska (Vojvodine) began massacring the Magyar population. The *Honveds* quickly moved in to rescue Kossuth's precarious situation.

With 10,000 men, General Bem restored order in Transylvania, while Generals Damjanich and Perczel crushed the Serbian insurrection. General Gorgey retook Pest on April 24 and the fortress of Buda on May 21. Once again, the Imperial forces appeared to be defeated. With his power and popularity at a pinnacle, Kossuth hoped to follow his military victory with a political one. On April 14, 1849, on the initiative of the radical deputy Madarasz, the Hungarian parliament at Debrecen (reduced to barely a quarter of its members) proclaimed Hungarian independence, the deposition of the Habsburgs and the election of Kossuth as Regent. In the days that followed, a series of reforms were enthusiastically voted in.

The decision of the Hungarian Parliament prompted Emperor Franz Joseph to act on the advice of his entourage, who were pressing him to accept the offer of assistance from the Czar of Russia. In June, 1848, Nicholas I had offered Austria his services in putting an end to the revolutions. His offer had been politely declined. In early summer of 1849, however, the situation had changed radically enough to lead the Austrians to reconsider Nicholas's offer. Kossuth's actions were seen as leading to the secession of Hungary from the Empire; something which, clearly enough, the Austrians were unwilling to allow. Russian intervention was accepted. In July, a Russian army of over 200,000 men commanded by Marshal Paskievitch, responsible for putting down the Polish revolution of 1830-1831, invaded Hungary from the north and east. Simultaneously, the Austrian army of Marshal Haynu attacked from the west. Kossuth was in open conflict with General Gorgey and found himself increasingly isolated. He attempted to rally various ethnic groups to his cause by passing a liberal law intended to benefit them, but it was too late; no friends of the Magyars, they waited until the end of the war to take sides. At the battle of Segesvar on July 31, the *Honveds* were defeated, and among the fallen was the poet Petofi. On August 9, virtually abandoned on all sides, Kossuth decided to go into exile in Turkey, where he was very well received. Kossuth left General Gorgey in power. On August 13, 1849, at Vilagos, the Hungarian Army surrendered, although certain strongholds held out longer. Arad held until August 17, and the last to surrender was Komarom on September 25, 1849, when its commander,

General Klapka, was offered honorable terms.

The Austrians dealt harshly with the defeated nation. Hungary was put under marshal law under Marshal Haynu, called the Hyena of Brescia for his harsh suppression of the Italian revolution. Haynu organized military tribunals to punish those who had participated in the insurrection. Prince Batthyany, head of the first independent Hungarian government, was shot on October 6, 1849 in Pest, while on the same day in Arad, 13 Hungarian generals were executed. They were recorded in Hungarian history as the martyrs of Arad. Only General Gorgey was spared, escaping the death penalty with a heavy prison sentence. Gorgey won his reprieve by merit of always having tried to temper the more radical elements in the government and army. In total, more than a hundred executions were carried out, and thousands received prison sentences of varying length in Hungary and Austria. While the Magyars were harshly punished, the other ethnic groups that had challenged Austrian hegemony received similar treatment.

The Hungarian revolution that began with such hopes in March, 1848, ended in blood in August of 1849. It was the longest of all the European revolutions of the mid-19th century. Its failure was due mainly to the fact that its leaders, in spite of idealism and liberal ideas, had not found a solution to the problem of nationalism. Inspired by a romantic patriotism and blinded by their own enthusiasm in creating a Hungarian state both national and independent, they alienated the ethnic minorities who were themselves awakening to their own national identities. In their rush to destroy the traditional structures, the revolutionaries put a match to the powder keg of central Europe and cleared the way for open conflict between the different nationalities. In the short run, the revolutions of 1848 appeared to have failed without exception. The framework created by the Congress of Vienna appeared to have remained intact, despite the absence of Metternich. Viewed from a different angle, however, the revolutions left their mark. Some important reforms passed by the revolutionary regimes remained: feudalism was definitively abolished and the equal rights of all Austrian subjects proclaimed. And a problem that had never troubled the Habsburgs before had been raised. The questions of relations between the different nationalities and of nationalism itself were to trouble the Austrian Empire up to its dissolution.

Chapter 9

The Search for New Structures

In spite of their apparent defeat by the forces of counter-revolution, the revolutions of 1848-49 profoundly affected the peoples of Eastern Europe, even those who were only indirectly involved in the events themselves. Governments were also affected: the revolutions had demonstrated the importance of nationalism, and while some deplored or even directly opposed it, others sought to use it to their expansionist ends. Nationalism became an important element in the foreign policy of the major powers.

THE POWERS AND THE QUESTION OF THE OTTOMAN EMPIRE

Perhaps the first nation to feel the full force of nationalism was the weakened Ottoman Empire, which by 1850 was considered "the sick man of Europe." The awakening of the Balkan nations had already led to independence in Greece and autonomy in Serbia, and the vacuum developing in southeastern Europe soon became a great concern for the major powers. Diplomatic opinions regarding what should be done ranged from simply propping up the Empire to a solution suggested by the Russian ambassador to his British colleague in January 1853: complete dismemberment. Due in part to conflicting national interests, the major powers remained in disagreement. While European nations were aware of the oppressed Christian peoples in the Ottoman Empire who were eager to be free of the Turks, concern for their own interests caused them to remain inactive.

The Russians had long supported dismemberment. Not only did Czar Nicholas I see himself as the protector of the Orthodox Christians in the

Balkans, but was also eager to break the Turkish "lock" that closed the Straits of Bosporus to the Russian fleet, and that prevented all direct access to the Mediterranean. For internal political reasons, Napoleon III also demonstrated concern for the Christian communities of the Ottoman Empire from the beginning of his reign. One of the main tenets of his foreign policy was the *principal of nationalities*, and in its name Napoleon supported the emancipation of the Balkan peoples, albeit with the full consent of the British; another tenet of the Second Empire's foreign policy rested upon cooperation with Britain. Unfortunately, the British wanted the Ottoman Empire to remain intact in order to serve as an obstacle to a Russian presence in the eastern Mediterranean. The Austrian Empire, however, considered the Balkans its natural outlet to the sea, and accordingly favored maintaining the status quo. It was also alarmed that its Serbian and Rumanian subjects might be attracted to the new states that would rise from the ruins of the Ottoman Empire.

The first serious international crisis linked to the Ottoman question broke out in 1853, and rapidly developed into the conflict known as the Crimean War. The dispute began in Jerusalem over the use of the Holy Places. Roman Catholic churchmen, mostly French, had progressively extended their influence in Jerusalem at the expense of Orthodox monks. The Russian government felt that the ousting of the Orthodox clergy was unjust, and decided to take the matter to the Sultan of Turkey, who had jurisdiction of Palestine. In February 1853, Czar Nicholas I sent a mission under Prince Menchikov to Constantinople, with the intention of obtaining permission to protect the Orthodox Christians of the Ottoman Empire. Backed by the knowledge that he was supported by the British, the sultan refused the request. The refusal culminated in the departure of Menchikov and his mission in May and in a clear break in relations between Russia and the Empire. The Russians responded by sending troops into Moldavia and Wallachia, and in November 1853, the sultan declared war on Russia.

The Crimean War lasted nearly two years and saw the participation of virtually all major powers. France and Great Britain entered on the side of the sultan in March of 1854, and Austria, while ostensibly neutral, clearly favored the allies. The war ended in a Russian defeat. The **Treaty of Paris** of March 1856 attempted to reconcile the principle of keeping Ottoman territory intact with the interests of the Balkan peoples as supported by France, and was considered a diplomatic success. The independence and integrity of the Ottoman Empire, a principle firmly supported by the British, was solemnly confirmed and guaranteed by the powers, while Serbian autonomy was ratified and "an independent and national administration" was also extended to Moldavia and Wallachia. The Treaty of Paris was the result of a number of compromises. Napoleon III suggested uniting the principalities of Moldavia and Wallachia into a single Rumanian state to increase their power: an idea to which the sultan, the British, and especially the Austrians were firmly opposed. The compromise settled upon declared Moldavia and Wallachia to be the United Principalities, possessing the same legal and judicial systems but remaining two distinct states, each with a *Hospodar* elected for life. The main victim of the treaty was Russia; not only was the Ottoman Empire strengthened at its expense, but the Black Sea was also neutralized. In closing, the peace conference also succeeded in agreeing on the internationalization of the Danube.

NAPOLEON III AND THE BALKAN QUESTION AFTER THE TREATY OF PARIS

> "The government of the Empire has always been characterized by a dichotomy of thought regarding the Balkans. While it has tried to assure the independence and maintenance of the Ottoman Empire in accordance with the political interests of France and Europe, it has also had as a constant concern the improvement of the conditions of the Christian peoples living under the sovereignty and suzerainty of the sultan. It considers one of the more fortunate results of its policy and the efforts of its armies to be a contribution to the easing of conditions for these numerous populations by obtaining for them the rights and advantages of religious freedom..."
>
> Official statement of the French government published in the **Monieur** of February 5, 1857.

In the years following the Treaty of Paris, Napoleon III quietly continued with his policy of promoting a united Rumania. The French consuls assigned to Bucharest and Jassy (Messrs. Blondel and Place) advised the Moldavian and Wallachian assemblies to circumvent the intentions of the treaty by electing a common *Hospodar*. On January 24, 1859, the two assemblies elected Alexander Ion Couza, who took the title of Prince of Rumania. This went unchallenged by the European nations, and the sultan himself recognized it two years later. The Rumanian state was born.

The state suffered its first interior crisis on the night of February 10, 1866, when a military conspiracy led by conservative Boyars forced Prince Couza to resign. The Boyars accused him of taking excessively dictatorial powers, but in reality the plot was motivated by resistance to Couza's social policy, which clearly benefited the lower classes. In his brief reign Prince Couza pursued a number of major reforms. In 1863, monasterial properties were secularized, and shortly thereafter he abolished the *corvee* system of serf labor, restoring in the process full property rights for peasants—a measure that affected nearly 400,000 families. Couza also supervised the lowering of the property qualification for the ability to vote, as well as the creation of free and compulsory primary education. In this light, the reasons for Couza's fall are much more clear.

Napoleon III was concerned with who would succeed Couza to the throne, favoring Prince Charles of Hohenzollern-Signaringen, who was a cousin of King William I of Prussia through his father, and of Napoleon III himself through his mother. Prince Charles entered Bucharest in May, 1866, and, through the efficiency of the French ambassador to Constantinople, was quickly recognized by the sultan as hereditary prince of Rumania. His descendents reigned until the communist takeover in 1947.

Polish Illusions

Russian-controlled Poland remained calm throughout the revolutions of 1848. It remained calm not because national sentiment had disappeared, as both the clergy and nobility made clear, but because of the Russian repression imposed after the uprising of 1830-31, which made any revolutionary action impossible. The first hint of a thaw appeared in 1855 with the death of Czar Nicholas I, symbol of the most intransigent absolutism. His death was greeted with relief by the Poles, who saw in his son, Czar Alexander II, someone more open to progressive ideas. However, when the new Czar received the deputies from the Polish nobility in 1856, he informed them that he intended to continue the policies of his father and that there was no question of restoring the Constitution of 1815. Nevertheless, he appointed Prince Gorchakov as viceroy of Poland in place of his authoritarian predecessor, Paskievitch. Upon his arrival in Warsaw, the new viceroy published a degree of general amnesty and restored confiscated properties to the rightful recipients, thereby raising Polish hopes of a more permissive political atmosphere.

In the climate of relative freedom that began to settle over Poland, a hesitant and cautious political life was reborn. The Agronomic Society was founded in 1855 by Count Zamoyski, and included several thousand landowners, most of them nobles. It quickly became the rallying point of the liberal and national opposition to support an independent Poland linked to Russia only by a common sovereign. These relatively moderate liberals that formed the White Party were flanked on the left by members of the radical Red Party composed of students, the lower classes of Warsaw, and some members of the gentry. The Red Party demanded the total independence of Poland within its historic borders.

The success of the united Italian movement of 1859-60 was greeted with enthusiasm by Polish patriots. They noted with joy that Napoleon III had supported the Italians in their fight for independence, and were convinced that he would do the same for Poland. As his minister of foreign affairs was none other than Count Walewski, son of Marie Walewska and Napoleon I, their hopes were further encouraged. The Poles also knew that Napoleon III was an enthusiastic supporter of the principle of nationalities; a fact which he had just reiterated by supporting the Moldavian and Wallachian Rumanians in their fight for independence.

By early 1860, Poles were confident about their future. Hadn't Czar Alexander instituted liberal reforms, abolishing serfdom on lands owned by the crown in 1858? And wasn't he about to extend them to all of Russian territory? The time seemed ripe for action. The first demonstrations in Poland began on November 29, 1860, the anniversary of the uprising in Warsaw of 1830, and flared up again on February 25 and 27, 1861. While the demonstration of November 29 was peaceful, those of 1861 were marred by brutality, as Russian troops fired into the crowd killing several demonstrators. The Agronomic Society was anxious to avoid the repression and bloodshed that a new revolution would bring, and thought it best to present a petition demanding freedom from Russian occupation to the viceroy. The viceroy responded by dissolving the Society and exiling Count Zamoyski, only to be himself removed by Alexander II. The czar was clearly uncertain about what policy to pursue regarding Poland, and his hesitancy was reflected by his exchange of viceroys several times.

In Poland the Reds and Whites quickly renewed their conflict. The liberal leader, Wielopolski, attempted to work out an agreement with the czar, but was immediately accused of treason by the Reds. To prevent further disturbances, Wielopolski advised the authorities to call the young men of Warsaw up for active duty, but no one answered the call for mobilization. Instead, the situation deteriorated further, and on January 22, 1863, the Revolutionary Central Committee directed by the leaders of the Red Party called for a general insurrection. A similar committee was formed at Vilna, and on March 31, declared Lithuania an integral part of Poland. By the end of April, all of Poland was in a state of insurrection, including the provinces directly administered by Russia. The Central Committee was now recognized as the provisional government, and began to appeal to foreign powers for assistance. Napoleon III, to whom the provisional government had delegated General Mieroslawski, wrote the the czar personally to ask him for the restoration of the Constitution of 1815 and for the appointment of his brother, the Grand-duke Constantine as viceroy. The czar's answer was negative, and requests to the British produced no better results. Austria pursued the neutral position it had taken during the Crimean War, but again favored the insurgents. Prussia, however, gave its full support to the czar, and Bismarck closed the Polish-Prussian border to prevent Polish insurgents from using Prussian territory as a refuge.

Polish troops were quickly recruited and assembled, and led by commanders such as generals Wysocki and Poradovski, attempted to paralyze Russian troop movement. The fight, however, was unequal and the size of the Russian armies was quickly felt. In May 1863 General Mouraviev reoccupied Lithuania, which was immediately put under military rule: Russian was made the official language and most of the Catholic clergy was deported to Siberia. In the parts of Bielorussia where the disturbances took place, the Uniate Church was severely repressed and reinstated under the control of the Orthodox Church. In Poland, Warsaw was surrounded by General Berg's army and was forced into surrender. Members of the provisional government were arrested, condemned to death by a court martial, and hanged in August 1864. Tens of thousands of insurgents were deported to Siberia and their properties confiscated. All surviving Polish institutions were abolished, and Russian became the compulsory language of the government and the university. The Polish nobility, which as a rule had supported the insurrection, was heavily fined. And in order to pit the peasants against the nobles, the Russian government decided in March 1864 that the peasants on lands of the crown, church, or nobility would become full owners of the land they worked, and that all traditional rents and obligations would be abolished. This pro-peasant measure did not succeed, however, in winning them over to the side of the Russian occupants as it had been designed to do. Finally, the Catholic Church, which had always been the guardian of national traditions as well as a new focus of nationalism, suffered dearly under the repression. All bishops, without exception, were arrested and departed to Siberia (in 1870 all the episcopal seats were still vacant). Most of the convents were closed in 1864, and church property was secularized the following year.

Poland paid a heavy price for its bid for freedom. Despite the repression, the Poles succeeded to a great extent in passively resisting the policy of "Russianization" imposed on them, particularly in the local schools and administration. The force of the Russian repression and the inaction of the European powers demonstrated, once and for all, that the era of romantic resurrection was over.

From Austria to Austria-Hungary

The failure of the 1848-49 revolutions in Austria as well as the subsequent repression did nothing to resolve the problems the Empire faced. The escalation of liberal ambitions and of national movements continued. Emperor Franz Joseph, true to his word upon his ascension to the throne, attempted to find a workable solution which would take both into account without either weakening the privileges of the crown or jeopardizing the interests of the Empire.

In the years immediately following the revolution, Franz Joseph appeared to heed the advice of his conservative entourage, and in particular to that of his mother, the Archduchess Sophia. He first entrusted the position of minister of the Interior to a general, Prince Schwarzenberg, and after the prince's death in 1852 to Alexander Bach, who also performed many of the duties of prime minister. The "Bach years," as the ten-year period was later called, were characterized by a return to an authoritarian regime in the tradition of Metternich, with several distinguishing characteristics. The government resumed the old Habsburg tradition of close alliance with the Catholic Church that had been undermined by the reforms of Joseph II; the concordat signed with Pope Pius IX in 1855 gave the Catholic Church a privileged position in the state, and far more responsibility for education. The Bach government also brought back the Germanizing policies of Joseph II, in which the different provinces of the Empire were provided mainly with German-speaking civil servants and administrators who enforced the imposition of German in the schools and local governments. This policy was backed by an underlying theme of idealism. In the minds of the leadership, the most effective way to promote peaceful coexistence between all the nationalities was to impose a common language on them. But at the same time, to gain the goodwill of the peasants, Bach left the social reforms of the revolution in place: feudalism, along with feudal rights and labor taxes were definitively abolished, and the equality of all subjects reaffirmed.

Bach's policies met with mixed results, and its failures, as demonstrated in Italy in 1859 and in the passive resistance of non-German subjects—in particular the Hungarians—led Franz Joseph to take control of public affairs personally in order to reorganize the monarchy along a new set of principles. In March 1860, the emperor called together a Great Council of the Empire, composed of both elected members and citizens appointed by the emperor. Two major political currents were represented. One group of delegates favored unity, and wanted the Empire to become a liberal state with a constitution and a central government responsible to the parliament. Others, including the Croatian, Hungarian, and Czech delegates, favored a form of federalism which would reestablish the former historic states and expand their national governments.

The federalistic October Diploma proclaimed on October 20, 1860, was a result of Franz Joseph's concern for reconciling the unity of the Empire with the diversity of its peoples. In each province of the Empire, an elected diet was to have major legislative powers, and would send delegates to the imperial council (*Reichsrat*), which was responsible for matters that the provinces had in common. All of the nationalities were put on an equal footing, and all citizens were eligible for all occupations. Furthermore, in each state, the local language was to be the official language—a matter of no small importance to the provinces. Proclamation of the October Diploma was followed by the election of deputies to the various national diets everywhere. Due to opposition from liberals and conservatives alike, only a few months later, on February 26, 1861, Franz Joseph revoked the October Diploma, replacing it with the February Patent. The February Patent was centralist in nature, and constituted a reversal of Franz Joseph's position. It left the local diets intact, but some of their functions were transferred to the *Reichsrat*, which essentially became a parliament to which the ministers were responsible. It was made up of two houses, the House of Lords appointed by the sovereign, and the House of Deputies which included 340 deputies elected by the diets.

As the Hungarians had been the most demanding of the nationalities in 1848-49 and were very supportive of the October Diploma, it is not surprising that they were very dissatisfied with the February Patent of 1861. Ferenc Deak, leader of the opposition since Kossuth's exile, demanded a return to a strict adherence to the original constitution, while the Magyar deputies flatly refused to attend the *Reichsrat*. Their actions led to the dissolution of the diet. In Bohemia, the February Patent was no better received, but the Czech deputies did agree to attend the *Reichsrat* at which they presented demands for reform.

The situation remained at an impasse for four years. In 1865, however, Franz Joseph began to negotiate with the Magyar opposition, and at the opening of the diet, he announced that the old constitution be restored, but with the interests of the Empire safeguarded. With the support of Count Gyula Andrassy, who was exiled in 1848 and later granted amnesty, Deak agreed to negotiate. While it is possible that an agreement would never have been reached, Austria's defeat at Koniggratz against the Prussians and the personal intervention of Empress Elizabeth in favor of the Hungarians facilitated an agreement between the emperor and his Hungarian subjects.

Signed on February 18, 1867, the agreement was called the Austro-Hungarian Compromise (*Ausgleich*), and was actually two documents. The first was a constitutional statute which redefined the relationship between Austria and its dependencies, while the other was a constitutional pact between Franz Joseph and the Hungarian nation. The Habsburg possessions became a dual monarchy consisting of the Austrian Empire (Austria, Bohemia, Moravia, Slovenia, Carniole, Istria, and Galicia), and of the Kingdom of Hungary (Hungary proper, Transylvania, Croatia-Slavonia, and Fiume). Each state had its own institutions, its own administration and its own laws, but the two parts were united under the scepter of a common monarch—Franz Joseph, emperor in Austria and king in Hungary. The coronation of Franz Joseph as King of Hungary on June 8, 1867, symbolized the reconciliation of Hungary and the dynasty.

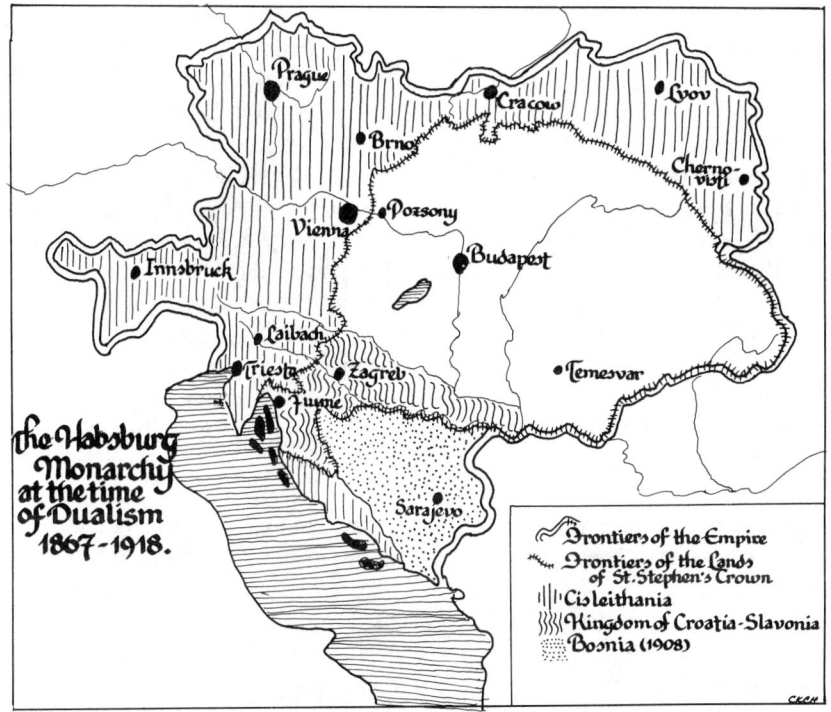

In Austria, legislative power stemmed from an Imperial Council (*Reichsrat*) made up of two houses. The House of Lords consisted of princes, prelates, 53 hereditary peers, and 100 members appointed for life by the emperor. The House of Deputies consisted of members elected for six-year terms by voters from several different social groups. 85 of the 353 deputies represented the large landowners, 137 the commercial elite and the cities, and 131 rural communities. This system was weighted in favor of the Germans and the Poles. The government, however, was not answerable to these assemblies.

In Hungary, the Parliament also included two assemblies. The composition of the High House resembled that of the House of Lords in Austria, and the Lower House the House of Deputies. The lower house was made up of 447 deputies, 337 for Hungary proper, 75 for Transylvania, 34 for Croatia-Slavonia, and one for Fiume, all elected by voters meeting property requirements. But unlike Vienna, the government in Hungary was answerable to the assemblies.

For what was declared the "common interests of Hungary and the other countries of His Majesty," three joint ministries were created—those of

Foreign Affairs, War, and Finance. Their ministers were under the supervisory authority of two delegations of 60 deputies, each elected by the parliaments of Vienna and Budapest. Expenses linked to joint affairs were paid for by a financial arrangement that assessed Hungary for 30 percent of the expenses and Austria for the rest. The Imperial and Royal Army belonged to both partners in the Empire, with German as the language of authority. But Austria and Hungary each still possessed their own territorial armies—the *Flandsturm* in Austria, and the *Honved* in Hungary, which were locally recruited and which used their national languages as the language of command. The Austro-Hungarian Compromise was completed in November 1868 by a Hungaro-Croatian compromise negotiated between the government at Budapest and the Diet at Zagreb. The agreement redefined the status of Croatia-Slavonia, making it an autonomous kingdom within Hungary with its own diet and local administration. The Budapest government was represented by the *ban*.

The reorganization of the Habsburg monarchy entrusted the development of the Empire to the two largest national groups, the Germans in Austria and the Magyars in Hungary. The question remained whether the other minorities would be content with this compromise, which did guarantee them equal rights, use of their own languages, and religious freedom, but which kept them out of certain high positions and discriminated against them in varying degress.

Chapter 10

The Austro-Hungarian Experiment
1867—1918

CONTEMPORARY VIEWS ON AUSTRIA-HUNGARY

After the signing of the *Ausgleich*, the compromise of 1867 that transformed the Austrian Empire into the Austro-Hungarian Dual Monarchy, the most immediate question that arose concerned the issue of nationalities. It was far from clear that the compromise would fulfill the expectations and aspirations that the ethnic minorities had expressed so violently in 1848-49. The question was the object of interminable controversy within, as well as without, the Dual Monarchy.

Within the Empire, there were those who believed that the compromise of 1867 was only the first step of a process that would lead to a true federalist system, with dualism evolving logically to include a third, and perhaps even a fourth, element. Others, however, particularly Hungarians with nostalgic memories of Kossuth, saw the compromise as nothing more than a temporary expedient, to be followed sooner or later by complete independence. It should be noted that these viewpoints corresponded more with the opinions of the intelligentsia and the politically aware than with the opinions of the typical citizen. Generally speaking, the various populations of the Dual Monarchy tended to remain faithful to the person of the sovereign himself as representative of the state, rather than to the prevailing constitutional system.

Attitudes differed outside the Empire. German nationalists were hostile to the concept of dualism from the beginning, and strongly opposed any evolution towards a federal system that would weaken the position of the Germans within the Empire. Instead, Pan-German proponents within Germany, with the strong support of politicized German-Austrians, envisioned integrating the Habsburg Empire—either with or without the Hungarian territories—into the framework of a vast *Mittel-Europa* governed from Berlin. For their part, the Russian court was well aware of the great number of Slavs in the Austro-Hungarian monarchy. Russians were also conscious of the advantages to be reaped should they succeed in separating the Slavs from Austria-Hungary, and at least in theory were willing to use ethnic ties to attract the young Slavic states of the Balkans. Pan-Germanism in the west was thus paralleled by Pan-Slavism in the east.

In France, a strict neutrality on Austria-Hungary was maintained in official circles, but academics such as Ernest Denis and Ernest Lavisse, such leftist politicians as Gambetta and Clemenceau, and anticlerical groups and freemasons considered the Habsburg monarchy to be a conservative and clerical state. Accordingly, they did not hesitate to denounce the Dual Monarchy, focusing on real as well as contrived oppression of the Slavic and Rumanian peoples. The **Franco-Russian Alliance of 1892** reinforced anti-Austro-Hungarian sentiments. Now aligned against Austria-Hungary by the need for military support from Russia in the case of a new Franco-German conflict, France embraced the principles of St. Petersburg concerning Austria-Hungary and the Balkans. In the name of Franco-Russian friendship, the point that the most oppressed nationalities of the early 1900s in eastern Europe were located in Russia was rather pointedly ignored. In Russia, the Polish, Baltic, Ukrainian, and Caucasian peoples weere already subject to a policy of intense Russification, which was to worsen in the communist era.

In the years between World Wars I and II, French historians severely judged the defunct Austro-Hungarian Empire. History textbooks used in secondary and higher-level education systematically oversimplified and caricaturized the Habsburg monarchy. A typical example is the remark alleged to the Austrian chancellor, Beust, on the subject of dividing peoples of the Empire in 1867; "Gardez vos hordes, nous garderons les notres," Beust is quoted as saying to Andrassy, president of the Hungarian Council. Translated as "Keep your hordes and we will keep ours," this oft-cited quote has never been documented and is used in conflicting forms by historians. Some believe Beust addressed these words to Andrassy, but others insist they were directed at Deak, the Hungarian chief negotiator of the Ausgleich of 1867. Recently, however, competent historians have been treating the issue with more care and accuracy. Regarding the treatment of ethnic minorities, V. L. Tapie writes in his *Monarchies et Peuples du Danube:*

"On the whole, conditions were reasonably tolerable, although they could not be expected to remain stable as national awareness within each ethnic group continued to grow... Marriages and migrations within the monarchy often meant a change of nationality, and although language remained the basic indicator of nationality, even that was not always conclusive. Foreign observers and members of the press only reluctantly acknowledged these subtleties that were revealed through direct contact with life in Austria-Hungary..."

In *L'Europe Central*, J. Droz comments on the attitude of the different nationalities during the first World War:

"To the amazement of a number of politicians, an authentic Austrian patriotism was clearly displayed in all strata of the population, and in all the ethnic groups of the Empire: the Slavs did their military duty just as willingly as the Germans and Magyars."

THE ETHNIC COMPOSITION OF AUSTRIA-HUNGARY

The Austrian part of the Empire contained the greatest variety of nationalities and with it the greatest confusion. Due in part to the diverse territorial acquisitions of the Habsburgs over centuries, the potpourri was also caused by population migrations within the territories themselves.

The populations of certain areas were all German; the Vorarlberg, the province of Salzburg, and the duchies of Upper and Lower Austria are examples. Other provinces contained German-speaking majorities, such as the German-speaking Tyrol, where the German-speaking population extended far beyond the present day Austro-Italian border to the town of Bozen (Bolzano). While Carinthia and Styria both possessed German majorities, they also hosted significant numbers of Slovenes—20 percent of the population in Carinthia and 29 percent in Styria. The capital city of Vienna was, of course, mainly German, but because of its role as the nexus of the Empire, all nationalities were represented. Of the approximately 2,000,000 inhabitants enumerated by the census of 1910, nearly 15 percent were Slavs, consisting mainly of 200,000 Czechs and over 100,000 Poles. Vienna was also home for about 200,000 Jewish refugees from rampant anti-Semitism in the Russian Empire and Rumania. To the south were the Italian and southern Slavic areas. Trentino was purely Italian with a population of 119,000, while the province of Gorizia boasted 154,000 Slovenes and 90,000 Italians. In Istria, 168,000 Croats coexisted with 147,000 Italians and 55,000 Slovenes. Dalmatia, acquired by Austria in 1815 from the French Napoleonic Empire (which in turn had acquired it from the Republic of Venice), was populated by 501,000 Serbo-Croatians and a minority of approximately 16,000 urban-based Italians. In general, the urban areas of the southern provinces were dominated by Italians and the countryside by Slavs, but this balance was in flux; the rural exodus caused by increasing industrialization was bringing a larger Slavic population into the urban areas.

The provinces north of Austria proper, the provinces of St. Wenceslas' crown, as they were called, contained a majority German population grouped in compact settlements throughout the mountainous country, along the borders with Austria and Germany, and in the cities of Karsbad, Marienbad, Reichenberg, Znajm, and Budweiss. However, in examining Bohemia-Moravia, it was discernable by the end of the 19th century that the Germans did not possess the majority that they had forty years before. In 1855, Germans made up 40 percent of the population in Prague, but by 1910 they were no more than seven percent. In the Moravian capital of Brno, their numbers declined in a similar fashion, as Czechs became the majority population throughout the Bohemian-Moravian basin in both rural and urban areas. And in the Teschen area of Silesia, Germans were included in a multi-ethnic society of Poles, Czechs, and Germans.

In western Galicia, the Poles held a slight majority, while they shared the east with a large Ruthenian minority. Jews were distributed nearly everywhere throughout Galicia, but the largest concentrations were found in cities such as Lemberg (Lvov). Similarly, the population of Bukovina was very mixed: it consisted of 300,000 Ruthenians, 273,000 Rumanians, 168,000 Germans, a large Jewish population for which no figures exist, and small minorities of Poles and Magyars.

Regarding religion in the Dual Monarchy and its provinces, over four-fifths of the inhabitants were Roman Catholics, an element which provided significant cohesion. The Roman Catholic majority was followed in declining order by the Uniates, the Orthodox, and the Protestants. Particularly numerous in Vienna and in the large cities as well as in Galicia and Bukovina, the Jews made up about five percent of the total population.

Ethnic distribution was more harmonious in the Hungarian Kingdom. Excluding Croatia-Slavonia because of its special status, the Magyars made up 54 percent of the population, and lived throughout the region. They dominated the plains on both sides of the Danube and Tisza rivers far beyond the present borders of Hungary. In 1910, 80 percent of Budapest was Magyar, followed by a fairly large German population of 97,000, as well as numerous Slovaks. The Magyars were a majority in all Hungarian cities except Pozsony (Pressburg), where the Germans slightly outnumbered the Hungarians by 38 percent to 35 percent.

Numbering about 2,000,000 in Hungary, the Germans were present in all of the cities, although in the urban setting they assimilated so well with

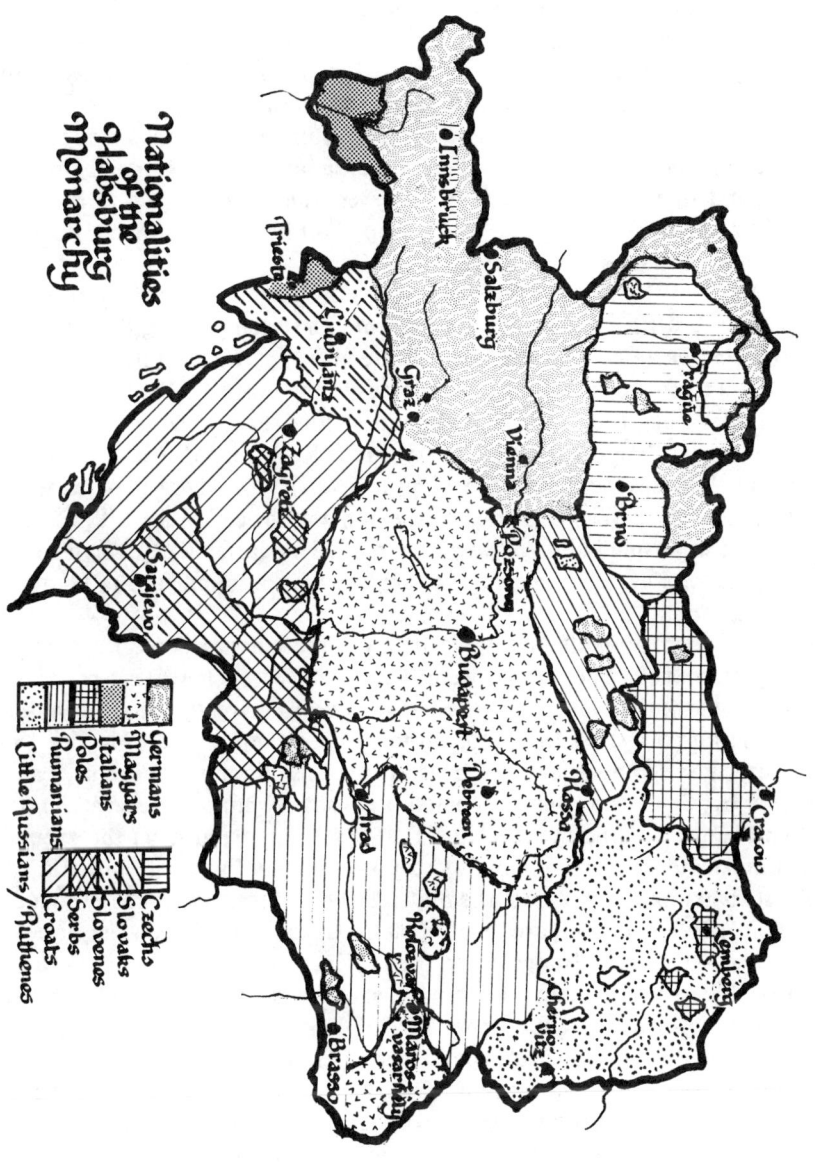

the Magyar population that the German-speaking proportion began to shrink: it declined from 13.6 percent in 1880 to 10.4 percent in 1910. Some closely-knit islands of Germans existed in various regions of the country. These were concentrated in the far west, in what is today the Austrian Burgenland, in Transdanubia, in the Banat, in the mining country of the northern Carpathians, and finally in southeastern Transylvania.

Some 3,000,000 strong in Hungary, the Rumanians made up about half of the populations of Transylvania and the Banat. They lived mainly in rural areas and small towns. Gradually, however, they became part of the rural exodus, and by the end of the 19th century had become significant minority groups in the larger towns of Transylvania.

Most of the 2,000,000 Slovaks in Hungary lived in the northwest mountains, although demographic pressure had been pushing them into the Danubian valleys from the mid-19th century onward. The Ruthenian population was concentrated in rural areas in the northern Carpathians, and like the Slovaks they began moving down toward the plains of the Tisza during the last half of the 19th century. In the Ruthenian districts, numerous Russian Jews also settled in the Magyar towns, with whom they tended to assimilate. The Serbs had settled on the Banat at the end of the 17th century, and were still living in the southern arm of the Hungarian Kingdom in closely knit groups. The Serbs shared the territory with an amalgam of Germans and Magyars.

The population of Croatia-Slavonia was more homogenous than that of Hungary proper. The Croats were a majority everywhere, except on the eastern side of the plain where the Drava and Sava rivers joined. There they were outnumbered by the Serbs, who came as refugees during the 18th century. For demographic and political reasons, the port of Fiume, called Rijeka by the Croats, was designated a *corpus separatum* (separate entity) from Hungary. Although the Croats attempted to claim it on the grounds that the population was originally Croatian, so many Italians from Istria and Trieste had moved there since the mid-1800s that the census of 1910 counted 24,000 Italians, as compared to 13,000 Croats and some 600 Magyars.

The Kingdom of Hungary and the province of Croatia-Slavonia boasted a wide diversity of religions. Roman Catholics were in the majority with 52.1 percent, followed by the Lutheran and Calvinist Protestants, and the followers of the Orthodox and Uniate churches. The Jews came in increasing numbers from Russia throughout the 19th century, and by 1910 represented five percent of the population. Many of them settled in Budapest—satirically termed "Judapest" in several anti-Semitic pamphlets—and in the rural areas of Ruthenia and northwestern Transylvania.

The annexation of Bosnia-Herzegovina in 1908 greatly increased the number of Slavs in the Dual Monarchy. Of the 1,800,000 inhabitants of this province, 96 percent were Serbo-Croatian and the remaining four percent was divided between Germans and Hungarians, consisting mainly of civil servants and their families. The Orthodox religion held a slight majority there of 51 percent, followed by a large Moslem minority of 30 percent and a smaller Catholic minority of 15 percent.

OPERATION OF THE SYSTEM

The *Ausgleich* of 1867 dividing the Habsburg Empire into two separate states each with extensive authority over its own territory was an interesting experiment in national sovereignty. In spite of linguistic and religious diversity, the Dual Monarchy managed enough coherence to function fairly well for half a century. The unity of the system was due first to the personality of the sovereign. No one could deny that, despite the events of 1848-1849 and the repression that followed, the emperor-king, Franz Joseph, knew how to evoke feelings of loyalty to the dynasty, feelings that lasted until his death on November 21, 1916. His long reign and his personal tragedies—the death of his only son and heir, Archduke Rudolph, in 1889 at Mayerling, followed by the assassination of his wife, Empress Elizabeth, by an Italian anarchist in 1898—earned him the respect and even the affection of his people. Loyalty to the dynasty was far from a mere rhetorical formula.

Another element providing unity was the Catholic religion, which brought together such diverse groups as Germans, Poles, Slovaks, Slovenes, Croats, and the majority of Hungarians and Czechs. It grouped them around the emperor-king, whose ancestors had been considered defenders of the Catholic faith since the time of Charles V. With nearly 40,000 lay priests and some 20,000 monks and nuns, the Catholic church was an important spiritual leader whose influence could be put at the disposal of the sovereign. High officials of the other Christian religions could play similarly influential roles, and served as representatives in the parliamentary assemblies.

The Imperial and Royal Army also served as a unifying factor in the Dual Monarchy. As the sole official language, German was understood by both officers and common soldiers alike, reinforcing cohesion among the soldiers and officers from different regions and of different nationalities. The officers' corps was considered a means of social advancement, since unlike the German army, access to the higher ranks was not an aristocratic monopoly. The army accelerated the process of assimilation and resulted in a sort of archetypical Austro-Hungarian, who, while not renouncing his own ethnic origins, felt more a part of the monarchy as a whole rather than of a particular region. This attitude was encouraged by opening up the higher command posts to all nationalities, not only the "dominant" ones. Officially, promotions were granted solely on competence and aptitude for responsibility. General Potiorek, governor of Bosnia-Herzegovina in 1914, was of Czech origin, and Admiral Horthy, last commander-in-chief of the Austro-Hungarian navy, was Hungarian. The Polish generals Sikorski and Rozwadowski, the Croatian Field Marshal Boroevic, and even a Rumanian like General Boeriu all held high commands during the First World War, and all were decorated with the Order of Maria Theresa—the military's highest honor.

A comparatively efficient and honest civil service with its numerous bureaucrats further reinforced the Empire's cohesion. Here also anyone who was competent and willing to take part in the system could hope for a brilliant administrative career. At least in principle, all ethnic groups were placed on equal footing. The state did not ask anyone to give up his national language or culture, but in addition to his own language, a candidate was required to know the official state language: German in the Austrian Empire and Hungarian in the Kingdom of Hungary. The Czechs took full advantage of the opportunities offered, and by 1914 filled a third of the posts in the joint ministries—a much higher proportion than they represented in the general population.

Unity was further served by common interests that the various nationalities shared in daily life as well as in economic matters. First, the population was fairly mobile, moving from region to region, and from the countries to the cities. This resulted in a cultural mingling; the Slovak peasant who moved to Budapest became Magyarized, while the Sudeten German who went to Prague became more Czech. A change of nationality within one or two generations was a frequent phenomenon, and such changes were accelerated by intermarriage. One example among thousands is the family of the composer, Franz Lehar. His family originally came from Moravia, and the composer's ancestors spoke Czech. His father was a military band leader, and as such was sent to Hungary where he adopted Magyar ways and married a Magyarized German. Lehar's brother, Anton, also moved to Hungary, married a Viennese woman, and had a brilliant military career leading to the rank of general, which he received in 1921. The composer himself moved to Vienna early in his career.

Economic explanations are just as relevant in accounting for stability and cooperation in Austria-Hungary. The various parts of the Empire and their inhabitants also had common economic interests. The Dual Monarchy functioned remarkably well as an economic unit, with different regions furnishing complementary agricultural and industrial resources. Grains came from the Puszta (the Hungarian plain), livestock from the Alps and the Carpathians, and sugar beets and hops from Bohemia. Coal came from Bohemia and Transylvania, iron from Austria and some mountainous ores of Bohemia, gold and silver from the Carpathians, bauxite and copper from

Croatia and Hungary, and so on. A well developed network of overland and river transport provided easy access to different parts of the Dual Monarchy, and the ports of Trieste and Fiume opened the way to Mediterranean and overseas destinations. The era of Franz Joseph was a time of economic prosperity for Austria-Hungary, as the growth and embellishment of Vienna, Budapest, Prague, Zagreb, and other cities attest.

Finally, in a century marked by sharp national conflicts, it must be noted that the Austro-Hungarian monarchy fostered the coexistence of different ethnic groups through an organization flexible enough to allow them each a place in the sun. Austria-Hungary was never a racist state: while Germans and Hungarians were the two dominant groups, other nationalities enjoyed much broader freedoms than their racial counterparts across the borders. Illiteracy was lower among the Rumanians and Serbs in Hungary than in Rumania and Serbia. All nationalities were protected equally by the law, and the *Ausgleich* guaranteed freedom of conscience and of religion. Most local government problems were settled by the provincial diets in the local languages, and each nationality had its own complete system of education. The Czechs had their university at Prague, while the Poles had theirs at Cracow and Lemberg, where Polish students from Russia came to study. In Hungary, the state provided primary and secondary schools in which the local languages were used, and churches were allowed to and often did open schools. All education was subsidized by the state. The only provision which can be interpreted as anti-ethnic in the Kingdom of Hungary was that all non-Hungarians in the Hungarian schools had to receive three hours of instruction in Hungarian a week. And, in contrast to the practice in Austria, higher education was almost exclusively in German or Hungarian. In the Hungarian provinces, only the Croats had their own university at Zagreb. On the whole, education was less liberal in Transylvania than in Austria proper, especially during the period between 1906 and 1910 when the nationalist Independence party, Kossuth's spiritual heir, governed the country.

POLITICAL CONFLICTS IN THE DUAL MONARCHY

Between 1867 and 1914, the two halves of the Dual Monarchy underwent a period of political instability.

The Austrian Empire

In the Austrian Empire, sometimes called *Cisleithania*, the major problem was interethnic relations. Although each province had its local diet which sent deputies to the *Reichsrat* in Vienna, it was only after the electoral reform of 1873 that these delegates were elected by universal suffrage. At the beginning of the Dual Monarchy, many deputies from Cisleithania hoped the

Empire would evolve into a three-state system. Hohenwart, the conservative president of the Austrian Council, conducted secret negotiations with the Bohemian Diet, and, with the agreement of Franz Joseph, drew up a proposal for reform that would have given Bohemia a status similar to that of Hungary. Such a reform was what Palacky, head of the Czech National party, had always desired. The proposal stipulated that Franz Joseph was to be crowned King of Bohemia in Prague. When the project was unveiled in October, 1871, however, it ran up against the opposition of Bohemian Germans who were afraid of becoming a minority. It was also opposed by Hungarian leaders such as Andrassy, who worried about the effects of such a project on the various ethnic groups: he foresaw Slovenes, Ruthenians, and others demanding similar status for themselves. Bowing to the opposition, Franz Joseph renounced the project, and Hohenwart resigned on October 30, 1871. Czech politicians were universally extremely disappointed, and different opinions on how to counter it caused a rift in the National party. The "old Czechs," centered around Palacky's son-in-law, Rieger, continued to search for a settlement with Vienna, seeing benefit for Bohemia in following a policy of cooperation with the government of Eduard Taaffe (1879-1893). This policy did bear results; the Language Act of 1880 made Czech the official language in areas with a German majority, where local government was bilingual. In 1882, Prague gained a Czech-language university alongside the older German-language one.

The Young Czechs, on the other hand, stubbornly resisted compromise with Vienna, and following the mounting of an active verbal opposition won the elections of 1891. Political activity increased with the laws of 1896 and 1906, which progressively introduced universal suffrage. Of the numerous parties that began to form, the National Catholics and the Social Christians were loyalists, while the Agrarians were fence-sitters. The National Socialists, however, as well as the Realists, favored an alliance with the Slovaks and other Slavic peoples. They were under the influence of Thomas Masaryk, a professor at the University of Prague, who led them to a position of systematic opposition that did not, however, completely reject the advantages of the system. The older parties, the dwindling Old Czechs, and the Young Czechs under Charles Kramarj, maintained a strong following in the business community because they favored Bohemian autonomy and an orderly conservatism. The Bohemian Social Democratic party had long been a branch of the Austrian Social Democratic party, and spoke for the rapidly growing industrial working class. In 1897, the various branches of this party became autonomous in their own countries, and in the 1911 elections, the Czech Social Democrats won 37 percent of the vote in Bohemia-Moravia. Their return placed them second to Kramarj's Young Czechs; they were clearly now a force to be considered. Demands for Bohemian autonomy intensified in the final years of the 19th century, and as tempers rose, a physical training society with nationalist tendencies, the *sokols* (hawks), began to turn to violence.

Faced with increasing Czech nationalism, German Bohemians worried about eventual domination by the Czech majority and resisted reform by every means possible. National rivalries often surfaced in skirmishes between student groups, despite the central government's goal of avoiding violence at any cost. It worked towards this objective by guaranteeing equal rights to both populations in Bohemia, but both populations did much to render reform difficult. When in 1897, for example, the government proposed a measure requiring all civil servants in Bohemia to be bilingual, the Germans systematically opposed it, as the measure favored the German-speaking Czechs. In the end, civil servants were required to know the languages of the area where they worked.

The Poles in Galicia presented far fewer problems. They enjoyed broad autonomy in local government and cultural affairs, and were grateful to a regime that guaranteed them equal right, much coveted by their compatriots in Prussia and Russia. Polish deputies to the *Reichsrat* were consistently part of the majority supporting the government, and Poles were often appointed to important posts. Two of them, Count Potocki in 1870-1871 and Count Badeni from 1895-1897, became presidents of the Austrian Council. In Badeni's cabinet were also two other Polish ministers. At the same time, another Pole, Count Goluchowski, served as joint foreign minister from 1895 to 1906. In early 1900, however, alongside the traditional conservative and populist Polish parties appeared two new parties inspired by ideas born in Polish Russia. They formed as the Polish Socialist party, under Joseph Pilsudski, and the National Democratic party, each having its counterpart in Polish Russia and Polish Prussia.

The generous treatment of Poles in the Austro-Hungarian system aroused the envy of the Ukrainians in Galicia and Bukovina, where the intelligentsia began demanding similar privileges, especially in cultural matters. In 1902, violent demonstrations took place in Lemberg for the creation of a Ruthenian university. Violence accompanied Ruthenian opposition during the next several years and in 1908, the Polish governor of Galicia was assassinated by a Ruthenian student. On the whole, though, the peasant masses did not sympathize with such extremist actions.

Among the southern Slavs, Slovene and Dalmatian politicians continued to search for development within the framework of the Empire. For cultural and religious reasons, they felt little attraction to the Orthodox Serbs, but what they feared most was Italian infiltration of the coastal region and Slovene towns.

Thus, most of the ethnic groups in the Austrian part of the Dual

Monarchy saw their future and that of the Habsburgs as inextricably linked. Paradoxically, some of the Dual Monarchy's most vocal opponents were German, preferring instead the concept of a "greater Germany" directed from Berlin.

The Kingdom of Hungary

Although Hungary possessed a long tradition of active parliamentary rule, it did not have universal suffrage. Since the electorate was made up only of financially qualified voters, the parliament reflected only a segment of the general mood of the country. In 1913, despite the lowering of property qualifications for the franchise, only a third of the adult male population was allowed to vote. Political thought was divided into two main currents, represented by the Liberal party and the Independence party. The Liberal party was led by Count Kalman Tisza, head of government from 1875 to 1890, and by his son Istvan, head of government from 1902 to 1905, and from 1910 to 1917. Both were disciples of Ferenc Deak, and were devoted to the principle of dualism. The Independence party was led by Ferenc Kossuth, son of the famous revolutionary leader of 1848-1849. Kossuth was later joined by such Liberal party dissidents as Counts Apponyi and Karolyi, who wanted total independence for Hungary. The Independence party governed the country from 1906 to 1910; its ultra-nationalist policies angered the non-Magyar nationalities and caused a conflict with the crown over the army. As in Bohemia, several new parties appeared alongside these in the late 19th century. The Christian People's party of Count Janos Zichy was opposed to the lay laws of 1892-1893; the Agrarian party sought to defend the interests of those in the agricultural sector; and the Social Democratic party championed the industrial workers. Due to the traditional parties refusal to introduce universal suffrage, however, these parties were unable to gain more than a few seats in parliament.

The official policies of the Hungarian state toward its non-Magyar minorities were closely tied to that country's domestic politics. In general, the Liberal party was more openminded regarding minority rights than was the Independence party. As soon as dualism was adopted, Deak negotiated the Hungaro-Croatian Compromise of 1868 with the delegates of the Zagreb Diet, granting the Croats broad autonomy regarding their own affairs. During the same year, Deak encouraged Hungarian parliament to pass a law on nationalities which kept Hungarian as the official state language, but which provided for equal opportunity for employment. The law also stipulated that "the parishes, churches, and local associations should select their own language of administration," and that "in the parish, town, and country councils, everyone may use his native language."

Taking advantage of the liberal provisions of this law, in 1881

Transylvanian Rumanians founded the National Rumanian party. Its immediate platform was a demand for Transylvanian autonomy, and for a separate Rumanian civil service in the areas populated by Rumanians. The leaders of the party petitioned Franz Joseph to the effect in 1892, using not his title of king of Hungary, but of emperor of Austria. Prosecuted by the Hungarian state not for their demands but for addressing them to the emperor, thereby denying that Transylvania belonged to Hungary, their 1894 trial received considerable attention abroad. George Clemenceau and Ernest Lavisse took the part of the accused, and were scandalized by the prison sentences given them. The petitioners were granted clemency the following year, but the Rumanian National party was banned until 1905. In the elections of 1905, 14 Rumanians were elected to the parliament. At their head was Jules Maniu, a lawyer who was to play an important role in Rumanian politics during the interwar period.

Among the Slovaks, political unrest appeared in the early years of the 20th century, instigated mainly by the intelligentsia and activist members of the lower clergy. A populist party was set up by a priest, Father Andreas Hlinka, who made cultural and administrative autonomy for Slovak areas a part of his program. Hlinka and his cohorts organized demonstrations against Apponyi's education policies, which increased Magyar language instruction in minority schools. These demonstrations degenerated into riots in October, 1907, and the military intervened in the small town of Csernova.

A different interest group favoring closer ties with Prague grew up around Milan Hodza and his newspaper, *Hlas* (The Voice). Protestant Slovak intellectuals gave it their support in favor of the overtly flamboyant clericism of Hlinka's followers. Slovak national protesters were relatively few in number, however, and Hlinka himself was disowned by his superiors. The ideal for many Slovaks was to become part of Hungarian society through assimilation, as did Father John Csernoch, who became Archbishop of Esztergom and Prince Primate of Hungary on the eve of World War I. The last king of Hungary was crowned by Cardinal Csernoch in December, 1916.

Despite the autonomy given them by the Compromise of 1868, the Croats had become strongly nationalistic, especially in political and intellectual circles. Since 1873, a movement to unite all the southern Slavs of the Dual Monarchy had been growing, and was given new impetus during the term of *Ban* Khun-Hedervary (1883-1893), whose mishandling of Croatian nationalists by supporting the Serbian minority against them only increased their fervor. The most outspoken proponents of this new Illyrism, as Croatian nationalism was termed, were Bishop Joseph Strossmayer and the historian Frano Ratzki. Another nationalistic movement, the Party of the Rights also appeared, led by Eugene Kvaternik. All agreed that Croatia should be a sovereign state, but within the Habsburg monarchy. The

Croatian nationalists also agreed that Croatia should join forces with the Slovenes, as the two shared the bond of a common religion. They disagreed, however, over uniting with the Serbs, due to the issue of the Serb's Eastern Orthodox faith. On this, no agreement was reached. At the Congress of Fiume in 1905, however, the partisans of Yugoslavism prevailed. It was not to Belgrade that they turned, but to Vienna and the heir Archduke Franz Ferdinand.

EXPECTATIONS FOR THE AUSTRO-HUNGARIAN MONARCHY BEFORE THE OUTBREAK OF WORLD WAR I

In 1914, no established group in Austria-Hungary thought seriously about destroying the Empire from the inside; the protesters only wanted to transform and modernize the system. They were aware of the advantages that a viable and coherent Habsburg Empire could offer its inhabitants. No one questioned the legitimacy of the dynasty represented by the strong yet aging Franz Joseph, even though Czech intellectuals such as Thomas Masaryk and Eduard Benes would have preferred a presidential system similar to the American one. The great majority of the people were sincerely attached to the imperial and royal family.

What the political leaders of the minority nationalities desired was a federalism evolving from dualism, toward first a tripartite and then a quadripartite system. They were opposed by others with a vested interest in the status quo. Even the socialists held similar views: Karl Renner, later to be president of the Republic of Austria, was quoted as saying "existing nations are forced to lead a common existence." For him, the transformation of the Empire was still the preferred solution.

A whole series of projects to reform the Empire were worked out in the years immediately before the war. In 1906, Aurel Popovici, a Transylvanian Rumanian, published *The United States of Greater Austria*, in which he advocated subdividing the Empire into autonomous provinces according to nationalities. Archduke Franz Ferdinand made no secret of his intent to transform the Empire when he succeeded his uncle. He intended first to restore the Kingdom of Bohemia, and then to coalesce the southern Slavs into an Illyrian state. In Belvedere Palace, his Viennese residence, the prince received numerous representatives of the various nationalities. His visitors included Charles Kramarj, head of the Young Czechs, the Slovak Milan Hodza, the Rumanians Jules Maniu and Aurel Popovici, the Croatian Frank, and also representatives of Austrian and Hungarian Social-Christian parties. The prince was trying to strengthen the ideological and spiritual ties that could unite the various peoples. In his opinion, social Christianism could provide a vehicle for rapprochement of the various ethnic groups, while for

Karl Renner, only an Austro-Marxism was capable of settling the question of nationalities properly—on the basis of class-consciousness. The archduke was particularly unhappy with German nationalists and the Magyars of the Independence party, whose excessive nationalism threatened stability and reform. Franz Ferdinand wished to ensure all the peoples of the Empire the freedom to expand culturally in a more equitable society, organized along the principles of social Christianism and within the framework of a decentralized state. To achieve these objectives, he opted for a policy of peace, which led to occasional clashes with the chief of the general staff, Konrad von Hotzendorf. The prince knew that without a lengthy period of peace, the Empire could not be transformed or even maintained, particularly in the face of the combined covetous designs of Germany and Russia. It is not difficult to see why Franz Ferdinand had become the man to eliminate in 1914.

Chapter 11

The Awakening of the Polish Nation
1870—1914

After the Poles failed in 1830-1831, and again in 1863, to win back their independence from Russia, they were subjected to harsh rule and a policy of intense russification. During the last part of the reign of Alexander II and under Alexander III (1881-1894), patriotic activity was paralyzed. Most of the leaders of the 1863 insurrection had been executed and their followers exiled to Siberia. Even the Catholic church was deprived of its leaders. While the situation eased somewhat with the ascent of Alexander III, the Polish church was still weighed down with the endless bureaucratic procedures involving the registration in the seminaries of candidates for the priesthood. Conditions among the regular clergy were even worse, since most of the monasteries were closed in 1864.

Even though the Polish language schools had been closed and other restrictions imposed, the national language endured and clandestine language teaching allowed young Poles to retain their national identity. In the early 1880s, the generation of romantic revolutionaries was superseded by a new generation of protesters from the new classes born of the industrial revolution, the working class and bourgeoisie, whose aspirations and methods of attaining them differed from those of their elders. Russian Poland had been industrialized since 1870, and the urban population had increased in proportion. Warsaw, for example, had grown to a population of 594,000 according to the census of 1897. While the aristocracy remained influential in the country, the new classes were beginning to make themselves felt in urban areas like Warsaw and Lodz. Karl Marx's ideas reached Russian Poland fairly early. In the early 1890s, two clandestine groups of socialists were already in existence: the Social Democratic party of Poland and Lithuania of Rosa Luxembourg and Felix Dzerjinski* and the *Bund* (General League of Workers), which was a Jewish organization from Lodz and a major part of the Russian Social Democratic party. The socialists were more interested in overthrowing the czarist regime and reforming the social and economic system than in Polish independence. Some militants concerned themselves with national interests, however, and held a meeting in Paris in 1892 which resulted in a new socialist movement, the Polish Socialist party of S. Limanowski. This party, which published a clandestine newspaper edited by a young radical, Joseph Pilsudski, grew much faster than its social democratic competitors. Patriotism was firmly entrenched in the Polish working class. Pilsudski moved to Galicia where he could easily maintain contact with Polish emigrants, and from there he flooded Russian Poland with clandestine socialist publications.

Alongside the workers, the Polish middle class had their own political organization, the National Democratic party, founded in 1897. It was a party of the moderate opposition, led by Jan Poplawski and Roman Dmowski, both of whom eventually had to flee to Galicia for asylum.

Events of 1904-1905 in Russia had their effect on Poland. Socialists of various leanings organized strikes and attacks on Russian civil administrators. The National Democrats tried to obtain a certain measure of autonomy for Poland out of the situation. Czar Nicholas' manifesto issued in October, 1905, promising a constitution and an elected legislative assembly or *duma* was greeted joyfully in Poland. Elections for the first *duma* were held in April, 1906. Despite a call for socialist abstention, the Poles voted overwhelmingly for the National Democratic party's moderate opposition which took all of the seats that year and again in the 1907 elections for the second *duma*. But the moderate and cooperative attitude of the Polish delegates did little good. Autonomy was refused. Even worse, the new electoral law for the third *duma* took away over half of the seats the Poles had a right to, considering their proportionate numbers in the Russian Empire.

However, due to the liberalization that followed the Russian revolution of 1905, the Poles recovered some of their freedoms lost in 1830, particularly those regarding use of the Polish language and education. But these concessions were not enough to satisfy a people who had never given up regaining their independence.

---

*Rosa Luxembourg then went to Germany where she was active in the Spartakist movement. She died during the Berlin riot of January 15, 1919. Felix Dzerjinski (1877-1926) remained in Russia after the October Revolution and organized the Tcheka (today KGB).

In the Prussian provinces, the fate of the Polish people had its highs and lows. An early difficult period paralleled the *Kulturkampf* (1871-1879) during which Bismarck tried to make the Catholic church toe the line. Polish Catholics, as well as German Catholics, were harassed by the authorities. Stubborn bishops were removed from their dioceses. Bismarck made a compromise with Rome in 1880, and conditions were temporarily ameliorated in Poland. But beginning in 1886, Bismarck embarked on a policy of Germanization in the formerly Polish provinces. He set up a colonization commission to assist Germans who wanted to move in to acquire land with help from the state. The ascension of William II briefly slowed the colonization policy, but it picked up again even more systematically in the early 20th century and numerous clashes ensued. At the Berlin Reichstag, Poland's fifteen deputies led by Albert Korfanty continually deplored this policy of German colonization of Polish land, but they were vastly outnumbered by the German deputies. Though slightly better off than their compatriots in Russia, by 1914 the Prussian Poles were just as aware of the need to unite all Poles into one independent state.

Austrian Galicia, however, was the focus of more activity for independence. It was from his base in Galicia that Joseph Pilsudski organized undercover groups ready to intervene actively in Russia when the opportunity arose. These groups became known officially as "Societies of Tir" in 1910. It was there that the decisive struggle for independence was shaping up, and the tensions in the Balkans in 1912-1913 were a forewarning of imminent action. A provisional government commission including the socialist Pilsudski, the populist Vincent Witos, and generals Sikorski and Haller, was ready to take over a liberated Poland in case war broke out with Russia.

Chapter 12

The Balkans Between the Great Powers 1878—1914

BEGINNINGS OF AUSTRO-RUSSIAN RIVALRY IN THE BALKANS (1870-1878)

In 1870, most of the Balkans were still under Ottoman control, with the exception of the few Balkan Christian groups who had managed to free themselves and form their own independent states. The Greeks were one of these groups, although independent Greece still only included the Peloponnese, Attica and a few of the Cycladian islands. The Serbs were another group, although autonomous Serbia far from included all of the Serbian people. Some Serbian refugees of the 17th and 18th centuries became Austrian or Hungarian subjects; others remained under Turkish rule. The Montenegrins had an independent patriarchal state, and finally, by means of the Crimean War, the Rumanians created an autonomous principality, although many Rumanians still lived outside of it in Transylvania and Bukovina. The Bulgars, the Albanians, numerous Macedonian and Bosnia-Herzegovinian Serbs remained Ottoman subjects.

Repeated intervention by the Great Powers in the Balkans during the first two-thirds of the 19th century was considered an encouraging sign by the Turkish-ruled populations. The United Kingdom was strongly opposed to the dismemberment of the Ottoman Empire, especially in any way that might allow the Russians access to the eastern Mediterranean. The British attitude hardened in 1869 when the opening of the Suez Canal made the Mediterranean the shortest route to India. Russia and, to a lesser degree, Austria-Hungary, watched everything that happened in the Balkans with great interest. Both hoped to see the Turks leave, in theory to liberate the Christian peoples, but also for other obvious political and economic reasons. For the Russians, the Balkans could open a gate to the sea. To the Austro-Hungarian monarchy, the Balkans seemed a natural geographic extension of the Empire. Part of the Empire's population had racial kin living in the Balkans, so Russian presence in the region threatened the cohesion of the Dual Monarchy; Russian-liberated Slavic states acted as magnets, attracting Slavs away from Austria-Hungary. Therefore, as far as Vienna was concerned, if the Balkans had to be liberated, better it be by Austria-Hungary than by Russia.

This conflict of interests, latent since the beginning of the century, began to develop into a pronounced rivalry in the 1870s. During that time, Russia appeared particularly interested in the Bulgarians. As we noted in previous chapters, national consciousness came late to the Bulgarians, but by 1870, Bulgarian patriots had become more active. Most of them were living in exile in Rumania, and under the leadership of Basil Levski (1837-1873) and Ljuben Karavelov (1834-1891), they began to pave the way for revolt. They were in contact with members of the Central Committee of the Bulgarian Revolution, a secret organization in existence since 1869. They also distributed subversive literature and organized terrorist attacks. Levski was caught participating in such an act, and was executed in February, 1873. The Russian government supported Bulgarian aspirations for independence, both through a committee to aid the Slavs created in 1856 in St. Petersburg, and through the diplomatic channels of Ambassador Ignatiev at Constantinople. One concrete result occurred in 1870; the Bulgarian church gained its independence from the patriarchate at Constantinople, and an independent Bulgarian exarchate was created with authority over Macedonia and all of Bulgaria proper. Then the Russian government began to feel the negative effects of Bulgarian activism within Russia, and hesitated to encourage further acts of terrorism.

Austro-Hungarian authorities had little interest in Bulgaria and made no effort to hinder Russia's actions there. They were attentive, however, to happenings in Bosnia-Herzegovina whose territory adjoined autonomous Serbia and Montenegro. The Austro-Hungarians hoped that the eventual liberation of Bosnia-Herzegovina would not lead to an expansion of Serbia toward the Adriatic, because Serbia's access to the Adriatic could eventually benefit Russia. In the spring of 1875, Emperor Franz Joseph took a trip to inspect the Dalmatian and Croatian border with the Ottoman Empire. The Slavic population of Bosnia-Herzegovina took this as a cue to rise up against the Turks, who were experiencing a serious political and financial crisis. Sultan Abdul-Aziz I (1861-1876) was again pressuring his subjects in the Ottoman Empire in order to cover interest payments on the foreign debt. Officially sanctioned extortion by Turkish tax collectors provoked an insurrection in a Serbian village of Herzegovina in July, 1875. Within a few weeks the unrest had spread throughout the province and into Bosnia. Volunteers from Serbia joined the revolutionaries. The Turks reacted violently, massacring the civilian population, but the insurrection left its mark. In April, 1876, Bulgarian revolutionary committees unleashed a general revolt. Bulgarian exiles from Rumania came to lend a hand to their compatriots under the leadership of Hristo Botev. The Great Powers intervened on behalf of the sultan, demanding payment of Turkish debts and an improvement of the lot of the Christian populations. This intervention, which came at a time when new revolts were breaking out everywhere, provoked a nationalistic reaction from the Turks; in Salonika, they assassinated the French and German consuls and harassed European residents.

Despite repression, the revolutionary movement gathered force in the Balkans. In July, 1876, Serbia and Montenegro entered the fray. These two countries hoped to share Bosnia-Herzegovina, and together were trying to contain any expansion of liberated Bulgarians to the west. The struggle against the Turks had not diluted ancestral rivalries between the Serbs and the Bulgarians. The Serbs were quickly defeated by the Turks, but the Montenegrins, commanded by the Russian general Tchernaiev, fared better.

The rapid deterioration of the Ottoman Empire led first to a palace revolt in Constantinople. In May, 1876, Abdul-Aziz was deposed by his nephew Murad, who went mad shortly thereafter and was deposed in turn on August 30, 1876, by his brother Abdul-Hamid II (1876-1909). In view of the mounting disturbances and the severe repression that resulted, Austria-Hungary and Russia agreed on an eventual joint intervention. In July, 1876, Count Andrassy met with his Russian counterpart Gorchakov in Bohemia, and the two diplomats worked out a division of the Balkans: the west, or Bosnia-Herzegovina, would go to Austria-Hungary, and the east, or Bulgaria, would become Russia's.

In Constantinople, agents of the Great Powers continued negotiations with the sultan. The British were anxious to humor the Turks and settled for vague promises that the lot of the Christians would be improved. But Russia, supported by Austria-Hungary, insisted on definite commitments from the Turks. The Turks replied with dishonesty and Turkish partisans proceeded to carry out new massacres in Bulgaria, provoking a Russian declaration of war on April 24, 1877. The Russians attacked on two fronts, in the Caucasus in the direction of Armenia, and in Bulgaria toward Constantinople.

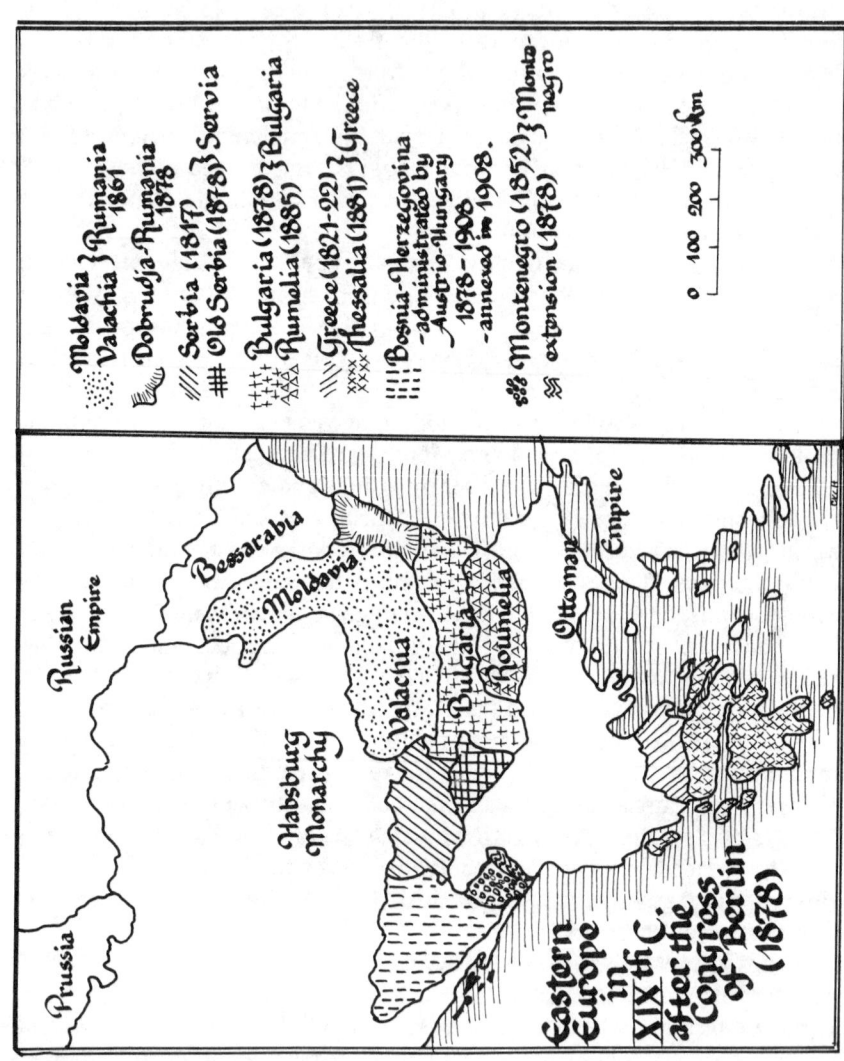

Armenia and Bularia were quickly liberated. The Turks requested an armistice on January 31, 1878, and signed the Treaty of San Stefano on the following March 3. The treaty represented a major victory for Russia and at the same time guaranteed the liberation of nearly all the Balkan peoples. States that were already autonomous, such as Rumania, Serbia and Montenegro, gained total independence and slightly expanded their territories. An autonomous greater Bulgaria, under Russian influence, came into being. Russia expanded its territory in Asia Minor with Kars Ardahan and Batum, then annexed Bessarabia, which had been ceded by Rumania. Rumania in turn received part of Bulgarian Dobrudja in compensation. As expected, Austria-Hungary took over the administration of Bosnia-Herzegovina.

Great Britain, and to a lesser extent, Austria-Hungary, reacted sharply to this Russian presence in the Balkans. Disraeli, the English prime minister, threatened to intervene and promised the Turks his support. (The Turks later reciprocated by ceding Cyprus to the English.) In view of the agitated emotional climate in Great Britain, Gorchakov agreed to the meeting of a European congress suggested by Bismarck. At the **Congress of Berlin** (June 13-July 13, 1878), Russia lost ground. Rumania, Serbia and Montenegro remained independent, but the latter two countries had to give up some of what they had gained from the Treaty of San Stefano. Serbia kept Vranje, Nish and Pirot. Montenegro kept the port of Antivari. Greater Bulgaria was dismembered with the south remaining in the hands of the Turks; Rumelia was proclaimed a Turkish province, but with a Christian government and an autonomous administration; northwestern Bulgaria, including Sofia, became an autonomous principality. Thrace and Macedonia, assigned to greater Bulgaria at San Stefano, remained Turkish.

For the peoples concerned, the Congress of Berlin was highly upsetting. It was a painful failure of Russian policy in the Balkans even though they had held on to Kars, Batum and Bessarabia. Relations between St. Petersburg and Vienna, already deteriorating, suffered even more when Austria-Hungary retained control over certain areas. Its presence in Bosnia-Herzegovina and in the sanjak of Novi Pazar separated the Serbs from Montenegro and thus from all possibility of access to the Adriatic coast. For the Serbs, Austria became a potential adversary just as formidable as the Turks. The Bulgars, whose human losses had been considerable, were far from satisfied in losing Thrace and Macedonia. Once again, the Great Powers had looked after their own interests first when deciding the fate of the Balkan peoples.

DEVELOPMENTS WITHIN THE BALKAN STATES UP TO THE CRISIS OF 1908

Rumania

The coronation of Prince Charles of Hohenzollern in 1866 marked the beginning of independent Rumania. A constituent assembly elected by landholders and the bourgeoisie adopted a constitution in 1866 which made Rumania a constitutional monarchy with a bicameral legislature. The senate had 120 members elected by the wealthier citizens, while members of the chamber of deputies were elected by quasi-universal suffrage. Until World War I, Rumanian politics were dominated by the Boyars and the large landowners, and by the Liberal party of John Bratianu which defended the interests of the bourgeoisie.

Matters of foreign policy played a major role throughout this period. The Rumanian parliament took advantage of the Russo-Turkish war to declare total independence on May 21, 1877, which was ratified by the Treaty of San Stefano and the Congress of Berlin. The Rumanian army also fought alongside the Russians in the war for Bulgarian liberation. Shortly thereafter, in 1881, Prince Charles took the title of King of Rumania. His long reign (1881-1914) coincided with Rumania's entry into international politics. With family ties to the Hohenzollerns of Germany, King Charles had a natural preference for the central empires. In 1883, on the advice of most of his ministers, he made a secret agreement with Austria-Hungary and remained faithful to this alliance despite public opinion, which tended towards France.

Throughout this period, most of the politically aware and the population as a whole demonstrated a kind of uncompromising nationalism which surfaced in two forms. The first, irredentism, represented a desire to gather all Rumanians together within a single state. Territories they considered *irredenta*, or belonging to them because they contained a large proportion of Rumanian inhabitants, were Bessarabia, ceded to the Russians in 1878, and Transylvania. Transylvania had been Hungarian since the time when the ancestors of the Rumanians were still in Albania, but the Rumanians had been moving there gradually since the 13th century, eventually making up half of the population. Nationalist elements in Bucharest financed the activities of the National Rumanian party in Transylvania, and offered scholarships to Rumanians on the outside who wanted to come and study in Bucharest. The Cultural League, founded in 1890, strengthened the links between Rumanian intellectual circles in Rumania and Transylvania.

The second type of Rumanian nationalism took shape as anti-Semitism. This anti-Semitism was facilitated by legislation; as late as 1888, the Court of Appeals still denied Rumanian nationality to Jews, even those born in

Rumania. This was contrary to the resolutions of the Congress of Berlin which had given equal rights to all the inhabitants of the newly independent countries. The only way for Jews to escape subjugation was to request naturalization, but between 1880 and 1900 only 200 naturalizations were granted. Moreover, there were hundreds of pogroms which were met with complicity by the authorities. Parisian academics were quick to lash out against Austria-Hungary during the trial of the petitioners in 1894, when several Transylvanian Rumanians were condemned to prison and freed the following year; but these same academics remained strangely silent on the matter of the daily persecution of Jewish victims in Rumania, and were willing to sacrifice the 100,000 Transylvanian Jews to Rumanian irredentism.

Socially, Rumania was particularly traditional. Most of the people were poor peasants. In spite of the poorly managed agrarian reform of 1864, the peasants' condition deteriorated because available plots of land became inadequate to meet the rapidly increasing population. Demands on the land grew and were joined by heavy taxation, made even heavier by a corrupt administration. Two major peasant revolts broke out, one in March, 1888, and a more serious one in February-March, 1907. The latter uprising was brutally supressed by the army under General Avarescu. In the Giurgiu region, the army resorted to artillery to subdue unruly villages. In the closing years of the 19th century, the birth of industry built on extraction of resources (oil from Ploesti, for example), and on processing of agricultural products, led to the formation of the Social Democratic Workers' party of Rumania in 1893. This party sought to improve the harsh living conditions of the workers and to obtain universal suffrage. The Russian revolution of 1905 and the Rumanian uprising of 1907 reinforced the socialist movement which reorganized in 1910 to become the Marxist-inspired Social Democratic party.

Serbia and Montenegro

The Congress of Berlin had recognized Serbia's independence, but the country was still small and archaically organized, with a population of a little over two million inhabitants. (Belgrade, the capital and the only major city, had less than 30,000 inhabitants.) With no access to the sea and no railroad—the Belgrade-Nis line was only completed in 1881—Serbia consisted of peasants with small- and medium-sized holdings devoted principally to raising grains, trees, shrubs and pigs. The few existing industries specialized in processing agricultural products.

A long tradition of struggle against the Turkish occupying forces had hardened the Serbian peasants, who used their primitive tools as weapons with ardor. Even such arms were precious while the liberation of the Serb populations were still not complete. Some Serbs were still subjects of the Ottoman Empire while others were subjects of Austria-Hungary, and Serbia had not forgotten them. In addition to the Turks, the Serbs saw another enemy in Bulgaria who, like Serbia and Greece, had eyes on a key passageway between the worlds of the Danube and the Aegean: Macedonia.

Since the early 19th century, Serbia had been almost exclusively governed by princes from the Obrenovitch family. Michael (1859-1868), the son of Miloch, frequently visited western Europe. He knew his country was backward and hoped to modernize it, but his attempts at changes within the regime provoked opposition. After his assassination on June 10, 1868, possibly by a supporter of the rival Karageorgevitch dynasty, power went to a 14-year-old, French-educated nephew, Milan Obrenovitch. During Milan IV's reign (1861-1889), Serbian institutions were liberalized. The constitution of 1869 made the country a constitutional state in which, at least in principle, major freedoms were guaranteed. The prince, who took the title of king in 1882, retained executive powers but shared legislative powers with a parliament, the *Skupshtina*, which was composed of 160 delegates, 120 of them elected by the people and the rest appointed by the prince. There were two political parties. The liberal party was actually conservative, favoring alliance with Austria, and had the support of the wealthy peasants who saw Austria-Hungary as the natural market for agricultural surpluses. The radical party spoke for the poor peasants and favored closer ties with Russia. In the September, 1883 elections, the radicals won, but the king continued to rule with the conservatives. This led to a major peasant uprising which was severely suppressed. Milan IV provoked further conflict with his subjects when he divorced his immensely popular Russian wife, Natalie, in 1888. Faced with a mounting wave of discontent, the king brought out a new, more liberal constitution in 1888, in which all of the delegates to the parliament were to be elected.

Suddenly, on March 6, 1889, the king abdicated in favor of his 12-year-old son, Alexander, for whom he appointed three regents. The regents adopted a policy of extreme dependence on Austria-Hungary, and bloody political confrontations multiplied. King Alexander momentarily resolved the crisis when, on April 13, 1892, he made it known he was personally taking over the reins of government. The radicals, who held a majority in parliament, expected a lot from the young king, but were quickly disappointed. In 1894, Alexander abolished the constitution of 1888 and reverted to the more authoritarian one of 1869. In fact, Alexander I ruled as an absolute monarch, while his wife Draga, who was divorced from a Serbian officer, engaged in a variety of intrigues. Over 80 percent of Serbian trade was with Austria-Hungary, and these growing ties added to the general discontent. During the night of June 10, 1903, a military plot, organized by the brother of Queen Draga's ex-husband, resulted in the assassination of the king, the queen, all members of the Obrenovitch family and several ministers and court dignitaries. Several days later, the parliament unanimously decided on Peter Karageorgevitch as king. Thus the descendant of George the Black, hero of the uprising of 1804, became King Peter I.

The new sovereign had spent most of his life abroad. Peter I had fought in the French army under General Bourbaki in 1870-1871, and had distinguished himself at the battle of Villersexel. His coronation marked a decisive change in Serbia's foreign policy. Under Peter I, pro-Russianism took hold, and the king entrusted Nikola Pashitch, the head of the radical party and staunch supporter of alliance with Russia, with considerable power. The king immediately reinstated constitutional rule, and the elections brought in a solid radical majority.

Peter I turned to France for financial credit which he used to buy military equipment from Creusot. Austria-Hungary countered in 1905 by closing its border to Serbian agricultural products which were then sold to France. As a result of the *coup d'etat* in Belgrade, Russia reversed its defeat at the Congress of Berlin.

In Montenegro, a tiny state of 3470 square miles and 236,000 inhabitants, independent since 1878, development was peaceful. Prince Nicholas (1860-1918) tried to modernize the country, reorganize the administration, and put an end to the patriarchal and tribal system that had characterized the country up until then. Economic progress led to the formation of an embryonic socialist party in 1903, under the direction of Jovan Hajdukovitch. Simultaneously, a liberal party favoring union with Serbia was created in educated circles, whose numbers had increased under the more open policy of the prince. Having proclaimed himself king of Montenegro, Nicholas gave his subjects a constitution in 1905, although he actually retained exclusive power and gave parliament only a minor role. Nevertheless, the majority of Montenegrins looked toward Belgrade for direction, rather than to their king.

Independent Bulgaria

The Congress of Berlin had created an autonomous Bulgarian principality of two million inhabitants, subject to the Ottoman Empire. Eastern Rumelia, with its 800,000 people, was made into an Ottoman province headed by a Christian governor at Plovdiv (Philipponpolis) chosen by common consent of the Great Powers and the sultan.

In conformance with the resolutions of Berlin, the Russians were responsible for setting up a government in the Bulgarian principality. A Constituent Assembly was elected and met at Tirnovo on February 22, 1879. Despite opposition from the conservatives supported by Russian authorities, the liberal majority in the assembly voted to adopt a constitution that granted power to a National Assembly, *Sobranje*, elected by universal suffrage. The office of chief of state was unanimously entrusted to Prince Alexander of Battenburg, a nephew by marriage of the Czar and an officer in the Prussian army. On July 31, 1879, the prince moved to Sofia, which was proclaimed the capital city.

Prince Alexander knew that he had the support of Russia behind him when he began to set up a reign of personal power in Bulgaria. In April, 1881, he suspended the constitution. The Russians felt that through Prince Alexander, who was loyal to them, they could make the young Bulgaria a vassal principality. They were in for a disappointment because the prince wanted to retain his new authority and keep his country independent. In 1884, the Czar and his nephew broke off relations and the Russian advisors were sent home. In order to gain the popularity of the Bulgarian people—who disliked his authoritarian regime—Prince Alexander appealed to national pride by promoting Bulgarian unity. The National Assembly and the Rumelian population were pleased. On September 18, 1885, led by the writer Zachary Stojanov, Rumelians who wanted to unite with Bulgaria seized power at Plovdiv. Two days later, Prince Alexander triumphantly entered the capital of Rumelia.

After five centuries of Ottoman domination, the Bulgarian people were reunited within an independent state of 3,500,000 inhabitants. Unified Bulgaria remained fragile, however; Turkey refused to recognize the forceful takeover, and Serbia, faced with the disquieting prospect of a powerful state at its borders, took the offensive and attacked. The Serbian army was easily beaten at Slivnitza on November 5, 1885, and only the mediation of Austria saved Serbia from an even greater catastrophe. An international conference held at Constantinople recognized the *de facto* union of the two Bulgarian principalities. This personal triumph of Prince Alexander, the "hero of Slivnitza," provoked the wrath of the Czar. A regiment led by officers sympathetic to Russia invaded the royal palace and forced Alexander to abdicate on August 9, 1886. The Bulgarian people fought back, and the president of the National Assembly, Stefan Stambulov, called back the sovereign to whom the Bulgarians owed their unification. Prince Alexander then returned to his capital, while the Russian government continued to demand his resignation.

Stambulov, who held the reins of power and had popular support, became the spokesman for Bulgarian nationalism confronting this Russian interference. Russophile elements were weeded out of the army, and elections held in late 1886 resulted in a wide majority for the anti-Russian nationalists. Stambulov then began his search for a prince to reign over Bulgaria, for in late-19th century Europe it was inconceivable for an independent state to become a republic. After long negotiations with the Great Powers, Prince Ferdinand of Saxe-Coburg was called to the throne on July 7, 1887, by an overwhelming majority in the Bulgarian assembly. Until then, the new prince had served as an officer in the Austro-Hungarian army. He came from a family that had given Belgium its first king, Leopold I, and had given England a husband for Queen Victoria, Prince Albert. His maternal grandfather was none other than King Louis-Philippe. Thus, the coronation of Prince Ferdinand was generally considered a victory for Austria-Hungary and Germany, and a second setback for Russia in Bulgaria. The Russian government refused to recognize the new prince for a long time. Russia came out of the affair embittered; it had assisted in the emancipation of Bulgaria in the hope of acquiring a subordinate state, but twice successively Bulgarians and their chosen princes had refused to substitute the Russian yoke for Ottoman domination.

During the first years of Ferdinand's reign, Stambulov was the power behind the throne. He resigned in May, 1894, and in July of 1895 was assassinated. From that time on, Prince Ferdinand himself governed with the support of a coalition of conservatives and liberal Stambulists. As the century drew to a close, new political groups began to form alongside the traditional parties. The Social-Democratic party, champion of the budding working class, was founded secretly in 1891 by Dimitri Blagoev (1856-1924). It was later strengthened by Georgi Dimitrov (1882-1949) with the creation of the first Socialist Union in 1904, and by the Agrarian Union in 1899 which promoted agrarian reform and the abolishment of peasant debts. The Bulgarian working class was small in number, and the effects of its Social-Democratic party were correspondingly weak. Under the leadership of Alexander Stambolijski (1879-1923), the Agrarian Union made rapid progress among the peasants and managed to obtain 29 percent of the vote in the 1911 elections.

Despite all the political activity, Bulgaria was still theoretically under Ottoman rule. Autonomy was not independence, regardless of the similarities. This equivocal situation was settled on September 22, 1908. Taking advantage of the Ottoman Empire's internal difficulties and of the international crisis provoked by the Austro-Hungarian annexation of Bosnia-Herzegovina, Prince Ferdinand declared the kingdom of Bulgaria independent and proclaimed himself Czar of the Bulgarians, a title once used by his medieval forbearers.

At the dawn of the 20th century, three Balkan states gained control of their destinies. They had much in common politically, socially, and economically, with their authoritarian monarchies and essentially peasant societies. Foreign policy, however, divided them and even put them in opposition. Some were proteges of Austria-Hungary (Serbia and Bulgaria, and then Bulgaria alone), while others were dependent on Russia (Rumania, Montenegro and Bulgaria at first, then Rumania, Montenegro and Serbia).

At that moment in history, the Great Powers were divided into two antagonistic factions, the Triple Alliance of Germany, Austria-Hungary and Italy, and the Triple Entente of France, Britain and Russia. Clearly, there was some danger in reproducing these divisions on a small scale in the Balkans, even more so since there were numerous quarrelsome elements among the Balkan people, and the slightest dispute could generate a conflict.

THE EXPLOSIVE SITUATION IN THE BALKANS (1908-1914)

By the beginning of the 20th century, the unstable Balkan peninsula had become a jousting field for Austria-Hungary and Russia, who confronted each other through the Bulgarians and the Serbs. Meanwhile, many ambitions were aroused by the progressive vulnerability of the Turkish Empire still controlling the Christian populations of Macedonia, Thrace and Albania. These were to flare up violently in the years preceding World War I.

The Macedonian Problem

The Congress of Berlin had left Macedonia to the Turks, to the great disappointment of the Greeks, Serbs and Bulgarians, each of whom claimed legitimate rights to the territory. Before the Turkish conquest, the area belonged to the Byzantine Empire and was frequently under Bulgarian and Serbian attack. By the early 20th century, Macedonians numbered about three million, living in the Vardar Valley and the surrounding mountainous regions. They were divided into three main nationalities: a Greek majority lived on the Aegean coast with the port city Salonika, with islands of Turks and Bulgarians; Serbs were present throughout the interior of the country, with a high concentration around Skopje, but were usually a minority in the interior compared to the Bulgarian population; Bulgarian influence was great, and strengthened noticeably with the creation of an independent Bulgarian exarchate in 1870, with jurisdiction over all of Macedonia. Besides these three major nationalities making up roughly four-fifths of the population, there were a multitude of other ethnic groups: Albanians and Vlachs in the mountainous regions, and Turks, Armenians and Jews in the cities.

The liberation of Bulgaria in 1885 raised great hopes in Macedonia at a time when local intellectual circles were becoming more and more conscious of a "Macedonian" entity. Bulgarian influence grew even stronger with the formation in 1893 at Salonika of IMRO, the Interior Macedonian Revolutionary Organization. IMRO organized sporadic terrorist attacks and assaulted Turkish authorities. As the century opened, the entire interior was ripe for insurrection. On August 2, 1903, IMRO launched a massive uprising known as the Saint Elias' Day (Ilinden) rebellion. It involved all of

Macedonia and extended into Thrace. The Turks reacted with brutality, and thousands of Macedonians fled into Bulgaria. The Great Powers were divided on the Macedonian question: Great Britain wanted to see major reforms in Macedonia; Austria-Hungary and Russia, who were attempting to mend their relationship, agreed at Murzteg not to intervene but to ask the sultan for a few token reforms. Bulgarian neutrality on this matter led to dissent within the IMRO and a splintering along ethnic lines. Some of the Macedonian revolutionaries turned toward Belgrade, and in 1910 at Skopje founded a Macedonian socialist group advocating a Balkan federation with room for an independent Macedonian republic. Others remained faithful to Bulgaria, making the Macedonian question yet another subject of contention between Serbia and Bulgaria.

The 1908 Crisis in Bosnia

Since 1878, Austria-Hungary had governed Bosnia-Herzegovina as well as the sanjak of Novi Pazar in the name of the sultan. The half-civilian, half-military administration was competent and efficient; roads and railroads had been built, but there had been no changes in the social structures inherited from the Turks. The Austro-Hungarian government depended on the Catholics and Moslems to reinforce its authority, while the Orthodox followers remained openly sympathetic to Serbia.

In early 1908, in order to demonstrate its intention to remain in Bosnia-Herzegovina, Austria-Hungary arranged with the sultan to construct a railroad between Bosnia and Macedonia. When the project was announced, Russia and its Serbian allies were highly suspicious, and considered intervening with France on the side of the Macedonians. In the Ottoman Empire, the reaction was a heightened nationalism. The "Young Turks," hostile to any concession made to the Great Powers, staged a revolution in July, 1908, and forced a liberal constitution on Sultan Abdul-Hamid. The Young Turk revolution, further weakening the Ottoman Empire, brought a new wave of hope to Macedonia, Serbia, Bulgaria and Greece.

To prevent Serbia from taking advantage of the situation and re-questioning the status of Bosnia-Herzegovina, Austria-Hungary simply annexed the province on October 5, 1908, leaving Novi Pazar to the Turks. Serbia protested vigorously, but like Russia, whose army was still reorganizing after the Russo-Japanese war, was not able to intervene militarily and had to accept the new situation. Austria had earned the bitter resentment of the Serbs, a fact demonstrated in Bosnia-Herzegovina with the proliferation of secret pro-Serbian societies financed and supported by Serbian military circles and by a flurry of anti-Austrian propaganda.

The Balkan Wars of 1912-1913

The Turkish revolution of 1908 had so weakened the Ottoman Empire that unrest spread throughout the occupied territories. The sultan, who had tried to seize absolute power in 1909, was deposed by his brother, Mohammed V (1909-1919). The Young Turks took over and restored state order with expedient brutality—in the name of the unity of the Empire. Despite constitutional guarantees assuring all races their equality, the new power was used arbitrarily against non-Turks. The victims were mainly Armenians, Greeks, Macedonians, and Thracian Bulgarians.

Although they had always been loyal subjects of the sultan, the Albanians supported the Young Turk revolution of 1908. The Albanian people had begun their period of national awakening in the late 19th century. A league for the defense of the Albanian nation had been founded, which promoted numerous schools and an Albanian language press. In 1908, Albanians hoped to obtain autonomous status and formed a political organization around Ismail Kemal Vlora, who was in close contact with the Young Turks. But the nationalistic attitude of the Young Turks left no room for Albanian aspirations. Anti-Turk uprisings broke out in Albania in 1909-1910, while Vlora and the 25 Albanian delegates spoke for the autonomist movement in the parliament at Constantinople.

Along with the trouble in Albania, the Turkish government became embroiled in armed conflict with Italy over Tripolitania (1911-1912). The Turks lost Cyrenaica and Tripolitania (Lybia), Rhodes and the Dodecanese islands to Italy. The Ottoman Empire appeared so vulnerable that the Balkan states decided to liberate Macedonia. Russia, ever conscious of its interests in the Balkans, advised the Serbs and Bulgarians to unite against the Turks. An alliance was formed in February, 1912. Greece joined it in May, and Montenegro in October. This Balkan League of Christian Peoples was determined to expel the Turks from eastern Europe. Each of the participants in the alliance had to contribute a military contingent to the common struggle: 300,000 men from Bulgaria, 150,000 men from Serbia, 120,000 men from Greece. Bulgaria, which supplied the largest contingent, expected to be amply repaid for it.

In the summer of 1912, the Turks found out about the plot and sent military reinforcements. On October 8, Montenegro opened hostilities by declaring war on the Ottoman Empire, marking the beginning of the first Balkan War. In the days that followed, Turkey retaliated by declaring war on Bulgaria and Serbia, but not on Greece. However, this did not stop Greece from keeping its agreement with the Allies. The Balkan coalition was quickly victorious. On October 24, the Serbian army under General Putnik and crown prince Alexander defeated the Turks at Kumanovo, then entered Skopje and Monastir a few days later along with Montenegrin reinforcements. The Greeks, doing their part, liberated Thessalia and Epirus, then lay siege to Janina (Ioannina). That day the Serbs won at Kumanovo, while the Bulgarians battled the Turks at Kirk-Kilisse then at Lule Burgas. From there, they marched on Constantinople; along the way they attacked Adrianople (Edirne) and finally took it on March 23, 1913.

The Greeks and Serbs entered Albanian territory as they advanced. Ismail Kemal Vlora mistrusted the intentions of the Balkan League countries and decided to take the Albanian cause before international opinion. At Valona he called together representatives of all the Albanian peoples, Moslem, Orthodox, and Catholic. This assembly declared Albanian independence on November 28, 1912. Vlora formed a provisory government, then went to London to attend a conference of the Great Powers arranged to consider the situation created by the Balkan War.

At the conference, Austria-Hungary and Italy favored an independent Albanian state, but were opposed by Russia and France who backed Serbian and Greek claims on the country. After long negotiations, the preliminaries of the London conference were produced May 30, 1913. These were to serve as a basis for future peace in the Balkans. Turkey was only allowed to keep Constantinople and its immediate surroundings in Europe. An independent and neutral Albania was set up under the protection of the Powers, who would also select a prince. Macedonia was to be divided up among Bulgaria, Greece and Serbia, who were to come to an agreement on the division by themselves.

The division of Macedonia in 1912 quickly set allies against each other. Bulgaria had hoped for the largest share of the province, but was thwarted by an agreement between the Greeks and the Serbs. Bulgaria retaliated on June 23, 1913, by attacking its former allies. Czar Ferdinand's initiative ended in failure, as he had against him not only the Serbs and Greeks, but also the Rumanians. Even the Turks, in trying to limit their losses, opposed his efforts.

The **Treaty of Bucharest** concluded the second Balkan War on August 10, 1913. Turkey regained Adrianople and part of eastern Thrace, now called European Turkey. Rumania received a small part of Dobrudja that Bulgaria had refused to cede in 1878, a region with a Bulgarian majority and a continuing source of tension between the two countries. Greece got the Macedonian coast with Salonika (Thessaloniki) and Chalcidique (Kavalla), the island of Crete and several central Aegean islands. Serbia obtained most of western and central Macedonia with the towns of Skopje, Ochrid and Bitola, thus incorporating Bulgarian and Albanian populations into her territory. Serbia also received a piece of the sanjak of Novi Pazar, the rest going to Montenegro. With this, Serbia's authority extended over a territory of 34,600 square miles and over more than 4.5 million people. Montenegro, through acquisition of the sanjak of Novi Pazar, had a common border with Serbia. Bulgaria gained only a little on the western border, but in the south reached the Aegean by annexing part of Thrace with the port of Dedeagatch (later Alexandroupolis).

The Balkan wars left deep scars. The loss of human life was heavy; 156,000 Bulgarians, 71,000 Serbs, 68,000 Greeks and some 10,000 Montenegrins fell in the fratricidal wars. The division of conquered Turkish territory also caused bitterness, especially among the Bulgarians who felt poorly compensated for their efforts, and, after their defeat, found themselves totally isolated in the midst of hostile neighbors. On the international level, Austria-Hungary was extremely concerned about Serbia's advance, with its territory now adjoining Montenegro's. Even more disquieting was the ever shriller anti-Austrian propaganda in the Serbian press and the increasing activity of secret societies such as the Serbian officer-led "Black Hand."

Austria-Hungary could no longer count on any country in this part of Europe except Bulgaria and Albania. Even Germany, its ally since 1872, was pressing harder to bring the Ottoman Empire into its own system of alliances. The Albanian question nearly brought Austria-Hungary and Serbia into conflict in September of 1913, when Serbia refused to withdraw from Albanian territory. The Serbs ultimately bowed to international pressure, and in December, 1913, the Great Powers agreed on definitive borders for Albania. Independent Albania had a territory of 10,800 square miles, contained 800,000 inhabitants, and was given a German prince, Wilhem of Wied, as sovereign. This was victory for the Central Powers. The Albanian state blocked Serbia's—and therefore Russia's—direct access to the Adriatic Sea. Albanians remained dissatisfied with their borders, because 400,000 of their compatriots had been incorporated into Serbia by the Treaty of Bucharest.

The Balkan wars marked an apparent victory for the indigenous Christian populations in eastern Europe, gaining independence in the wake of retreating Turkish domination. On the other hand, the Great Powers' involvement in the wars intensified nationalism and rivalry between neighboring peoples with race and even religion in common, dividing the region by fostering divergent allegiances. In fact, the Balkan peoples did not realize they were not masters of their own fate, but that decisions concerning them were being made in St. Petersburg, Vienna, London or Paris.

Chapter 13

Epilogue: The First World War

Europe in 1914 had much cause for tension. In the West, Franco-German antagonism had been bottling up since the war of 1870-1871 and was ready to explode at the least incident; the 1911 Agadir crisis nearly provided the spark. No one dismissed the probability of impending war, even though the French elections of April, 1914, in which anti-war elements gained, had been reassuring. In the East, Russian imperialism in the Balkans and Constantinople had been colliding with Austro-Hungarian interests since 1908. Anti-Austrian propaganda from Belgrade directed toward the Slavic subjects of the Austro-Hungarian empire merely accentuated the antagonism.

The annexation of Bosnia-Herzegovina by Austria-Hungary in 1908 and the Balkan wars of 1912-1913 had made a veritable powder keg of eastern Europe and had aggravated rivalries and antagonisms among the recently liberated Balkan peoples. Peace was further threatened by alliances that the various warring factions in the Balkans had made with the Great Powers. Serbia and Montenegro knew they had Russia's support, especially since Peter Karageorgevitch had taken the throne. Russia had been a military ally of France since 1892. Russia had also normalized its relations with Great Britain in 1906, and Great Britain had reconciled with France in the Entente Cordiale of 1905. Serbia thus had reason to think that Russia, France and even Great Britain—the countries of the Triple Entente—would back it up in case of conflict with Austria-Hungary. Bulgaria, on the other hand, was deeply disturbed by its losses in the second Balkan War, and looked to

Austria-Hungary for support. To exacerbate matters, Austria-Hungary was alarmed by the expansionist ambitions of Serbia and its Russian ally. Since 1872, Austria-Hungary had maintained close ties to the German Empire and to a lesser degree, Italy, through an agreement known as the Triple Alliance. Rumania was in a special situation. The Rumanian people and most politicians, especially those of the Liberal party, were Francophiles and Irredentists. They hoped to create a Greater Rumania by annexing Hungarian Transylvania and Austrian Bukovina. But their king, Carol I, was personally committed to the Germans and, on the advice of most of his ministers, signed an alliance with the Central Powers.

In the year between the end of the second Balkan War and the outbreak of World War I, Austro-Serbian relations deteriorated rapidly. In close contact with the Russian embassy at Belgrade and Serbian military headquarters, Serbian nationalist and secret societies stepped up their anti-Austrian propaganda—under cover in Bosnia-Herzegovina, but openly in Serbia, where they had the scarcely concealed support of the Serbian prime minister, Nikola Pashitch. By far the most important of these secret societies was the Black Hand, led by Colonel Dimitrievitch of the royal Serbian general staff and a highly placed secret service agent. Dimitrievitch was in close contact with young terrorist groups operating in Bosnia-Herzegovina.

At the instigation of the Black Hand, Bosnian students decided to stage a terrorist attack in Bosnia-Herzegovina during maneuvers of the Austro-Hungarian army in June, 1914, when the heir to the throne of Austria-Hungary, Archduke Franz Ferdinand, would be present. Terrorists went to Sarajevo from Serbia, and it was there on June 28, 1914, that the student Gavrilo Princip and his accomplices shot and killed the archduke and his wife, the Archduchess Sophia. In assassinating Franz Ferdinand, the murderers and those who recruited them were after the heir to the Austro-Hungarian throne; but even more importantly, they wanted to eliminate the man who made no secret of his intent to coax the Slavic population of the Empire back to Vienna from Belgrade. In this, the archduke posed a special threat to Serbia and Russia, for if the Habsburgs succeeded in winning over the Slavs, it would put an end to Russian hopes for hegemony in the Balkans and along the Adriatic.

In Vienna the military chief of staff, Marshal Konrad von Hotzendorf, with the strong support of his German counterparts, called for quick military action to settle the Serbian affair once and for all. Emperor Franz Joseph and the Hungarian prime minister, Istvan Tisza, feared that such action would provoke a Russian reaction and set off a European war. Russia had in fact assured Serbia of total support from the beginning, and in late July, the president of the French republic, Raymond Poincare, accompanied by most of his ministers, made an official visit to St. Petersburg to reinforce the

Franco-Russian alliance. After long debates in the crown council, during which Tisza tried to play a moderating role, Austria-Hungary sent an ultimatum to Belgrade on July 23, 1914, requiring total acceptance within 48 hours. The ultimatum included the demand that Austria be allowed to participate in the investigation of the assassination. On July 25, the Serbian government refused to accept the ultimatum that would have allowed Austrian police on Serbian soil. Austria-Hungary immediately broke off diplomatic relations with Serbia. Serbia decided on full mobilization of its troops, and Austria-Hungary began a partial mobilization. Despite English offers to mediate, Austria-Hungary knew it had the unconditional support of Germany, and exactly one month after the assassination at Sarajevo, on July 28, 1914, declared war on Serbia, making it known to all the powers that this was to be a localized conflict. But the Russian government could not let Serbia be crushed without losing credibility in the eyes of France, and mobilized at once. From then on, the situation became a test of alliances. The German government, also a partisan in the localized war, insisted that Russia stop preparations for war and that France declare neutrality. St. Petersburg refused, as did Paris, and the result was quasi-general warfare. Great Britain hesitated, then joined in on August 4, when German troops violated Belgian neutrality. Later, on November 1, the Ottoman Empire sided with the Central Powers and joined Germany and Austria-Hungary in battle in hopes of keeping Russia out of the Dardanelles Straits. The alliance game had thus made a European war out of the Austro-Serbian conflict. The people of eastern Europe, whose rivalries and antagonisms had been at the root of the conflict, found themselves involved in a larger struggle in which they were the stakes.

World War I had a profound effect on the fate of the peoples of central and eastern Europe. Although split into two opposing camps, the divisions between the people were not always clear. Austro-Hungarians fought for the Central Powers with an energy and a loyalty that lasted until the summer of 1918, while the Serbs and the Slavs of southern Austria-Hungary fought the Serbs of Serbia, their brothers, with no apparent second thoughts. The Rumanians from Transylvania were Hungarian subjects as well, and beginning in the summer of 1916, pitted themselves against the Rumanians from Russia who had sided with the Triple Entente. Even stranger was the situation in Poland. Those Poles who were German or Austro-Hungarian subjects found themselves face to face with brothers who had been taken into the Russian army. At first, the people generally showed a loyalty to the flag under which they fought. On September 9, 1914, the commander-in-chief of the Russian army, the Grand Duke Nicholas, attempted to win the Poles over to the Russian cause, promising in the name of the czar to restore Poland to an autonomous state "under the scepter of the Russian emperor." At the

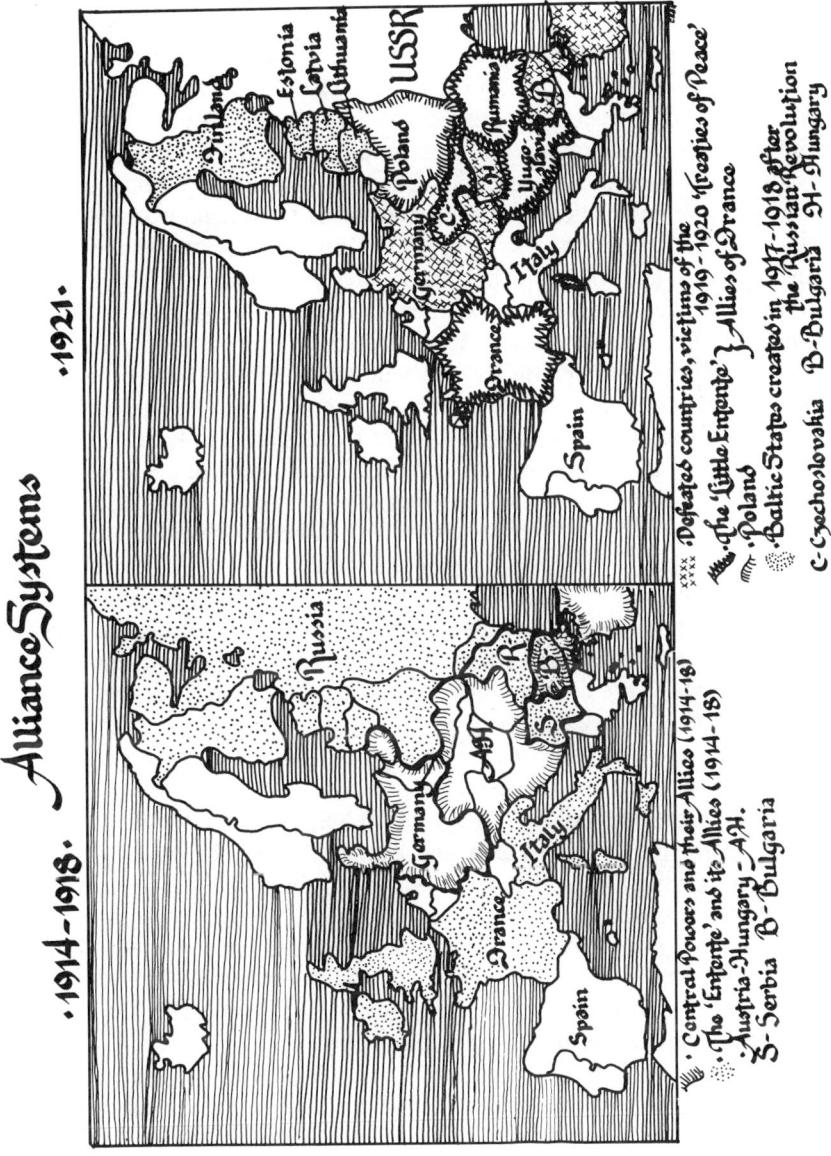

same time, Austria-Hungary was organizing along with its Polish contingents a legion to liberate Poland from the Russian yoke! After the successful summer campaign of 1915, the German and Austro-Hungarian authorities allowed an embryonic Polish state to develop under their protection.

In the camp of the Triple Entente, Serbia carried the heaviest load of the war. In spite of a few early victories, the Serbian army was in an awkward position when the Bulgarians went over to the side of the Central Powers and invaded, or "liberated," Macedonia. The remnants of the Serbian army fled along with the government and King Peter, first to Albania where they were clearly unwelcome and then to the island of Corfu—escaping the Austro-Hungarian troops who had occupied all of Serbian territory and were preparing to do the same with Albania. In principle, Albania maintained neutrality, but was nonetheless soon involved in the conflict. After being pillaged by what was left of the Serbian army, Albania was occupied by Austria-Hungary. But Albania had already been destined for sacrifice by the countries of the Triple Entente; in a secret treaty signed in London in April, 1915, bringing Italy into the war, Italy and Serbia were to get key bases in Albania!

Until early 1918, the war seemed to be balanced in favor of the Central Powers. Rumania, whose new king, Ferdinand, had entered it into war on the side of the Allies in 1916, was beaten after six weeks of combat and was nearly totally occupied by German, Austro-Hungarian and Bulgarian troops. After much hesitation, the Rumanian government agreed to sign the Treaty of Bucharest with the Central Powers on March 16, 1918. The Serbian army was powerless in refuge on Corfu, and Montenegro had given up fighting in 1916. Poland, under Austro-German protection, was supposed to have gained territory won from Russia.

When the revolutions in Russia broke out in 1917, the Russian army was caught up in the turmoil. Lenin and the Bolsheviks, in power since the October revolution, wanted peace at all costs. Thus, a separate treaty was signed by Soviet Russia with Germany at Brest-Litovsk on March 3, 1918. The Russians gave up all of their western possessions, namely Finland, which had declared its independence in December, 1917, the Baltic provinces of Estonia, Latvia and Lithuania, Poland, and also the Ukraine and a large part of White Russia (Bielorussia).

With the successes of the Central Powers in early 1918, a new political geography was beginning to take shape in central and eastern Europe; there was the proposed restoration of a Greater Poland loosely linked to Austria-Hungary, a Greater Bulgaria as master of the Balkans, and an Austria-Hungary supervising the Serbian state. Many of those in Austria-Hungary who had hoped for a union of all southern Slavs within a renovated Empire, now pinned their hopes on the young emperor, Charles, who had succeeded Franz Joseph in November, 1916. It appeared as though the young sovereign would adopt the policies that Franz Ferdinand had advocated. In early 1917, the Club of Southern Slavic Delegates of the Empire meeting in Vienna had presented the emperor with a petition requesting the union of all southern Slavs into an Illyrian state within the Empire. Profound changes were expected of the new emperor. He had, after all, ordered Prime Minister Tisza to resign for opposing reforms, and had just pardoned certain Czech nationalists condemned to death for treason, among them, Kramarj, head of the Young Czech party.

A breath of hope seemed to fill the Empire, to the despair of the Pan-Germanists. A *Pax Austriae* could reasonably be expected. But actually, the outcome of the war was far from settled. The Triple Entente, even after the defection of Russia, still held a few trump cards: the United States had entered the war in 1917; frequently reinforced French expeditionary troops were in Salonika; Greece followed Italy and Rumania in entering the war on the side of the Triple Entente; and finally, the Central Powers had no decisive victories on the western front. The war was not yet over.

In Rumania and Serbia the local populations under Austro-Hungarian and German occupation hoped for liberation, counting on a victory of the Triple Entente on the western front to redress their unfortunate situation.

The Austrian and Hungarian leadership seemed certain of victory and were backed by the leadership of the various nationalities; they were already confidently planning the reorganization of central and eastern Europe. Others were less certain, foreseeing a possible victory by the Triple Entente, and so they tried to keep their options open in case their hypothesis proved true.

In Hungary, the majority of the politically aware supported the government, but a few members of the Independence party, grouped around a liberal aristocrat, Count Mihaly Karolyi, made no secret of their Francophile sentiments, even at the risk of appearing to be traitorous.

There were certain Czech and southern Slav politicians as well, who kept in contact with the Entente in order to escape the common fate should the Central Powers lose. The Croatians and Serbs who had left the Empire when war broke out and who had started a Yugoslavian committee in London in April, 1915, made contact with the Serbian government in exile on Corfu. These contacts led to the July 7, 1917, Declaration of Corfu, signed by the delegates of the committee in London, by Pashitch, head of the Serbian government, by the Croatian Ante Trumbich and by the Dalmatian Frano Supilo. This document stated that in case of an Entente victory, the Croatians, the Slovenes and the Serbs would unite to form a Yugoslavian state under the Karageorgevitch family. The Montenegrin delegates also agreed with the provisions, despite the opposition of their king, Nicholas.

But acts like those of the Yugoslavian committee of London were rare. Most of the empire's southern Slavs could imagine no outcome other than remaining within some sort of reworked Habsburg framework.

Even more significant were the activities of Czech emigrants. During the first years of the war, Bohemia seemed to be calm, and most Czech soldiers fought loyally, though they did have a few more desertions and surrenders than other groups. In November, 1914, however, one of the leaders of the Czech opposition, Professor Masaryk, left Prague and went via Italy to France and then to England. He was joined by his friend and disciple Eduard Benes. Together they instigated the Czech National Council in France in 1916, which brought a young Slovak officer living in France, Milan Stefanik, over to their cause. The idea of a Czechoslovakian state began to take shape. The Czech emigrants presented it to the Allies, Aristide Briand and Lloyd George in particular, with such success that early in 1918, the dismemberment of Austria-Hungary had become one of the Entente's objectives for the war. These emigrants proved to be valuable aides to the Entente because they were able to provide the Allies with first-hand information through their highly-placed connections in the Austro-Hungarian administration.

The Polish leadership began to adopt a similar policy. Inside the country, they collaborated with the Central Powers to assure that they would create a Polish state in case they won the war. Outside, Polish emigrants made contact with the Allies in order to obtain the same advantages from them should the Entente win the war.

The leaders of nationalities not yet fully independent thus practiced a double policy through the rest of the war. Those who remained inside demonstrated their loyalty to the Dual Monarchy so that this loyalty would be repaid if the Central Powers won the war. On the other hand, those who emigrated and sided with the Entente worked at convincing the Allies that their people were with them in spirit and had nothing in common with Austria-Hungary. In this way, they were in a good position to obtain their country's independence if the Allies won. The people of the Empire generally remained loyal to it. Although the initial enthusiasm for the war had disappeared by early 1918 and was replaced by signs of serious discontent, this was due more to war weariness and difficulties of day-to-day existence than from a desire to overthrow the government.

The year 1918 marked a decisive turning point in the history of the peoples of central and eastern Europe. As the American troops arrived, new hope surged through the countries of the Entente. They now took more interest in plans worked out by Czech and Yugoslavian emigrants outlining the dismemberment of Austria-Hungary. The Allies became ardent defenders of an independent, reorganized Poland, no longer restrained by the need to humor Russia—which had withdrawn from the war. The Congress of Oppressed Nationalities was held in Rome in April, 1918, instigated by France and Italy. It ended with a vote to dismember Austria-Hungary and free the Slavic, Rumanian and Italian nations. The fate of the eastern European peoples hung on the balance of the war. If the Central Powers won—and until July, 1918, this was still possible—Austria-Hungary would dominate the Danubian and Balkan regions of Europe; the nationalities of the Empire would be given autonomous status within a reorganized federalist Empire as envisioned by the Emperor Charles, and Poland would regain its independence, or at least wide-ranging autonomy under a Habsburg king. If the powers of the Entente won, however, Austria-Hungary would be dismembered into as many states as there were nationalities, with the southern Slavs gathered into a large state ruled by the Serbian dynasty, and the Czechs and Slovaks united into a Czechoslovakia. Poland was to be an independent state in this case as well, a buffer between Germany and the Soviet Union.

The war turned around rapidly as the Allies began to win on the western front in wake of the failed offensives at Ludendorf. The French Marshal Foch began a counter-offensive on August 8, 1918, and another one was launched from Salonika by the Allied army under General Franchet d'Esperey. Within a few weeks, hopes for victory changed sides. On September 29, Bulgaria became the first nation to lay down its arms, quickly followed by Turkey; the allied army was now permitted to occupy Bulgaria and the Straits, and to liberate Serbia and Rumania from where they could directly attack Austro-Hungarian territory. Simultaneously, Italian troops under Marshal Diaz began an offensive which led to an armistice with Austria-Hungary on November 4, 1918, followed by armistice with Germany one week later.

In autumn, 1918, the victory of the Entente powers seemed to be a victory of the people over the monarchs. Three great empires, those of the Habsburgs, the Hohenzollerns and the Romanovs, had crumbled in the turmoil.

The people of these empires were about to become masters of their own fate. But would they be able to assume this weighty legacy? Could they live as good neighbors, forgetting their differences and working to build a future of peace and fraternity in this part of Europe? Or, on the contrary, would national antagonisms and various rivalries set them against each other?

Part III

An Era of Confrontation

Chapter 14

Political Changes in Central and Eastern Europe After the First World War

The defeat of the Central Powers (Germany and Austria-Hungary) and their allies (Bulgaria and the Ottoman Empire) precipitated the fall of the governments and regimes they had directed during the war. Meanwhile, leaders of nations suddenly liberated by the defeat of their guardian powers made the most of the circumstances and created their own independent states. Profound political changes were taking place amid a climate of revolutionary agitation and feverish activity; countries were jockeying for positions of leverage at the opening of the peace talks. Among the vanquished peoples, however, political agitation turned to revolution.

THE FIRST WAVE OF REVOLUTION IN THE DEFEATED COUNTRIES

From the beginning of autumn, 1918, when the Allies launched their great offensive, there was no longer any doubt that the war was lost for the Central Powers.

The Bulgarian Revolution

The first country affected by the defeat was Bulgaria. On September 18, 1918, the Eastern Army, under General Franchet d'Esperey, broke through

Bulgarian lines and liberated the Serbian territory occupied by Bulgaria since the end of 1915. To avoid being encircled, Bulgarian troops pulled back toward their national territory. News of this retreat caused consternation throughout the country. On September 23, some of the regiments mutinied, and the rebellion spread to nearly all units. The rebels took the city of Radomir where they blocked off the general headquarters of the army. Government leaders in Sofia immediately sent a delegation to the commander of the Allied army at Salonika to conclude an armistice quickly. Simultaneously, they sent the two agrarian leaders, Stambolijski and Daskalov, to Radomir to try and pacify the mutinous soldiers. Stambolijski was immensely popular because he had been arrested toward the end of 1915 for his strong opposition to the war and seemed to be the only man able to halt the rebellion. He gladly accepted this mission, afraid that revolution would further weaken Bulgaria and leave it entirely at the mercy of the Allies. His attempts to calm the rebels were thwarted by Daskalov, who had other ideas. Daskalov had adopted some of the Bolshevik ideas that had been seeping into Bulgaria since the October Revolution and used the occasion to join the rebels, take charge of a Republic of Radomir, and begin a march on the capital. Daskalov's foolish escapade lasted only a few days; he was arrested at the gates of Sofia by loyalist troops. The armistice of September 28 brought some relief to the starving civilian population, which had been forced to provide food supplies to the German army of Marshal Makensen stationed in Macedonia and Rumania. Conditions of the armistice included the complete retreat of Bulgarian troops to behind the borders of 1913, the occupation of part of the country and right of passage for the armed forces of the Entente. On the strong advice of the Allies, Czar Ferdinand abdicated on October 3, 1918, in favor of his son, Boris III (1918-1943).

The Bulgarian defeat, along with a range of economic problems, such as rising prices and food shortages, created an atmosphere ripe for revolution among the civilian population. While Stambolijski's Agrarian party and the urban middle-class parties hoped mainly for a more democratic country and for some agrarian reform, others took much more radical positions. The Bulgarian Socialist party adopted Bolshevik tenets and sent their delegates to the Moscow conference that produced the Third International in March, 1919.

King Boris was prudent and let the Agrarians govern, with Stambolijski at their head, in order to prevent a more detrimental party from taking power. The main task for the government was to establish a minimum amount of order in preparation for the problems certain to arise from the signing of a peace treaty.

The Austro-Hungarian Revolution

News of Bulgaria's surrender echoed resoundingly throughout Austria-Hungary, and affected the leadership as much as the common people. On October 1, 1918, the new head of the Austrian government, Baron Hussarek, made an effort to calm the various Austrian nationalities by announcing that Austria was to be restructured along federalist lines to assure the different national groups administrative and political autonomy. At the same time, Baron Burian, Minister of Foreign Affairs in the Dual Monarchy, sent President Wilson a diplomatic note aimed at opening peace talks on the basis of Wilson's Fourteen Points. The Allies, not wanting to disassociate the Austro-Hungarian problem from the German problem, delayed their response. Meanwhile, in a manifesto on October 16, Emperor Charles announced to his subjects that "The Empire will become a federal state in which each ethnic group will form its own political community within its own territory...." The measures announced in the Imperial Manifesto applied only to Austria, but they also guaranteed Czechs, Poles, Slovenes and other southern Slavs satisfaction of some, if not all, their requests. The emperor hoped that the leaders in Budapest would have the wisdom to accord their peoples the same rights.

Unfortunately, the emperor's Manifesto came too late. The emperor and his former cabinet chief, Count Polzer-Hoditz, had finished it by the beginning of 1917, but certain Austrian political groups had done everything in their power to delay its publication. When it finally appeared, the time had passed. Leaders of different ethnic groups, who saw defeat coming and realized the consequences for those who remained with the Empire, turned down the Manifesto and opted instead for the kind of independence that their national councils in exile had been demanding since 1916.

In Bohemia, Czech delegates to a national council took up the idea of an independent Czechoslovakia, which Masaryk and Benes had advocated since 1916. In a reply to the Imperial Manifesto, drafted at a meeting on October 19, the delegates stated the only solution was total independence. The night before, in Washington, D.C., Masaryk had declared the independence of Czechoslovakia and its complete alliance with the Entente. The Habsburgs had lost Bohemia. A delegation from the National Council, equipped with official passports issued by the Austrian authorities (in itself an example of the usual Austrian liberalism), left Prague for Geneva in order to make contact with Benes and emigrant representatives. On October 28, exuberant crowds rejoiced in the streets of Prague at the proclamation of a republic, and there was no reaction from the authorities even though they had the means to enforce order. Instead, the imperial administrators relinquished power to the provisory authorities in a quasi-official manner. On October 30, a Czech delegation headed by M. Tusar went to Vienna to settle the various formalities for independence.

The example set by Prague was contagious. In Bukovina on the same day, a national council decided to rejoin their province to Rumania. On October 29, the Diet at Zagreb broke all ties linking Croatia to Austria and Hungary, and then reluctantly admitted the possibility of a "common sovereign and national state of Slovenes, Croatians and Serbs." On October 31, the Slovene diet did the same at Ljubljana. Meanwhile, the Polish national council took charge of Galicia without completely breaking with Austria.

In the Hungarian half of the Dual Monarchy, the situation was somewhat different. News of the Bulgarian surrender gave rise to a heated debate in the Hungarian parliament. A deputy from the Independence Party, Marton Lovaszy, publicly declared himself as "a friend of the Entente" and demanded immediate peace. At the instigation of Count Mihaly Karolyi, several members of the bourgeois opposition and of the Independence party, as well as the Socialists, formed a national council to prepare for Hungarian independence on October 25. At that point, however, Karolyi's influence in parliament was weak. Also, the Hungarian people seemed to be largely faithful to the old regime, with the exception of the workers in Budapest who were responsive to pacifist and socialist propaganda. Emperor Charles and his wife were counting on this loyalty of the Hungarian people when they decided to go to Hungary. The royal couple stayed in Hungary from October 22 to 27, and had the impression that as far as the people were concerned, nothing had been lost. The sovereign even tried to come to an agreement with Mihaly Karolyi, but the members of the national council wanted a radical change in policy and demanded total independence from Austria. Paradoxically, the national council remained completely deaf to the demands of non-Magyars. The idea of secession catching on among several of the diverse ethnic groups clearly upset the Magyars. Bad news from the front along with the Croatian decision to break with Hungary caused a stir that the national council was quick to exploit. On the front, the Italians had launched a major offensive in the Dolomites on October 24; the Austro-Hungarian troops under the Hungarian general Kovess and the Croatian general Boroevic withstood the attack until October 26, but that day some Hungarian units refused to go to the line and asked instead to be returned to defend Hungary under attack from the east. A few days later the front collapsed and negotiations for a truce began.

The news of a truce caused riots in Budapest. On October 28, there were demonstrations in the capital, and police and gendarmery fired into a crowd which was moving toward the parliament. The disturbances doubled in intensity. There were strikes in factories and workshops, and workers' councils, modeled on those of the Russian soviets of 1917, sprang up here and there. Finally, in the evening of October 30th, a large crowd including rebel soldiers took over the official buildings; the governor then relinquished power to the national council. The following day, Karolyi gained two offices. By telephone from Vienna, the Emperor, Charles I, invested him with the power of president of the Hungarian council, and then in Parliament Square the people granted him full powers by acclamation. On the same day, Count Istvan Tisza, who had done all he could to prevent the war in July 1914, was assassinated by rebel soldiers who accused him of causing the war!

Hungarians who cheered Karolyi on and who expected him to preserve Greater Hungary were overly optimistic. Leaders of the various ethnic groups were coming out in favor of independence. They knew that the conditions for peace would be hard on those who lost and that it was time to take advantage of Hungary's situation. Meeting on October 30 at Turoc-Szent-Marton, the Slovaks declared their independence and their desire to join the Czechs within a federal state. On the following day, the leaders of the National Rumania party at Arad formed a national council that demanded immediate self-determination for the Rumanian people and the rejoining of Transylvania to Rumania, none of which prevented them from simultaneously negotiating with a delegate from Budapest, Oscar Jaszi. Throughout the Rumanian-dominated communities of Transylvania, the Rumanians took over local government. In the Vojvodine, the Serbs adopted the same attitude in early November—after the region was occupied by Serbian troops. A local assembly, representing less than half the population, announced at Ujvidek on November 25 that the province would be joined to the kingdom of Serbs, Croatians and Slovenes.

And as in Cisleithania (Austria), the ethnic groups in Transleithania (Hungary) rejected the old structures. The Habsburg Empire was coming apart at the seams. Each nationality had chosen independence and a severing of ties with a centuries-old community. Two fixed points remained, however: the army and the Emperor. In the first days of November, the army withdrew from the scene. In signing the armistice of November 4 and giving the order to halt combat even before the cease-fire, the military commanders marked the end of the Empire. Only the Emperor remained. On November 11, in a message to the delegates of the Assembly of German Austria, which since the beginning of the month had taken charge of plans for the German-speaking provinces, Emperor Charles made known his intention to retire from "all participation in the affairs of state," and then withdrew to the Chateau of Eckartsau. The Republic of German Austria was announced in Vienna on the following day. At the same time in Hungary, Mihaly Karolyi, at the head of a cabinet of socialists, radicals and representatives of the Independence party, was loudly demanding the sovereign's abdication. On November 13, a delegation from the Hungarian parliament led by the primate, Cardinal Csernoch, went to Eckartsau. The sovereign gave the Hungarian delegates a document similar to the one he had given to the representatives of the Austrian parliament two days earlier.

From then on, German Austria and Karolyi's Hungary each had to work alone in erasing the past. The nationalities who had broken away from them had won, and the age of nationalism had begun.

THE SITUATION AMONG THE VICTORS

The defeat of the Central Powers and the upsetting of the Austro-Hungarian Empire benefited the peoples and states that had fought against it or had defected in time.

Triumph For the Small Nations: Serbia and Rumania

Serbia had supported the war effort from the beginning and had suffered considerable human and material losses, but ultimately gained from the ordeal. The Austro-Hungarian, German and Bulgarian armed forces evacuated its territory. The Serbian army and allied contingents from the Eastern Army had forced them to retreat in the second half of October. Even better, the Serbians had received permission from the Allied high commander to occupy not only Croatian and Slavonic territories, some of whom had shown a desire for union with Serbia, but also the Vojvodine and certain points of southern Hungary with the city of Pecs.

In Belgrade, the Pan Serbian policy of Pashitch gained approval. Tiny Serbia of 1914 had thus gathered together all the southern Slavs under the authority of its sovereign. Even Montenegro, who since 1914 had fought alongside Serbia, decided to join in after a vote of the national assembly on November 13. The old king of Serbia, Peter I, had been ill since the beginning of the war and had entrusted his son, Prince-Regent Alexander, with the leadership of the new state to be called the Kingdom of Serbs, Croatians and Slovenes. It became the Kingdom of Yugoslavia in 1931.

This union of southern Slavs into one state actually owed its existence to a misunderstanding. The Croatian and Slovene representatives who accepted the idea of uniting with the Serbs had imagined this union as an egalitarian federation. That was clear when organization began for the new state. A provisory assembly met in Belgrade on March 1, 1919; it was composed of Serbian deputies elected to the parliament at Belgrade in 1912, most of them radicals who favored a single, centralized state, and of non-elected Croats and Slovenes sent by the various national councils. The national minorities were not invited to send representatives. Even without the German, Hungarian and Albanian national minorities—totalling some two million people—the new state contained a wide diversity of ethnic groups. There were six million Orthodox Serbs living next to over four million Croats and one and a half million Slovenes, all Roman Catholics. These people were brought closer together by language, but were separated by religion, traditions, and by different levels of cultural and economic development. The Yugoslavian borders were not finally drawn until the treaties of Saint-Germain-en-Laye and Trianon.

Despite the separate treaty Rumania had been obliged to sign with the Central Powers in March, 1918, it returned to battle on the side of the Entente countries during the Allied army's offensive. For this, Rumania became one of the victors, and its leaders intended to make the most of it. National councils in Russian Bessarabia, in Austrian Bukovina and in Hungarian Transylvania made their desires to join Rumania clear. On December 1, 1918, at Gyulafehervar, the assembly of the National Rumanian party announced that Transylvania had joined Greater Rumania, thus anticipating by a few days the Allied decision authorizing Rumania to occupy most of Transylvania. The borders would not be final until the peace conference, however.

The Birth of the Czechoslovakian State

The national council at Prague had taken over the former kingdom of

Bohemia on October 28 and quickly announced a republic. The old chief of the opposition, Kramarj, returned from Vienna where he had met with Benes, to set up a provisory government on October 31. Benes became minister of foreign affairs, and as such went to Paris to take part in the peace conference.

On November 14, the National Provisory Assembly met in Prague. It was made up of 201 Czech deputies and 69 Slovak deputies recruited by co-option. In fact, only the Czech deputies were representative, since they were designated proportionate to the size of the different parties that represented the Czechs at the *Reichsrat* elected in 1911. The 69 Slovak deputies were chosen arbitrarily, weighted so as to encourage union at the expense of autonomy. There were no representatives from the minority ethnic groups making up 40 percent of the population. At its first seating, the provisory national assembly announced the dethronement of the Habsburgs and appointed Professor Thomas Masaryk, who was at the moment still in the United States, as president of the republic. The assembly then turned to the drafting of a constitution which was finally adopted on February 29, 1920.

Poland's Difficult Renaissance

For some time, there had been agreement both within and without Poland for the need to restore the Polish state and grant it full independence. President Wilson's Thirteenth Point called for the creation of an independent Polish state with access to the sea. Throughout the war, Austro-Hungarian Poles fought under the Polish flag as military units. These legions of volunteers were led by Polish officers under the command of Joseph Pilsudski and generals Haller and Sikorski. The leaders now called on the Poles in Russia to rebel. Polish deputies to the Russian *Duma* had maintained a loyalist attitude toward Russia since August 8, 1914, but the success of the great Austro-German offensive in summer, 1915, which liberated almost all of Russian Poland, presented the Polish problem in a different light. The Polish Legions liberated Lublin while the Germans were entering Warsaw on August 5, 1915. The Poles sincerely believed that the Central Powers would grant them independence. The Central Powers hesitated to take a stand, however, which provoked the resignation of a disappointed Joseph Pilsudski. Not until the following year, on November 5, 1916, did the German and Austro-Hungarian governments issue a manifesto announcing their intention to create an independent Poland with Russian Polish territories. The Polish Legions were immediately placed at the disposal of a provisory state council with Pilsudski responsible for military matters. The Russian revolution of 1917 slightly altered the attitude of the Poles. As long as the empire of the Czars existed, it remained a danger and an enemy to most Poles, and so the

Central Powers were their only hope. But Russia in full-scale revolt was no longer a threat to Poland. Germany, however, made no secret of its imperialist ambitions in eastern Europe and intended to keep the Polish territories it had held since the end of the 18th century. Germany had become the more immediate danger. Consequently, the provisory Polish authorities began to resist some of the German occupants' demands. When von Beseler, the governor of Warsaw, tried to place a German officer in charge of the Polish Legions, Pilsudski and most of the Polish officers resigned and were immediately imprisoned.

In Russia, the Poles who had remained in the Duma expected no more from the Central Powers than the little they had expected from the Russian provisory government. Instead, they made contact with the Allies. A Polish national council in exile was even set up in Paris with a National Democrat, Dmowski, as president. It also benefited from the support of Polish Americans rallied to the national cause by the pianist, Ignac Paderewski. Faced with the threat of Poles defecting to the Allied cause, the Central Powers became more understanding of the Polish viewpoint. A regency council was created with Cardinal Kakowski, the archbishop of Warsaw, as president, assisted by some conservative aristocrats. The Polish administration had very limited powers; all important issues were settled by the authorities of the German occupation. The representatives of Prussian and Galician Poles at the parliaments in Berlin and Vienna made no attempt to hide their desire to construct an independent Poland. But they had few opportunities to act before the defeat of the Central Powers appeared certain. Then, on October 7, 1918, the Regency Council declared the country's independence and formed a national government union made up of Socialists and National Democrats. The defense of Polish interests among the Allies was entrusted to the National Council of Paris.

As the Central Powers crumbled, the process of setting up an independent Polish state accelerated. In Galicia, the Poles took over all administrative offices, and on October 7 at Lublin a socialist, Daszyniski, became head of a provisory government of the Republic of Poland. Daszyniski appointed Joseph Pilsudski, still a prisoner of the Germans in the fortress of Magdebourg, as his minister of war. Several days later in Warsaw, the Regency Council conferred the command of all Polish forces to Pilsudski, who by then had been liberated. Pilsudski thus found himself supreme commander of an army made up of such disparate elements that in the course of the war they had worn different uniforms and had fought on opposing sides. In addition to his military responsibilities, Pilsudski was appointed chief of state and given full powers by both the Regency Council and the government at Lublin.

Pilsudski's task was by no means easy. Poland thus far existed only on paper. There were no fixed borders, no single currency, no common laws. The country was threatened on the west by the German Corps Francs who were trying to retain the Reich's eastern provinces, and also on the east by Soviet Russia who had not completely renounced the territory it had lost in the Treaty of Brest-Litovsk. Pilsudski first set about laying the foundation for his administration, and in particular for a national army with what remained of the Legions and the army that General Haller had put together in France. He then organized elections by universal suffrage on November 28 for a constituent assembly. Wishing to devote himself entirely to his military duties, Pilsudski on January 16, 1919, made Paderewski, back from the United States, leader of a Cabinet-council for national union and sent Roman Dmowski to represent Poland at the peace conference.

Several days later, the assembly met and adopted a provisory constitution, and also retained Pilsudski as chief of state and commander of the armed forces. After 130 years of obliteration, the Polish state was reborn from territory which had often served as a battlefield during the long war—a war which ended in the defeat and ruin of the three countries that had partitioned Poland in 1772.

Albania's Struggle For Freedom

On the eve of World War I, Albania had just obtained its independence, and on March 7, 1914, its new sovereign, the German Prince Wilhem of Wied, had arrived on Albanian soil. Several months later, war broke out and the prince, who had been incessantly caught up in a revolt of Moslem peasants who resented a Christian ruler, left the country on September 3. The young Albanian state, though neutral, quickly became the object of Greek, Italian and Serbian attention. After the Serbian defeats in the winter of 1915-1916, Albania was occupied in the south by the Italians who controlled the Vlora, and by the French who controlled Korca, while in the north and center, the country was held by the Austro-Hungarian armies. Immediately after the Bulgarian armistice was declared, French, Italian and Serbian troops took the place of the departing Austro-Hungarians.

The various occupations left deep wounds; though a non-belligerent people, over 70,000 Albanians were killed in the course of the war and their country devastated. At the end of the war, a national congress was held in the Italian zone at Durres. The result was a provisional government led by Turhan Pacha and supported by Albanian emigrants living in the United States. Turhan Pacha immediately went to Paris to plead the case of his country, which had been divided up between Italy and Serbia by the Treaty of London in April, 1915. The Italians were aggressive, trying to make Albania into a protectorate, but the Albanians reacted with a wave of patriotism; anti-Italian riots took place in Valona in November, 1919. On January 21,

1920, a group of leading citizens met and renounced the Durres government, judged to be too accommodating to the Italians. Asserting Albanian's desire for independence, a regency council composed of representatives of the different communities began to govern from Tirana. But the country remained under occupation until the end of 1920. The Albania with borders of 1913 did not become an independent and sovereign state until its admission to the League of Nations on December 27, 1920.

ATTEMPTS TO BOLSHEVIZE EASTERN EUROPE

Since the October revolution of 1917, Russia had been governed by a council of commissars, a small elite group of the Bolshevik party presided over by Lenin. Soviet Russia's new leaders, Trotsky in particular, made known their intention to export their brand of political philosophy to other countries. Prisoners of war from the Central Powers watched the revolutionary events unroll before their eyes and often took part in it themselves. Then after they were freed by the Treaty of Brest-Litovsk, most of them returned to their own countries. Deeply impressed by what they had seen in Russia in October, 1917, some of them began to spread Bolshevik ideas. Since the end of the war, all European socialist parties had been wrestling with the problem of what stance to take on the Bolshevik revolution: should they continue to remain loyal to the tradition of parliamentary reform, or follow Russia to work toward revolution to install a dictatorship of the proletariat? Supporters of the Bolshevik model met with Lenin in Moscow on March 2, 1919, and laid the foundation for the Third Socialist International. Socialists from countries ruined and defeated by the war were the most receptive to the Bolshevik solutions, and tried to adapt them to their own situations.

The Hungarian Soviet Republic and Its Failure (March-August, 1919)

Hungary was the first eastern European state to attempt the Bolshevik experiment at any length. The bourgeois revolution of October 31, 1918, had instated Count Mihaly Karolyi at the head of a government supported by a coalition of liberal bourgeois, Kossuthist nationalists, and socialists.

The government quickly ran up against several problems. The economic situation was disastrous and getting worse every day. High inflation was weakening the currency and an influx of bureaucrats and private citizens from territories occupied by neighboring countries did nothing to ease the task for the new leadership. Social tensions set the stage for extremists grouped around Bela Kun, a socialist journalist and an ex-prisoner of war in Russia. Though liberated by the February revolution, he remained in Russia until April, 1918, to participate in Bolshevik activities. Many socialists disappointed in the ineffective Karolyi government turned to Bela Kun, and with them he organized the Hungarian Communist party on November 24, 1918. In January, 1919, hoping to repeat what had been so successful at Petrograd, Bela Kun tried to incite the Budapest garrison to revolt and seize power. The attempt failed, and he was arrested. But Karolyi's cumulative problems allowed Bela Kun to regain lost ground. Czech and Rumanian troops, impatient to take over territory promised them by the Allies, shattered Karolyi's attempts to foster a favorable image. Karolyi was expected to be able to save the country through his supposedly good relations with the French leadership. As the Hungarian government grew weaker, however, Allied demands increased. On March 20, 1919, President Karolyi received an ultimatum from Lieutenant Colonel Vyx, the Allied representative in Budapest, demanding that the Hungarians evacuate more territory than agreed upon in the terms of the armistice. Karolyi resigned in protest on March 21, leaving power "in the hands of the Hungarian proletariat." Was his action a result of blackmail on the part of the Allies, or the last gesture of a disappointed patriot? Whatever the reason, it left Bela Kun and his supporters in charge of the country.

The Hungarian Soviet Republic was born. A commissariat of the people made up of communists and left-wing socialists with Eugene Landler, Matyas Rakosi, Tibor Szamuelly, and Jozef Pogany was formed under the presidency of Bela Kun. They decreed a radical agrarian reform, the nationalization of banks and industries, and the separation of church and state. Opponents of the regime were systematically eliminated by the Hungarian *Czeka*, or "Lenin's Boys." Hundreds of summary executions took place. The main victims were the wealthy public figures, the priests and the peasants who resisted the forceful takeovers. Anxious to protect the revolution from foreign enemies and to guard national territory against invasion, Bela Kun appealed to the patriotic sentiment of the people. With help from officers of the former imperial and royal army under the command of General Aurel Stromfeld, Bela Kun created a Red Army that successfully fought off the Czechs, retook some Czech-occupied sites and sponsored a short-lived Slovak Soviet Republic in the Presov region.

The Rumanians were responsible for striking the decisive blows during this period of Communist experimentation in Hungary. With the tacit support of Clemenceau, and in spite of the terms of the armistice, Rumanian troops invaded what was left of Hungary, systematically pillaging the countryside. At the same time in June of 1919, a counter-revolutionary government was formed in the south of the country in the French-occupied city of Szeged. Under Admiral Horthy, former commander of the Austro-Hungarian fleet, several thousand former soldiers gathered into a National Army. The Rumanian march on Budapest led to the departure of

Bela Kun and most of his Bolshevik followers on August 1, 1919, after 133 days of rule. Two days later, the Rumanians occupied the Hungarian capital, and a counter-revolutionary government was formed in conjunction with the government of Szeged. But Hungary's condition was catastrophic. The economy was in ruins and food stocks and fuel were alarmingly low due to neighboring countries' economic blockades. In addition, national territory was divided *de facto* into two zones: the Rumanians controlled the east and the center, including Budapest, and Horthy's national army held the south and west. Finally, a third zone, the far south, was occupied by French and Serbian troops. Firm Allied protest led to Rumania's evacuation of Budapest and the rest of the country in early November, and Admiral Horthy's troops entered the capital on November 16. The counter-revolution was victorious, but the country was in ruins.

The Failure of Bulgarian Bolshevism

In Bulgaria, unrest following the armistice was deftly channeled by King Boris III who had entrusted the agrarian leader, Stambolijski, with the government. But the new head of state inherited some thorny economic problems. Inflation, unemployment, and general confusion among the population had created a climate ripe for revolution. Most Bulgarian socialists chose, in March, 1919, to join the Third Socialist International, and during the congress they held from May 25 to 27, they changed the party into a Bulgarian Communist party with Basil Kolarov as secretary general. The unions, led by Georgi Dimitrov, gave the Communist movement their full support. In the first elections after the war, held in August, 1919, the Communists won 45 seats and polled 20 percent of the vote. After the Soviet Republic failed in Hungary, the Comintern did all it could to support the Bulgarian Communist party so it could make Bulgaria Moscow's outpost in the Balkans. In autumn of 1919, the Communists stirred up a wave of social protest throughout the country, particularly fostering strikes in transport and industry. Stambolijski, bolstered by support from the king and a sizable agrarian representation in the parliament, decided to call up the reserves. Peasant volunteers were given the responsibility for keeping order and for preventing an eventual general strike. Communist agitation momentarily came to a halt. Here, as in Hungary, the attempt to bolshevize had failed.

The Russo-Polish War

A barely revived Poland had to confront Soviet Russia on the issue of their common border. Here, however, the Bolshevik threat took a different form from that in Bulgaria and Hungary. To begin with, Poland had a common border with Soviet Russia, a border that was still hazy in early 1919.

Many Poles still cherished the hope of returning to the historical borders of Greater Poland of the 18th century, but in this their interests ran counter to those of the young Baltic states born from the ruins of old Russia. However, as the German troops gradually evacuated Russian and Baltic territories they had occupied in 1915-1916, the Red Army took their place and began attacking the armies of the young Baltic republics and of Poland. From April to August, 1919, General Pilsudski counter-attacked vigorously, retaking Brest-Litovsk, Grodno, Wilno and most of White Russia from the Soviets. The Allies were divided on the question of Poland's eastern borders. The English opted for the Curzon line proposed by a British diplomat. The line generally corresponded to the former eastern edge of the Congress Kingdom, and in January, 1920, Lloyd George strongly advised the Poles to come to an agreement with Moscow. France, on the other hand, feared the encroachment of Bolshevism in eastern Europe, and looked more favorably on Poland's position, advising the leaders in Warsaw to act prudently.

The Red Army's victories in the Russian civil war and the reconquest of the Ukraine were seen by Poles as a direct threat to their country. Trotsky made no secret of his hostility to the new Polish government, and the Polish revolutionary Dzerjinski's presence on the People's Council of the Commissariat was no reassurance to Warsaw. General Pilsudski decided to thwart Russian plans by throwing his support behind the Ukrainian leader, Simon Petliura, who had fled to Poland after the Red Army's victory. On April 25, 1920, Polish troops attacked in the Ukraine and took Kiev on May 6. The Red Army's reaction was overwhelming. On May 30, the Soviets mounted a major offensive, and in a matter of a few days reoccupied all the territory Pilsudski had gained since 1919. Galicia itself was directly threatened.

Given the gravity of the situation, on July 10, 1920, in the presence of both parties, Lloyd George proposed an agreement based on the Curzon line. The Russians rejected the idea of British mediation, but while in Warsaw, they were asked for an armistice by a cabinet-council of national union led by the agrarian Witos. Poland was geographically isolated from its western allies, and only Hungary, who had just experienced a run-in with bolshevism, was willing to help. A French military mission conducted by General Weygand arrived in Poland on July 26. Despite fierce resistance by Polish combat troops, the Soviets continued to advance. In early August, they arrived on the right bank of the Vistula, across from Warsaw. Pilsudski decided to resist. On August 14, he began a counter-offensive in which the Poles made a spectacular comeback. This "miracle of the Vistula" led to a collapse of the Red Army, and the taking of 50,000 prisoners. The Reds retreated and within a few days had given up over 250 miles. The Polish government, now in a position of strength, agreed to negotiate. Talks opened on September 18 and resulted in a preliminary agreement on October 12 which was ratified by the Treaty of Riga on March 12, 1921. Historic Poland was nearly restored, although Lithuania as well as the other Baltic states were not included.

Thus, while peace talks were taking place in Paris, a kind of stabilization had begun to take shape in eastern Europe based on the existence of national states. Some of these states, considered losers in the war, had still managed to weather the Bolshevik storm; Austria, Bulgaria and Hungary were examples. Other states, who had been linked to the Allies from the beginning like Serbia and Rumania, or who joined them later like Poland and Czechoslovakia, were on the side of the victors, and expected to profit from the situation when the treaties were settled.

Chapter 15

Eastern Europe in the Aftermath of the War

The peoples in eastern Europe were trying to reorganize as national states with varying degrees of success. The victorious countries were sending representatives to Paris to work on the peace settlements beginning January 18, 1919, but Germany, Austria, Hungary, Bulgaria and the Ottoman Empire were not invited to take part. Representatives did come, however, from the new countries born of the disintegration of the central empires and from Russia, Poland, Finland, the Baltic republics, Czechoslovakia, Serbia, Rumania and the smaller states in southeastern Europe that had fought with the Allies. And some of these countries' representatives made themselves heard, in particular the Czech delegates, Eduard Benes and his assistant, Stephan Osuky.

THE PEACE SETTLEMENTS

At the outset of the war, the Allied leaders had no plan for postwar territorial modifications in the Danubian and southeastern areas of Europe. No one seriously thought of destroying the Austro-Hungarian Empire; many French and British diplomats considered it a stabilizing element in the heart of Europe. At the most, they considered making a few border alterations in order to give Serbia access to the Adriatic. No one had a precise idea of what to do about Poland. Some felt the Prussian Poles and the Poles of Galicia should be brought into an enlarged and autonomous Poland within the

Russian empire, something the Czar had suggested in August, 1914, and the Allies were still discussing during a conference held in December, 1916. As for the future of the Ottoman Empire, however, Russia had sharply defined ideas, making known its intention to occupy Constantinople. This did not appear to offend the British.

Gradually, as the conflict evolved, the shape of future peace terms emerged. In the **Treaty of London**, signed on April 26, 1915, by France, Great Britain, Russia and Italy—by which Italy became a co-belligerent— the Powers agreed to give Italy the provinces of Trent and southern Tyrol, Trieste and Istria as well as part of the Dalmatian coast with several islands. Moreover, Italy was promised a zone of influence in Albania and Asia Minor. This treaty apparently bore little resemblance to the "theory of nationalities" that was constantly invoked by French and English politicians to justify their traditional support for the "oppressed" nationalities of Austria-Hungary. The Treaty of London actually offered to liberate far fewer Italians than it promised to deliver into Italian hands non-Italians, Austrians in south Tyrol, Slovenes in Istria, Serbs and Croatians in Dalmatia, and Albanians. The following year, diplomatic arrangements preceding Rumania's entry into the war led to an agreement on August 17, 1916, in which victory would assure Rumania Transylvania and the Banat of Temesvar. The question of Austrian Bukovina was left unsettled due to Russia's opposition.

Beside the official preparation for future settlements, Czech emigrants who had left Austria-Hungary at the beginning of the war, such as Thomas Masaryk and Eduard Benes, persuasively and effectively lobbied French and British leaders behind the scenes. The same kind of activity was practiced by Serbian diplomats assigned to Paris and by Serbian and Croatian emigrants. They all worked to convince the Entente powers that Austria-Hungary had to be destroyed and replaced with nation states. These ideas began to attract the attention of a number of politicians and diplomats responsive to the real or assumed Francophilia of these refugees. In 1916, Benes published a pamphlet entitled *Destroy Austria-Hungary!* clearly stating the author's goal. Benes' ideas were generally shared by many well known French academics such as the historians Ernest Denis, Ernest Lavisse and Louis Eisenman (the latter on military duty in the information service of the ministry of war), the geographer Emmanuel de Martonne, and the philosophers Emile Durkheim and Celestin Bougle. Also in agreement were influential journalists like Andre Tardieu, Charles Loiseau, Jules Sauerwein and Paul Louis, leftist or center-leftist politicians like Albert Thomas, Franklin-Bouillon, and influential pressure groups like the League of Human Rights and the Freemasons. Masaryk and Benes reinforced their circle of Parisian friends through valuable diplomatic contacts made socially in the salon of the parents of Madame Louise Weiss. Through them, Benes met people who introduced him to influential diplomats of the Quai d'Orsay, Philippe Berthelot, Jules Laroche and Pierre de Margerie—the very men who, among other tasks, were drawing up the future peace settlements. While Benes lobbied in Paris, Masaryk worked to turn Anglo-Saxon policy in their favor. He was in frequent contact with English journalists, in particular with Henry Wickham-Steed, editor-in-chief of the *Times*, and with well known academics such as Professor Seton-Watson. With their support he launched the magazine, *New Europe*, on October 19, 1916, "meeting ground for all those who see the restructuring of Europe on the basis of nationalities, the rights of minorities, and geographic and economic realities, as the only guarantee against another repetition of the horrors of war." In addition, Masaryk was in contact with numerous influential groups of Czech, Slovak and Ruthenian emigrants in the United States.

Concerted pressure in influential places began to bear fruit. The concept of dismembering Austria-Hungary went from mere hypothesis to being one of the objectives of the Allies. When President Wilson asked the Allies to define their goals in his memorandum of December 20, 1916, Philippe Berthelot, Benes' friend, drew up the French reply dated January 10, 1917, and included a paragraph concerning the liberation of peoples under the rule of Austria-Hungary and the restoration of a Polish state. He left Poland's future status vague enough to avoid displeasing the Russians. The 1917 revolutions of February and October resulted in the Russian exit from the war, and the armistice signed by the Bolsheviks gave the Allies free rein in Poland. In the spring of 1917, France and Great Britain began to make contact with Poles living in western Europe and the United States, asking them to join the Allied armies. When the United States entered the war in April, 1917, as an associate power, further discussion of projected settlement terms was necessary. The American point of view was set out in President Wilson's Fourteen Points, announced in an address to the U.S. Senate on January 8, 1918. Points X, XI, and XIII recommended "autonomous development" for the peoples of Austria-Hungary, restoration of the Serbian state with access to the sea, establishment of new relations between the Balkan states, and the creation of an independent Polish state which would include indisputable Polish territories and access to the sea. The American conditions for peace were not quite in alignment with the views of France, Britain or Italy. However, Wilson's message caused no more anxiety among those who wanted the dismemberment of the Austro-Hungarian Empire than the offers for separate peace made by the Austro-Hungarian emperor from March to May, 1917, or the memorandum from Pope Benoit XV dated August 9, 1917; they knew they had the strong support of the European Allies, even if London seemed hesitant. This was clearly apparent at the Congress of Oppressed Nationalities held in Rome on April 8-10, 1918, sponsored by France and Italy. The Pact of Rome signed at this meeting reaffirmed the rights of nationalities to their political and economic independence and restated the incompatibility of these rights with continued existence of the Habsburg Monarchy. It was then, in April-May, 1918, that the Allies definitively decided in favor of the policy extolled by proponents of the Austro-Hungarian Empire's destruction and recognized the Czechoslovakian National Committee of Paris as the official government. On June 5, the Allies also recognized Polish independence in advance.

When the Peace Conference began, all the Great Powers had to do was recognize the nation states created in the last days of the war and keep the promises made in the individual treaties and to emigrant committees. While major decisions regarding the peace settlements were made by the Council of Four (colloquially known as "The Big Four"), France, Italy, Great Britain and the United States, the particular problems of each state and the exact details of the new borders were worked out in special committees. As soon as the treaties were finalized, the defeated nations were asked to sign. In this way, the Treaty of Versailles was signed with the Germans on June 28, 1919, the Treaty of Saint-Germain-en-Laye with Austria on September 10, 1919, the Treaty of Neuilly with Bulgaria on November 27 of the same year, and the Treaty of Trianon with Hungary on June 4, 1920.

THE TREATIES

Once again, it is important to stress that the peace terms made between the allied and associated powers and the defeated countries were imposed, not negotiated. Consequently, while the states forced to sign the treaties submitted to the terms, they never accepted them. This fact significantly influenced the development of relations between the ex-antagonists in the war.

The Fate of the Defeated Countries

—Germany's New Borders

In the west, Germany was required to hand over Alsace-Lorraine to France and several bordering areas to Belgium, while Denmark took territory north of Sleswig, the latter case following a plebiscite. But it was in the east that German losses were most acute. The **Treaty of Versailles** was supposed to settle the border between Germany and the new Polish state, taking into account both Polish access to the Baltic and the alleged will of the populations involved. Germany had to relinquish to Poland the province of Posnania which had a Polish majority dominating in the countryside, as well as a piece of western Prussia with the predominantly Polish city of Thorn; the area was to form a corridor 25 to 55 miles wide to give Poland access to the coast. But since the coastline at the end of the corridor had no port, the Peace Conference decided to make the city of Danzig (Gdansk) and its immediate surroundings a free city under control of the League of Nations. The Poles were to have free access to this port. In this way, the primarily German population of Danzig and the area around it was separated from the Reich without being annexed by Poland. It was obvious that the division of eastern Prussia and the rest of Germany by the corridor presented ample invitation for incidents and conflicts. The Poles also wanted southeastern Prussia with the city of Allenstein, but were thwarted when the plebescite required by the treaty polled a majority in favor of Germany. In compensation for retaining Allenstein, the Germans had to give up the Memel territory with its rural population of Lithuanians and urban Germans on the far eastern side of Prussia. Memel was governed first by an International Commission under the auspices of the League of Nations, but in 1923, the Lithuanians took over by force and the League of Nations acquiesced before the accomplished fact. The last disputed territory, Upper Silesia, was rich in ferrous and non-ferrous minerals, and was claimed by both Poland and Germany. The required plebiscite took place on March 20, 1921, in an extremely tense environment. Germany won with 70 percent of the vote, but Poland challenged the results under the pretext that nearly 200,000 of the voters who had taken part in the election, though born in Upper Silesia, were now living in other regions. On May 2, a former Polish deputy to the Reichstag, Korfanty, instigated a Polish uprising in Upper Silesia and the Germans retaliated by creating the armed militia, "Corps-Francs." Finally, the League of Nations stepped in and divided the territory, giving two-thirds of it back to Germany and the rest, including the city of Kattowitz, to Poland. In all, Germany lost nearly four million people, counting the population of the free zone, to Lithuania and Poland.

—Austria and Hungary

The Austrian republic had shrunk to a territory of 32,300 square miles with a population of 6,500,000 inhabitants. The new Austria had to relinquish the old Habsburg acquisitions Bohemia-Moravia, Bukovina, Galicia, Slovenia, etc. These regions were accordingly Slavic, Rumanian or Italian but also contained nearly four million Germans living in fairly dense settlements. Austria was forced to give Italy the southern part of Tyrol south of the Branner Pass. Even though German inhabitants were in a majority in this region, it had been promised to Italy by the Treaty of London for essentially strategic reasons and without regard to the wishes of the populations concerned. Carinthia was claimed by the Kingdom of the Serbs, Croats and Slovenes, and a plebiscite was set up for October 10, 1920. The

Klagenfurt area polled a majority for Austria, but the results were challenged by Yugoslavia. The **Treaty of St. Germain**, however, gave Austria a slice of western Hungary, its former partner in the Dual Monarchy. This territory under Austrian authority was the province of Burgenland, and had an 80 percent German majority with the remaining 20 percent divided about equally between Hungarians and Croats. At the Peace Conference, the Czech delegates had hoped to see this territory divided up between Czechoslovakia and Yugoslavia in order to make the two Slavic states contiguous, but the Allies resisted. The treaty finally awarded the territory to Austria, thus creating a bone of contention between the two former allies. The Hungarians were unwilling to cede the Sopron region with its Hungarian majority to their neighbors and sent groups of armed men to prevent the Austrians from moving in. Italy offered to mediate, and set up a plebiscite on December 14-15, 1921, at Sopron and the surrounding area. Two-thirds of the votes were cast for Hungary. Thus the Sopron region remained Hungarian, but the rest of Burgenland, including the city of Eisenstadt, became Austrian.

Hungary fared badly by the **Treaty of Trianon** which deprived it of two-thirds of its thousand-year-old territory. The country was reduced to 35,900 square miles from its previous size of a respectable 125,660 square miles, and contained a population of 7,600,000 inhabitants, over 90 percent of them Magyar. Through this action, Hungary became a nation state with a homogeneous population. There were only two minority groups of any consequence: 400,000 Germans and about 100,000 Slovaks. But over three million Hungarians outside the new borders found themselves absorbed into neighboring states.

And so, the two pillars of the former Austria-Hungary were hard hit by the treaties, giving the advantage to their neighboring "succession states" who now had authority over four million Germans and three million Hungarians. The problem of nationalities was merely replaced with the problem of national minorities.

—Bulgaria

In the **Treaty of Neuilly**, Bulgaria lost the meager territorial advantages it had gained in the Balkan wars. Bulgaria emerged from the peace settlements with a territory of 42,800 square miles and about 5,500,000 inhabitants, all of them Bulgarian. Bulgaria had to give Serbia the Macedonian districts which it still holds, but even more painful was losing the Aegean coast to Greece. Bulgaria thus lost its only access to the sea; the Bulgarian port of Dadeagatch became Greek under the name of Alexandropolis. In all of these lost territories, Bulgarians constituted the majority of the population, just as they had in Dobrudja previously. Here again, the terms imposed on the defeated country were far from founded on the principle of self-determination.

The Beneficiaries of the Treaties

—Poland Restored

While the treaties of Versailles and Saint-Germain quickly established the southern and western borders of Poland, it was not until March, 1921, that the Polish-Soviet border was settled. Poland, as restored in 1921, covered a territory of 149,922 square miles—smaller than the old Poland of the Jagiellons, since Lithuania was not included, but more extensive than the Poland of today. With 27 million inhabitants, the Polish state was the most populous country of central-eastern Europe. Its territory included Posnania, the "Polish corridor" and Upper Silesia taken from Germany, Galicia which had been under Austrian rule since the end of the 18th century, the former Congress Kingdom governed by Russia since 1815 along with a few more districts taken from the USSR in 1921. In this new state, the Poles accounted for about 65 percent of the total population. Inversely, according to Polish sources, nearly 200,000 Poles were still living inside the new borders of

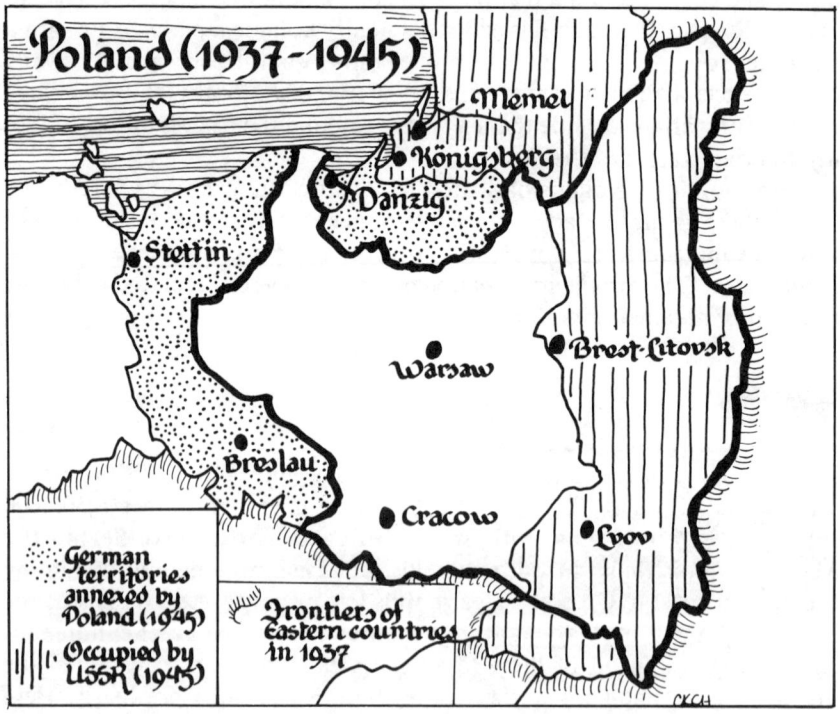

Germany, and over 100,000 of them were also in the Teschen region of Czechoslovakia. The Czechs had occupied the Teschen at the time when Poland was fighting off the Red Army which created a climate of mistrust, even hostility, between Prague and Warsaw throughout the interwar period.

The Population of Poland in 1930

Poles	20,000,000	65.5 %
Jews (mainly Polish)	2,300,000	7.5 %
Ruthenians/Ukranians	5,400,000	17.8 %
Germans	1,250,000	4.1 %
White Russians	1,000,000	3.4 %
Other (Lithuanians, Russians, etc.)	555,000	1.7 %

(from *Les Slavs* by R. Portal)

—Czechoslovakia

Unlike Poland, which had been a homogeneous state for seven centuries and whose restoration put an end to 130 years of unjust foreign domination, Czechoslovakia was an entirely artificial creation, made up of three distinct regions. In the west were the kingdom of Bohemia and the principality of Moravia ruled by the Habsburgs since 1526. Here the population was two-thirds Czech, and one-third German. Concentrated along the borders with Germany and Austria, the German populations tried to secede in 1919. At the Peace Conference, however, Benes called up the historic unity of Bohemia to justify incorporating this sizable German population into Czechoslovakia. The second region within the Czech state was Slovakia, which had been a part of the kingdom of Hungary since the 10th century when the Hungarians had conquered the Slav ancestors of the Slovaks. Benes laid claim to a territory that far exceeded the area inhabited by the Slovaks, not for historical reasons this time—the Slovaks had never been part of the kingdom of Bohemia—but for economic and strategic reasons. The new state needed access to the Danube and Marshal Foch regarded the Danube as an easily defendable border. With Foch's support, Benes' reasoning succeeded, and Czechoslovakia annexed the city of Pozsony despite its Germano-Hungarian population and the entire left bank of the Danube populated solely by Hungarians. The third region of Czechoslovakia was Carpathian Ruthenia which had been Hungarian since 895-896, and whose Ruthenian majority dated from the 13th century. The Treaty of Trianon had provided for the autonomy of this region, but nothing was done until 1938.

Czechoslovakia thus became a multinational state, covering 54,190 square miles and inhabited by a population of nearly 14 million, 40 percent of whom were neither Czech nor Slovak.

Czechoslovakia Between the World Wars

Area: 54,190 square miles (140,397 km^2)
Population: 13,613,000 as of February 15, 1921

Nationalities

Czechs	6,661,000	48.9%
Slovaks	2,100,000	15.4%
Germans	3,124,000	22.9%
Magyars	745,000	5.5%
Ruthenians	462,000	3.4%
Poles	76,000	0.6%
Other	445,000	3.3%

Religions as of 1930

Roman Catholics	10,800,000
Lutheran/Calvinist	800,000
Czechoslovakian Church	800,000
United Brotherhood	300,000
Jews	250,000
Atheists	1,750,000

—"Greater" Rumania

The treaties of Saint Germain and Trianon also benefited Rumania, whose territory grew from 50,000 square miles in 1913 to 113,450 square miles in 1920, and whose population expanded from seven to over 15.5 million. The following territories were annexed by the former Rumania: Bessarabia from the Russians, Bukovina from the former Habsburg Austrian Empire (Cisleithania), Transylvania and most of the Banat from Hungary. The new borderline between Hungary and Rumania became the object of lively debate in which economic and strategic motives carried far more weight than ethnic composition. A strip of land about 13 miles wide was assigned to Rumania despite its predominantly Hungarian population simply to give the Rumanian state control of a strategically important railroad. For the same kinds of reasons, the Hungarian cities of Szatmar-Nemeti, Nagyvarad and Arad became Rumanian along with their immediate surroundings. Drawing the border just 13 miles to the east would have avoided such a situation. The division of the Banat, claimed by both the Rumanians and the Serbs, opened up confused negotiating among the Allies. The total population of Rumanians and Serbs in the area was clearly less than the German and Hungarian majority. The former Regat (Rumania before World War I), populated exclusively by Rumanians and a small sprinkling of Bulgarians of Dobrudja, expanded into a "Greater" Rumania in which foreigners made up over a third of the population.

Rumania as of December, 1930

Area: 113,870 Square Miles (295,000 km^2)
Population: 18,057,000

Nationalities

Rumanians	12,981,000	71.9%
Magyars	1,425,000	7.8%
Germans	745,000	4.0%
Jews	728,000	3.9%
Ruthenians	582,000	3.2%
Russians	409,000	2.2%
Bulgarians	366,000	2.1%
Gypsies	262,000	1.4%
Turks	154,000	0.8%
TOTAL Rumanians		71.9%
TOTAL National Minorities		28.1%

Religion

Orthodox	73%
Catholic Uniate	7.6%
Roman Catholic	7.5%
Lutheran/Calvinist	6.9%
Jewish	4.0%
Muslim	1.0%

—The Kingdom of Serbs, Croats and Slovenes: Yugoslavia

The old kingdom of Serbia also gained from the peace settlements. First under the name of the Kingdom of Serbs, Croats and Slovenes, then as Yugoslavia in 1931, the state extended over a large territory of 95,400 square miles. The population of 12 million was composed largely of South Slavs, though national minorities accounted for 15 percent of the total population. Yugoslavia was made up of the old Serbian territory enlarged at the expense of Bulgaria, Montenegro and the former Hungarian Vojvodina (Bacska) and further expanded by the addition of the ex-Austrian Slovenia and Dalmatia, Hungary's Croatia-Slavonia, and the former Bosnia-Herzegovina.

Yugoslavia Between the World Wars

Area: 95,980 Square Miles (248,665 km^2)
Population: 11,245,000 as of January 21, 1921

Nationalities

Serbs	5,365,000	47.7 %
Croats	2,834,000	25.2 %
Slovenes	1,024,000	9.1 %
Germans	513,000	4.7 %
Magyars	472,000	4.0 %
Albanians	441,000	3.7 %
Bulgarians	274,000	2.7 %
Turks	236,000	2.3 %
Rumanians	72,000	2.3 %
Italians	14,000	0.6 %

Religion

Orthodox	48 %
Roman Catholic	37 %
Muslim	11 %
Other	4 %

In summing up the political and territorial restructuring of central and eastern Europe that followed in the wake of World War I, the following facts emerge:

First, the peoples never had the right of self-determination. Their fate was decided in Paris, London or Rome according to the economic and political interests of the Great Powers, though often with the complicity of certain national leaders. Some countries were able to benefit somewhat because their representatives were effective in lobbying the Great Powers and talked them into maximizing economic advantages or military agreements for their respective nations, even though these countries may have played only a very minor role on the Allied side in the war. The defeated countries were harshly treated, though paradoxically Germany fared better than the rest.

Second, it must be noted that the principle of self-determination used by the Allies to legitimize the war in the eyes of the various populations was applied in a highly arbitrary manner. The new political borders only rarely coincided with the ethnic ones, and linguistically homogeneous populations were frequently cut in half by an arbitrary line. Except for a few limited cases, the populations concerned were never consulted. In the few plebiscites that were organized, the treaties' beneficiaries came out behind, leading these states to oppose any new requests for plebiscites. The consequence of this policy was that after the signing of the treaties, the victim states worked to have the terms revised, with outside help if necessary, while the beneficiary states appeared ready to sacrifice almost anything to hold onto their advantages. In addition, the beneficiary states contained large numbers of national minorities determined to rid themselves eventually of their new masters, thus setting the stage for future problems in the new states.

Finally, nothing was done to facilitate a minimum of economic agreement and cooperation among the states that had long formed an economically coherent group.

Chapter 16

Political Struggle and Internal Conflict
1919—1939

The eastern European states born or restored in the wake of World War I evolved within considerably different political structures. Diverse national traditions and character played as much a part as the politics involved; the differences, however, should not eclipse the fact that a number of similarities did exist in most, although not all, of the emerging states.

POLITICAL CONSTRAINTS

The evolution of the eastern European countries was affected from the outset by the proximity of the Soviet Union. The October Revolution of 1917 unquestionably influenced their internal politics, and on two occasions shortly thereafter, bolshevism came uncomfortably close. The first lasted from March to August, 1919, when Hungary became a soviet republic, attempting in the process to pull Slovakia in the same direction. The second took place during the summer of 1920, when the Red Army advanced deep into Poland. These two events made a lasting impression upon the eastern European regimes, and all with the exception of Czechoslovakia responded by banning their Communist parties. The Party organizations immediately went underground, and Party leaders who were not arrested went into exile, usually in the USSR. Some of them, like the Bulgarian Dimitrov and the

Hungarian Rakosi, waited patiently there for events to turn in their favor. Others, such as Bela Kun, organizer of the short-lived Hungarian Soviet Republic, perished in the Stalinist purges. Again with the exception of Czechoslovakia, the regimes either barely tolerated or banned socialist parties remaining loyal to the Second International, and strictly controlled or fettered all union activity. It should be noted that in these countries the relatively low level of industrialization would not have encouraged a strong union movement in any case, which explains the continued exception of the more developed Czechoslovakia.

One constant in eastern Europe was the existence of authoritarianism; all of the east-central governments, whether monarchies or republics, practiced repression to some degree. Even in Czechoslovakia, considered an exemplary democracy, the president of the republic retained considerable authority, firmly establishing himself as the seat of the government. With the exception of Hungary and Czechoslovakia, the heads of state never hesitated to use force in applying their personal definition of power.

Due in part to the geographical boundaries set by the peace treaties, most of the eastern European countries contained populations of diverse nationalities. Accordingly, the leaders sought to encourage the theme of unity, and many thought that this was best accomplished through strict centralization. Centralization was the rule in Poland, Rumania and especially in Czechoslovakia and Yugoslavia, and abuses committed in its name fueled separatist tendencies which were often encouraged from without.

The combination of economic crisis and fascistic influence in the early 1930s fostered the growth of extremist movements inspired by the German and Italian models. These political groups attempted to destabilize the governments in power, relying on nationalist and anti-Semitic sentiments, and on financial support from Rome or Berlin. Groups such as the Iron Guard in Rumania and the Hungarian Arrow Cross were valuable auxiliaries in Hitler's expansionist plans.

DIVERSITY BETWEEN THE NATIONS OF EASTERN EUROPE

Czechoslovakia: A "Westernized" Imitation of Democracy

To many observers, Czechoslovakia seemed to be the only exception to authoritarianism in this part of Europe. It was the only country governed, at least outwardly, according to the standards of western democracies. Just after independence, the provisory constituent assembly drew up a constitution that was adopted on February 29, 1920. According to this constitution, legislative powers belonged to a national assembly composed of two houses, the chamber of deputies and the senate, both elected by suffrage that was universal, direct, secret, and mandatory. The members of parliament voted on the budget and legislation, as well as supervising the operation of the government and selecting the president of the republic. The president was head of the executive branch, and was elected for seven years by the members of the national assembly. He possessed extensive powers, notably the right to veto and the right to dissolve both houses of the national assembly. He was head of the armed forces, designated civil service officers, and appointed the president of the council. Professor Thomas Masaryk, the most important architect of the Czechoslovakian state, was elected to be its first president on May 27, 1920, and was reelected in 1927 and 1934. Masaryk retired for reasons of health in December, 1935. His closest associate, Eduard Benes, succeeded him in the presidency until October 5, 1938, when he resigned in protest over the agreements of Munich between Hitler, Chamberlain, Daladier, and Mussolini. The strong personalities of these two statesmen lent much more authority and prestige to the office of president than had been anticipated by the constitution.

Political life in Czechoslovakia was first and foremost characterized by a multiplicity of parties, both national and those formed to represent minorities. The vote was split among more than 20 parties. The government was made up of coalitions formed and reformed amid bitter debate between party leaders, creating sharp divisions among the national parties. On the right, the National Democrats represented the financial and industrial sectors, the Agrarians spoke for the countryside, ranging from large landowners to small farmers, and the Populists represented the large bloc of Catholic voters. In the center, Benes' National Socialists tended to identify closely with the viewpoint of the state government, and constantly served as a foundation upon which each governmental coalition was built. Finally, on the left the Social Democrats and the Communists enlisted support from the working class in Bohemia and Moravia. Apart from these national parties, the Slovak autonomists were represented by Father Hlinka and Monsignor Tiso, while the various German, Hungarian, and Ruthenian parties helped make or break a government depending on their abstention or opposition during crucial debates.

Following the strong showing of the left and far left in the elections of 1920, blamed partly on postwar economic difficulties, centralist coalitions ranging from the Social Democrats to the National Democrats were most continually in power. Heading these coalitions were the Socialist Tusar (1920-1922), and the Slovak Agrarian Hodza (1935-1938). For years, the Communists systematically adopted a stance of opposition to the Czech governments. Until 1935, they denounced Prague's policies towards the national minorities as oppressive, and incorporated into their party platform support for minority autodetermination. After 1935, however, the Communists' attitude changed radically, and in 1938 the Communist secretary-general Klement Gottwald became a staunch defender of a republic plagued by the secessionist attempts of national minorities. Just as the Communists began to take a more active role in the government, however, a fascist movement composed of middle class and rural members dissatisfied with the established parties was gathering momentum. Victims of the economic crisis, they formed a national assembly (FR), but until 1938, their movement had only limited appeal.

The problem that plagued the politics of the First Czechoslovakian Republic was the relationship between the two dominant nationalities; 2,600,000 Slovaks lived alongside 7,100,000 Czechs counted in the survey of December 1, 1930. The union of these two peoples, advocated during the war by most Czech politicians and holding the blessing of the American Slovak community, should have resulted in a federal state in which Czechs and Slovaks had the same rights and duties. These were the provisions of the agreement signed in Pittsburgh on May 30, 1918, by Masaryk and representatives of the North American Slovaks. According to the agreement, Slovakia was to have its own administration and legislative diet. But at the end of the war, in spite of a resolution put forward by the Slovak Assembly at Turoc Szt. Marton, the Czechoslovakian state was set up as a single and centralized structure. On January 1, 1919, soldiers of the new "Czechoslovakian" army and their Sokol auxiliaries occupied Bratislava (formerly Pozsony) and the Slovak countryside. Slovakia was treated as conquered territory, while its "liberators" behaved more like conquerors than brothers. They systematically assaulted not only everything associated with the old Hungarian regime, but also the religious beliefs of the Slovaks. Hundreds of traditional calvaries were broken and Church statues mutilated. The anticlericism of the new regime, which claimed Jan Hus as its patron, deeply offended the conscientiously Catholic Slovaks. They were further shocked by their Protestant compatriots' cooperation with the iconoclasts of Prague.

From the beginning Slovakia was administered by Czechs, to the profound disappointment of the Slovaks who had hoped to occupy the positions vacated by Hungarian civil servants. As Slovak perceptions of inequality persisted, the local clergy, which had staunchly defended the rights of its flock under the Hungarian regime, resumed its opposition. Father Hlinka, one of the leaders of the resistance against Hungarian centralism in 1907, went to Paris with the intention of defending the rights of his countrymen at the Peace Conference. He was able only to file a long memorandum, in which he set out the grievances of the Slovaks against the Czechoslovakian government. However, the influence of the Czech leaders carried such weight in Paris that Hlinka was deported after two weeks. The Paris episode demonstrated the organization and resources of the Czechs: Benes' agents were everywhere.

Memorandum Presented by the Slovak Autonomists to the Paris Peace Conference of September, 1919

"...Instead of obtaining autonomy, we have fallen under Czech hegemony. We have come to Paris in order to claim what we were solemnly promised.... Slovakia has become a Bohemian colony and is treated as such. We are being exploited by the Czechs... They mean to wrest our Slovak soul from us. In our schools, those who teach the Slovak language are Czechs who cannot speak it... Another matter that sets Slovaks against Czechs is religious intolerance. The heresy of Jan Hus, unknown until now in Slovakia, is avidly preached by the Czechs... The soldiers, the Sokols, and Czech government employees deride the piety of the Slovak people. Many statues of saints have been mutilated and many churches profaned... The Czechs want to use us, without consulting us, and against our will. There is no Czechoslovakian nation; there is a Czech nation and a Slovak nation. We are not Czechoslovaks; we are Slovaks, and wish to remain so... In order to demonstrate to the Peace Conference that all we have said is the pure truth, we venture to request a plebiscite in Slovakia, which will reveal the true sentiments of the Slovak nation. But this plebiscite can only take place under the protection of the Entente."

Dr. Frantisek Jehlica, Deputy
Monsignor Andrej Hlinka, Head of the Autonomist Party

(Quoted from F. d'Orcival, *Le Danube Etait Noir*)

Once back in Czechoslovakia, Father Hlinka organized the autonomist movement into a Slovak Populist party which enjoyed the support of the Slovak Catholic church. As the main element of its political platform was Slovak autonomy, the party was opposed by conservatives and members of the Protestant minority. Despite vigorous campaigning by the opposition in the elections of 1925, the Populist party polled 34 percent of the vote. In the years that followed, the Party managed to hold its own, and in 1938 they won in a landslide victory. In the 1938 elections, the Populists obtained more votes than all parties favoring union with the Czechs combined, and if the votes for Hlinka's party were combined with the other parties opposed to centralization—the German Slovak parties and the Slovakian Communists—the result would be a clear majority for an autonomous Slovakia. The Slovaks' desire for autonomy was not, as the government in Prague claimed, a matter of a few "obscurantist priests," but rather the wish of an entire people.

The Slovak question was of extreme importance to Czech authorities because if the Slovaks were given the autonomy and freedom to decide their own future, it would be the end of Czechoslovakia. President Masaryk was clearly aware of this: in an interview with the *Berliner Tagblat* on July 26, 1930, he unhesitatingly stated, "We cannot give the Slovaks autonomy because they will separate from us and join Hungary." Masaryk's statement reveals not only the mentality of Czech statesmen of the time, but also a curious interpretation of self-determination, as it implied that Slovaks preferred the old Hungarian "oppression" to Czech "liberation." For the leaders in Prague, there were only two possibilities: either accept the secession of Slovakia or keep the Slovaks in the state by force. From the beginning, the Prague government chose the latter policy and stubbornly held to it despite the risks and strains that it entailed. From that point on, the Slovaks were considered untrustworthy and were systematically denied important positions in government. An examination of job distribution in the government of 1938 shows that equality between Czechs and Slovaks was only a myth. Out of 140 high-ranking officers, only one was a Slovak, and among the 13,000 subordinate officers, only 420 Slovaks were to be found. In the ministry of foreign affairs, the numbers were 33 to 1,246, while within the central administration only 130 Slovaks were employed out of a total of over 8,000 civil service positions. The situation was identical in Slovakia itself, where in the railway offices, for example, 90 percent of the administrators were Czech and 70 percent of the subordinate employees were Slovak. Such ratios were far from coincidental, as the Czechs did everything in their power to maintain their position. A glaring example was the import of over 170,000 Czech "colonists" into Slovakia between 1921 and 1925, where they were the main beneficiaries of the agrarian reform. While it would appear that this state of affairs would have alarmed those who contributed to the creation of the Czechoslovakian state, the Prague governments proved so adept at manipulating influential journalists that the perception persisted that they had been the acolytes of Czechoslovakian "democracy." This was far from true; Slovakia was nothing more than a colony of the Czechoslovakian state, and one run entirely by and for the Czechs. Overwhelmed by rampant Czech nationalism, the Slovak nationalist movement seemed to become yet another disappointed and bitter element of destabilization in Danubian Europe. This was confirmed in 1938-39 by Slovakia's pro-German behavior during the German occupation of Czechoslovakia, support which Germany rewarded with the creation of an independent Slovakian state.

To conclude, we have demonstrated that the image of Czechoslovakia as a democracy was an illusion. While the constitution was democratic and the parliamentary government was based on the principle of universal suffrage, these liberal institutions benefited only one segment of the population. Even if a liberal law was adopted, it was applied only at the discretion of Czech administrators that were all too often overzealous supporters of Czech centralization. The Slovak minority was not the only minority to suffer discrimination. The German, Hungarian, Ruthenian, and Polish minorities were also not considered brothers of the Czechs, and were discriminated against both directly and indirectly. We will examine these minorities in greater detail later.

Poland: From Parliamentary Democracy to Military Dictatorship

The restoration of the Polish state, the Republic of Poland, took place under particularly delicate conditions. Until 1921, the new state possessed largely undefined borders, particularly on the Soviet Russian side. Moreover, the founders of the new Poland were faced with the serious problem of trying to combine within a single state provinces that for over a century had been separated from each other, and that had been living under regimes with radically different political and social structures.

After the constituent assembly elections, however, the new state had a provisory constitution which granted power to the president of the Republic, Joseph Pilsudski. His considerable power was increased by his parallel role as commander-in-chief of the armed forces; a duality made necessary by the war against Russia which lasted until the armistice of October 12, 1920. While Pilsudski was leading Polish troops to victory, the deputies in the constituent assembly were working on the final draft of a constitution. Their task was made difficult, however, by the civilian government's lack of popularity next to the prestigious hero of the Vistula. After long debates between a right wing favoring parliamentary rule to counter Pilsudski's personal power (led by the Populist Witos), and a left desiring presidential rule, the assembly adopted a definitive constitution on March 17, 1921. The constitution set up a bicameral parliament with a diet elected by voters over the age of 21, and a senate by citizens age 30 and over. For both houses, the voting was direct, secret, and representatively proportional. At the head of the executive branch, the constitution provided for a president to be elected by the members of both houses meeting as a national assembly, and granted him a term of seven years. The president had nearly the same powers as delegated to the president of the French constitution of 1875; like the French president, he was given the right to dissolve parliament with the agreement of three-quarters of the senators.

The new institutions were established by November, 1922. Marshal Pilsudski, widely considered to be the most popular candidate for president, found presidential power too limited and refused to run. Following a close election, the Socialist candidate, Narutowicz, assumed office on December 9, 1922. His election, however, created a storm of protest; the right and the

Nationalists condemned his Jewish background and his membership in the Freemasonry. Less than two weeks after coming to power, Narutowicz was assassinated by a Nationalist, and General Sikorski was named provisional head of government. Sikorski managed to restore peace, and proceeded with new presidential elections.

On December 20, 1922, Stanislas Wojciechowski was chosen by the national assembly as president with Pilsudski's support. His right-of-center government had to contend with a number of pressing issues, namely a falling currency, social unrest, and difficult relations with an army unhappily confined to its barracks while aware of its prestige. The temporary retirement of Marshal Pilsudski in May, 1923, seemed to solve the latter problem, but the Marshal had no intention of staying out of public affairs. Less than three years later, following the return of his old adversary Witos, Pilsudski was moved to action by a fear that the new chief of state might remove those generals and officers who supported him. On May 12, 1926, troops loyal to Pilsudski marched on Warsaw, to be resisted by loyalist troops under orders from General Rozwadowski. But on May 14, the sedition triumphed. While the right sanctioned resistance to the forceful takeover, the Socialists, who still believed Pilsudski to be one of their own, called a general strike in his support. President Wojciechowski and his government resigned *en masse* to put an end to the fratricidal conflict that had already caused the death of several hundred civilians. After an interim period, the national assembly agreed to name Pilsudski as president of the Republic. To the surprise of everyone, he refused, supporting instead the election of a Socialist friend, Professor Ignace Moscicki. The Marshal settled for the titles of Minister of War and of Inspector General of the Army.

In reality, with the support of the army, Pilsudski was the real power behind Moscicki's government, encouraging legislative reform that would benefit his later plans. The constitution of 1921 was modified to increase presidential powers; the president of the Republic was given the unrestricted right to dissolve parliament, and could adopt a budget by decree if the assemblies could not do so during parliamentary session. Elected to the presidency with the help of the Socialists, Pilsudski gradually began to engineer a break with them. With the support of a block within the government devoted to ultra-nationalist policies, his personal appeal, and sharing his hostility to the established parties, Pilsudski established a virtual dictatorship. The opposition, composed of Socialists now hostile to Pilsudski, Wito's Populists, and Korfanty's Christian Democrats, decided to join forces. During the congress held in Crakow on June 29, 1930, the opposition leaders demanded Pilsudski's removal and an end to the dictatorship in "defense of the law and the freedom of the people." Pilsudski reacted violently, dissolving both houses of parliament and arresting the principle leaders of the opposition. The Communists, few in number because Poles regarded them as having a close association with Russia, remained as semi-clandestine as they had been since 1926.

The elections of November 16, 1930, were far from free. Under strong pressure from the authorities, the Pilsudski government obtained an absolute majority despite the abstention of one quarter of all eligible voters. Once again, the constitution was amended to boost authoritarian powers, and even after Pilsudski's death on May 12, 1935, Poland remained an authoritarian state. The Marshal's dictatorship was replaced by a dictatorship of colonels. President Moscicki, re-elected for seven years in 1933, theoretically retained the powers of chief of state, but the government was actually controlled by the military. Colonel Beck, minister of foreign affairs from 1932 to 1939, and General Smigly-Rydz, Pilsudski's replacement as Inspector-General of the army, possessed the most authority.

In the face of such power, the opposition parties on the right and left alike were reduced to silence; their leaders were imprisoned or confined to their homes. Leaders of parties representing the numerous national minorities received equal treatment. Most of the Communist leaders fled to the USSR, but so many of them were eliminated in the Stalinist purges that in 1938 Moscow dissolved the Polish Communist party. The only tolerated form of opposition that remained was absention, although sporadic rioting occurred, particularly in rural areas. In June, 1936, the peasants of Myslenice revolted, and in August, 1937, agricultural workers went on strike in various parts of the country. This unrest, compounded by occasional striking in Lodz and Warsaw, was a strong indication that the country was not in agreement with the reign of colonels. While Pilsudski's prestige had facilitated acceptance of his dictatorship, his successors possessed no such popularity.

A Kingdom Without a King: Hungary Under Admiral Horthy

After the Hungarian Soviet Republic was removed by the joint forces of the Entente, the Rumanian army, and the Hungarian national forces, power was first exercised in Budapest by a coalition cabinet led by Huszar—a Populist with Christian-Democratic leanings—under the close supervision of Horthy's National Army in the summer of 1919. Huszar's cabinet called general elections in January, 1920, to be conducted under the principles of universal suffrage and secret ballot. The 1920 elections gave a clear majority to the Smallholder's party and the National Christian party, respectively considered the moderate and conservative parties. Both were staunchly opposed to socialist-communist ideas. These two parties were themselves split over the question of royalty; the Smallholders were hostile to the Habsburgs and desired an elected national monarchy, while the National Christians supported the restoration of the emperor, King Charles, who had resided in exile in nearby Switzerland since the spring of 1919. Because the allied countries, at the request of Czechoslovakia, had made it clear that they opposed any attempt to restore Habsburg rule in any of the Danubian countries, the national assembly selected Admiral Horthy as Regent of Hungary on March 1, 1920.

Soon after June 4, 1920, the Hungarian government was compelled to sign the Treaty of Trianon, an act which immediately restored the country's sovereignty. Within Hungary, the government took decisive steps to quell the aftereffects of the Bolshevik revolutions of 1918-1919. Leaders of the Hungarian Soviet Republic who did not find refuge outside of the country were tried and some executed, while lesser members were issued heavy prison sentences. Count Karolyi was also judged in absentia and his goods confiscated. Alongside the official and legal repression, unofficial nationalist groups sprang up, whose members conducted summary executions and acts of terrorism against anyone with connections to the Bolsheviks. Termed the "White Terror" and often exaggerated by the media, it lasted until the end of 1920. The terror often took an anti-Semitic twist, partly due to the large numbers of Jews who had played important roles in the Soviet Republic. Out of 45 commissars of the people, 32 had been Jewish, including Bela Kun himself.

The election of Admiral Horthy as regent was considered by many a temporary solution that would last until the international situation permitted a restoration of the monarchy. But Horthy and his entourage of young nationalist officers were reluctant to accept the king's return. They made this clear in April and again in October, 1921, when the Habsburg King Charles tried to return to Hungary. The regent's hostile attitude backed by Council President Count Istvan Bethlen and the threats of armed intervention by Czechoslovakia, Rumania and Yugoslavia, caused the attempted restoration to fail. At the express request of the Allies, the Hungarian Parliament passed the "dethronement" law on November 6, 1921, barring the Habsburg family from the throne and giving the country the right to elect the sovereign.

From then until October, 1944, Hungary was a constitutional monarchy in which the powers of head of state rested with the regent. The legislative power remained, as before 1918, with a parliament made up of two assemblies: the upper house was restored in 1926 and included representatives of the church, the nobility and the general population. The house of deputies was elected by universal suffrage. Elections were by secret ballot in the urban areas, but by public vote in the rural constituencies. This last restriction was eliminated for the 1939 elections. Unlike Poland under Pilsudski and the colonels, Horthy's Hungary was a conservative state with authoritarian tendencies, but one in which an opposition was permitted and tolerated. Although the Communist party was banned and went underground as a result of its role in the Soviet Republic, a Social-Democratic party existed with representatives in parliament who, like their colleagues, enjoyed parliamentary immunity and did not hesitate to criticize the government. Freedom of the press as well as freedom of assembly were guaranteed by the constitution, although parties on the left were selectively subjected to harassment.

Under the direction of Count Bethlen, prime minister from April, 1921, to August, 1931, the major political concern was the moral and economic reconstruction of a country devastated by war and by the amputation of two-thirds of its territory. Economic recovery began with the stabilization of the currency in 1926, but was upset by world crisis in 1930-1931. The depression was first felt on the political level by causing a split within the party of small land owners, the Smallholders party, which was part of the ruling government coalition. The left wing of this party formed a new group under Zoltan Tildy and Bela Kovacs, the Independent Smallholders party. The governing party then swung further right and assumed a more authoritarian stance, notably pronounced under Gyula Gombos who was prime minister from 1932-1936. As a result of the exterior crisis, the extremist parties gathered strength. On the left, the clandestine Communist party organized workers' demonstrations against unemployment. On the extreme right, discontented nationalists, judging the government policies as too soft, joined various radical movements. These came together in 1937 to form a single group known as the Arrow Cross party under the leadership of Ferenc Szalasi, an anti-Semitic admirer of national-socialist Germany. Anti-Semitism spread in the governing party as well. In April, 1938, the cabinet under Prime Minister Kalman Daranyi (1936-1938) instituted a law limiting the number of Jews in certain professions to 20 percent. That cabinet's successor, the Imredy cabinet, wanted to lower the percentage of Jews allowed in the liberal professions to six percent, but came up against the opposition of the High Chamber. Cardinal Seredi, the primate of Hungary, became the spokesman for adversaries of the project, which was then abandoned by the government itself. The elections of May, 1939, were the only truly free elections of the Horthy era besides those of 1920. The governing party again obtained 180 of the 260 seats. The Social Democrats and the Independent Smallholders won about 15 seats each, but the far right managed to elect some 40 deputies, 31 of whom were of the Arrow Cross party. As the honest and conservative Count Paul Teleki took over the helm of government in February, 1939, Hungary stood out as a rare example of constitutional and parliamentary rule in a part of Europe dominated by dictatorships.

THE BALKAN DICTATORSHIPS

Unlike Hungary, Czechoslovakia, or even Poland during the interwar period, the Balkan states were characterized by dictatorial regimes which, by their attitudes and repressive systems, resembled the Ottoman Turkish regime more closely than the western democracies. Each of these states was a unique case.

From Tribalism to Royal Dictatorship: Albania

Between independence in 1920 and annexation by Italy in April, 1939, Albania experienced an active political life and underwent rapid changes. This situation was partly due to the tardy awakening of nationalism among the local elite and to the constraints of traditional tribal structures, reinforced by powerful religious antagonisms between Muslims, Catholics and Orthodox followers. Another constraint was the illiteracy rate, which was at this time over 90 percent. In addition, Albania suffered foreign interventions by Italians, Greeks and Yugoslavs.

In the April, 1921, elections, the vote was split between the northern conservatives under the direction of Shevket Verlazi, who opposed any agrarian reform, and the Populist party representing the southern bourgeoisie and the intellectuals under the leadership of Bishop Fan Norli, a Harvard graduate and the Albanian American's delegate. But the most prominent personality was Ahmed Zogu, a 25-year-old chieftain from a fierce central Albanian tribe. In a country where vendettas and tribal warfare were the rule, the real power lay with whoever possessed the military means to impose his authority. Ahmed Zogu possessed those means, and had often distinguished himself in battle at the head of his warriors. With the support of his tribe, the Mati, he seized power and declared himself head of state on December 22, 1922. In the elections held the following year, Zogu's partisans emerged the victors. His adversaries, however, led by Fan Norli, persevered. In January, 1924, Zogu was wounded in an assassination attempt and a general uprising followed. Zogu fled to Yugoslavia to await the right moment

Population of Albania

Inhabitants:
1923	817,000
1937	1,038,000

Religion:
Muslims	764,000 (68%)
Orthodox Followers	229,000 (20.7%)
Roman Catholics	104,000 (10.4%)

to return. On June 16, 1924, Fan Norli took over the government and began the process of reforming Albania into a democratic state. Meanwhile, the exiled Zogu was actively preparing a comeback. Within six months, supported by his warriors and the remnants of Wrangel's army in refuge in Yugoslavia, Zogu reappeared in Albania and ejected Fan Norli's government from Tirana.

After assuming the office of president of the Albanian Republic on January 21, 1925, Ahmed Zogu became a virtual dictator. In order to establish his authority and augment the country's coffers, he turned to Mussolini's Italy and in December, 1926, and December, 1927, signed agreements which essentially made Albania an Italian protectorate. Though an Italian vassal, Zogu was assured of his power at home. A constituent assembly elected under more than suspect conditions in August, 1928, unanimously granted him the hereditary title of King of Albania. King Zogu behaved like an oriental potentate as he attempted to modernize his overwhelmingly backward country. Despite his inclinations towards independence, the country's financial difficulties forced him to guide his policies by the wishes and interests of Italy. Then, Mussolini, fearing Albania's eventual rapprochment with neighboring Yugoslavia and the western democracies, put a brutal end to Zogu's reign with an invasion at dawn on April 7, 1939. Three days later, the entire country was in the hands of the Italians, and Victor Emmanuel III was declared King of Albania on June 3 by an assembly of Zogu's former adversaries. Albania's flirtation with independence had been brief.

From the "Green" Dictatorship to the Royal Dictatorship: Bulgaria

As head of state after the elections of August, 1919, and March, 1920, which gave his supporters 40 percent of the vote, Alexander Stambolijski tried to establish a "Green," or Agrarian party, dictatorship within the framework of the monarchy. King Boris III had remained discretely in the background from the beginning of his reign, and let Stambolijski govern. The prime minister particularly tried to please the peasants who represented three-quarters of the population. With the agrarian reform of 1922, he limited private property to 30 hectares and abolished peasant debts. But at the same time he demanded total submission of the peasants and obligatory labor, designed to provide inexpensive manpower for the construction of major public projects.

Stambolijski appeared to be making peace with the Communists, with whom he had fought so bitterly when he first took office. At a conference at Genes in 1922, a political rapprochement was initiated between Bulgaria and the USSR. Meanwhile, within Bulgaria the police began jailing White Russian refugees who had been there since the end of the Russian Civil War.

Fear of an eventual bolshevization of Bulgaria brought the bourgeois parties together in a bloc against the Agrarians. Nationalists, grouped around the League of Officers and Professor Alexander Tsankov's National Entente, decided to take action against the Stambolijski regime. They denounced the agreement signed with Yugoslavia in April, 1923, which opposed IMRO and the Komitadji groups who were fighting for the liberation of Macedonia, as a betrayal of the Bulgarian homeland. The presence of 300,000 Macedonian refugees opposing any compromise with Belgrade furnished the Nationalists with additional power. Stambolijski countered the mounting opposition by creating the Orange Guards, made up of peasants devoted to his cause. Their intervention during the violence-frought elections in the spring of 1923 secured 216 of the 245 seats for the Agrarians.

The opponents responded to these rigged elections with a *coup d'etat*. During the night of June 8, 1923, the garrison at Sofia took over key points in the capital and arrested government ministers. King Boris III, who had not taken part in the plot, requested Alexander Tsankov to form a new government. Stambolijski, in his native village under the protection of militant peasants, was finally captured by the military after fierce resistance, and put to death on June 14 under exceptionally barbarous conditions. The Ottoman ways had not yet disappeared in Bulgaria. The Communists, who had supported Stambolijski on occasion, waited until after the *coup* to act. In August, 1923, the clandestine Central Committee under Georgi Dimitrov and Basil Kolarov advocated, despite opposition from some of the members, an armed uprising to be supported by the Agrarians. The government, however, was warned of the preparations and responded by arresting thousands of militant Communists and Agrarians. A general strike protesting these arrests as well as revolt in certain rural regions in the Balkan mountains September 20th to 30th were of only limited success. The cities did not join the movement. The repression that followed was harsh, and there were rumors that several thousand fell victim to the "White Terror." The Communist party was banned, but its leaders had already fled the country.

Tsankov's conservative and nationalist government organized elections in November of 1923, which gave 185 seats to the Democratic Entente of the bourgeois and nationalist parties. The opposition on the left garnered 62 seats from members of the early peasant and worker parties. Even though present in parliament, this opposition was nonetheless under constant police surveillance. The government's paranoia may have been well-founded, as on several occasions isolated elements tried to overthrow the government by force. The most spectacular terrorist act was the explosion set off in the cathedral at Sofia on April 16, 1925, shortly before the king's arrival. A hundred people were killed and over 300 wounded. Using this as an excuse, the government hardened its position, and fanatical private groups organized their own forms of violent vengeance. All that the terrorist attempts succeeded in accomplishing was alienating the majority of the population, who hoped for peace and tranquility after ten years of war and upheaval.

King Boris III, disturbed by the excesses of the White Terror, turned the government over to a Macedonian, Andre Liapchev in January, 1926. While moderates flocked to the new government, IMRO terrorism did not abate. Ivan Mihajlov and the most determined members of IMRO stepped up their terrorist activities both in Bulgaria and in Macedonian Yugoslavia, in conjunction with Croatian nationalists. The economic crisis of the late 1920s was fatal to Liapchev's government, and the Agrarian opposition and the moderates of the Democratic party carried the elections of June, 1931. The new leaders, Malinov and the Democrat Muchanov, established a more liberal regime.

The rise of Nazism in Germany in the early 1930s inspired nationalist fervor in Bulgaria as well. Tsankov's Popular Social Movement which favored Germany, and the Zveno group, "the Link," led by the republican officer, Colonel Velchev, became the spokesmen of militant nationalism. On May 19, 1934, the Zveno group seized power and relegated the king to a position as a mere figurehead, once again putting Bulgaria under a dictatorship. This new military power embarked upon a completely unexpected foreign policy; while representing themselves as ultra-nationalists on the one hand, they opened negotiations for entente with Yugoslavia and reestablished relations with the Soviet Union on the other. King Boris did not allow them to remain in power for long. He dismissed Colonel Velchev in January, 1935, and soon afterward had him tried for attempting to overthrow the government. From then on, the king governed as an authoritarian through compliant politicians, while foreign policy became more closely aligned with that of Germany, Bulgaria's most important trading partner in the economic crisis. The new leaders, however, attempted to counterbalance German influence by signing agreements with Yugoslavia and the other Balkan countries. In 1938, like the other Balkan states, Bulgaria was governed by a royal dictatorship.

From Corruption to Palace Revolts: Rumania

Rumania between the first and second World Wars was a nation characterized by violent political clashes between various factions and by quarrels within the royal family. The addition of new provinces as well as the adoption of universal suffrage in 1919 caused upheaval in the political life of the country. The Treaty of Versailles in May, 1919, gave Rumania the provinces of Bessarabia, Bukovina, and from Hungary, the Banat and Transylvania. New political parties sprang up in answer to the new voting population. The Conservative party disappeared, a victim of its former pro-German policies. Its place on the right was filled by two parties, the Liberal party of Ionel Bratianu, a staunch defender of the interests of the urban middle class, and by the People's League led by General Avarescu. Avarescu was supported by former soldiers who hoped for a more authoritarian regime.

Beginning in 1920, several fiercely anti-Semitic and ultra-nationalist factions broke away from the People's League to form the National Christian party led by Alexander Cuza, and the National Christian Defense League of Corneliu Codreanu. In the center of the political spectrum sat the Peasant Czarist party of Ion Mihalache and the former Transylvanian National Rumanian party, led by Jules Maniu. These two parties later united as the National Peasant party. On the left, the Socialist party enjoyed a burst in popularity brought on by the economic difficulties caused by the war and by a failing currency. The Socialists, however, also suffered from splintering: in May, 1921, a large number of its militant members joined the Third International and formed the Rumanian Communist party.

Until the death of King Ferdinand I in 1927, Rumania was subjected to a series of governments that distinguished themselves by a penchant for rigging elections in their favor and by the violence and pressure they exerted on their opposition. The elections of November, 1919, were the first and the only elections to take place under nearly fair conditions, even though the Hungarian, German, and Macedonian national minorities—making up over 20 percent of the population—could not participate. The elections resulted in a majority for Mihalache's Peasant party and Maniu's Transylvanian party. The Transylvanian Vajda-Voevod, a former deputy to the Hungarian Parliament, formed a mixed cabinet, but the king dismissed it after three months because of growing peasant and worker unrest.

Power passed to the energetic General Avarescu. Avarescu quickly dissolved the chamber of deputies, and organized new elections which, after careful preparation, gave his party 224 of the 369 seats. Despite bad memories he had left in the countryside after his repressive tactics during the peasant uprisings of 1907, Avarescu believed he could resolve the peasant problem through agrarian reform. The reform, which affected the large landowners in Transylvania more than the Boyars in the older provinces, did succeed in appeasing the peasantry. The dictatorial nature of Avarescu's government, however, caused increasing discontent. Avarescu was removed by the king in January, 1922, and was succeeded by Ionel Bratianu's Liberals.

The new government of Bratianu repeated the pattern set by its predecessor, setting up elections that resulted in an overwhelming majority for the Liberals, who took 260 seats with the remaining hundred distributed among all the other parties. The new parliament adopted another constitution in 1923, which allowed the king to retain sweeping executive powers. Parliament was divided into two chambers exercising legislative power; the senate was elected by a two-step ballot and included hereditary members, while the representatives of the chamber of deputies were elected to four-year terms by universal male suffrage. The same parliament passed a new electoral law which automatically gave half of the seats to the party obtaining 40 percent of the votes, with the rest distributed proportionally among the other parties, including the majority party. This assured the party with 40 percent of the vote of possessing at least three-fifths of the seats. The electoral law went into effect in time for the 1927 elections, and helped the Liberals to a resounding victory—despite the union of the two peasant parties into the National Peasant party, led by Jules Maniu. The elections themselves were nearly worthless. Never before had such pressure been exerted by the authorities; never had opposition candidates been so crudely abused by the police; never had electoral violence attained such a level. These methods shocked Maniu and the other Rumanian politicians of Transylvania, who were accustomed to the honest and efficient Hungarian administration of only a few years before.

Rumanian politics became even more complicated after the death of King Ferdinand on July 20, 1927. Ferdinand had come to power upon the death of his uncle Carol I, founder of the dynasty in 1914. He played a decisive role in Rumania's entry into the war on the side of the Allies, and had sent his wife, Queen Marie, to defend the interests of the country before Clemenceau, with the intention of assuring that Rumanian interests would prevail at the Peace Conference. Throughout his reign, Ferdinand was a major political force through his advisor, Prince Barbu Stirbey, who had close ties to the Liberal party. Stirbey was, in fact, the brother-in-law of Ionel Bratianu. The crown, by process of succession, should have gone to Prince Carol, the son of the deceased king. But the Prince's dissolute private life and his indiscrete relationship with a promiscuous Jewess, the famous Helene Lupescu, led King Ferdinand to pressure Carol into renouncing his rights to the throne in January, 1926. The rights of succession passed to Michael, Carol's young son by his legitimate wife, Queen Helene. Accordingly, at the age of six, Michael became king under a regency composed of his uncle Prince Nicholas, the Orthodox Patriarch Miron Cristea of Transylvania, and the president of the high court of appeals, Gheorge Buzdugan.

The National Peasant party chose to use the regency period to move against the Liberals. Circumstances seemed favorable as Ionel Bratianu had died on November 24, 1927. But Bratianu's death changed little since his brother succeeded him at the head of the government. Persecution of the opposition intensified. In January, 1928, for example, the Transylvanian deputy Vajda-Voevod was barred from parliament for 30 seatings for having dared to protest the methods of those in power and for comparing the new Rumanian regime with the former Hungarian regime in Transylvania. The National Peasant deputies boycotted parliament, and in March, 1928, organized large protest demonstrations in the streets of the capital, Bucharest. At the same time, the nationalist far-right increased its activities, most notably the brutal persecution of Jewish minorities. The streets became an arena for clashes between various political groups. The regents reluctantly agreed to withdraw from the Liberal cabinet, and on November 10, 1928, Maniu formed an entirely National-Peasant cabinet, with Transylvania prominently represented by Vajda-Voevod as minister of the interior, and Popovici in charge of the finance ministry. On December 15, 1928, Maniu's supporters emerged victorious from the elections with 78 percent of the votes and 348 seats, compared to the Liberals' ten. Maniu quickly conformed to prevailing political customs and proceeded to use the same tactics employed by his adversaries. Monetary problems brought on by the fall of the *lei* also confronted him, but by February, 1929, he had managed to stabilize the currency through foreign loans. A serious social crisis then began in the country, provoked by a renewed outbreak of Communist agitation: there were strikes in Bucharest, in Timisoara (formerly Temesvar), and in the coal-mining area of the Lupeni valley. In October, 1929, the old tradition of nepotism reappeared with the death of the regent Buzdugan; Maniu had him replaced with Constantine Sarateanu, brother-in-law of Vajda-Voevod and a relative of Popovici.

Maniu's systematic takeover of the positions of power was motivated by his plan to recall Prince Carol from his exile in Paris eventually, and to have himself declared the sole regent governing the country in the king's name. On June 5, 1930, Carol arrived by airplane in Transylvania and on June 8, parliament declared him King of Rumania as Carol II. His return just as the country was beginning to feel the effects of the world-wide depression was ill-timed. Maniu withdrew in October following a disagreement with the sovereign, and was followed by a succession of cabinets headed by the diplomat Titulescu, the historian Iorga, and the Transylvanian, Vajda-Voevod. Each proved as inept as the next in solving the country's problems: peasant unrest because of falling prices in agriculture and the price of land, and discontent among the workers because of growing unemployment. In 1931, several bank failures destroyed the savings of the bourgeoisie, and the middle classes began to join the ranks of the discontented. Moreover, parliament was dissolved three times—in 1931, 1932, and 1934—and electoral fraud continued, contributing to the growing gap between legal and popular representation.

The clearest manifestation of popular discontent was in the rise of extremist movements. Primarily nationalistic and anti-Semitic, these movements gained power at the expense of the established parties. In the early 1930s, Corneliu Codreanu dominated the nationalist far right. Head of the National Christian Defense League, Codreanu's resume included organizing a wave of anti-Semitic violence in Rumania in 1923. Accused of participating in a political assassination, Codreanu was arrested and tortured in May, 1924, along with several of his supporters. He retaliated by assassinating the police commissioner of Jassy, responsible for his torture, and was again arrested. After acquittal in a jury trial, Codreanu renamed his movement the Legion of the Archangel Gabriel, which after merging with several other nationalist movements became the Iron Guard. An outspokenly ultra-nationalist, violently anti-Semitic, and blatantly fascist movement, the Iron Guard possessed a paramilitary force called the Guardists, who wore a green-shirted uniform and adopted the fascist salute. Their acts of violence prompted Maniu to ban them; a policy followed by succeeding governments. This did not dim the ardor of the militants, however; they joined forces with Transylvanian German "cultural associations" and were further influenced by pan-German propaganda. Upon election in 1934, Premier Duca had many Guardists arrested, and many perished under torture in prisons. The Guardists retaliated by assassinating Duca on December 29, 1934, and King Carol II promptly appointed a Liberal named Georgi Tatarescu as premier. Tatarescu had the conspirators of the assassination arrested and tried along with Codreanu; the assassins were condemned to life in prison, but Codreanu was acquitted for lack of evidence.

By 1935, anti-Semitism and nationalism were rampant in the country. Jews were barred from some professions—for example, in 1937, lawyers, doctors, and pharmacists moved to exclude their Jewish colleagues. Under these pressures, the established parties split into factions, breaking from or joining with the increasingly popular Iron Guard. In 1935, a segment of the National Peasant party under Vajda-Voevod negotiated an alliance with Codreanu, while the remainder under Maniu sought an agreement with Tatarescu's Liberal government. By 1937, however, the alliances had shifted: Maniu and Codreanu joined forces for the elections of 1937 against the Liberals and Vajda-Voevod. These elections resulted in an unworkable assembly, and King Carol II personally took over the reins of government, producing a new constitution in February, 1938. It passed overwhelmingly in a referendum: 4,289,000 voters accepted it next to 5,483 dissenting.

By 1938, King Carol had become a virtual dictator. First he attacked the far right, arresting Codreanu and hundreds of Guardists in May, 1938. A few months later, during the night of November 29, Codreanu and 14 Guardist prisoners were killed during an alleged escape attempt. Carol had not singled out the far right for punishment alone, for simultaneously numerous militant

Socialists and Communists were jailed. King Carol used his newly acquired constitutional powers to abolish all political parties in favor of a one-party system, named the National Renaissance Front. From this point onwards, he was absolute master of the state. This did not put an end to nationalist agitation, however, which was marked by numerous political assassinations as it grew. Here again, Balkan custom persisted.

The Greater Serbian Dictatorship: Yugoslavia

The union of all the southern Slavic peoples into the Kingdom of the Serbs, Croats, and Slovenes on December 1, 1918, quickly turned into a Serbian annexation of the other minorities living in Yugoslavia. From the very beginning, the Serbs played a dominant and dominating role in the new state: the throne belonged to the Serbian Karageorgevitch dynasty, high government officials were almost without exception Serbian political figures, and the officer corps of the new army was filled with officers of the former Serbian army. Furthermore, each government from 1918 onwards pursued similar policies of centralization, Serbian nationalism, and authoritarianism. This was hardly surprising, as the new regime had immediately refused to instate the federalism promised the Croats and Slovenes in order to separate them from Austria-Hungary during the war. The first Serbian regime fought not only the federalist desires of the new provinces, but also for the Socialist Workers party promoting the Third International. This party became the Yugoslavian Communist party in June, 1920, with a splinter reformist party breaking away in late 1920.

The radical Serbian party of Pashitch, in power since King Peter's accession to the throne in 1903, continued to dominate the political scene. Even after Pashitch's death in 1926, the Radical party continued in strength with the support of two other Serbian parties, the Democratic and Agrarian parties. With the electoral laws in their favor, the three Serbian parties carried the elections held for the constituent assembly in 1920. Their opposition consisted of the Communist party, which obtained some 50 seats, and several political groups representing the new territories. Most notable of these were Mehmed Spaho's Organization of Yugoslavian Muslims, Father Korosec's Popular Slovene party, and Stephan Raditch's Croatian Peasant party, whose 58 deputies refused to take their seats in protest of broken promises for a federalist state. The Hungarian and German minorities were not permitted to take part in the elections, and later were deliberately excluded from the assemblies.

The pan-Serbian majority adopted the authoritarian and centralizing *Vidovdan Constitution* on June 28, 1921. The resulting regime was a dictatorship marked by corruption and electoral coercion, scarcely disguised by its parliamentary trappings. In August, 1921, the Communist party was the first to be abolished, as a result of a series of Communist-inspired strikes during the preceding year. In 1924, it was the Croatian Peasant party's turn, and Raditch was arrested for a brief time. Raditch had dared to demand self-determination for the Croatian people, and even had the audacity to stand up in the middle of parliament and state—to the great indignation of the Serbian deputies and the loud applause of the Croatian and Slovene deputies—that "the Croats were not slaves under the Habsburg monarchy" and that the Serbs "were never their liberators." These impassioned but unfortunate words earned him a term in prison for treason.

Parliament became the arena for more and more violent confrontations between the Serbian parties and the parties from other regions of the kingdom. The point of no return was reached on June 20, 1928, when during a full session of parliament a Montenegrin deputy, Punitsa Ratchich, aimed his revolver at the Croatian Peasant's party and pulled the trigger several times, instantly killing two deputies and gravely wounding Raditch, who died a few days later. Such violence did not prevent the Peasant party, led by Raditch's former secretary Vladko Matchek, from continuing the fight for Croatian autonomy. However, the crisis provoked by the events of June 20 resulted in the establishment of a royal dictatorship. King Alexander (1921-34) dissolved parliament on January 6, 1929, and abolished the Vidovdan Constitution of 1921. Individual freedoms and freedoms of the press—what was left of them—were suspended, while all local elected assemblies were replaced by commissions appointed by the Central Powers. Then in 1931, King Alexander promulgated a new constitution even more centralizing than the preceding one. The constitution abolished the historic provincial divisions, and changed the name of the country to Yugoslavia, now divided into nine *banovinas* (territories). The role of parliament was reduced to that of a rubber stamp as the ministers answered only to the king. The constitution also banned all regionally-based parties. Accordingly, the Croatian, Slovene, and Macedonian parties, as well as those parties representing national minorities, joined the Communist party (banned in 1921) in illegality. Most of the national political leaders were arrested along with thousands of underground militant Communists.

The royal dictatorship succeeded in radicalizing groups opposed to greater Serbian nationalism. Active Croat nationalists formed a secret society, the Ustasha, led from Rome by an exiled lawyer, Ante Pavelitch. Law-abiding Croats from the Peasant party attempted to take measures to save the situation. In late 1932, they asked the king to restore suspended freedoms as well as equality among the three ethnic groups of Yugoslavia. Their reasoning was sound: in the Yugoslavian army of 1932, there was only one Croatian out of 116 generals, and similar proportions existed throughout all branches of higher administration. The king's response was emphatically negative. Furthermore, he had the principal leaders of the Croat Peasant party arrested. From this point onwards, direct action seemed to be the only effective way of making Croatian voices heard. The pan-Serbian terrorism which had enjoyed the tolerance, if not the complicity, of the government from 1919 to 1929 was almost completely superceded by anti-Serbian terrorism by 1933. And it was, in fact, a Macedonian IMRO terrorist recruited by the Ustasha who assassinated King Alexander along with the French Minister of Foreign Affairs, Louis Barthou, in Marseille on October 9, 1934.

Paradoxical as it may seem, the attack in Marseille helped release some tension. King Peter II, son and successor to Alexander, was still very young, and so Prince Paul, the deceased king's cousin, took over as regent. The new prime minister, the Serbian Milan Stojadinovitch, released Matchek and other Croat Peasant leaders, and attempted to isolate the IMRO and Ustasha extremist movements through diplomatic agreements with Italy and Bulgaria. In order to partially satisfy the Croats and the Slovenes, at least in the area of religion, Stojadinovitch signed a concordat with the Holy See, formally placing Catholicism on an equal footing with Orthodoxy. This concession unleashed the furor of Orthodox Serbians, who demonstrated noisily in Belgrade and ransacked several Catholic churches; religious tolerance was still foreign to the Yugoslavian peoples of this era. Stojadinovitch's successor, Cvetkovitch, followed his example in attempting to settle the Croat problem. In August, 1939, Cvetkovitch concluded an agreement with Matchek's Peasant party, providing for an autonomous Croatian *banovina,* and bringing Matchek into the Yugoslavian government as vice-premier. These concessions, which came so late and so reluctantly, appeared to many Croats as motivated more by opportunism than by sincerity. The concessions did not succeed in checking the terrorist activity of the Ustasha, whose declared objective was total Croatian independence with the support of the Axis powers if necessary.

Like Czechoslovakia, Yugoslavia never managed to achieve either a spiritual or political unity of its various populations. Both countries were artificial creations born of the imaginings of politicians isolated from the common people. Both were soon to suffer the consequences.

Chapter 17

Interwar Economics: An Impossible Balance

The significant changes in territorial boundaries in central and southeastern Europe as prescribed by the treaties of 1919-1920 resulted in the breakdown of existing economic systems. The birth of new states eager to protect their independence resulted in tighter border controls, with economic controls not far behind. Unwieldy customs and currency restrictions, magnified by tariff wars, caused a variety of problems in the years immediately following the war for private citizens as well as for countries.

One of the most striking features in the economic situation of eastern Europe after the war was the unequal economic development of the various countries. In terms of industrial development, Czechoslovakia was roughly equal to the industrialized nations of western Europe, and resembled Germany in the relatively small role that agriculture played. The other east-central European countries, however, were heavily dependent on agriculture. In Hungary, 51 percent of the work force was employed in agriculture, while in Albania the figure reached 80 percent, with the other countries falling somewhere in between. Even among these predominantly agricultural states however, Hungary and Poland had sizable industrial sectors which distinguished them from their Bulgarian, Rumanian, Yugoslavian, and Albanian neighbors. Nearly everywhere at this time, large estates employing many farm workers and seasonal laborers coexisted with numerous small farms that did not always make a viable profit, although in

Bulgaria and former Serbia medium-sized and family-owned farms were more successful.

Energy and mineral resources were also unevenly distributed. Coal was abundant in Czechoslovakia and Rumania, as was lignite in Hungary. Hydro-electric potential was most evident in the Slovakian and Transylvanian Carpathians, while Rumania's potential energy base was petroleum. Ore was unequally distributed as well; Czechoslovakia and Poland possessed iron, but Hungary and Yugoslavia had bauxite. Gold and silver, the precious metals that had once made the fortunes of Bohemia and Hungary, were exhausted with the exception of a few remaining traces in Czechoslovakia and Transylvania.

After the war, all of the states of central and southeastern Europe desired economic self-sufficiency, for both ideological and financial considerations. Attempting to protect their weaker sectors with customs duties and other protectionist measures, they also attempted to minimize their external debt by confining themselves solely to their national resources. Such policies quickly led to reduced trade between countries as well as a reorientation of business and commerce to a form considered more suitable for the new national boundaries. The result was economic stagnation, which worsened as economic relations between the nations deteriorated. Czechoslovakia imposed high customs duties on agricultural imports from Hungary and Poland, and Hungary and Poland reciprocated, attempting to protect their barely-competitive industries from foreign competition.

The new borders had been settled upon without full consideration of the economic dislocations they would cause. This was most evident in the countries carved out of the former Austro-Hungarian Empire, as the new boundaries separated regions with complementary economies and resources. In several cases the borders separated regions producing ore and energy from the industrial regions that used them: the partition of Upper Silesia in 1921, for example, left the coal mines and metallurgy factories in German possession, while Poland obtained the copper and iron mines.

The Great Powers deftly turned such situations to their own advantage, investing heavily in eastern European countries. As few limitations on the use of foreign capital existed at this time, they were able to take control of mining resources. French and English capital was concentrated in Rumania, Czechoslovakia and Yugoslavia; Poland was dominated by German, Austrian, and English capital; and Hungary was controlled mainly by German and English capital.

The new borders also disturbed the traditional worker migration patterns. The Ruthenian and Slovak mountain peoples, who had always gone to neighboring Hungary as seasonal agricultural workers in the summer, abruptly lost their job opportunities. Consequently, social and economic conditions in eastern Slovakia and Carpathian Ruthenia worsened progressively, and the population emigrated in increasing numbers to western Europe since Bohemia was not able to provide enough work. This is only one of the many examples of the peace treaties' failure to provide for a measure of economic cooperation and coordination between countries.

The war's losers were not the only ones to suffer economic dislocations and troubles in the 1920s. It was more than a simple "reconversion crisis"; the prewar monetary system was completely disorganized, and the rapid depreciation of several linked currencies—the Austro-Hungarian crown, the German mark, and the Russian ruble—put a lasting damper on economic activity. In some countries, like Poland, there were as many as three different currencies in circulation in 1919-1920.

After 1920, however, the east-central nations began, more or less successfully, to put their monetary systems in order. One by one, currencies were stabilized with the help of foreign loans, often obtained through the efforts of the League of Nations. However, as the nations still followed the precepts of the gold standard, their currencies were valued at a figure far below their prewar level. The new states' problems were not all monetary: nations were faced with massive unemployment and popular discontent, as hundreds of thousands of demobilized soldiers sought to return to the work force. The problem was most severe in the defeated countries, whose military forces were strictly limited by treaty, and who also had to absorb thousands of government employees and private citizens expelled from areas annexed by the victorious countries. Despite quota laws imposed by the United States in 1921 and 1924, emigration eased the unemployment problem somewhat. The mainstream of labor refugees went to France, which was plagued by a shortage of laborers needed for reconstruction. Thousands of Poles, Slovaks, Ruthenians, Hungarians and Yugoslavs settled in France well into the 1920s.

All postwar eastern European governments attempted to address the serious issue of dismantling large land holdings. Systematic land reforms were adopted in Czechoslovakia in the winter of 1918-1919, and in Rumania as well as the new Yugoslavian territories in 1921. In all three countries, the reforms were specifically aimed at eliminating the German and Hungarian estate holders. In Czechoslovakia, the law limited the size of property to 250 hectares, while one million hectares confiscated from the large property owners were to be redistributed to small farmers and farm workers. But only the German property owners in Bohemia and the Hungarian owners in Slovakia and Ruthenia were affected by the land reform, as large estate owners of Czech origin were able to reclaim their lands after a period that generally did not exceed two years. The Rumanian land reform act of 1921 had the same nationalist slant. The law limited the maximum estate size to 500 hectares, and this limit was further reduced to 270 in the newly annexed territories in order to affect the Hungarian estate owners in Transylvania more than the Boyars in Moldavia and Wallachia. Elsewhere, land reform policies pursued similar measures, but more slowly and in piecemeal fashion. Poland in 1920 and 1925 and Hungary in 1920 and 1923 were examples of such incomplete reforms as in both of these countries the landed aristocracy retained nearly a third of all cultivated land in 1930.

During the 1920s and 1930s, each country pursued an independent course of industrial development, but their customs barriers so slowed trade between neighboring countries that acquiring markets outside of eastern Europe was necessary. However, despite salaries low by western European standards, the prices of products manufactured in Hungary, Poland and even Czechoslovakia were not competitive because of outdated and inefficient production techniques. With the exception of a few specialized products, like Bata shoes or the machine tools and heavy machinery produced by Skoda in Czechoslovakia or Hungarian Tungsram lights, eastern European exports consisted of raw materials. The Danubian and Balkan countries exported grain, meat, and tobacco, while Bulgaria, Hungary, Poland and Yugoslavia produced minerals. Rumania's primary export was oil.

Economic cooperation between the eastern European countries would certainly have hastened postwar reconstruction. But the exaggerated nationalism of the treaties' beneficiaries and the bitterness of the defeated countries prevented attempts to unite for trade and customs purposes, even though limited trade between them had been established as early as 1920-1921. National chauvinism dominated this era in eastern Europe; although the countries of the Little Entente were closely united by political and military links, they refused to extend this cooperation to the economic arena.

The worldwide depression of the early 1930s severely damaged the tentative and fragile economic recovery that had begun in east-central Europe. The economic crisis affected all the countries in the region without exception. Markets were saturated with agricultural products and prices collapsed, buying power evaporated through inflation and the standard of living tumbled. In Hungary, the price of a quintal of wheat fell from 33 to nine *pengo* between 1928 and 1932, while in Rumania it fell from 500 to 180 *lei*. Raw materials followed a similar course, and the export of agricultural products and raw materials became increasingly unprofitable and hazardous. The large established exporters in the United States and Canada were better organized to sell their agricultural surpluses, and increased their market shares at the expense of the east-central nations. Because of this and a low demand for raw materials due to the industrial slowdown, protectionist measures proliferated everywhere, excluding eastern European producers from nearly every export market. Protectionism resulted in an unequal balance of trade and balance of payments, and the failure of the Viennese Kreditanstalt bank in May, 1931, followed by several German banks closely linked to eastern European banks, dealt yet another blow to the weakened currencies.

Unemployment had remained latent in these countries since the early 1920s due to the tempering effect of emigration. As traditionally open countries closed their doors one after another to both immigrants and guest workers, unemployment shot up, cutting a wide swath through the work force; all fields, ranging from farm and industrial workers to office employees, felt the impact. In Poland in early 1933, 780,000 of the 1,800,000 workers usually employed in industry were permanently laid off, and industrial production was 50 percent of the 1929 level. In Hungary, a third of the industrial work force was either partially or completely unemployed, and most young graduates of higher education found themselves in similar circumstances. Even Czechoslovakia, previously considered a viable industrial force, suffered; in 1932-33, unemployment reached nearly one million, while exports fell by nearly two-thirds.

Protectionism and isolationism did not arise unchallenged. Despite popular pressures for such measures, some political leaders sought to establish a minimum of cooperation between countries that had formerly been part of the Austro-Hungarian Empire. Under the aegis of the League of Nations, the French government presented two plans, the most famous of which was the **Tardieu Plan**. The Tardieu Plan called for the progressive lifting of customs barriers between the Danubian countries, and the creation of an economic bloc made up of Austria, Czechoslovakia, and Hungary, to be followed later by Yugoslavia and Rumania. The idea was not new; the Hungarian economist Elemer Hantos had written profusely and delivered numerous addresses in favor of a Danubian common market.

All the attempts to form a customs union ended in failure for a multiplicity of reasons. First, political tension between the victorious and the defeated nations hindered negotiations, while the thorny question of national minorities posed a major obstacle to any rapprochement between old enemies. For Hungary, improving the conditions for Hungarian minorities in the countries of the Little Entente was a stipulation for any opening of negotiations. The countries of the Little Entente, however, had no intention of altering their policies affecting minorities until after an economic agreement had been reached. In addition, Italy and Germany did not see the Tardieu Plan as working in favor of their ambitions and interests, and did all in their power to subvert the Plan. For Germany in particular, eastern Europe was a vital zone for the supply of foodstuffs and raw materials, as well as serving as a market for German manufactured products defined by barter agreements. From 1933 on, the German government sought and concluded trade agreements with most of the Danubian and Balkan countries with such efficiency that by 1937 Germany had become the primary trading partner of every country in east-central Europe. Germany had realized that economic ties were the most effective mechanism to bring them into its sphere of influence instead of France or Great Britain.

To conclude, it was the inability of ultra-nationalists in eastern Europe to find a *modus vivendi* between themselves and other interest groups that opened eastern Europe to Germany's national socialist hegemony. Once again, the void left by the disappearance of the Austro-Hungarian Empire was all too apparent: it was a void that Hitler would not hesitate to fill.

Chapter 18

International Relations between the Wars

In the wake of the First World War, it was evident that the Great Powers—responsible for the territorial restructuring of eastern Europe—had no intention of remaining out of eastern European affairs.

Immediately after the war, the three victorious European powers of France, Great Britain, and Italy made political and economic inroads into the eastern European arena, each taking advantage of Soviet isolation and the temporary eclipse of Germany. For western Europe, the eastern countries provided an excellent buffer zone between Germany and the Soviet Union. As the war ended, the West feared an eventual rapprochement between Moscow and the defeated countries, Germany in particular. The communist Spartacist agitation in Germany during the winter of 1918-1919 and the attempted bolshevizing of Hungary under the Bela Kun government of 1919 only increased their fears, and they took little comfort in the Russian overtures to the Weimar Republic which led to the signing of the **Treaty of Rapallo** on April 16, 1922. To counter the possible alliance between Germany and the Soviet Union, the Allies adopted the *cordon sanitaire* policy, intended to separate the two countries with a block of countries aligned and integrated into the Western defense system. France was the most enthusiastic supporter of this program and strove to win the support of the other Allies, while the English were most reluctant to accept it.

The second attraction eastern Europe held for the Western powers was purely economic. With their economies in ruins from the war, and with a wealth of mineral and agricultural resources, the eastern countries presented definite economic opportunities. As technological innovation and economic growth lagged behind the western nations, it was evident that most of these countries could serve as exceptionally important markets for English, French, and Italian investment and manufactured goods. Great Britain made the most use of this sort of economic cooperation, as did France and Italy though to a lesser extent. The French were enjoying a period of prestige in Europe due to their recent military victories, and the eastern European countries they had backed in the peace negotiations constituted a major zone of interest.

The British initially proceeded with caution. To London, the idea of a *cordon sanitaire* seemed vague at best, and in the name of realism the English were the first to open trade relations with the new Soviet state. A considerable amount of British capital was invested in Czechoslovakia, Hungary, and Rumania. By 1920, British businessmen in Prague, Budapest, and Bucharest were already laying the groundwork for commercial and financial agreements. The agreements were quickly accepted and signed, and chambers of commerce founded for Anglo-Czech, Anglo-Hungarian and Anglo-Rumanian interests.

France played only a secondary role in economics and finance, due partly to its limited funds. However, France played a major role in political and military affairs. Those in charge at the Quai d' Orsay, Philippe Berthelot in particular, gave full support to the young states who owed their independence or their expanded territories to the French. With these states, a politico-military alliance system was quickly ratified. The treaties signed aimed to establish a security system for France on Germany's eastern borders from 1920 to 1925 dependent on military alliances between France and each of the friendly eastern European states, and were intended to be protection against both Germany and the Soviet Union. The system was first put to the test in the short war of 1919-1920 between the Soviet Union and Poland, which led to French support of Poland. Paris viewed a sufficiently large and powerful Poland as a doubly stabilizing factor in northeastern Europe, countering both the Germans and the Soviets. Franco-Polish military cooperation was a keystone of French foreign policy until the final crisis of August-September, 1939. This did not, however, prevent Colonel Beck, the Polish foreign minister from 1932 to 1939, from complementing what he considered a dubious treaty with France with the signing of non-aggression pacts with the Soviet Union and with fascist Germany.

French policy toward the Danubian countries was hesitant after the war, as leaders were undecided between supporting all of the young states' demands unconditionally, or pushing for a Danubian federation led by Hungary. A Danubian federation would require changing several inappropriate clauses of the Treaty of Trianon, and Alexandre Millerand's letter as president of the Peace Conference to the Hungarian delegation left the door open for a possible revision of the treaty's harsh terms. During the year of 1920, the anti-Soviet former ambassador to Russia, Maurice Paleologue, now the new secretary general of the Quai d'Orsay, seemed to favor a policy of rapprochement with Hungary. The Teleki government in Budapest received this news with pleasure. The new secretary general had little sympathy for Czechoslovakia, which he felt was initiating a policy of flirtation with the USSR, and which had consistantly refused French convoys the right to cross Czech territory to aid Poland when it was about to fall to the Red Army. Czechoslovakia was also the first eastern European country to establish diplomatic relations with Soviet Russia. Paleologue therefore favored a pro-Hungarian orientation, and a Franco-Hungarian treaty was negotiated and signed between May and June, 1920. The treaty stated that in exchange for certain economic advantages extended to French financial and industrial groups, France would press for the revision of certain provisions in the Treaty of Trianon. The policy's confirmation came in the summer of 1920, when Hungary volunteered to join France in aiding Poland.

In September of 1920, Paleologue was replaced as secretary general by Philippe Berthelot, a personal friend of Masaryk and Benes. From then on, the pro-Hungarian policy was abandoned, and Paris returned to abiding strictly by the terms of the treaties of 1919-1920 and of cooperating with the successor states to Austria-Hungary. This did not prevent Aristide Briand, prime minister in 1921, from entertaining the idea of restoring the Habsburgs in Hungary, and perhaps in Austria as well. With his control of foreign policy, Berthelot forestalled this policy, and it was definitively abandoned in November, 1921, for a closer alliance between France and its Danubian "clients" of Rumania, Czechoslovakia, and Yugoslavia. These three nations formed the **Little Entente**, agreeing in 1921 to hinder attempts to restore the Habsburgs in Hungary, and to oppose Hungarian revisionism. France gave its full support to the Little Entente and soon signed military treaties with each of the member countries. French generals took over in Prague, Bucharest, and Belgrade in order to reorganize the armed forces of the Entente nations. The Little Entente remained the pillar of French policy in the Danubian countries until 1938.

Italy was also active in eastern Europe, and disapproved of the attempted Franco-Hungarian rapprochement of 1920 as well as of the treaties between France and the Little Entente. The Italian government was involved in a major dispute with Yugoslavia over Fiume (Rijeka), and as a result turned its attention to Yugoslavia's rival neighbor, Albania. Having failed to annex this state during the peace conference of November, 1921, Italy managed to gain recognition from the powers as a protector of Albania in case of Greek or Yugoslavian aggression. Italo-Albanian relations grew even closer with Mussolini's rise to power, particularly when Ahmed Zogu became king. Mussolini was the first to recognize Zogu after his successful takeover. In exchange, Italy gained certain privileges in Albania. The Banca Nazionale d'Albania established in Rome, in September, 1925, was created with the heavy financial support of the Italian Society for the Economic Development of Albania, and was given the task of issuing Albanian currency. Such financial inroads paved the way for an Italian takeover of Albania. The Tirana Pact signed on November 26, 1926, was the first step, and the following year a new treaty not only strengthened the "links of friendship and security" between the two countries, but also gave Italy control of the Albanian armed forces. Economic problems tied to the depression of 1929 tightened Mussolini's grip on Albania. Ahmed Zogu, ruling as King Zog I, wanted to be free of the Italians, but Mussolini ordered an invasion on April 7, 1939. Albania was then annexed as part of the Italian Empire.

Albania was not the only object of Italian ambitions. While France depended on the eastern European countries who had benefited from the treaties, Italy courted the treaties' victims: Hungary and Bulgaria, both of which had suffered heavy losses under the treaties' terms, and who had been quarantined by their neighbors. By 1921, Italian support won Hungary the right to hold a plebiscite at Sopron, which turned in Hungary's favor. Budapest was very responsive to Italy; as Hungarian leaders had made revision of the treaties a cornerstone of their foreign policy, they played along readily with Mussolini. In 1925, the two countries signed a trade agreement as a prelude to political entente. Count Bethlen, head of the Hungarian government, signed a friendship pact with Italy in Rome on April 5, 1927. While the Hungarians sincerely believed that Italy would support their demands for revision of the Treaty of Trianon, Mussolini was only trying to counterbalance French influence with the Little Entente. Italy did aid a secret, though very limited, rearmament of Hungary, but Mussolini had no intention of upsetting the balance of power in this region.

Mussolini pursued a related policy with Bulgaria, which was also involved in territorial disputes with the Little Entente. Bulgaria had bickered with Rumania over the Dobrudja, with Yugoslavia over Macedonia, and with Greece over Thrace. Yugoslavia and Greece were also on bad terms with Italy, a fact which should have facilitated Italo-Bulgarian rapprochement; but the only concrete result of Italian overtures was the marriage of the king of Italy's daughter with King Boris III of Bulgaria. Sofia was hesitant of becoming involved with Italy, and sought instead to improve relations with its neighbors. Treaties drawn up in 1927 with Yugoslavia and in 1938 with the countries of the Balkan Pact allowed Bulgaria to regain equal rights in military matters.

The worldwide depression of 1929 combined with Hitler's rise to power on January 30, 1933, profoundly altered the balance of power in eastern Europe. The German economy was involved in most of the east-central nations. For Hitler, this part of Europe was both a market for German manufactured goods and a source of raw materials and foodstuffs. By 1933, a number of treaties had been drawn up between the German government and the various eastern European states. Despite their close political ties to France, the countries of the Little Entente responded to Hitler's advances. Benes himself was among the first to send his congratulations when Hitler was named Chancellor of the Reich. Hitler's primary objective in this part of Europe was to establish German hegemony by means of the *Anschluss*, joining Austria to the Third Reich. Mussolini feared this, sensing that a powerful Germany at Italy's northern border was far more dangerous than a small, practically unarmed Austria, particularly since Italy had annexed the German-speaking southern Tyrol in 1919. Mussolini wanted to consolidate Austria and Hungary in order to prevent the *Anschluss*. The *Roman Protocols* were signed on March 17, 1934, with the intention of maintaining Austrian independence against Germany's expansionist inclinations. Shortly thereafter, on July 25, 1934, Chancellor Dollfuss of Austria was assassinated, and Austrian Nazis pressed for the *Anschluss*. The French minister of foreign affairs, Louis Barthou, reinforced the anti-German treaties with the countries of the Little Entente and Poland, and even attempted to incorporate the USSR and Italy. Italy hoped that Hungary would join as well, but Barthou ignored this possibility in order to please the Little Entente, thereby facilitating a Berlin-Budapest rapprochement.

The October, 1934, assassination in Marseille of Barthou and King Alexander of Yugoslavia—who had come to France to reconfirm his opposition to Hitler—had serious consequences. Hungary was immediately accused of organizing the assassination, although it was quite clear that it was an internal Yugoslavian affair. As a result, Hungary moved a little closer to Germany politically. Paradoxically, the new leaders of Yugoslavia under the pro-German regent Prince Paul began to seek entente with Germany. Rumania simultaneously began a similar policy, albeit for economic reasons. Czechoslovakia remained the only country in the Little Entente determined to stand in the way of German imperialism in the Danubian region, although it lay geographically in the direct path of the German threat. Italy opposed the *Anschluss* in 1934, but by 1936 began to change its attitude since Hitler had given Italy full diplomatic support during the conquest of Ethiopia, and the two states then cooperated in the Spanish civil war. Little by little, the Rome-Berlin axis was created, the existence of which allowed Hitler to carry out the *Anschluss* in March of 1938.

Czechoslovakia was in a delicate position. While Hitler was preparing to make his claims on behalf of the German minority in Bohemia, Czechoslovakia was almost unanimously deserted by its allies of only a few years before. Hitler believed he could count on Hungarian support in this matter because of the existence of a Hungarian minority in Czechoslovakia. But Budapest, despite strained relations with the countries of the Little Entente, preferred to pursue the issue through negotiation with diplomatic support from Italy and hopefully, Great Britain, than through military action.

By 1938, Germany and Italy had become the major powers in eastern Europe. France—the nation that had dominated the area since 1920 through the Little Entente—was gradually ousted. France was displaced partly as a result of the depression, but more importantly because of diplomatic failures beginning in 1935. France's inability to prevent the return of compulsory military service in Germany and the rearmament of the Rhineland in 1936 hurt its credibility in the eyes of the countries of the Little Entente and of Poland. At the same time the countries of the Little Entente were distancing themselves from France, the Entente itself was degenerating into nothing more than a formal alliance between states united only by their hostility for Hungary. Their disunity showed in their contrasting responses to the confrontation by Hitler according to the dictates of differing national interests. The revisionist states of Hungary and Bulgaria believed that the rise of the Axis would favor their own territorial ambitions, while in fact they were only being used as tools for German and Italian interests.

By 1939, hope for peace and prosperity in eastern Europe had turned sour. Frustrated nationalism fed by injustice and bitterness reigned; the hour of reckoning was soon to come.

Chapter 19

National Minorities: A Source of International Tension

Since the political borders drawn up by the victorious powers seldom coincided with ethnic boundaries, millions of men and women were separated from their kinsmen and unwillingly placed in the borders of countries favored by the treaties. These populations became known as the "national minorities," defined as an oppressed group of individuals having ethnic or religious characteristics different from those of the majority of the population of the state which they inhabit. Eastern Europe between World Wars I and II was in many ways a Europe of minorities.

As the terms of the treaties were being worked out, France, Great Britain, Italy, and the United States were divided between the necessity of satisfying their allies in eastern Europe and the desire to adhere to the Wilsonian principle of the right to self-determination, one of their original grounds for going to war. They were also aware of the threat to peace posed by the numerous uprooted populations within the new states. While conforming to the usual requirements of peace treaties, the Great Powers demanded the beneficiaries sign agreements promising to protect the rights of these "foreign" peoples. Obtaining signatures to these treaties for the protection of minority groups was not always an easy matter. While Czechoslovakia and Yugoslavia agreed to sign without much protest and were subsequently just as ready to violate the agreement, Rumania and Poland refused to sign until pressured. These agreements were guaranteed by the League of Nations as equally as the peace treaties themselves, and the signatories were required to write the terms into their constitutions. With such guarantees, the powers were confident that the provisions would be respected.

The main provisions of the **Treaty on the Protection of Minorities** signed by Rumania and the principle Allied powers on September 9, 1919, pledged Rumania to "extend to all inhabitants full protection of life and liberty without regard to birth, nationality, language, race, or religion" (Article II). Rumania recognized "as Rumanian nationals, with full rights and without further ceremony, all persons residing, on the date the treaty becomes effective, within Rumanian territory, including annexed territories and territories that may be ultimately annexed, unless on said date the persons claim nationality other than Austrian or Hungarian" (Article III). Rumanian nationality was equally granted to "persons of Austrian or Hungarian nationality born in territories given to Rumania if their parents are residing there, even if on the date the treaty becomes effective, they are not themselves residing there" (Article IV). Rumania in turn promised not to enact "any restriction upon the free usage of any language...." "In spite of the Rumanian government's adoption of an official language, reasonable facilities will be made available to nationals of languages other than Rumanian to use their languages, oral and written, in the courts" (Article VIII). Minorities received the right to "create, direct, and control, at their own expense, charitable, religious or social institutions, schools and other educational establishments with the right to use their own language and to observe their religion freely" (Article IX). The treaty also stipulated that "the Rumanian government will grant cities and districts with proportionally large numbers of nationals with languages other than Rumanian the appropriate facilities to assure that in elementary school, children will receive instruction in their maternal language. This stipulation will not prevent the Rumanian government from making Rumanian language instruction mandatory in the aforesaid school" (Article X). And finally, Rumania pledged to grant the Transylvanian Saxons and Szekelys local autonomy in religious and educational matters (Article XI).

Poland, Czechoslovakia, and Yugoslavia signed treaties for the protection of minorities containing similar resolutions. In principle, the League of Nations' guarantee meant that the treaties would be strictly observed. In order to assure effectiveness, the Council of the League of Nations detailed a procedure for minorities to complain by petition. Sir Eric Drummond, the English secretary general of the League, appointed a Norwegian, Erik Colban, as head of the minority section. Helmer Rosting, a Dane, and Pablo de Azcarate, a Spaniard, were appointed as assistants. The procedure was to be as follows:

—Determination of the secretary general of the petition to the members of the council, with remarks of the government involved;

—Examination of the petition and the remarks of the government by three (or on occasion five) members of the council appointed by the president of the minority section, for the purpose of deciding whether to call the council's attention to an infraction or impending infraction of the treaty as stated in the petition;

—Negotiation between the section on minorities and the government in question. If negotiations lead to a satisfactory result, the matter is closed; if not, the members of the council put the matter on their agenda;

—Examination of the question by the council; appointment of an advocate; negotiation between this advocate and the government concerned; vote on a resolution by the council.

This rather lengthy procedure made any intervention by the League of Nations uncertain at best in case of mistreatment of minorities, particularly since the government in question could take advantage of a series of procedures to delay the action—for example, by requesting more time to deliver its remarks. In addition, what negated the system of minority protection was that the states most likely to disobey the resolutions were linked by treaties of alliance to the powers dominating the Council of the League of Nations. This was clearly the case with France and the nations of the Little Entente. Hungary complained to the council on March 15, 1923, about the Hungarians of Transylvania who chose other citizenship and were thus stripped of their possessions—in direct violation of Article III of the treaty described above. In a memorandum of April 6, 1923, addressed to the political section of the Quai d'Orsay, the French department of the League of Nations summarized the Hungarian position and noted that Rumania was counting on French support. The head of the political section wrote the following remark at the bottom of the memo:

> The Hungarians have a legal complaint, but the Rumanians are our friends. My government means therefore to support the Rumanians, while indicating to Monsieur Titulescu (the Rumanian delegate to the League of Nations) that he should refrain from pushing the matter too far.

The principle victims of political repression by the new states were the German minorities in Poland, Czechoslovakia, and Yugoslavia, as well as the Ruthenian minorities in Poland and Czechoslovakia. The Albanian and Bulgaro-Macedonian minorities in Yugoslavia also suffered considerably. These minorities had a singular trait in common; they were on the losing side in 1918 and had no allies to forward their cause. But they were not the only victims. The Poles of Czechoslovakia, the Rumanian minority in Yugoslavia, and the Serbian minority in Rumania had the same problems. Nationalism continued to reign in eastern Europe—a far cry from the Wilsonian ideals of international cooperation.

The archives of the League of Nations in Geneva are full of petitions and complaints citing various treaty violations, a few trumped up and unjustified, but the vast majority backed by overwhelming evidence against the accused states. It is not difficult to understand the bitterness and despair of the peoples who were arbitrarily uprooted from their countries and delivered to foreign states.

Rumania, Czechoslovakia, and Yugoslavia were the worst offenders against national minorities. The leaders of these countries quickly realized that the Powers, in giving them such large numbers of non-native people, had bestowed them with a dangerous gift. They were well aware that these new subjects would remain attached to their old countries—how could it be otherwise? The new states were thus faced with assimilating or eliminating these minorities, despite the resolutions they had signed.

The tactics designed to deal with the minorities followed common patterns: a prolonged state of siege in the annexed territories; physical and moral cruelties wherever the minority group was small; other tactics when the group was larger and formed a tighter community. Occasionally an entire population was expelled, as in the case of the Bulgarians driven from the western shores of the Aegean Sea by the Greeks. This eliminated the Bulgarian minority in Greece, but 300,000 destitute Bulgarians had to be absorbed by a ruined and exhausted Bulgaria. Elsewhere, only the elite were expelled—lawyers, journalists, teachers, and religious leaders—depriving the minority of its natural leaders. All civil servants who had served in preceding regimes were expelled and replaced with others usually less competent and often less honest. The Transylvanians of both Hungarian or Rumanian origin quickly learned that any new arrivals were sent wherever the ethnic composition of an area needed to be changed to benefit the state of Rumania. A report from the French minister at Bucharest dated September 10, 1920, eloquently states:

> Hungarians in particular are targeted by the rapid, intensive Rumanization plan adopted by the government in Bucharest. Thanks to regulations they have adopted, the authorities have the means to rid themselves of all those whose position seem worth taking. On August 21, 50 families from Kolozsvar (Cluj) were sent to Hungary, on August 28, 75 families, and last week 53 families.... There is no need to emphasize the conditions under which these evacuations took place...

The French military attache confirmed his colleague's observations: "Even in the Rumanian villages (in Transylvania) there are complaints of abuses..." A similar policy was used in Czechoslovakia. In 1927, Eduard

Benes explained to William Martin, a Swiss journalist, how he went about altering the ethnic composition of Czech towns and cities:

> The dominant power always has the means to modify the ethnic character of towns by stationing troops, civil servants, commerce, banks in them...we have done this.... This experiment has worked in Brunn (Brno) which was almost entirely a German city when we took it, and in which the German minority is now disappearing. The same is happening in Kassa (Kosice), which was a Magyar city and now is nearly all Slovak.

The political rights of national minorities were systematically ignored in the early days and eliminated later. Despite the treaties, the national minorities in Rumania and Yugoslavia were refused the right to vote until 1926. The minorities in Czechoslovakia made up nearly 40 percent of the total population by *official* estimates, but the constitutional assembly responsible for legislation regarding language usage and agrarian reform did not include a single representative from the national minorities. And when the minorities were finally allowed to participate in elections, their parliamentary reprsentation was diminished by manipulation of voter registration. In Prague, a 90 percent Czech city, one deputy represented only 38,000 people while in Karlsbad (Karlovy-Vary), a 95 percent German-speaking city, one deputy represented 47,000. In Slovakia, the unequal treatment was even more obvious; in Ersekujvar (Nova Zamky), a 90 percent Hungarian city, a deputy represented over 53,000 inhabitants and in Ungvar (Oujgorod), a Hungaro-Ruthenian city, one deputy represented over 63,000. The same disproportions were found in Rumania and Yugoslavia. In the rare occurrence when minorieties were allowed to participate in Yugoslavian elections, the Hungarians were allowed three deputies, although numerically they should have had twelve.

To further weaken the minorities, the states tried to impoverish them through biased land reform. In Czechoslovakia, the German and Hungarian estate owners were the only ones adversely affected by the reform, while the Czechs actually benefited. In Ruthenia, out of 162,000 hectares confiscated from Hungarian property owners, only 22,000 hectares were distributed to Ruthenian peasants, with the remainder distributed to Czech ex-soldiers enlisted to *colonize* the region. In Poland as well, only the large German estates were affected by the new agrarian laws. In Rumania, the land reform of 1921 impacted Transylvania much more severely than the older provinces: the Rumanian Boyars were allowed to keep 500 hectares, while the Transylvanian property owners were permitted only 260 hectares and were given only half the compensation. The League of Nations deliberated this matter in 1921, but did not reach a verdict in favor of the Hungarian petitioners until 1927, and even then it was incomplete. In Yugoslavia, discriminatory fiscal land laws deprived the German and Hungarian minorities of their property in favor of Serbian colonists, while Croatian property owners received the same treatment as the Germans and Hungarians.

Beginning in 1925, however, upon advice from France recommending moderation and prudence, a certain standardization of treatment appeared, although in all but word the national minorities remained second-class citizens. Cultural and lingistic discrimination remained frequent. Considered a model of democracy, Czechoslovakia in many ways exemplified policies pursued by the new nations between 1925 and 1938. A 1920 law permitted the use of minority languages in local administration and the courts of districts in which minorities comprised at least 20 percent of the population. But in the following year, administrative shuffling of district boundaries reduced the liberal intentions of the 1920 law to near-zero. Then in 1926, a decree stated that "the administrative authorities could always require the use of the official language when the public interest was at stake;" their willingness to do so resulted in the Czech language being used exclusively in local administration and courts of law, even in districts with German, Hungarian, Polish, or Ruthenian majorities. The methods used in taking the censuses which served as the basis for applying the language law were questionable. A census taken in 1930 in Czechoslovakia illustrates the corrupt methods used: in Bohemia-Moravia, the head of the family filled out the census forms, but in Slovakia and in Ruthenia the census taker himself completed them, giving him ample opportunity to alter the information. The census takers were hand-picked, and in the district of Bratislava with its numerous German and Hungarian residents, not a single one of the 300 census takers was either German or Hungarian. The petition presented to the League of Nations by representatives of the German and Hungarian minorities was met with no reaction, as could be expected. In Rumania and Yugoslavia, policies regarding minority groups were even harsher than in Czechoslovakia. With examples such as these, it is easy to see why the minority question poisoned international relations in this part of Europe.

Adolph Hitler's rise to power and Germany's support for the German minorities convinced some states to adopt a more liberal policy toward their national minorities: Transylvanian Germans, for example, gained special status in 1935. Nevertheless, Konrad Henlein's German Party of the Sudetenland claimed, but was not granted, autonomy, and by 1937 was clearly oriented toward Berlin and national-socialism. After Hitler seized Austria in 1938, Rumania and Yugoslavia liberalized their treatment of national minorities. A Rumanian ordinance dated August 4, 1938, finally guaranteed non-Rumanian groups the use of their own languages in public assemblies in areas where they were in the majority, and the post office finally agreed to deliver letters addressed in languages other than Rumanian and to rescind the exorbitant surcharges on telegrams in German or Hungarian. Primary and secondary school were also reopened. At the same time, Czechoslovakia began making overtures to its minorities. The minorities could only greet initiatives from men such as Benes and Titulescu—who had purposefully undermined the minorities' justifiable complaints to the League of Nations—with disbelief and mistrust.

In 1938, concessions granted or promised to minorities came too late; the victims of 20 years of mistreatment were no longer willing or able to forget. Instead, these minorities, backed by the governments of their respective countries of origin, demanded with increasing insistence a revision of the treaties and the reparation of their countrymen. Paradoxically, it was Hitler who championed the rights of these peoples to self-determination, and it was to him that the Germans, Hungarians, Slovaks, Croats, and even Poles looked for assistance.

Chapter 20

From Munich to Yalta
1938—1945

Hitler's annexation of Austria on March 15, 1938, creating the "greater" Germany that had been the leitmotif of all German nationalist movements since 1848, was the first sign of weakness in the structure created by the victors of World War I. The *Anschluss* allowed the *Wehrmacht*, the German army, to move into the heart of Danubian Europe. From Vienna, German influence could spread at leisure throughout this part of Europe in preparation for conquest. Germany could count on a vast network of sympathizers in this area. First, there were sizeable groups of German minorities nearly everywhere, thoroughly steeped in national-socialist propaganda. Second, Germany had the support of national-socialist inspired political movements within most of the Danubian countries (Arrow-Cross in Hungary, Iron Guard in Rumania, National Gathering in Czechoslovakia), and also of the Croat and Slovak autonomist movements. In addition, Germany could exert considerable pressure through finance and trade agreements made with all of the Danubian and Balkan countries. Finally, Germany could count on a cooperative attitude from both the defeated countries, who hoped one way or another to have the treaties of 1919-1920 revised, and also from certain beneficiaries of these treaties, like Rumania and Yugoslavia, who wanted Germany to prevent any such revision.

Italy, who had played a major role in these regions between 1925 and 1935, was no longer in a position to dictate policy since Italian armed forces had been weakened by the war with Ethiopia and participation in the Spanish civil war; Italy itself was counting on Germany for military aid.

THE END OF CZECHOSLOVAKIA

Czechoslovakia in the mid-1930s was rightly considered the most powerful and best-armed state in the Danubian area, as well as a faithful spokesman for French interests in the region. Its own armament industry combined with generous military assistance from France consolidated its military strength. There were, however, latent weaknesses behind this image of power. The minority groups which made up nearly 40 percent of the population were becoming more strident in their calls for separatism, particularly in the Slovak and Ruthenian regions, and successive governments took care to hide these threats through a policy of authoritarian centralization.

But the security and even the independence of the Czech state was threatened by increased German military strength after Hitler's rise to power, by the hardening of President Benes' attitude toward the non-Czech populations, by the progressive weakening of France beginning in 1936, and particularly by the *Anschluss*. In early spring, 1938, the different national minorities led by the German Sudeten party under Konrad Henlein joined with the Slovak autonomists of Father Josef Tiso as a bloc to demand concessions from the Prague government. Shortly after the *Wehrmacht* entered Austria, the German Sudeten party deputies, who had won 70 percent of the German votes in the 1935 elections, demanded internal autonomy for areas with German-speaking populations. A similar claim was formulated on April 24, 1938, during the party congress held in Karlsbad (Karlovy-Vary) according to a program worked out between Henlein and the German leaders. Hitler knew very well that Benes would refuse to give in and there would be an excellent pretext to intercede militarily on behalf of the Sudeten Germans. Germany was counting on Hungary's cooperation in eventual military action against Czechoslovakia, and promised restitution of Hungarian territory lost in the Treaty of Trianon in return. Hungarian leaders wanted to avoid a war with Czechoslovakia; they knew they were militarily inferior and were still hoping for revision through peaceful means. Hitler was unable to obtain anything from them even during a visit to Germany by Admiral Horthy and his ministers on August 21-26, 1938.

Far from making concessions to the German minority as France and Great Britain had suggested, Benes decided to use force. Using the pretext of German troops amassing along the border, he began to call up the reserves on May 21. He halted this action a few days later, while Paris and London tried to induce both sides to restrain themselves. The French, at the same time, were investigating Soviet interest in helping Czechoslovakia in case of German attack. Maxime Litvinov, head of the Soviet diplomatic service, agreed in principle to assist Czechoslovakia in accordance with a treaty the USSR had signed on May 16, 1935, but on the condition that Soviet troops could cross Poland and Rumania. Both countries, Poland in particular, objected. Consequently, Czechoslovakia could no longer rely on Soviet military assistance in case of German aggression, leaving only France in a position to intervene. Benes, who was kept informed of these transactions, softened his position slightly on urgent advice from the British, and on September 7, 1938, initiated negotiations with representatives from the German Sudeten party. But on the same day, violence broke out between the Germans and the Czech police at Morawska-Ostrava. Though the situation remained tense, negotiations continued and an agreement was pending. Unfortunately, on September 12 in Nuremburg, Hitler gave a fiery speech denouncing Czech cruelty towards the Sudeten Germans and demanded their autodetermination. In the days that followed, rioting broke out in Sudetenland. Knowing he had Hitler's support, Henlein demanded that the Sudeten Germans be allowed to join the Reich.

In view of the seriousness of the situation, the British prime minister, Neville Chamberlain, went to Berchtesgaden on September 15 to meet with Hitler. During their conversation, the two agreed on the advisability of letting regions with German majorities join the Reich. London and Paris accepted the compromise reluctantly. Only Prague had to be persuaded to accept the Chamberlain plan. Would Benes, at the request of his allies, be willing to give up the territory that these same allies had offered him in 1919? On September 21 a French-British memorandum was sent to him; if Prague refused to accept the agreement made between Chamberlain and Hitler, Czechoslovakia could no longer in any circumstances count on aid from the Allies. Benes was forced to submit, particularly since the Soviets had let him know that they would not intercede either; the treaty of 1935 promised Soviet action only in conjunction with France. On the same day, the Czech cabinet led by Milan Hodza resigned in protest. Benes asked General Sirovy, the commander of the armed forces, to form a National Union government. In principle, everything seemed settled.

Encouraged by the Czech agreement, Chamberlain left Germany on September 22. During his interview with Hitler at Bad-Godesberg, Chamberlain was presented with new demands. Hitler wanted the same sort of agreement for the Hungarian and Polish minorities, and he was adamant about permitting emigrants to vote in the plebiscites to be held in zones with mixed populations. These new demands alarmed France and Great Britain, and both adopted a firmer stance. On September 23, Czechoslovakia began a general mobilization, France called up the reserves, and Great Britain put its fleet on alert. War seemed inevitable, especially after Hitler's violent speech of September 26, and his announcement to Chamberlain that Germany would begin mobilizing on the 28th. Chamberlain made another effort to preserve the peace. On the morning of September 28, he suggested an international conference to Hitler and Mussolini. Mussolini took credit for the idea, and it was accepted by all.

At the conference held in Munich on September 29, Hitler, Mussolini, Chamberlain and Daladier agreed to give Germany the German-speaking Sudeten territories of Czechoslovakia before October 10, in an agreement known as the **Munich Pact**. In a document attached to the agreement, France and Great Britain pledged to guarantee the new Czech borders; Germany and Italy did the same, but on the express condition that the matter of the Hungarian and Polish minorities be settled within three months through direct negotiation between the concerned parties. The terms of the Munich Pact were then imposed on Czechoslovakia by the Great Powers, two of whom were allies who had taken part in its creation in 1919. Czechoslovakia's partners in the Little Entente, Rumania and Yugoslavia, made no effort to assist their ally.

Immediately after the agreements were signed, the German authorities escorted by the *Wehrmacht* took over the ceded territories amid great enthusiasm from the local populations. Just before the conference in Munich, Poland revealed the treaty signed with Czechoslovakia in 1925, and claimed the Teschen territory in an ultimatum addressed to Prague on September 30. Then on October 2, Polish troops moved in to occupy this 386-square-mile territory whose population of 200,000 was 70 percent Polish. In Prague on October 5, Benes resigned in response to the Munich agreements, and left for London. He was replaced as president by Emil Hacha, a modest and honest magistrate, while the leadership of the government was taken over by Rudolf Beran, an Agrarian who headed a center-right coalition. The pro-Germanic Frantisek Chvalkovsky became head of foreign affairs. The Czechs were bitterly disappointed in the attitude of their foreign "friends," but after a few protest demonstrations, anger gave way to resignation. To stop the break-up of the country, Prague finally decided to grant the Ruthenians and Slovaks a measure of autonomy on October 6. The Slovak diet at Bratislava chose Father Tiso to head the local government, and Father Augustin Volisin took over that function for the Ruthenians.

The Hungarians thought that the moment had come to press for revision of the territorial clauses in the Treaty of Trianon. In accordance with the agreements of Munich, direct negotiations opened on October 9 at Komarno between a delegation from the Hungarian government and a Czechoslovakian delegation led by Father Tiso. The negotiations closed in failure on October 13. The two parties both agreed to ask Germany and Italy to arbitrate. In the First Arbitration of Vienna in November, 1938, Hungary regained 4670 square miles with 1,030,000 inhabitants, 830,000 of them Magyar and only 143,000 Slovak, and the towns of Kassa, Komarom and

Munkacs (Munkatchevo). Between November 4 and 11, Hungarian troops marched into this territory and were universally welcomed as liberators. The Hungarians had hoped for more, but Hitler, who wanted to take charge of the Slovaks, had not meant to grant more. From a purely ethnic viewpoint, the new border was nearly perfect, with only 66,000 Hungarians under Czechoslovakian rule.

Although Czechoslovakia still existed in November, 1938, dismemberment had taken its toll. The defense system was in complete disorder, with mountain heights and Bohemia all in the hands of the Germans. The population, however, was far more homogeneous than before. The remaining minorities constituted an insignificant percentage of the population. The Ruthenians and the Slovaks seemed content with the autonomy granted to them, and Hitler had just declared that he had no more ambitions for expansion in that direction. From November, 1938, Czechoslovakian policy underwent a change. The democracy organized by Masaryk—with the limitations mentioned earlier—rapidly evolved into an authoritarian system. The Communist party was banned and the opposition in parliament, composed of Socialists and friends of Benes, was reduced to silence. In Slovakia, the autonomists wanted more than autonomy, and Tiso made no secret of his desire to turn Slovakia into an independent and sovereign state. The Slovakian elections he had called in 1935 gave him an overwhelming majority in the diet and bolstered his intentions. Ruthenia was jointly coveted by Poland and Hungary, both desiring a common border to fend off the German threat.

In early March, 1939, tensions within Czechoslovakia brought another German intervention. The pretext was renewed conflict between the central government and the Slovaks. Prague took a dim view of Tiso's ardently defended calls for independence. On March 10, President Hacha dismissed Tiso's Slovak government and declared a state of siege throughout the country. In Bratislava, the people reacted to these measures with violent demonstrations organized by German agents from Vienna. A former leader of the Catholic party, Karol Sidor, formed a transition government, but Slovak agitation quickly overwhelmed the authorities. The Germans were quick to act. On March 13, they sent two emissaries to Tiso to persuade him that it was time for Slovakia to become independent. The same evening, Tiso went to Berlin, where he met with the German foreign minister, Joachim von Ribbentrop, and then with Hitler, who advised him to declare Slovakian independence at once; according to the Germans, Hungary was only waiting for the right opportunity to invade the country. When the Slovak diet convened the following day, Karol Sidor presented his resignation and then urged the deputies to confide power to Father Tiso. With applause from the deputies, Sidor ended with: "Long live the Slovak nation; Long live free

Slovakia!" Slovakian independence was promptly declared, carried by 57 out of 63 votes.

Slovakian independence marked the beginning of the end of the Czechoslovakian state, and the end came quickly. Acting on the suggestion of Chvalkovsky, the Czechoslovakian minister of foreign affairs, Hitler called President Hacha to Berlin; during a dramatic and stormy interview on March 14, 1939, Hitler demanded that what was left of Czechoslovakia, meaning Bohemia and Moravia, be placed under the protection of the Reich. The German protectorate of Bohemia-Moravia was born. On March 15, Czechoslovakia ceased to exist. German troops immediately marched into the country and disarmed the Czechoslovakian army. At the same time, Hungarian troops were moving into Carpathian Ruthenia, which had been part of their territory for over a thousand years, thus establishing a common border with its ally, Poland.

One of the key elements in the system set up by the Entente in 1919 to defend their interests in Danubian Europe had crumbled. Germany's aggression and the inaction of the Allies, along with Czechoslovakian internal problems such as the multinational nature of its state and its oppressive centralizing policy toward non-Czechs, were largely responsible for the downfall of this artificial state. Neither Rumania nor Yugoslavia lifted a finger in its aid; both adopted the same passive stance as they had at Munich. But this time, in London and in Warsaw, there was a sudden realization that Germany would not be appeased and Poland would be next to serve German ambitions in eastern Europe. On March 22, Germany seized the port of Memel, which was officially Lithuanian but populated by Germans. Paradoxically once again, in Memel as in Sudetenland, Hitler made himself out to be a veritable champion of the people's right to self-determination. Thanks to him, the Germans and the Czechoslovakian Hungarians, the Poles in Teschen, the Slovaks, and the Germans in Memel had recovered their freedom!

THE FOURTH PARTITION OF POLAND

Until the summer of 1938, Germano-Polish relations had been polite on the whole, particularly after the signing of the non-agression treaty in 1934. It was only natural that Poland had taken advantage of Czechoslovakia's troubles to retake Teschen, coveted since 1919. But there were latent sources of tension with Germany. Foremost was the problem of Danzig and the corridor. The "Free City" had been in Nazi control since 1935, and the city made no secret of wanting to return to Germany. At any moment a minor incident in the corridor could provoke a crisis, and the presence of over 1,200,000 Germans in Posnania and Upper Silesia only complicated the situation. Members of the German minority were organized in cultural associations directed from Berlin, having the potential to initiate a wave of disorder that the Polish authorities would feel compelled to put down. Germano-Polish relations began to deteriorate in October, 1938. On October 24, 1938, Foreign Minister Ribbentrop proposed a new treaty to the Polish ambassador in Berlin. By this new agreement, he argued, Danzig would be returned to Germany and Germany would be granted extraterritorial rights to build a highway and a railroad through the corridor. In exchange for these major concessions, Poland could keep a free zone in the port of Danzig and could use the extraterritorial railroad. Also, the non-aggression pact signed in 1934 would be extended from ten to 25 years, assuring the mutual borders.

However, the response of the Polish foreign minister, Colonel Beck, was that returning Danzig to Germany was out of the question. But diplomatic relations were not broken, and Beck was invited to meet with Hitler on January 5, 1939, at Berchtesgaden. A few days later, Ribbentrop went to Warsaw to celebrate the fifth anniversary of the Germano-Polish treaty of 1934. Officially, nothing seemed to have changed between the two countries except that the subject of Danzig had been broached. Within Poland, however, friction between Poles and Germans was increasing, though not reaching the level of violence in Sudetenland the preceding year.

After the dismemberment of Czechoslovakia on March 15, 1939, German-Polish relations suddenly entered a new phase of tension. A few days after the occupation of Prague, the German government again demanded Danzig, and on March 27, the German navy staged maneuvers near the mouth of the Vistula. Beck held his ground, and the British government backed his resistance in view of Hitler's successive failures to keep his promises. On March 31, in a speech to the Commons, Chamberlain announced that Britain would stand beside Poland if its independence were threatened and the Poles chose to resist. A few days later, Beck went to London to sign a treaty of alliance. On April 13, the French government took the same firm stand, and Poland also expected some support from Hungary with whom it had shared a common border since March 15. Meanwhile, Hitler was completing his plans for attack and reinforcing his links to Italy with a defensive and offensive military alliance treaty signed on May 22, the Pact of Steel. Incidents of violence between Poles and Germans were increasing in Upper Silesia and in the corridor. Common people on both sides vented feelings of extreme nationalism, while Polish authorities hardened their position.

In view of the German threat, France and Great Britain, who chose to support Poland, turned to Russia. In mid-summer 1939, at the instigation of the French, political negotiations opened in Moscow, followed by opening of military negotiations on August 11. But relations were strained, and two major obstacles made signing of a treaty highly unlikely. First, Poland did not want Russian troops to cross its territory in case of war with Germany; second, the Soviets continued to introduce new counter-projects and additions as if to prolong the talks. In fact, while negotiating with the French and British, the Soviets were also holding discussions with the German Ambassador von Schulenburg on the advantages of a political agreement between the two countries. The Western Powers were in for a shock when on August 23, a German delegation led by Ribbentrop arrived in Moscow to sign a non-aggression pact.

By this **Russo-German** pact, valid for ten years and in immediate effect, the two countries agreed to abstain from any act of aggression against each other and to refrain from entering into any system of alliances that could pit one against the other. Even more importantly, the document secretly provided that, in the event the Polish situation changed, the USSR could take over the eastern Polish provinces up the Narew-Vistula-San line, as well as Estonia, Latvia, Finland, and even Rumanian Bessarabia. Despite French and British efforts to work out a compromise between Berlin and Warsaw, the dice were cast; Hitler had decided to settle his differences with Poland by force.

On September 1, 1939, at 5:45 in the morning, the German army invaded Poland. On the same day, the Danzig senate announced the rejoining of Danzig to the Reich with Gauleiter Forster, head of the local Nazis, already chosen on August 23 to lead the free state. The German invasion of Poland provoked an outraged reaction. In the evening of September 1, French troops were ordered to mobilize; on the following day, the Polish government urged its allies to respect their obligations. On September 3, after Berlin rejected a Franco-British ultimatum demanding withdrawal of German troops from Poland, Great Britain and France declared war on Germany. The Danubian and Balkan states, along with Italy and the USSR, declared neutrality.

For Poland, the war began under disastrous conditions. Isolated from its western allies, Poland had easily defendable natural borders with friendly Hungary and Rumania, but on the sides where danger lay, to the west as well as to the east, there were only wide open plains with over 900 miles of border to be defended. Moreover, despite the bravery and heroism of its soldiers and officers, the Polish army was composed mainly of cavalry, and lacked the motorized units necessary to face a well-trained and well-equipped enemy. At the outset of the war, the small Polish air force was destroyed on the ground by the *Luftwaffe*. Major railway intersections were also attacked from the air by the Germans, and even more demoralizing to the Poles was the bombardment of civilian populations. From the beginning of the war, the German minority within the country behaved as a fifth column, actively preparing to welcome their "liberators." Polish authorities brutally reacted to any sabotage attempts, sometimes resorting to summary executions as on September 2, when 150 German civilians were shot at Bydgoszcz. In retaliation, German troops increased the number of civilians executed in villages where they met resistance.

The Polish army under Marshal Smigly-Rydz was scattered around the country, making effective defense more difficult. On September 14, less than two weeks after hostilities began, Warsaw was surrounded. The city was under constant artillery fire and attack from the air, and was then cut off from water and food supplies. The German invasion was soon joined by a Russian invasion. On September 9, Foreign Affairs Minister V.M. Molotov advised the German government that the Soviet army was about to occupy eastern Poland according to the provisions of the Russo-German Pact of August 23. On cue, the Soviet press unleashed a violent campaign against Poland, with accusations of oppressed White Russian (Bielorussian) and Ukrainian populations within Polish borders. Then on September 17, just as the already outnumbered Polish army neared exhaustion, the Soviets launched a rear attack. The Soviets had two excuses ready to justify their aggression: first, the Polish state had practically ceased to exist, and so the non-aggression pact signed with it in 1934 was void, and second, the USSR fully intended to protect the White Russians and the Ukrainians in Poland. The Red Army concentrated on the southern borders of Poland in order to prevent the remnants of the Polish army from crossing into Hungary and Rumania. The Polish government and the high command had already fled with President Moscicki into Rumanian territory. Despite the difficulties, thousands of civilians and soldiers managed to reach the Hungarian and Rumanian Carpathian mountains, and escape the misfortune besieging their country.

The *Blitzkrieg* in Poland was a total success for the *Wehrmacht*. Warsaw capitulated on September 27, after a 17-day resistance led mainly by civilians, and the Germans and the Soviets controlled nearly all of the country. The last islands of resistance around Gdynia fell on October 2. One month of war had put an end to Polish independence once again; Poland lost 300,000 men, 450,000 prisoners were in the hands of the Germans, and 200,000 were taken by the Soviets.

The will of the country had still not been broken. President Moscicki, tainted by association with the colonels' regime, resigned in exile on September 30, and a National Union government was formed in Paris under the leadership of General Sikorski—committed to continuing the struggle with the Allies. Former members of the army, found in Hungary and sent to France through Yugoslavia, were organized into a Polish Legion.

The fate of occupied Poland was already sealed. On September 22,

Germans and Soviets agreed on the fourth partition of Poland. Germany took over all the territories to the west of the Bug as stipulated in the Russo-German non-aggression pact. As compensation, Lithuania went to the Soviets. The new borders were set on September 28 by a treaty of "delineation and friendship" in which each party pledged to "tolerate no Polish agitation on their part of the territory liable to upset order in the other part." This condemned any Polish resistance in advance.

Both of the co-partitioners began to organize their new acquisitions. Germany simply annexed the regions it supposedly ceded to Poland in 1919; these were Posnania, Danzig, the corridor, and Upper Silesia, which for administrative purposes became the Incorporated Territories of the East. The German-speaking citizens were its elite, and were reinforced by German colonists from inside the Reich and by Germans repatriated from the Baltic area. Alongside them, the Poles who were not expelled were subjected to a policy of Germanization, reduced to the ranks of second-class citizens and relegated to menial jobs. The remaining Polish territory became the *General-Gouvernement* of occupied Polish provinces under the authority of the German governor, Hans Frank. The *General-Gouvernement*, populated by around 12 million Poles with Cracow as its capital, was in a reality a huge occupied zone with a partially Polish local government under close surveillance by the Germans. Polish occupied territories furnished the Reich with a large reservoir of manpower as well as with a considerable amount of food stocks and raw materials. The Jews, who were numerous in the cities and towns, were the first to feel the effects of Poland's new status. By the end of September, they had been re-enumerated and were forced to wear the yellow star; by the end of 1939, they were being pushed into ghettos.

The situation was no better in Soviet-held territories. These regions were annexed as part of the Socialist Republics of Bielorussia and the Ukraine, after a pretense of consulting the public. Citizens of Polish origin were stripped of their rights and placed under the constant surveillance of the Soviet authorities. Over a million Poles—a million and a half according to Polish General Wladyslaw Anders—were deported to the USSR between October, 1939 and June, 1941. Over 200,000 of these perished in Soviet prison camps. The principal victims of these deportations were the middle class and the liberal professions. Also included were prominent personalities: priests, intellectuals, former military officers, politicians and union leaders, in short, the people important to society. Even more characteristic of Soviet behavior in eastern Poland was the persecution of Jews who had fled German-occupied territory. Two members of the Jewish socialist organization, BUND, Henryk Ehrlich and Victor Atler, fled Warsaw in September, 1939, for refuge in eastern Poland. They were arrested there in 1941, even though they had formed a Jewish Anti-Hitlerian Committee at the request of

Soviet authorities. When the Germans attacked the USSR in June of 1941, the Committee was evacuated to Moscow and then to Kouibychev. After that, in December, 1941, no more was heard of them: Ehrlich and Atler simply disappeared. Later, it was learned that they had been executed for anti-Soviet activities. Theirs was not an isolated case; the two partners in Poland's partition exhibited strangely similar behavior.

CHANGES IN THE DANUBIAN AND BALKAN AREA, 1939-1941

In accordance with the pacts signed with Germany, the USSR began to move into the Baltic republics. Governments of those countries were forced to sign treaties of mutual assistance which included the surrender of naval bases and air fields to Soviet-manned garrisons. Finland refused these Soviet terms, and was invaded on November 30, 1939. Though finally overcome, the determined resistance of the Finns at least enabled them to salvage their political independence. Estonia, Latvia and Lithuania were less fortunate. In June, 1940, the Soviets used the pretext of local acts of aggression against the Red Army for direct intervention in these countries, setting up Communist-dominated governments subservient to Moscow. Elections held on July 14 resulted in over 90 percent for the pro-Soviet single list of candidates, and gave a semblance of legality to the takeover of the three Baltic republics. Baltic independence, regained in 1917, had hardly lasted longer than Poland's.

The events of August-September, 1939, the Russo-German pact, and the liquidation of the Polish state under joint assault by Stalin and Hitler, clearly demonstrated to the still independent Danubian and Balkan countries who the true masters of Europe were at this time. Each state began its own system of reorganization in view of the new conditions.

Hungarian Neutrality and Revisionism

For the Hungarian leaders, who since 1919 had based their policy on the struggle against bolshevism, the signing of the pact between Molotov and Ribbentrop came as a shock, and even more of one since in January of 1939, they had agreed to sign the German-sponsored **Anti-Comintern Pact** against the USSR. Their indignation intensified when in early September, 1939, Hitler requested permission to transport German troops across Hungarian territory to attack the Polish army from behind. Count Teleki, the Hungarian prime minister, categorically refused, giving further instructions to the border guards to assist fleeing Polish soldiers and civilians crossing the border. Teleki had to act with care, however; he had to avoid directly offending Germany in view of the two countries' disproportionate military forces and he also knew perfectly well that if Hungary wanted to obtain its revisionist goals in Transylvania, support of the Axis powers was a necessity. Teleki attempted to turn to his other ally, Italy, to counterbalance German influence, but Mussolini's policy had grown progressively more dependent on Hitler's since 1939. Without abandoning his policy of strict neutrality, Teleki accelerated the rearmament begun by his predecesor in 1938 to prepare for any opportunity to retake territory lost in 1920. The opportunity arose in 1940, when the USSR demanded surrender of Bessarabia and northern Bukovina from Rumania. The Axis countries' maintained a neutral stance in this affair, encouraging the Hungarian government to ask Rumania to open negotiations in Transylvania. Talks began at Turnu-Severin, but quickly bogged down. Germany and Italy stepped in to mediate once again, and in the Second Arbitration of Vienna on August 30, 1940, Hungary was awarded the north of Transylvania, a territory of 17,000 square miles and 2,500,000 inhabitants, over 1,100,000 of them Magyar. The acquisition included the towns of Kolozsvar, Nagyvarad as well as the entire Szekely country.

The return of part of Transylvania to the "motherland" was greeted enthusiastically by the Hungarian people. It was a clever move on Hitler's part, because, as he hoped, it created a rivalry between Hungary and Rumania for Germany's attentions, in one case in order to obtain the rest of Transylvania, and in the other, to recover the part lost. Count Teleki was aware of Hitler's motives. Straining to maintain neutrality, Teleki initiated rapprochment with his southern neighbor, Yugoslavia; the two countries signed a friendship pact on December 12, 1940, pledging to settle their differences through negotiation. But Teleki was the first to realize the limited extent of his freedom. Germany was victorious on all fronts and more powerful than ever, and in late November, 1940, Hungary was forced to comply when Hitler invited it to endorse the **Tripartite Pact**, a defensive agreement Germany, Italy, and Japan had signed on September 27, 1940. Thus, while still officially neutral, Hungary was being drawn into the new European order.

The Fascistization of Rumania

The establishment of the royal dictatorship in Rumania in early 1938 had little effect on the country's problems. Codreanu and the main leaders of the Iron Guard were eliminated, but their followers continued to agitate under Horia Sima. In addition, the different nationalist populations increased their demands for secession despite a relatively liberal statute granted them on August 4, 1938. The Bulgars in southern Dobrudja rose up in May, 1939, and were severely repressed, increasing the tension between Bucharest and Sofia. The situation was scarcely better in Transylvania where the Hungarian minority was increasingly impatient to be returned to

Hungary, and where the German minority, under the influence of intense national-socialist propaganda, was setting up a state within a state with the barely disguised support of Berlin. Finally, in Bessarabia and Bukovina, Communist propaganda encouraged by Moscow inspired separatist demonstrations among the Russian and Ukrainian populations. To all of this was added country-wide political agitation by the old parties, now formally dissolved. The winter of 1939-40 was particularly difficult because of the economic repercussions of the war; Rumania was principally affected by sudden rises in prices and food shortages caused by existing trade agreements with Germany, which required supplies.

The crisis came to a head during the summer of 1940. On June 26, 1940, a Soviet ultimatum demanded surrender of Bessarabia and northern Bukovina within 24 hours. Rumania gave in, since Germany, when asked, refused to stand up for Rumanian rights. Then came the crisis with Hungary that the German-Italian arbitration settled in Vienna by giving Hungary the western half of Transylvania. And finally the Bulgars demanded western Dobrudja; bilateral negotiations held at Craiova resulted in an agreement on September 7, by which southern Dobrudja was restored to the Bulgars. These actions marked the end of the "great" Rumania granted by the treaties of 1919-1920, but it was also the birth of a new Rumania, smaller of course, but with a more homogeneous population and closer to the principles of nationalism. This new Rumania no longer had Bulgars, Russians, or Ukrainians; the only national minorities were some 500,000 Hungarians and an equal number of Germans, comprising scarcely seven percent of the total population. The public, however, nourished since 1919 on the dream of a "great" Rumania extending from the Tisza to the Dniester, had trouble accepting these territorial adjustments. Popular discontent grew, and after the loss of western Transylvania, the public turned against King Carol II, who was subsequently accused of treason. The discontented elements and the pro-German nationalists pinned their hopes on General Ion Antonescu, minister of war and general chief of staff, who had objected to the successive capitulations of the sovereign. Under pressure of public opinion, the king relinquished power on September 4, 1940, to the general—who then took the title of *Conducator* (Supreme Guide). The next day, Antonescu asked the king to step down, and Carol II abdicated in favor of his son, Michael, who had already held the scepter from 1927 to 1931.

General Antonescu established a military dictatorship, a move supported by the fascist Iron Guard, and stripped King Michael of most of his powers; Antonescu then reinforced ties between Rumania and Nazi Germany, with the intention of benefiting his country, and on October 8, authorized German troops to set up bases on Rumanian territory. Rumania became a fascist state, called the National Legionary State. The new regime was violently anti-Semitic. Thousands of Jews and political opponents were arrested and their property confiscated. The Guardists who ran the country kept their own police alongside the official police for the purposes of extortion and vengeance. During the night of October 26, 1940, in the same Jilava military prison where exactly two years before Codreanu was shot by the police, the Guardists massacred 64 well-known supporters of the old regime, including General Marinescu and Professor Nicolas Iorga, known for their anti-German sentiments.

General Antonescu, anxiously holding on to his authority, quickly realized the threat to the country posed by the uncontrolled Guardists. After meeting with Hitler and assuring him of Rumania's total loyalty, Antonescu rid himself of the most radical Guardist elements. The Guardist police and the Green Shirts were dissolved; their leader, the vice-premier Horia Sima, was dismissed and escaped to Germany where the Germans kept him in reserve in case Antonescu became less cooperative. The country welcomed this purge. Though rid of the Guardists who had helped him to power, the *Conducator* stuck to his policy of personal rule. Rumania remained a totalitarian fascist state with a foreign policy completely aligned with the Reich, as demonstrated by its eager acceptance of the Tripartite Pact on November 23, 1940.

Ambiguities in Bulgaria

Like Hungary, Bulgaria had managed, though with difficulty, to stay out of the international crisis of summer 1939, and to adopt a stance of strict neutrality when war broke out. Despite personal sentiments favoring the Axis powers, King Boris III tried to keep his country out of the conflict for as long as possible. The policy adopted in the early 1930s was not altered when a Germanophile, Bogdan Filov, became head of the government; Bulgaria remained an authoritarian state with a neutral foreign policy. Neutrality, however, did not prevent the Bulgarian government from taking advantage of Rumanian difficulties and taking back the southern Dobrudja Rumania had annexed at the end of the Second Balkan War. Bulgaria was able to obtain part of its revisionist goals peacefully.

During the winter of 1940-41, just as Germany was preparing plans for invading the USSR, Hitler tried to bring Bulgaria into his fold as an ally, or at least to secure Bulgarian neutrality and economic cooperation. He asked Bulgaria to join the Tripartite Pact, and promised restoration of the Aegean coast it had lost in 1910—as soon as Greece, who had been at war with the Axis powers since October 28, 1940, was defeated. Meanwhile, the USSR, viewing Germany's political evolution with growing alarm, made diplomatic overtures to Bulgaria, even offering a pact of friendship and mutual assistance on November 25, 1940. Approached by the two greatest powers of the time, Bulgaria hesitated to take sides. Public opinion traditionally preferred the Russians because of the decisive role Russia played during the war of independence; however, Russian advances were carefully refused, avoiding a diplomatic break. Boris III took his time in responding to the Germans, but on March 1, 1941, Bulgaria submitted and joined the Tripartite Pact. The next day, German troops from Rumania arrived in Bulgaria to set up bases for a counter-offensive against Greece, following the setback for the Italian expeditionary corps.

The End of the Yugoslavian State

After the assassination of King Alexander, Yugoslavia began to pull away from its traditional alliances in favor of Germany. This new policy was primarily the work of the regent, Prince Paul. During the two Czechoslovakian crises in 1938-1939, and during the German attack on Poland, the Belgrade government adopted a neutral stance, though Yugoslavian leaders realized their country's independence was threatened by the danger of growing German domination in the Danubian area. It was in part to offset this threat that they normalized relations with Hungary by signing a friendship pact in 1940. Hitler was planning to invade the USSR, and wanted Yugoslavia to join the Tripartite Pact in order to strengthen his alliances. After lengthy hesitation, Yugoslavia accepted, and on March 25, 1941, in Vienna, representatives of the Belgrade government signed their country into the Tripartite Pact. When this news reached the Yugoslavians, it caused a wave of protest among the pro-French and anti-German Serbian populations. There were violent demonstrations in Belgrade. On the night of March 26, Serbian officers opposed to the regent's policies and secretly aided by British agents, seized power, removed Prince Paul from office, and declared Prince Peter, son of the deceased King Alexander, of age. At the request of King Peter II, the Serbian general, Duchan Simovitch, formed a National Union government. To the disappointment and anxiety of the Croats and Slovenes, it was dominated by Serbs. Simovitch completely revised Yugoslavian foreign policy. He established contact with the British, and prepared a friendship treaty with the USSR, signed on April 5.

In only a few days, Yugoslavia had moved towards the Axis' adversaries—less than two months before the date Hitler planned to attack the USSR. German retaliation was swift. On April 6, the *Luftwaffe*, the German air force, bombed Belgrade, and German ground troops poured into Yugoslavia from all sides: from Austria, from Bulgaria, and also from Hungary. The day after the *coup d'etat* in Belgrade, Hitler had asked for the Budapest government's military collaboration in exchange for the Vojvodine territory lost by Hungary in 1920. Count Teleki was very cautious; he felt bound by the friendship treaty signed with Yugoslavia the preceding winter, and would only agree to military collaboration if Croatia proclaimed independence and the Hungarian minorities were threatened. The Hungarian chief of staff, General Henrik Werth, had in fact already agreed to Hitler's offer; on April 3, when Teleki learned that the *Wehrmacht* had begun deployment across Hungarian soil, he chose to commit suicide rather than break his word. Teleki's death removed the last obstacle to Hungary's military participation, particularly since the new head of state, Laszlo Bardossy, was enthusiastically pro-German. Augmented by Hungarian and Italian contingents, the *Wehrmacht* quickly occupied Yugoslavia. In Zagreb on April 10, Croat nationalists took advantage of the new situation to take over the government. On the same day in Jellachich Square, Colonel Kvaternik declared the independence of the National Croat State, and on April 15, Ante Pavelitch, supported by the Croat fascist group, the Ustaschians, became the leader, *the Poglavnik*, of independent Croatia. Later there were plans to give the crown of Croatia to an Italian prince, the Duke of Spoleto. In Serbia, the Yugoslavian army tried to resist, but was rapidly overwhelmed, and surrendered on April 17. King Peter II and his government fled to London, where on April 22 they called for a general uprising.

Yugoslavia had disappeared under the joint forces of its neighboring countries and Croat separatism. In its place there was an independent Croat state, enlarged by Bosnia-Herzegovina on April 23, 1941, but deprived of Dalmatia, which went to Italy. At the center was a small Serbian state, occupied first by the Germans alone, and then by both Germans and Bulgarians. The rest of Yugoslavia was divided up among its neighbors: Germany annexed northern Slovenia along with the Maribor region, and had direct rule over the Yugoslav Banat despite protests from Hungary and Rumania; Italy took southern Slovenia along with Ljubljana, and made a protectorate of the former Montenegro; Hungary recovered most of the Vojvodina including the towns of Szabadka and Ujvidek, while Albania, under Italian sovereignty since April, 1939, annexed Kosovo and part of Albanian-populated Macedonia. The Bulgarians received most of Macedonia including the town of Skopje, and at the same time, the defeat of Greece allowed them to retake the Aegean coast. Again in this case, despite the aggressive action of the *Wehrmacht* and its allies, the new borders were closer to the aspirations of the people than the old unified kingdom of Yugoslavia had been. But there was no room for idealism; Germany and Italy were not acting according to Wilsonian principles, but were only trying to establish their political and economic hegemony.

Just before the invasion of the USSR, postponed due to the events in Yugoslavia, the Reich and its allies were in a strong position in Danubian and Balkan Europe. All of the countries in this region, by choice or by force, were in the German sphere of influence.

THE EASTERN EUROPEAN COUNTRIES DURING THE GERMAN-SOVIET WAR, 1941-1945

At dawn on June 22, 1941, German troops unleashed Operation Barbarossa, planned since December, 1940, and invaded the Soviet Union from several points. On the same day, Rumania, Slovakia and Croatia declared war on the USSR. Budapest had not been asked to take part in the "Crusade against Bolshevism," but the Hungarian chief of staff wanted Hungary to participate in order to maintain good relations with the Reich. The bombardment of the Hungarian town of Kassa by apparently Soviet—but more likely German or Slovak—planes furnished the needed pretext, and on June 27, Hungary also declared war on the Soviets. Of all the Reich's allies, only Bulgaria remained neutral. From then on, however, directly or indirectly, all eastern European countries, by choice or by force, occupied, neutral or allied with the Reich, would be affected and drawn into the German war effort. And all of them, allies as well as victims, would suffer the consequences.

Germany's Allies

Incontestably, Antonescu's Rumania showed the greatest enthusiasm for the war against the USSR. The *Conducator* first saw it an an excellent occasion to make a show of loyalty to Hitler. Interior policies were already aligned with Germany's, particularly policy regarding the Jews, who were at best sent to concentration camps and assigned to public works, or at worst murdered during bloody pogroms such as those that took place at Jassy and in Bukovina. But above all, Rumania saw the war as a way to recover land lost in 1940, and in effect, Bessarabia was reoccupied and brought back into Rumania in July, 1941. King Michael immediately awarded Antonescu the title of "Marshal of Rumania" for his successes. Later, Rumania was given all the Soviet territory between the Dniester and the Dnieper, or the province of Transistria with its capital, Odessa. Since 1848, Rumanian nationalists had considered this region part of their national territory, using dubious arguments to prove it. The new region was thoroughly pillaged and Rumanian colonists sent to "Rumanianize" the local populations. By 1941, 20 Rumanian divisions, over 700,000 soldiers, were fighting on the Russian front beside the *Wehrmacht*. In addition, Rumania delivered large quantities of food and nearly all the oil it produced to Germany.

Hungary participated on a smaller scale. Up until mid-1942, there were scarcely more than 40,000 Hungarian soldiers engaged in military operations in Russia. The war was unpopular among both the opposition, which organized a peace demonstration in front of the statue of Petofi in Budapest on March 15, 1942, and among state leaders, including Nicolas Kallay, the country's prime minister as of March 9, 1942, and Vice Regent Istvan Horthy, son of the Admiral, all of whom were looking for a way out of the costly and unpopular conflict. Kallay made overtures to the Allies, who had broken off relations with Hungary in December, 1941, but these efforts were blocked by pro-German military command. To placate the Germans, who were aware of the Hungarians' double game, Kallay had to send the Second and Third armies to the front on the Don, bringing Hungarian military participation up to 250,000 men by the end of 1942. Hungary also sent Germany increased food supplies and most of its limited petroleum. By contrast, of the other countries in the war, Croatia and Slovakia sent only about 20,000 men each, and Bulgaria put only its economy at the service of the German war effort.

Slovakia and Croatia, like Bulgaria and Rumania, modeled their institutions and interior policies on those of Germany. In Slovakia, Father Tiso, with the support of the majority of the population, followed an ultra-nationalist line in regard to the Czechs who were interned or deported to Bohemia-Moravia; he also discriminated against the Jews. On September 10, 1941, the Slovak diet unanimously adopted a *codex judaicus* that limited to four percent the number of Jews who could hold public office or enter the liberal professions. A Slovak *SS*, called the Hlinka Guard, was established to maintain order. The Slovak regime was much less radical than those in neighboring countries, however, because of the Christian principles guiding the leaders. In Croatia, for example, Ante Pavelitch's government was known for its brutality and authoritarianism, with the state organized according to the *Fuhrerprinzip*. The regime distinguished itself in anti-Serbian and anti-Orthodox policy. The Croats, who had suffered 20 years of Serbian dictatorship, took violent revenge under the leadership of Ante Pavelitch. With the support of fascist Croats and Muslims from Bosnia, Pavelitch embarked on a campaign of systematic persecution of the 1,900,000 Orthodox Serbs who lived within the confines of the Croat state. Nearly 300,000 of them perished between 1941 and 1945, either because they had taken up arms to fight in resistance groups, or simply because they refused to give up their religious beliefs.

The Defeated Countries

While the countries described above had some independence beyond their close ties to Germany—ties which also gave them certain privileges—the countries occupied by Germany through annexation or defeat in war suffered a fate none would envy.

The protectorate of Bohemia-Moravia became part of the Great German Reich on March 15, 1939. Baron von Neurath, former foreign minister, was appointed protector, and Reinhard Heydrich became chief of police. By the end of 1939, the universities with young students full of patriotic sentiments were closed, and the Sokol groups dissolved. The population as a whole adopted a wait-and-see attitude, although isolated resistance groups acted with the Benes government in exile in London, or with the underground Communist party. Bohemia-Moravia's industry was actively engaged in the German war effort and also furnished manpower for German factories. In early 1943, nearly 300,000 Czechs were employed in factories in Germany. Until then, the population had remained calm and were secretly appreciative they had escaped Poland's fate and were still fully employed. The assassination of Heydrich, however, who had just succeeded von Neurath as protector, brought a wave of repression that radically changed popular feelings. On May 29, 1942, an assassin sent from England had struck down Heydrich, who always traveled with a small escort. Immediately afterwards, the two villages of Lidice and Lezaky were totally razed by the *SS* and their populations were massacred in reprisal. Thousands of arrests were followed by deportation to Germany. The entire population was under suspicion; the time of "collaboration" had passed.

Nothing could compare with the Polish situation. From the beginning, Poland was treated as a defeated enemy country. Governed directly by authorities of the occupation, the Poles lost nearly all of their rights. Hardest hit were the Jews, who were immediately penned up in overcrowded ghettos. Beginning in February, 1942, these ghettos were progressively emptied of their occupants who were sent to concentration camps. In September, 1942, the Warsaw ghetto of over 400,000 Jews began to feel the effects of the Nazi exterminations; the resulting revolt in early 1943 only accelerated the liquidation. A total of over *3,000,000* Polish Jews were exterminated. The German authorities also undertook a liquidation of the Polish elite. Intellectuals, artists, priests, monks, teachers, and members of the liberal professions were systematically interned or simply executed. The Polish nation suffered through yet another tragedy.

The German-Soviet war brought no changes, only the Polish territories annexed by the USSR in 1939 were amalgamated into the *General-Gouvernement*. The Poles realized that the fate of their compatriots who fell into Soviet hands was hardly better than their own. They had further proof of this when on April 13, 1943, the Germans discovered in the forest of Katyn near Smolensk, eight enormous common graves containing the bodies of thousands of Polish officers taken prisoner by the Soviets at the end of September, 1939, and executed in the spring of 1940. The Soviets, like the Germans, clearly demonstrated their determination to destroy Polish society.

Poland was forced to participate in the German war effort; its agricultural and industrial output were requisitioned by Germany, and civilian manpower was sent to work in German factories, where in early 1943 there were over 1,600,000 civilian workers, 527,000 of them women.

In the Balkans, the countries occupied by the Germans and their allies were subjected to a systematic exploitation of their resources. Serbia, under the puppet government of General Neditch, furnished only manpower and raw materials to Germany, but even these were limited by growing popular hostility. The Italian position was even more tenuous in regions they held; even in Albania they met active opposition from the local populations.

1943—THE TURNING POINT OF THE WAR

German military setbacks in the winter of 1942-43, marked by the Anglo-American landing in North Africa on November 8, 1942, and the surrender of the Ninth German army at Stalingrad on February 3, 1943, completely changed the course of the war. German allies began to wonder if they had made the right choice, and resistance movements within most of the occupied countries took new hope and intensified their action against the occupying forces.

Rumania's Sudden Change of Allegiance

The example of the Italian king who, on July 24, 1943, turned his back on Mussolini and signed an armistice with the Anglo-Americans on September 3, gave Germany's allies food for thought. In Rumania, the *Conducator*'s namesake, Foreign Affairs Minister Michael Antonescu, noted the changing situation on the Russian front, and had been trying to establish contact with the Allies since summer of 1943. Antonescu's adversaries increased their efforts to persuade King Michael to dismiss the dictator and ask the Allies for an armistice as the king of Italy had done. In April of 1944, Prince Barbu Stirbey was secretly sent to Cairo to open armistice negotiations. Peace supporters joined together into a National Democratic Front formed on June 20, 1944, which included Bratainu's Liberals, Maniu's National Peasants, Titel Petrescu's Socialists, and even Patrascanu, a representative of the clandestine Communist party. The deteriorating military situation led them to act. The Soviets had crossed the Dniester on August 18, and were dangerously close to the Rumanian border. King Michael, who had given his full support to Antonescu's opponents, had Marshal Antonescu and Michael Antonescu arrested in the Royal Palace on August 23. The king then appointed a new cabinet led by General Sanatescu, and including members of all of the National Democratic Front parties. The

German troops occupying the country were interned, though some units managed to flee to Hungary.

By changing sides at the last minute, the Rumanians expected to be treated as allies. However, Soviet troops immediately moved in and treated the country as a conquered land. The civilian population again had to endure the pillage of the new occupying forces, while the local police were disarmed by the Soviets. Despite the Rumanian government's urgent request to the Anglo-Americans, the Soviets refused to sign an armistice until September 12, 1944. Rumania, who had been the first eastern European state to enter the war, was also the first to leave it.

Bulgaria's Attempts to Negotiate

The Rumanian about-face had immediate repercussions in Bulgaria. Bulgaria was not at war with the USSR, but had economically contributed to the German war effort, causing a break with the Allies. In July, 1942, the underground Communist party appealed to all democratic opposition parties to join in a "Fatherland Front" to fight the pro-German policies of the government. After Stalingrad, the number of guerillas began to grow, and by 1944, they were at least 10,000 strong. Since the tragic disappearance of King Boris III on August 28, 1943, an event blamed on the Germans, a regency council of Prince Cyril, the deceased king's brother, Bogdan Filov and General Milov, administered state affairs in the name of the young king, Simeon II. The regents retained the pro-German policy at first, but in view of growing public discontent and Allied victories, they asked the diplomat Ivan Bagrianov, on June 1, 1944, to form a government capable of opening negotiations with the Allies. Events in Bucharest accelerated changes in Bulgaria. On August 26, Bagrianov stated that Bulgaria, having just revoked its alliance with Germany, intended to remain neutral as it had always been, particularly in the German-Soviet conflict, and as a gesture of Bulgarian goodwill, he ordered troops to evacuate Yugoslavian Macedonia. To please the Anglo-Americans, the regents replaced Bagrianov's government with another led by the Agrarian, Muraviev, nephew of the Agrarian movement's historic leader, Stambolijski, who had been killed by reactionaries in 1923. The appointment was made too late, and did not conform to the Moscow-supported plans of the Bulgarian Communists. The Communist party had ordered its partisans to stand ready on August 26 for a general insurrection in conjunction with the Soviets. On September 5, the USSR declared war on Bulgaria, and on September 8, Soviet troops from Rumania crossed the Danube and entered the country. On the same evening, the Fatherland Front unleashed a general insurrection, seizing the regents and cabinet members. The Bulgarian leaders who had planned to keep their country out of the German-Soviet conflict and step out of a tight spot with a minimum of damages, were badly rewarded for their efforts. The Soviets, who were in a position of strength in the summer of 1944, were not going to let such a strategically placed country escape their influence.

The Failure of Hungary's Diplomacy

Hungarian leaders too, after Stalingrad and the decimation of the Second Army, wanted out of the war. They had also tried to negotiate with the Allies after 1942, and were hoping for an Allied landing in the Balkans or on the Adriatic that would keep them out of a direct confrontation with the Soviets. As a gesture of goodwill toward the Allies, the Kallay government made every attempt to limit Hungarian contributions to the war effort in 1943. Deliveries of supplies were reduced to less than in 1938. The Germans, who were perfectly aware of the secret negotiations, decided on military occupation. On March 15, 1944, Regent Horthy was summoned by Hitler and ordered to increase Hungarian participation, and to form a new, more pro-German government. During these interviews, in the night of March 18, German troops moved in to occupy Hungary and began arresting all those known for anti-German sentiments. Under pressure from Hitler, Horthy confirmed the change worked in his absence and formed a new pro-German government led by Dome Sztojay "to fight the common enemy, particularly bolshevism." But Hungarian diplomats stationed in neutral countries also received orders to maintain contact with the Anglo-Americans. The new government increased Hungarian contributions to the war effort enough to satisfy German demands by supplying German troops still occupying Soviet territory. Relations between German generals and their Hungarian counterparts were difficult, particularly since they held differing concepts of the war. For example, while the German high command ordered captured Russian partisans to be treated like bandits and shot, General Lakatos, commander of Hungarian troops in Russia, told his officers to treat them "with courtesy and humanity."

The presence of the German army in Hungary radically altered the position of the Jews. With the exception of the pogrom of Ujvidek in 1942 in which a thousand Serbians and Jews died, and for which the instigators were publicly reprimanded and punished by the government, Hungary's 800,000 Jews had been relatively well treated. By March, 1944, some 70,000 foreign Jews had fled persecution for refuge in Hungary. The German occupation abruptly and brutally changed their situation. On April 27, the Sztojay government decided to group Jews together in ghettos, and then on orders from the SS officer, Adolf Eichman, began the first conveyances to Germany in mid-May, 1944. Intervention by the Vatican and by Catholic and Protestant churches, and diplomatic protests from neutral countries led to the suspension of these deportations by early July. The Jews were then put to work on local projects.

As the German grip tightened on Hungary, the opposition parties met secretly with encouragement from official circles and agreed, despite their reservations, to join forces with the underground Communist party. During the summer of 1944, as the Red Army's advance was dangerously close, Regent Horthy relieved the Sztojay government of its duties and replaced it with General Lakatos' government which was much cooler toward the Germans. After the signing of the Soviet-Rumanian armistice, Horthy secretly sent an official delegation to the Soviet government to obtain a similar armistice. Such an agreement was signed in Moscow on October 11 and was to go into effect on the 16th. But when on October 15, Admiral Horthy went on the radio to announce that he had just signed an armistice and that Hungary was quitting the war, the Germans invaded the Royal Palace in Budapest and arrested Horthy and his ministers. Then before taking Horthy to Germany, where he was detained until the end of the war, they forced him to name Ferenc Szalasi, head of the Arrow-Cross party, as chief of state. Hungary had come close, but ultimately failed to leave the war.

RESISTANCE MOVEMENTS DURING GERMAN OCCUPATION

As the eventual German defeat became clearer, the various resistance movements in the occupied countries intensified their efforts.

In Bohemia-Moravia, resistance activity was fairly weak—even after German repression following the assassination of Heydrich—and was limited to sabotage, to isolated attacks on "collaborators" and German officials, and to strikes. Resistance groups working with the exiled Benes government in London were heavily infiltrated by members of the underground Communist party, particularly since summer of 1941. The Czech resistance was hardly visible until the last weeks of the war, after American troops had already liberated Pilsen and Soviet troops were already at the gates of Prague. On May 5, 1945, the resistance led a general uprising in the capital directed primarily at German civilians, since the German military had already been evacuated. On May 9, the Red Army entered Prague.

In Slovakia, the resistance began to organize in 1942 in the mountainous regions where Slovak army deserters formed guerilla groups, and were joined by local Communists, autonomists disappointed in Father Tiso's regime and some 1,700 escaped French prisoners of war. At the end of December, 1943, a National Slovak Council was secretly formed in the mountains of central Slovakia by representatives of the Slovak Communist party, such as Gustav Husak, and Protestant members of the Democratic party led by Joseph Lettrich. The goal of this council was the liberation of the country and rebuilding of a Czechoslovakian state in which Czechs and Slovaks would be treated equally, which had not been the case in the first Czechoslovakian republic. In early 1944, the resistance became more aggressive and gained control of vast sections of Slovakia, alarming the government in Bratislava, which called in German troops to restore order. On August 24, 1944, a German convoy containing General Otto, head of the German military mission in Bucharest, was ambushed near Turciansky Sv. Martin (formerly Turoc Szt. Marton). This was the signal for revolt. On August 29, the insurgents seized the city of Banska-Bystrica and its radio station, from which they called for a general insurrection. Regular units of the Slovak army joined them. General Csatlos, Tiso's minister of war, tried to escape but was captured by the insurgents and handed over to the Russians who executed him. For nearly two months, 60,000 Slovak partisans managed to hold several German divisions at bay. They were finally crushed by the weight of numbers, and on October 27, their last center of resistance, Banska-Bystrica, surrendered. The Slovak revolt had cost over 25,000 lives. Isolated groups, badly organized and demoralized, held out here and there, but most of the country was again under German control. Soviet troops fighting in nearby eastern Hungary had made no effort to support the Slovak revolt. They would not make their appearance in Slovakia until the beginning of March, 1945.

In Poland, the spontaneous resistance to German occupation had the backing of almost the entire population. It was directed from London by the Polish government in exile led first by General Sikorski, and after his accidental death on July 4, 1943, by the peasant leader, Stanislaw Mikolajczyk. The behavior of the Soviets between September, 1939, and June, 1941, made the Polish resistance suspicious of Soviet overtures after the outbreak of the German-Soviet conflict. Polish prisoners of war interned in the USSR since September, 1939, who had endured 18 months of Soviet concentration camps, nearly all refused the Soviet offer to fight in the Red Army. After an agreement between generals Anders and Sikorski and the Soviet authorities, the prisoners were transferred to Iran beginning in the summer of 1942, and from there to Egypt, where they were taken into the British army. But thousands of officers and soldiers were still missing, and the slow, evasive Soviet responses to questions about the disappearances only intensified Polish distrust. The men in question had in fact died in the concentration camps. Out of 10,000 Poles interned in the camp at Kolyma, only 583 left it alive. And this is only one example among many. The discovery of the mass grave in the forest of Katyn added even more poison to the already bad relations between the Polish government in exile and the Soviet leadership.

The Polish resistance remained independent of the Soviets, and answered only to London, the only government recognized by the resistance. Its activities were carried out by the Interior Army or *AK (Armia Krajova)* created in 1941 and numbering 380,000 men by 1944. In the country, this army was under the command of General Bor-Komorovski, and operated under orders of an underground parliament, the National Unity Council. The council was presided over by the Socialist, Puzak, and represented by the four democratic opposition parties in the time of the colonel's regime: the Polish Socialist party, the Peasant party, the Christian Workers and the Nationalists.

Beside this "national" resistance, Polish Communists from the USSR who escaped the purges of 1938 were also in Poland trying to counter the activities of the *AK*. In early 1943 they organized a clandestine Polish Worker party within Polish territory. Its resistance fighters were known as the Popular Army or *AL (Armia Ludowa)* commanded by General Rola Zymierski. Its numbers never reached 40,000, a tenth of the *AK*'s.

The record of Polish resistance successes between January 1, 1941 and June 30, 1944, is impressive: 6,930 locomotives and 19,058 railroad cars destroyed, 732 derailments, and nearly 6,000 German officials killed or wounded. But the most spectacular success was the Warsaw uprising on August 1, 1944. At that time, Soviet troops had already advanced deep into Polish territory, accompanied by a unit of Polish volunteers, the Kosciuszko Division. A National Liberation Committee formed in Lublin and led by the leftist Edward Osobka-Morawski and the Communist Boleslaw Bierut, declared itself the "only source of power in the state" on July 22. This power play was strongly resented by the *AK* and the Polish government in exile, and was probably what pushed the *AK* to act. On August 1, *AK* fighters and the citizens of Warsaw began the Warsaw uprising. For 63 days the *AK* and civilians held off German troops, turning every house into a fortress. Although the Soviet army under Marshal Rokossowsky arrived on the right bank of the Vistula in early September, they made no effort to help, even though they were only a few kilometers from the struggle. The Soviets actually refused to allow English and American planes trying to parachute arms and supplies to the fighters to use Russian-held airfields. The head of the Polish government in London, Mikolajczyk, was in Moscow to discuss Poland's future with Stalin, but was unable to convince the Russians to assist the Poles in Warsaw. On October 3, short of ammunition and facing starvation, the freedom fighters surrendered. One hundred thousand of them had died in combat. The *AK* and civilian survivors were deported to Germany and the city was destroyed. When the Red Army took over on January 17, 1945, there was nothing but piles of rubble and deserted ruins.

The Soviets had clearly wanted the Polish resistance to be crushed. While the Poles may have rushed into the uprising, it is almost certain today that on July 29, Radio Moscow broadcast a call to revolt. At any rate, once the fight had begun, the Russians simply stood by and watched. This attitude was certainly not adopted casually; it was deliberately planned. The major goal of the Soviets was less to rid Warsaw of the Germans than to see that the Polish resistance was crippled. Eliminating the *AK* was a prerequisite to setting up a regime more sympathetic to the USSR. In the eastern regions of the country controlled by the Red Army, *AK* members were purposefully hunted down by the Soviet military police. Over 50,000 of them were deported to the USSR and very few returned. It was a strange behavior for the "liberators" of a supposedly "allied" country. When the Red Army took over all of Poland in early 1945, the resistance, which had largely contributed to pushing out the Germans, was almost totally wiped out, and the country was left exhausted and in ruins.

There were similarities between the Yugoslav and the Polish resistance movements: both were able to call up large numbers of fighters who then played a major role in liberating their country. But the similarities ended there. From London on July 22, 1941, King Peter II called for a popular uprising against the occupying forces. In answer to his appeal, General Draga Mihajlovitch, a Serbian appointed as minister of war by the king, organized the first combat groups of the "Chetnik" movement in the mountains of Serbia as the first contingents of a national army to aid the Allies when they landed. The Chetniks waged a cautious kind of guerilla war in hopes of avoiding German reprisals such as the massacre in the Serbian village of Kragujevac in October, 1941, in which the Germans shot 7,000 civilians in reprisal for a guerilla ambush. The Chetniks were devoted to the idea of a "greater" Serbia and to Orthodoxy, and were more likely to quarrel with the Croats and Muslims of Bosnia for the common cause than with the Germans and Italians. On occasion, they even collaborated with the occupants against their rival resistance fighters.

The Chetniks were not the only resistance movement in Yugoslavia. A partisan movement, the communist and federalist inspired National Liberation Front, was founded in late April, 1941, by the secretary general of the party, Josip Broz, nicknamed "Tito." After the Germans invaded Russia, the Partisans called for a national uprising on July 12, 1941. Even though Tito was of Croat origin, the Serbian regions answered his call for resistance most enthusiastically. Mihajlovitch also found most of his followers in Serbia. In late 1941, Tito's Partisans already numbered 80,000 men; by the end of 1943, there were 300,000 of them; and at the end of the war there were 800,000. The Partisans essentially waged a war of attrition and harassment. From their mountain strongholds, they descended into the valleys to sabotage travel routes and communications and to ambush enemy convoys.

At first, the two resistance movements tried to find common ground. Tito and Mihajlovitch met in September, 1941, but failed to come to terms due to the profound political differences between the two, one an old monarchist officer and the other, a Communist revolutionary militant. They also differed on how to fight the occupying forces, and from then on, Tito viewed Mihajlovitch as a traitor. The British tried to bring the royalist resistance and the popular resistance back together, but after Tito's military victories in the field, they withdrew their support from the Chetniks at the end of 1943, and backed only the Partisans. King Peter II actually disavowed his own general after Tito's Partisans managed to liberate almost half of the country, a spectacular feat in that it had been accomplished without outside assistance.

While leading the resistance against the Germans, the Partisans were also planning Yugoslavia's future. At Bihac on November 27, 1942, the anti-fascist Council of the National Liberation of Yugoslavia was created as a provisory government, in preparation for a postwar social democracy. It was designed along the lines of a federal state in which the different nationalities would enjoy equal rights. This underlined, once again, the unequal treatment of certain nationalities in the former Yugoslavia. After Italy's defection in September, 1943, the Partisans recovered some of the war material, weapons and ammunitions abandoned by the Italians, and were able to step up their offensive. In the summer of 1944, Serbia, Macedonia, Montenegro and Bosnia-Herzegovina were almost entirely under the control of the Partisans. Only the areas of Belgrade and the Vojvodina, Croatia and Slovenia still eluded them. The combined forces of the Red Army and the Partisans led to the liberation of Belgrade on October 20, 1944, and to the expulsion of Hungarian troops from the Vojvodina. German troops and the Croat fascists held out in Croatia and Slovenia until early May, 1945. There again, despite assurances from Tito on the future equality of the various peoples, the Croats—and to a lesser degree the Slovenes—were conspicuously absent in the resistance movements. Many Croats were unable to believe Tito's promises.

In Albania, the resistance within the country was somewhat similar to Yugoslavia's in that it achieved liberation. Albania had been part of the Italian Empire since 1939, and Victor-Emmanuel III had replaced Zog I on the throne. At the outset of Italian occupation, a government of conservatives presided over by Shefret Verlaci, an old enemy of Zog, ruled under supervision of the Italian high commissioner, though it quickly incurred growing popular hostility. The Albanians deeply resented the massive influx of Italians preparing for an upcoming attack on Greece, using Albania as a point of departure. After Yugoslavia disappeared and Greece was occupied by the *Wehrmacht*, the Italian government planned to regain public favor by flattering patriotic sentiments through the creation of a "greater" Albania. Kosovo and a few Greek districts with Albanian populations were in fact added to the Albanian state. In December, 1941, the Italians chose a middle-class nationalist, Mustafa Kruja, as head of the Albanian government. But such measures did not placate the opposition. The resistance was already organizing in the mountains. One group was formed by King Zog's former followers, led by Abas Kupi, and supported by the English. The other group, under the aegis of the Communist party, was born at Korca in 1930, and met secretly in Tirana from November 8-14, 1941. They elected a young French-educated intellectual named Enver Hoxha as head of its central committee. The Communists joined the National Liberation Front, open to all enemies of fascism, and from there organized the first groups of partisans who fought the Zogist troops in a veritable civil war beginning in 1943. After the Italian occupying forces were replaced by the Germans in September 1943, the National Liberation Front intensified the battle for liberation. They fought in a similar style to the Yugoslav partisans, with whom they were cooperating actively. As soon as an area was liberated, militant Communists took control, and a provisory government was formed by Enver Hoxha on May 24, 1944. The last of the fighting occurred in October and November, and Hoxha's triumphal entry into Tirana on November 28, 1944, marked the achievement of independence.

The liberation of Albania, like that of Yugoslavia, had been the sole work of the Partisans. Though they had received arms and material from the Anglo-Americans and to a lesser degree from the Soviets, they were loosely organized and had always acted independently without direction from outsiders. It was a unique case in eastern Europe, and the consequences strongly influenced the political development of both countries.

THE END OF THE WAR IN CENTRAL AND EASTERN EUROPE

At the beginning of the winter of 1944-45, the Soviets were about to occupy Hungary, Czechoslovakia and the west of Poland, and they expected to finish with Germany before the end of the winter. They already had a firm grasp on Bulgaria and Rumania as well as the eastern half of Poland, and in Albania and Yugoslavia, Communist-led resistance movements controlled the country.

Only Germany's old allies, Hungary, Croatia and Slovakia, continued to struggle. In Hungary, the abortive attempt for a separate peace and the German dismissal of Regent Horthy had brought Ferenc Szalasi and the extremist Arrow-Cross party to power. Once in power, they turned the country into a police state whose first victims were the Jews. At the same time, Hungary rapidly became a vast battlefield where the *Wehrmacht* and

Hungarian contingents fought the Red Army for nearly six months. Typical of the hard-fought battles was the siege of Budapest, begun by the Soviets on December 25, 1944, and lasting until February 13, 1945. Fighting continued until April 4 in western Hungary, though by then most of the country was under Soviet control. The Szalasi government fled to Germany, and was replaced by the pro-Soviet provisory government formed in late December at Debrecen, one of the first large towns taken by the Red Army.

During the first few months of 1945, German troops were also expelled from the other east European territories. After the fall of Warsaw, on January 17, 1945, the west of Poland was quickly occupied by the Red Army, which then advanced deep into Germany toward Berlin. The capital of the Reich was surrounded on April 19, and fell into Soviet hands on May 2. Further south, the Soviet army was slowed by German resistance in Hungary. At the end of March, Slovakia was finally liberated. Banska-Bystrica, the center of the Slovak uprising of August, 1944, was taken on March 25, and Bratislava, capital of the short-lived independent Slovakian state, fell in turn in early April. Before adjourning its last seating on January 23, 1945, the Slovak parliament expressed the wish that Slovakia be able to maintain its identity in the future. Just before the Red Army entered Bratislava, Father Tiso and several of his ministers crossed over into Austria where they were taken prisoner by the Americans who turned them over to the new Czechoslovak authorities in October, 1945. On April 3, President Benes and his government had already returned to the country they had left in October, 1938, moving into the first sizeable town to be librated, Kosice, known by its old Hungarian name of Kassa from 1938 to 1945. On the following day, Benes announced the Kosice Program which gave a general description of the new Czechoslovakia: the new state would be for Czechs and Slovaks only, implying that the old national minorities would be eliminated. Even further south, Yugoslav Partisans continued the struggle against Ante Pavelitch's fascist Croatian troops and their *Wehrmacht* backers. The Croats resisted tenaciously, and the last battles in northern Slovenia and the northeast ended with the final surrender of Germany on May 8, 1945. To escape the Partisans, the last Croat units surrendered to the Americans holding Austria, but were turned over to Tito.

CONCLUSION: YALTA

In May of 1945, 25 years after the end of the First World War—a war which had completely upset political borders and marked a new beginning for the peoples of eastern Europe—the course of history was redirected. The Wilsonian dream of a Europe of nations in which all peoples, great and small, could live in peace and security, enjoying a spirit of cooperation, had vanished after the treaties of 1919-1920 were signed. Eastern Europe had been politically and geographically restructured according to principles that had little to do with the principles for which armies had fought, leading to frustration, rivalry and heightened antagonism between countries and to a rise in nationalism, to internal instability, and to increased interest in foreign support, support which always came with strings attached.

Twenty years after the end of a bloody and ruinous war, disastrous for all, another even more disastrous war began, leaving in its wake an eastern Europe that was nothing more than a rubble-strewn battlefield. Even more than in 1919, the fate of the people of this part of Europe was in the hands of the victorious powers. Germany's allies and victims alike had decisions imposed on them by the powers of the moment. The Munich Conference had been a prelude to the Second World War, when the Great Powers had decided the future of Czechoslovakia without even consulting its government, and had then imposed a judgement which largely served to open the door for Hitler to the Danubian region. It ended in decisions made in January, 1945, during another international conference, this time at Yalta. Here the new powers, the United States, the United Kingdom and the USSR, decided to place the eastern European countries within the Soviet sphere of influence, and once again ignoring the wishes of the populations. Eastern Europe* as we know it today was born at Yalta. This Eastern Europe includes the Danubian and Balkan states, Poland, and the Russian-occupied part of the former Reich which became the German Democratic Republic in 1949. From Yalta on, Eastern Europe was to live in the shadow of Moscow.

---

* Western and Eastern Europe are capitalized after they become actual political entities at Yalta in 1945.

Part IV

In the Shadow of Moscow

Chapter 21

A Warning

By the end of the war, the USSR had extended its authority over all of Eastern Europe through the presence of its military forces in territories conquered or occupied by Soviet troops after 1944, or through the dominating influence of Soviet ideology in the resistance movements which liberated Albania and Yugoslavia. The USSR had persuaded the Allies to recognize this exceptionally favorable position during diplomatic talks in Teheran and Yalta, and immediately after the war began efforts to consolidate and reinforce it.

Once the Soviets gained this foothold in Eastern Europe, Eastern European history became dominated by the problematic relationships between the governments of its countries and the Soviet Union. In order to understand the policy of the USSR toward all of these countries after 1945, two basic principles of Soviet political philosophy must be kept in mind:

First, as a state, the USSR considered itself under constant threat, real or imagined, from the Western capitalist states—a phobia dating back to the October Revolution, but reinforced by the German invasion in 1941. As a result, the security of the entire stretch of borders facing the Western countries was an overriding priority. To the Soviets, the best way to guarantee this security was to create a wide defensive glacis, a viewpoint which was advanced and successfully argued by Soviet diplomats during negotiations with Hitler before the signing of the Russo-German Pact, and also with the Western Powers during and after the war.

Second, as the first socialist state and the founder of world Communism, the USSR's intention was to extend the politico-economic system it adopted in 1917 to the rest of the world, in particular to those countries forming its "zone of security;" whether this view was publicly stated by the Soviets or dissimulated for various opportunistic reasons, it was a cornerstone of Marxist-Leninist principles, an underlying fact never denied by Kremlin leaders. With these conditions in mind, the Soviets encouraged or imposed Communist-led governments in Eastern Europe. These governments were to be maintained at all costs, against the will of the people and by force if necessary. It also clearly followed that any Communist leader who did not demonstrate unconditional loyalty to the Soviet party line, was stripped of power. The East European Communist leaders implicitly accepted this point of view, this unconditional imperative, sometimes sacrificing their careers and even their lives in the name of the higher interests of the Party and the Soviet state. The baffling behavior of certain East European Communists, which bordered on the masochistic at times, is impossible to explain or understand without taking these given principles into account. Only blind loyalty and an unconditional obedience to Moscow can explain the self-sacrifice of the victims in the trials during the 1950s, who confessed whatever they were asked to confess in the interest of the Party. This behavior was exemplified by the resigned docility of the Czechoslovak Party secretary, Dubcek, who humbly admitted his errors and destroyed his own work in order for people to accept his self-criticism more easily.

The principle of absolute loyalty to the USSR was written into law during the secret meetings held at Szklarska-Poreda from September 22 to 27, 1947, out of which emerged the Cominform (Communist Bureau of Information). Communist party leaders from nine European countries—the USSR, France, Italy, Poland, Hungary, Bulgaria, Czechoslovakia, Rumania and Yugoslavia—unanimously accepted the principle of total, unconditional loyalty to the Soviet Union. From then on, being Communist implied acceptance of Soviet leadership and guidance.

In a few cases Soviet leaders and socialist countries appeared to tolerate some deviation from the principle of absolute fidelity to Moscow, as in Tito's Yugoslavian schism in 1948 or the break in relations with Albania under Enver Hoxha in 1960, but there was no actual show of leniency or change in principles. The explanation for these exceptions lies elsewhere. Neither Yugoslavia nor Albania were under direct Soviet military authority, and therefore the Soviets and their allies did not deem it wise to intervene militarily—as they did in Budapest in 1956 or in Prague in 1968. Such an operation might have had international repercussions. The Soviets, however, never gave up hope of bringing these countries back into the "family." The principle of unconditional loyalty to Moscow and to the socialist camp was still very much in force. For a brief time, it appeared that the relative tolerance of Poland's trade union, Solidarity, lasting for over a year, was an indication that something was changing in the Kremlin. The events that took place in Poland after December 13, 1981, abruptly ended these hopes.

Chapter 22

The New Status of Eastern Europe

The German invasion of Russia brought the Soviet Union into the Second World War, where it became an active and successful participant in military operations against the Reich, and also the most directly affected country in the territorial reorganization of Eastern Europe. In 1919-1920, France played a determining role, imposing its views on its partners; in 1945, it was the USSR who dictated the rules for the peace settlement in Eastern Europe.

IN PREPARATION FOR THE FUTURE STATUS OF EASTERN EUROPE

By the summer of 1941, Great Britain and the United States saw the USSR as an ally and full partner in the struggle against the Axis powers. In their initial meetings with the Allies, the Soviet leaders made it very clear that there would be no question of giving up territory gained in the Russo-German Pact—the three Baltic republics and eastern Poland—nor did they attempt to hide their wish to guarantee their own security as well as East European security against any future German aggression. From 1942 on, the Soviets declared their interest in dividing Germany, and in redistributing part of Italy to Yugoslavia and taking part of Rumania for themselves.

The western Allies were evasive about the question of the Russian border with Poland; the Poles had been an early ally, and France and Great Britain had entered the war for Polish territorial integrity in September, 1939. Thus, no precise provisions were made on the Polish-Soviet border question until 1943. After the victory at Stalingrad, which heightened Soviet prestige, the Anglo-Americans became less antagonistic to Soviet propositions and began to exert pressure on the Polish government in exile to give up claims to the eastern provinces. In return, the USSR was ready to compensate Poland with territory in the west to be taken from Germany. The Polish government firmly refused to abandon the principle of territorial integrity and hardened its position after the discovery of the mass grave at Katyn. When General Sikorski asked for an inquest of the matter by the International Red Cross, the Soviets broke off diplomatic relations with Poland, to the acute embarrasment of the Anglo-Americans. Sikorski's accidental death on July 4, 1943, relieved the pressure on the western Allies, particularly since his successor, Mikolajczyk, seemed more flexible. But attempts to reestablish contact with Moscow remained in an impasse, as Mikolajczyk steadfastly refused to give up the eastern Polish provinces.

At the **Teheran Conference** of November 28 and 29, 1943, Churchill, Roosevelt and Stalin—known as "the Big Three"—discussed the problem of Germany and agreed it was necessary to divide the country. They also spoke of Eastern Europe. The West acknowledged Stalin's hold on the Baltic states and listened again to his views on the Polish border question. Stalin argued that if Poland were to gain Pomerania and Silesia in the west, Danzig in the north and part of eastern Prussia, it was only fair that the Poles should give up the territory beyond the Curzon line. Roosevelt seemed to accept Stalin's arguements, but Churchill was more reticent. Churchill finally agreed to Stalin's demand, provided the Poles found it acceptable. During the same conference, Stalin, supported by Roosevelt, turned down British plans to open a second front in the Balkans. The idea of an Anglo-American landing in the Balkans was totally out of step with Russian plans for expansion in Eastern Europe. The Soviets scored a clear victory when the project was abandoned. Just after the Teheran conference, the Soviets scored another diplomatic coup with the signing of a friendship treaty in Moscow on December 4, 1943, with the Czechoslovak government in exile. In his conversations with Stalin, Benes promised that the Communists would play an important role in the future government of a liberated Czechoslovakia. Benes also insisted that the Soviets erase feudalism in Hungary and Poland; his hatred for these neighboring countries caused him to promote an active Soviet presence in Eastern Europe.

Soviet victories beginning in early 1944, and the Red Army's occupation of Bulgaria, Rumania and part of Poland, convinced the Allies to let the Soviets have their way in all matters concerning Eastern Europe. The Polish question resolved itself when the Soviets set up a national council, which was an actual government based in Lublin in direct defiance of the Polish government in London. The failure of the Warsaw uprising did not help matters for the Poles in London. In October, 1944, Mikolajczyk went to Moscow accompanied by Churchill, and was compelled to accept the borders Stalin demanded as well as the fusion of the London government and the Lublin Committee. Mikolajczyk was disowned by his colleagues and replaced as head of the government in exile by Tomasz Arciszewski, a socialist dedicated to preserving the territorial integrity of his country. But this change of leadership had no effect on the course of events. The Great Powers had decided to settle the Polish question without the Poles.

The **Yalta Conference**, from February 4 to 11, 1945, was the first to deal with the fate of Germany, whose territory was divided into zones of occupation under each victorious power. In Poland, the initial Soviet plan was accepted using the Curzon line as the new Polish-Soviet frontier, and giving Poland territorial compensation at Germany's expense. Churchill managed to assure Poland, however, that a Polish national union government would be formed with members from the Lublin Committee to prepare for the election of an assembly to organize the new Poland. At Yalta, the Big Three put together a document which emphasized their own responsibilities in the future organization of the "liberated states and the former satellite states of the Axis powers in Europe;" the Allied powers pledged to encourage the formation of "governments by representatives of all democratic elements of the population, that would organize free elections as soon as possible to establish governments responsive to the will of the people." In actuality, expressions like "democratic elements of the population" and "free elections" did not hold the same meaning everywhere. The Anglo-Americans were certainly aware of this, but taking into account the Red Army's presence in Eastern Europe at the time, it was difficult for them not to give the Soviets *carte blanche* in those areas they already occupied. Thus, the Big Three divided Europe among themselves at Yalta.

Less than three months after the German defeat, the **Potsdam Conference** (July 17—August 2, 1945) completed the arrangements made at Yalta. The Allied foreign affairs ministers were asked to draw up peace treaties with Germany's former allies, while the treaty with Germany itself was to be drawn up later. Major policy decisions regarding Germany were made and the exact lines of the different zones of occupation set. The Anglo-Americans and the Soviets finally ratified their Yalta agreement on Poland's new borders with the USSR. Once again, the peoples of Eastern Europe had had their fate decided for them.

THE NEW TERRITORIAL FRAMEWORK OF EASTERN EUROPE

Sanctions Against the Defeated Countries

Bulgaria and Rumania, despite their change of allegiance toward the end of the war, were considered defeated countries just like Hungary. The conditions of the armistice signed by the new leaders just as the fighting ceased was premonitory; the armistices returned the borders to the lines of 1937 with a few adjustments. Germany's three former allies first had to make restitutions to their victims in gold or merchandise: Rumania, 300 million dollars, but 200 to the Soviet Union and 50 each to Czechoslovakia and Yugoslavia; Bulgaria, 70 million, with 25 going to Yugoslavia and the rest to the USSR—despite the fact that Bulgaria had only been at war with the USSR for a few days, and not even that by choice! The Soviets used these reparations as an indirect method to further weaken the countries they occupied, continuing this strategy by demanding deliveries of foodstuffs and raw materials. All German assets in defeated territory automatically became the property of the USSR—and Germany had invested heavily in Eastern Europe. Through confiscated German assets, the Soviets came into control of large and key sectors of the economies of Hungary, Bulgaria and Rumania. These three countries were also to be placed under occupation by Soviet troops until the signing of the peace treaties. For the duration of the occupation, an "Allied Commission" was responsible for "regulating and supervising the execution of the terms of the armistice under the leadership of the Soviet Commandant and with the participation of representatives of Great Britain and the United States."

After several meetings of the Allies, the defeated countries were invited to Paris to sign the peace treaties on February 10, 1947. Bulgaria did fairly well territorially; it kept the southern Dobrudja that Rumania had ceded in 1945, but had to relinquish the Greek and Yugoslav territory occupied in 1941. Hungary was returned to the Treaty of Trianon borders with the exception of three villages on the Danube across from the city of Bratislava, which were ceded to Czechoslovakia. Hungary thus lost all the territory regained between 1938 and 1941. Rumania recovered the northern part of Transylvania that it lost to Hungary in 1940, but had to surrender all claims to Bessarabia and Bukovina, territories which the USSR had taken at the same time in 1940. Restitutions set by the terms of the armistice were confirmed by the peace treaties. The three countries were all restricted militarily, and the USSR planned to bring them into the Soviet security system. The treaties also authorized the Soviet Union to maintain troops in Hungary and Rumania so that it was assured of contact with its zone of occupation in Austria.

Countries of the Victors

The new Polish borders were drawn according to the decisions made at Yalta and Potsdam. For the western Allies, these borders were only provisory, and in their eyes, they would be legally finalized only by the peace treaty with Germany; until the agreements signed by Willy Brandt and the Polish government, the "new Polish provinces" were considered to be under "provisory Polish administration" by the western Allies. The Soviets and the Poles on the other hand, considered the borders to be final.

In the west, the border between Poland the Soviet zone in Germany followed the Oder River and its tributary, the Neisse. Poland gained substantial advantages such as a broad maritime coast stretching from the mouth of the Oder to the mouth of the Vistula, the rich farmlands of Pomerania and Prussia, and especially Silesia with one of the richest coal beds in Europe. In the east, however, Poland lost everything east of the Curzon line except for the city of Przemysl, which it kept, and shared eastern Prussia with the USSR. Looking at the total picture, Poland in 1945 was 30,880 square miles smaller than in 1938, had shifted westward with an off-centered capital, and had a better balanced economy with sizeable industrial potential in Silesia and a much more extensive maritime coastline than the narrow Danzig corridor.

Albania and Yugoslavia were also subject to border realignment. Albania returned to its borders of 1939, but Yugoslavia made some gains on its western border: Italy surrendered Istria, except for the city of Trieste, a large part of Julian Venetia, and the port of Fiume which became Rijeka.

The Soviet Union was really the main beneficiary in the war, as its borders moved noticeably westward. Already at Teheran and Yalta, the USSR had garnered official recognition of its sovereignty over the Baltic republics of Estonia, Latvia and Lithuania—acquired first in 1940, then occupied by the Germans from 1941-1944, then reacquired during the winter of 1944-1945. The USSR also annexed the north part of eastern Prussia with the city of Konigsberg, renamed Kalingrad. This push to the west was also at the expense of its official allies. The USSR was not satisfied with eastern Poland, and despite promises to Benes to respect Czechoslovakian territorial integrity, forced Prague to surrender Carpathian Ruthenia after stirring up the local population. On January 29, 1945, a Russo-Czechoslovak agreement officially marked the withdrawal of Czechoslovakia from the area. The USSR then held both sides of the Carpathian mountain chain, putting an end to the common border between Rumania and Czechoslovakia and advancing deep into the Hungarian plain. It was a major strategic position: ethnically, the region was mainly Ruthenian, but had a sizeable Hungarian minority.

Expulsion of Germans from Eastern Europe (1945-1947) and exodus of German citizens from GDR to GFR (1945-61)

NATIONAL MINORITIES AND POPULATION TRANSFERS

The new political makeup of Eastern Europe increased the number of national minorities. The Great Powers responsible for the new organization were aware of the problem; to minimize the risks, they allowed countries acquiring new territories to expel whole populations. At the Potsdam Conference, the deportation option was extended to include all populations foreign to Eastern Europe. The main victims of these relocations were the Germans, Poles and Hungarians. Germans in eastern Prussia and in regions acquired by Poland were promptly and indiscriminately deported to Germany in the winter of 1945-1946. For the government in Czechoslovakia, the option to expel minorities sanctioned by the Allies was advantageous, as it happened to coincide with the Kosice Program which limited the Czechoslovakian state to Czechs and Slovaks only. Between May and

August, 1945, 800,000 Germans were deported to Austria, and after the Potsdam Conference, the 2,500,000 Germans remaining in Czechoslovakia were driven out under particularly harsh conditions. Only 155,000 anti-Nazi, or reputedly anti-Nazi, Germans were allowed to remain in the country. The other Danubian states also expelled Germans who had lived in certain areas for centuries. Out of the 600,000 Germans in Hungary, only 250,000 were allowed to stay, and over half of the 780,000 Germans in Rumania were deported. But the fate of the Yugoslav Germans was the most tragic. Apart from 80,000 who were sent to Germany in 1943, 450,000 remained in Yugoslavia in 1945; out of these remaining, from 140,000 to 260,000 (depending on the source), were massacred during the deportation, while the rest suffered great hardships arriving in Austria.

The Soviets treated the two million Poles within their annexed territories similarly, deporting them to Poland where they were resettled in the western regions just vacated by the Germans Simultaneously, the Polish government invited Polish emigrants to return and fill the void left in the wake of war. Nearly two million of them answered the call.

The only national minorities unaffected by mass relocation were the Albanians and the Bulgaro-Macedonians in Yugoslavia, and most of the Hungarians who had already been placed under the authority of neighboring states in 1919. Czechoslovakia would have liked to eliminate the Hungarian minority in southern Slovakia. Several thousand Hungarians were in fact deported to Hungary in 1945, and then on February 27, 1946, an agreement between the Hungarian and Czechoslovak governments authorized an exchange of Hungarian "war criminals" and "traitors to the Czechoslovak homeland" for Hungarian Slovaks who wanted to move to Czechoslovakia. About 30,000 people were exchanged in this way. Tens of thousands of Hungarians considered to be undesirable in Slovakia but also necessary to the Czechoslovak economy were moved to the Sudetenland to replace the recently deported Germans. They were not able to return to their own villages until 1948-1949.

The ethnic map of Eastern Europe of 1947 was much less complicated than that of 1938. The German minorities had nearly entirely disappeared as a result of the population transfers, a better term for which would be "deportations," considering the conditions under which these transfers took place. Thousands of destitute men, women and children were forced to travel, usually on foot and in the dead of winter, over hundreds of miles. The national minorities had become less numerous, but the cost of achieving this objective was very high, perpetuating national hatreds.

CONCLUSION

At the close of the Second World War, the Soviet Union emerged as the main beneficiary of the changes in Eastern Europe, and was the only country to make major territorial gains. The Soviets were able through their acquisitions to accomplish the major policy goal of establishing a defensive glacis to the west; the Red Army was on guard from the North Sea to the Adriatic, from the Baltic Sea to the Danube. The Soviet military presence gave Moscow extraordinary means of pressure on the Eastern European governments. Soviet take-over of German assets in countries formerly allied with Germany gave the USSR major economic advantages, advantages reinforced by the integration of East Germany into the Soviet system. For the victorious countries such as Czechoslovakia or Poland, the military power of the USSR appeared to offer the most effective protection against the possibility of yet another German aggression. Thus, the postwar era began with the Soviet Union's overwhelming influence on the direction of Eastern European affairs.

Chapter 23

The Birth of Popular Democracies

Following the military crippling of the Reich and its allies, the political regimes linked to Germany were eliminated and the German-occupied territories liberated. Then, the major problem became filling the political voids left by the ousted powers with governments capable of the political, economic and moral reconstruction of the war-torn countries of Eastern Europe.

AN ENVIRONMENT FAVORABLE FOR THE COMMUNISTS

There are two factors to be considered when tracing the progress of the Communists from an initially weak force to one which managed to take control of the governments of Eastern Europe: the omnipresent Red Army and the Communist-dominated resistance movements. Legitimized by the Soviet Union's status as a victorious power, the Red Army occupied Rumania, Bulgaria, Hungary, eastern Austria and the German territories between the Elbe and the Oder-Niesse line unresisted; it moved into Czechoslovakia and Poland as a co-belligerent and ally. Only Albania and Yugoslavia escaped occupation by Soviet troops, as they had been liberated and were still held primarily by indigenous Communist resistance fighters.

The presence of the Red Army had a definite influence on the selection of the new leadership in the Eastern European countries. The local commander-in-chief was in a position to support or dismiss the local authorities and to intervene in the interior affairs of the country. The occupiers controlled the media, and were in a position to authorize or censure any publication until the signing of the peace treaties. For nearly two years, these occupied countries were essentially controlled by Soviet authorities. Moreover, any activity contrary to Soviet interests could be legally construed as "anti-Soviet subversive activity" and the perpetrators arrested by the all-powerful Soviet military police. This method was frequently used to eliminate influential journalists or politicians who did not choose to collaborate with the Communists. The arrest in February, 1947, of the Hungarian peasant leader Bela Kovacs by the Soviet military police for anti-Soviet activities is but one example of these direct interventions in the interior affairs of the defeated states. The same tactics were also employed in supposedly friendly countries. Numerous high officers of the Polish Interior Army, including Puzak, a socialist who had presided over the clandestine parliament during the war, were arrested in early 1945 and secretly sent to Moscow, where they were tried (June 18-21, 1945) for "planning military action against the Soviet Union in conjunction with Germany." The accusation was ludicrous in view of the heavy tribute the Polish resistance had paid to the Nazis. But the Polish resistance was not of much value to the Soviets, since it was not dominated by the Communists. In Puzak's case, as in Kovacs', the Soviets were simply eliminating capable and popular politicians who were known for their anti-Communist sentiments.

Another method the Soviet military authorities used to make their presence felt in occupied countries was to tolerate, even encourage, extortion of the civilian population by Red Army units. In countries considered to be allies such as Poland or Czechoslovakia, or in defeated countries being treated carefully like Bulgaria, the behavior of Soviet soldiers was beyond reproach, but in Rumania, Hungary, Ruthenia, and especially in Germany, extortion and violence were the rule during the first few months of the occupation. Between August 23 and September 12, 1944, the Soviet troops went on a rampage of looting and raping through Rumania, a country which had voluntarily admitted the Red Army. Thousands of civilians were kidnapped and sent to the USSR, where they were forced to work on reconstruction projects, not to be repatriated until 1947 or even later. In Hungary, the behavior of Soviet soldiers was just as brutal. On Good Friday, 1945, the bishop of Gyor, who was defending a group of women taking refuge in his church, was killed by Soviet soldiers. In Budapest, thousands of civilians were taken away to work in the Soviet Union until 1947. Even the Swedish diplomat Raoul Wallenberg, who had intervened on behalf of the Jews during their persecution, was kidnapped by the Soviet military police and never seen again. Such tactics revealed a deliberate intent to demoralize the population and to nip any resistance in the bud, preparing public acceptance for changes to come.

In Yugoslavia and Czechoslovakia, the Partisans committed the acts of violence. Yugoslavian Croatia was treated as a defeated country and thousands of Croats died in the Partisan-led punitive campaigns. Thousands of Hungarians and Germans were massacred in the reconquest of the province of Vojvodina. In Czechoslovakia, the Slovak "collaborators" and members of the German and Hungarian minority were victimized. The ulterior motive of the Soviets or Partisans in permitting or perpetrating the violence was to create a climate of terror in areas where their political plans might meet with resistance. The population was being bombarded simultaneously with propaganda by the local Communists, who offered collaboration as the only way to put an end to the violence.

Another element contributing to Communist success was the ruined economy of the Eastern European states. While Czechoslovakia and Bulgaria were relatively well-off, other countries were devastated. Human loss had been heavy everywhere, and industrial potential as well as transportation and communication systems were barely functional. In Germany and the defeated countries, what had not been destroyed was dismantled and carried off as reparation. Moreover, the battles that took place on Hungarian, Polish, and German territory badly impaired agricultural potential, resulting in practically yieldless harvests in 1944 and 1945. Shortages of food added to the hardships. By clever manipulation of propaganda, large property-owners and speculators were made the scapegoats for the economic problems, while providentially stocked markets were attributed to the generosity of the Soviet liberators. Economic difficulties meant high inflation everywhere, particularly in Rumania and Hungary, where it surpassed all records in monetary history—including the German inflation of 1923.

In addition, massive population shifts caused by the deportation of thousands of prisoners-of-war to the Soviet Union—more than 300,000 from Hungary alone—as well as the return of Polish emigrants to Poland, led to a sociological upheaval so great that normal political life was all but impossible. Finally, the civilian populations everywhere were so physically and morally exhausted by the five terrible years they had just lived through, that they were ready to accept any changes as long as they included a return to normal living conditions.

THE ESTABLISHMENT OF NEW REGIMES

The political transformations that took place between 1944 and 1948 in Eastern Europe all resulted in takeovers of the governments by the local Communist parties—under the guidance of the Soviet Union. "Popular democracies" or "people's republics" emerged in all of these countries. The Soviets thus achieved their goal of having the Western Allies recognize Russian dominance over this part of Europe with a bare minimum of conflict.

In the beginning of the postwar period, the Communist parties in Eastern Europe were small, with the exception of Czechoslovakia whose prewar Communist party membership had already been high. In general, the indigenous Communist parties had either been decimated by Nazi persecutions—as in Germany—or were opposed by existing social structures and attitudes stemming from historic unpopularity. In many cases, the links between local Communist parties and the Soviet Union added to their unpopularity. Despite these handicaps, the Communists had gained control of all of the governments in Eastern Europe by 1948. Their ascent to power varied country to country, as they compensated for their relatively small numbers with careful strategy. In some countries, the governments were rapidly and expediently transformed, while in others, the change took place in states, often by turning a coalition government into a single-party system.

The Method of Expedience

—Bulgaria, Albania and Yugoslavia

In Bulgaria, Albania and Yugoslavia, the Communist ascent to power was rapid; by the end of 1945, Communist regimes were firmly in place. The Soviets were particularly interested in Bulgaria, a Slavic country with a strong pro-Russian tradition dating back to its first days of independence. The country's revolutionary tradition in 1919-1920 was distinguished by both a strong agrarian movement and by its Communist party, whose secretary general, Georgi Dimitrov, was a highly respected figure in the Communist world. The Communists had taken over the resistance movement with the cooperation of Agrarians like Nicolas Petkov, and Social Democrats through the Fatherland Front formed in 1942. When Soviet troops invaded Bulgaria on September 8, 1944, the Fatherland Front led a general uprising involving the whole country and took over the government the following night. Provisory authorities were put in charge throughout the land. A provisory government was formed in Sofia under Colonel Georgiev, an ex-military man from the extreme-rightest Zveno group, who had gone over to the Communists. The Georgiev government immediately signed an armistice with Marshal Tolbuhin, commandant of the Soviet troops, and committed the Bulgarian army to the military struggle against Germany. While the army was kept busy outside the country after October 8, the Fatherland Front's militia moved in to police the country.

The new government immediately instigated a radical purge of "war

criminals" for its own expedience. The regents, numerous bourgeois party deputies, many high civil servants and other leading citizens, and any government officials in power since 1941, were arrested and taken before the people's courts. The official purge affected nearly 11,000 persons, and was followed by 2,138 executions, including those of the three Regents, Prince Cyril, Bogdan Filov and General Milov, as well as the former prime minister, Bagrianov. Looking ahead to the elections planned in late 1945, the Communists were able to eliminate the conservative right and the bourgeois party leaders with the assent of their Fatherland Front allies. Moreover, through their takeover of municipal administrations, they controlled the electoral lists. The non-Communist parties in the Front consisted of the Agrarian Union of Nicolas Petkov, the People's Union, the Zveno group and the Socialists. They were divided between presenting a single list under the Front banner and drawing up separate lists. Those favoring a single list won out, and those who favored separate lists regrouped around Nicolas Petkov. In the election of November 18, 1945, the single list of the Fatherland Front polled 88 percent of the votes. Suspecting fraud, the opposition called in vain for new elections. Bolstered by their success, the new government began to rework the country's institutions. Following the referendum of September 8, 1946, in which 92.7 percent of the Bulgarians voted for a republic, the monarchy was abolished and on September 15 the Communist Basil Kalarov became prime minister of the Bulgarian republic. The next month, elections for a constituent assembly began. The Front list polled 70 percent of the votes and gained 362 seats, including 275 for the Communist party. Petkov's opposition polled 30 percent of the votes, but won only 99 seats. With an absolute majority in the assembly, the Communists began to undermine Petkov, whose power base was centered in the countryside. He was accused of treason, arrested, condemned to death and quickly hung on September 23, 1947. After the elections, in October of 1946, Georgi Dimitrov became premier. The process begun on September 9, 1944, had led to absolute control of the state by the Communists. The constitution adopted on December 4, 1947, declared the country the Bulgarian People's Republic, confirming officially what Bulgaria had been in fact since the end of 1944.

In Albania, the establishment of a popular democracy was the direct result of the National Liberation Front's victory. Despite British support of the Zogist resistance, the National Liberation Front was already in control of half of the country by the end of the war. On May 24, 1944, a congress was held at Pernet, the first city to be liberated, to form a provisory parliament; a provisory government was also formed and called the Antifascist Committee, with Enver Hoxha, secretary general of the Albanian Communist party, as president. After the last German troops were expelled, Hoxha controlled all of the country except for a few mountainous districts held by supporters of King Zog. In early December, the Communists began to hunt down the Zogists and any national opposition. Hundreds were condemned to death by popular tribunals and summarily executed. Having eliminated the potential opposition, Hoxha called elections for December 2, 1945. The single list of candidates presented by the Democratic Front under Hoxha polled 93 percent of the votes. The constitution of 1946 then sanctioned these transformations and made Albania a popular democracy.

The resistance army's victory in Yugoslavia put Tito and the Antifascist

Council of the National Liberation of Yugoslavia (AVNOJ) in an excellent position to take control of the government. According to a compromise signed at the time of liberation by Tito and Ivan Subachitch, a representative of King Peter, Yugoslavia was to be a federal and democratic state. A constituent assembly was to decide whether the monarchy would be retained or abolished. When Tito signed this agreement in December, 1944, he was well aware that he risked nothing as he possessed a considerable advantage with his 800,000 soldiers. On March 7, 1945, in accordance with the agreement, Tito formed a government which included representatives of the royal government such as Soubachitch in foreign affairs, but which was dominated by Communist allies of Tito from different Yugoslav nationalities; the Slovene Edward Kardelj, the Serb Alexander Rankovitch, and the Montenegrin Milovan Djilas were most prominent among his highly-placed allies. Of the 28 ministers, 23 were Communist. The real power in the country was in the hands of Tito's supporters, who were placed strategically throughout the country. They controlled local governments, purged the legal system and the civil service, and dispensed summary justice through official and officious popular tribunals to eliminate "collaborators," or, more simply, political opponents. In addition, non-Communist newspapers were banned, and political meetings of non-Communist movements were impeded. The ministers who had come from London resigned in protest, while the opposition asked voters to boycott the elections. The only candidates were members of the People's Front, a vast organization that had replaced the National Liberation Front. It was directed by Tito and the Communists, and included a variety of groups such as the unions and the Young Communists. The elections were held on November 11, 1945, with all Yugoslavs invited to participate except for the several hundred thousand whose names had been crossed off the polling registers for political reasons. The People's Front won 90.48 percent of the vote. Over 11 percent of the voters heeded the advice of the opposition and did not vote.

The first decision of the constituent assembly in its opening meeting on November 29, 1945, was to announce the Federal People's Republic of Yugoslavia. Its organization was then detailed in the constitution of January 30, 1946—modeled after the Soviet constitution of 1936. In 1946, the Communist world saw Tito as one of Stalin's most faithful disciples; he had certainly demonstrated that he'd learned how to purge and eliminate his adversaries. Tens of thousands of his opponents were physically eliminated in 1945 and 1946. The Croats were particularly targeted, even though Tito himself was of Croat origin. He came down hard on any of his compatriots who had cooperated with Ante Pavelitch, the Ustashian leader, or had served in his army or government. Over 100,000 Croat soldiers who had taken refuge in Austria were extradited by the Anglo-Americans and given over to

Tito. Thousands were executed. It was not enough to track down the "collaborators" of independent Croatia or occupied Serbia; the Chetniks were also persecuted. They had fought the Germans since the early days of the war, but Tito quickly accused them of "collaboration." Their leader, General Mihajlovitch, was condemned to death and executed in June, 1946. The Catholic Church was also hard hit, as hundreds of priests in Croatia, Vojvodina and Slovenia were summarily executed in 1945. The Archbishop of Zagreb, Father Stepinac, was accused of "collaboration" and condemned on October 11, 1946, to 16 years in prison, despite the fact that he had persistantly played a moderating role, urging the Croat leaders to use restraint in Croatia.

—The Deception of Poland

At the end of the war, Poland was unique in being considered a friend and ally of the Soviet Union, and in having a legal government in exile with armed forces under its command. Some 100,000 of these soldiers, commanded by General Anders, fought alongside the Allied forces in the liberation of Italy. The others, in the Interior Army or *AK*, were engaged in a constant struggle against the German occuping forces within Polish territory. To stir up matters, the Soviets established a National Liberation Committee in Lublin made up of Communists and Communist sympathizers. On July 22, 1944, it declared itself the only legal government of Poland. After the failure of the Warsaw uprising and the elimination of the survivors of the Interior Army by the Soviets, the Lublin-based committee had ample opportunity to establish its own government in each area as it was liberated. In this way, the Communists and their sympathizers gained control of all the towns. At the Yalta Conference, the Big Three had recommended enlarging the National Liberation Committee to include representatives of the government in exile. The Poles in London, however, refused to cooperate with the Committee members. Despite opposition from the heads of the government in exile, the Socialist Arciszewski and General Anders, Stanislaw Mikolajcyk agreed to return to Poland on personal grounds. On June 29, 1945, a Provisional Government of National Unity was formed by Edward Osobka-Morawski, a pro-Communist Socialist, in which Lublin committee members held 17 of the 21 posts. Mikolajczyk and Gomulka were made deputy premiers, with Osobka-Morawski as president. Another Communist, Boleslaw Bierut, remained president of the provisory parliament, called the National Home Council. Most of the ministers were Communists or men with pro-Communist leanings.

The major accomplishment of the Polish Communist leaders and the Soviets during the period of the National Liberation Committee in Lublin, had been to instigate the creation of political parties that did not seem to be

Communist. These parties used acronyms similar to traditional democratic parties, but were actually led by opportunists who had deserted the traditional parties for the Communists, and acted as fronts for the Party. To counter the Socialist party led from London by Arciszewski, Lublin set up a Polish Workers' party of Socialists led by Osobka-Morawski, which assumed the London-based party's name on September, 1944. A dissident Peasant party and a dissident Democratic party were created in the same way. The names of these new political groups were deliberately chosen to resemble those of recognized parties and thus confuse the population.

The provisory government should have organized elections immediately, but instead pushed the date back to January, 1947. A single list of candidates was prepared by the Polish Worker party (the Communist party) with the approval of the dissident parties from Lublin. Mikolajczyk was offered a quarter of the seats if he would only agree to the single list principle. He refused, but the die had already been cast. For an entire year before the voting, the government had been systematically undermining the traditional parties' efforts to reorganize; their publications were banned and their public meetings sabotaged. A smear campaign was mounted against the London members of the government who for the most part had refused to return to Poland under the circumstances. Survivors of the Interior Army were also targeted. They were accused of anti-Soviet activities, since some of them had tried to organize underground resistance fighting groups in the south of the country. It was, to say the least, a tough electoral campaign. The "official" candidates of the "democratic bloc" led by the Communists were given every opportunity to present their program to the voters. This was not the case, however, for the Independent Socialists and friends of Mikolajczyk, whose candidacy had to be requested in writing by 1,000 voters in each district. Communist-dominated municipal authorities disqualified over a million voters from the registers for trumped-up reasons, and consequently, the signatures of these disqualified voters were declared void on the opposition candidates' lists. In this way, 246 Peasant party candidates were eliminated and 149 of them arrested. Even more Independent Socialists were disqualified. After the ballots were cast, hardly any representatives of the opposition were allowed to observe the counting of the votes. Under these conditions, the January 19, 1947, elections resulted in a 90 percent landslide for the Communist block parties. The opposition was only able to elect 28 deputies, 27 of them from Mikolajczyk's Peasant party, and one Independent Socialist, Zulawski, from Cracow. At the first seating of the new parliament, Zulawski denounced the tactics used, daring to state, "The elections were not free; in reality, there were no elections at all, only an organized terrorism of the voter and his conscience." His speech was censured, as was one in a similar vein delivered by Mikolajczyk, who soon gave up the struggle and fled the country the following October.

In the four cases just examined—Bulgaria, Albania, Yugoslavia and Poland—only minor differences caused by local conditions differentiated the expedient process by which the Communists rose to power. In the first stage, the Communists took control of key posts, aided by the groups they had infiltrated and supported by the Red Army and Communist-led resistance fighters. These infiltrations occurred at all levels of the police, the army and the secret police, and took place as soon as a real or provoked power vacuum occurred. Then, in the second stage, in control of the government, courts, and police, they called elections to legalize the new power structure *a posteriori*.

The Progressive Method

—Rumania: From Constitutional Monarchy to Popular Democracy

Rumania's progression from dictatorship to Communist regime by seemingly democratic steps, was a special case. Ion Antonescu's dictatorship was eliminated by the August 23, 1944, *coup d'etat* by a National Democratic Front formed by the Liberals, the Social-Democrats, the Peasant Party and the Communists, under the initiative of King Michael. In its place, a short-lived national union government was formed under the leadership of General Sanatescu.

The new government immediately came up against a variety of difficulties caused by the onerous and costly presence of the Red Army, social tensions linked to galloping inflation, food shortages, peasant unrest instigated by Petru Groza's Communist Plowmen's Front, and worker unrest excited by the Communist-led *Apararea Patriotica*. (The latter group, composed of armed workers, had received aid for use against the Germans and Antonescu's Partisans at the time of the August 23 events.) The opportunity was ripe for the Communists to increase their strength: Rumanian Communist leaders in exile in Moscow were liberated and returned, such as Secretary General Gheorgiu-Dej, Anna Pauker, and Vasile Luca—all three carefully selected and indoctrinated for their return to Rumania. In addition, numerous former supporters of Antonescu wishing to clear themselves joined the ranks of the Communist party *en masse*. The Communist party was consequently strengthened in numbers and influence. From October, 1944, onward, the Communists united to establish the National Democratic Front as the dominant political force. The established parties reluctantly joined, and soon found themselves thrown in with Communists and Communist-controlled mass organizations in the reconstruction of a new independent Rumania that had to be protected from the "enemies of democracy." Under these circumstances, General Sanatescu resigned on November 6, 1944, and formed a new government in which the Communists were given an increased number of ministerial posts. Gheorgiu Dej became Minister of Transportation, Lucretiu Patrascanu became Minister of Justice, Nicolai was appointed Minister of Social Affairs, and, most importantly, Georgescu was made under-secretary of state. Lack of a common point of view created discord in the cabinet, particularly in the face of recurring Communist-instigated rioting by workers. After only one month in office, the second Sanatescu government was dissolved and was replaced on December 5, 1944, by one led by the openly anti-Communist General Radescu. The Communists, however, retained all their previous ministerial posts. Rioting intensified throughout the country with demonstrations against high prices, and in favor of agrarian reform and nationaliations. Throughout this time, the Communists Petrescu and Georgescu concentrated on "purifying" local governments, courts and police through purges. The army, which had joined the Soviets in fighting the Germans, was out of the country, but the few units stationed within Rumania did not escape the purge.

In early 1945, the Communists began to reap the fruits of their labors. They had managed to attract many of the discontents to their side, including the Hungarian minority party *Madosz*, the Hungarian People's Union, which had been harshly treated when the Rumanian authorities regained northern Transylvania. The Communists accused General Radescu of favoring reactionary elements in the country, and unleashed a country-wide campaign calling for his resignation. As in Poland, the Communists had infiltrated the non-Communist parties in order to sow discord and confuse the general population. The namesakes of the Liberal and National Peasant parties sprang up alongside the originals, under the leadership of Georgi Tatarescu and Alex Alexandrescu respectively.

The political situation became more and more confusing. On February 24, 1945, the Communists organized mass demonstrations against fascism and the Radescu government in Bucharest. The Red Army provided trucks and gasoline to transport the demonstrators. Shots were exchanged that evening. The Communists blamed Radescu, who in turn broadcast his reply on the radio blaming:

> ...the stateless foreigners without God or country... ...horrible hyenas, the Jewess Anna Pauker and the Hungarian Vasile Luca, foreign by their nationalities to the aspirations of the Rumanian people.

At that point, the Soviets decided to intervene directly. The Soviet vice-minister of foreign affairs, Andrei Vychinsky, arrived in Bucharest on February 27 and demanded to see the king immediately to call for a new government. When King Michael refused, Vychinski ordered the new commandant of the Soviet forces in Rumania, General Sussaykov, to disarm the gendarmerie and the Rumanian police as well as the garrison at Bucharest. The following day he repeated his demand as an ultimatum. The king hoped to placate the Soviets by replacing General Radescu with Prince Stirbey. Vychinski refused the offer during a stormy interview, and the king yielded to pressure, appointing the Communist Petru Groza as premier. On March 6, 1945, the Communist-dominated Groza cabinet took office. The liberal dissident Georgi Tatarescu, discredited by his collaboration with the dictatorship under King Carol II, became minister of foreign affairs. A short time later, Moscow sent Marshal Malinovsky to Rumania, officially to dismantle a so-called military plot against the Soviets supposedly hatched by Radescu and his friends. Nevertheless, the situation slowly began to ease. Under pressure from the British and the Americans, the National Peasant and Liberal ministers were even brought back into the government. The Communists, however, were in control of all key posts throughout the country in both the national and local governments. Knowing that they could always rely on the Soviets, they began tightening their grip on the state. In control of the judicial system, they were able to initiate purges, weeding out "collaborators" who refused to support the new government. The dictator Antonescu was tried at the end of May, 1946, and was immediately executed. Prominent members of the preceding regime were "rehabilitated."

Most of 1946 was spent paving the way for the November 19 elections. The electoral campaigns took place in a climate of tension and oppression. National Peasant and Liberal candidates who, along with Petrescu and the Socialist left, had refused to join with the Communists in preparing the list, were all but prevented from taking part in the campaign at all. Many of them were arrested and beaten by a police force that was once again brutal and unprincipled. The election results were not made public until four days after the polls had closed, and during this time the ballot-boxes had been in the hands of municipal authorities loyal to the Communist party. It came as no surprise, then, that the government bloc polled over 5,800,000 votes—or 71 percent of the vote—while the combined opposition polled 1,200,000 votes and was magnanimously granted 34 out of the 414 seats. This was still too much for the Communists. They decided to completely eliminate the opposition. The National Peasant party was declared illegal in August 1947; shortly beforehand, on July 14, one of its leaders, Ion Mihalache, was arrested and charged with high treason as he was preparing to flee the country. The other Peasant leader, Maniu, along with several different party officials, were also arrested. Following a trial in front of a people's tribunal presided over by Colonel Alexander Petrescu, the former director of prisons and concentration camps under Antonescu, Jules Maniu and Ion Mihalache were condemned to hard labor for life.

The long march to power drew to a close near the end of 1947. King Michael, who was progressively isolated and becoming more of a nuisance to the Communists, went to England in October for the wedding of Princess Elizabeth, heiress to the throne. He extended his stay to the delight of the Rumanian leaders, who discreetly let him know that his return was undesirable. The king, however, returned to his country on December 21. A few days later on December 30, the head of the government, Groza, came to the royal palace and demanded the king's abdication. The royal guard and the king's counselors had already been disarmed and placed under arrest. On January 3, 1948, King Michael and his entourage left the country. In February, the Social-Democrats and the Communists merged to form the Rumanian Workers' party, and, together with the Plowmen's Front and the Hungarian People's Union, presented a single list for the new elections under the name of the People's Democratic Front. The elections on March 28 of that year gave the People's Democratic Front 405 of the 414 seats. The first act of the new assembly on April 13 was to adopt a new constitution for the Rumanian People's Republic.

—The Illusion of Democracy in Hungary

As in the other Eastern European states, the communist presence in Hungary was also initially small, with a membership of barely a few thousand in the clandestine Communist party in 1938. Hungary was unique, however, in that the Soviets allowed a limited democracy to develop briefly; as soon as it turned against them, it was brutally stifled.

The sequence of events began in the last months of the war. At the time Szalasi, the fascist Arrow Cross party leader, seized power with German support in November, 1944, the east and the south of Hungary were already occupied by the Red Army. The National Independence Front was then quickly organized at Szeged by leftist members of the opposition, including parties of the left, union leaders, and representatives of the resistance. A coalition government was formed which then appointed a provisory government on December 21, in Debrecen. It was presided over by General Miklos of Dalnok, and included well-known members of the Horthy government like Geza Teleki and General Voros, along with representatives from the Independence Front parties: the Smallholders, National Peasants, Socialists and Communists. Even though the provisory government declared war on Germany immediately after taking office, according to the terms of the armistice the country was technically placed under the control of the Allied Control Commission, headed by the Soviet military under Marshal Vorochilov. Once Hungary had been liberated, the provisory government moved to Budapest and began working quickly to protect their ruined and demoralized country.

In order to create a legal base for its actions, the new government decided to call elections as quickly as possible. Electoral laws restricted eligible parties to those of the National Front alone, while "collaborators" were excluded. Despite these limitations, the elections were relatively free. The municipal elections in Budapest were a first test. The most moderate party of the Independence Front, the Smallholders, obtained an absolute majority in the capitol. This tendency carried over into the general elections held on November 4, 1945, when the Smallholders, with 57 percent of the vote, obtained 245 seats to the Communists' 70, the Socialists' 69, the National Peasants' 23 and the Democratic party's 2. The Smallholders' victory stemmed largely from their being the least leftist of the authorized parties, and thus attracted votes from the right and center-right. What the voters did not realize, however, was that this party had already been infiltrated by pro-Communists such as Istvan Dobi (who later became chief of state), Gyula Ortutay, the minister of public instruction and culture, Erno Mihalyi, Lajos Dinyes and other cabinet ministers. The Communists had also succeeded in infiltrating the National Peasant and Socialist parties.

Pressure from the president of the Allied Control Commission, Marshal Voroshilov, and the indecision of the victorious party leaders, Nagy and Tildy, brought about the formation of a coalition government which included the Communists—despite the fact that a clear majority of the voters were against the Communists, who only garnered 17 percent of the vote. In the Tildy cabinet formed on November 15, 1945, the Communists secured the Ministry of the Interior—which controlled the police—with the appointment of Imre Nagy, and of council vice-president and deputy prime minister with the appointment of Matyas Rakosi, secretary general of the Communist party. A far-reaching purge was then instigated with the complicity of the majority party. People's courts passed death sentences on Szalasi and most of his ministers, as well as on diverse officials from the Horthy era such as prime ministers Imredy and Bardossy. Other public figures were imprisoned or deported to Siberia, as was Count Istvan Bethlen, who had been prime minister in the 1920s despite his unflagging opposition to the government's pro-German policies since 1933. The purge also reached into the administration and into the army, whose ranks were thinned by nearly 14,000 members between 1945 and 1948. Also affected were the police, as the gendarmerie was disbanded and a number of its members prosecuted for "war crimes." The Smallholders did nothing to oppose these measures; they were afraid of being overrun from the left by the Communists who often used mass demonstrations as pressure tactics, and they felt that once the peace treaty was signed and the Soviet occupying forces had left, things would take care of themselves.

At the request of the Communists and the Socialists, the majority party—the Smallholders—voted in favor of a government-sponsored bill creating a republic. Tildy was then elected president of the Republic, and replaced as head of the government by his friend Ferenc Nagy. The constitution accepted on February 6, 1946, provided for a single assembly to be elected by universal suffrage through a direct and secret ballot, which would then appoint and supervise members of the government. Although the Smallholders held both presidential offices—of the Republic as well as the prime ministry—and a majority in the assembly, their power was visibly eroding. Taking advantage of popular discontent arising from economic difficulties and galloping inflation, the leftist bloc of Communists, Socialists and National Peasants began to step up mass demonstrations against the majority party in March, 1946, accusing the Smallholders of sabotage. The most violent attacks were directed at the party's right wing under Bela Kovacs. Anxious to maintain the coalition, Ferenc Nagy pressured his colleagues to expel reputedly anti-Communist elements from the party. Infiltration of the Smallholders by pro-Communists began to pay off as 23 deputies were expelled. Ferenc Nagy brought in a law dictating heavy sentences for "enemies of democratic order" and replaced Minister of the Interior Imre Nagy, judged to be too moderate, with a hardline Communist, Laszlo Rajk.

By autumn, 1946, people began to feel the effects of these measures. Anti-Communist newspapers first found their paper supplies cut off, and were soon shut down altogether while the leftist bloc escalated its attack on the Smallholders. It was the beginning of "Operation Salami," as it was called by Rakosi at a January, 1952, session of the Communist party Political Academy. At the academy session Rakosi explained how the Communists managed to take over by devouring the opposition "slice by slice," beginning with the Smallholders. Through Rajk, the Communists gained several important posts. The *AVO (Allamvedelmi Ostaly)*, a political police force or state security authority directed by the Communist Gabor Peter, and a political section under General Palffy-Oesterreicher in the ministry of defense were put in charge of the struggle against the "enemies of the people." In December, 1946, the political section announced that a plot implicating members of the Smallholders had been uncovered, in particular the primary Communist adversary Bela Kovacs. Even though parliament refused to annul his parliamentary immunity, Kovacs was arrested by the Soviet military police in February, 1947, and his "confession" led to further arrests. Ferenc Nagy was one of those compromised, and while on a private visit to Switzerland was requested by telephone to resign, since proof of his collusion with the "plotters" had just been discovered. Nagy resigned on May 30, 1947 and Lajos Dinnyes came in as head of the government. Although he was also a Smallholder, he was in better graces with the Communists. As a result of the arrests, resignations, and defections, the ranks of the Smallholders were decreased from 246 to 184 in the assembly, and thus lost their absolute majority.

After dismantling the principal non-Marxist party in the country, Laszlo Rajk announced that parliament would be revived and set the elections for August 31, 1947. The atmosphere was tense; the uncovering of "plots" weighed heavy on many minds, and the recent institution of preliminary authorization and censorship effectively muzzled the press. The electoral law of July 24, 1947, decreased the number of eligible voters by over 500,000. In addition, parties other than those of the Independence Front could present candidates only by petition. Despite the risks involved in signing such petitions, there were enough signatures to allow six opposition parties to field candidates, but this had the unfortunate effect of splitting the non-Communist vote. The electoral law stated that absent voters could cast their ballots wherever they might be. The Communists, in charge of the police and the elected local governments except in Budapest, encouraged their supporters to vote several times on the absentee voters' "blue ballots." Despite these conditions, the Communists polled only 21.8 percent of the vote, giving them 97 deputies. The Smallholders suffered the greatest loss with only 15.2 percent of the vote—due mainly to their indecision and passivity in the face of Communist demands. The National Independence Front remained the dominant force with 60.2 percent, but the Communists were slowly taking the Front over from within. On the other side, the small opposition parties with nearly 40 percent of the vote obtained only 142 seats to the Front's 269. Though the Communists were far from holding a majority with their 97 deputies, they had two major advantages in the presence of the Red Army and the lack of cohesion among their adversaries.

After the elections, the Communists continued their attacks on the opposition and turned their attention to the "reactionary elements within the Socialist party." The discovery of a "fascist plot," allegedly including the head of the right wing of the Socialist party, Karoly Peyer, as well as the leaders of the bourgeois opposition parties, set off a new wave of arrests. At Rajk's request, Peyer's parliamentary immunity was withdrawn on November 22, 1947. The centrists of the Socialist party, Anna Kethly and Antal Ban, were in turn denounced as "reactionaries." The leadership of the party expelled them to avoid further complications, preparing the way for a merger with the Communist party. The merger was accepted in principle at the Socialist Party Congress held from June 11 to 13, 1948, and soon after, Socialists and Communists joined under the common banner of the Hungarian Worker's party. Matyas Rakosi became its secretary general. The last obstacle to establishment of a popular democracy was the president of the Republic, Tildy. The discovery of a "plot" implicating his son-in-law precipitated his resignation on July 30, 1948; his replacement was Szakasits, president of the Hungarian Workers' party. The pseudo-democratic experiment had been short-lived.

Czechoslovakia and the Communists

Like Poland, Czechoslovakia had maintained a government in exile throughout the war, headed by President Benes in London. But unlike its Polish counterpart, the Czechoslovak government deliberately chose a policy of *entente* with the Soviets, there being no outstanding disagreement between the two countries. The policy of entente with the Soviet Union was confirmed on December 4, 1943, with the signing of a treaty of friendship and alliance based on the principle of non-interference in the other's internal affairs. During a visit to Moscow, Benes reached a political agreement with the secretary general of the Czechoslovak Communist party, Klement Gottwald; upon liberation, they decided, a united government would be formed under the direction of the left, and free and secret elections would be held as soon as possible. The resulting government would be led by the head of the most numerous party. In signing, Gottwald was certain that the Communists would win the first election.

When Benes returned to Czechoslovakia and temporarily settled in Kosice on April 3, 1945, he appointed a Socialist, Zdenek Fierlinger, as head of the government. In his cabinet, the Communists received eight of the 25 ministries. In addition to the post of deputy prime minister given to Gottwald, the Communists obtained two key ministries: the Interior, which meant control of the police and local administrations, and Information, which meant supervision of the press and the radio. The parties of the government in exile, the different underground organizations of the resistance, and the unions immediately formed the Czech and Slovak National Front, while on the local level the Communist-dominated resistance committees took over as each territory was liberated. On April 5, Fierlinger's government published its political platform, called the Kosice Program. This document provided for the continuance of the special alliance with the Soviet Union while internally, it ordered the punishment of traitors and collaborators. In addition, the program gave Slovakia special status, initiated a wide-sweeping land reform, and nationalized all banks, mines, and industries employing more than 500 salaried workers.

These measures went into effect after the government's move to Prague at the end of May, 1945, and the formation of a provisory parliament with delegates of the National Front. As expected, the special tribunals set about judging "traitors" and "collaborators" from June, 1945, until 1948. The victims of this purge were leaders of the German and Hungarian minorities charged with treason, and members of Father Tiso's Slovak government.

Tiso's trial, which took place in Bratislava from December 3, 1946, to April 15, 1947, provoked angry protests as five of the seven tribunal judges were avowed Communists. Tiso was sentenced to death and executed on April 19, 1947, despite his immense popularity with his countrymen and appeals for clemency from the Czechoslovak episcopacy and from Joseph Lettrich, head of the majority Slovak Democratic party. His execution was deeply resented by a large portion of the Slovak population. In total, out of 20,000 trials held during the political purge, there were 365 executions. The purge also reached into the administration, the courts, and the police. With the help of the purges, and having control over the interior ministry, the Communists were able to place their own men at virtually all levels.

The awaited elections were held on May 20, 1945. Five parties were authorized to participate: the Communist party with its Czech and Slovak sections, the Social Democratic Party, the National Socialist party (closely tied to Benes), the Czech Populist party of Father Sramek with Christian Democratic tendencies, and the Democratic Slovak party. The Communist party won 38 percent of the vote; its support came more from Czech areas (40 percent) than from Slovak (30 percent). The social Democrats polled 13 percent of the vote, giving an absolute majority to the Socialist-Communist coalition. The Communist victory is quite understandable in light of the role they played in the resistance and by the activities of the Party's membership, which had grown from 80,000 in 1938 to over 500,000 by the end of 1945. This victory can also be explained by the key positions the Communists held in the city governments, and also by the noticeable decline of the Social Democratic party compared to its position before the war. Against this coalition of the left, the bourgeois parties won 49 percent of the votes for their candidates—the National Socialists holding 18 percent, the Populists 16 percent, and the Slovak Democrats 15 percent. The crucial point to be noted in these elections is that while at least three out of five voters were not Communist, the Communists had nevertheless become the major political force in the country. In accordance with the agreement made with Benes, Gottwald formed a new government with the National Front parties on July 2, 1946. The Communists gave themselves nine ministries, including those of the interior, justice, and information; the other parties were given 13 ministries, including that of foreign affairs appointed to Jan Masaryk, son of the former president of the Republic. The post of national defense minister was given to the professedly apolitical General Ludvik Svoboda.

The Communist party's victory at the polls and the efforts made by Communist supporters in the reconstruction of the country raised the party's influence and prestige. Its membership rose to 1,300,000 by 1948. The new Central Committee, whose secretary general was now Rudolf Slansky, was composed of men completely devoted to Moscow and to Gottwald. Through the intermediary local governments, the Communists controlled over half of the town governments, primarily in Bohemia: they were less influential in Slovakia. Since 1945, the Communists had controlled the Revolutionary Unionist Movement—the only authorized union—directed by Antonin Zapotocky, a member of the Central Committee of the Communist party. Furthermore, they had gradually infiltrated all of the other parties, including the left wing of the Social Democratic party under Fierlinger. They even entered the Populist party with Father Plohjar, who was to play a leading role in the Priests for Peace movement. They could also count on the army, whose chief of staff, General Svoboda, was a party admirer. Svoboda had wanted to join the Party in 1945, but was dissuaded by Gottwald himself, who pointed out that by remaining "apolitical" he could be "of greater service to the party." Until 1947, the Gottwald government encountered little opposition in implementing the economic terms of the Kosice Program. But as the Communists slowly worked their way into the sectors they did not yet control, leaders of the bourgeois democratic parties began to sense the danger more than Benes himself could.

The first signs of tension within the ruling coalition appeared in July, 1947, when it was necessary to decide whether Czechoslovakia would participate in preliminary meetings on an implementation of the Marshall Plan. Designed by the United States Secretary of State, George C. Marshall, the plan provided substantial credit to European countries to assist in the reconstruction and modernization of their economies, with the condition that the funds were to be controlled by representatives of the United States. On July 4, the Czechoslovakian cabinet unanimously approved the principle of participation in these meetings, but Gottwald suggested having the decision approved by Moscow. In the meantime, the USSR had publicly rejected the Marshall Plan. Gottwald's suggestion was not made as head of an independent government, but rather as the devoted and faithful spokesman of the Soviet leadership. This was no secret in Moscow, and was directly evidenced when the non-Communist Minister of Foreign Affairs, Masaryk, was practically excluded from talks held between Gottwald and his Minister of Commerce, Loebl, with Stalin. The Soviets made it clear that acceptance of the Marshall Plan would be considered a hostile act against the USSR. On July 10, the entire Prague government, and Benes as well, stepped into line with the Soviet position to decline the American offer. The non-Communist ministers then realized that it was Moscow—through Gottwald—that was determining both domestic and foreign policy in Czechoslovakia. Accordingly, they initiated a policy of resistance.

The second phase of the crisis occurred almost simultaneously in Slovakia, when the secretary general of the Slovak Communist party, Gustav Husak, launched a virulent attack against the Democratic party led by

Joseph Lettrich, accusing it of having been infiltrated by former followers of Father Tiso and of promoting nationalist agitation in the country. Numerous active Democrats were arrested, and the deputy Urisny was implicated in the plot. In Prague, the non-Communist ministers denounced Husak's methods; Husak retorted on November 5 by coordinating a general strike in Slovakia demanding a purge of the Democratic party. These proceedings had begun to alarm the non-Communist opposition. The Social Democratic Party Congress in progress at Brno was aware of the growing influence of the Communists, and refused a proposal to join forces with them. This provoked Gottwald into denouncing them as "foreign-supported reactionaries" opposing the establishment of socialism in Czechoslovakia.

From that moment on, the Communist attitude hardened progressively. The unions increased their mass demonstrations and warning strikes. Meanwhile, poor harvests were causing continuing food shortages, high prices, corrupt trade practices, and accompanying worker discontent. At the end of 1947, the unions revived the popular militia that had been disbanded after the war; the official reason given was that the Republic needed defense against reactionary elements. At the same time, tension mounted with the announcement that a major plot had been uncovered at Most-na-Labe. The Communist Minister of the Interior, Vaclav Nosek, took advantage of the situation to conduct a purge of the police. As the situation evolved, non-Communists began to take alarm, particularly since general elections were set for the following May. The Communist party platform for these elections recommended extended nationalization of all firms with over 50 salaried employees, as well as intensified agrarian reform.

The bourgeois parties, counting on support from President Benes, decided to take the offensive. On February 13, 1948, the National Socialist ministers demanded the reinstatement of several high-ranking police officers dismissed by Nosek; their request was granted. Pushing for more, the non-Communist ministers decided to resign *en masse*, hoping that Benes would refuse their resignations and that the Gottwald cabinet would be forced to resign. On February 20, they presented their resignations, but contrary to their expectations, General Svoboda and Jan Masaryk refused to follow, and the Social Democrats judged the ministers' actions to be "inopportune." In the midst of the bourgeois parties themselves, pro-Communist elements criticized the resignations; it was too late, however, and the fate of the country was now in the hands of the president of the Republic. Aware of the danger inherent in the ministerial crisis and in the calling of free elections in which the "silent majority" could potentially side with the former ministers, the unions mobilized their forces. When it was clear that a crisis was in the making, Josef Smrkovsky, deputy commander of the popular militia, mobilized his troops. In a meeting in Prague on

February 21, Gottwald announced the discovery of an imperialist plot. On the following day, the unions called an hour-long general strike. During the night of the 22nd, at the instigation of Gottwald and Nosek, a number of military officers and ranking civil servants judged to be unreliable were arrested, while the bourgeois party headquarters were searched. The crisis escalated. Supported and surrounded by the armed militia called up by Pavel and Smrkovsky, thousands of demonstrators descended upon Prague, brought in by special trains from the working class suburbs and provincial villages. The first demonstration took place on the 23rd, accompanied by a general strike. Tensions peaked on the 25th, when 300,000 militant Communists assembled on Wenceslas Square demanding that Gottwald be kept on as head of state. Benes was unable to secure the support of the Social Democrats and, abandoning his associates, gave in to the crowd's demands. On the evening of the 25th, he agreed to replace the ministers who had resigned. Out of 20 ministers in the new Gottwald cabinet, 12 were Communist. Along with Masaryk and General Svoboda—who retained their portfolios—the non-Communists were represented by three Social Democrats from the party's left wing, one dissident Populist and two maverick Slovak Democrats. The Prague *coup* had succeeded with Benes' reluctant cooperation. The mob, armed and mobilized by the Communist party, had imposed its will. Several days later, during the night of March 9, Jan Masaryk died. Although the official verdict was suicide, a rumor persisted that he was thrown out of his office window.

Parliament set to work on the constitution which was still pending. They accepted the new constitution on May 9, 1948, before adjourning. In the general election held on May 30, the single list of candidates sponsored by the National Front polled 6,430,000 votes out of 8,000,000 registered voters: over 1,500,000 voters abstained or submitted a blank ballot. President Benes, in poor health for some time, resigned on June 7, never having given his official confirmation to the new constitution. He died soon thereafter, on September 3, 1948. Immediately after his resignation, the assembly unanimously selected Klement Gottwald as the new president of the Czechoslovak Repulic. Czechoslovakia had become a popular democracy.

The Birth of the German Democratic Republic

Germany under Soviet occupation was another special case; with the fall of the Reich on May 8, 1945, and in accordance with Allied decisions, the German state had ceased to exist as a political entity. It was governed by authorities of the occupying military forces, each in their respective zones. The Soviet occupying forces deftly exploited a number of factors: these included the absence of prisoners of war (not liberated until 1947), the oppressive presence of the Soviet army, the disorientation of the civilian population in a country devastated by battles and bombing, and finally, the demoralization caused by defeat. The National Socialist (Nazi) regime had eliminated political parties so effectively since 1933 that the Soviets had ample room to operate. During the war, the Soviets had promoted a Committee for Free Germany in Moscow, presided over by Walter Ulbricht. Ulbricht was a Communist who ran a newspaper titled *Freies Deutschland*, through which he forwarded his opinions of how Germany should evolve for the future. By May 1, 1945, German Communists who had fled to Moscow were already returning to Berlin and reorganizing the party. Once the war was over, the Soviet military government set up a provisory local government made up of members of the parties disbanded in 1933, though preference was given to the Communists. In the summer of 1945, the Soviets agreed to permit the reformation—or creation—of a number of political parties. Apart from the Communist party of Ulbricht and Wilhelm Pieck, the reorganized parties included the Social Democratic party under Otto Grotewohl and Frederic Ebert, the son of the former president of the Reich, the Christian Democratic party under Otto Nuschke, and the Liberal party with Johannes Dieckmann. These parties decided on July 14, 1945, to form the United Front of the Antifascist and Democratic parties, in order to fight the vestiges of Hitlerism, imperialism and militarism, and also to reconstruct the country along democratic lines. The Communists and the Social Democrats immediately opened negotiations leading to a common convention held in April, 1946, in Berlin. At the convention, they formed the Socialist Unity Party of Germany—the *Sozialistische Einheitspartei Deutschlands*, or SED. The SED boasted 1,300,000 members and became the first political group in the zone of Soviet occupation.

Even before the SED was formed, the *Laender*, or new administrative districts, were in place. The local provisory government had initiated profound governmental restructuring, agrarian reform, and nationalizations. These changes were ratified by popular referendum. In October of 1946, the first provincial and municipal elections were held. The SED won 48 percent of the vote, and the Liberals and the Christian Democrats 24 percent each. A little later, two new political parties appeared: the Democratic Peasant party and the National Democratic party. Gradually, the Soviets returned the responsibility of local government to the Germans. In March, 1948, as the result of a people's congress that brought together representatives of the political parties and new constitution. The opening of the Cold War and the resulting deterioration in relations between the Western powers and the Soviet Union affected the eastern segment of Germany profoundly. After the U.S. and Britain set up a German Economic Council in the Western occupied zoned of Berlin in June of 1948—instigating a monetary reform—the Soviets decided to retaliate by creating a 25-member economic commission, and later decided to seal off Western access to Berlin by land. These crises accelerated the establishment of a communist East German state. On May 30, 1949, a new meeting of the people's congress approved the constitution drafted by the people's council. The provisory congress then adopted the name of the "People's Chamber," and on October 7, 1949, appointed Otto Grotewohl as head of the provisory government of the German Democratic Republic (GDR)—just as the Federal Republic of Germany (FRG) was being organized in Bonn. Through its political orientation and its leaders, the GDR would soon become a full-fledged member of socialist Europe.

Thus, with the exception of the GDR where the transformation came later, all of the Eastern European countries had become popular democracies by 1948. The Communist parties became the dominant political force in each of these countries, with a marked determination to pattern their country's political, economic and social life on the Soviet model. The Soviet bloc had come into being.

Chapter 24

The Age of Stalin
1948—1953

For the people of Eastern Europe, the five years that elapsed between the winter of 1947-48 and the death of Stalin comprised the darkest and most difficult period after the end of the war. Internationally, these years were marked by the cold war and by the establishment of close ties between the Eastern European countries and Moscow. Only Yugoslavia managed to break these ties with the Soviet Union. Internally, dictatorial systems were put in place during these years just after the war reached its zenith; opponents of the new regimes were put on the defensive and became victims, as were many Communist leaders themselves. Economically, the years 1948-1953 witnessed the irreversible establishment of the planned socialist economic system.

MOSCOW AND THE EASTERN EUROPEAN COUNTRIES

The establishment of popular democracies in Eastern Europe coincided with the cold war in the international arena. After 1946, the entente between the allies of the Second World War, which had prevailed up until then despite some localized friction, began to deteriorate as relations cooled between the leaders of the Western and Soviet blocs, or the US and the USSR. The causes for the cold war are linked primarily to the differences in political and economic tenets of the two blocs. During the war, these differences had been discreetly set aside in the interests of confronting a common enemy; once peace returned, however, they reappeared with a vengeance, especially since President Roosevelt's successor, Harry S. Truman, seemed much less disposed than his predecessor to grant further concessions to the Soviets. In addition, the means by which the Communists had come to power in Eastern Europe provoked serious reservations in western countries accustomed to pluralistic parliamentary democracy. The Western powers quickly came to the conclusion that Stalin had got the better of them at Yalta.

President Truman's clearly stated intention of containing the Soviets provoked a hardened reaction—notably revealed in the organizational meeting of the Cominform in September, 1947. Considering Eastern Europe indispensable for security reasons, the Soviets decided to close it off to the exterior world. Accordingly, the Soviet leaders prohibited Eastern European countries from making any political or trade agreements directly with Western countries. Czechoslovakia's refusal, following orders from Moscow, to accept aid from the Marshall Plan, clearly illustrated Moscow's desire to keep the upper hand in Eastern European foreign affairs. Moreover, the USSR hurriedly concluded an economic agreement advantageous to Czechoslovakia. Other trade agreements were signed in the months that followed with other popular democracies. Even though these countries had previously traded mainly with Western Europe, the USSR was to become their primary trading partner. At the same time, trade agreements were signed among the popular democracies. For a country like the German Democratic Republic, which had always been part of the vast economic ensemble of Germany, the new orientation necessitated a radical overhaul of economic activities in order to meet the needs of the new trading partners.

These economic agreements were matched by political treaties of alliance, friendship and mutual assistance that reinforced each country's links with the USSR as well as with each other, strengthening the bonds of the "Soviet bloc." These treaties provided for instructors and technical experts to be sent to each country by the USSR, and gave the Soviet military the responsibility of reorganizing the armed forces in each country. The ultimate goal was to form a group of countries united among themselves and definitively bound to the Soviet Union—as both the center of world communism and as a state. The principle of these privileged ties with the USSR, based on the strict adherence of all Communist parties to the party line from Moscow, was solemnly confirmed at the Szklarska-Poreda conference. By the end of 1947, the countries of Eastern Europe had begun to resemble a homogenous bloc with close ties to the Soviet Union, which was militarily present in Hungary, Poland, Rumania and in the German Democratic Republic. At this time, Yugoslavia under Tito appeared to all as closest to the USSR politically and ideologically. It was undoubtedly for this reason that Belgrade was chosen as the seat for the Cominform. However, less than one year later, on June 28, 1948, the Cominform condemned Tito's policies and called upon the Yugoslav Communist party to change directions.

The Yugoslav Schism

The break between Yugoslavia and the Soviet bloc in the summer of 1948 caused the first serious crisis in the socialist world. It was difficult to imagine that the most Stalin-like of the Eastern European leaders would suddenly turn rebellious. Tito had faithfully based Yugoslavia's institutions on the Soviet Union's, and the Yugoslav constitution of 1946 strangely echoed Stalin's constitution of 1936. The secret police, the *UDBA*, under the direction of Alexander Rankovitch, had used Stalinistic zeal when they eliminated various opponents. In foreign policy as well, Yugoslavia had always been aligned with the USSR in attacking American imperialism, and furthermore, was actively supporting Communist guerrillas who were waging a veritable war on the Greek government. Weren't these signs evidence enough of Tito's unswerving loyalty? The leaders in Moscow didn't think so, finding aspects of Tito's behavior disquieting. First of all, since Tito's own armies had liberated most of Yugoslavia's national territory, Tito felt less dependent on the Soviets than other Eastern European leaders. This Yugoslav nationalism didn't seem to bother the Soviets until early 1948. Affairs became more complicated when Tito began planning a Balkan federation under the direction of Belgrade, gathering Albania and Bulgaria around Yugoslavia. Since the end of the war, Yugoslavia had been conducting an intense political and economic campaign in Albania, resulting in an agreement of cooperation and mutual assistance, signed in July, 1946, and reinforced by a customs and monetary agreement in November of the same year. The two countries decided to dispense with customs and adopt a single monetary unit. Simultaneously, hundreds of Yugoslav technicians, both civilian and military, descended upon Albania. The presence of these Yugoslav instructors, who often behaved arrogantly toward the local populations, provoked violent disagreements within the Albanian Communist party. Some Albanian leaders were under the impression that Tito intended to make Albania the seventh republic of the Yugoslav federation. The leadership of the Albanian Communist party insisted on maintaining close ties with Yugoslavia up until early 1948, when Tito tried to place the Albanian armed forces under Yugoslav control and station his troops in Albania "to defend Albania from the threat of Greek monarchist-fascists." Enver Hoxha, despite a large pro-Yugoslav faction within the Albanian Communist party, decided to take action and notified Moscow of Tito's intentions. By May, 1948, relations between Tirana and Belgrade had begun to deteriorate.

Moscow was doubly alarmed by Tito's expansionist views, since Bulgaria was also targeted. Relations between Belgrade and Sofia had been cordial since the meeting between Tito and Dimitrov and the agreement of Euxinograd on November 27, 1947, in which Yugoslavia gave up demands for Bulgarian reparations in exchange for Bulgarian withdrawal of claims to Macedonia. Plans for a Balkan federation were also discussed. Then, in early January, 1948, Dimitrov mentioned the possibility of such a federation—which could include other Eastern European countries like Hungary, Poland, Czechoslovakia and even Greece—and was criticized on January 28, by the Soviet government newspaper *Pravda*. He retracted his words a few days later. All this was too much for Moscow; if Tito wanted to annex Albania and group the Balkan and Danubian countries around him, it could eventually threaten Soviet hegemony in the area. Moscow tried to obtain a self-criticism from the Yugoslavs and appeared to be succeeding on February 11, when Yugoslavia signed a document in Moscow agreeing to consult the USSR in all matters regarding foreign affairs. In spite of this apparent show of good will, Tito had no intentions of relinquishing control. The central committee of the Yugoslav Communist party met on March 1, and adopted a firm line regarding the Soviets. Moscow retorted on March 18, by recalling Soviet military advisors from Yugoslavia on the pretext that they had been poorly treated and were under close surveillance by the Yugoslav secret police. Tito retaliated in a long letter to Soviet Minister of Foreign Affairs Molotov, justifying the surveillance of the Soviet advisors—who had been engaged in espionage. Step by careful step, Yugoslavia was heading for a break, but no one except select insiders knew what was going on. The USSR made a last attempt to bring Tito into line by asking the anti-Titoists in the Yugoslav Communist party, Colonel General Joujovitch and Andre Hebrand, president of the Planning Committee, to denounce the Party's policies. The maneuver failed; Joujovitch and Hebrand were expelled from the Party in April, then arrested. Tito, with Party leaders Djilas, Kardelj, and Rankovitch all firmly behind him, stubbornly stood up to Moscow, and in so doing had the unanimous support of the Party. After expelling the Joujovitch-Hebrand group from the Party, Tito still attempted to justify his actions to Moscow. In a letter dated April 13, addressed to the leaders of the Soviet party, he reminded them that "inaccurate and slanderous information" about the Yugoslav party and its policies had been furnished by Joujovitch and Hebrand, who had been expelled for their attempts to splinter the party. Tito spelled out in detail his position on relations with the USSR, emphasizing the fact that "whatever love each of us may have for the USSR, the leader of socialism, we do not love our own country—which also honors socialism—any less."

Until that moment, the rank-and-file members had no idea what was taking place. The first public indication of the crisis occurred on May 17, 1948, on the celebration of Marshal Tito's birthday. Neither the USSR nor Albania sent the traditional congratulatory messages. Tito, on his part, had just refused the Kremlin's proposal of arbitration by "brother parties." When the Cominform convened in late June, 1948, the leaders condemned Tito's policies. In their resolution of June 28, they denounced the nationalists' takeover of the Yugoslav Communist party and called upon the "authentic Communists" of Yugoslavia to "impose a new political direction." Immediately, the central committee of the Yugoslav Communist party called upon militants and members of the People's Front to continue the work of enlightened socialism.

Positions had been taken, and the break came quickly. On July 1, Albania was the first of all the Eastern European countries to renounce treaties signed with Yugoslavia. Then, on July 4, Yugoslavia was expelled from the Cominform. In Yugoslavia itself, Tito had the firm backing of the Fifth Party Congress and refused to budge; he denied all accusations of deviation and nationalism directed at the leadership of the Yugoslav Communist party, and appealed to the entire population to support its leaders.

The USSR made a last ditch effort, attempting a military *coup* against Tito. The Soviets could count on the chief of staff, General Jovanovitch, but the army did not seem inclined to follow the plot leaders. Jovanovitch decided to flee the country, but on August 11, he was shot down by the militia as he was about to cross the Bulgarian border. His accomplices were arrested shortly thereafter.

Yugoslavia was immediately quarantined; the "brother countries" practically set up an economic blockade. Socialist countries' ambassadors posted in Belgrade were recalled, leaving only the deputies in the Yugoslav capital. Simultaneously, Moscow reinforced its hold on the faithful Eastern European countries. In 1949, in order to tighten its hold on the popular democracies, the Soviet Union created a Council of Mutual Economic Assistance (COMECON), designed to establish close economic cooperation between member countries through multilateral treaties. However, COMECON was slow to become effective; it was only after the death of Stalin that it became a reality. Regular meetings of the ministers of foreign affairs in the Eastern European countries were organized, and military cooperation was strengthened under the strict control of the Soviet Union. There was no question of allowing another Yugoslavian experiment to develop. When the Polish leadership seemed to hesitate, Poland was placed under the sharp surveillance of Marshal Rokossowsky—a man of Polish origin, but a Soviet citizen and marshal in the Red Army—who was named head of the Polish army as well as Minister of Defense. The Yugoslav schism brought about a definite hardening of positions within the popular democracies and rigorous alignment with Moscow.

EVOLUTION OF THE POPULAR DEMOCRACIES DURING THE STALIN ERA

Government Organization

All the Eastern European countries have been governed by popular democracies since 1948. The Communist party rose to power everywhere, imposing its political objectives on the populations and making communist ideology the inspiration for new legislation. The Soviet constitution of 1936 was the model for constitutions adopted by Rumania in April 1948, Czechoslovakia in May of the same year, by Hungary in August 1949, and by the German Democratic Republic—East Germany—in October. Constitutions already in force in Albania and Yugoslavia since 1946, and in Bulgaria and Poland since 1947, were all based on the Soviet example. The Yugoslav constitution most closely resembled the Soviet model because of its six federated republics and two autonomous territories; like the USSR, the popular assembly was composed of two houses, the Federal Council, made up of deputies elected proportionately one for each 50,000 inhabitants, and a People's Council which represented the different nationalities. This Popular Assembly, which was analogous to the Supreme Soviet of the USSR, voted on laws, appointed governmental officials and elected the presidium—the collective leadership of the state in which the president, in this case Marshal Tito, held major powers.

In the other non-federated popular democracies, power was held by a single assembly (the Chamber of the People in East Germany, the Diet in Poland, the Great Assembly in Bulgaria and Rumania, the National Assembly in Hungary and in Czechoslovakia, and the Popular Assembly in Albania); the government and the presidium, also sharing in power, were elected by the assembly. The president of the presidium was the head of state in each country. All representatives, local and regional counselors and assembly members, were elected by a suffrage of men and women over 18 on a direct and secret ballot (although what took place in the polling sites was suspect) through a single list of candidates. The lists were drawn up before the elections by the leadership of the popular or patriotic fronts gathered around the communist parties, and the unions and other mass organizations linked to the Party. In principle, the voter could choose to approve the list, or turn in a negative or blank ballot, or abstain from voting. The system was so well organized that the total of blank or negative votes never exceeded five percent of the registered voters! All of the constitutions claimed in one form or another that the popular democracy was the "state of the workers and peasants" and most of them clearly mentioned the leading role of the Communist party. The constitutions officially guaranteed the principal freedoms: freedom of the press, of assembly and of religion. The gap between theory and practice, however, was large.

At least until the mid-1950s, all of these provisions were only theoretical formulas. In fact, the real power lay with the Communist party, or more precisely with the leaders of the Communist party who were in constant contact with the leaders of the Soviet Communist party. The true power holder was the Communist party's secretary general, a position which was frequently combined with head of state or of government. Thus, Matyas Rakosi was both secretary general of the Hungarian Worker's party and prime minister; Walter Ulbricht was both president of the State Council of East Germany and first secretary of the United Socialist party, just as in their respective countries Enver Hoxha and Tito headed both the state and the Party. After being elected president of the Republic, Klement Gottwald ceded leadership of the Party to Rudolf Slansky, but retained a supervisory role. In a similar fashion, the leadership of state and of the Party in Poland were separate. In all of these countries, Party bureaucracy always took precedent over the state.

The communist state's absolute power was reinforced by the unions and mass organizations, and was propped up universally by a political police force which practically constituted a state within a state—charged with ferreting out opponents both within and outside of the Party. The all-powerful political police introduced an atmosphere of mistrust and suspicion, infiltrating all levels of society.

Political Purges in the Eastern Bloc States

Following the Yugoslav schism, Soviet leaders called upon the leadership of the various Eastern European communist parties to increase their vigilance against any infiltrating "class enemies," or anyone whose behavior could be interpreted as pro-Tito. By summer, 1948, communist parties had all begun to scrutinize the activities and attitudes of every active member, particularly those in high positions. It was an enormous undertaking, since the ranks of the Party members had swollen greatly after the establishment of popular democracies; many opportunists had joined for reasons of self-protection or ambition. Thousands of members were expelled, officially for pro-Titoism or anti-Sovietism, but more often for demonstrating slight tendencies of thinking independently about Party matters. Taking all the Eastern European countries into consideration, it has been estimated that nearly a quarter of the parties were expelled or striken from the rolls, and seven to eight percent of these former members were later arrested.

Dismissal from the Party carried serious consequences at the time, adversely affecting the victim's employment opportunities and social life. The overall effect of these purges on the countries involved was considerable. The Yugoslavian people were not spared either, but there, the pro-Soviet elements were flushed out.

Throughout Eastern Europe, public attention was focused on the large public trials, often broadcast over the radio, during which high-ranking Party officials, feared or respected by those around them, were accused of a series of crimes ranging from simple treason or espionage for the imperialist countries, to trafficking in foreign currency. To the public's amazement, the accused, pale and contrite, willingly confessed to the crimes they were accused of and more.

The Polish Communist party was the first to attack prominent members, and the earliest and most famous victim of their purges was Wladislaw Gomulka, secretary general of the Polish Worker party since 1943. Accused of "nationalist and rightist" deviation during the meeting of the Polish central committee in September, 1948, Gomulka was immediately replaced by Boleslaw Bierut, a true Stalinist who was already chief of state. Gomulka was dismissed from the Party in November, 1949, at the same time as the long-standing leader of the Popular Army, General Spychalski, was dismissed. Spychalski's arrest in May, 1950, on charges of attacking the security of the state, followed by Gomulka's the next year, did not result in the type of large show trial becoming customary in the other countries.

Elsewhere in Eastern Europe, large show trials were staged to impress the public and to bolster Party support. Typical of these trials was the trial of Laszlo Rajk and his codefendents, which took place in Budapest from September 16 to 24, 1949. The accusation was:

> "Rajk and his followers intend to tear Hungary away from the defenders of the peace..." and are accomplices "of Tito, who with his cohorts has deserted socialism and democracy...and has made Yugoslavia into a satellite of the imperialists.... Behind Rajk's work, there is American imperialism which has already assembled its pack of ringleaders in the zone of Austrian occupation—the officers of the Arrow Cross, fascists, Horthyists, and former gendarmes—who hope to bathe in the worker's blood...."

These accusations were outrageous given that Rajk and his principal codefendent, Palffy-Oesterreicher, had been among those who had played particularly decisive roles in the Communists' rise to power in 1947-1948, and were personally responsible for the establishment of the repressive apparatus now being used against them. Rajk and two of his companions were condemned to death and executed; the others were given heavy prison sentences. Rajk's trial was in reality a trial of Tito, and his confession instigated a chain reaction in the other popular democracies.

In Czechoslovakia, a first wave of purges struck certain Slovak Communist leaders accused of "bourgeois nationalism and deviationism." At the instigation of Rudolf Slansky, acting in concert with the Soviet security forces, a group of government officials was arrested in February, 1951, including the minister of foreign affairs, Clementis, the president of the Slovak Commissary Council, Gustav Husak, the commissioner of education, Novemesky, and the commissioner of culture, Holdos. Soon afterward, Rudolf Slansky was himself targeted; he was relieved of his functions as head of the Party in September of the same year, and arrested on November 24 in company with other prominent personalities—most of whom were also of Jewish origin. The trial took place behind closed doors in November, 1952. Slansky and those he had had arrested were seated side by side on the defendants' bench. Eleven of the 14 defendants, including Clementis and Slansky, were condemned to death and executed. Two of the survivors, Arthur London and Eugene Loebl, later spoke of the physical and moral coercion suffered by the defendants. All of the accused first claimed innocence and loyalty to the Party, but during the interrogation, they were promised their lives would be spared in exchange for the confessions necessary for the Party to unmask the true enemies of socialism. They all agreed to betray their best friends in the interests of the Party or to save their own skins.

Besides the Slansky and Rajk trials, dozens of other trials were held in Hungary and Czechoslovakia. Men like Janos Kadar of Hungary and Gustav Husak in Czechoslovakia, who later held high offices in their respective countries, were condemned and tortured in Stalin's prisons. Ironically, it was at the request of the Soviets that these men took over leadership under dramatic circumstances: Kadar after the revolt in Budapest was crushed in 1956, and Husak after the failure of the "Prague Spring" in 1968. Why, after their treatment during the purges, these men agreed to do this is hard to explain, except perhaps out of unconditional loyalty to the Party and to the Soviet Union. Albania, Bulgaria and Rumania also conducted purges which victimized persons who had made contributions to the consolidation of Communist power in their countries; Traiko Kostov in Bulgaria, Lucretiu Patrascanu and Anna Pauker in Rumania, and Koci Xoxe in Albania had all been long-time Party activists who were then put on trial.

The victims of these widespread purges had a common trait; they were more nationalistic and less devoted to Moscow than those who eliminated them. Some, like Slansky or Anna Pauker, were Jewish; almost all of them had fought in the resistance inside or outside of their countries; and others had served in the international brigades during the Spanish civil war. It was because of contacts that they might have made outside their countries that they appeared less dependable to the Kremlin, regardless of proof of their loyalty. All had participated in, though perhaps not personally organized, the elimination of opponents of the new political order. And paradoxically, men like Rajk and Slansky were later decorated as martyrs, though they were in reality the first victims of the repressive system which they themselves had worked so hard to create. Outside of the automatic outcry raised by Western journalists, it is doubtful that the thousands of innocent people thrown into prison by Rajk, Slansky and others, seriously bemoaned the fate of their one-time prosecutors.

Besides the well organized, propagandistic "show trials," there were millions of victims of the Stalin era whose trials and misfortunes were fairly unknown. Only after the 20th Party Congress in 1956, where Khrushchev openly admitted the police brutality and injustices committed against millions, did the world learn what had actually taken place in the years 1948-1956 in all the Eastern European states after the Communists seized power.

Following the Soviet precedent, a man-hunt began for so-called "reactionaries, fascists, capitalists, conspirators, counter-revolutionaries, spies and for any enemies of the proletariat." Millions were arrested, tortured in the cells of the secret police and, in most cases, sentenced in secret trials to hard labor in prison or in camps. Thousands were executed for "political crimes." In many cases, the accusations were based on false denunciations; in others, the secret police fabricated conspiracies and plots which the accused first learned about during their interrogation or in their trial. The treatment of those arrested was so barbaric that many died from torture, from beatings during interrogation, or simply from hunger. In Hungary in the years 1948-1956, not less than 400,000 people were arrested and sentenced, and over 1500 were executed or tortured to death—solely for political reasons.

The victims at the beginning were mostly from the former ruling classes and others whose loyalty to the order of things was suspect: officers, military personnel, former government employees, intellectuals, priests, landowners, businessmen—members of the middle class. Later they also victimized workers, peasants and students who had started to protest against the terror and the tumultuous economic situation.

Although millions were sent to jail, thousands of these "undesirables" were exiled from the cities and sent to the country or to forced labor camps. They were picked up by the secret police at night-time, given one hour to pack their most needed belongings—100 pounds per person—and had to leave everything else, home and possessions, behind forever. In Hungary, in May-June, 1951, nearly 100,000 of these undesirables were evicted from Budapest and deported to collective farms in the east of the country. Similar methods were used in Czechoslovakia at about the same time, and numerous opponents of the Rumanian regime were assigned to forced labor on the Danubian delta.

The Struggle Against the Church

The attitude of the Communist power toward religion and the church varied from country to country. In Bulgaria and Rumania, where the populations were primarily Orthodox, the new power tried to bring church leaders over to the cause, playing on a long-standing antagonism with Rome and on the necessity of siding with the patriarch of Moscow, who was devoted to the Soviet state. From the beginning, the Serbian Orthodox clergy adopted a submissive position towards Tito's regime. Everywhere the recalcitrant members of the Orthodox clergy were removed from their parishes with the cooperation of church hierarchy and relegated to monasteries where they became virtual prisoners. The Orthodox church became one of the main forces behind the regime, and as such, reaped the benefits. In Rumania, the government forcefully brought the Catholic Uniates back into the fold as a recompense. The Uniate Church had been separate since the end of the seventeenth century, and its abolition in 1948 was deeply resented by its followers and clergy, who continued their practices secretly, often under persecution.

In the Catholic countries, the situation was different. The Catholic church was a force to be reckoned with because of its ties to Rome and its centralized structure. Unless neutralized or at least controlled by the state, it was seen as a potential rallying point for dissidents. As early as 1945-1946, numerous priests and monks as well as prominent Catholics were arrested and sentenced for "collaboration" and "anti-Soviet activities." Officially, the church as such was not targeted, although under the pretext of "collaboration" such well-known personalities as Josef Stepinac, the archbishop of Zagreb, were eliminated. Similarly, the agrarian reforms that affected church property were not specifically directed against the church, but by depriving it of its patrimony, the church became dependent on the state for survival. Where Catholics were a minority, as in Albania, the church was eliminated by 1945, but elsewhere, persecution did not begin until 1945-1947. The Catholic press was dismantled step by step beginning in 1946, with the exception of Poland, which was granted a reprieve until 1949. By that time, the independent Catholic press was essentially eliminated in the rest of Eastern Europe. Next came nationalization of educational institutions operated by the church and abolition of mandatory religious instruction, measures which were in effect everywhere but Poland by 1948. All Catholic associations, youth and adult, and all Catholic action movements were dissolved. These actions were protested by the local church officials, often accompanied by demonstrations by followers. The ruling powers retaliated through the Communist press, violently attacking the Vatican "agent of American imperialism" and the bishopric. More insidious procedures were also employed; the state might encourage minority movements of Priests for Peace, led by "progressive" priests on friendly terms with the communists—men like Father Horvath in Hungary and Father Plohjar in Czechoslovakia. The state also openly supported Catholic movements receptive to new ideas; one such movement was the Pax group in Poland, led by a former leader of a far-rightist party before the war named Count Boleslaw Piasecki, who had been arrested by the Soviets in 1944, then liberated as a Communist. Attempts were made to play the lower clergy against the higher clergy, but with only limited success. As an example, the "open mind and cooperative attitude" of Cardinal Stefan Wyszynski in Poland was contrasted with his "reactionary" colleagues, Cardinal Mindszenty in Hungary and Father Beran in Czechoslovakia, who were both accused of being agents of the Vatican—called the "center of international fascism" by the Orthodox Council held in Moscow in July, 1948.

Repeated public protests by the Catholic church against the attacks on religious freedom, against the encroachment of the temporal upon the spiritual and against the abuse of power by the regime, led to the physical persecution of numerous priests in late 1948. The Communist state grew increasingly intolerant of this moral force commanding such a large audience. The thousands of Hungarians who crowded in to hear sermons by Cardinal Mindszenty and the hundreds of thousands of Poles who thronged around the sanctuary at Czestochowa, only strengthened the Communist leaders' resolve to strike quickly. Cardinal Mindszenty was arrested on December 26, 1948, and accused of plotting against the Republic, of spying, and of dealing in foreign currency. His appearance in court, physically broken, and his faltering confession of his "crimes" for which he was condemned to prison for life, provoked a wave of protest in the country. In order to avoid a serious uprising, the Hungarian bishopric capitulated; on April 30, Archbishop Grosz agreed to sign an agreement with the government which officially guaranteed freedom of religion and financial aid to the church, in exchange for the church's recognition and pledge of loyalty to the socialist state. The agreement was in fact blatant deceit. One week later, the Hungarian government dissolved nearly all religious orders: over 10,000 priests and nuns were dispersed, many of them sent to work camps. At the beginning of the following year, Archbishop Grosz was arrested in turn and sentenced to 15 years in prison. In the same year in Czechoslovakia, the bishops that had not been arrested in 1950 were rounded up, including Archbishop Beran of Prague on March 10, 1951. In Poland that year, the police arrested Bishop Kaczmarek of Kielce, and the former archbishop of

Lvov, Basiak. Also that year, every Catholic bishop remaining in Rumania was imprisoned. The high clergy was not the only victim of these physical persecutions; the lower clergy was continually harassed, as priests were arrested and seminaries closed. In the early 1950s everywhere in Eastern Europe, the Catholic church had become a "church of silence." Poland remained the only fortunate exception, but not for long. Cardinal Wyszynski, who had gone ahead and signed an agreement with the government despite the serious reservations of the Holy See, was targeted anyhow and restricted to his quarters in September, 1953.

While the hierarchy was being dismantled, the state assumed greater control of the church by creating an Office for Ecclesiastical Affairs in all Catholic countries, responsible for the assignments and nominations of all priests made by the bishops who remained. With the ability to veto or approve certain candidates for certain posts, the Communist state was in fact in full control of each diocese. In addition, when a bishop died, his Rome-appointed successor could not take office without prior government approval. Because of their opposition to the government, many appointed bishops were not allowed to carry out their duties and their dioceses were placed under the direction of apostolic administrators chosen by the government.

The Protestant churches in general experienced fewer difficulties, with the exception of East Germany where the Protestant majority posed a potential threat. In other countries, Protestants were in the minority, so the state's only tactics were to eliminate troublesome pastors and bishops considered to be hostile, and to attempt to pit the Protestant minority against the Catholics. Protestants often joined the government, as did Janos Peter, a Hungarian Protestant bishop, when he became Minister of Foreign Affairs. More commonly in these Catholic countries, a Protestant would be appointed head of the Office of Ecclesiastical Affairs.

Economic and Social Tranformations

At the end of the war, the new governments in Eastern Europe instigated bureaucratic reorganizations that would lead, several years later, to the establishment of a planned socialist economy. The first steps taken concentrated on agriculture, with the object of definitively eliminating large private landholding in Eastern Europe. The agrarian reforms first set a maximum limit on private property, limits which ranged from five hectares in Albania, to 20 hectares in Bulgaria (except for a 30 hectare limit in the Dobrudja), 45 hectares in Yugoslavia (with a maximum of 20 to 35 hectares for arable land according to region), 50 hectares in Rumania and Czechoslovakia, 57.5 hectares in Hungary, 50 to 100 hectares in Poland according to region, and 100 hectares in the German Democratic Republic.

Land reclaimed in this way was redistributed among small farmers or to landless peasants. The largest property transfers took place in Poland and in East Germany. In Hungary, over 2,900,000 hectares, or 34.6 percent of the land, was divided among some 642,000 farmers, most of whom had extremely small plots. In Poland, 4,500,000 hectares reclaimed in the ex-German western provinces were given out in lots of seven to 15 hectares to 440,000 peasant families, while in the older provinces, 1,100,000 hectares filled out the small plots of 440,000 families. In East Germany, the large aristocratic estates of the Prussian *junkers* disappeared; 559,000 beneficiaries shared 2,190,000 hectares, 40 percent of which was distributed in lots of seven hectares to agricultural workers. Part of the confiscated land was not redistributed, and formed the first state farms modeled on the Soviet *sovkhozes*.

As soon as the popular democratic regimes were firmly in place, the leaders encouraged the peasants to form collective farms modeled on the Soviet *kolkhozes*. In 1945, the Bulgarian government began encouraging cooperative work farms, which by 1948 already numbered 579 and covered 190,000 hectares. Yugoslavia and Albania had adopted identical policies in 1945. Elsewhere, collectivization of land was delayed in order to avoid upsetting rural order. 1949 was a decisive year in agricultural collectivization; landholdings were pooled, supposedly by voluntary contributions from the farmers, but actually accomplished by the same type of coersion used in the USSR in the 1930s. The tensions caused by the land collectivization surfaced as passive resistance by the peasants, or, in East Germany, by massive emigration to the Federal Republic of Germany (West Germany). By 1953, the process of collectivization was well underway. Yugoslavia had given the peasants some choice fairly early, but in 1953 lowered the maximum size of individual farms to ten hectares. Collectivization in the other countries was complete in the 1960s, with the exception of Poland where the peasants were able to leave the cooperatives after the events of 1956—which most of them did.

In other sectors of the economy, changes went deeper and were more radical. During the years 1945-1958, the banks were nationalized, as were foreign trade, mining, transportation and basic industries. In some countries like Albania and Bulgaria, industries were totally nationalized from the beginning. Other countries accomplished nationalization in stages, beginning with companies with over 500 employees, then in companies with over 100 workers, until in 1949 nearly the entire industrial sector and even some craft sectors were nationalized. Retail trade was also affected by nationalizations, although in certain countries like Hungary, East Germany and Yugoslavia, part of the retail business remained in the private sector.

These changes completely upset social structures. The independent worker, the artisan, the businessman and the small shopkeeper, all became salaried workers in a production cooperative. The medical professions were bureaucratized and the pharmacies nationalized. Other liberal professions, like notaries and court clerks, were bureaucratized, while lawyers were organized into professional cooperatives. In order to more effectively erase the past and open certain "noble" professions to the new rising classes, entry into institutions of higher learning was restricted to students from only the worker and peasant classes—a policy which had drastic implications for the countries. All the major alterations which took place in the Stalin era were at first instituted by force, and later maintained with more flexibility.

The entire economic system in the Eastern European countries was determined by rigorous mandatory plans, plans with more emphasis on production than on consumption and revenues. Beginning in 1950, after the initial short-term plans aimed at postwar reconstruction were concluded, five year plans were universally adopted. As in political matters, Eastern European leaders followed the Soviet model in drafting their economic plans. Heavy industry and equipment took priority over consumer needs. Urbanization accompanied industrialization, and workers began to outnumber peasants everywhere except in the less economically developed countries like Albania, Bulgaria, Rumania and Yugoslavia. The push to develop heavy industry required massive investments possible only through great sacrifice on the part of the people; the production of consumer goods was sharply limited, leading to market shortages of many basic items. These scarcities, combined with problems in the system of distribution and insufficient family incomes at the lower levels—despite the increase in women workers—fostered an atmosphere of discontent which lay dormant, waiting for the right moment to explode.

Chapter 25

Eastern Europe During Destalinization
1953—1968

The death of Stalin on March 5, 1953, five years after popular democracies had been established throughout Eastern Europe, was the first major test the new leaders had to confront. Just as they had followed Stalin's every instruction during his reign, these leaders followed instructions from the new men in the Kremlin with the same docility. Only a month after Stalin's departure, on March 27, the new leadership headed by Georgi Malenkov initiated a policy of reform with the publication of a liberal decree of amnesty, quickly followed by an assault on the security forces (the *KGB*) and its director, Lavrenti Beria, who served as the scapegoat. By eliminating Beria in July, the new Soviet leaders gave the strong impression that they intended to make a break with certain practices of the past. Malenkov and his team established a collective leadership of the state and of the Party in order to avoid repeating the over-personalization of power under Stalin. A breath of liberalism seemed to warm the Kremlin, but would it reach the satellite-country capitals? There was every reason to believe so, since during a July meeting of the Cominform in Moscow the Soviet leaders advised that the "brother parties" universally adopt collective leadership and make certain concessions to the people.

Thus, changes in Moscow were to set an example for the other popular democracies to follow, altering the pro-Stalin attitude of the leaderships and easing the daily life of the people.

WARNING STORMS BEFORE 1956

The First Explosion: Berlin 1953

At the time of Stalin's death, the German Democratic Republic was in particularly difficult straits. In addition to the economic problems then common to all of the Eastern European countries, East Germany was confronted with a wave of discontent called, colloquially, "voting with the feet." Thousands of East Germany citizens—agricultural workers angered by the collectivization of land, factory workers disappointed in the regime and unhappy with their low wages, professionals young and old—began taking advantage of the policy of unrestricted travel between the different parts of the former *Reich*. With a simple subway ticket, East Germans in dangerously accelerating numbers were going from the Soviet sector to the Western sectors, and from there, by air to West Germany where work was plentiful and the living standard higher. The departures only aggravated an already suffering economy. Ignoring signals from Moscow to moderate policy, Walter Ulbricht issued a decree on May 28, 1953, raising quotas for production—ostensibly to avert an economic crisis—and was met with a backlash. The Soviets disclaimed him, raising opposition against him in the SED and forcing him to back down. On June 11, the Party newspaper, *Neues Deutschland*, announced certain measures were being taken to improve the quality of life for the people, including an end to university discrimination aimed at the youth of the middle classes. Nonetheless, the decree of May 28 remained in force, and the people reacted by rising *en masse*.

On June 16, demonstrations took place in the streets of East Berlin protesting the raised quotas for production; the announcement of its suspension at the end of the day was not enough to calm emotions. The next day, on the 17th, a general strike took place in Berlin, Leipzig, Dresden, Rostock, and in most of the other industrial centers of the country. In Berlin, the demonstrators quickly got out of hand, overstepping the bounds of order by attacking official buildings and Party headquarters, and then burning the Soviet flag flying over Brandenburg Gate, the symbol of divided Germany. The worker demonstration had degenerated into an anti-Soviet demonstration. That afternoon, the Soviet army took action. A state of siege was declared and Red Army tanks rolled through the streets, shooting into the unarmed crowds. The following repression was harsh; in addition to the hundreds of victims of the street fighting, the Soviet military tribunals had over 40 people executed immediately. There were over 20,000 arrests, and thousands of people were sentenced to heavy prison terms.

The true beneficiary of the events in Berlin was Ulbricht, who was able to persuade Moscow that he alone was capable of bringing about order in East Germany. Until his death in 1973, he ruled over the German Democratic Republic with a heavy hand.

Destalinization in Hungary and Its Limitations

In Hungary, the first consequences of the Kremlin's new orientation was a brief eclipse of Stalin's most faithful Hungarian disciple, Matyas Rakosi. The office of secretary general of the Hungarian Workers' party that he occupied was taken over by a directorship of three secretaries, but Rakosi himself remained as one of them. Simultaneously, Rakosi ceded his post as prime minister to Imre Nagy, who had been in semi-disgrace since 1950. On July 4, 1953, Imre Nagy presented his platform to the parliament. In the economic sphere, he announced a slowdown in agricultural collectivization and offered a means for dissolving collectives if a majority of members so desired. What most impressed the public, however, was the announced liberalization of the regime. "The agents of power," Nagy declared, "should take care to see that every citizen is able to enjoy rights stipulated in the constitution. Enforcement of the law is one of the most urgent tasks of the government." A partial amnesty was immediately declared and several concentration camps were closed. Furthermore, several thousand "undesirables" evicted from Budapest were allowed to return to the capital. But Imre Nagy had to reckon with the Stalinists still numerous in the Party. "Nagyists" and "Rakosists" confronted each other violently during the congress held in March, 1954, but the new political line followed by Nagy was ultimately approved. The conflict between "liberals" and "Stalinisits" flared up again soon thereafter, and during the March 9, 1955, meeting of the central committee, the "Rakosists" once again gained the upper hand. They denounced the "rightist deviation of Comrade Nagy," relieved him of his duties and replaced him on April 4 with a Rakosi loyalist, Andras Hegedus. Nagy was dismissed from the Party in November.

It was difficult for the new leadership to retract the liberalization policies initiated by Nagy, because an atmosphere of thaw had already begun to pervade the country. People had begun to speak openly again, to discuss issues and to criticize policy; prewar political leaders like Anna Kethly, Bela Kovacs and Zoltan Tildy had been liberated; peasants left collective farms in droves and returned to their old farms; and in Budapest, students and intellectuals gathered together for increasingly open discussions through an organization known as the Petofi Circle, named for the revolutionary poet of 1848. The circle publicly demanded the return of Imre Nagy, who in less than two years had become immensely popular in the country. Within the Party itself, the old militants began to demand the rehabilitation of Laszlo Rajk and his friends, and were successful after a long and persistent struggle when he was released on March 27, 1956. By then, the real defendent in the Rajk trial, Tito, had himself been publicly rehabilitated by the new leaders in the Kremlin.

The Moscow-Belgrade Reconciliation

The death of Stalin removed the major obstacle to improved relations between the USSR and Yugoslavia. On June 6, Molotov suggested that embassies replace the diplomatic missions that had taken care of diplomatic relations between the two countries since 1949, an offer Tito quickly accepted. Then the Soviet press, followed by the press in the popular democracies, slowly stopped attacking Yugoslav leaders. Border incidents with Albania, Hungary and Rumania—so numerous in the early 1950s—nearly ceased. But the major event, which took place just after Bulganin and Khrushchev took charge and stabilized power in the USSR, was the trip these new Soviet leaders took to Yugoslavia. Nikita Khrushchev, first secretary of the COSU (Communist Party of the Soviet Union), accompanied by Premier Nikolai A. Bulganin and president of the presidium, Anastas I. Mikoyan, arrived in Belgrade on May 26, 1955. Khrushchev publicly expressed his regrets for what had happened in 1948 and astutely blamed much of the errors on Beria; he further recognized the Yugoslav Communist party as an authentic Marxist-Leninist party. The address Khrushchev delivered to Tito at the Belgrade airport on May 26, 1955, follows:

Dear Comrade Tito,

"... The people of our countries have long been united by ties of fraternal friendship and by common struggle.... We sincerely regret what has happened.... We have carefully studied the documents on which the grave accusations and the grave offenses directed against the leaders of Yugoslavia were founded. Facts prove that these documents were complete forgeries...."

The communique published as a result of the visit stressed the validity of "different forms of socialist development." After this diplomatic mission, the other Eastern European countries, one by one, normalized relations with Yugoslavia. Only Albania seemed to harbor certain reservations; Enver Hoxha had not forgotten Tito's imperialist designs on Albania. For the time-being, however, Yugoslavia had become a full-fledged member of the "socialist family" despite the fact that its leaders had not renounced any of their independence.

Destalinization in the Other Eastern European Countries

The revolt in East Berlin and the internal struggles within the Hungarian Workers' party prompted leaders in the other countries to act with caution. In Czechoslovakia action was limited to the establishment of a collective leadership. After Gottwald succumbed, on March 14, 1953, to an acute flu virus he contracted during exposure at Stalin's funeral, Antonin Zapotocky became president of the Republic and was replaced as head of government by Villiam Soroky, a Slovak. Meanwhile, the Party, separated at least in principle from the state, was put under the leadership of Antonin Novotny. In early June, 1953, a monetary reform including a change in currency which devalued personal savings, led to rioting; the harsh repression that followed indicated that Stalinist tendencies remained strong in Czechoslovakia despite changes in government and Party personnel. Those who favored the hard line continued to govern for another 10 years, and little by little, the first secretary of the Party, Novotny, became the leading figure in the system. Rehabilitating the victims of the great trial of 1951-1952 was never even considered.

In Rumania, destalinization was limited to a small-scale amnesty. Gheorgiu-Dej, Rumania's "best son" and the secretary general of the Rumanian Communist party since 1945, kept his office despite a minor eclipse in 1953, while Petru Groza remained president of the Republic. In Bulgaria as well, the changes were limited. A few outcasts, such as Kostov who was executed in 1949 for Titoism, were rehabilitated. Vulko Chervenkov remained as secretary general of the Bulgarian Communist party and as chief of state until 1956, when he relinquished his leadership to Todor Zhivkov, his assistant and a fellow Stalinist. The situation in Albania was similar: Enver Hoxha remained leader of the Albania Workers' party but entrusted the government to Mehmet Shehu, a man who had organized the anti-Titoist purges of 1948-1949.

In Yugoslavia, it seemed absurd to speak of destalinization since Tito had in fact been Stalin's first victim. However, the methods of Tito's government even after the break with Moscow had remained Stalinist. The wind of liberalism that had swept over most Eastern European countries after 1953 had reason to affect Yugoslavia as well. The major changes came in the economic sector with the development of decentralization initiated in 1951, and marked by decollectivization of farmland in 1953. The year 1953 also witnessed a measure of liberalization in the government when a few political prisoners were set free, but, on the whole, the government remained dictatorial. A long-time companion of Tito, Milovan Djilas, president of the Federal Assembly, was sharply reminded of this fact when he was excommunicated from the League of Communists for having criticized the bureaucracy and for demanding the democratization of the government.

When Djilas repeated his charges in a *New York Times* article published in December, 1954, and added to them by calling for the creation of a second political party, he was relieved of all his public duties and put under surveillance.

Poland initially remained impervious to the changes taking place in the neighboring countries. In Poland, charges of "violating socialist legality" had been less numerous and had come later than elsewhere. As in the other countries, however, the Party and the state were separated in March, 1954. The Stalinist Bierut kept his control of the Party, but relinquished his post as president of the state council to Alexander Zawadski. The socialist Jozef Cyrankiewicz took over as the ministerial council president, serving from 1947 to 1952. The following August, the new government decided to liberate several thousand political prisoners including the former secretary general of the Polish Workers' party, Gomulka; it also announced that it would re-examine the cases of parliament members unjustly accused. Warsaw appeared to be hastening to correct the errors of the past, but their reforms were tempered with actions such as placing Cardinal Wyszynski under house arrest. Nevertheless, as in Hungary, even what was judged to be insufficient liberalization provoked a mood of renewal in intellectual circles, and political discussions raged openly.

Despite its shortcomings, the first phase of what is called destalinization began a process with ramifications soon felt by the leaders of certain countries, Poland and Hungary in particular. The Soviets, who had originated this destalinization, had not altered their views on their hegemony in Eastern Europe. To better weld the diverse components to Moscow and to each other, and also to alert the Western powers to the limits of the thaw beginning to appear in East-West relations, the Soviets organized a meeting of all Eastern European leaders in Warsaw from May 11 to 14, 1955. It was at this meeting that the treaty of friendship, cooperation and mutual assistance known as the **Warsaw Pact** was signed. The pact was officially drafted as a response to the rearmament of West Germany; however, its purpose was above all to reinforce ties between the socialist countries. A unified military command was created and immediately assigned to the Soviet marshal, Ivan S. Konev, who held the post until 1961. All of the Eastern European countries took part in the Warsaw Pact with the exception of Yugoslavia—even after its reconciliation with Moscow.

THE CRISES OF 1956

Even though it may appear astonishing, it was the 20th Soviet Communist Party Congress held in Moscow in February, 1956, that unleashed the crises brewing in certain countries. During the congress,

Nikita Khrushchev read a secret report behind closed doors and in the presence of only the highest command of the Soviet Party. The Khrushchev report denounced the extremist cult of personality developed under Stalin, ennumerated his crimes and abuses of power, and detailed the methods used in the Stalinist era to incite a veritable terror in the country. Khrushchev also mentioned the persecutions that had victimized certain peoples of the Soviet Union both during and after the war, and analyzed the dominant versus dominated character of relations between the USSR and the popular democracies.

The Polish leadership received the Khrushchev report during March, and were the first to reveal its contents at the urgent request of the Party—causing a great stir in the country. The contents of the document were soon known to Eastern Europeans everywhere because Western radio stations diffused the information in their broadcasts directed at the Eastern bloc. The broadcasts understandably invoked skepticism in the minds of ordinary citizens, and caused Party activists a good deal of mental turmoil. On the other hand, Yugoslavs were delighted with this *a posteriori* justification for their conduct in 1948, and the April, 1956, announcement that the Cominform was to be disbanded only confirmed their position.

The people in the Eastern bloc countries had their own interpretation of the Khrushchev report. For them, the report symbolized a challenge to the entire system which had been imposed on them in 1945, not just questions of theory reserved for policymakers to deliberate over. The public assumed that the next step, logically, would be the departure of the present leadership which had so blindly followed orders from Moscow; they felt that eventually the operation of the government would have to be reconsidered; indeed the government itself would have to be put under scrutiny. The strongest reactions against the existing governments took place in Poland and Hungary, both Catholic countries with Western traditions and more developed national awarenesses.

The Illusion of Liberalization in Poland

In Poland, where the first phase of destalinization had been slow to begin, the outcome of the 20th Congress was the appointment of a "centrist," Edward Ochab, to succeed the Stalinist, Bierut—who had died in Moscow March 12—as head of the Party. Ochab considerably broadened the scope of the liberalization previously initiated; 30,000 political prisoners from a variety of backgrounds were granted amnesty in April, and former Communist leaders, given conditional liberty at the end of 1954, were granted total freedom—though not rehabilitation. Such was the fate of Gomulka and his associates. On the other hand, prosecution began against the major directors of the security forces for "violating socialist legality."

The general population raised much more concrete problems. Low salaries and increases in production quotas had caused deep discontent among the workers in late 1955. Tensions rose sharply during the International Fair at the end of June, 1956, but the situation had been ready to explode for several months. When workers from Poznan sent a delegation to Warsaw to present their complaints and had their demands rejected, they declared a strike and took to the streets. On June 28, to the astonishment of the participants and foreign visitors at the fair, the workers demonstrated, shouting slogans which were not limited to economic and social affairs: "Down with the USSR! Freedom of religion! Freedom for Cardinal Wysynski!" The crowd seized several police commissariats and set arrested protestors free. The Polish authorities called in the army, and Polish army tanks and security forces brutally cleared the streets. When it was over, order once again reigned in Poznan, but hundreds had been arrested, and, by official counts, the casualty toll stood at 54 dead, hundreds wounded. The authorities denounced the "armed provocateurs" they held responsible for the action, and accused "agents of American imperialism" of interference. Feelings of discontent ran deep throughout the population; the leaders of the Communist party had changed, but nothing had been settled.

At the plenary meeting of the central committee held in Warsaw, July 18-20, 1956, Stalinists and moderates clashed. The liberals could not get past the Soviet veto in their efforts to obtain the rehabilitation of Wladislaw Gomulka, who enjoyed a certain measure of popularity with his status as a victim of Stalinism, and seemed to be the only person able to rekindle confidence in the country.

Destalinization continued to proceed cautiously. The atmosphere of latent discontent led the Polish leaders to make certain concessions, but all within an established framework. Meanwhile, the situation grew more critical daily. The Catholics demanded freedom for their primate and made this demand known in a dramatic fashion during the national pilgrimage to Czestochowa. There, on August 15, prominently placed on the stage, was an empty chair—a visible symbol of the absence of Cardinal Wyszynski.

In order to placate public opinion with a gesture, the Diet met in an extraordinary session and voted to reform the penal administration, restricting the rights of the police. Tension mounted at the end of September when the Poznan demonstrators were put on trial. During the trial, the government, its methods and its inability to solve real problems, were denounced without hesitation. When the verdict was passed down, it was clear that the atmosphere had changed; sentences were lenient, indicating an effort on the government's part to avoid more trouble.

The government had to act quickly because public opinon was growing more and more impatient. The Polish leaders wanted to keep Poland in the socialist camp while simultaneously appeasing the people. After a long hesitation, the central committee decided in early October to recall Gomulka; on October 13, in the presence of Gomulka, the politburo worked out an elaborate program of reforms to be ratified at the central committee meeting called for the 19th. The Stalinists among the Party leaders were disappointed in this turn of events and attempted a forceful takeover supported by the army; they knew they could rely on Marshal Rokossovsky and on General Witaszewski, but their plans were thwarted when subordinate officers and enlisted men refused to participate. The planned military *coup*, intended to arrest Gomulka and other liberals sometime between October 15 and 19, never took place.

The Polish leaders realized that only an intervention by the Soviets could alter the course of events. In fact, on the morning of October 19, 1956, Khrushchev, Molotov and Mikoyan accompanied by Marshal Konev and an impressive military delegation, arrived in Warsaw. At the same time, Soviet troops semed ready to converge on Warsaw from throughout the country. Despite these threats, the central committee met and began their affairs by naming Gomulka to the post of first secretary. Gomulka, whose confidence was bolstered by the firm backing of the Party leadership, led a delegation from the Polish central committee that met with the Soviet delegation. During the night of October 19, Poles and Soviets argued passionately while the population was kept informed by radio, readying itself for the worst. On the morning of October 20, the Soviets left for Moscow, and tension eased slightly.

The Soviets' motivation to recognize Gomulka in his new office did not come from a fear of a hostile reaction by the Polish people; they had more than the means to suppress any attempts at resistance at their disposal. On the contrary, what led them to "give in" was Gomulka's reassurance that he and his entourage would retain "essentials," which for Moscow included continuing the socialist form of government and maintaining alliances with the USSR and the socialist camp. Gomulka made no secret of his intentions to this effect when he gave a speech before the central committee in Poland on October 20, declaring, "We will not permit anyone to profit from the process of democratization at the expense of socialism. At the head of this process of democratization is our Party." For Gomulka, there was never any question of jeopardizing "the cause of socialism in Poland."

Such words could not help but reassure the Soviets. During the same session, Gomulka announced several measures calculated to placate a suspicious public. He made it known that the peasants would be allowed to leave the cooperatives—which most of them rushed to do—and that religious freedom would be respected, provided the church supported the popular government. On October 21, Cardinal Wyszynski was liberated. Shortly afterwards, a combined church/state commission began work on outstanding problems. The peasants and the Catholics, who made up the majority of the Polish people, seemed to have been satisfied. For the workers who had instigated the chain of events, Gomulka promised higher wages as well as the democratization of the official unions.

Were these concessions merely opportunistic measures concocted to win the support of the people and the church, or were they the beginnings of a new route towards socialism? No one in Poland seemed to be asking such questions at the end of 1956. Everyone trusted Gomulka, believing he had just saved the country from Soviet military intervention—an issue of major concern for the Poles. They were especially sensitive to it since they had just seen, from not so far away, that same Soviet army crush the insurrection in Hungary.

The Hungarian Revolution of 1956

The first phase of destalinization in Hungary ended with the elimination of its principal author, Imre Nagy, and the return to power of the Stalinist forces led by Matyas Rakosi and his friends. Nagy's brief stay in power had fueled hopes for change, not just within the population but within the Communist party itself. The "Nagyist" Communists now felt it necessary to bring their leader back to power and establish a true social democracy. For many private citizens who had forgotten the role he had played in 1945 as Minister of the Interior, the name Imre Nagy evoked images of the decollectivization of land, partial political amnesty, greater freedom in the country, and the beginnings of real change. Feeling pressure from the growing discontent of the population and worried by the events in Poznan, Rakosi finally decided to step out of the political limelight, and on July 18, 1956, asked to be "relieved of his duties" because of "errors in creating a cult of personality and in violating socialist legality." However, one of Rakosi's closest allies, Erno Gero, replaced him at the head of the Party. Several others, who never belonged to the Rakosi clique, were also admitted to the central committee; these comrades, such as Gyorgy Marosan and Janos Kadar, had been victims of the Stalinist purges. But with Gero at the head of the Party and Hegedus still at the head of government, Rakosi's friends remained in control.

Nevertheless, the Petofi Circle in Budapest and other intellectual circles were demanding Imre Nagy's return, while people throughout the country were watching the evolution of events in Poland with great interest. During the October 6th funeral services for Laszlo Rajk and other victims of the 1949 trials, the first major public expression of a desire for change surfaced. During the ceremony, Imre Nagy publicly expressed his sympathies to the widow of the former minister of the interior. It was a strange ceremony, one in which the "mourners," the opponents of the regime, came more to demonstrate their hostility to the Rakosi regime than to pay their respects to the dead. Gomulka's return to power in Poland inspired a wave of enthusiasm in Hungary, an atmosphere heightened by the October 14th announcement by the central committee that Nagy was to be rehabilitated. Joyful demonstrations were held throughout the country, celebrating a future which suddenly appeared brighter. Around October 19, taking advantage of regained freedoms, students in Szeged, Debrecen and especially Budapest, formed independent associations outside of the official associations controlled by the Party. The Budapest student group immediately drafted a manifesto of 14 points including demands for the withdrawal of Soviet troops, for free and secret elections with more than a single list, freedom of the press and of artistic expression, freedom for political prisoners, and above all, the reinstatement of Imre Nagy as head of government.

On October 23, the leaders of the Communist party—Gero, Hegedus and Kadar—returned from an official visit to Yugoslavia, only to find their capital in a state of agitated excitement. The students had organized a demonstration of solidarity with the Poles which was to be held in front of the statue of General Bem, the Polish hero of the Hungarian Revolution of 1848-49. At first, the demonstration was prohibited, but later it was authorized to proceed for that afternoon. The students were soon joined by workers from the suburbs and people passing by, and the crowd proceeded to assemble in front of the state radio building. Suddenly, while the students were asking that their demands be broadcast, the *AVH* (secret police) fired into the crowd. The moment constituted a turning point, changing a peaceable demonstration into a violent uprising: the *AVH*, already intensely unpopular and universally feared by the Hungarians, had attacked a defenseless crowd. The demonstration quickly turned riotous, and Hungarian soldiers who were sent to reestablish order distributed their guns to the crowd instead. Flags were raised with the Communist red star torn out of the center. The crowd, which had swelled to around 250,000 people, was surging towards the parliament where Imre Nagy was desperately attempting to calm them. When the old leader began to speak, he used "Comrades!" to address the crowd, which provoked angry boos. The crisis was no longer a problem within the Party, but was developing into a revolt against the government itself. That evening on the radio, Gero denounced the "threatening forces which weighed against socialism" and reprimanded the activists who were "attempting to break the bonds between our Party and the glorious Communist party of the Soviet Union." The speech angered the demonstrators still in control of the streets. During the night, a mob attacked the Communist buildings and Soviet bookstores, set fire to portraits of

Communist leaders, and began destroying the giant statue of Stalin. During this time, radio broadcasts were warning the people of "fascists and reactionary elements" that had risen up against the socialist order. In the early hours of the morning on October 24, Imre Nagy, as newly appointed prime minister, announced the imposition of martial law and appealed to the demonstrators to put down their arms. He also made it clear that he favored the development of a "socialism with a national character," but these words were not enough to restore peace, and revolt spread to the rest of the country.

Before resigning as head of the Party, Gero asked for assistance from the Soviets. On the 24th, Soviet tanks began to crawl through the streets of Budapest, but did little else; there were even a few instances of Soviet fraternization with the crowds. That evening, a Soviet delegation led by Mikoyan and Mikhail Suslov arrived in Budapest and immediately met with Imre Nagy at Party headquarters. Nagy seemed to have received a *carte blanche* from the Soviets to act on his own discretion, and in fact, the replacement of Gero on the 25th by Janos Kadar as the head of the Party, was interpreted as a gesture of appeasement. The new first secretary announced that "once order is reestablished, there will be negotiations with the USSR for a fair and just settlement of outstanding matters between the two socialist countries." The insurgents appeared to have won the first round, but the revolt was far from over. The general strike, begun in Budapest on the 24th of October, had spread rapidly throughout the country. New Revolutionary Workers' councils were established in preparation for the creation of a genuinely democratic system of government; members of the councils were elected, and took over all functions from the Communist bureaucracy with little or no resistance. On occasion the *AVH* fought back, as in Mosonmagyarovar, where they fired into the crowd and killed over a hundred civilians. This sort of violent resistance by the *AVH* provoked the anger of the revolutionaries, and a number of the political police were massacred in retaliation, especially after torture cells—used in the not-so-distant past—were discovered in Budapest. The Revolutionary Workers' councils were one of the most characteristic features of the uprising, representing the first practical steps towards restoring order in the country and reorganizing the Hungarian economy on a socialist basis, only this time, without Communist party control.

Imre Nagy was being swept away by the magnitude of the movement. To appease the people, he invited Bela Kovacs and Zoltan Tildy, formerly of the Smallholders' party, to join his government on the 27th. The Revolutionary Workers' council and non-Communist members of the government only recognized Nagy as the head of a national union government; the one-party system had been unanimously rejected. On October 28, Nagy appeared to be siding with the revolutionaries: "the government refuses to consider this massive popular uprising as a counter-revolution.... The grave crimes committed in the course of these last years of our history have precipitated this vast movement," he declared in a radio broadcast. He also announced that an agreement had been reached with the Soviets on the withdrawal of Soviet forces from Budapest, and that negotiations on the withdrawal of troops from the entire country were underway.

Nagy's speech was well received. At that point, the situation in the country was as follows: in Budapest, the official government was in the hands of Imre Nagy under the watchful eyes of diverse movements, associations and parties—which had been revitalized by the atmosphere of regained freedom. In the country, the real power was in the hands of the Revolutionary Workers' councils, whose philosophies varied according to region; the west of the country, Transdanubia, clearly leaned towards anti-communism, while the Council of Miskolc, in the east, represented "national communism." In Budapest, as in the country, a newly organized national guard maintained order with the regular police force. Despite the wide spectrum of opinions, there was agreement on two points: Soviet withdrawal from Hungarian soil, and the establishment of true democracy.

On October 28, Nagy's government ordered a ceasefire, and fighting stopped largely on the insurgents' terms. At the Kilian barracks in Budapest Hungarian army units had fought on the side of the revolutionaries against Soviet forces. In fact, except for the secret police, there were no recorded instances of Hungarian troops fighting on the side of the Soviets against their own countrymen. The army units fought under their new leader, Colonel Pal Maleter—who had been instructed to fight against the insurgents, but joined their forces instead.

The "freedom fighters" were primarily workers, students and other young Hungarian men and women, fighting in small groups with crude weapons. They were the first to use the "Molotov Cocktail," named after the Soviet foreign minister, which was a remarkably effective homemade bomb consisting of a loosely corked bottle filled with gasoline, designed to explode when thrown against a tank. The Soviet forces were also hampered by insufficient infantry support and a poor fighting moral within the ranks of the Russian soldiers, who disliked the task assigned them. About 300 Soviet soldiers actually fought on the side of the insurgents, and were later executed in the Soviet embassy yard in Budapest under the orders of Yuri Andropov—who was at that time Soviet ambassador.

For a few fleeting days, Hungary experienced a climate of exceptional liberty. All political prisoners were liberated, dozens of newspapers appeared and the political police was dissolved. Cardinal Mindszenty, symbol of the resistance in 1948, was liberated by soldiers of the regular army and on October 30, the Nagy government published a decree absolving him of all accusations against him. He was given a triumphant homecoming upon his return to Budapest on October 31.

These moments of freedom did not last long. On October 31, new Russian units, mainly from central Asia, entered the country. The capital was slowly being caught in a vice. On the evening of November 1, in a radio broadcast, Nagy criticized the Soviets for having broken their promises by sending in more soldiers; he then announced Hungary's intention to withdraw from the Warsaw Pact and become a neutral country, and in so doing committed the unpardonable in the eyes of the Soviets. Janos Kadar and several of his friends, probably acting on Tito's advice, broke with the Nagy government and took refuge in subcarpathic Ruthenia in Soviet territory. Meanwhile, the Red Army continued to pour into Hungary, despite the Hungarian government's protests to the Soviet embassy in Budapest and to the secretary general of the United Nations, Dag Hammarskjold. On November 3, the Soviet army was in control of most of the country; the Austrian border, open since October 24, was again closed off. In Budapest, Imre Nagy filled the vacancies left in his government by the departure of Kadar's associates with leaders of the former democratic parties, naming General Bela Kiraly as commander of the national guard and Pal Maleter, now a general, as Minister of Defense. As such, Maleter was to take part on the same day in negotiations with the Soviet high command to organize Soviet troop withdrawal. The meeting with the Soviets turned out to be an ambush. On the night of November 3, Maleter and members of the Hungarian delegation were arrested by the head of the Soviets, the *KGB*'s General Serov. That evening, Cardinal Mindszenty gave a radio-broadcast speech calling for national unity, a theme later subverted by official propaganda. The next morning, November 4, Budapest was attacked. Heavy artillery and an air force battered the city from the air, and tanks began entering the city from all sides. Despite the determined resistance of the national guard and civilian fighters, Soviet soldiers took control of most of the city in 48 hours. Within the next few days, the last pockets of resistance were crushed.

Order was restored by November 13. Government leaders who had not fled the country took refuge in foreign embassies. Nagy and his ministers went to the Yugoslav embassy. Despite assurances by the Yugoslavs of their safety, they were arrested by the Soviets as soon as they left the embassy. Cardinal Mindszenty found refuge in the United States embassy, remaining there until 1971.

November 4 marked the end of Hungary's brief encounter with freedom. That same day, Hungarians learned by radio that Janos Kadar had formed a "Hungarian Revolutionary Worker-Peasant Government." The new regime announced that it intended "to protect the progress made through socialism, to raise the living standard of the workers, to crush the harmful reactionary forces, and to restore peace and order with the help of the Soviets." Curious as it may seem, the men Moscow entrusted with the task of taking over Hungary were men like Janos Kadar and Gyorgy Marosan, who had themselves spent time in Rakosi's prisons for pro-Titoism.

Excerpts from Addresses Made in Hungary on November 3 and 4, 1956

Cardinal Mindszenty's Address—November 3, 1956

"We desire to live in complete friendship with all peoples and all countries.... We want to live on friendly terms with the great United States as well as with the all-powerful Russian empire, and we want to be good neighbors to Prague, Bucharest, Warsaw and Belgrade.... We are neutral. We have given the Soviet Union no reason for bloodshed.... Now we need free elections, without corruption, in which all parties can field candidates. These elections should be held under international supervision.... I summon all of my authority to caution Hungarians against any party quarrels or any misunderstanding after these days of magnificent unity..."

Appeal by Imre Nagy—November 4, 1956, 4:20 AM

"This is Prime Minister Imre Nagy. Today at dawn, Soviet troops launched an attack on the capital with the obvious intention of overturning the legal government of democratic Hungary. Our troops are resisting. The government is at its post. I am informing the Hungarian people and the entire world of these facts."

Janos Kadar's Address on the Morning of November 4, 1956

"...Even though much progress has been made during the last twelve years, the Rakosi-Gero clique have committed grievous errors and have seriously violated the law. All of this has rightly angered the workers. Reactionaries are now trying to use this discontent for their own purposes.... By exploiting the mistakes made in the construction of our popular democratic system, reactionary elements have misled a number of honest workers, particularly the young—who joined the movement with the best of patriotic intentions.... We must put an end to the excesses of the counter-revolution...."

Hungarian Writers' Union Appeal—November 4, 1956, 6:56 AM

"This is the Hungarian Writers' Union! To all writers of the world, to all groups of scholars and academicians, to all scientific academies and associations, to the intelligentsia of the world, we ask aid and support from each of you. There is not a moment to be lost. You know what is happening; it is useless to describe it in more detail. Help Hungary! Save the writers, the workers, the peasants of Hungary, and our intelligentsia! Help us! Help us! Help us!"

The Worker and Peasant Government's Appeal—
November 4, 1956, 9:00 PM

"The events of November 4 have brought about the total eclipse of reactionary forces in Hungary. The government of Imre Nagy, which opened the door to the counter-revolution, has crumbled and no longer exists.... The socialist forces of the Hungarian people, in conjunction with the Soviet troops called in to defend them, are dedicated to the tasks undertaken by the revolutionary worker and peasant government...."

Source: Horay, Pierre. *La Revolte de la Hongrie*, Paris, 1957. Excerpts from speeches broadcast on Hungarian radio in October-November, 1956.

The Hungarian revolution of 1956, when compared to events taking place at the same time in Poland, clearly demonstrated the extent of Moscow's tolerance. For Moscow, it was out of the question for any socialist country to leave the "system," regardless of the opinion of a majority of that country's inhabitants. A few reforms in the satellite countries might be acceptable, but for any member of the Warsaw Pact to renounce its alliances and take a neutral stance was absolutely intolerable.

Moscow viewed the uprising in Hungary as a security problem, a problem even more unnerving in light of the fact that France and Great Britain had chosen to launch the Suez expedition against Nassar's Egypt—then an ally of the USSR—at precisely the same time. The Soviets were under the impression that the events were related and part of some strategy. The Hungarian revolution, however, had been brewing for several years and was spontaneous—provoked by a regime which had imposed itself upon the people and had brought them nothing but misery and servitude.

The repression following the Hungarian revolution was harsh. Thousands were arrested and sentenced to long prison terms or captured by the Soviets and deported to Siberia; hundreds more were sentenced to death after quick military trials. The principal defendants, including Nagy and Maleter, were condemned to death after a secret trial and were executed June 17, 1958. According to the former chief of police in Budapest, Kopacsy, who witnessed the events, the Soviets required that Kadar attend the executions of the men he had once collaborated with. If Kopacsy's testimony is true, it proves that the Soviets wanted to issue a serious warning to the new Hungarian leaders, alerting them to the dangers of attempting similar experiments.

The crisis in Poland and Hungary in 1956 seemed to leave their countries in quite different circumstances. In Poland, destalinization appeared to have succeeded without bloodshed. Gomulka, with the blessings of Cardinal Wyszynski, had kept the socialist regime intact by allowing a few concessions, such as agricultural decollectivization and greater religious freedoms. Gomulka had actually reinforced ties with the USSR, signing an agreement on a visit to Moscow in November, 1956, in which he sanctioned continuing Soviet military presence in his country in exchange for economic favors. But in 1957, with the strong support of the Polish people who saw in him a successful negotiator with ideas for improvement, Gomulka was able to limit the effects of the concessions made. Nevertheless, he was unable to solve his country's economic problems; the problems which had been at the root of the crisis in Poznan in June, 1956, were no different from those which faced Poland in 1960.

In Hungary, despite the apparent failure of the revolution in 1956, the new leaders quickly realized that nothing could remain as it had been before the uprising—something they had to keep in mind while revising their political strategy. The Soviets made the first wave of repression more harsh than the Hungarian authorities desired, but it was followed by a period of relative detente. Ten years after the events of 1956, Janos Kadar's Hungary had become the envy of the other Eastern European countries with its relatively high standard of living and relative liberty.

In 1956, Gomulka and Kadar played decisive roles in their respective countries: Gomulka was then the most popular man in Poland, and Kadar, by contrast, the man most disgraced in Hungary. Ten years later, the tables had been turned. Gomulka had become the hard-liners' champion within the socialist world, deeply disappointing his people, while Kadar, using a successful economic development policy and downplaying heavy ideology, had won over many of those who had opposed him. Gomulka was driven from power by the 1970 workers' revolt in the Baltic ports, but Kadar remained the uncontested leader of his country until 1988.

FROM CRISIS TO CRISIS: EASTERN EUROPE FROM 1956 TO 1968

The events in Poland and Hungary in 1956 prompted changes in all the Eastern European countries; the leaders tried, either collectively or individually, to take measures which would prevent the recurrence of such crises.

New Directions in Eastern Bloc and Soviet Policy

The events in Poland and Hungary forced the USSR and its allies to redefine their relationship to one another. The military intervention in Hungary clearly demonstrated that no Warsaw Pact country was free to leave the socialist bloc or to organize its foreign relations as it pleased. The USSR obviously meant to maintain the protective glacis constructed along its western borders, and concentrated on keeping it intact. Revitalizing the Council of Mutual Economic Assistance (the CMEA or COMECON) created in 1949 was another move to promote cohesion within the socialist bloc. Until the mid-1950s, COMECON existed to develop trade relations between the member states and with the USSR. Beginning in 1955, its prevailing goal was to coordinate the economic plans of each country and institute specialization according to each country's potential. In June, 1962, the countries adopted the fundamental principles of the International Socialist Division of Labor, according to which, in theory, each country would receive a monopoly or at least a major share of the market in the production of some specific item—for both domestic consumption and export to partner countries. Only the USSR, with its variety of resources and its relatively advanced level of economic development, was exempt from the specialization rule. The true objective of these measures, however, was to increase economic interdependence among the various states. In order to avoid payment problems with COMECON, a bank for international economic cooperation was created. Based in Moscow, it began operation on January 1, 1966. At the same time, cooperation between socialist countries was extended to domains other than trade, such as transportation, technological exchange, joint construction of pipelines and nuclear power stations. The objective remained constant: to weld the various members of the socialist community closer together.

The Soviet leaders, under Khrushchev initially and then under Leonid Brezhnev after October, 1964, were beginning to embark on a policy of *detente* with the West about this time. The policy led to a development of trade between the Western countries and the Communist world and also border openings to foreign visitors. These new economic and political orientations were to have significant consequences within the socialist world.

A Note of Discord: Albania

From the beginning, Albania showed the least enthusiasm of all the popular democracies for the new direction set by Moscow after the crises of 1956. Enver Hoxha and the Albanian leadership approved of the Soviet military intervention in Budapest without reservation, but simultaneously renewed their attacks on Yugoslavia. They accused the Yugoslavs of having encouraged Imre Nagy's liberalization policies. Later, Hoxha let it be known that he thought the Khrushchev report and the new orientations of the 20th Congress were responsible for provoking the counter-revolutionary movements in Poland and especially in Hungary. Hoxha repeated his charges to Khrushchev himself on a visit to Moscow in April, 1957. Nevertheless, Hoxha continued on apparently friendly terms with Moscow even though he held firm to hard-line policies at home. Hoxha never missed an opportunity to mention the positive role Stalin had played in the history of socialism until finally, in the year 1960, relations between Moscow and Tirana began to show signs of strain. The Albanians increased their attacks on the "Yugoslav revisionists," and thus indirectly attacked their real target, Khrushchev. Invoking their national independence, Albania became more reticent in accepting Moscow's philosophy on the international division of labor, and outright refused to condemn the stance taken by Beijing in the ideological conflict pitting the Chinese against the Soviets. In fact, the Albanian head of state, Haxhi Kieshi, took advantage of his official visit to Beijing in June, 1960, to publicly endorse Mao Tse-tung's philosophy. Meanwhile, Enver Hoxha was conducting a purge of the Albanian Workers' party, expelling all pro-Soviet members from the central committee. The Moscow-Beijing conflict thus echoed in the Balkans. The Soviets recalled their technicians from China, and refused to send Albania a promised shipment of grain. Both sides were preparing for a break, which finally took place in Moscow in November, 1960, at the Party Congress. Enver Hoxha attacked Khrushchev's revisionist positions, condemned the policy of rapprochement with Yugoslavia, and publicly praised Stalin and the Chinese leadership. The Albanian delegation left Moscow before the conference was over. Until 1978, Albania was the spokesman of Chinese communism in Eastern Europe. Chinese technicians moved into Albania to help develop the country's natural resources and economy. With the support of the Chinese, Albania did not fear intervention by any of the Warsaw Pact countries.

The Evolution of Yugoslavia

Yugoslavia normalized relations with the other socialist countries of Eastern Europe in 1955. The Soviet intervention in Hungary clouded these relations somewhat, particularly since Tito's position throughout the affair was ambiguous, but neither the Yugoslavs nor the Soviets were in a position to make an issue of it. The USSR had its problems with China, and Tito had his hands full in Yugoslavia with internal tensions. Milovan Djilas, the one-time Partisan and Communist party leader, had intervened again in protest of the rapprochement policy with the USSR. He was arrested for his criticism and sentenced to another term in prison. Yugoslavia was struggling with economic problems essentially brought on by hesitating between a policy of complete decentralization and the centralized socialism advocated by Rankovitch. In addition, continuing regional disparities between the more developed western republics like Croatia and Slovenia and the underdeveloped eastern regions like Macedonia and Kosovo revived traditional tensions between the Croat and Slovene faction and the Serbs. Liberal policies prevailed in the political sphere beginning in 1965-1966—although a contentious academic, Professor Mihajlov, was arrested after publishing a book in the West in which he harshly criticized the USSR. Political liberalization was confirmed by the June 1966 dismissal of the all-powerful secret police chief, Rankovitch, who had been the spokesman of pan-Serbian nationalism in the government. Rankovitch was accused of conspiracy and of abusing power, but was never prosecuted. In connection with the Rankovitch affair, the secret police force, the *UDBA*, was purged and decentralized. Another component of liberalization was expanding the powers of local assemblies and democratizing their operation; they became more vocal, and less unanimous in their voting. The same kind of *detente* began to appear in the strained relations between the church and the regime. On June 25, 1966, Father Casaroli, acting for the Holy See, signed an agreement with the president of the Commission on Cults, Moratcha, reestablishing full freedom of religion and an open communication between the Yugoslav church and Rome. The agreement was the prelude to Yugoslavia's resumption of diplomatic relations with the Vatican.

"Kadarism" in Hungary

Despite the shadow of its origins, the Kadar government managed to reconcile a relatively liberal policy with the existence of a popular democracy. This development was the personal work of Janos Kadar, the first secretary of the Socialist Workers' party beginning in 1956, and leader of the government from 1956 to 1958, and from 1961 to 1964. In his first term, Kadar primarily worked to reassure the USSR and the other socialist countries of Hungary's allegiance by tightening political and military ties through the Warsaw Pact and by taking full advantage of the economic cooperation offered by COMECON. Domestically, Kadar attempted to justify Soviet intervention in a May 9, 1957, report to parliament; "the counter-revolution tried to bring down the legitimate government of the Hungarian People's Republic, as well as its social order... in order to install in its place the most reactionary of bourgeois dictatorships, the fascist dictatorship." On the other hand, Kadar also recognized that "the mistakes made by Rakosi and his group played an important role in the events of 1956" (from a report to the Socialist Worker Party Congress, November 30, 1959).

From 1959 on, the Hungarian government embarked on a policy of considerable liberalization. A partial amnesty released political prisoners, and a new political slogan replaced an old one by reversing it. Rather than the Stalinist, "Those who are not with us are against us," it now read, "Those who are not against us are with us." In keeping with this motto, former government officials dismissed in 1949 were reinstated. Border restrictions were progressively lifted in both directions, and in 1964, 200,000 Hungarian tourists were allowed to travel in the West.

A similar flexibility was adopted in relations with the Catholic church. While the state kept control of ecclesiastical appointments, an agreement was finally reached on September 15, 1964: the Holy See was allowed to fill a certain number of vacant episcopal seats. The case of Cardinal Mindszenty, in refuge in the American embassy, was not settled until 1971 when Pope Paul VI asked the prelate to leave the country and thereby go into exile. The nomination of a new primate, Cardinal Lekai, seemed to put an end to the friction between Budapest and Rome.

The economic policies of the Kadar government were also distinguished by a desire for efficiency and pragmatism. Economic reform was in full force after July 1, 1968, giving business wide freedoms and introducing a veritable free-market economy. The priority of developing heavy industry had been abandoned after 1953, and was now replaced by a focus on modernization and the development of trade between all countries. A result of this policy—already obvious in the late 1960s—was a relatively high living standard, particularly in comparison with neighboring socialist countries. Ten years after the failure of the revolution of 1956, Kadar's Hungary was already a happy exception within the socialist camp.

The "Neo-Stalinists"

Bulgarian and Rumanian leaders took advantage of the events of 1956 to end the limited destalinization policy that they had begun. In Bulgaria, Todor Zhivkov continued to benefit from the concentration of power. He held the office of secretary general of the Communist party from 1956 on, and in 1962, added to it the office of prime minister. Under Zhivkov, Bulgaria aligned its policies rigorously with the USSR's. With its strategic position between Rumania and Yugoslavia, it became the Soviet Union's most faithful and zealous ally in the Balkans. In Rumania, the period after 1956 was also marked by a return to rampant Stalinism. The first victims were the Hungarians in Transylvania; they had welcomed the events in Budapest and were thus considered suspect once again, losing the few concessions they had gained in 1950. But the Hungarian minority was not the only group brought to a heel. Out of fear of potential agitation, the whole population was placed under close surveillance by the militia and the secret police. Communist party power, incarnated by Gheorgiu-Dej until his death in 1965, passed on to First Secretary Nicolae Ceausescu who has remained as head of state since December, 1967. Ceausescu, Rumania's "best loved son," cleverly built up an international image to garner affection from the West of an open-minded leader who occasionally defied Moscow; he objected to the small role Rumania was assigned in COMECON, increased Rumania's agreements of economic cooperation with Western countries, and took advantage of the Moscow-Beijing rivalry to play both sides against each other. In reality, Ceausescu combined this show of nationalism with repressive Stalinism and nepotism.

In Poland, Gomulka was returned to power with the support of the liberals and the church, and with the enthusiastic approval of the people. Much to their dismay, however, he began to restrict the progression Kadar was following in Hungary. His demeanor toward the church was indicative of his change in political orientation. Officially, the agreements of 1957 granting the church special status were maintained, but beginning in 1958-1959, local problems increased. The state made it difficult for parents to enroll their children in catechism, and at other times denied authorization for thee construction of new churches, even when all expenses were to be paid by followers. In each case, Cardinal Wyszynski intervened and won, but only after long and painful negotiations. The church/state conflict reached its height in 1965-1966 when the Polish bishops began communicating with their colleagues in East Germany, hoping to reconcile the two peoples. The Polish government interpreted these actions as treason against Poland. Cardinals Wyszynski and Wojtyla responded by publicly denouncing the harassment endured by church followers.

Hopes for the economic improvement which Gomulka had promised were quickly shattered. While salaries did rise more than 35 percent between 1956 and 1959, inflation soon reduced gains to zero. Purchasing power for all workers remained very low and, as in the past, the unions continued to play the mediating role between the political powers and labor. Low productivity and high net cost of industrial products slowed exports even to the COMECON countries, while imports of equipment increased. The result was growing foreign trade deficit and high foreign debt both to the USSR and to Western countries. Beginning in 1962, accelerating inflation accentuated the latent dissatisfaction among the workers. Only the peasants had benefitted from the Gomulka regime; they left the collective farms in great numbers and managed to raise their incomes with higher productivity. But elsewhere economic problems, periodic shortages of basic goods, and the disillusionment brought on by false hopes, all contributed to the low morale of the workers which surfaced in alcoholism, violence, vandalism and corruption. To ward off outbreaks of public discontent, Gomulka began to harden his policies in 1959, and to tighten censorship. He accused certain intellectuals of being too receptive to Western influences, and dismissed the likes of the Minister of Education, Brankowski, who were considered too liberal. Gomulka himself was becoming more and more authoritarian. A group of Party leaders formed around him, made up of General Spychalski, General Moczar, the minister of the interior, Edward Ochab, his predecessor as head of the Party, and former socialists Jozef Cyrankiewicz, the prime minister, and Adam Rapacki, minister of foreign affairs. The members of this group shared traits in common: the firm desire to maintain alliances with the socialist bloc, a suspicion of Western countries—particularly West Germany—a preference for strict order and a hostility towards intellectuals. They stood by the USSR in 1968, determinedly criticizing the Czechoslovak experiment with liberalization. Gomulka's personal prestige was slowly affected by this change in political direction, and his unpopularity grew because of his rule's personal character.

In East Germany, Walter Ulbricht's neo-Stalinist policies continued unfalteringly. Sealing off East Berlin from West Berlin by the Wall in August, 1961, ended the flow of discontented emigrants. But the East German leaders nevertheless attempted to avert potential discontent by improving the standard of living. Because of a high level of industrial development and massive exports, East Germany began to experience a high growth rate in the 1960s. Its role in COMECON was similar to West Germany's role in the European Economic Community (the EEC). Consumer goods were produced to satisfy the needs of a population whose standard of living by 1968 was already the highest in Eastern Europe. The economic success of the socialist government thus compensated for the conservatism of its leaders.

In Czechoslovakia, where there had been no destalinization *per se*, the situation was somewhat different. The Czechoslovak Communist party had been one of the first to condemn the events in Hungary and Imre Nagy's policies, and to applaud the intervention by Soviet tanks. The crisis caused the regime to harden its stance; Novotny and his conservative following were not going to take any risks in their own country. They implemented a system that served as a model for discipline in the socialist bloc. In 1960, the new constitution ratified the stricter policy, and Czechoslovakia went beyond the stage of a popular democracy to become a socialist republic.

It was only in 1962 that Novotny took some steps toward amnesty and announced the creation of a commission to review political trials of the 1950s. The commission began its work in early 1963 and examined 480 cases. The rehabilitation of Slansky on August 21, 1963, was the first of its kind, although it was posthumous and only partial because he remained expelled from the Party. Others, like Clementis in 1964 (posthumously), then Gustav Husak, Arthur London and Eugene Loebl, were reinstated completely. All of the bishops arrested in 1950 were released in the summer of 1963, but they were not awarded the right to rehabilitation. They remained under surveillance and were not allowed to resume their duties. Archbishop Beran of Prague, who had been imprisoned in March, 1951, was released in October, 1963, but confined to his residence. He was finally allowed to leave the country for Rome in February, 1965. It was also during the years 1963-1964 that the country began to allow visits by Western tourists, giving the impression that a thaw had indeed come to Czechoslovakia. Censureship became less stringent, and people began to feel the changes.

The first releases of prisoners and the rehabilitations provoked contradictions within the Party. While liberal elements were demanding explanations, the conservatives grouped around Novotny, re-elected to the presidency in 1964, and Prime Minister Jozef Lenart, to attempt to retard the already slow process of liberalization. The situation developed rapidly despite their efforts because of a number of accumulating unsolved problems. The greatest of these was the catastrophic state of the Czechoslovak economy. Collectivization was completed in 1959-1960, but a combination of passive resistance by the peasants and climatic uncertainties brought on serious supply shortages in the cities. In industry, the massive weight of the bureaucracy held back production, while COMECON's international division of labor policy caused disorganization within certain branches of industry by eliminating certain products. Economists like Otak Sik and Eugene Loebl recommended administrative reform and greater decentralization of business in order to revive the economy. After long debates within the Party, Novotny accepted their suggestions in 1967. About the same time, The Slovak Communists under Dubcek and Husak asked for justice for their countrymen, and that Czechoslovakia become a federated state. Intellectuals led by the Slovak novelist Ladislav Mnacko demanded the truth about the major trials with greater boldness and criticized the rehabilitations as expedient methods for government officials to clear their consciences. Czechoslovakia seemed ripe for crisis in 1967; though a bastion of Stalinism, the country had many similarities to Poland and Hungary in 1956.

The Prague Spring in 1968

To better understand the events that took place in Czechoslovakia in 1967-1968, the international context at the time should be considered. These were the years of student demonstrations in Western Europe, particularly in Italy, West Germany and France, which culminated in the May, 1968 riots. In China at the time, the cultural revolution was at its height. The authorities in Moscow and in most Eastern European capitals looked with great suspicion upon the anarchistic demonstrations and took steps to avoid any repetition of the furor in their own countries. The Six-Day War of 1967 between Israel and the Arab countries caused further East-West tension, since the USSR and all the socialist countries except Rumania formally condemned Israel's action and denounced American imperialism for its collusion with Zionism.

It was in this context that the crisis brewing in Czechoslovakia suddenly came to a fore. The IVth Writers' Congress which opened in Prague on June 29, 1967 became a forum for protest; numerous speakers strongly denounced the anti-Israeli campaign being waged by the Czechoslovak leadership. During the Congress, participants demanded freedom of the press, and the novelist Ludvik Vaculik denounced the regime's abuses of power. Then in July, another writer named Ladislav Mnacko left the country for Israel to protest the anti-Semitism of the Czechoslovak government. Participants who were Party members were expelled if they protested, and the publication of the Writers' Association journal, *Literarni Noviny*, with a circulation of over 600,000 was suspended.

In a central committee meeting on October 30, Novotny demanded more severe sanctions against the intellectuals, but was opposed by Czech liberals and by Slovaks led by Alexander Dubcek, the first secretary of the Slovak Communist party. The clash between Dubcek and Novotny was a conflict between a liberal and a conservative, but also a product of the ongoing rivalry between the Czech and Slovak factions within the Party. The next day, October 31, students from the Prague Technical College demonstrated for better living conditions, but were brutally beaten by the police under orders from the government; their protests began to take on an increasingly political character. The liberal current in the Party only served to make Novotny all the more unpopular. He took measures to avoid further confrontations on advice from Brezhnev, who visited Prague on December 8, 1967. Brezhnev had no desire to see Czechoslovakia, strategically located in central Europe, weakened by internal strife.

The central committee meeting of December 19 to 21 was distinguished by a new confrontation between Novotny and the hard liners, and the coalition of Czech liberals and Slovaks led by Dubcek. No concrete decisions were reached during the three-day melee of free debate. Taking advantage of a lull during the end-of-the-year festivities, Novotny planned a military *coup* with the support of General Sejna who served under Miroslav Mamula, the head of the Communist apparatus in the ministry of defense and the popular militia. The plot failed because General Vaclav Prchlik heard of the plan and warned Dubcek. By the time the central committee met again in early January, 1968, Novotny's position was seriously shaken. The committee reached a compromise after much debate; Novotny remained president, but resigned as head of the Party. During the night of January 4, Dubcek was chosen to be first secretary of the Czechoslovak Communist party, marking the first time a Slovak became the political leader of the country. The coalition of Slovaks and liberal Czechs had overcome the conservatives, electing not only a Slovak, but a member of a new generation.

Changes were quick in coming. On March 5, Dubcek announced that censorship would be suspended. Political discussions, which up to then had taken place in private or in small circles of friends, could now be taken up in newspaper columns, on the radio and on television. Political debate raged openly, with full participation of the public—constituting a hitherto unheard of situation in the country. The church took advantage of the new climate to demand the religious freedom guaranteed by the constitution but never observed or enforced. On March 12, the episcopate, at the request of seminary students and followers, removed Father Plohjar from his office in a Communist cover organization known as the Peace Movement of the Catholic Clergy, the "peace priests." This puppet movement was dissolved and reorganized under a new name in order to continue its activities. Delegates from religious orders which had been dissolved in 1950 began asking the ministry of culture for justice for past persecution and for permission to resume their work. Bishop Frantisek Tomasek of Prague, speaking for the episcopate, demanded the total rehabilitation of condemned priests, particularly that of Archbishop Beran in exile in Rome. The bishops already released were authorized to return to their dioceses, but the case of Archbishop Beran remained in suspense.

Dubcek and his associates took advantage of their newly won freedom to find rapid solutions to the numerous problems facing the country. In March, Dubcek promised the Slovaks that a special statute would put them on equal footing with the Czechs in the framework of a federal state. President Novotny's resignation on March 21 and the ensuing exodus of "Novotnyites" opened the doors for the liberals at all levels of government. On the 30th of that month, the National Assembly chose General Svoboda to succeed him as president by an overwhelming majority, 282 out of 288 votes. A new state leadership composed of men well disposed to the new orientation of the Party was formed under the Czech liberal, Oldrich Cernik, with new ministers Jiri Hajek in foreign affairs, General Dzur in the defense ministry and Ota Sik in charge of economic reform. On April 18, the National Assembly chose another liberal, Josef Smrkovsky, as its president. The central committee ratified the new "action program," subtitled *The Czechoslovak Road to Socialism*, on April 4 and 5, providing for: "a wide alliance of progressive forces in the cities and countryside headed by the worker class, and the unity of the Czech and Slovak nations." They recalled that "the Party is founded, and will continue to be founded, on the working class," and that "the goal of the Party is not to become a universal administrator of society...or to impede all social life with its directives.... The policy of the Party should never lead non-Communists to believe that they have been deprived of their rights and their freedom by the Party...." During March and April of 1968, a period known as the "Prague Spring," socialism had indeed taken on a human face.

It is interesting to note that the instigators of the Prague Spring were men who had pledged unconditional loyalty to the Party and to Moscow throughout their careers. These "liberals" had all played decisive roles during the Prague *coup* of 1948 bringing the Communists to power, and had held responsible positions throughout the Stalinist era. Josef Smrkovsky, who was made the likeable hero of the Prague Spring by the Western press, was the same man who had mobilized the workers' militia to support the ultra-Stalinist Gottwald in February 1948, thus assuring the success of the *coup*. Oldrich Cernik had climbed the ladder of *cursus honorum* from a good *apparatchik* during the Stalinist era, first as party secretary, then as secretary of the central committee, minister of planning, council vice-president in the Lenart cabinet, and finally as a member of the presidium under Novotny. In 1948, General Svoboda had given Gottwald the unconditional support of the army, an army he had also purged of non-Communist elements; though he was removed from power in the early 1950s, Svoboda still led the comfortable life of a retired high official during the time of the purges. Dubcek himself was the product of a Communist upbringing. His family had lived in the USSR from 1925 to 1938, and he had become active in the clandestine Communist party in Czechoslovakia from 1939 on, then participated in the Slovak insurrection of August, 1944, and went on to a brilliant career within the Party. He was a member of the central committee of the Slovak party in 1951 at the same time that Husak, Clementis and other Slovak Communist leaders were being persecuted; Dubcek, however, was sent to the political academy in Moscow from 1955 to 1958 because of his zealous devotion to the Party. He returned in the midst of the Novotny era and continued up the Party ladder until he became first secretary of the Slovak party in 1963.

As their backgrounds indicate, those responsible for the Prague Spring were far from liberal. Why then did they attempt to take the Czechoslovak party in such a new direction? Undoubtedly they acted more out of a desire to salvage a system to which they were deeply attached than to end the abuses of that system. But they were walking a fine line. In giving their pledge of goodwill to the intellectuals and to a public hungry for freedom, Dubcek and his colleagues were risking the displeasure of the leaders in the USSR and the other socialist states. On April 13, *Pravda* commented on the events in Czechoslovakia, denouncing the "anti-Socialist elements indulging in attacks against the Party." Czechoslovakia's neighbors were anxious as well. In Dresden at the end of March, Walter Ulbricht warned the Czechoslovak leaders of the risks they were undertaking and Gomulka in Poland ventured the same opinion. In Hungary, however, Kadar seemed to look approvingly on the Dubcek experiment, noticing its similarities to the policies he himself had applied to Hungary since the early 1960s.

The Prague Spring was becoming more and more of a concern to the entire socialist camp. By the end of August, diverse movements were created or reappeared within the country, taking advantage of lifted restrictions and hoping to obtain still greater freedoms. The Sokols, banned since 1930, were reorganized and portraits of Masaryk and Benes began to reappear everywhere. Former political prisoners organized associations to demand justice for themselves and punishment for those officials responsible for their imprisonment. Former political party members, Socialist and Populists, began to ask for a voice in the administration of public affairs. The church was anxious to reform the youth movements, and began publishing church newsletters.

On June 27, liberal intellectuals who had originated the revival tried to accelerate the process of liberalization by publishing a statement written by Vaculik called *2,000 Words*. This manifesto pointed out the differences between true liberals and those who, like Dubcek, were running the government and the Party, and also harshly criticized the Communist party's misuses of power since 1948. It denounced the threats leveled against the revitalization efforts within the country, declaring "Let us establish committees to defend freedom of expression, let us have marshals to maintain order at our meetings and support the security organs when they prosecute genuine criminal activity.... Let us stand firm in the face of threats from the outside and not initiate conflict." Moscow reacted sharply, and the Czechoslovakia party leadership itself realized it had unleashed a tide it could not control. Attempting to curb the movement, Dubcek increased his warnings to the people. He told the workers' militia on June 13, that the Party was "committed to fighting the anti-Communist phenomenon and all the excesses which were endangering the process of democratization." When the *2,000 Words* manifesto was published, the authors were sharply criticized by Communist party leaders. Smrkovsky spoke of "political romanticism" in the *Rude Pravo*, and Jiri Hajek denounced the text as liable to furnish supporters of the hardline with arguments. Dubcek and the new leadership meant to follow a median course; they had no intention of returning to political pluralism or of questioning the Party's authority to decide on the future direction of the country. An extraordinary Congress had been called for the following September in order to define major future policy.

Dubcek quickly encountered increasingly hostile reactions from other socialist countries. Moscow and the "brother countries" were extremely uneasy with the good-natured anarchy which was growing in Czechoslovakia and which threatened to spread to other Eastern European countries, carried by the thousands of Czechoslovak tourists traveling through them. An ill-timed statement by the minister of foreign affairs, Hajek, approving economic cooperation with Western countries while continuing close ties with COMECON countries, was interpreted in Moscow as the beginning of a shift in foreign policy. On May 3, as Dubcek, Cernik and Smrkovsky traveled to Moscow to explain their policy to the Soviets. The Polish press violently attacked the Prague leadership, accusing them of wanting to collaborate with West Germany. The East German press minced no words on the subject of Dubcek's policy either. The Soviets were more reserved; they did not seem to have lost hope of retrieving Dubcek peacefully, or if necessary through intimidation. On May 17, the head of the Soviet government, Aleksei Kosygin, accompanied by the commander in chief of the Warsaw Pact armies, Marshal Andrei Gretchko, paid a brief visit to Karlovy-Vary— officially for the therapeutic value of the warm waters. Dubcek met with him there. The Soviet leaders warned him once again of the risks he was undertaking in allowing the policy adopted in March to continue. During the interview, they agreed that Warsaw Pact military maneuvers would be held in the near future in Czechoslovak territory. These maneuvers, in which Soviet, Czechoslovak, East German, Hungarian and Polish troops participated, began on May 30. The soldiers were to leave at the end of June, but it was not until mid-July that the last Soviet units left the country. This prolonged foreign military presence coinciding with intense diplomatic activity between Moscow and the Eastern European capitals should have prompted leaders in Prague to take certain precautions. Instead, they adopted an attitude of complacent optimism, blaming *agents provocateurs* for the growing unrest of the population. Once again, how could this strange behavior be explained? Did Dubcek truly believe that nothing was happening? Or had he decided to let the Soviets act, and if so, why?

In early July, 1968, the Soviets decided not to allow the Czechoslovak Communist party to continue on its new path. Brezhnev began to gather his allies together into a common front. He could count on the Poles, the Germans and the Bulgarians, but the Hungarians were less dependable. During Kadar's visit to Moscow in early July, Brezhnev clearly spelled out his position, "The USSR cannot be and will never be indifferent to the fate of socialist structures in the other countries, as well as to the common cause of socialism and communism in the world." Kadar was forced into line with Moscow's position, completing the "coalition of five." Rumania still refused to condemn the Dubcek experiment. On July 14, the Communist leaders of the five countries met in Warsaw to "examine the upsurge in aggressive imperialist activity that is undermining the socialist regime in certain countries through diversionary tactics, and is weakening the ties of ideology and cooperation which unite the socialist states." They addressed a letter to Czechoslovak party leaders in which they announced their acute concerns: "We cannot allow foreign powers to lead your country from the path of socialism and to put Czechoslovakia in danger of being separated from the socialist community. This is a problem relevant to all communist and workers' parties.... Powers who are opposed to socialism together with revisionist powers have taken over the press, the radio and the television in your country.... Reactionary forces were thus able to publish their platform in the document entitled *2,000 Words*—which constitutes open opposition to the Communist party and a call to fight against the constitutional government." To end this situation, "the five" demanded "a determined and courageous offensive against the anti-socialist forces of the right..., the suspension of all political organizations that have taken a position against socialism..., closing the Party ranks around the principles of Marxism-Leninism in order to maintain democratic centralism and continuing the struggle against those who use enemy forces in their activities." The warning was clear, and only a blind man or an accomplice could ignore the veiled threats in the letter. The presidium of the Czechoslovak Communist party answered the letter with a long declaration: the Communist leadership did not feel socialism was endangered in Czechoslovakia, and "if such a situation should arise, the leadership would employ every means to defend the socialist system. Our policy is based on alliance and cooperation with the Soviet Union and with the other socialist countries.... We would never allow the accomplishments of socialism and the security of the peoples within our country to be threatened, nor would we allow imperialism, whether by force or by peaceful means, to break the socialist system by subverting a relationship of power in its favor." The declaration recalled that the leadership of the Czechoslovak party had unanimously condemned the *2,000 Words* and that "the Czechoslovak Communist party is trying to prove that it is capable of exercising political leadership by means other than bureaucratic and police force, such as the power of Marxist-Leninist ideas, the Party program, and a fair policy supported by the entire population." It closed with regrets that the Czechoslovak Communist party had not been invited to the meeting in Warsaw.

The polemic intensified in mid-July. While the Hungarian press was still relatively moderate in tone, the Soviet, East German and Polish newspapers were particularly inflamatory. There was news of a cache of arms discovered in Czechoslovakia; West German tourists, who had flocked to Prague when visas were granted liberally, were accused of coming to assist the "counter-revolutionaries" as a fifth column. Although confronted with these increasingly direct attacks, Dubcek continued his attitude of naive insouciance, even going so far as to state on July 28 that there was absolutely no cause for alarm. However, that same evening, an impressive Soviet delegation led by Brezhnev, Kosygin, Podgorny and Suslov arrived at the small Czechoslovak-Slovak border station of Cierna-nad-Tisou to meet Dubcek and a large Czechoslovak delegation. The conversations that took place between July 29 and August 1, turned to confrontation; the "amiable and broad exchange of opinion" mentioned in the final communique led to another meeting between "the five" and the leaders of the Czechoslovak Communist party in Bratislava on August 3rd. Once again, socialist unity was stressed: "the maintenance, consolidation and defense of what has been attained at the price of heroic efforts and self-denial of the people, is the common international duty of each of the socialist countries." The final communique of the Bratislava meeting emphasized the priorities of concerted action for European security and peace, and a strengthening of the Warsaw Pact. The crisis seemed to abate and the risk of military intervention diminished, to the great relief of a population that was less optimistic than its leadership.

Dubcek's unawareness of the situation, whether feigned or real, brought the matter up again. Tito and Ceausescu both met with him in Prague, the first from August 9 to 11, and the second on the 15th. Both men received triumphant welcomes, which was too much for the Soviets. The Prague-Bucharest-Belgrade rapprochement looked too much like the beginning of a new Little Entente to them, and their reaction was quick.

During the night of August 10, armed forces of the Warsaw Pact entered Czechoslovakia from all sides; Soviet airplanes landed at the airport in Prague, deplaning units of shock troops that immediately took control of the capital, occupying public buildings and the central committee headquarters. There, the Soviets took Dubcek, Cernik and Smrkovsky prisoner and sent them immediately to the USSR, while President Svoboda was isolated in his Hradschin palace. The absence of basic precautions had greatly facilitated the Soviets' task. Dubcek drew up an appeal to the central committee as soon as he learned of the Soviet intervention, protesting "this act contrary to the fundamental principles of relations between socialist countries." Both Dubcek and General Svoboda appealed to the population to remain calm.

On the morning of August 21, 1968, the entire country was occupied by Warsaw Pact forces. The Czechoslovak army remained passive throughout, and the population limited itself to a few demonstrations and instances of rock throwing—nothing like the demonstrations in Budapest twelve years earlier. The next day, Communist militants held a secret meeting in a factory on the outskirts of Prague, naming a new central committee and a new presidium, while retaining Dubcek in all of his offices. The new leadership called a one-hour strike for the following day in what would be the only concrete demonstration of resistance.

President Svoboda hoped to diffuse the crisis by going to Moscow on August 23; he was accompanied by General Dzur and Gustav Husak, who had kept his distance from Dubcek in the final days. Svoboda was recieved as a head of state, but he refused to negotiate until Dubcek and his colleagues were released. The Soviets conceded. In exchange, the full Czechoslovak leadership headed by Svoboda and Dubcek signed the **Moscow Accords** on August 26, which "normalized" the situation. The leaders from Prague had totally capitulated: they admitted that the presence of Soviet troops was justified because of the threats to socialism in Czechoslovakia, threats Dubcek himself admitted he had underestimated.

The Prague Spring ended with a permanent Soviet military presence in Czechoslovakia. A treaty signed on October 16 spelled out the status of the Soviet armed forces, stating that most of the 500,000 men who had participated in the invasion would be withdrawn, but that several Soviet divisions would remain indefinitely. The "liberals" of the Prague Spring were the first to assist in the "normalization" procedures, to the great disappointment of those citizens who had placed their trust in them. Dubcek remained head of the Party until April, 1969, when he was replaced by another Slovak, Gustav Husak. Dubcek was then expelled from the Party in June, 1970. Josef Smrkovsky was relieved of his duties as president of the National Assembly when the new constitution took effect on January 1, 1969, and despite his display of self-criticism, was also expelled from the Party in 1970. General Svoboda continued as president of the Republic, and remained head of state until his death in 1975. Hundreds of intellectuals and thousands of private citizens traveling outside the country at the time of the Soviet invasion chose not to return. Dubcek's so-called "friends," Tito and Ceausescu, had raised a few objections initially but then they too accepted the normalization.

The only true beneficiaries of the Prague Spring were the Slovaks and the Soviet Union. The Slovak intellectuals and the leaders of the Slovak Communist party had played an important role in instigating the mechanics of change, and as a result, finally saw the transformation of Czechoslovakia into a true federation of Czech and Slovak states. The events of 1968 granted the Soviets the opportunity to station their troops in Czechoslovakia in the quadrilateral area of Bohemia that juts far into West German territory. Dubcek had done them a favor in providing a pretext for intervention; ultimately, he did not fare badly himself. Imre Nagy had not been so fortunate.

At the end of the 1960s, despite the crises of 1956 and 1968, the Eastern Europe countries remained socialist states in which the Communist party retained exclusive control over the government; all foreign policies—except for Albania's and to a lesser degree, Yugoslavia's—were faithfully aligned with Moscow's. Through COMECON the Eastern European nations formed an integrated and powerful economic bloc; nevertheless, they all remained dependent on the USSR for raw materials, for their energy supply and also for their export market—though they tried to expand their trade relations with the industrialized capitalist countries and with the Third World.

Economic integration never succeeded in erasing the inequalities in levels of economic development within the bloc. Some countries such as East Germany and Hungary were able to raise their living standards because of their advanced technology or the flexibility of their organization. Others, like Poland and Czechoslovakia, despite their abundant natural resources, were not able to overcome the economic problems confronting them, primarily because of their weighty bureaucracies and low agricultural and industrial productivity. Agricultural countries like Bulgaria, Rumania and Yugoslavia met with varying degrees of success. Bulgaria and Rumania did fairly well, but only at the expense of the living standard of their populations. Yugoslavia, however, was plagued with a hesitant economic policy and inefficient administration despite its associate membership in both COMECON and the EEC, and its status as the only Eastern European country to possess a convertible currency. Although partially hidden by the emigration of part of its work force to Western Europe, Yugoslavia's problems with inflation and unemployment were serious.

The crises of 1956 and 1968, differences in foreign and domestic policy, differences in the levels of economic development and in standards of living, all contributed to changing the image of a homogenous Eastern bloc that prevailed in the early 1950s. The 1968 crisis and the invasion by the Warsaw Pact troops caused an involuntary resurgence of a certain nationalism that had its hour of glory between the two world wars. National diversities which had lain dormant slowly reappeared. The entry of East German troops to Bohemia evoked memories on both sides of historical antagonisms between Czechs and Germans, and in southern Slovakia, the Hungarian minority enthusiastically welcomed the Hungarian troops taking part in the Warsaw Pact invasion on August 21, 1968. The Slovaks took advantage of the situation to demand the autonomy they had been waiting for since 1919. And everywhere, through the events of 1956 and 1968, the "church of silence" demonstrated that its following remained as strong as always, despite official atheism and persecution. A continuity of tradition was exposed by the crises of 1956 through 1968; these upheavals took place only in East Germany, Poland, Hungary and Czechoslovakia—all countries with cultural traditions closest to those of the West, and with the most developed national consciousnesses.

Chapter 26

From the Prague Spring to Solidarity
1968—1981

The failure of the Dubcek experiment in Czechoslovakia demonstrated once again that Eastern European leaders would be prohibited from deviating too far from the Moscow line, both in their internal affairs and more understandably in matters of foreign policy. In what became known as the Brezhnev Doctrine, Moscow considered intolerable any actions which might undermine socialism or the integrated system of defense established in 1955 by the Warsaw Pact. The Soviet troops stationed in Czechoslovakia following the Prague Spring made it clear that this fundamental principle of Soviet policy was not to be compromised.

GENERAL TRENDS OF THE 1970s

The international context changed in the 1970s, and the socialist world was compelled to change as well in its thinking, spawning new problems and new solutions. Internationally, trade between Eastern Europe and the capitalist countries increased considerably, but for certain socialist countries, this new growth translated into a chronic trade deficit with the West. Intermediate or long-term loans covered the deficit, but created a sizable foreign debt in several countries. Poland led the Eastern bloc countries into the 1980s with a record-setting debt to Western countries on the order of $26 billion. The economic crisis affecting the Western world after the 1973-1974 energy shortage, along with the accompanying inflation and the sudden rise in the price of energy and certain raw materials, also affected the Eastern European countries. Equipment and supplies normally purchased in the West became more expensive, and oil prices on the Soviet market were raised to reflect OPEC prices. Inflationist tendencies infiltrated the socialist bloc. Prices rose despite government attempts to camouflage inflation with subsidies to keep the price-tags on certain products artificially low. Often, governments were forced to completely withdraw high-priced items from the market, replacing inflation with scarcity; the items would then resurface on the black-market at much higher costs. After a certain point, governments would be left with no choice but to adjust prices. The shock of sudden and drastic price increases on the people in the Eastern European countries, with their meager salaries, often created backlashes against the system. The most notable examples of these reactions were in Poland—in 1970, 1976, and 1981. East Germany and Hungary, on the other hand, generally practiced a policy of true pricing, instituting gradual increases which did not provoke such adverse reactions.

Another major change in the 1960s was a relaxation of border restrictions for western tourists. Yugoslavia, Hungary and Rumania received the most tourists, but the other countries, with the exception of isolationist Albania, were also affected. Besides the foreign currency visitors brought in, western visitors exposed Eastern Europeans to different standards of living, different customs, ideas and freedoms. Inversely, Eastern European nationals from most countries began travelling to the West in growing numbers. These two-way exchanges brought new understanding to the peoples concerned, broadening perspectives for people who had lived in such isolation. The era of *detente* facilitated the opening of doors to the West, which led to certain changes in the behavior of the people in the socialist states. Younger generations of students and intellectuals often traveled to the West, or at least studied it. As a result, they became increasingly indifferent to the official ideology, at times challenging it openly.

Each Eastern European country developed its own body of dissidents. For some, the growing disaffection with the promises of the communist ideology led to violence, vandalism, or alcoholism; for others, disillusion compelled them to look elsewhere for answers, especially to more traditional beliefs. In all the Eastern bloc countries, whether of Catholic, Protestant, Orthodox or even Muslim tradition, there was a tremendous resurgence of interest in religious ideology, especially among the young who had been educated to be atheist. Catholicism persisted in Poland, even when the church was persecuted, and was strengthened by Cardinal Wysynski's personal influence and the 1978 election of the Polish Pope, Wojtyla. Eastern Europe was experiencing a religious revival despite continuing harassment and persecution—to the consternation of officials. Making every effort to appear indifferent, the impressive Eastern European delegations sent to the funeral of Paul VI and to the enthroning ceremonies for John Paul I and II in 1978 were nonetheless indicative of the importance Eastern European leaders actually gave the issue of religion.

The attitude shift among the policy makers in Eastern Europe also fomented a universal desire for greater freedom, especially after the signing of the Helsinki Accords in 1975. The Accords were signed by 35 nations, including t..e Soviet Union and all the Eastern European countries with the exception of Albania, with goals of strengthening European security, cooperation, and the promotion of "fundamental freedoms including freedom of thought, conscience, religion, and belief." In many Eastern European countries, intellectuals set up committees for the defense of human rights to keep vigil over the principles of Helsinki. The committee in Poland was named the *KOR* (Workers' Defense Committee); in Rumania and Czechoslovakia, the *Charter 77* movement was formed after 500 people signed a document requesting freedom of expression and conscience. These committees were generally composed of intellectuals, writers and poets, philosophers and artists. Many members came from the ranks of the Communist party, including Ota Ornets, who signed the *Charter 77*, and the Rumanian writer, Paul Goma. The committees published regular appeals and circulated *szamizdat* literature, the Russian word for clandestine publications usually typed and circulated by dissident writers.

Alongside these activist committees, independent trade unions sprang up spontaneously, shadowing official unions which served the interests of the "working-class government" rather than the workers themselves. The Solidarity movement in Poland is the best-known example. Independent trade unions were formed in Rumania after the harsh repressions of the miner strikes in Transylvania, and also in East Germany and in Czechoslovakia. These "free" unions were greatly hindered by the authorities; most Rumanian independent union leaders were interned in psychiatric hospitals, while their East German and Czechoslovak counterparts were imprisoned.

In Hungary, Kadar maintained a conciliatory policy towards activist groups, despite the hardening of policy elsewhere. The official unions actually developed a role in defending the workers' interests. Hungary seems to have escaped the protest movements, with a few exceptions: the "leftist" writer Miklos Haraszti took the government to task in his book, denouncing the negative aspects of assembly line work in factories, and a few sociologists of the "Budapest School" tried without much success to begin a protest movement.

Hungary remained, despite foregoing reservations, a country without violent confrontations, primarily because its leaders were economically effective and politically flexible. The other Eastern European countries, however, protected themselves from internal violence through their firm-handed policy against dissension; Zhivkov in Bulgaria, Honecker in East Germany, Ceausescu in Rumania, and Husak in Czechoslovakia all maintained a hard line and an unconditional alignment with Moscow after the failure of the Prague Spring. Their success in suppressing internal strife was not matched everywhere, especially on the Adriatic coast and on the shores of the Baltic.

THE "ENFANTS TERRIBLES" OF THE ADRIATIC: ALBANIA AND YUGOSLAVIA

In the post-1968 era, Albania and Yugoslavia were the two particularly sensitive sectors within the socialist world. The two countries were similar in several ways. Both were led by men who had held power since 1945; Albania's Enver Hoxha and Yugoslavia's Marshal Tito had both been leaders in the resistance movements fighting the occupation, and had both managed to free their respective countries without aid from the Soviet army. Both Hoxha and Tito had been militant Communists since their youth, and both, through different circumstances, were led to reject Moscow's protection in favor of national independence. And both, after breaking with Moscow, looked for outside support. For a short time, Tito accepted aid from the Western powers, essentially to prepare for potential aggression by neighboring countries. After his reconciliation with the Soviets in 1955, Tito played the Third World card and became the champion of the "non-aligned countries" until his death in 1980. Hoxha turned to the Chinese after his break with the Kremlin, and with Chinese technical and military assistance was able to maintain Albania's political independence while modernizing the country. Both countries claimed to be authentic socialists, but each took its own nationalist road to socialism. Finally, both countries held the distinction of occupying strategic positions on the Adriatic coasts, able to offer excellent shelter to a friendly war fleet. Facing the Italian coast and in close proximity to the eastern Mediterranean, they offered a tempting advantage to any country with whom they were on good terms.

The major differences between Albania and Yugoslavia were equally significant, and remain sources of contention in the 1980s. A small country, Albania is poor in resources, isolated by its terrain but homogenous in its population. Yugoslavia, by contrast, is vast, open on all sides, with a multi-national population and varied, though unevenly distributed, natural resources. Politically, Albania continued to maintain the rigid structures of the Stalin era, to the extent that Stalin remained the object of official veneration. In contrast, the Yugoslavian regime adopted the principal of decentralization in the early 1950s and became progressively more liberal—especially after the 1966 crisis eliminated the hardliners from the Party. Economically, while decentralization perpetuated regional disparities and social inequalities in Yugoslavia, Albania's authoritarian and rigid planning led to economic development with an egalitarian society.

Albania's foreign policy began to shift at the end of 1976 just after the death of Mao Tse-tung, "the great friend of the Albanian people." The leaders in Tirana began to worry when the new Chinese leaders denounced the crimes of the "Gang of Four." Their anxiety increased when in September, 1977, Tito—the distinguished adversary of the Albanian Communist party—took a long tour of the USSR, China and Northern Korea. By the end of 1977, the Albanian press began to publish articles criticizing the dangerous policies of Hua Guofeng and Deng Xiaoping— labeled "opportunists" for the occasion. The tone of the criticism became more and more acerbic, and the Chinese leaders were soon denounced as "traitors and renegades of Marxism-Leninism." The Chinese took note of these attacks, and on July 7, 1978, the Beijing government announced that it was recalling its technicians immediately and was suspending all credit agreements with Albania. The Chinese technicians returned home by the end of the month, and Albanian trainees in China did the same. To the leaders in the Albanian capital, Tirana, China was "a revisionist, imperialistic and chauvinistic superpower."

The visit of Hua Guofeng to Yugoslavia in August, 1978, less than a month after the break between Albania and China, solidified Hoxha's position. For the Albanians, the Chinese, just like the Russians, were nothing but "villainous revisionists." Tito was still the object of the most virulent attacks; in a brochure distributed by the Albanian embassy in Belgrade just after the visit of Hua Guofeng, Enver Hoxha deplored the "dominating, expansionist and hegemonic tendencies" of Tito, whose experiment with decentralization had led his country to "anarchism," and who "was selling out completely" to foreign capitalists by granting them the right to invest in Yugoslavia. Hoxha also denounced Tito's policy towards religion, considered by the Albanians to be too tolerant.

Marshal Tito's death on May 4, 1980, momentarily quieted the customary attacks of the Albanian press on Yugoslavia. It was even possible to think that with the leadership in Belgrade, relations between the two countries would improve. This was the case until the end of the summer of 1980, when signs of unrest began resurfacing. Suddenly, in April, 1981, violent demonstrations by the Albanian minority in Yugoslavia escalated tension. A particularly prolific community of about 1,300,000 Albanian nationals were living in Yugoslav territory, primarily in the autonomous territory of Kosovo in the Federated Republic of Serbia. There, Albanians constituted nearly three-quarters of the population, while the Albanian minority in the Federated Republic of Macedonia numbered about 17 percent.

Until the 17th century, the population of Kosovo was exclusively Serbian, but after the Serbian population emigrated to Hungary to escape Turkish persecution, the country was repopulated with Albanian Islamic converts. In 1913, Serbia recovered Kosovo through the Balkan Wars and began to re-Serbanize the region by bringing in Serbian colonists. By the 1930s, however, the Serbs represented only 20 percent of the population.

The Albanian population had provoked riots in Kosovo before; in November and December, 1968, they asked that Kosovo become the seventh republic within the Yugoslav federation, causing a commotion. Belgrade refused their demand, but made a few economic and cultural concessions. Calm returned for a period, but beginning in 1975-1976, tension rose again. In February, 1976, Albanian "irredentists" were accused of plotting to undermine territorial integrity and were harshly penalized. Latent unrest took on a much more overt character in early March, 1981. For over a month, the region of Kosovo was rocked with violence which peaked in early April at Prichtina, the capital of the region. According to Yugoslav authorities, demonstrators cried out for Albanian nationalism; they were in fact demanding that Kosovo become part of Albania. This agitation was accompanied by a general strike throughout the province. The official tally from the Kosovo riots cited nine deaths (eight demonstrators and one of the peace-keeping forces) and hundreds of wounded on both sides, but eye-witnesses speak of dozens of dead and thousands of wounded. The area was sealed off by the army and the militia, and order was re-established in mid-April. New demonstrations broke out again in the first days of May when the demonstrators went on trial. In total, over 2,000 persons were arrested and charged for participating in the riots. The Yugoslav authorities decided to hit hard; the judges, gathered on April 21 under Federal Prosecutor Goutchevitch, received instructions to "condemn the enemies of the country with vigor." In addition, the leadership of the League of Communists of Kosovo was purged "because of its incompetency and its inertia." At that point, over 500 persons "who had attempted to assault the constitutional order, the integrity and the sovereignty of Yugoslavia" had been sentenced to long prison terms.

The Kosovo affair had natural repercussions on relations between Albania and Yugoslavia. On April 8, 1981, the Albanian Communist daily, *Zeri I Popullit* rose to the defense of the Albanians in Kosovo, "who asked to be liberated from Serbian rule." Yugoslavia, on the other side, denounced Albanian interference in Yugoslavia's internal affairs and suspended cultural agreements between Kosovo and Albania. Belgrade blamed the Kosovo trouble on a clandestine Albanian Marxist-Leninist party founded in 1973 with the support of the Tirana government.

The effects of what had taken place in Kosovo extended beyond the Balkans. On July 14, 1981, an attempt was made on the life of the Yugoslav ambassador in Brussels, and other malevolent acts were directed at Yugoslav establishments in Belgium. Yugoslav officials blamed these acts on Albanian nationals, but no one was able to prove it.

The events in Kosovo, whatever their origin, demonstrated the fragility of the Yugoslav Federation, a fragility which became even more apparent after the death of Tito. The problems facing the country had existed for a number of years, but the political void left by Tito only exacerbated them. Nationalism persisted within the country, primarily in Croatia, a region with a past tied to the Austrian-Hungarian monarchy and to Western tradition, and ill at ease in a Serbian-controlled state. The Croat problem had been latent since before 1945, during the interwar period, but sharpened noticeably after 1971. Croat terrorism intensified in 1971, both within and without the country. The most spectacular act was an assassination attempt on the Yugoslav ambassador in Stockholm on April 9 of that year; it was the first in a string of terrorist attacks on diplomats.

Terrorist activity within the country consisted primarily of Croat student agitation, and was much tamer. The 30,000 students at the University of Zagreb launched a general strike from November 23 to December 3, to protest Serbian imperialism in Croatia. They were supported by the *Matica Hrvatska*, an association led by a Catholic intellectual, Professor Marko Veselica, a defender of the Croat people's cultural rights who was later imprisoned. The authorities reacted to the protest by arresting strikers and purging the Croat Communist party, accusing it of being too lax in its treatment of the nationalists. Relatively popular local Communist leaders such as Tripalo and Haremuj were dismissed, but these actions did not pacify the student strikers. Although the revolt had not succeeded in bringing in the workers who had been given a few economic concessions by Tito, most of the Croat population and the Catholic church were solidly behind the students. Serbian control over the Croat people indeed became the rule; over 80 percent of the police force in Croatia was Serbian, and the proportion was even higher in the upper echelons. Similar proportions existed in higher administrations and in the army.

Macedonia, one of Yugoslavia's six federated republics, lies at the other end of the country from Croatia. With 1,700,000 inhabitants—1,200,000 of whom are considered "Macedonian" by the census—Macedonia constituted another factor of instability in Yugoslavia. The Yugoslavs tried to create a Macedonian nation and to erase all vestiges of Bulgar tradition. At the end of 1978, the *Memoirs* of Madame Drogoitcheva, a member of the Bulgarian Communist party, were published, reviving the quarrel between Sofia and Belgrade because of her insistence that "Macedonians are Bulgarians." Inversely, in the name of Macedonian nationalism, the Yugoslavs accused the Bulgarians of assimilating the "Macedonians" living in Bulgarian territory.

The second serious problem Yugoslavia grappled with was its economy. The country was deeply affected by the economic crises in the West during the 1970s. The foreign trade deficit, always large, ballooned when the prices of oil and other raw materials increased. Disorganized decentralization, a policy of raising salaries, the reparation of currency spent by Yugoslav tourists outside of the country and the large budgetary deficit accumulated by the Tito regime, all contributed to inflation. The foreign debt grew to around 17 billion dollars by 1980. Devaluation and a policy of austerity entailed a lower standard of living for the population. These measures were undoubtedly necessary in order to recover an equilibrium lost during the years in which the country lived beyond its means, but risked provoking discontent. Unemployment was also high: over 800,000 were affected in 1980, and unemployment compensation was ridiculously low. Sending surplus man-power abroad was practically impossible since most West European countries closed their borders to foreign workers. Even West Germany urged their *gastarbeiter* (guest-workers) to return to their own countries, including several hundred-thousand Yugoslav workers.

Yugoslavia's economic crisis was compounded by regional disparities and antagonisms. Rich regions like Croatia and Slovenia became less and less disposed to share with the poorer republics in the eastern regions of the country.

The political void left by the death of Marshal Tito did not simplify matters. The position of the president of the republics was officially defined in the Constitution of 1974 specifically for Marshal Tito during his lifetime. On May 15, 1980, the system of joint leadership provided for in the constitution for the post-Tito period was established. The presidency was transferred from one person to a collective leadership of eight individuals, each representing a republic or an autonomous province. Each member of the presidency now serves for a year as the head of the "collective presidency of the Federal Republic of Yugoslavia." The rotation of politicians as head of state undeniably weakened the political power of the position. The League of Yugoslav Communists came under the direction of a group of hardliners led by the Serb Dusan Dragosavac and the Slovene Stane Dolanc. The politically aware in Yugoslavia recognized the inconveniences of the joint system of leadership, and worked to substitute a more efficient organization.

After the death of Tito, the supporters of the hardline—afraid of the risks involved in a break-up of the federation and of smoldering social tensions—were clearly in the process of taking over and making their own views policy. Slovene writers who asked for a little more publishing freedom were sternly reprimanded by the official press. Seven professors at the University in Belgrade, released in 1975 for ultra-leftist activities in collusion with outside enemies, were recalled. The Serbian poet Gojko Djogo was accused of having presented Yugoslavia in one of his last books "in a false and malevolent light" and of having "offended Tito's memory;" he had written that Yugoslav society was a society without freedom. For these offenses he was arrested and sentenced to two years, but numerous Serbian intellectuals and academics petitioned for their colleague, and were able to obtain his release.

A religious revival in Yugoslavia did not please Tito's successors, and a new polemic developed between the Catholic church and the state. During a meeting of the leaders of the League of Yugoslav Communists, one of the presidium, Branko Pouharitch, violently attacked the Croatian hierarchy, declaring that "the highest dignitaries of the Catholic church of Croatia are turning the church into a refuge for dissidents and the politically desperate" and condemned all requests for the rehabilitation of Cardinal Stepinac. The Archbishop of Zagreb, Kouhanitch, had in fact just publicly demanded the rehabilitation of his distant predecessor. In response to these attacks, the episcopate replied at Eastertime in a pastoral letter demanding that the freedom of worship be observed.

The state adopted the same rigid attitude toward the Muslim community. The religious revival was also widespread there, and the dozens of mosques in Sarajevo were visited with increasing frequency. Several Muslims were condemned for "war crimes" committed when Bosnia was part of Ante Pavelitch's Croatian state.

This hardening in interior policies coincided with a noticeable reinforcement of Soviet influence in Yugoslavia. Relations between Belgrade and Moscow became more steady: Soviet warships called more and more frequently at Yugoslav ports and a certain military cooperation developed between the two countries.

POLAND IN CRISIS

The whole world watched Poland after the summer of 1980, and the names of a few newsmakers in that country, Gierek, Jaruzelski, Kania, Walesa, Wysynski, and of course Pope John Paul II (Wojtyla), became household words. Several events took place in Poland which were then

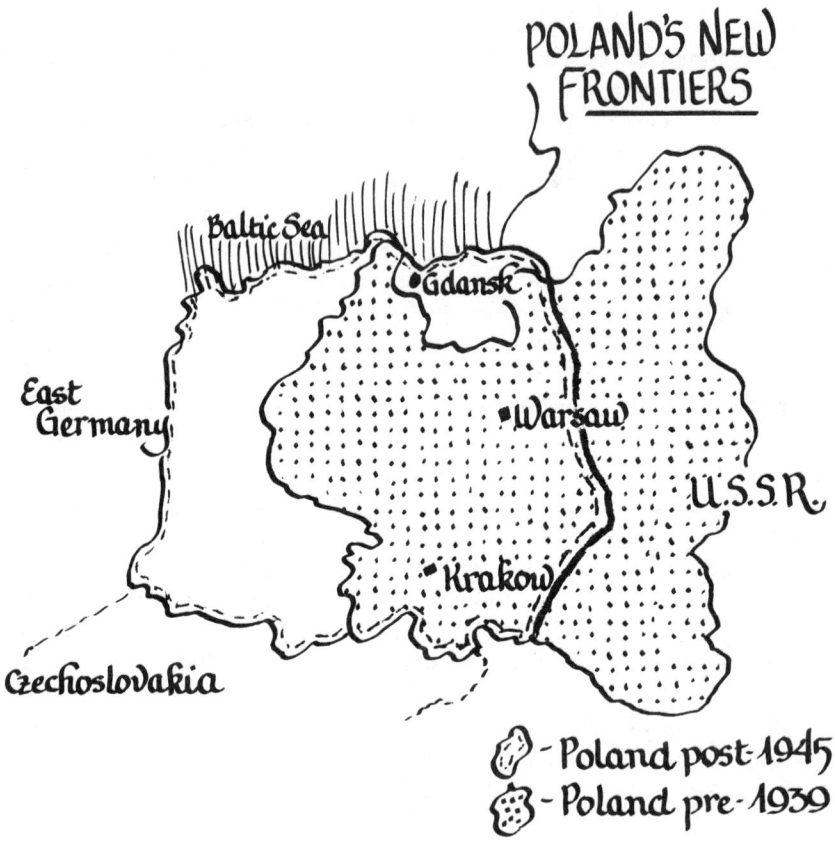

unique in the East European countries: several hard-fought strikes were successful; a cardinal spoke on equal terms with a Communist party chief; animated debate within the Communist party resulted in decisions taken without unanimous consent; and a Party first secretary was unsure for days whether he would be re-elected.

These unusual events were preceded by a long succession of political, economic and social crises that began with the 1956 workers' revolt in Poznan. It was thought that returning the national and so-called liberal Communist, Gomulka, to power would settle the country's serious problems, but this was not the case. Gomulka's term was marked by a progressive hardening of the regime, by a total alignment with the USSR during the events in Prague in 1968, and by the continuation, even aggravation, of the economic conditions underlying the crisis of 1956. In December, 1970, a new uprising of the worker class ended Gomulka's stay in power. The economic crisis had been provoked in the beginning by rising inflation and artificially low prices of certain commodities. A government decision on December 12, 1970, to sharply increase the price of food in order to halt inflation sparked the revolt. Although these measures were necessary, their sudden imposition just before the Christmas holidays provoked an equally sudden reaction from the public. On December 14, 1970, in the Baltic ports from Gdansk to Szczeczin, spontaneous strikes broke out. Thousands of workers from the naval shipyards gathered in demonstrations that quickly degenerated into riots; local Party headquarters were burned, and members of the militia attacked. Gomulka called in the army and asked General Korczynski to restore order. In the night, the entire coastal region was cut off from the rest of the country and occupied by Polish army tanks.

The country was unaware of what was happening on the Baltic. When the government gave its version of the events two days later, it blamed "bums" and "vandals," but these statements were not at all well received. Demonstrations began again in earnest. On December 17 at Gdynia, troops fired on workers in the shipyard who had returned to work after three days on strike; on the same day the police fired shots at Szczeczin. Officially, about 50 died and hundreds more were wounded. Unofficial tallies were much higher. Throughout the country—in Poznan, in Warsaw, in Silesia—people demonstrated their solidarity with the workers in the shipyards. In the Baltic ports, the workers went on strike again and occupied their worksites. Democratically elected representatives of the workers opened negotiations with the local authorities. It was under these circumstances that a young electrician by the name of Lech Walesa was elected president of the strikers' committee in Gdansk. Talks led to the withdrawal of army units, and work began again on December 22, 1970.

The immediate consequence of these worker strikes was the departure of Gomulka. The Polish politburo met immediately without Gomulka, who was officially ill, and asked Edward Gierek, a former miner who had once worked in the mines in northern France, to assume duties as first secretary of the Polish Worker party. Gierek enjoyed a certain popularity among the miners of Silesia who had elected him. Like Gomulka in 1956, he seemed to want to re-direct Polish politics, attempting to open a dialogue with the different segments of Polish society. He suspended the obligatory deliveries of quotas for the peasants; for the workers, he cancelled the price increases announced by his predecessor and promised that the official unions would be democratized. Just as Gomulka had done, Gierek opened a dialogue with the church, which had as extensive an influence in the country as ever. The tension rapidly diffused, and in the elections set for March 19, 1972, the voters were allowed to alter the order of the candidates on the official list; Gierek and his followers were elected while Gomulka's colleagues brought up the end of the list. Despite this auspicious beginning, the new leadership team led by Gierek proved to be just as incompetent as its predecessor in solving Poland's problems.

Politically, the critical situation which had existed since 1970 worsened. The foreign trade deficit from trade with COMECON countries as well as capitalist countries grew. Trade imbalances were aggravated by increases in the prices of energy and raw materials, by low industrial and agricultural productivity, and by the artificial and unrealistic pricing of goods within the country. The government tried to address these difficulties, but the June 1976 attempt to raise prices without corresponding increases in workers' salaries provoked new demonstrations and strikes, forcing the government to back down.

The discontent of a growing number of Poles was accentuated by the obvious scarcity most people in the country were experiencing, contrasted with the abundance and waste of government dignitaries and profiteers. The gap between the real country, represented by the immense majority of the population, and the governing class, made up a few thousand privileged individuals and their clientele, grew wider and wider. This widening gap between classes, compounded by an increasingly ubiquitous black market, created the explosive situation of the summer of 1980.

Two unequal forces confronted Gierek's government: first, as a result of the movements of 1956 and 1970, a clandestine unionism made sporadic appearances, scattered but active. Lech Walesa had been dismissed from his job by the insidious repression that followed the worker agitation of June, 1976, and led the difficult life of an unemployed worker; nevertheless, he maintained contact with his former worker friends who held him in high esteem. In April, 1978, he helped found a clandestine newspaper, *The Coastal Worker*, which became the voice for underground unions. Similar groups sprang up around the country, in particular the Workers' Defense Committee, or *KOR*, led by a Warsaw academic named Jacek Kuron. For the first time, the worker movement had the support of the intelligentsia.

Next to these constantly harassed clandestine groups, another even greater force began to arise, openly counteracting government abuses of power. This force was the Catholic church, which had long played a moderate and conciliatory role in Polish politics. The church supported Gierek's reforms in 1970 much as it had done for Gomulka in 1956, but quickly realized that the new leadership intended to restrict the religious freedoms the church had struggled to acquire in 1956. It also realized that the people's disappointment in the government was leading to more uprisings. From 1974 to 1980, the Polish episcopate under Cardinal Wyszynski led the fight in defense of the rights of the people and of religious freedom, while at the same time trying to contain the growing popular discontent. In June, 1974, Cardinal Wojtyla did not hesitate to publicly denounce attempts to undermine religious freedom: "Catholics do not want to be treated like second-class citizens," he declared to over 100,000 followers assembled in Cracow.

While it is true that the Polish church held a privileged position in the state in comparison with other Eastern European countries, the government nonetheless used every opportunity to attack it. From 1974 to 1980, the church-state relationship alternated between periods of tension and calm. In 1976, for example, the state minister in charge of religious affairs, Kazimierz Kakol, said "Just as I am obliged to smile in my duties as state minister in order to inspire confidence in the people, so will I as a Communist ceaselessly fight religion and the church. We must never allow the religious education of children. I am ashamed when Communists from other countries ask me why so many Poles still attend church. If we cannot annihilate the church, we should at least prevent it from doing damage." Several months later, in seeming contradiction, Cardinal Wyszynski received bouquets of flowers from the Polish government for his 75th birthday.

The Catholic Church in Poland (1981)

Population—95 percent Roman Catholic
18,000 priests and 30,000 monks and nuns
500 to 600 priests ordained every year
2 cardinals: Cardinal Macharski and Cardinal Glemp
A Catholic University in Lublin
A Faculty of Theology in Warsaw
27 Dioceses
27 Seminaries

The church did not hesitate to defend the moral and material interests of the Polish people whenever it judged it necessary to do so. Confronted with economic difficulties, the primate spelled out the church's position. In a pastoral letter in 1977, Cardinal Wyszynski felt duty-bound to remind the authorities of the simple fact that "men must eat every day, and for that to be possible, there must be convenient places to buy bread, meat and milk without wasting so much time and energy." The cardinal was clearly alluding to the difficulties in obtaining supplies and to the long waiting lines in stores.

The election of Cardinal Wojtyla as Pope John Paul II on October 16, 1978, heightened the church's considerable prestige. The government was forced to alter its position to adjust to the church's increased strength. This change was obvious in November, 1978, when Cardinal Wyszynski, in the presence of the same minister, Kakol, jokingly demanded freedom of expression: "It would be enough if you would give the censors good pensions and thank them for their work." The Pope's triumphant visit to his native country in June, 1979, as well as his open stance in favor of human rights and religious freedom before members of the government and Communist party officials, furthered the influence of the Church, even among atheists. With the strong support of the Pope, the church took a public position in support of jailed dissidents. On May 7, 1980, the episcopate requested that the authorities cease the prosecution of "those citizens holding nonconformist views...in the interests of internal peace." The message went on to declare, "we are filled with anxiety by the recently intensified reprisals because they are aggravating existing tensions." These warnings were issued in May of 1980. The events of that summer confirmed the accuracy of the Polish bishops' predictions.

A sudden announcement of a price increase for the end of July, 1980, set off the powderkeg. On July 1, the first strike broke out in a tractor factory at Ursus, a suburb of Warsaw, and another at Gdansk, again in the shipyards. Everywhere, workers demanded wage increases and the cancellation of the announced price hikes. Gierek refused to back down, claiming his decision was necessary to fight inflation, and so provoked further strikes. By the end of July, a hundred businesses were affected; in August, the movement spread to all branches of the economy. The transportation workers in Warsaw and most major cities, textile workers in Lodz, miners in Silesia, all stopped working. But it was in Gdansk, in the Lenin shipyards, that the strike was at its most obstinate. It was led by Lech Walesa and another activist in the independent trade union, Anna Walentynowicz, who had just been laid off for her union activities. The 16,000 shipyard workers began their action on August 14; they organized at the worksite, setting up an inter-company strike committee. They rapidly drafted a list of demands, including professional requests, rights to religious freedoms and the radio broadcast of a mass every Sunday. By the end of August, the entire region around Gdansk was paralysed by strikes: 100,000 strikers occupied their factories and their worksites.

At first the government seemed to adopt a firm policy. The head of the government, Edward Babiuch, and his deputy prime minister, Tadeusz Pyka, did not want to back down. On August 20, a repression began, not against the workers, but against about 15 members of the *KOR* who were arrested along with a few dissident intellectuals. The workers added the liberation of these detainees to their list of demands. The government was unnerved by the rapprochement between its political opponents and the workers, and softened its stance. The first secretary of the Party in Gdansk, Tadeusz Fiszbach, contacted the strikers. The government dismissed Pyka and replaced him with a liberal, Mieczyslaw Jagielski. Talks between the strikers committee and Jagielski finally led to a formal agreement on August 31. In the meantime, the Party made a gesture of appeasement by replacing

Prime Minister Babiuch with a liberal, Jozef Pinkowski. The church tried to promote calm, to the point that the bishop of Gdansk, Kaczmarek, advocated the workers return to work if their demands were recognized. In a communique on August 27, the Polish episcopate stressed the need for the workers' freedom to "organize into associations which they create for themselves and which defend their interests," thus echoing a right demanded by the Gdansk workers.

In the other Eastern bloc countries, there was a general outcry after the governments recovered from their initial surprise. The hardliners in the socialist camp—the East Germans, the Czechoslovaks, the Bulgarians and the Rumanians—denounced the anti-socialist activities taking place in Poland and called for vigilance. Only the Hungarian and Yugoslav moderates displayed any sympathy for the Polish strikers. The USSR first limited its action to scrambling Western radio signals, then the Soviet press denounced Western agents' activity in the outbreak of strikes in Poland. In September, Soviet critics grew more aggressive, and *Pravda* recalled that "the true sovereignty and independence of popular Poland are only guaranteed by its fraternal union with the other socialist countries." In early October, Soviet troops were first noticed massing along the eastern Polish borders.

The evolution of the Polish crisis must be examined on three levels, beginning with the unions. The independent unions had been organized openly and outside of the Party and official organizations in a matter of weeks, and numerous Communist party members joined them. During the strikes in Gdansk, Lech Walesa and the members of the strikers' committee laid the foundations for the Solidarity union, and in the August 31 agreement with the government, the principle of independent unionism was officially recognized. After drawing up the statutes, Solidarity leaders presented them to the government tribunal in Warsaw to be legalized. The first shock for the new union came on October 24; the tribunal had taken it upon themselves to alter certain points in the statutes, profoundly changing their original intent. Lech Walesa, while trying to calm the militants, appealed to have the offending changes omitted, and this time won. On November 10, the Supreme Court restored Solidarity's statutes to their original form.

For the first time in an Eastern European country, an apolitical union, with no ties to the Party or the state, was formed and officially recognized by the Communist government. Its millions of members had all joined of their own free will, not because the government had coerced them to join as had been the case with the official unions. Immediately after the official recognition, Solidarity guaranteed the accords made at Gdansk to the workers. Its first actions, on January 10 and 24, 1981, were to obtain the promised Saturdays off.

Lech Walesa had the solid support of the Polish church, which was able to channel the energy of certain active members. In an audience granted on January 15, the Pope congratulated Walesa for forming an independent union in Poland, declaring that "men who are active in the same type of work have the right to join together freely...for the purpose of determining the benefits that this work is entitled to. This is a fundamental personal right." He then recalled that the matter was "strictly internal to Poland" and that Solidarity should be "guided by justice and love" in its actions. The Pope concluded his declaration with the words, "May the same courage that you demonstrated at the beginnings of your initiative, and also the same prudence and moderation, accompany you always."

The example set by the workers in Polish cities was followed by the peasants in the country. The creation of a rural Solidarity movement caused concern among the authorities, who initially refused to register it. But finally on May 12, the statutes of Rural Solidarity were officially recognized. The landed peasants also formed an independent union, just as apolitical as the worker's union. From then on in socialist Poland, the government and the Party had to deal with a serious, responsible and greatly representative organization. Despite government provocation and with the exception of a few thoughtless local acts, the leadership of Solidarity proved both effective and prudent in avoiding any major conflict with the government. They accomplished this without relinquishing any essential points.

The Polish crisis must also be examined on the level of internal politics. The events in July-August, 1980, caused a profound shake-up in the government and Party agencies. The Sixth plenum of the central committee meeting on October 4 and 5, proceeded to evict Gierek's associates, and the former first secretary—suffering from heart trouble, according to official reports—was himself ousted. A new Party leadership was established with Stanislaw Kania as first secretary, surrounded by moderates like Stefan Olszowski and Kazimierz Barcikowski, the avowed liberal Mieczyslaw Rakowski, and by General Moczar. The new leaders drew up their program during the plenum of December 1; the slogan "yes to renewal, no to anarchy," was indicative of the new Party line. When, on December 16, the highest state authorities attended the dedication of a monument to the victims of the repression during the 1970 strikes at Gdansk, it was obvious that something had changed in Poland. But the limits of this change were also clear when the liberal Pinkowski was replaced as head of the government by General Wojciech Jaruzelski. With Kania leading the Party, and Jaruzelski at the head of government, the centrists were victorious. In a statement to the Diet on February 12, 1981, General Jaruzelski announced: "the government will labor honestly and reasonably for socialist renewal, for socialist democracy." Those who "committed errors in the past will be prosecuted," and "the hand of the government will remain continually outstretched, in all sincerity and goodwill, to all patriots of good faith." Recalling the serious economic difficulties of the moment, he appealed to the unions for a truce of 90 days while pledging that commitments made would be kept. Jaruzelski concluded his speech by reassuring the other Eastern European countries that, "the place of popular Poland is and will remain in the midst of the socialist forces...Poland will remain a member worthy of the confidence of the politico-defensive alliance which is the Warsaw Pact."

The attitude of the other Eastern bloc countries caused serious anxieties within Poland as well as in Western Europe. On at least two occasions, at the end of 1980 and in March-April, 1981, it was feared that the Warsaw Pact forces would intervene as they had in Czechoslovakia during the Prague Spring. The first warning was issued on December 5 during a surprise meeting of the Warsaw Pact leaders in Moscow. In fact, the meeting, which took place according to the official communique "in an atmosphere of comraderie, mutual understanding and agreement," ended more positively than had been predicted. The participants declared themselves convinced "that the Communists, the working class and the Polish workers would be able to surmount the difficulties that had arisen and would guarantee the country's future development in the socialist path;" they reiterated that the Polish Communists "could rely on the fraternal solidarity and support of countries who had signed the Warsaw Pact."

Despite continual attacks in the Soviet, East German and Czechoslovak press, the situation seemed to ease a little in early 1981. Tension rose again suddenly when on March 19, police forces beat rural union activists at Bydogoszcz; then in late March, Warsaw Pact maneuvers known as *Soyuz '81* began on Polish territory, coinciding with a hardening on the part of the Polish government towards dissidents. The abnormal prolongation of the maneuvers and the resurgence of social tension after the Bydogoszcz incident seemed to foreshadow a tightening of governmental power in conjunction with Soviet military intervention.

Verbal attacks on Polish leaders became more virulent. This was most obvious at the opening of the Czechoslovak Communist party congress on April 6, 1981. In the presence of Brezhnev, in Prague for the occasion, the first secretary of the Czechoslovak Communist party, Husak, castigated "the anti-socialist and counter-revolutionary forces threatening socialism in Poland." He warned that "the socialist community will not watch passively as the Polish Communist system is threatened." In mid-April, the situation eased again with the completion of the *Soyuz '81* maneuvers. The impromptu visit of the Soviet party theoretician, Mikhail Suslov on April 23 and 24, just before the opening of the 10th plenum of the Polish Communist party, prompted new concern. The visit, however, did not deter the Polish Party leadership from announcing democratization of Party operations in preparation for the 9th extraordinary congress set for July 14. Kania continued to steer a course somewhere between Moscow and Solidarity.

The assassination attempt on the Pope on May 13, followed 15 days later by the death of Cardinal Wyszynski, brought about a kind of truce in relations betwen the government and Solidarity. Tension rose again on June 5, when the Soviet Communist party issued a solemn warning to the leaders of the Polish Worker's party. The letter laid the blame for Poland's problems on "the counter-revolution hiding in the midst of Solidarity" and sternly criticized the government's successive concessions. "It is now a matter of mobilizing all the healthy forces of society in order to block this class enemy and to fight the counter-revolution. The Party can and must find within itself the energy to reverse the course of events and to set them right before the Congress." This call to order ended with the reminder that, "We will not allow socialist Poland to be attacked and will not abandon a brother country in its misfortune." The letter was reminiscent of the letter Dubcek received in 1968 from the five Warsaw Pact first secretaries.

The reprimand from the Soviet Communist party influenced the meeting of the central committee held on June 10, 1981. Kania essentially recognized that "conscious counter-revolutionary actions threaten socialism and national life." For him, "Poland is and will remain a socialist country and a link in the defensive coalition of the treaty of Warsaw and of COMECON." Nevertheless, he felt that Solidarity and the church also had their place in the evolutionary process.

Just before the opening of the 9th Congress, a visit by Andrei Gromyko, the Soviet minister of foreign affairs, slightly eased tension caused by the June 5 letter. The joint communique issued on July 5 stressed, once again and in the familiar manner, that "Poland has been and always will be a lasting link in the chain of socialist communities."

On a social level, the situation remained critical after 40,000 dockyard workers on the Baltic held a warning strike on July 8, when salary negotiations between Solidarity and the government failed. The next day, employees of the airline, *LOT*, observed a non-working day because the government refused to confirm the employee's election of a new director. New strikes set for July 23 were canceled when a last-minute agreement was reached.

The extraordinary Congress took place as planned from July 14 to 20, attended by over 2,000 delegates elected in free elections by members of the 105,000 Communist party cells. The attentive delegates from the other Eastern bloc countries were led, interestingly enough, by second-ranking officials. The Soviet delegation was led by the first secretary of the Party from the Moscow region, Grichine. As an opening declaration, Grichine stated,

"It is up to the Poles alone to settle their problems. The Polish Communists are capable of recovering the confidence of their own nation. We are confident that the Polish Workers' party will know how to surmount this awkward crisis and repel the counter-revolution." In the wake of Gromyko's conciliatory visit to Poland just before the Congress, Grichine's statement made sense and also seemed to indicate that for the time being, the USSR was willing to let the Poles settle their own differences.

The Congress decided by a large majority in the first session that the higher offices of the Party would be elected by secret ballot at the end of the Congress. After procedural matters were settled, Secretary Kania read his report. Kania felt that the Polish situation combined the "struggle for socialist renewal" with the "struggle against the enemies of socialism," thus justifying his faction's centrist position. He denounced the "reactionary and extremist groups trying to turn Solidarity into a political party in opposition to the socialist government." He also condemned all dissident movements including the *KOR* and the *KPN* (Confederation of Independent Poland), which he contended were supported by "Western centers that specialize in the subversion of the socialist community." Kania asked for a reinforcement of the "alliance of reasonable people," of which the church was party, to counter the serious problems facing the country.

In the days that followed, various speakers took part in the debates; after each commentary by one of the liberals, such as Fiszbach, first secretary from Gdansk, or Rakowski, deputy prime minister in charge of relations with Solidarity, the participants applauded enthusiastically. Rakowski, whose apparent popularity threatened Kania's power, proposed a wide alliance between the Party, the Solidarity movement and the church, in order to regain public confidence and to act effectively. In the evening of July 16, the Congress initiated the election of the 200 members of the central committee. With Jaruzelski, Kania, Barcikowski, Olszowski and Rakowski elected by nearly three-quarters of the vote, the centrists gained the most ground in the central committee. Meanwhile, the ultra-liberals such as Fiszbach and most of the ultra-conservatives were eliminated.

At the end of the Congress on July 19, Stanislaw Kania retained his position as the first secretary with 1,311 votes, or over two-thirds of the vote. The centrist tendency was also reflected by the majority of the 15 members elected to the politburo, although a few conservatives were also voted in. These included Albin Siwak, the notorious adversary of Solidarity. Inversely, the liberal Rakowski did not receive enough votes to be elected. The Congress also announced the expulsion of Gierek and his associates, and asked the party leadership to begin proceedings against them.

There was something strange about this Congress, where the delegates openly applauded the liberals, but in the secret voting, excluded them from office. This secret vote, which was considered by many as an obvious sign of democracy, worked against the liberals by the pressures exerted on the delegates at the time of the vote. In his closing speech, Kania once again emphasized his zeal for the policy of socialist renewal, but also underscored the importance of the struggle against the adversaries of socialism. He advocated a "wide alliance of responsible citizens" to fight the dramatic problems facing the country. To reassure the "brother countries," Kania concluded by re-emphasizing Poland's loyalty to the socialist bloc and to the Soviet Union.

Despite all the commotion made over the Congress, none of the problems at the root of the Polish crisis had been solved; the economic crisis, the uneasy relationship between Solidarity and the state, and the food shortages all remained as before. This failing did not go unnoticed. The Congress had hardly closed before a new wave of strikes and demonstrations swept the country. Despite the moderating stance of Solidarity leaders and the church, people staged hunger walks throughout the country to protest the new price hikes and further rationing. Thousands of women marched to cries of "We are hungry!" in the streets of Lodz, Szczeczin, Kutno, Wroclaw and Warsaw. In the capital, mass transit workers and taxi drivers paralysed the city August 3 to 5 by parking their vehicles in the city center. Two weeks later, the printers refused to print the Communist newspapers in order to push their demands. Only an intercession by Lech Walesa and Cardinal Glemp prevented a confrontation with the government.

The Solidarity congress opened in Gdansk in the first days of September, 1981. Solidarity activists did not mince words in their criticism of union leaders they judged to be too conciliatory towards the Communist government. They voted for a motion to support all movements in Eastern Europe and the USSR attempting to form independent trade-unions. Lech Walesa's re-election on October 2, by only 55 percent of the vote, clearly indicated that although the average worker still had confidence in the man who had spearheaded the workers' revolt of the previous summer, they wanted more assertive action. The final motion of the Congress demonstrated that the members wished to "create living conditions with dignity in an economically and politically sovereign Poland, and to create a life free of poverty, fear, exploitation and lies, in a lawful and democratically organized society." They also demanded decentralization of the economy, including the right of workers to control companies as well as union access to the media. With ten million members, the support of the immense majority of the population and the approval of the church, Solidarity was aware of its representation relative to the state and the Workers' party, which had lost one-third of its numerous members.

A serious crisis within the Worker party erupted in the meeting of the plenum of the central committee from October 16 to 18. Stanislaw Kania was replaced as first secretary by General Wojciech Jaruzelski, who was already head of the government. A few days prior to the plenum, rumors spread that the Polish army was preparing to seize power, but the authorities had simply decided to extend military duty by two months for all soldiers whose tours of duty were ending. One of the first measures Jaruzelski took was to assign these soldiers to alleviating the problems of the economy and of waste, and to improve transportation. The new first secretary, whose nomination was well-received in Moscow, clearly demonstrated his intent to widen the base of power to include everyone willing to help, as long as they had some respect for basic socialist principles.

On October 21, Cardinal Glemp returned from Rome where he had met with Pope John Paul II, with Jaruzelski and then with Lech Walesa. The idea of a national *entente*, supported from the beginning by the church, began to take shape. A few days later, on October 29, the Solidarity leadership, despite criticism from militant members, appealed to all of its members to cease any strikes in progress. This gesture of goodwill after the discord caused by the worrisome decisions of the October plenum brought about a certain *detente*. On November 11, for the first time since the war, Warsaw freely and officially celebrated the independence of 1918, and linked it by name to Marshal Pilsudski, who had been deleted from Polish history since 1945. Even more heartening in the days that followed, representatives of the government and of Solidarity began negotiations to work out the details of a national *entente*. After long discussions held "in an atmosphere of sincerity and understanding," an agreement was finally reached on November 18, between Solidarity Vice President Wadolowski and Ciosek, the minister in charge of union relations. A national *entente* finally appeared feasible.

The End of Illusions

Any hopes raised by the November 18 agreement were quickly dispelled. While negotiating with Solidarity, the government and the Worker party were secretly planning a takeover. The Poles had become accustomed to tumultuous ups and downs since the summer of 1980, and so did not seem overly concerned by the disquieting signs on the horizon. They had had several brushes with disaster since the mad Gdansk summer of 1970, but things had always fallen back into place. Now, at the end of November, 1981, the situation was rapidly deteriorating. First, on November 22, the internal security forces (*ZOMO*) roughly searched the home of Jacek Kuron, head of the *KOR*, accusing him along with other Solidarity members of trying to create "a political organization hostile to the socialist state." The media then launched a major smear campaign against certain Solidarity leaders, accusing them of "counter-revolutionary and anti-socialist scheming" which was aggravating the country's economic plight.

Poland's perilous position was pushed to new heights during the meeting of the Polish Worker party on November 27 and 28. General Jaruzelski announced that the politburo, of which he was the first secretary, had commanded the government, of which he was the leader, to present to the Diet a project proposal for a "law on extraordinary means of action in the interest of protecting citizens and the state." The emergency legislation was to "put at the disposal of the government of Poland the full powers indispensible in effectively opposing the acts of destruction ruining the country and its economy, threatening the socialist state, order and public safety." This was a far cry from the words of the national *entente*, effectually eliminating the gains the workers' had struggled for in the summer of 1980, beginning by revoking their right to strike.

Jaruzelski had completed an about-face; he announced in no uncertain terms that the time for discipline had arrived. Solidarity quickly felt the effects of this new government position. On December 2, police brutally evacuated striking students from the military firefighters' academy in Warsaw. Confronted with such government provocation, Solidarity leaders called together a presidium in the little town of Radom. Stating that "the government has nullified the possibilities for a national *entente* by choosing a path of force, and has thus rejected the chance of a dialogue with society," the Solidarity leadership decided by a wide majority that if the Diet granted the full emergency powers requested by Jaruzelski, Solidarity would initiate a general, nationwide strike. Lech Walesa, always careful to avoid confrontation, voted against the general strike proposal.

Two days later, on December 7, three events further charged the already explosive atmosphere. The church, for the first time, very clearly took Solidarity's side against the Party; Cardinal Glemp unhesitatingly asked the deputies in the Diet to reject Jaruzelski's request for a law granting emergency powers. On the same day, Polish government leaders received a message from their Soviet counterparts notifying them that the time had come to put an end to Solidarity's activities. Finally, still on December 7, Polish radio began broadcasting speeches by Lech Walesa and other Solidarity leaders secretly taped during the meeting at Radom. An extract was broadcast in which Walesa said, "I don't believe in anyone who has collaborated with this system since 1970. They want to swindle us. They realize that if we put our program into action, if we distribute farmland to the deprived peasants and create committees for self-administration, we will topple their system." This was too much for the Party leaders, especially because certain Solidarity leaders, convinced that they and their ten million followers represented the true country, had suggested holding a referendum on the methods and means of the present government.

A confrontation was inevitable. Solidarity could neither back down nor make new concessions without looking like a substitute for the old official unions. The church issued continual appeals for peace, but was also unable to back down because the soothing words it had issued since the beginning of the crisis might be interpreted as a sign of collusion with the government. Jaruzelski and the Workers' party leaders, on the other hand, could not allow such a referendum to take place, since from all appearances, the results would be a public affront to the Party and an undeniable demonstration of its unpopularity. Action had to be taken, and quickly. Once more, the Kremlin was growing impatient. On December 11, the *Tass* news agency accused Solidarity of wanting to "upset both the executive and the legislative branches in popular Poland" and gave assurances that the measures announced by Jaruzelski would have full Soviet support.

In the night of December 12, while the national commission of Solidarity at Gdansk recommended that the referendum mentioned above be held before February 15, 1982, General Jaruzelski decided to crush the gathering using the armed forces. Within a few hours, the army and the militia were in control of the country, and in Warsaw, tanks patrolled the streets in the early hours of the morning. In a radio message, Jaruzelski announced that the country was in a state of war and under martial law, that a Military Council of National Salvation (*WRON*) had been created to direct the government, and that Solidarity leaders had been arrested along with Gierek and several other Communist party leaders.

On December 13, the country had been cut off from the rest of the world: telephone service was suspended, Telex lines cut, and the borders sealed. The meager news being broadcast over Polish radio and television confirmed that Solidarity leaders had been arrested, mentioning as many as 1,000 arrests. A curfew from 10 P.M. to 6 A.M. was announced, the right to strike was suspended, the work week was restored to its six-day length, and annual vacation time was cut in half. Most importantly, key industries were taken over by the military; employees of public transportation, mines, electrical power stations and steel plants, were essentially drafted. Any strike or act of disobedience was subject to prosecution under the military code. Undaunted Solidarity members threatened strikes anyway, but were discouraged by the primate of Poland who advocated patience and calm, even though he condemned the army's seizure of power. He was echoed by the Pope, who urged his compatriots "not to shed any more Polish blood."

After the initial shock that followed the army's takeover, the workers began to react. In major industrial centers, Gdansk, Szczeczin, Katowice, and Silesia, striking workers locked themselves in their factories. Attempts by the army and the militia to dislodge them led to numerous and often violent clashes. On December 16, ten miners were killed in the Wujek mine in Silesia when the armed forces intervened. Workers and students organized passive resistance throughout the country, despite the harsh repression. There was talk of several thousand arrests and at least 200 dead. Most of the Solidarity leaders, including Walesa, were held in a villa near Warsaw.

On Christmas Eve, 1981, ten days after the proclamation of a state of emergency in Poland and the institution of martial law, the future of the country looked very bleak. The majority of the Polish people remained passive during this time, not because of the harsh behavior of the military and the militia, but because they knew that resisting Jaruzelski's forces would give the Soviet army and the Warsaw Pact forces the right to intervene in Poland as they had in Czechoslovakia in 1968. They also knew that without help from the West, any confrontation would be senseless. The example of Hungary in October 1956, when the Western nations forgot their promises to aid the revolutionaries, was still in the memory of the Polish people. Thus, General Jaruzelski was able, with relatively little risk, to end Polish hopes for a better society.

Chapter 27

The Age of Gorbachev

GORBACHEV AND THE REFORM PERIOD

The political and economic problems of the socialist countries of Eastern Europe became increasingly serious after 1981, forcing the Communist leadership in each country to make concessions to its people. While borrowing heavily from Western nations, they desperately began to look for new economic policies. Brezhnev's death on November 10, 1982, and the ensuing crises of succession in the Soviet Union were sure to have repercussions on the satellite countries.

The designation of the ex-KGB chief Yuri Andropov as Soviet Party leader was considered a victory for the reform-minded. During his short term, he attempted to "clean up" the Party bureaucracy and called for greater efforts to decentralize the economy. In his first major address to the central committee as general-secretary, Andropov announced his plans for government reform. Condemning the "old ways," he recommended new steps to mobilize the Soviet economy. Andropov became the first Soviet leader to speak of experimental reform, of more independent and vocal management, and of the possibility of learning from the outside world. In agriculture, he encouraged farmers to use more initiative. He also insisted that state enterprises should better reflect state investment with their output. Andropov revealed no drastic changes in Soviet foreign policy at first, but at a Warsaw Pact meeting in Prague two months after taking office (January 1983), he presented a proposal to ease tension between East and West.

Andropov's health was failing, and during his prolonged illness he became increasingly dependent on a younger member of the Politburo—Mikhail Gorbachev. Gorbachev also had the support of Mikhail Suslov, a long-time Politburo member. When Andropov died in February 1984, he was succeeded by his old friend Konstantin Chernenko, a confidante of Brezhnev's. During Chernenko's fourteen months as Party leader, he reverted indirectly to Brezhnev's policies, restoring central planning to the economy, making the Party a haven for bureaucrats, and renewing a critical relationship with the Eastern European nations.

The selection of Gorbachev as general secretary was announced only four hours after Chernenko's death on March 4, 1985. After three physically feeble and ineffective leaders, the majority of the Politburo members were more than ready to vote for Gorbachev, who at fifty-four became the youngest man to ascend to the secretary-general's position since Stalin came to power in 1924. He was also the only Soviet leader besides Lenin to come from an intellectual background. With Gorbachev, not just a new leader, but a new generation moved into the Kremlin.

In the first four months in his new position as general-secretary, Gorbachev showed a great deal of political strength. He undermined his chief rivals, Romanov and Gromyko, and brought to power allies such as Shevernadze, the foreign affairs minister, Nikolai Rizkhov, the prime minister, Viktor Chebrikov, the KGB boss, and Yegor Ligachev, the ideology chief. These changes in the politburo and the secretariat were the most extensive in fourteen years, replacing the old, hard-liners and entrenched bureaucrats with men with reputations for hard work and efficiency.

After Gorbachev had secured his position, his attention turned to the Soviet economy, which had been steadily losing momentum. His new economic and government reforms were guided by a policy called *perestroika*, literally, the "restructuring." The reforms included changing the planning and pricing systems, establishing a new policy for financing industry and agriculture, initiating a new system for distributing basic industrial materials, reorganizing different specialized government ministries and changing the communal system of local government.

Glasnost, the policy encouraging openness and public debate in Soviet society, was the other key to Gorbachev's reforms. Gorbachev realized that an amount of criticism from the rank-and-file Party members would be healthy for the country, and also the only force which would encourage greater involvement of the public in the system. He saw that a society without internal judgment, unable to recognize or voice its own problems, would stagnate. It soon became clear, however, that the new "openness" had its limitations; for example, criticism of the local Party secretary and factory management was permissable, but voicing discontent with the Communist party leadership itself was still taboo.

Although Eastern Europeans believed something significant was happening in the Soviet Union, they responded to Gorbachev's reforms with skepticism. From experience, they were more realistic about the promises of his policies. *Glasnost*, they knew, was still a far cry from the open society the West envisioned, a society with complete freedom of speech and publication. The publication of a few previously forbidden books was met with an enthusiastic response from the West, but as Joseph Brodsky, the 1987 Nobel prize winner in Literature said, "This literature belongs to the people. It was stolen. When the thief returns it, why should I be grateful to him?"

After more than forty years of Soviet domination, the peoples of Eastern Europe realized that the Soviet Union would never grant them complete independence. Gorbachev confirmed their belief in a speech to the Polish Party Congress in June 1986; he repeated that the USSR would not tolerate any Eastern European country rejecting Communist party rule or leaving the Warsaw Pact. On the other hand, he has said that the forcible interference of one country in the affairs of another is unacceptable. While Gorbachev acknowledges the ties of mutual interdependence between the Eastern European countries and the Soviet Union, what he would do in the case of another East Bloc insurrection "endangering socialism," previously a justification for Soviet military intervention under the Brezhnev Doctrine, is unclear.

Eastern Europeans know too from experience that drastic economic reforms can only be put into effect at tremendous cost to the masses. By the mid-eighties several signs in their own countries already warned them of this possibility: prices rose at extreme rates, especially in food and rent, supposedly guaranteed in Marxist society. A personal income tax was introduced and a new bankruptcy law ratified, ending state subsidies for inefficient factories and eliminating millions of jobs—violating the Marxist promise of guaranteed employment. Even if Gorbachev succeeded with his new policies in the Soviet Union, Eastern Europeans were aware that the effects of his reforms on their own bureaucratic systems and entrenched leaders would be slow, and perhaps not even beneficial.

The Continuing Economic Crisis in Eastern Europe

Eastern Europe's most serious problem is the state of its economy. Although differing in specifics, the nations all share in the problems wrought by central planning and a failure of the system to take the world market or domestic demands into consideration. East Bloc industry and agriculture are inefficient and suffer from bad management and low worker morale. The countries remain dependent on one another and on the Soviet Union for food, commercial goods, and energy resources, yet as a whole bloc they are still not self-sufficient. Under the pressure of run-away inflation and burgeoning foreign debts and trade deficits, the nations of the East Bloc recognize the need to make radical changes in their Marxist-inspired economic systems.

With the exception of Hungary and East Germany, the Eastern European nations suffer from constant food shortages. The shortages are brought on by a lack of modern farm equipment and insufficient chemical fertilizers, and compounded by forced labor practices on the state-owned farms or *kolkozes*. Governments aggravate food shortages by exporting the best agricultural products to Western countries in exchange for hard currency. In Czechoslovakia and Poland, it is common to see men and women standing in long lines for basic food items such as bread and meat. "Luxury items" like coffee, wine and chocolate are only available in special western currency stores.

In Rumania, food shortages have been particularly severe. Forty years after the Second World War, Rumanians must still buy food with food-stamps. In parts of the country basic food items such as milk and cooking oil, not to mention meat or other sources of protein, are scarce; children and elderly people die regularly of malnutrition. According to official sources, Rumanian President Nicolae Ceausescu declared that "Rumanians are used to eating too much," and in an article published in the *Scinteia* on July 14, 1982, recommended that Rumanians reduce their caloric intake by 300 to 500 calories a day to alleviate the food shortages.

Hungary was able to meet the demands of its domestic market by giving peasants the permission to farm their own small plots in addition to working on the collective farms. The policy, initiated in 1968, was a success; farmers contributed 35-40 percent of all domestic food from their private plots, and Hungary became the first Eastern European country to export food. Bulgaria soon followed suit, and found that almost 30 percent of its total agricultural output came from the 13 percent of agricultural land lent to the peasants.

Inflation is the second malady afflicting the economies of countries in Eastern Europe. Poland set the East Bloc record for inflation in 1982, when prices for food went up 300 percent and still fell short of real market costs. Yugoslavia's inflation rate in 1986 was 140-150 percent, a rate the government attempted to control with renewed foreign credit; despite their efforts, by 1988 inflation had rocketed to 215 percent while wages failed to keep up.

To add to inflation, East Bloc economies are burdened by growing foreign debts to western creditors. In mid-1988, Poland owed close to $40 billion, followed by Yugoslavia owing $20 billion in debt, Rumania $6 billion, the GDR $13.5 billion, Hungary $18 billion, Bulgaria $5.5 billion, and Czechoslovakia trailing at a mere $4 billion. During the years 1980-81, every single Eastern European country had to reschedule their loan repayments. Most are able to fulfill their current payments only by imposing austerity programs on their citizens.

Eastern Europe's trade deficit with the West is also enormous, causing problems with credit worthiness. According to a report by the Organization for Economic Cooperation and Development, the OECD, the deficit was in excess of $3.5 billion in 1986. The East Bloc's trade towards the East is not much better; records from 1986 show that the Soviet Union had a $2 billion surplus of exports to the Eastern European market.

Integral to Eastern Europe's economic crisis is the shortage of energy resources and basic industrial materials. Most Eastern European countries must import the greater part of the gas and petroleum they consume from the USSR. They are required to pay a much higher price to the Soviets than the world market price, despite the fact that they financed the bulk of the Soviet pipe-line construction. Rumania could be much more self-sufficient, as it produces more than 11 million tons of petroleum and 28 billion cubic meters of gas yearly, but it is obligated to export an important part of its production to its neighboring Bloc countries because of COMECON agreements.

Other Bloc countries depend on the Soviets for additional resources. Poland, the GDR and Hungary get much of their electrical power from the Soviet Union. Most of the factories for heavy industry, built during the Stalin era, depend on Soviet iron ore. The biggest Hungarian steel mill in Dunaujvaros, for example, gets its ore from the Ukraine, transported over more than 1,500 miles of waterway. In spite of different COMECON agreements, the Soviet Union is not able to service all the energy needs of its Warsaw Pact allies. To pay for grain and modern technology, it exports much of its energy resources to western countries.

Eastern European countries have no choice but to initiate conservation policies, find alternative energy sources and somehow acquire the technology to make their countries more independent of Soviet energy sources. Such efforts are marked by the hydro-electric dam being constructed between Czechoslovakia and Hungary, the drastic energy restrictions in Rumania, and the development of nuclear energy plants in Bulgaria and East Germany.

Gorbachev's economic reforms in the Soviet Union have run up against great obstacles, obstacles Eastern European leaders also face in attempting to improve their own economic systems. Eastern Europeans remain skeptical that changes in the Soviet Union, even in the unlikely instance of unequivocal success, will favorably affect their own systems. Greater economic freedom without accompanying political freedom and changes in the hegemony of the Communist party will be ineffective and will not enable East Bloc nations to recover from their economic straits.

The Minority Problem in Eastern Europe

In his last years, Lenin vigorously fought against any nationalist sentiments in the Soviet Union. He was well aware that in a multi-national state, any kind of "nationalism" could lead to civil war. According to his Marxist-Leninist doctrine, all nationalities in a communist state should have the right to live in their own cultural settings, to keep their languages and traditions intact, and to have equal access to all government positions. Unfortunately, theory and practice diverged greatly. Stalin, who was a Georgian, praised the "Russian" people after the war with Germany but at the same time cruelly forced the Tartars and the Volga-Germans along with some tribes in the Caucasus to relocate to different parts of the Soviet Union—accusing them of collaborating with the Germans during the war. There are 1.2 million Poles, 170,000 Hungarians and 2.9 million "Moldavians" (formerly Rumanians) presently living under Soviet rule, but little is heard of them; no East European government would dare to confront the Soviet Union about its minorities.

After the Second World War, the victorious powers reinstated the old boundaries of the 1918-1920 treaties in Eastern Europe, again cutting off millions of people from their homelands and creating new minorities in foreign countries. Since then, the problem of the national minorities has become progressively more apparent in the region.

—The Hungarian Minorities

Hungary, which lost two-thirds of its territory after the First World War, has minorities in all of its surrounding countries, especially in Rumania, Czechoslovakia and Yugoslavia. Until 1982, the issue of the Hungarian minorities in neighboring countries was rarely spoken of in Budapest's official circles, and then only with caution.

The more than two million ethnic Hungarians living in Transylvania (Erdely) has been a source of ongoing tension between Rumania and Hungary. For many years, Hungarians were aware of Ceausescu's Rumanization policies and the extreme economic hardships to which the Hungarian minority was being subjected. In Transylvania the use of the Hungarian language was abolished for education or any official use even in the areas where Hungarians formed a majority. Hungarian history was eliminated from school curriculum, and the established Hungarian grammar schools and universities such as the famous university in Cluj (Kolozsvar), were closed. Finally, the Rumanian government instated a policy forcing Transylvanian Hungarians to move to different parts of Rumania, thereby dividing families and dispersing the Hungarian population.

The arrest of several well-known Hungarian leaders in Rumania in November, 1982 (the author Geza Szocs, the philosopher Ara-Kovacs, and

Professor Karoly Toth), provoked a reaction in Hungary. At the initiative of the author Gyula Illyes, a letter signed by 70 members of the literature and arts community in Hungary was sent to Prime Minister Gyorgy Lazar, asking for his intervention. For the first time, the Hungarian government dared to express openly its dispute with Rumania over the situation of the Hungarian minorities in Transylvania, and furthermore allowed the press and radio to cover it. Two leading members of the Hungarian Communist party, Gyorgy Aczel and Peter Varhonyi, travelled to Bucharest to meet Rumanian authorities. Nothing came of the meeting or from similar talks held in Debrecen. Ceausescu, in a speech in December, 1984, declared that the minority issue had been "solved," adding that questioning post-war frontier settlements was tantamount to siding with "vengeful and irredentist forces," threatening the "peace and security of Europe."

During the years 1985-1988, the situation became increasingly volatile as accusations of misconduct came more frequently from both sides of the Hungarian-Rumanian border. The Soviet *glasnost* policy gave the Hungarian government the freedom to act more openly against the Rumanian regime. In 1987, over 2,000 ethnic Hungarian refugees escaped Rumania by crossing the border into Hungary. The Hungarian government granted them permission to stay, and the number of refugees fleeing Rumanian persecution increased steadily. In the first six months of 1988, an estimated 10,000 refugees fled Rumania into Hungary, and in spite of drastic measures by the Rumanian government to close the borders between the two countries that summer, Transylvanian Hungarians continued to arrive in Hungary in great numbers.

In 1988, the differences between the two Warsaw Pact allies reached a high point with the disclosure of Ceausescu's plan to destroy 7000 Hungarian and German villages in Transylvania. The plan entails "bulldozing" entire villages—leveling to the ground historic churches, cemeteries, and traditional Erdely buildings—in order to clear new land for agriculture and modernize the peasantry. Village populations will be forced to evacuate their homes and move to newly-built government tower blocks where several families share a common kitchen and bathroom. Torn from their traditional societies, they are to work in large "agro-industrial complexes."

Ceausescu's "village extermination" plan was greeted with cries of outrage in Europe. The Hungarian Parliament in June 1988, condemned the destruction of the Hungarian villages in Rumania and the resettlement of ethnic Hungarians, accusing the Rumanian government of attempting to wipe out the Hungarian population. In Budapest on June 27, 1988, for the first time in the history of Communst rule in Eastern Europe, over 100,000 people demonstrated against Rumanian policy, calling it "genocide." In retaliation, the Rumanians accused the Hungarians of "chauvinistic, nationalistic, anti-Rumanian and anti-socialist" action, and closed the Hungarian Consulate in Cluj. They also evacuated a building in Bucharest which was rented by a Hungarian Cultural Center, and accused the Hungarians of interfering in Rumanian internal affairs.

Protests were held against Ceausescu in other European countries, and the European Parliament called on the Rumanian leader to end his village destruction policy. Hungarian Prime Minister Grosz said in an interview with a western journalist that he wanted to talk with the Rumanian leader, warning against drawing conclusions about the future course of Hungarian-Rumanian relations. He traveled to Moscow to obtain support from Gorbachev, but at the July 1988 Warsaw Pact/COMECON meeting, the issue was never raised; not only is the Soviet Union too absorbed in domestic problems to concern itself with external squabbles, but it has less influence in Rumania than most of the other East Bloc countries.

The Hungarians in Rumania are not the only Hungarian minorities to be victimized by the renewal of nationalism. The situation of 650,000 Hungarians living in southern Slovakia has become increasingly difficult since 1970. In 1982, the arrest and interrogation by police of several members of the Hungarian intelligentsia in Slovakia demonstrated lingering persecution of minorities in the region. The fate of the 450,000 Hungarians in the autonomous Vojvodina region of Yugoslavia may become a matter of controversy; Tito's constitution secured the right of all nationalities to use their languages and keep their cultures with autonomy, but the Serbian Republic wants to annex the small province where the Magyar live.

—**Minority Problems in the Balkan States**

Of all the East Bloc countries, the issue of divided nationalities is nowhere so problematic as in Yugoslavia, a state comprised of seven distinct national groups, often conflicting with one another, and maintaining ethnic ties to other nations.

The most serious problem revolves around the Albanian minority living in the autonomous province of Kosovo in the Yugoslav Republic of Serbia. By 1987, the Albanians in Kosovo numbered about 1.7 million, still comprising over three-quarters of the population there. Disgruntled with their status in Yugoslavia, they had erupted in protest regularly since the federation was established. The demonstrating renewed in 1980 had not abated by 1988. Numerous protests, terrorist attacks and attempts to destroy public buildings continued throughout the eighties. Incidents like the three bombings in Pristina in November of 1982 were common, and resulted in the imprisonment of many hundreds of Kosovo Albanians charged with connections to terrorism. Government repression in Kosovo was directed at not only the separatists accused of collusion with Albania, but the "culturalists" who want to protect the Albanian language and culture in Kosovo. The disturbances occasioned the exodus of numerous Serbs living among a majority of Albanians.

Yugoslavia has watched neighboring Albania's reactions to the situation in the Kosovo region with trepidation, but Hoxha and now Alia have done little more for the Albanians in Yugoslavia than issue verbal attacks against the government in Belgrade. However, new agitation of the Yugoslavs, especially the Serbs, in the late eighties to abolish the autonomous status of Albanian Kosovo and make the province part of Serbia, could lead to active differences between the two countries.

In Bulgaria, the government began a campaign to assimilate the Turkish minority of over 800,000 people. The government ordered Turkish schools to merge with Bulgarian, the elimination of instruction in Turkish, and in 1984-85, forced the Turkish population to "Bulgarize" their surnames. According to Amnesty International reports, during a forced resettlement in 1985, more than 100 Turks died in the villages, although the causes were never made known. The Bulgarian authorities insisted that there had been no Turkish minority in Bulgaria, and that the Bulgarian citizens who changed their names did so voluntarily, "rediscovering" their true Slavic identities.

There is no Eastern European country without a nationality problem either within or outside of its borders. The Gorbachev policy of *glasnost* has opened one of the most dangerous doors to conflict between these nations—the door of nationalism responsible for starting both world wars.

A CHANGING EASTERN EUROPE

In the era of radical transformation in the power structure of the Soviet Union, the solid leadership of Mikhail Gorbachev, and the successful meetings between the leaders of the two superpowers, Eastern Europeans knew that some reform in ther own countries was inevitable. Each nation, depending on its leadership and economic and political history under Communist rule, reacted differently to the example of "liberalization" coming from the guardian to the East.

Albania: Opening to the World

Albania under the leadership of secretary general Enver Hoxha pursued a policy of ultra-isolationism unparalleled in the Communist world. With Hoxha's death on April 11, 1985, an era spanning 41 years came to an end. No other communist leader had ever attempted to affect such comprehensive changes on the social, political, religious and economic structures of a nation. Under Hoxha, Albania was transformed from a feudalistic society into a "Marxist" state where all citizens were considered equal and became faithful members of the Communist party. Everyone worked for the state and all private property, including the Church's, was confiscated. Hoxha dissolved all religious institutions, and in 1967 he launched a purge of religious leaders, both mullahs and priests, and sent them to labor camps. That same year, he proclaimed Albania the first truly atheist state.

Hoxha made Albania a bastion of Stalinist orthodoxy. Considering Albania the only authentic socialist state, he pursued a policy of national self-reliance, cutting off virtually all ties with other nations. In 1948, he quarreled with Tito and broke off diplomatic relations with Yugoslavia; in 1961, he ended relations with the Soviets in protest over Khrushchev's destalinization policies; in 1978, when the Chinese began instituting reforms, Hoxha ended Albania's ties to the Communist regime in Beijing.

Hoxha came to believe that all political and economic troubles in Albania were caused by outside powers desiring to overthrow his regime. He accused the Yugoslavs of sending Albanian immigrants to invade the country. In November of 1982, Hoxha revealed that Albania's former prime minister Mehmet Shehu—who had served the Party loyally for twenty-seven years—had been a spy for the CIA up until his "suicide" in December of 1981. Friends and acquaintances of the ex-prime minister who regarded the suicide with suspicion were expelled from the Party and some were then arrested, indicating that Shehu probably died at the hands of Hoxha's secret police.

It was not until after Hoxha's death, in 1985, that Albania began to show slight deviations from its policies of extreme isolationism and orthodox Stalinism. Mr. Ramiz Alia, Hoxha's successor as general secretary of the Albanian Communist party, was regarded at first as a Hoxha man who would continue his policies faithfully. However, under Alia the economy has moved away from strict centralization, and concepts like initiative, self-motivation, and pay incentives for increased production—unthinkable several years ago—have been introduced. Alia has openly criticized poor management, inefficient methods, and low working morale; he is concerned about the large technical gap with the rest of the industrialized world that he knows Albania must close. Fortunately, Albania has no foreign debt because its constitution outlaws acceptance of foreign credits.

The Albanians began building huge hydro-electric plants around the 1960s. The biggest plant is at Koman, and was begun with Chinese assistance and completed by Albanian technology when the Chinese withdrew all economic aid. Before 1945, only one-third of the population had electric light; by 1970, not only did all of Albania have electric power, but it exported energy to neighboring countries. Albania became the world's third largest chrome producer, and mined copper, nickel and petroleum for export. But Albania lags behind in technological development, and Alia is aware of the industry's desperate need for outside stimulus. He has felt the necessity of discarding Hoxha's unequivocal stand of absolute self-sufficiency; under Alia during 1987-88, Albania expanded economic and cultural links with Italy and France, signed a friendship treaty with Greece, and extended diplomatic relations to Canada and West Germany. In February of 1988, Albania took part in a multi-lateral Balkan conference in Belgrade with the other Balkan states, namely Greece, Turkey, Rumania and Yugoslavia. The aims of the conference were to begin the denuclearization of the Balkans, and to increase trade and cooperation. The Albanians maintained that they were the only nation involved independent of Bloc ties and pressures from the superpowers.

By the late eighties, the Soviet reforms of *perestroika* and *glasnost* had affected little change on the political life in Albania. The reforms are regarded as dangerous and unwise departures from orthodox ideology. Albania's "opening to the world" consists of limited trade and transportation agreements with its neighbors and several West European countries, and a slight easing of border and tourism restrictions, not a democratization of the system or any concessions to the absolute authority of the Communist party leadership.

Yugoslavia: A Fragile Federation

In neighboring Yugoslavia, the Communist party leadership faces difficult problems with both the Yugoslav economy and with escalating tensions between its constituent republics. In 1988, Yugoslavia was in its worst economic crisis of four decades. The national debt by official accounts totaled $20 billion, but experts suggested a figure closer to $25 billion would be more accurate. More than 11½ percent of the national budget repays the interest on the debt alone. The yearly inflation rate for the 1980s was between 150-200 percent, and in 1988 reached 215 percent. Unemployment hit 15 percent, a number which will double if the government pushes through a "dissolvement program" which went into effect in July of 1988. The law refers to an estimated 7000 firms and factories which must be shut down because of maintained losses over the last few years—industries which employ over one and a half million workers. The state-controlled union agreed to the "dissolvement program" but requested that new jobs be provided for the workers. The union accused the government of heavily taxing the factories while simultaneously supporting an enormous bureaucratic apparatus administering the economy.

A massive scandal in the Republic of Bosnia-Herzegovina dealt one of the country's biggest economic enterprises a major blow. Mr. Jamdija Pozderac, Bosnia's representative to the Yugoslav state presidency (in line to become president in 1988), resigned and several high-ranking managers were arrested for their connection to corruption involving bribes and money transfers. The event was a sign for the news media, which for years had demanded that the Party should be answerable for the failure of the country's economic system.

In June, 1988, at a meeting of the League of Yugoslav Communists, the 786 delegates requested new economic reforms better reflecting *perestroika*, the use of more market-oriented policies and private incentives for foreign trade. That month, more than 10,000 Yugoslavs demonstrated in Belgrade, calling on the government to resign and for an end to the new economic austerity program. After weeks of strikes and massive protests in Serbia, Bosnia-Herzegovina and Macedonia over economic and ethnic problems, the 1988 Party president, Stipe Suvar, called a meeting of the central committee in October. He urged the delegates to unite behind the Party and the government, finishing with a warning: "All of us in this country are faced with a choice, either we resolve the crisis together, or we all head to destruction." By the end of the meeting, Suvar declared that "Yugoslavia will not fall apart," and reported a "virtual consensus on profound changes." These changes were manifested in the decision to "purge" one-third of the 165-member Central Committee and the resignation of five of the 23-member presidium.

Many Yugoslavs demand constitutional changes that would reduce the power of the country's autonomous republics and reestablish federal authority over the economy. But Slovenia and Croatia refuse to accept any restrictions on their independence. Their resolve is strengthened by the Republic of Serbia's agitation for greater authority, spearheaded by the Serbian Party leader, Slobodan Milosevic. Milosevic became a hero among the Serb populations for his demagogic speeches favoring the annexation of the Vojvodina province with its Hungarian minority and the Muslim-Albanian dominated province of Kosovo. In reply to Stipe Suvar's demand that "reckless confrontations and mass rallies" be put to an end, Milosevic protested any ban of meetings, something "unacceptable for the Serbs." In mass rallies, mostly Serb nationalist, crowds clamored for the return of these provinces to create a greater Serbia, to give the Republic more weight in Yugoslavian politics. "Serbia," Milosevic declared, "has no claims to the territory of other republics, but does have claim to territory in its own republic." Non-Serb nationalities fear that Milosevic's drive would create an imbalance of political power between the seven republics by giving Serbia, already the largest republic, additional status.

The world-wide prediction that Yugoslavia would fall apart as a federation after the death of Marshal Tito is slowly becoming a reality. The delicate balance necessary for unity between the divergent republics is increasingly difficult to maintain; conflicting interests between the prosperous Croat and Slovene republics and the impoverished Serbs and the rest of the country, all serve to weaken the federation. The force holding the "Yugloslav" state together as an entity is the Serbian-dominated military, which is not an adequate replacement for the unifying effect of Tito's charismatic leadership.

Rumania: Legacies of the Ceausescu Dynasty

Before the Communist takeover in 1947, Rumania was a prosperous country, considered the "bread-basket" of the region and rich in oil and minerals. Rumania in the 1980s is the poorest country in Eastern Europe with the possible exception of Albania. The Rumanian economy, still governed by the orthodox system instated by Stalin in the Soviet Union in the 1930s, is now Eastern Europe's most glaring failure.

The capitol of Rumania, Bucharest, once called the Paris of the East, is today a devastated city. On President Ceausescu's orders, the old city was razed; the monasteries and churches dating back three to four centuries along with Bucharest's only Sephardic synagogue were not spared. Historic houses and famous buildings are being demolished to make room for Ceausescu's dream of a new socialist city, built in a Stalinist monolithic style. Plans include a palatial headquarters for the Communist party, various ministries and state committee buildings, and a palace for the president and his family, dubbed "Palatu Ceausescu" by the Rumanian people. The estimated cost of the grandiose project is about $1.5 billion dollars, spent at a time when the country faces a widespread shortage of food and fuel. The plight of his countrymen does not seem to concern Ceausescu, as the construction of the new "Ceausescu Bucharest" continues uninterrupted.

The *Conducator* ("leader"), the nickname Nicolae Ceausescu was given in 1965, holds the nation's three most powerful positions: head of state, general-secretary of the Communist party, and commander in chief of the army of about 200,000 soldiers. The ubiquitous and feared Rumanian secret police, the *securitate* are also under his direct command. With the aid of this Gestapo-like organization and a network of thousands of informers, Ceausescu has absolute control of the country.

Surrounding himself with loyal advisors, most of whom are family members, Ceausescu's position appears impenetrable. His wife Elena holds the positions of first deputy prime minister, chairman of the National Council of Science and Technology, and is in charge of the Party personnel department. Their youngest son Nicu, who turned thirty-eight in 1988, was the former head of the Communist youth organization and is now first secretary of the Sibion region in Transylvania. Altogether, thirteen immediate family members occupy important government and Party positions, and Nicolae and Elena's birthdays are national holidays. In the Communist world, only North Korea comes close to Rumania's level of nepotism.

In May of 1987, Mikhail Gorbachev visited Rumania, marking the first such official visit by a Soviet leader since 1976. In a televised speech before 4,000 Rumanian Party members, he expounded on his hopes for *perestroika* and *glasnost*. Gorbachev then turned to the state of Rumania's economy, pointing out the severe food and energy shortages and the "difficulties Rumanians endure in their everyday lives." He went on to criticize Rumania's mistreatment of minorities, and said that it clashed with Lenin's policy on nationalities. The nepotism of the Ceausescu family was also alluded to as he stressed the importance of Party decision-making over decisions made by individuals.

Gorbachev's speech marked the first instance the Rumanian public heard of the political and economic reforms taking place in the Soviet Union and in other East Bloc countries; Rumania forbids the publication of literature from other socialist countries, and not even the Soviet paper *Pravda* is for sale in Bucharest.

The first open rebellion in Rumania was catalyzed by the municipal elections in November of 1987 in Brasov, Transylvania. About 20,000 angry workers—fed up with the government's severe austerity program—went on a four-hour rampage, storming the city hall and Party headquarters, and setting them on fire. They protested the new pay and power cuts along with worsening living conditions, shouting, "We want bread!" and "Kill Ceausescu!" The government sent 1,000 policemen and military tanks to restore order. Later the *securitate* arrested hundreds of workers for their participation in the rebellion.

The tragic fate of the Rumanian people, living in cold and in hunger, is the responsibility of Ceausescu's chaotic leadership. In the 1960s, he decided to industrialize Rumania, completely neglecting the country's reliance on its healthy agricultural sector. In 1969 alone, 200 new industrial sites were built, including a giant refinery which has never produced more than one-third of its capacity. The new industries fared poorly; their products weren't competitive and couldn't find markets in the West. Ceausescu was forced to turn to the Soviets for oil, minerals and other energy sources for which the Russians cleverly requested payment in dollars.

The United States Senate finally cancelled the Rumanian's most-favored-nation trade status because of its dismal human-rights record. The loss to Bucharest of American business comes to nearly $350 million a year.

Over time, the biggest tragedy caused by the industrialization policy was the abandonment of the agricultural sector. For almost 20 years there was no serious investment, modernization, or new technology put into agriculture.

The result was already apparent in the 1970s as food shortages became more and more serious. Ceausescu ordered a radical austerity program to counteract the effects of the shortages. Basic foods such as bread, cooking oil and sugar are rationed, and staples such as milk and butter are rare in shops. For four winters in the mid-1980s, the electricity use for a family was limited to a single 40-watt bulb. Heaters and other electric appliances were strictly forbidden. In some cities, electricity was blacked out for hours at night—killing newborn babies in hospital incubators—while factories were floodlit to keep them in operation 24 hours a day.

The Rumanian people know that there is no hope for change in their lives as long as Ceausescu and his family remain in power. But the "sick man of communism" as *The Economist* (October 26, 1985) called Ceausescu, displays no intention of changing his policy or stepping down. Unlike Poland or Hungary, dissident groups and reform-demanding writers remain underground and seem to have little impact on the system. A question is how long Gorbachev will tolerate Ceausescu's Stalinist leadership in his new Communist Europe.

Bulgaria: The Good Satellite

Often referred to as the 16th Soviet Republic because of its strict adherence to Soviet policy, Bulgaria is the Soviet Union's most favored ally in the Eastern Bloc. Anti-Soviet sentiment among the Bulgarians is minimal compared to the rest of the Bloc, stemming in part from historical loyalties and alliances.

Since Gorbachev's rise to power in the Soviet Union, Todor Zhivkov, the Bulgarian party's general-secretary since 1954, has worked to prove his readiness for reform, for more democracy in the system and better planning and management of the economy. At the Central Committee meeting in July, 1987, the aging general-secretary presented a radical reform plan designed to drastically alter Bulgarian life. He dissolved the Council of State and the Council of Ministers, replacing them with a new department, the National Coordinating Board. His plans for the economy included giving market forces a greater role, more "realistic" valuations of the country's currency, the *Leva*, and more attention to exports and tourism. Factories and businesses were granted more autonomy in their organization, prizes established for production and salaries set according to performance, Zhivkov did not allow for any major changes in the political life of the country, except to give parliament, the National Assembly, a more important role in decision making.

In January 1988, six months after the congress, Zhivkov had to call a special Party conference to clear up the effects of his proposals. The new reforms, which had changed so frequently, confused not only the economic management but the population as a whole. At the meeting, the young Party members requested more organized and progressive reform proposals, and a greater share for themselves in leadership. In reply, Zhivkov suggested that all high-ranking Party leaders be limited to a term of two or three years to allow younger Party members to move into more powerful positions. Of course, the new law is to go into effect in 1991, giving Zhivkov several more years in power.

In March of 1988, Prime Minister Grisha Filipov resigned and was replaced by an old Party organizer, Georgi Atanasov. Although not an expert in economic affairs, Mr. Atanasov's primary responsibility is to supervise an industrial reorganization. In January of 1988, all ministries responsible for the country's industrial and agricultural management were disbanded and replaced with one super-ministry. By completely overhauling the economic organization, Zhivkov was attempting to follow Gorbachev's *perestroika* initiatives and reduce the overstaffed industrial and trade ministries.

Hungary: Window to the West

In all of Eastern Europe, the most visible effect of *Glasnost* was the ouster in Hungary of Janos Kadar, who had served as Party general-secretary for thirty-two years. In an extraordinary Party Conference in May of 1988, Kadar and his followers were removed not only from the most important government positions, but also from the Central Committee. Kadar's popularity had waned in his last years in office; he was considered weak and his calls for moderation and a slower pace were interpreted as resistance to reform.

The Central Committee voted in Hungary's first secret ballot to elect a new party boss, Prime Minister Karoly Grosz. At a comparatively young fifty-seven, Grosz had a reputation for being a good administrator and a disciplined, faithful Party member. He announced in several speeches that the Communist party would continue to be the only governing party and that alliances with the Soviet Union and the other socialist countries would remain as before. Nevertheless, after his election, Grosz selected several popular and progressive co-workers to initiate a period of reform. These men included Imre Pozsgay, Janos Berecz, and a previous economic reformer Rezso Nyers, who was expelled from his position during the Brezhnev era for his western orientation. Grosz declared his intention to push through several new economic policies, warning his countrymen to tighten their belts because they had been living beyond their means for years.

Hungary's human rights record improved under the new government. It tolerated criticism of the Stalin-Rakosi era, recognizing that during that time hundreds of thousands of Hungarians had been thrown in prison and thousands had been executed on fabricated charges. Travel restrictions to non-communist countries eased significantly after January 1988. Finally, the administration introduced a law to parliament allowing the formation of independent political "associations" as long as they did not become political parties.

The source for most of the reforms was a government-sponsored organization, the Patriotic People's Front, chaired by Pozsgay, the most reform-minded member of the Politburo. Pozsgay spoke of a new system for elections where candidates would not have to belong to the Communist party, and also advocated freedom for the press and for writers and artists.

In September of 1988, over 350 intellectuals—primarily writers, artists and sociologists—drafted the constitution for a new independent organization called the Democratic Forum. According to this constitution, the primary goal of the Forum was to become the spiritual and social guide for Hungary's democratization. The founders comprised many of Hungary's most popular writers: Sandor Csoori, Istvan Csurka, Sandor Lezsak, Zoltan Biro, Gyula Fekete, and others. The Grosz government has kept silent about the new movement, and will probably continue to look the other way as long as the Forum doesn't question the absolute hegemony of the Communist party. The regime is aware that it needs the support of the writers for the success of many of its new reforms; the Hungarian dissident movement and its publication of *Szamizdat* literature is one of the most active in Eastern Europe, and reaches the population in a way the government is unable to.

Hungary introduced economic and social reforms as early as 1968, reforms far more radical than any Mr. Gorbachev has proposed for the Soviet Union. Despite the outward successes of many of Hungary's reforms, the effects of "goulash communism"—a market-oriented, decentralized, yet state-controlled economy—finally caught up with the country. The economic prosperity of the early 1980s in Hungary was supported by tremendous borrowing, totalling over $17.7 billion of debt by 1988.

The new leadership faces enormous economic difficulties. Hungary has the highest debt per person in all of the East Bloc and an inflation rate which rose from 14 to 20 percent in 1987, to over 25 percent in 1988. The stagnating economy, a trade deficit rising over $1 billion a year, and an economic growth rate hovering around one percent a year, confronted the Grosz government when it took office. Grosz, instated as prime-minister in 1986, attempted to counter these problems by introducing reforms hitherto unheard of in Communist countries. Hungarians were faced with "western" innovations such as personal income tax, wages based on performance, reduced subsidies for transportation and living supplies, and an end to support for factories unable to make a profit.

In July of 1987, Hungary introduced the first bankruptcy law known to the Communist world, and was soon followed by Poland and Yugoslavia.

Subsidies for steel mills, coal mines, and hundreds of other out-dated industries cost these countries more than $1 billion a year. Already responsible as "socialist states" for subsidizing food, housing and transportation, the artificial support of profitless industries had become too much of a financial burden. Reducing subsidies in the social sector or raising prices to more realistic levels was considered risky; Poland had attempted such solutions in 1956 and in 1970, but in so doing catalyzed the strikes responsible for ousting Party leaders Gomulka and Gierek. Socialist states realize they must shut down unprofitable and inefficient factories, but are then faced with the dilemma of millions of unemployed workers in a system where employment is guaranteed. Hungary and other socialist countries can introduce reforms such as the bankruptcy law, but find it almost impossible to put them into effect.

To alleviate its energy problems, Hungary agreed to a joint Hungarian-Czechoslovakian project for a large hydro-electric dam. The plan was signed and put into effect in September, 1986, while Kadar was still in office. The dam, already being built at Bos-Nagymaros on the Danube with Austrian loans, is under fire from the Hungarian public because it will destroy a large, beautiful area in northern Hungary. The dam will only supply a minimum of energy to Hungarian industry but Grosz and the new leadership know that cancellation of the disastrous project at such a late date will cost almost $1 billion—far too much for the already indebted country. The government and the Patriotic Front have suggested a national referendum on the dam in 1989, but the probability of cancelling the project is slim.

It is critical for Hungary to import necessary goods and technology from the West, but new credits from different countries and institutions are limited. Hungary received 13 credits from the World Bank between 1983 and 1987. The last two credits signed in July of 1988 brought the country's total debt to the World Bank to $1.5 billion. In July 1988, Mr. Grosz visited the U.S. to get financial support for his economic programs. He was not accepted with open arms by either the U.S. government or the business community, but was somewhat more successful with the EEC. In June of 1988, Hungary became the first East Bloc member of COMECON to sign an agreement with the Community, giving it the right to export food and industrial products to Community members. The EEC also agreed to eliminate all its trade quotas on Hungarian goods by 1995.

In spite of an atmostphere of *glasnost* and waning fear of the police apparatus, most Hungarians are suspicious of the new government; they are afraid that a new economic policy without corresponding social, cultural and political changes will be unsuccessful. They demand more political and religious liberty, greater freedom of speech and the abolishment of state organizations responsible for censorship. But the new leadership, like the one it replaced, continues to require that all reforms and final decisions come from the Party.

East Germany: COMECON's Wealthy Member

The economic and political experiences of the German Democratic Republic under socialism has been different from any of the other East Bloc countries. Enjoying the highest standard of living in Eastern Europe, East Germany is comparatively a prosperous country. There is little unemployment, plenty of food and no strikes or protests. The East German industry functions well, and exports goods with a fair rate of success to the rest of the world. "Why institute reforms?" the government asks, when everything appears to be working just fine. The leadership considers Gorbachev's reforms of *perestroika* and *glasnost* to be doomed to failure.

Eric Honecker, who has been the head of state and general secretary of the communist Socialist Unity party since 1971, keeps a strong hold on the political and economic life of the GDR; he maintains that the country's tightly-run economy needs no changes, ignoring the enormous financial assistance it receives from West Germany.

The political life in the GDR also appears to be more relaxed in comparison to other East Bloc states. The people live far more normal lives than in neighboring Czechoslovakia or Poland. Mr. Honecker continues to staunchly defend the heavy state subsidies which insure that rent, food and transportation remain inexpensive.

Relations between the two Germanies improves every year. Mr. Honecker's official visit to the West in September of 1987, the first such visit made by an East German leader in 40 years, did not come as a complete surprise. The visit was planned in August 1984, but Honecker was requested to "postpone" his trip by the Soviets. The Soviet Union had threatened West Germany that inter-German relations would suffer if Germany agreed to station Euromissiles on their territory. The talks and subsequent agreements between the two superpowers to reduce nuclear missiles in Europe made it possible for Honecker to meet with the German chancellor, Helmut Kohl, in Bonn. The visit was followed with great interest by both the Communist Bloc and the West; the fear of a German reunification, altering the balance of power in Europe, was still strong. Without West Germany, NATO defense would be considerably weakened, while in Poland, Czechoslovakia and the Soviet Union the memory of Hitler's Germany was still very much alive. But Honecker silenced any rumors of a reunification with a speech in which he compared the two country's economic and political systems to "fire and water." This was direct retort to Mr. Kohl's earlier remark that "Germans suffer from their separation."

The two German leaders agreed to set up a joint economic commission and approved agreements on the environment, radiation control, and science and technology. Honecker also agreed to ease travel between the two states, allowing for one million East Germans under retirement age and more than two million pensioners to visit West Germany each year. Bonn agreed to pay East Germany nearly $550 million a year for the street use and postal services necessary for transit through the GDR to Berlin. The West Germans also agreed to give $100 to every East German visiting the West. Bonn promised a "swing credit" to finance East German trade and duty-free exports to the European Community. An unofficial outcome of the meeting was Honecker's promise to rescind the order for East German border guards to shoot-to-kill people attempting to escape East Germany.

After his successful visit in West Germany, Honecker made an official visit to Paris in January of 1988. The French government wanted to underscore the importance of French and European involvement in the countries behind the Iron Curtain, and became the first NATO country to recognize the GDR. The visit marked an important advance in the GDR's drive for international acceptance.

East Germany's relationship with the Soviet Union continues to be cordial and deferring, but is no longer one based on complete understanding. the East German leaders mistrust *glasnost*, believing it could undermine the power of the Communist party. Honecker believes in hard work, discipline, and has little tolerance for public criticism at home. Gorbachev's plan to limit the tenure of elected Party officials to two five-year terms is out of the question for East German politicians. Out of the 22 members of the Politburo, 12 have been members for longer than a decade. Honecker himself has belonged since 1958, while his prime minister, Willi Stoph, has been a sitting member since 1953.

The East Germans also feel they need no lessons from the Soviet Union in running their economy. As Honecker has said, "Present Soviet developments have arisen from Soviet needs" and "we intend to continue in our previously proven way." Gorbachev has himself praised East German industry and its high-quality production. Although the COMECON members demanded that East Germany export first to Eastern Europe and the Soviet Union, East Germany was able to export enough to the West after fulfilling trade agreements with the East to earn hard currency surpluses. As a result, the country's national debt has come down from $11.7 billion in 1981 to $4 billion in 1988.

Honecker and the leadership in East Germany are attempting to move away from a "vassal-state" relationship with the Soviet Union to one based on partnership and trade. The bitter disappointment of the East German's when Honecker's visit to the West was postponed and they were forced to withdraw their Olympic team (one of the best in the world) from the games in Los Angeles did not help their image of the Soviet Union. Gorbachev has realized the detrimental consequences of such decisions and their potential for jeopardizing the Soviet Union's relationship with Eastern Europe; unlike his predecessors, he approaches East Bloc leaders with a semblance of friendliness and equality.

Czechoslovakia 1969-1988: Husak's Solution

Gustav Husak came to power in the wake of the Warsaw Pact tanks that crushed the Prague Spring in 1968. In April of 1969 he was elected to the position of Czechoslovak first secretary and by 1970 had garnered the presidency. Brezhnev was instrumental in instating Husak and the rest of the leadership in Czechoslovakia after the invasion, including Prime Minister Lubomir Strougal and the hardline chief of ideology, Vasil Bilak. When Gorbachev took office in 1985, these men had already been in power for sixteen years; they paid little attention to his criticism of the Brezhnev years in the Soviet Union or to his reform policies. Husak had always been a faithful ally to the Soviet Union, but Gorbachev's reform initiatives directly contradicted the leadership style he had developed after the Prague Spring. Husak had virtually banished all thought of reform in Czechoslovakia—the word itself was taboo after Dubcek's attempt to "reform" Communism in 1968. Czechoslovakians knew that as long as he remained in power, they couldn't expect to see any real changes in their system.

As far as Husak and the other Communist party leaders were concerned, Czechoslovakia was in no need of reforms or guidance by the Soviet Union. Before the Party Congress in March of 1986, government figures showed an economic growth rate of 3.2 percent. At the Congress, Husak acknowledged a degree of failure for the measures taken in 1981, but carefully avoided any suggestion of economic or political reforms as a solution.

In April, 1987, Gorbachev made an official visit to Prague. In contrast to his visits to Poland and Hungary, where he openly praised General Jaruzelski and Janos Kadar for their advancement of reforms, Gorbachev reminded the Czechoslovak leaders of the Soviet experiments in self-criticism, economic reorganization, and the democratic elections of Party officials. He referred to the Soviet Union's unresolved problems and the difficulties involved in putting reform into action, without ever directly mentioning Czechoslovakia's struggling economy and stagnating political system. The Czechoslovakian people nonetheless understood the meaning behind Gorbachev's words—the subtle criticism of Husak's resistance to reform—and gave him a warm welcome.

In December of 1987, after finding it difficult to adapt to Gorbachev's call for reforms, Husak stepped down as secretary general of the

Czechoslovak Communist party. Retaining his largely ceremonial position as president, he was still the first Eastern European leader to fall victim to "Gorbachevism." The Party leadership was taken over by another hardliner, Milos Jakes, a long-time Politburo member educated at the Moscow Party College. Jakes was considered an opportunist for having first supported the liberalism of 1968 and then, after the Soviet and Warsaw Pact invasion, becoming the overseer for purges of Party members for their behavior during the Dubcek era. Not a Gorbachev-style reformer, Jakes has done little to initiate *perestroika* and *glasnost* in Czechoslovakia. Although he has endorsed a limited restructuring of the economy, he will not make a wholesale commitment to reforming the sluggish industrial and agricultural sectors. Following in Husak's footsteps, Jakes has also discouraged any liberalization of the nation's political and cultural life.

The human rights organization, Charter 77, has emerged as the locus for increasing disenchantment with the regime. Most Czechoslovakians are more inclined to listen to this organized source of unofficial information than to official publications. The movement is concerned with the environment, with the economy, and is the only serious group to challenge the political repression imposed on the Czechoslovak people in the name of "normalization" after the Soviet invasion. When Charter 77 was founded in 1977 by writers, artists and others, its members never sought mass endorsement and disavowed any political activity. Their aim was simply to be the monitoring group for the Helsinki Accords on Human Rights. Yet the movement has had its effect on the people and the regime, galvinizing people to voice their discontent as they did in Prague on December 10th, 1987, "Human Rights Day." Despite an authorized ban on meetings, over 1000 young people assembled in protest, shouting "Husak out!" and calling for reform. The Czechoslovak press remained silent, but Husak was ousted a week later. Beginning in 1987-88, Charter 77 also established contact with other East Bloc dissident movements like the Hungarian Democratic Forum, Solidarity in Poland and East German church-sponsored groups for human rights.

The instatement of Milos Jakes as the new Communist party leader dashed hopes that Gustav Husak's departure would open the door to Soviet-initiated reforms in Czechoslovakia. Nevertheless, there are signs that the Czechoslovak people, who have remained silent for so long, are regaining the voice they lost in 1968 and will exert pressure on the government to abandon its inflexible resistance to change.

Poland: Solidarity's Resurrection

General Wojciech Jaruzelski's decision to impose martial law and crush the Solidarity movement on December 13, 1981, was well received by the governments of the other Communist countries. East Germany and Czechoslovakia in particular feared that their own populations would be contaminated by the Polish example and applauded the "lesson" taught the Polish dissidents. Other countries like Hungary and Yugoslavia were concerned that a need for Warsaw Pact troop intervention in Poland would create tensions with the West, and were relieved that the crisis was resolved internally.

The West was outraged by the declaration of martial law and Solidarity's defeat; huge protest marches were staged in capitals and other major cities around the world. The U.S. government suspended Poland's most-favored nation trade status, barred the Polish airline *LOT* from landing on U.S. territory, blocked Polish membership to the IMF (International Monetary Fund), and suspended Polish fishing rights in U.S. waters. Many European governments adopted the U.S. sanctions imposed against the Jaruzelski regime.

In two years of power, General Jaruzelski was able to restore order to Poland and strengthen the Communist system without using excessive force. He began to suspend, but not abolish, the extraordinary measures taken after the crackdown in December of 1981. He felt secure enough in his position to run the risks of liberating Lech Walesa on November 12, 1982, of closing most of the camps where about 10,000 Solidarity activists had been interned, and of allowing the Pope to visit Poland for a second time.

Most of the nearly ten million Poles who joined Solidarity during the years 1980-81 became passive and apathetic after the crackdown. Although faithful to the spirit of Gdansk, they were afraid of the consequences of participating in active opposition. According to official reports on the first year of the "state of war" or *sztatarium* after martial law was imposed, 15 people were killed and 991 injured. Demonstrations took place all over Poland but especially in Warsaw, the towns on the Baltic Sea and the industrial districts in Silesa; they were followed by severe repression by the infamous police unit *ZOMOS*. Great courage was demanded of participants risking arrest, and many were deterred from protesting.

The Polish episcopate was consistently opposed to violent action, and attempted to channel popular discontent into other means of expression. Cardinal Glemp negotiated with the government unceasingly to find a compromise which would respect basic human rights and the liberty of the Church, but would comply with Party stipulations. In November, 1982, Glemp met with Jaruzelski, and the result of the meeting—that Pope John Paul would visit Poland in the Summer of 1983—was announced with great fanfare. At the meeting Jaruzelski also agreed to release Walesa and to suspend martial law before the end of the year. These concessions were announced right before the beginning of a big strike called for November

10th by the clandestine Solidarity movement, effectively diffusing the strike to the great advantage of the authorities.

Cardinal Glemp's conduct during 1981-82 came under fire from younger priests in Polish industrial centers and the Vatican for being too cooperative with the Jaruzelski regime. In fact, the concessions Glemp obtained in the name of the Church were far from minimal. The Pope's visit from June 16-23 was a clear sign to the world of the importance of Catholicism in Polish society despite Communist ideology. Jaruzelski did take advantage of the opportunity to prove his ability to maintain internal peace in Poland, a status that certainly increased his credibility with foreign powers and no less importantly the Kremlin's leaders.

The extent of the "freedom" granted to Lech Walesa, however, was limited. Although no longer under arrest, he was constantly watched by the police. In 1983, when he was awarded the Nobel Peace Prize, Walesa was unable to go to Oslo to accept the distinction for fear of being prevented from returning to Poland.

Suspension of martial law on December 30th, 1982, was also limited. General Jaruzelski and the military council remained in control of the state, and retained special "emergency" powers. Solidarity was outlawed by a large majority of the Polish parliament on October 8, 1982. The independent trade union's possessions were seized by the state, and ex-members of the movement continued to suffer constant harassment by the police and were discriminated against in employment. Of the 10,000 persons confined to camps after the imposition of martial law, many were liberated but many were accused of conspiracy and transferred to prisons. Some were retained until as late as 1984-85. In a show of strength, police burst in on a February 1984 meeting of Solidarity leaders, arresting seven including Bogdan Lis and Adam Michnik. They were tried and spent several years in prison for their Solidarity and *KOR* (Worker's Defense Committee) activities.

The visit of Pope John Paul II, once Cardinal Wojtyla of Cracow, in June of 1983, reawakened national and anti-government sentiments throughout Poland. A wave of demonstrations and protests against the regime and for the legalization of Solidarity swept the country. In Cracow, John Paul II celebrated a mass for over two million people, many of who waved illegal Solidarity banners. The Pope met with Jaruzelski twice, and had a private interview with Walesa, remarking that "everyone was pleased" with the outcome of the meetings.

Then in October of 1984, four officers of the Polish Secret Service kidnapped and brutally murdered Father Jerzy Popieluszko, a pro-Solidarity priest. The outburst of protest and demands for retribution from the Polish people were so vehement that the government decided, after long hesitation, to put the four accused men on trial. On December 27, 1984, the world was able to witness not only a detailed account of the murder, but the methods used by the secret police to undermine the Church and to infiltrate everyday Polish life. Since Tito's dismissal of his chief of security Rankovitch in 1966, no Communist country had lifted the veil of secrecy from the operations of its security organization. The trial lasted two months, during which both the government and the Church accused each other of interfering in one another's affairs. The normally cautious Cardinal Glemp spoke out about the dangers of cooperating with the government after learning of secret service infiltration in Church life. Jaruzelski attempted to put the Church on the stand with the accused, remarking that if the Church had occupied itself with strictly Church affairs instead of involving itself with politics as Father Popieluszko had, the entire crisis could have been avoided.

In October of 1985, Poland held a parliamentary election, the first in five years. The underground Solidarity called a boycott of the elections, but failed to reach the masses. With a 78.8 percent rate of participation, Jaruzelski considered the result a victory over Solidarity. He felt that both inside and outside of Poland, the people and the media accepted him as the legitimate leader in Poland. In November of that year, Jaruzelski stepped down from his position as prime minister but retained the Party leadership—the position of real power in the Communist world—which he had held for four years. He also took over the chairmanship of the Council of State, the position of President of Poland. Mr. Zbigniew Messner, an economist and a close associate of the General's, became the new prime minister.

The following year, in September of 1986, the Polish government declared a blanket amnesty for the remaining 225 Solidarity political prisoners, including Zbigniew Busak, the former head of the Solidarity underground, and Adam Michnik, leader of the *KOR*. In response to the amnesty, the U.S. lifted almost all of its sanctions and several European countries actually offered the Polish government loans—Austria bidding $40 million.

Poland's economy suffers from a foreign debt reaching nearly $40 billion in 1988, a skyrocketing inflation rate, poor export earnings, frequent food, oil and consumer good shortages, and a poorly paid, apathetic work-force. At the October 8th, 1987, central committee meeting, General Jaruzelski announced a new economic reform. His proposal included instituting a new competitive banking system, diminishing the role of central planning, setting up a stock market, and expanding the private sector. He warned his countrymen to expect their standards of living to fall because of wage-freezes and price increases; a 110 percent price hike was predicted for food, although actual prices only rose 40 percent, and 140 to 200 percent inflation predicted for fuel, energy, transportation, etc. Jaruzelski decided to diffuse discontent by letting the Polish people vote on a referendum, asking for support for his new economic reforms. The Poles, knowing from experience that any "reform" would begin with price increases, voted an emphatic "No" to Jaruzelski's plans on November 27, 1987. Solidarity had issued a statement on November 10, warning against the vote: "Huge price hikes with unclear guarantees of compensation... could well push broad circles of society into poverty and intensify feelings of hopelessness." The government went ahead with its plans despite the clear wishes of its citizens to the contrary.

The influence of Solidarity's voice on the referendum proved that seven years after the Jaruzelski regime's attempt to crush the movement, it was still alive. A new generation of workers moved into the underground structures of the union, organizing strikes in the coal mines, factories and shipyards. In August and September of 1988, the new strike leaders showed that they had more in mind than wage increases and better working conditions: the strikers now included demands for the legalization of Solidarity. The differing opposition groups, such as the former radical labor leaders, intellectuals agitating for democratic reform and Catholic activists, all agreed on Lech Walesa as the leader of a new strike movement. The choice was significant, as over the years differences in policy and goals had developed between the opposition. The greatest split within the labor movement occurred between younger, more radical strike leaders like Alojzy Pitrzik (37) and Jacek Merkel (34), and the veteran Solidarity leaders.

A wave of strikes catalyzed by the government measures broke out in April and again in August in the mines in Silesia and the shipyards on the Baltic Sea. The workers demanded the legalization of Solidarity and Lech Walesa stepped in to negotiate. The minister of the interior, General Kiszczak, promised that if the debilitating strikes ended, the government would be ready to talk with Walesa about the future of a new independent union. Walesa decided to cooperate with the government even though he had received no guarantee of legalization for Solidarity, to the dismay of younger Solidarity leaders. "Walesa took a tremendous risk in agreeing to end the latest strikes without any guarantees," said the historian Bronislaw Geremek, a Walesa advisor. The official talks between Walesa and Kiszczak were frustrated at every turn by the Jaruzelski faction which presented new demands unacceptable to the workers. It became obvious that the government had no intention of making concessions to Solidarity, but wanted to buy time and escalate divisions between the different Solidarity factions.

On September 19, 1988, the government of prime minister Zbigniew Messner resigned after strong criticism of its management of the economy. For the first time in Polish history, the entire cabinet, all nineteen ministers, stepped down. The new prime minster, Mieczyslaw Rakowski, was against restoring Solidarity's status as the only independent labor union in Eastern Europe, and declared that Poland's political and economic problems would not be solved by cooperation with the union. A few days later, the official Polish news agency, *PAP*, announced that the Lenin shipyard in Gdansk would be closed in December according to the new bankruptcy law. The government's decision to close the shipyard was decidedly political. The Gdansk shipyard was far from the least profitable yard in Poland and had been improving its performance—actually logging back-orders, including orders from the Soviet Union, and was predicted to make a profit in 1989. The real motive in closing down the yard was that it was the birthplace of Solidarity in 1980 and was still a symbol of resistance to the regime; Walesa worked there with 30,000 other workers, comprising an unusually disciplined and united work-force for the independent union. Rakowski anticipated the reaction of the shutdown: "Based on experience, I know this will lead to huge political turmoil..." Solidarity's negotiations with the government were essentially crippled by the announcement, and by the end of 1988, prospects for its reemergence as a legal force in Poland were dim.

Despite the setback for Solidarity, Poland has again demonstrated that it is Eastern Europe's most spirited country in the struggle against repressive regimes. With its courageous and relatively free press, an abundance of *szamizdat* publications, the unifying force of the Catholic church and many fledgling opposition organizations, Poland continues to push for a more democratic, pluralistic society, even within the confines of Communism's one-party system.

Conclusion

At the end of this foray into the history of eastern Europe, certain observations come to mind. First, after a close examination of the diverse peoples in the region—their origins, religious beliefs, traditions, and the political and economic forces they have been subjected to—distinct and permanent cleavages between them appear. The dividing line between the Orthodox Balkan countries and the other eastern European countries with their western, Christian traditions, remains as clear today as it was in the past. The line is the same as the one which once divided the regions long under Ottoman domination from those that were directly or indirectly under the political and cultural influence of the Habsburg Empire.

A second observation arises from the first, namely the importance of religion as a factor in delineating and preserving the civilizations of eastern Europe, despite persecution of religious organizations throughout the ages. In the absence of political power, or when political power became oppressive, the Church spearheaded national struggles and served as a strong force in unifying peoples. The clergy were leaders in the efforts to retain national languages and cultures when these have been threatened. The best example today is the activity of the Catholic church in Poland.

Finally, although the countries of eastern Europe were united into the same political, military and economic bloc in 1945, it is striking to note that in the ensuing period the different nations have not only retained their cultures and national identities, but also their old antagonisms and rivalries. Despite the existence of a "fraternal community of socialist countries," nationalism, provincialism and ethnic interests are still very much alive. The surviving national minorities created by border divisions after World War II are as oppressed as they were during the interwar period. The Hungarians and Rumanians continue to quarrel over Transylvania, the Bulgarians and Serbs over Macedonia. The Czechs and the Slovaks still harbor age-old suspicions of one another despite the fact that they are now united into one political state; at the same time, they agree on the administration of the oppressed Hungarian minority under their authority since 1920. The Yugoslav federation's different nationalities continue to clash, while its Albanian and Hungarian minorities endure Belgrade's centralism with increasing discomfort. Hard feelings still exist between East Germany, Poland and Czechoslovakia over territory between them which has changed hands over the years as borders shifted.

Almost seventy years after the treaties of 1919-20 were signed, this part of Europe still suffers from the traumatic upset of the territorial revisions: national groups were separated from their respective "homelands," from countrymen, suddenly becoming minorities in states with different languages, traditions and historical ties. The harmful consequences of the treaties were aggravated by their rewriting after the Second World War, and the peoples and states of Eastern Europe are still living with the increased tensions and never-ending problems they created.

In the era of Communism in Eastern Europe, resistance movements became a force to be reckoned with after 1970, and their activities have escalated since Gorbachev took power in 1985. In the beginning, the effects of the different protest movements were limited because of the heavy-handed repression governments used against the people who participated in them. The lack of communication with and awareness of dissident movements in other countries forced them to act separately. Later, as the spirit of *glasnost* spread throughout most of Eastern Europe—Albania and Rumania excepted—it became a duty to criticize the past, delve into history and the mistakes committed by former dictators, and to find new directions for the future. The dissident movements began to move more openly, less fearful of the consequences of their actions. They began demanding more political freedom and greater participation in the political process without the requirement of membership in the Party. Could these groups work together and on occasion speak out in a unified voice, supporting each other across national boundaries? Such action has already been seen, as at the Solidarity Union Congress in September of 1981, when leaders declared that all workers in Albania, the GDR, Bulgaria, Hungary, Czechoslovakia and Rumania could count on the support of the Polish workers if they chose "the difficult route of fighting for an independent trade union." If protest movements are able to organize on an international level, they are in less danger of disintegrating because of fractures among their own ranks, apathy among the populace, or government assimilation.

For more than forty years, Eastern European nations have attempted to realize Marx's vision of a socialist economy: a system motivated by ideological principles rather than incentives of individual profit, and all capital state controlled and owned. The serious economic crisis in Eastern Europe today has forced Communist leaders to acknowledge the failure of "Marxism" as it has been applied to Eastern European economic systems. Party reformers have attempted to reinterpret the ideology and have incorporated western ideas such as incentive systems to motivate workers, free-market competition of products and decentralization. There is no longer a lingering faith in the socialist economic system which Nikita Khrushchev predicted would "outstrip capitalism."

Gorbachev's ascension to power in the Soviet Union heralded a new age for Eastern Europe of radical transformations of Communist ideology and its organizational structures. Most of the new reforms contradict orthodox Marxist-Leninist principles simply by bringing in systems and ideas from the capitalist world: bankruptcy laws, personal income tax, stock markets, private enterprise for profit. Changing a system based on ideology drummed into the psyches of populations for decades carries with it enormous risks. Gorbachev's efforts could result in economic chaos throughout the Soviet Union and the Eastern Bloc, and spark a revolution within the Communist party. It would be a supreme irony if Gorbachev's ambitious policies of *glasnost* and *perestroika* were thwarted by the Eastern Europeans; his attempts to reconcile Communist authority with *glasnost* might unravel first in Budapest, Warsaw or Prague rather than in Moscow. Eastern European populations are confronted with collapsing economies, shortages of food and consumer goods, and energy-related troubles. They are frustrated at every turn from improving their situation by the daunting bureaucratic apparatus of the socialist state. As state repression eases, signs indicate that the populations will emerge from their passivity and despondency.

Communism's greatest failure in Eastern Europe was not its economic policy, but that Communist ideology was unable to win the hearts and minds of the people. The Parties in each country promised a new society based on equality with guaranteed food, shelter and employment; they issued ceaseless propaganda about the evils of the West, censured all publications to protect the people from corrupting information, and even resorted to force and terror. Yet they were unable to convince the masses to accept Marxist-Leninist principles or to create a new generation of "communists." The youth in Eastern Europe today was born after Communist rule was established. They were raised within the confines of the socialist state, taught the doctrines of Marxism-Leninism, and warned about the evils of Capitalism and religion. Despite their upbringing, they have turned away from Communist ideology, scorning it, towards alternative philosophies. They are the new voices for reform, for the Church, and against the regimes.

Another disappointment for the Communist leadership was the realization that the greatest threat to their hegemony was the working class—precisely those people who were supposed to be most benefited by Communism.

Under Gorbachev, the Brezhnev Doctrine has changed, but no one has yet tested its limits. The Soviet Union is engrossed in its own economic and political problems, and concerned with unrest between the non-Russian populations within its own borders. The Soviet leadership is tired of the financial burden of supporting the East Bloc countries and the responsibility of disciplining their internal affairs. An old system has been replaced with a new one in the Soviet Union, allowing Eastern Europeans greater security in their personal freedoms. However, the changes are a long way from producing true democratic structures complete with free, multi-party elections, and political and economic independence from Moscow. Gorbachev's reforms and the drastic changes he is trying to push through Soviet and East European societies are often misinterpreted in the West. It is doubtful that the Communist world has any intention of dissolving the Warsaw Pact or of allowing political pluralism to undermine the ultimate power of the Communist party.

The relationship of the Western states, especially Great Britain, France and the United States, with Eastern Europe has been critical and continues to be of importance. The tragic fate of the Eastern European nations in the 20th century began in 1945 at Yalta, when the superpowers agreed to let the Red Army occupy the eastern half of Europe to aid those ravaged countries in their postwar recovery. There has been much literature written about the agreement at Yalta, pro and con, but no nation in Eastern Europe would hesitate to accuse Roosevelt and Churchill of knowingly delivering them into Stalin's empire.

Since the Communist takeovers backed by Soviet occupying troops, Eastern Europeans have learned repeatedly that the words "self-determination" and "in the interests of the people" exist only in the vocabulary of western diplomats, not in actual plans for action. This bitter lesson was reinforced during the Hungarian Revolution in 1956, when the West was distracted by the crisis of the Suez Canal and the chaos of the world situation, and turned a deaf ear to the Hungarians' pleas for help. During the Prague Spring, and later during the Polish uprisings, promises of aid never materialized. The peoples of Eastern Europe realized that the West had relinquished its military right to interfere in what it perceived as the Soviet sphere of influence, and that any freedom they obtained would have to be won by their own power. Nevertheless, the diplomatic pressure of the Western countries on Soviet and Eastern European governments can continue to be influential in bringing the two Europes closer together.

It is well known today that neither Communist ideology nor the dictatorial power of the Soviet Union has been able to bring the countries of Eastern Europe together in friendly cooperation. Throughout this history, we have looked at differences characterizing the lives and ideologies of these people, differences which have been in place for centuries. Will Eastern Europe, after the trials of the 20th century, ever be able to stop the quarrels, prejudice and hatred among themselves to make economic and political peace—possibly building a future together? Is there any chance that these diverse and individualistic nations can form a united Eastern Europe something like the European Community of the West? Lajos Kossuth, the spiritual leader of the Hungarian revolution in 1848, called on the people of the Danube valley to unite in a Danubian confederation; almost 150 years later, his imperative has become more critical than at any other time in history.

—1988—

Appendix A

Overview of Eastern European Nations—1988

ALBANIA
Area: 11,097 square miles (28,489 kms^2)
Population: 2.9 million
Ethnic groups: Albanian 95%, Greek 2.5%
Languages: Albanian, Greek
Religions: (*historical*) Muslim 70%, Orthodox 20%, Roman Catholic 10%
Major Cities: Tirana (Capital), 300,000; Durres, 130,000; Vlore, 90,000; Shroder, 80,000 (1986 est.)
Government: Communist, 1976 Constitution
Political Party: Albanian Worker's Party
General-Secretary: Ramiz Alia
Economy: GNP $2.1 billion (1979)
Natural Resources: gas, oil, coal, chromium
Agriculture: wheat, corn, sugarbeets, cotton, tobacco
Industry: textiles, timber, fuels, semi-processed minerals
Member of the United Nations

BULGARIA
Area: 42,823 square miles (110,912 km^2)
Population: 8,990,000 (1986)
Ethnic groups: Bulgarians-Macedonians 85%, Turks 9%, Gypsies 2%
Languages: Bulgarian, Turkish, Greek
Religions: Orthodox 70%, Muslim 9%
Major Cities: Sofia (Capital), 1,100,000; Plovdiv, 310,000; Varna, 260,000
Government: Communist
Political Party: Bulgarian Communist party
General Secretary: Todor Zhivkov
Economy: GNP $25 billion (1985)
Natural Resources: lead, bauxite, coal, zinc, oil
Agriculture: grains, fruit, corn, tobacco, potatoes
Industry: chemicals, machinery, textiles, leather goods, vehicles
Member of the United Nations, Warsaw Pact, COMECON

CZECHOSLOVAKIA
Area: 49,378 square miles (127,899 km^2)
Population: 15.4 million (1983)
Ethnic groups: Czechs 64%, Slovaks 30%, Hungarians 5%, Germans, Poles
Languages: Czech, Slovak, Hungarian
Religions: Roman Catholic 65%
Major Cities: Prague (Capital), 1,900,000; Brno, 370,000; Bratislava, 350,000
Government: Communist
Political Party: Communist Party of Czechoslovakia
General Secretary: Milos Jakes
Economy: GNP $83.9 billion (1984)
Natural Resources: coal, brown coal, timber, natural gas
Agriculture: potatoes, grapes, fruit, livestock
Industry: steel, machinery, textiles, paper, autos, chemicals
Member of the United Nations, Warsaw Pact, COMECON

EAST GERMANY (German Democratic Republic)
Area: 41,612 square miles (107,774 km^2)
Population: 16.8 million
Ethnic groups: German
Languages: German
Religions: Protestant 80%, Roman Catholic 11%
Major Cities: East Berlin (Capital), 1,140,000; Leipzig, 563,000; Dresden, 515,000; Karl Marx Stadt, 316,000
Government: Communist, Constitution April 1968, amended 1974
Political Party: Socialist Unity Party (*SED*)
General Secretary: Eric Honecker
Economy: GNP $90 billion
Natural Resources: lignite coal, potash, uranium
Agriculture: grain, sugarbeets, potatoes, meat, dairy products
Industry: steel, chemicals, electrical and precision engineering products, fishing vessels
Member of the United Nations, Warsaw Pact, COMECON

HUNGARY
Area: 35,921 square miles (93,036 km^2)
Population: 10,685,000 (1983)
Ethnic groups: Magyar 93%, Gypsies 3%, Germans 2.5%, Slovaks
Languages: Hungarian, German, Slovak, Gypsy
Religions: Roman Catholic 65%, Calvinist 20%, Lutheran 5%, Jewish 1%
Major Cities: Budapest (Capital), 2,070,000; Miskolc, 205,600; Debrecen, 195,000
Government: Communist
Political Party: Hungarian Socialist Worker's party
General Secretary: Karoly Grosz
Economy: GDP $21 billion (1981)
Natural Resources: brown coal, bauxite, uranium
Agriculture: wheat, corn, wine, fruit, vegetables
Industry: electrical equipment, textiles, transportation equipment
Member of the United Nations, Warsaw Pact, COMECON

POLAND
Area: 120,727 square miles (312,683 km^2)
Population: 36,556,000 (1983)
Ethnic groups: Poles 98%, Germans, Ukrainians, Bielorussians
Languages: Polish
Religions: Roman Catholic 90%, Protestants 1.5%
Major Cities: Warsaw (Capital), 1,620,000; Lodz, 820,000; Cracow, 710,000
Government: Communist, Constitution, 1952
Political Party: Polish United Worker's party
General Secretary: General Wojciech Jaruzelski
Economy: GNP $110 billion (1984)
Natural Resources: coal, copper, silver, zinc, sulphur, iron
Agriculture: grain, potatoes, sugarbeets, tobacco
Industry: shipbuilding, textiles, chemicals, wood products
Member of the United Nations, Warsaw Pact, COMECON

RUMANIA
Area: 91,699 square miles (237,499 km^2)
Population: 22.4 million
Ethnic Groups: Rumanians 85%, Magyars 9%, Germans 2%, Serbo-Croatians, Gypsies, Ukrainians, Greeks, Turks
Languages: Rumanian, Hungarian, German
Religions: Orthodox 80%, Roman Catholic 9%, Calvinist, Lutheran, Jewish
Major Cities: Bucharest (Capital), 2.1 million; Constanta, 300,000; Iasi, 285,000; Timisoara, 285,000; Cluj, 265,000
Government: Communist, Constitution, August, 1965
Political Party: Rumanian Communist party
General Secretary: Nicolae Ceausescu
Economy: GDP $116.5 billion (1980)
Natural Resources: oil, timber, natural gas, coal
Agriculture: corn, wheat, oil seed, potatoes
Industry: mining, forestry, metal production, chemicals
Member of the United Nations (IMF), Warsaw Pact, COMECON

YUGOSLAVIA
Area: 99,000 square miles (256,409 km^2)
Population: 23.1 million (1985 est.)
Ethnic groups: Serbs 36%, Croats 20%, Bosnian Muslim and Serbs 11%, Slovenes 8%, Albanians 8%, Magyar 2%
Languages: Serbo-Croatian, Slovenian, Macedonian, Albanian, Hungarian
Religions: Orthodox 50%, Roman Catholic 30%, Muslim 10%
Major Cities: Belgrade (Capital), 1.3 million; Zagreb, 700,000; Skopje, 400,000; Sarajevo, 400,000; Ljubljana, 300,000
Government: Federal Republic, Constitution, 1974
Political Party: Communist League of Yugoslavia
President/General Secretary: Stipe Suvar (1988), rotates every year
Economy: GNP $46.3 billion (1984)
Natural Resources: coal, copper, bauxite, timber, iron, chromium, asbestos
Agriculture: corn, wheat, tobacco, sugarbeets, livestock
Industry: wood, processed food, nonferrous metals, textiles
Member of the United Nations, COMECON (observer status) and OECD (Nonaligned Movement)

Appendix B

Gallery of Faces

1200—1848

(L. to R.) Rudolph I, Habsburg (1218-1291), Emperor of Austria, King of Hungary and Czech-Moravia *and* Leopold I, Habsburg (1640-1705), King of Hungary and Bohemia

(L. to R.) Maria-Theresa (1717-1780), Queen, Austro-Hungarian Empire *and* Klemens von Metternich (1773-1859), Prince, Chancellor of the Habsburg Empire

Photos courtesy of Hungarian National Museum, Picture Gallery

1848—1914

(L. to R.) Lajos Kossuth (1802-1894), Leader of the Hungarian Revolution of 1848 (photo courtesy of Hungarian National Museum, Picture Gallery) *and* Franz Joseph I (1830-1916), Emperor of Austria-Hungary (photo courtesy of *Beruhmte Kopfe*, C. Bertelsmann, Verlag, Germany)

(L. to R.) Alexander II (1818-1881), Czar of Russia and Poland *and* Nicholas II (1868-1918), Last Czar of Russia (photos: courtesy of *Beruhmte Kopfe*, C. Bertelsmann Verlag, Germany)

Reproductions: Adam Balogh

1914—1945

(L. to R.) Boris III (1894-1943), Last Czar of Bulgaria (1818-1943), Carol II (1895-1953), King of Rumania, *and* Miklos v. Horthy (1868-1957), Admiral, Regent of Hungary (1920-44)

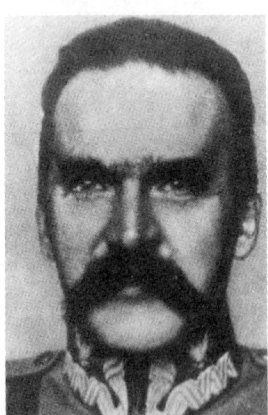  

(L. to R) Joseph Pilsudsky (1867-1935), Marshall, Polish Dictator (1916-35), Jozef Stalin, Soviet General-Secretary (1926-53), *and* Eduard Benes (1884-1948), Founder and President of Czechoslovakia (1935-38) and (1945-48)

Photos courtesy of *Beruhmte Kopfe*, C. Bertelsmann Verlag, Germany

1945—Present

(L. to R.) Mikhail Gorbachev, USSR, and Eric Honecker of East Germany (1987); Gorbachev and Nicolae Ceausescu of Rumania (1987)

(L. to R.) Janos Kadar of Hungary and Gorbachev (1986); Gorbachev and General Jaruzelski of Poland (1986)

(L. to R.) Nikita Krushchev and Tito (1956); Pope John Paul II and Lech Walesa (1987)

Photos courtesy of *The Economist Magazine, Newsweek,* and *World of Communism.* Reproductions by Adam Balogh.

Index of Names

Abdul-Aziz I, sultan, 133
Abdul-Hamid II, sultan, 133, 143, 144
Aczel, Gyorgy, 373
Adalbert, Saint (Vojtech), 27
Alaric, Visigoth chieftan, 18
Albert Jagiellon, king of Poland, 54
Albert of Brandenberg, 55
Albert of Habsburg, 43
Alboin, Lombard, king, 19
Alexander I, czar of Russia, 80, 82, 85
Alexander II, czar of Russia, 106, 107, 128, 405
Alexander III, czar of Russia, 128, 140
Alexander Jagiello, king of Poland, 54
Alexander, Karageorgevitch, of Serbia, 83
Alexander, king of Yugoslavia, 218, 242
Alexander, king of Serbia, 144, 165, 206, 207
Alexander of Battenberg, prince of Bulgaria, 140
Alexander, king of Poland, 54
Alexandrescu, Alex, 282
Alexis, czar of Russia, 69
Ali-Pascha Telepeleni (of Jannina), 82
Alia, Ramiz, 375, 376, 377, 399
Anders, General Wladyslaw, 237, 251, 279
Andras II, king of Hungary, 32
Andras III, king of Hungary, 35
Andrassy, Count Gyula, 110, 114, 122, 133
Andropov, Yuri, 322, 367, 368
Antoine, prince of Radziwill, 84
Antonescu, General Ion (Conducator), 240, 241, 244, 247, 281, 283

Antonescu, Michael, 247
Apponyi, Count, 124, 125
Ara-Kovacs, 372
Arciszewski, Tomasz, 266, 279, 280
Arpad I of Hungary, 22, 28 35
Arsenije III, patriarch of Pec, 61
Asen I, Bulgar emperor, 34
Asen, John II, Bulgar emperor, 34
Asparuk, Bulgar khan, 21
Atanasov, Georgi, 382
Atler, Victor, 237, 238
Attila (the Hun), 18, 19, 22
Audoin, Lombard, king, 19
Augustus, Roman emperor, 16
Augustus II (the Strong), king of Poland, 69, 70
Augustus III, king of Poland, 70
Aurelian, Roman emperor, 18
Aurelius, Marcus, Roman emperor, 17
Angelus, Isaac II, Byzantine emperor, 32, 34
Avarescu, General, 137, 201

Babiuch, Edward, 356, 357
Bach, Alexander, 109
Badeni, Count, 123
Bagrianov, Ivan, 248, 276
Balescu, M., 95
Ban, Antal, 287
Barbarossa, Admiral Frederick, 32
Barcikowski, Kazimierz, 358, 361
Bardossy, Laszlo, 243, 285
Barrot, Odilon, 87
Barthou, Louis, 207, 218
Basarab, Matei, prince of Wallachia, 60
Basiak, archbishop of Lvov, 307

Basil II, Byzantine emperor, 28, 29, 34
Batory, Stefan (Istvan), king of Poland, 56
Batthyany, Count Lajos, 97, 99, 102
Batu (son of Ghengis Khan), 34
Bayan, Avar khan, 19
Bayezid, sultan, 47
Beatrice of Aragon, queen of Hungary, 45
Beck, Colonel Jozef, 194, 234
Bela III, king of Hungary, 31, 32
Bela IV, king of Hungary, 34, 35
Bem, General, 94, 100, 101
Benes, Eduard, 126, 232, 337, 406
   and Communists, 250, 256, 265, 288-89, 291, 292
   exile government, 246, 250, 256, 265 288
   independence, 162
   National Council in France, 154, 216
   and national minorities, 223-24, 226, 229, 230, 256
   Peace Conference, 166, 174, 181
   president, 188, 231
   return from exile, 256, 288
   and Socialist party, 188, 232, 288-89
   and USSR, 265, 268
   and Western powers, 175, 176
Benoit XV, Pope, 176
Beran, archbishop of Prague, 306, 332-33, 335
Beran, Rudolph, 231
Berecz, Janos, 382
Berg, General, 108
Beria, Lavrenti, 310, 313
Berthelot, Philippe, 176, 215, 216
Bethlen, Count Gabriel, prince of Transylvania, 63, 65
Bethlen, Count Istvan, 195, 196, 285
Beust, chancellor, 114
Bibescu, George, prince of Wallachia, 84, 95
Bierut, Boleslaw, 252, 279, 302, 315, 316
Bilak, Vasil, 387
Biro, Zoltan, 383
Bismarck, Otto von, 107, 130, 135
Blagoev, Dimitri, 141
Blahoslav, Bishop Jan, 50
Bleda (brother of Attila the Hun), 18
Blondel, Consol, 105

Boeriu, General, 120
Boleslas I (the Cruel), duke of Bohemia, 27
Boleslas II (the Pious), duke of Bohemia, 27
Boleslaw (the Valiant), Piast, 27
Bonfini, 19, 44
Bor-Komorovski, General, 252
Boris III, king of Bulgaria, 406
   and Agrarians, 161, 171, 198, 199
   and White Terror, 200
   marriage, 217
   WW II, 241, 242, 248
Boris, prince of Bulgaria, 22, 28
Boroevic, General, 120, 163
Botev, Hristo, 133
Bougle, Celestin, 175
Bouillon, Franklin, 175
Bourbaki, General, 139
Brandt, Willy, 268
Brankowski, 331
Bratianu (brother of Ionel), 202, 247
Bratianu, D., 95
Bratianu, Ionel, 201, 202
Bratianu, John, 136
Brezhnev, Leonid, 327, 334, 338, 339, 367-68, 387
Briand, Aristide, 154, 216
Brodsky, Joseph, 369
Broz, Josip (*See* Tito)
Buda (son of Attila), 18
Bulganin, Nikolai A., 313
Burian, Baron, 161
Busak, Zbigniew, 391
Buzdugan, Gheorge, 202, 203

Callixtus III, Pope, 48
Calvin, 55
Capistrano, John, 48
Carol I, king of Rumania, 149, 202
Carol II, king of Rumania, 202-205, 240, 406
Casaroli, Father, 329
Casimir III Piast, king of Poland, 40
Casimir IV, king of Poland, 53, 54
Catherine II, czarina of Russia, 70, 71, 72
Ceausescu, Elena, 379
Ceausescu, Nicolae, 407
   dissent, 346

Ceausescu, Nicolae, *continued*
 food shortages, 370, 379, 381
 in power, 330-31, 379-81, 401
 minorities in Transylvania, 372, 373
 nepotism, 379-380
 Prague Spring, 338, 340, 341
 village destruction policy, 373-74
Ceausescu, Nicu, 379
Cernik, Oldrich, 335, 336, 338, 340
Cesarini, 47
Chamberlain, Neville, 188, 230, 231
Charles I, Austro-Hungarian emperor, 152-53, 155, 161-64, 176, 194, 195
Charles III, king of Hungary, 67
Charles IV, king of Bohemia, 38, 39, 41
Charles IX, king of France, 55
Charles of Hohenzollern-Singaringen, king of Rumania, 106, 136
Charles of Liechtenstein, 63
Charles V, Habsburg, 48, 49, 119
Charles X, king of Sweden, 69
Charles-Albert, king of Piedmont, 98, 99
Charles-Robert, king of Hungary, 39, 40
Chebrikov, Viktor, 368
Chernenko, Konstantin, 368
Chervenkov, Vulko, 314
Chlopicki, General, 86, 87
Chmielnicki, Bogdan, 69
Choiseul, 70
Chopin, Frederick, 87
Churchill, Winston, intro, 265, 266, 279, 397
Chvalkovsky, Frantisek, 231, 233
Ciosek, Stanislaw, 363
Clemenceau, 114, 125, 170, 202
Clementis, 303, 332, 336
Codreanu, Corneliu, 201, 204, 239, 241
Colban, Erik, 221
Coloman, king of Hungary, 31
Comenius (Jan-Amos Komensky), 63
Comnenus, Manual, Byzantine emperor, 31, 32
Condillac, Etienne Bonnot de, 76
Conducator, *See* Antonescu, General Ion or Ceausescu, Nicolae
Constantine, Roman emperor, 18
Constantine, viceroy of Poland, 80, 85, 86, 117
Copernicus, Nicholas, 54, 56

Corvinus, Matthias (Matyas Hunyadi), king of Hungary and Bohemia, 43, 44, 45, 48
Couza, Alexander Ion, prince of Rumania, 105-106
Cristea, Miron, patriarch of Transylvania, 202
Csak, Matthias, 39
Csatlos, General, 251
Csernoch, Cardinal John, 125, 164
Csokonai, Mihaly, 90
Csoori, Sandor, 383
Csurka, Istvan, 383
Cuza, Alexander, 201
Cvetkovitch, 207
Cyrankiewicz, Jozef, 315, 332
Cyril, Prince, 248, 276
Cyril, Brother, 22
Czatoryski, Prince Adam, 71, 80, 85

D'Alembert, 76
D'esperey, General Franchet, 155, 159
D'orcival, F., 190
Daladier, Edouard, 188, 231
Damjanich, General, 101
Daranyi, Kalman, 196
Daskalov, 160-161
Daszyniski, 167
de Azcarate, Pablo, 221
de Margerie, Pierre, 176
de Martonne, Emmanuel, 175
Deak, Ferenc, 90, 91
Decebale, Dacian, king, 16
Dembrowski, Edward, 88
Deng Xiaoping, 347
Denis, Ernest, 63, 114, 175
Diaz, Marshal, 155
Diderot, 76
Dieckmann, Johannes, 293
Dimitrievitch, Colonel, 149
Dimitrov, Georgi, 141, 171, 186, 199, 275, 277
Dinyes, Lajos, 285, 286, 298
Diocletian, Roman emperor, 18
Disraeli, Benjamin, 135
Djilas, Milovan, 278, 298, 314-15, 328
Djogo, Gojko, 351
Dmowski, Roman, 129, 167, 168
Dobi, Istvan, 285

Dobrovski, Father Joseph, 77, 89
Dobrowski, General, 94
Dolanc, Stane, 350
Dollfus, Chancellor, 218
Dombrowski, 77
Doukas, Michael VII, Byzantine
    emperor, 31
Dozsa, George, 48
Draga Obrenovitch, queen of Serbia, 138
Dragosavac, Dusan, 350
Drgislav, king of Croatia & Dalmatia, 28
Drogoitcheva, Madame, 350
Droz, J., 115
Drummond, Sir Eric, 221
Dubcek, Alexander
    confession, 262
    failure of policies, 343, 387
    first secretary, 334
    Prague Spring, 335-341
    Slovak cause, 333, 334
Duca, premier of Rumania, 204
Dumouriez, General, 70
Durkheim, Emile, 175
Dusan (Stephan Nemanja), 46, 47
Dzerjinski, Felix, 129, 172
Dzur, General, 335, 340

Ebert, Frederic, 293
Ehrlich, Henryk, 237, 238
Eichman, Adolf, 249
Eisenman, Louis, 175
Elizabeth, empress of Austria, 110, 119
Erkel, 90
Ernuszt, Clement, 44
Eugene, prince of Savoy, 66

Fan Norli, Bishop, 197, 198
Fekete, Gyula, 383
Fekete, Janos, 77
Felix of Ragus, 45
Ferdinand, Habsburg, of Austria, 88, 96, 97, 100
Ferdinand I, Habsburg archduke, 49, 52, 53
Ferdinand I, king of Rumania, 152, 201, 202
Ferdinand II, king of Bohemia, 62, 63, 64
Ferdinand III, king of Bohemia, 64

Ferdinand of Saxe-Coburg, czar of
    Bulgaria, 141, 145, 161
Fierlinger, Zdenek, 288, 290
Filipov, Grisha, 382
Filovv, Bogdan, 241, 248, 276
Fiszbach, Tadeusz, 356, 361
Foch, Marshal, 155, 181
Forster, Gauleiter, 235
Francis I, king of France, 48, 49
Francis II, Habsburg, of Austria, 79, 88
Francis II, Rakoczi, prince of
    Transylvania, 66
Frank, 126
Frank, Governor Hans, 237
Franklin-Bouillon, 175
Franz-Ferdinand, archduke of Austria,
    126, 127, 149, 153
Franz-Joseph, emperor of Austria, 94,
    100, 101, 108-110, 119, 121-122, 125, 126,
    405
Frederick I, king of Prussia, 63
Frederick II, of Prussia, 67, 70
Frederick III, Habsburg emperor, 43, 44
Frederick William IV, king of Prussia,
    93-94

Gaj, Louis, 90
Gambetta, 114
Geoffrin, Madame, 76
George of Podebrady, king of Bohemia,
    44
George (the Black), king of Serbia,
    139
Georgescu, T., 282
Georgiev, Colonel, 275
Geremek, Bronislaw, 392
Gero, Erno, 319, 320, 321, 324
Geza of Hungary, 28
Ghengis Khan, 34
Ghengis Khan, 34
Gheorgiu-Dej, Gheorghe, 281, 282,
    314, 330
Ghica, Alexandru, prince of Wallachia,
    84
Ghica, Gregory, prince of Wallachia, 83
Gierek, Edward, 351
    and church, 354
    ousted, 358, 361, 384
    secretary-general, 353-54, 356

Gisela of Bavaria, queen of Hungary, 28
Giskra, Karl, 98
Glemp, Cardinal Jozef, 362, 363, 364
  and Jaruzelski government, 389, 390 391
Goluchowski, prince of Poland, 94, 123
Goma, Paul, 345
Gombos, Gyula, 196
Gomulka, Wladislaw, 279, 336
  and church, 353-54
  economic problems, 331-32, 352
  liberation, 315, 316, 317
  ouster, 352, 384
  purged, 302
  recalled, 318, 319, 320, 325, 331-32, 352
  USSR, 326, 331-32, 352
Gorbachev, Mikhail
  Brezhnev Doctrine, and, 397
  Ceausescu, and, 374, 380, 381, 407
  East European leaders, and, 368, 374, 387, 407
  in power, 368, 381, 387, 395, 396
  reforms, 368, 369, 371, 380, 383, 386, 396, 397
  USA, talks with, 375
  Warsaw Pact, on, 369
Gorchakov, 106, 107, 133, 135
Gorgey, General Arthur, 100, 101, 102
Gottwald, Klement
  Communist takeover, 288-292, 301
  death of, 314, 336
  secretary general, 189, 288
Goutchevitch, 348
Gretchko, Marshal Andrei, 338
Grichine, 360-61
Gromyko, Andrej, 361, 368
Grosz, archbishop, 306
Grosz, Karoly, 382, 383, 401
  dam, 384
  reform, 382
  and Hungarians in Rumania, 374
Grotewohl, Otto, 293, 294
Groza, Petru, 281, 283, 284, 314
Gyarmathi, 77

Hacha, Emil, 231, 232, 233
Hadik, General Andras, 67
Hajdukovitch, Jovan, 139
Hajek, Jiri, 335, 337

Haller, General, 130, 166, 168
Hammarskjold, Dag, 323, 337,
Hantos, Elemer, 212
Haraszti, Miklos, 345
Haremuja, 349
Havlicek, 89
Haynu, Marshal, 101, 102
Hebrand, Andre, 298
Hedwig, of Jagiello, 53
Hegedus, Andras, 312, 319, 320
Helene, queen of Rumania, 202
Heltai, Gaspar, 51
Henlein, Konrad, 225, 229, 230
Henry, Count of Luxembourg, 37
Henry III, emperor, 31
Henry of Valois, king of Poland and France, 55, 56
Hess, Andreas, 45
Hitler, Adloph
  Anschluss, 218, 225, 227
  and Bulgaria, 240, 241
  and Czechoslovakia (Sudetenland), 188, 218, 229, 230, 231, 232
  expansionism, 187, 213, 218, 230, 232
  and Hungary, 218, 219, 229, 231, 238, 239, 242, 243, 249
  and Italy, 218, 231, 238
  and Jews, 237
  Munich agreements (1933), 188, 230, 257
  and national minorities, 219, 225, 226 230, 233
  pacts, 234, 236, 239, 241, 242
  and Poland, 233, 234, 236, 237, 238
  rise to power, 218, 225, 229
  and Rumania, 236, 241, 244, 261
  USSR, invasion of, 242, 244
  and Yugoslavia, 218, 242
Hlinka, Father Andreas, 125, 188, 189, 190
Hodza, Milan, 125, 126, 188, 230
Hohenwart, 121, 122
Holdos, 303
Honecker, Eric, 346, 385-86, 400, 407
Honius III, Pope, 32
Honterus, John, 51
Horthy, Admiral Miklos, 120, 170, 171, 406
  regency, 194-196
  and Hitler, 229, 249, 250, 255

Horthy, Vice-regent Istvan, 245
Horvath, Father, 306
Hosius, Stanislas, bishop of Varmy, 55
Hoxha Enver
  atheism, 376
  and China, 346, 347, 376
  death of, 375-76
  destalinization, 327-28, 376
  isolationism, 375-76, 377
  and Kosovo, 375
  secretary-general, 255, 277, 301, 314
  and Tito, 297, 313, 346, 376
  USSR, schism from, 262
Hua Guofeng, 347
Hunyadi, Janos, 47, 48
Hunyadi, Matyas (Matthias Corvinus), 43, 44, 45, 48
Hus, Jan, 41-43, 50, 64, 189
Husak, Gustav
  in power, 303, 341, 387
  Prague Spring, 336, 340, 341, 387
  purged, 303
  rehabilitation, 332, 333
  repression of dissent, 346
  resistance to reform, 387-88
  Slovak Council, 250
  Solidarity, 359
Huszar, 194

Ignatiev, Ambassador of Bulgaria, 132
Illyes, Gyula, 373
Imredy, Bela, 196, 285
Iorga, Nicolas, 203, 241
Istvan I (Saint Stephen), king of Hungary, 28, 31, 32
Ivanko (Boyar rebel), 34

Jagielski, Mieczyslaw, 356
Jakes, Milos, 388, 400
Jaroslav of Martinic, 63
Jaruzelski, General Wojciech, 351, 401, 407
  and Church, 390, 391
  elections, 361
  and Gorbachev, 387
  in power, 358, 363, 389
  martial law, 364-366, 388, 389, 390
  Solidarity: (1980) 358-59, 361, 363-66, 390; (1988) 391-92

Jaszi, Oscar, 163
Jehlica, Frantisek, 190
Jellachich, Colonel (ban of Croatia), 97, 99, 100
Jensensky, Jan, 63
Jerome of Prague, 42
John (the Blind), king of Bohemia, 37
John (the Fearless), king of Burgundy, 47
John Paul I, Pope, 345
John Paul II, Pope (Wojtyla) (*see also* Wojtyla), 5, 351
  assassination attempt, 360
  election, 345, 355
  martial law, 365
  and church, 363
  visit to Poland (1978), 355-56; (1983), 389, 390
  and Walesa, 358, 407
John the Pannonian, 44
John V, 46
John VI, of Cantacuzene, Byzantine emperor, 46
John-Sigmund (Zapoljai), Prince of Transylvania, 53
Jokai, Mor, 96
Joseph I, Habsburg emperor, 66
Joseph II, emperor of Austria, 67, 82, 109
Joseph Poniatovski, prince of Poland, 71
Joujovitch, General, 298
Jovanovitch, General, 299
Jungmann, Joseph, 89
Justinian, Roman emperor, 19

Kaczmarek, archbishop of Kielce, 306
Kaczmarek, General, 357
Kadar, Janos
  and activist groups, 345
  dam agreement, 384
  and Gorbachev, 387, 407
  ouster, 382
  Prague Spring, 336, 338
  purged, 303, 319
  reform policies, 326, 329-30, 387
  1956 Revolution, 319-326
  secretary general, 303, 319, 326, 329
Kakol, Kazimierz, 355
Kakowski, Cardinal, 167
Kallay, Nicolas, 245, 249
Kalmancsehi, Martin, 51

Kalojan, Bulgar tsar, 34
Kalorov, Basil, 277
Kania, Stanislaw, 351, 358, 360, 361, 362, 363
Kara, Ladislas, 45
Karadjitch, Vuk, 90
Karageorge (Petrovitch, George), 80, 81, 82
Karavelov, Ljuben, 132
Kardelj, Edward, 278, 298
Karolyi, Count Mihaly, 124, 153, 162, 163, 164, 169-70, 195
Kaunitz, Chancellor, 67
Kazinczy, 77
Kemeny, Janos, prince of Transylvania, 65
Kethly, Anna, 287, 312
Khrushchev, 396, 407
  Albania, 327-28
  destalinization, 376
  detente, 327
  Poland, 318
  in power, 313
  20th Party congress, 304, 316
Khun-Hedervary, ban of Serbia, 125
Kieshi, Haxhi, 328
Kisfaludy, Alexander, 76
Kissilev, General, 83, 84
Kiszczak, General Czeslaw, 392
Klapka, George, 100, 102
Kohl, Helmut, 385
Kolarov, Basis, 171, 199
Kolcsey, Ferenc, 90
Kollar, 90
Komensky, Jan-Amos (Comenius), 63
Konev, Marshal Ivan S., 315, 318
Kopacsy, 325
Kopczynski, 77
Kopitar, Jernej, 78, 90
Korczynski, General, 353
Korfanty, Albert, 130, 178, 193
Korosec, Father, 205
Kosciuszko, General Tadeusz, 71, 72, 76, 77
Kossuth, Ferenc, 124
Kossuth, Lajos, 398, 405
  exile, 110
  minorities, 97, 98, 99
  nationalism, 90, 91, 96
  nationalist party, 113, 121, 169
  War of 1848, 100-102

Kostov, Traiko, 303, 314
Kosygin, Aleksei, 338, 339
Kouhanitch, archbishop of Zagreb, 351
Kovacs, Bela, 196, 273, 286, 312, 321
Kovess, General, 163
Kramarj, Charles, 122, 126, 153, 166
Kruja, Mustafa, 255
Krukowizcki, General, 87
Kun, Bela, 169, 170-71, 187, 195, 214
Kupi, Abas, 255
Kuron, Jacek, 354, 363
Kvaternik, Colonel Eugene, 125, 243

Ladislas I of Bohemia (Ladislas V of Hungary), 43
Ladislas II, Jagiello of Poland, 53
Ladislas III, Jagiello of Poland and Hungary, 53
Ladislas Piast (the Short), of Poland, 40
Ladislas, Saint, king of Hungary, 31
Lafayette, General, 76, 87
Lakatos, General, 249, 250
Lamarque, General, 87
Landler, Eugene, 170
Laroche, Jules, 176
Laszlo, G., 21
Lavisse, Ernest, 114, 125, 175
Lazar, Gyorgy, 373
Lazar, Prince of Serbia, 47
Leczynski, Stanislas, king of Poland, 69, 70
Lehar, Franz, 120
Lekai, Cardinal, 330
Lemberg, General, 99, 100
Lenart, Jozef, 333, 336
Lenin, Vladimir Illyich, 152, 169, 170, 368, 372, 380
Leopold I, Habsburg emperor, 61, 65, 66, 404
Leopold I, king of Belgium, 141
Lettrich, Joseph, 289, 291
Levski, Basil, 132
Lezsak, Sandor, 383
Liapchev, Andre, 200
Ligachev, Yegor, 368
Limanowski, S., 129
Lis, Bogdan, 390
Liszt, Franz, 90
Litvinov, Maxime, 229
Lloyd George, David, 154, 172

415

Loebl, Eugene, 290, 303, 332, 333
Loiseau, Charles, 175
London, Arthur, 303, 332
Louis II, king of Hungary, 48, 49, 50
Louis, Paul, 175
Louis (the Great) d'Anjou, king of Hungary & Poland, 39, 40, 53
Louis XIV, king of France, 65, 66
Louis-Philippe, of France, 87, 141
Lovaszy, Marton, 162
Lubecki, Count of Poland, 85
Luca, Vasile, 281, 282
Lupescu, Helene, Queen of Rumania, 202
Lupu, Prince Vasil of Moldavia, 60
Luther, Martin, 49-51, 57
Luxembourg, Rosa, 129

Macharski, Archbishop of Cracow, 355
Madarasz, 101
Makensen, Marshal of German Army, 161
Malenkov, Georgi, 310
Maleter, Colonel Pal, 322, 323, 325
Malinov, 200
Malinovsky, Marshal, 283
Mamula, Miroslav, 334
Maniu, Jules, 125, 126, 201, 202, 203, 204, 247, 283
Mao Tse-tung, 328, 347
Marguerite, queen of Hungary, 31
Maria-Theresa, queen of Austria, 67, 404
Marie, queen of Rumania, 202
Maria, queen of Hungary, 43, 50
Marinescu, Gyorgy, 319, 324
Marshall, George C., 290
Martin V, Pope, 42
Martin, William, 224
Martinovics, Ignac, 78
Marx, Karl, 129
Masaryk, Jan, 289-292
Masaryk, Thomas, 289, 337
   Czechoslovak democracy, 126, 162, 232
   National Council in France, 154, 175, 176
   President, 166, 188
   and Slovaks, 122, 191
Matchek, Vladko, 206, 207
Matthias, Habsburg emperor, 62, 63
Maximilian II, king of Bohemia, 52, 53

Menchikov, prince of Russia, 104
Merkel, Jacek, 392
Messner, Zbigniew, 391, 392
Methodius, 22
Metternich, Klemens von, Chancellor of Austria, 79, 88, 90, 91, 95, 96, 97, 102, 109, 404
Michael, king of Rumania, 202, 240, 244, 247, 281, 282
Michnik, Adam, 390, 391
Mickiewicz, Adam, 87
Micu, Innocent (Uniate bishop), 78
Mieroslawski, General, 107
Mieszko I, king of Poland, 27
Mihajlov, Ivan, 200
Mihajlov (professor), 329
Mihajlovitch, General Draga, 253, 254, 279
Mihalache, Ion, 201, 283
Mihalyi, Erno, 285
Miklos, General Bela, 284
Mikolajczyk, Stanislaw, 251, 252, 265, 279, 280-81
Mikoyan, Anastas I., 313, 318, 321
Milan IV, king of Serbia, 138
Milic, Jean, prelate, 41
Millerand, Alexander, 216
Milosevic, Slobodan, 378
Milov, General, 248, 276
Mindszenty, Cardinal Jozef, 306, 322, 323, 324, 330
Mircea (the Great), prince of Wallachia, 59
Mircea (the Old), prince of Wallachia, 47
Mnacko, Ladislas, 333, 334
Moczar, General, 331, 358
Mohammed, 81
Mohammed, II, 48
Mohammed V, 144
Molotov, V.M., 236, 238, 298, 313, 318
Moratcha, 329
Moscicki, Ignace, 193, 194, 236
Mouraviev, General, 108
Muchanov, 200
Murad, Sultan, 133
Murat I, Sultan, 46, 47
Murat II, Sultan, 47
Muraviev, Constantine, 248
Mussolini, Benito
   and Albania, 198

Mussolini, Benito, *continued*
  and Bulgaria, 217
  dependence on Hitler's policy, 239
  and Germany, 218
  and Hungary, 217
  and Italy, 247
  Munich agreements, 188, 230-31
Nagy, Ferenc, 285, 286
Nagy, Imre
  execution, 325
  Hungarian Revolution, 320-25
  ouster, 319
  Prime Minister, (1953), 312
  rehabilitation, 320, 321
Napoleon I, Bonaparte, 77, 78, 80, 107
Napoleon III, 95, 104, 105, 106, 107
Narutowicz, 192-93
Nassar, Gamal Abdel, king of Egypt, 325
Neditch, General of Serbia, 247
Nepomucene, Saint Jan, 64
Nicholas, grandduke (czar) of Russia, 150
Nicholas I, czar of Russia, 83, 86, 87, 94, 101, 103, 104, 106
Nicholas II, czar of Russia, 129, 140, 175, 405
Nicholas, king of Montenegro, 139, 153
Nicolai, L., 282
Nosek, Vaclav, 291, 292
Novomesky, 303
Novosiltzov, Count, 80
Novotny, 314, 332, 333, 334, 336
Nuschke, Otto, 293
Nyers, Rezso, 382

Obrenovitch, Alexander I, 138
Obrenovitch, Michael, prince of Serbia, 83, 138
Obrenovitch, Milan, 83
Obrenovitch, Miloch, prince of Serbia, 82, 138
Obrenovitch, Natalie, queen of Serbia, 138
Ochab, Edward, 316, 331
Olszowski, Stefan, 358, 361
Orda, Tartar chief, 34
Orkhan, Sultan, 45, 46
Ornets, Ota, 345
Ortutay, Gyula, 285

Osman I, Sultan, 45
Osobka-Morawski, Edward, 252, 279, 280
Osuky, Stephan, 174
Otto (the Great) or Otti I, Holy Roman Emperor, 27
Otto, General, 251
Otto of Brandenburg, regent of Poland, 30
Ottokar II (Premsyl-Ottokar), 30

Pacha, Turhan, 168
Paderewski, Ignac, 167, 168
Paisi, 84
Palacky, Frantisek, 89, 97, 98, 122
Paleologue, Maurice, 216
Palffy-Oesterreicher, 286, 302
Pashitch, Nikola, 139, 149, 153, 165, 205
Paskievitch, Marshal, 87, 94, 101, 107
Patrascanu, Lucretiu, 247, 282, 303
Pauker, Anna, 281, 282, 303
Paul, prince of Yugoslavia, 207, 218, 242
Paul II, Pope, 44
Paul VI, Pope, 330, 345
Pavel, 292
Pavelitch, Ante, 206, 243, 245, 256, 278
Pazmany, Cardinal Peter, 65
Perczel, General, 101
Peter (of Bulgar uprising), 34
Peter, Bishop Janos, 307
Peter (the Great), czar of Russia, 60, 69, 70
Peter, Bulgar tsar, 28
Peter, Gabor, 286
Peter I Karageorgevitch, king of Serbia, 139, 148, 152, 165, 205
Peter I, of Montenegro, 83
Peter II, of Montenegro, 83
Peter II, king of Yugoslavia, 207, 242, 243, 253, 254, 278
Peter of Chelcice, 43
Petkov, Nicolas, 275, 277
Petliura, Simon, 172
Petofi, Sandor, 90, 96, 101
Petrescu, Colonel Alexander, 282, 283
Petrescu, Titel, 247, 283
Peyer, Karoly, 287
Philip IV, of Valois, 37
Piasecki, Count Boleslaw, 306
Pieck, Wilhelm, 293

Pilgrim, bishop of Passau, 27
Pilsudski, Marshal Joseph, 363, 406
   in power, 192, 193-94, 195
   minister of war, 167, 168, 193
   Russo-Polish war, 172
   Socialist party, 123, 129, 130, 193
   WWI, 166
Pinkowski, Jozef, 357, 358
Pitrzik, Alojzy, 392
Pius IX, Pope, 109
Plohjar, Father, 290, 306, 335
Podgorny, 339
Pogany, Jozsef, 170
Poincare, Raymond, president of France, 149
Polzer-Hoditz, Count, 162
Poniatowski, General Joseph, 78
Popieluszko, Father Jerzy, 390, 391
Poplawski, Jan, 129
Popovici, Aurel, 126, 203
Poradovski, General, 108
Potiorek, General, 120
Potocki, Count Stanislas, 85, 123
Potocki, Ignac, 71
Pouharitch, Branko, 351
Pozderac, Jamdija, 377-78
Pozsgay, Imre, 382, 383
Prchlik, Vaclav, 334
Premysl-Ottokar (Ottokar II), 30
Premysl I, 29
Princip, Gavrilo, 149
Putnik, General, 144
Puzak, 252, 273
Pyka, Tadeusz, 356

Radescu, General Nicolae, 282, 283
Radetzky, Marshal, 99
Raditch, Stephan, 205, 206
Radoslav Nemanja, 32
Rajk, Laszlo, 286, 287, 302, 304, 313, 319-20
Rakoczi, Ferenc (Francis II), prince of Transylvania, 66
Rakoczi, George I, prince of Transylvania, 65
Rakoczi, George II, prince of Transylvania, 65
Rakosi, Matyas, 170, 187, 285, 286
   Hungarian Revolution, 319, 320, 324, 329
   secretary-general, 287, 301, 312

Rakowski, George, 84
Rakowski, Mieczyslaw, 358, 361, 392, 393
Rankovitch, Alexander, 278, 297, 298, 328, 329
Rapacki, Adam, 332
Rastko, Nemanja (St. Sava), 32
Ratchich, Punitsa, 206
Ratzki, Frano, 125
Renner, Karl, 126, 127
Repnin, Russian ambassador, 70
Ribbentrop, Joachim von, 232, 234
   Russo-German pact, 235, 238
Rieger, 122
Rizkhov, Nikolai, 368
Rochambeau, 76
Rokossowsky, Marshal Konstantin, 252, 299, 318
Romanov, 368
Roosevelt, Franklin D., president of the U.S., 265, 266, 279, 296
Rosting, Helmer, 221
Roth, 91
Rousseau, Jean Jacques, 76
Rozwadowski, General, 120, 193
Rudolph, Archduke, 119
Rudolph I, Habsburg emperor, 30, 404
Rudolph II, Habsburg emperor, 52, 62,
Rydz-Smigley, *see* Smigley-Rydz

Safarik, Paul, 89
Samuel, prince of Bulgaria, 28, 29
Sanatescu, General, 247, 281, 282
Sarateanu, Constantine, 203
Sauerwein, Jules, 175
Sava, Saint (Rastko Nemanja), of Serbia, 32
Schwarzenberg, prince of Austria, 109
Sejna, General, 334
Selim III, 81
Seredi, Cardinal, 196
Serov, General, 323
Seton, Watson, 176
Severus, Alexander, Roman emperor, 17
Severus, Septimius, Roman emperor, 17
Shehu, Mehmet, 314, 376
Sidor, Karol, 232, 233
Sigismund I of Poland, 54, 55
Sigismund III Vasa, king of Poland, 69

Sigismund, king of Bohemia and Hungary, 41, 42, 43, 47
Sigismund-Augustus of Poland, 54, 55, 56
Sik, Otak, 333, 335
Sikorski, General, 120, 130, 166, 193, 236, 251, 265
Sima, Horia, 239, 241
Simeon II, 248
Simovitch, Duchan, 242
Sirovy, General, 230
Siwak, Albin, 361
Skanderbeg, Prince of Albania and Epirus, 47
Skarga, P., 55
Skrznicki, General, 87
Slansky, Rudolf, 289, 301, 303, 304
    rehabilitation, 332
Smigly-Rydz, Marshal, 194, 236
Smolka, 94
Smrkovsky, Josef, 291, 292, 335-38, 340, 341
Sobieski, Jan, king of Poland, 66, 69
Sofroni, 84
Sophia, Habsburg archduchess, 109, 149
Soroky, Villiam, 314
Soubachitch, Ivan, 278
Sozzino, Lelio, 57
Spaho, Mehmed, 205
Spychalski, General, 302, 331
Sramek, Father, 289
Stalin, Jozef, 368, 372, 379, 406
    and Albania, 327-28, 346
    cult of personality, 310, 316
    Czechoslovakia, 265, 290
    death of, 295, 310, 313
    Poland, 252, 265-66
    purges, 187, 194
    Teheran Conference, 265
    Tito, 278
    Yalta, 266, 279, 296
Stambolijski, Alexander, 141, 160, 161, 171, 198, 199, 248
Stambulov, Stefan, 140, 141
Stanislas-Augustus Poniatovski, king of Poland, 70, 71, 72, 76
Stefan I, Prvovencani Nemanja, 32
Stefan Nemanja, Zupan of Racia, 32, 34
Stefan (the Great) of Moldavia, 59
Stefanik, Milan, 154

Stephan, Habsburg archduke, viceroy of Hungary, 97, 99
Stephen, Saint (Istvan I), king of Hungary, 28, 31, 32
Stephen II (Istvan II), king of Hungary, 31
Stephen VI, Uros II, Nemanja, of Serbia, 46
Stephen VIII, Uros III, Nemanja of Serbia, 46
Stephen IX Dusan, Nemanja, of Serbia, 46, 47
Stepinac, Josef, archbishop of Zagreb, 279, 305, 351
Stirbey, Prince Barbu, 202, 247, 283
Stojadinovitch, Milan, 207
Stojanov, Zachary, 140
Stoph, Willi, 386
Stromfeld, General Aurel, 170
Strossmayer, Bishop Joseph, 125
Strougal, Lubomir, 387
Stur, Louis, 89
Sturdza, Ioan, prince of Moldavia, 83, 94
Sturdza, Micael, prince of Moldavia, 84
Sulijman (the Magnificent), 49, 52
Supilo, Frano, 153
Suslov, Mikhail, 321, 339, 359, 368
Sussaykov, General, 283
Suvar, Stipe, 378, 402
Svoboda, General Ludvik, 289-92, 335-36, 340-41
Swatopluk, king of Moravia, 22
Sylvester II, Pope, 28
Symeon, Bulgar tsar, 28, 29
Szakasits, A., 288
Szalasi, Ferenc, 196, 250, 255, 256, 284, 285
Szamuelly, Tibor, 170
Szechenyi, Count Istvan, 90-91, 97
Szemere, 97
Szocs, Geza, 372
Sztojay, Dome, 249, 250

Taffe, Eduard, 122
Talleyrand, 79
Tamerlan, Mongol Khan, 47
Tapie, V.L., 115
Tardieu, Andre, 175, 212

Tatarescu, Georgi, 204, 282, 283
Tchernaiev, General, 133
Teleki, Count Paul
  and French, 216
  and Germans, 238, 239, 242-43
  neutrality, 239
  Prime Minister 196
  suicide, 243
  and Yugoslavia, 239, 242
Teleki, Geza, 284
Theodosius I, Roman emperor, 18
Thokoly, Emeric, prince of Hungary, 65, 66
Thomas, Albert, 175
Thurn, Count of, 62
Thuroczy, 45
Tiberius, Roman emperor, 17
Tildy, Zoltan, 196, 285, 287-88, 312, 321
Tilly, Count of, 63
Tiso, Father Josef, 188, 229
  P.O.W., 256
  and Slovak autonomists, 231, 232, 245, 250-51
  trial of, 288-89
Tisza, Count Istvan, 124, 149, 150, 153, 163
Tisza, Kalman, 124
Tito (Josip Broz), 300, 391, 407
  and Albania, 297, 313, 346, 376
  and church, 305
  death of, 347
  and partisans, 253, 254, 256
  and Prague Spring, 340, 341
  rehabilitation, 313
  rise to power, 277-79, 301
  West, aid from, 346
  USSR: schism from, 262, 297-300; loyalty to, 278, 296, 297
  rapprochment with, 313, 328, 346
  Yugoslavia after death of, 348, 349, 350, 351, 378, 379
Titulescu, Monsieur, 203, 222, 226
Tolbuhin, Marshal, 275
Tomasek, Frantisek, bishop of Prague, 335
Tomaslav, prince of Croatia, 22, 28
Toth, Karoly, 373
Trajan, Roman emperor, 17, 18
Tripalo, 349
Trotsky, Leon, 169, 172

Truman, Harry S., President of the U.S., 296
Trumbich, Ante, 153
Tsankov, Alexander, 199, 200
Tusar, M., 162, 188

Ulbricht, Walter, 293, 301
Urisny, Deputy, 291
Uros I, Nemanja, of Serbia, 34
Uros II (Stephan IV Nemanja), of Serbia, 46
Uros III (Stephan VIII Nemanja), of Serbia, 46

Vaculik, Ludvik, 334
Vajda-Vaevod, 201, 202, 203, 204
Vajk (St. Stephen), 28, 31, 32
Valens II, Roman emperor, 18
Varhonyi, Peter, 373
Velchev, Colonel Damian, 200
Verlaci, Shefret, 254
Veselica, Marko, 349
Victor Emmanuel III, king of Albania, 198, 254
Vlad the Impaler, 48
Vladimirescu, Tudor, 83
Vladislas I, king of Hungary and Poland, 47
Vladislas II, Jagiello, King of Bohemia and Hungary, 48
Vladislav Nemanja, of Serbia, 32
Vlora, Ismail Kemal, 144, 145
Vojtech (St. Adalbert), 27
Volisin, Father Augustin, 231
Voltaire, 76, 77
von Beseler, Governor of Warsaw, 167
von Hotzendorf, Konrad, 127, 149
Von Neurath, Baron, 246
Von Schulenburg, 235
Vorochilov, Marshal, 284, 285
Voros, General, 284
Vorosmarty, Mihaly, 90
Vychinski, Andrei, 282, 283
Vyx, Colonel, 170

Wacho, Lombard, king, 19
Wadolowski, 363
Waldhouser, Conrad, 41
Walentynowicz, Anna, 356

Walesa, Lech, 351
  arrest, 366, 389, 390
  and Church, 358, 363
  government negotiations, 362, 364
  Lenin shipyard, 354, 393
  Nobel Peace prize, 390
  and pope, 407
  Solidarity union, 353, 357
  Strikes, 356, 392
Walewska, Maria, 77, 107
Walewski, Count, 107
Wallenberg, Raoul, 273
Wallenstein, General, 64
Weiss, Louise, 175
Wenceslas II Przemslyde, of Bohemia, 30, 31, 35, 40
Wenceslas III Przemslyde, of Bohemia, 30
Wenceslas IV Przemslyde, of Bohemia, 41, 42
Wenceslas, Saint, duke of Bohemia, 26
Werth, General Henrik, 243
Weygand, General, 172
Wickham-Steed, Henry, 176
Wiclif, Jan, 41, 42, 50
Wielopolski, 107
Wilhem of Wied, king of Albania, 146, 168
William II, prince regent of Prussian Poland, 130
William of Slavata, 63
William, prince regent of Prussian Poland, 94
Wilson, Woodrow, President of the U.S., 161, 166, 176
Windischgratz, General, 99

Witaszewski, General, 318
Witos, Vincent, 130, 172, 192, 193
Wojciechowski, Stanislas, 193
Wojtyla, Cardinal Karol, 354-55, 390, *see also* John Paul II, Pope
Wrangel, General, 198
Wysocki, General, 86, 94, 108
Wyszynski, Cardinal Stefan, 306, 307, 351
  death of, 360
  house arrest, 315, 317
  influence, 344-45
  liberation, 318, 325, 331

Xoxe, Koci, 303

Ypsilanti, Alexander, 82
Zaliwski, 86
Zamoyski, Count, 106, 107
Zamoyski, John, 56
Zamoyski, Polish Chancellor, 70
Zapolyai, John, 48, 49, 50, 52, 53
Zapotocky, Antonin, 290, 314
Zawadski, Alexander, 315
Zdanov, Andrei, introduction
Zeliv, Jan, Minister, 42
Zhivkov, Todor, 314, 330, 346, 381-82, 399
Zichy, Count Janos, 124
Zizka, John, 42
Zog I, Ahmed, king of Albania, 197, 198, 217, 254, 255, 277
Zrinyi, Miklos, 65, 66
Zulawski, 280
Zvonimir, Croatian King, 31
Zymierski, General Rola, 252

Index of Subjects

Adrianople, Peace of (1829), 82
Agadir crisis (1911), 148
Akerman, Convention of (1826), 82
Albania
  and Austria-Hungary, 145-46, 152, 168
  in Balkan Wars, 144-46
  Byzantine empire and, 29, 32
  Communist party, founding, 255, 261
  economics, interwar, 208
  independence: (1912) 145-46
    (1920) 168-69, 197
  Italy, 168
    annexation by, 197, 198, 216-17, 243, 247
    independence from, 254-55
  Kosovo: Albanians in, 184, 222
    annexation of, 243, 255
  at London conference, 145
  in Macedonia, 142, 145, 243
  nationalism, 81, 144, 197
  origins of peoples, 20
  Ottoman Turks and, 47, 58-59, 81, 131, 144-46
  Serbia and, 145-46, 152, 168
  Tartar invasion, 34
  Treaty of Bucharest, 145, 146
  Treaty of London, 152, 168, 175
  USSR, occupation by, 255, 261, 262, 268
  WW I, 152, 168-69
  Young Turk revolution, 144
  Yugoslavia and, 243
  Zog dictatorship, 197-98, 277
Albanian People's Republic, 6, 399
  atheism in, 5, 347, 376
  China and, 328, 346-47, 376
  Communist takeover, 275, 277, 281
  destalinization, 327-28, 376
  Kosovo, Albanians in, 3, 347-49, 374-75 378, 395, 402
  Germans, expulsion of, 277
  isolationism, 344-45, 347, 375-77
  Stalinism, 347, 376
  Tito's death, 346-47
  USSR, break from, 262, 297, 327-28 346, 376
  Warsaw Pact and, 328
  Yugoslavia, break with, 297, 299, 313, 327, 328
Allies, WW II, 236, 242, 244, 247-48, 252, 254
  appeasement policy, 230, 233
  Cold War, 295
  principle of self-determination, 220
  USSR and, post-war, 261-62, 264-65
  at Yalta, 256-57, 261, 266, 296
Amnesty International, on Bulgaria, 375
Andrinople, *See* Adrianople
Anjous dynasty, 36, 37m, 39-40, 53
Anschluss, 218, 225, 227, 229-30
Anti-Comintern Pact (1936), 238
Anti-Semitism, *See* Jewish peoples
Arad, Martyrs of, 102
Armenians, 3, 4
  in Bulgaria, 34, 61
  in Macedonia, 142, 144
  Ottomans, liberation from, 133, 135
  Russian empire and, 86, 135
Arpadian dynasty, 22, 28, 31-32, 35, 39
Arrow-Cross party in Hungary, 187, 196, 227, 250, 255-56, 284
Atheism, policy of, 5, 342, 344, 396
  Albania, 347, 376
  Czechoslovakia, 182

Augsburg, Peace of (1555), 51, 52
Ausgleich of 1867, 110-13, 119
Austria, Republic of
  deportations of Germans to, 269m, 270
  formation of, post WW I, 160m, 178-79
  France and, 212, 216
  Germany, *Anschluss* by, 218, 225, 227, 229
  Italy and, 218
  USA, occupation by, 256
  USSR, occupation by, 267, 272
Austria-Hungary (1867-1918), 1, 147m
  Balkans, in, 132-35, 141-43,
    Wars (1912-13), 144-147
  Bosnia, annexation of, 135, 143, 148
  Congress of Berlin, 135
  disintegration of, 155, 160m, 161-64, 177-78, 213
  ethnic minorities in, 113, 114-21
    non-Magyars in, 124-26
    revolutions of, 161-64
    in WW I, 149-50
  formation of, 108-12, 113-24
  Great Council of, 109
  governing policies, 119-21
  political conflict, 121-26
  Russia, rivalry over Balkans, 131-35, 142-43
  Sarajevo assassination, 148-49, 150
  Serbia and, 137-39, 141-42, 143, 145-46, 148-50, 152-53, 164, 205
  WW I, 126-27, 148-49, 150-55
    defeat in, 159, 164, 173
    peace settlements, 174-77, 178-79, 181
    Triple Alliance, 149, 150, 151m
    See also Austrian Empire *and* Austria, Republic of
Austrian Empire (1806-1867)
  Austria-Hungary, creation of, 108-12
  the Balkans, 82
  Congress of Vienna, 79-81
  Crimean war, 104, 107
  empire formed (1806), 81, 121
  Habsburg monarchs, 76, 81, 88
  Holy Alliance, 81
  Hungary: rule of, 75, 78, 81, 90-91
    uprising of, 96-100, 100-02
    ausgleich with, 110-12
  Jews in, 115, 116, 118

multinationalism, 1, 75, 76, 78, 88, 94
nationalism, 88-92
Poland, takeover of Galicia, 72, 85, 88, 94, 123, 130
Revolution of *1848*, 95-100, 100-02, 108
Slavs in, 78, 88-90, 99
Thirty Years War, 62-64, 65
and Turks, 49, 53, 58, 65, 66, 68
  See also Holy Roman Empire *and* Austria-Hungary
Austro-Hungarian Compromise, 110-13, 119
Avars, 19, 21, 22, 24
Axis Powers, 207, 218, 264
  anti-Comintern pact, 238
  Tripartite pact, 239, 241, 242

Balkan Conference (1988), 377
Balkan Federation, 297, 298
Balkan League, 144, 145
Balkan Wars (1912-13), 144-6, 147m, 148, 149, 348
Baltaliman Pact (1849), 95
Baltic States, 75, 151m, 152, 172, 235, 238, 268
Balts, 16
Bankruptcy Law, 369, 384
Bar, Confederation of, 70
Battles, *See under* place names
Belgium, 141, 150, 349
Berchtesgaden Talks, 234
Berlin, Congress of (1878), 134m, 135, 136, 137, 139
Berlin Uprising (1953), intro, 311-12
Berlin Wall, 3, 332
Bessarabia, 9
  Congress of Berlin, 134m, 135
  Rumania, joined to, 165, 182, 200, 239-40, 244, 267
  Russia, ceded to, 135, 235
  Treaty of Versailles and, 200
  USSR and, 9, 239, 240
Black Death (the Plague), 36
Black Hand, Serbian society, 146, 149
Black Market, 344, 354
Bogomilian Heresy, 61
Bohemia, 178
  Austria-Hungary, 110
  under, 115-16, 120, 122-23, 124
  independence from, 166

Bohemia, *continued*
    Austrian empire, under, 81, 89, 95-99, 109-10
    Battle of White Mt., 63
    Catholicism, 44, 63, 64, 119
        counter-reformation of, 52, 62-64
    Christianity, conversion to, 25, 26
    Communist party of, 290
    Congress of Vienna and, 81
    Czechs in: origins of, 22, 25, 27
        nationalism of, 43, 89, 95
        revolution of, 97-99, 122-23, 162-65
    Czechoslovakia, 154-55, 162
        formation of, 165-66, 181-82, 189
    defenestration of Prague, 63
    Germans, 30, 41, 43
        nationalism of, 95, 98-99
    Germany, WW II protectorate of, 233, 245, 246, 250
    Holy Roman Empire,
        fief of, 25-27, 29-30, 35, 49-53
        heart of, 38-39, 41
        unrest in, 57, 62-64
    Hungary and, 30, 39, 43, 44, 62, 63
    Hussites and, 41-43, 64
    language act of 1880, 122-23
    Luxembourg dynasty, 36-39, 41
    Marconans, 16, 20, 21
    Pan-Slav Congress, 99, 152-53, 164
    Peace of Wesphalia, 64
    Poland, and, 27, 30, 31,
    Przemsyl dynasty, under, 25, 27, 29, 35, 36
    Reformation in, 49, 50, 51
    Revolutions of *1848*, 95-97, 99
    Slovak autonomists, 125
    Thirty Years War, 62-64
    Young Czechs, 122, 126, 153,
        See also Czechoslovakia
            and Germany
Bolshevik Revolution (1917), 151m, 152, 169, 176, 186, 195, 261
Bolshevism in East Europe, 160, 161, 163, 169-173, 186, 195, 199, 238
Bosnia-Herzegovina, 5, 33m, 48
    Austria-Hungary, annexation by, 118, 132, 134m, 135, 141, 148
    Balkan wars and, 132-33
    Croat republic, part of, 243
    Ottoman Turks, against, 132-33
    Serbs in, 61, 131, 143, 149, 182
    Turks in, 48, 59m, 131
    Yugoslavia, joining of, 183
        Partisans and, 254
        unrest in, 377, 378
        See also Yugoslavia
Boyars, 34, 60, 83-84, 136, 201, 211, 225
    conspiracy of, 105
Brandenburg family, 40, 55
Brest-Litovsk, Compromise of, 55
Brest-Litovsk, Treaty of, 152, 168, 172
Brezhnev Doctrine, 343, 369, 397
Bucharest, Peace of (1812), 80, 81
Bucharest, Treaty of (1918), 148
Budapest, foundation of, 18
Bukovina
    Austrian, 131, 162, 165, 178
    movement to join Rumania, 162, 165
    Rumania and, 178, 182, 200, 239-40
    Russia and, 136, 165
    Treaty of Versailles, 200
    USSR, 239, 240, 244, 267
Bulgaria
    Austria-Hungary and, 132, 141, 142-43, 146, 148
    Alexander, unification under, 140
    Balkan wars and, 144-46, 179, 241
    bolshevism in, 160, 161, 171, 173, 199
    Byzantine empire, 22, 28-29, 32, 34
    Communist party, 171, 186, 198, 199, 248, 262
        takeover, 275-77, 281
    Congress of Berlin, 133, 134m, 135, 139, 142
    dictatorships in, 198-200, 241
    Dobrudja and, 179, 217
        Bulgars in, 239, 241, 267
    early peoples, 2, 16, 20, 21, 22, 32, 34
    economics in, 208, 209, 211, 274
    Empires: First, 28-29, 35
        Second, 33, 34, 46
    Germany and, 141, 200, 219
        WW II, 241-42, 245, 248-49, 275
    Jewish immigrants, 34, 61, 142
    IMRO and, 142-433, 199, 200, 207
    nationalism in, 84, 132-33, 140-41
    Ottoman Turks and, 46, 47, 60-61, 81, 131, 132-33, 135
    Russia and, 132-35, 139-41, 142-43
    Treaty of Neuilly, 177, 179-80

424

Bulgaria, *continued*
  Treaty of San Stefano, 135
  USSR: control by, 267, 271
    occupation by, 255, 265, 267
    relations with, 198, 200, 241-42
    WW II with, 248-49, 267
  Vlachs in, 61, 142
  WW I: and Central Powers, 151m, 152, 155
    defeat in, 155, 159-161
  WW II, 248-49
    neutrality in, 241-42, 244, 248, 267
    peace settlements, 257, 267, 276m
  Yugoslavia, 184
    Macedonians in, 199, 200, 207, 217, 270
    occupation of, 243, 248
    See also Macedonia *and* Bulgaria, People's Republic of
Bulgaria, People's Republic of,
  agriculture, 209, 342, 370, 399
  Communist party, 248
    takeover, 275-77, 281
  economics, 342, 370
  purges, 275-76
  reforms, openness to, 381-82
  religion, 5, 28, 399
  Turkish minority, persecution of, 375
  USSR, occupation by, 272-73, 275
    loyalty to, 262, 330, 381
  Yugoslavia, conflict over Macedonia, 3, 349-50, 395
Byzantine Empire, 4, 21, 27-36, 33m
  decline of, 45-58
  Ottoman Turks and, 46-48
  sphere of influence, 28-29

Calvinism, 5, 51, 55, 182, 183
  See also Protestantism
Catalonie (Chalons), Battle of, 19
Canada, exports to, 211
Catholicism, *See* Roman Catholic Church
  and Greek Orthodox Church
  or Uniate Church
Celts, 16
Central Powers, *See* Triple Alliance
Chamberlain Plan, 230-31
Charter '77, 345, 388
China, 34, 328, 331, 346, 347, 376

Chios, Massacre of, 82
Christianity
  conversion to, 17, 22, 25-31, 36, 44, 49, 51, 53
  traditions of, 394
CIA, 376
Cimmerians, 15
Climate, 9
CMEA *See* COMECON
Cold War, 293, 295-96
Collectivization, 307-08, 312
  change from, 370
  Czechoslovakia, 333, 337
  Poland, 331
  Rumania, 342, 380
  USSR, problems with, 328, 331
COMECON, Intro, 10, 327, 341, 371
  Bulgaria, 399
  Czechoslovakia, 400
  East Germany, 332, 385, 386, 400
  Hungary, 329, 374, 384, 401
  Poland, 331, 354, 360, 401
  Rumania, 371, 374, 402
  USSR, 229, 327, 341, 371
  Yugoslavia, 342, 402
Cominform, 262, 296, 297, 299, 310, 316
Comintern, Intro, 171
Communism, 396
  disillusionment with, 344, 367, 390, 396
Communist parties in Eastern Europe
  activity around WW II, 171, 188, 189, 190, 198, 199, 247, 248, 252, 284
  banning of pre-WW II, 186, 194, 195-96, 199, 206
  formation of, 137, 171, 201, 203, 205-06, 255, 261
  government organization of, 300-01
  resistance movements and, 272-74
  Slovakia, 250, 333
  Soviet republics, 169-71, 195-96
  takeovers of, 272-73, 274-92, 293-94, 336
  USSR: aid in takeovers, 255-56, 261-62, 272-73, 274-75, 282-83
  loyalty, 262, 279
  policy leader, 295-97, 310-11, 343, 369, 396-97
  See also COMECON
  and Warsaw Pact

425

Compacta of 1436, 42
Concentration camps, 246, 251
Congresses, *See under* place names
Congress of Oppressed Nationalities (1918), 155
Cordon Sanitaire, 214, 215
Corfu, declaration of, 153
Council of Florence (1439), 47
Council of Trent, 51, 55
Counter Reformation, 51-52, 55-57, 62-64
Crimean War (1853-55), 103, 104, 107, 131
Croatia, 16, 37m, 78
  autonomy during WW II, 243, 245, 255, 256
  Catholicism and, 4, 89, 119
    persecution of, 279, 305
  early people, 20m, 21, 22, 24, 26m
  Hungary and, 31, 39
    autonomy under, 112, 124
    in Dual Monarchy, 111, 115-18, 121
    uprising against, 97, 99-100
  pan-Slavism in, 83, 90, 97, 109, 125-26, 153
  Serbs: anti-Serb policy, 245, 349
    domination by, 205-07, 242, 278-79, 328, 349, 378
  Tartars and, 35
  Tomislav, kingdom under, 22, 28
  Ustasha in, 206, 207, 245, 254
  Yugoslavia, 160m, 163-65, 183-84, 205, 254
    postwar purges in, 278-79
    See also Yugoslavia
Crusades: Wiclif and, 42, 44
  against the Turks, 32-34, 43, 45, 47, 48, 60
Curzon line, 172, 255-56, 264-66
Czech language, 2
  in Bohemia, 38, 42, 77, 122, 123
  rivalry with German, 64
Czech-USSR Treaty (Litvinov, 1935), 216, 229-30
Czechoslovak Socialist Republic, 4, 5, 6
  anti-Semitism in, 4, 334
  Charter '77, 345, 388
  Church and, 5, 289, 335
  collectivization of, 333, 377
  COMECON, 333, 337, 400

Communist takeover of, 288-92, 336
destalinization, 314, 332
dissidents, 334, 346, 388, 389
East Bloc, relations with, 336, 338, 339, 395
economics, 9, 291, 333, 342, 387
foreign debt, 370
hydro-electric dam, 371, 384
national minorities in, 3, 372, 374, 395
political prisoners, 333, 345
Prague Spring of 1968, 333-41, 343, 352, 366
reform, resistance to, 387-88
Slovaks in, 333, 341, 342, 395
USA and, 290, 296
USSR and, 289, 262, 387
  Moscow Accords, 340-41
Warsaw Pact, 315
  invasion by, 338, 340, 342, 359, 360, 388
Yugoslavia and, 340-41
Czechoslovakia, 182
  Allies and, 153-54, 173, 215
  Communist party: 186, 188, 189, 190, 232
  postwar rise, 274-75, 288-92
  Slovak party, 250
  USSR, aid from, 262, 271, 272-73
  conflicts, Czechs and Slovaks:
    First Republic, 181-82, 189-192, 245
    Second Republic, 250-51, 269, 334, 335, 341, 395
  Czech-Slovak union, 154-55, 162, 175
  democratization, 187-92
  economics, 188, 208-12, 215
    post-WW II, 274, 291
  First Republic, 165-66, 181-82, 189
    dismemberment, 228m, 229-233, 234
  France and, 175, 229, 230
  Germany: Bohemia-Moravia as protectorate of, 233, 245, 246, 250
    war with, 218, 219
    WW II and, 228m, 229-30, 232, 233
  Hungary and, 170
    annexation by, 181, 229, 232, 233
  industrialization, 10, 187, 208
  Kosice Program, 256, 269, 288, 290
  land reforms, 210, 224
  Little Entente, in, 151m, 216, 128, 231

Czechoslovakia, *continued*
London government in exile, 246, 250, 256, 265, 288
Marshall plan, 290, 296
Munich pact, 231, 257
National Council in France, 154
national minorities in, 166, 181, 182, 188, 192, 210, 220-26, 228m, 229, 256
expulsion of, 269m, 270
Red Army victims, 274, 288
peace talks WW I, 173-74, 189-190
Poland, occupation by, 228m, 231, 232
purges in, 288-89, 291
Rumania, and, 231, 233, 267, 340-41
Second Republic, 250-51, 256
Slovak autonomists, 188-91, 229, 232, 233
Slovak Soviet republic, 170, 186
Sudeten Germans, 181-82, 192, 224
and Hitler, 219, 225, 229-31, 270
USA and, 154, 166, 176, 189
USSR: relations with, 216, 229-30, 250-51, 265, 288
annexation of Ruthenia, 268, 273
Red Army occupation, 272, 273
Vienna Arbitrations, 228m, 231-32
Yugoslavia and, 231, 233
See also Bohemia, Czechoslovak Socialist Republic, Moravia, Slovakia

Dacia, 15, 16, 17, 18, 20, 78
Dalmatia (Croatia), 16, 17, 20m, 21, 28, 32, 35, 61, 115
Danubian Common Market, 212
Danubian Federation, 215-16, 256, 398
Debt, foreign, 367, 370-71, 376
GDR, 370, 386
Hungary, 370, 383, 384
Poland, 343-44, 370, 391
Yugoslavia, 350, 370, 377
Decembrist Conspiracy, 86
Democratic Forum, 383, 388
Demography (modern), 5-6, 7, 165, 346
Denmark, 17
Deportations of WW II, 3, 269m, 270
Depression of 1929, 211, 218, 219
Destalinization, 239-40, 310-11, 313-20, 327, 332-33
Detente, 327, 344, 367, 375

Dissidents in the East Bloc, 334, 344, 345-56, 370-71, 381, 388, 395
in Poland, 361, 388, 393
See also Charter '77, Democratic Forum, KOR, Solidarity
Dobrudja
Bulgaria and, 179, 217, 239, 241, 267
Rumania and, 134m, 145, 183, 217, 239, 267
Dual Monarchy, *See* Austria-Hungary
Dynasties, *See* under family name

East Germany, *See* German Democratic Republic
Economics in East bloc
central planning of, 309
comparisons of, 10, 342
interwar, 208-213
See also Foreign debts
EEC, 332, 342, 384
Energy shortages, 369, 371, 380, 391
Entente Cordiale (1905), 148
Estonia, 2, 15, 75, 151m, 152, 235, 238, 268
Ethiopia, 218
Ethnic minorities, *See* Minorities of each country
Exchanges, East-West, 344

February Patent (1861), 110
Federal Republic of Germany, 6, 308, 331
Albania and, 377
division of Germany, 3, 218, 242, 257, 264-66
East Germans, escape/immigration to, 3, 269m, 308, 311, 332, 386
East Germany (GDR), relations with, 308, 385-86
See also Germany
Final Act of 1815, 79
See also Vienna, Congress of
Finland, 2, 15, 75, 152, 174, 235, 238
First World War, *See* World War I
Fiume, Congress of (1905), 126
Food shortages, 355, 362, 370, 379, 380, 391, 396
Fourteen Points, 161, 166, 176
France, 17, 262, 325, 333, 377
Austria-Hungary and, 114

France, *continued*
  Balkan Wars, 143-45
  Congress of Vienna, 79
  cordon sanitaire policy, 214
  Crimean war and, 104
  Croatia & Istria, 79, 78
  Czechoslovakia: nationalism of, 154, 175, 176
    WW II and, 216, 229, 230-31
  dynasties of, 36-39
  Eastern Europe and, 209, 214-19, 397.
  Germany and, 148, 177, 218, 229-30
    Munich Pact of, 231
  Great Britain and, 148, 325
  Hungary, 47
    treaty with, 216
  immigration to, 210
  influence of thought, 67, 76, 77, 84
  Little Entente and, 151m, 216, 218, 219, 222
  Marsaille assassination, 207, 218, 242
  national minorities, treaties on, 155, 176, 220, 222, 225, 229
  Ottoman Turks and, 47, 48, 49, 104
  Poland: 69, 70, 71, 86-87
    ally against Russia, 172, 176
    WW II ally, 215, 234, 235, 236, 264-65
  Revolution of 1789, 76, 77, 86, 93, 95
  Russia and, 114, 148, 149, 150
  Serbia and, 139, 148
  Treaty of London, 175
  Treaty of Paris, 104-05
  Treaty of Saxony, 80
  Triple Entente, 142, 148, 150, 151m
  USSR and, 234-35, 325
  WW I and, 148, 150, 164, 264
Franco-Hungarian Treaty of 1920, 216
Franco-Russian Alliance (1892), 114
Francs, 17
French Revolution, 76-78, 93, 95

Galicia, *See* Poland
Gepides, 17, 19, 20m
Geography, 8, 9, 181
German Confederation, 81, 97, 99
German Democratic Republic (GDR)
  Berlin uprising, 311-12
  Berlin wall, 3, 332
  COMECON, 332, 386, 400

Communist party (SED), 293-94, 295, 300, 301
dissidents, 311, 345, 346
division of Germany, 3, 218, 242, 257, 264-66
economy of, 10, 296, 332, 342, 344
escape/emigration to West, 3, 269m, 308, 311, 332, 386
foreign debt, 370, 386
industry, 332, 342, 400
land reform, 307-08
Protestantism, 307, 400
reform, resistance to, 385-86
USSR, 371, 386-87
  military presence of, 296, 311
West Germany (FRG), relations with, 308, 385-86
Germano-Polish treaty, 234
Germany
  Austria-Hungary and, 146, 149, 150
  Bulgaria and, 141, 200
    WW II, 241-42, 245, 248-49, 275
  Communist party in, 186, 293
  confederation of, 81, 97, 99
  Croatia, 245, 279
  Czechoslovakia, WW II occupation of, 191, 228, 229-233, 246
  division of, 257, 264-66, 292
  early peoples, 16, 17, 22
  economics, 209, 212-13, 218
  France and, 148, 177
    WW II and, 229, 230, 234-35
  Germans in eastern Europe, 3, 184,
    in Czechoslovakia (Sudetenland), 181-82, 192, 224
    and Hitler, 219, 225, 226, 227, 229-31, 233
    deportations of, 3, 269m, 270
    in Poland, 181, 234, 235-36, 256
    in Rumania (Banat), 182-83, 270
  Great Britain and, 188, 230, 231, 235
  Hungary in WW II, 229, 232, 239
    allied with, 244-45, 249-50, 255-56
  Italy, allied with in WW II, 218-19, 228-29, 234, 239
  Jews, persecution of, 246, 249-50, 255
  Munich agreements, 188, 228m, 231, 257
  Nazism, rise of, 200, 246

Germany, *continued*
  Ottoman Turks and, 146, 150
  Poland and, 150, 152, 167, 177-78, 180
    resistance in, 250-55
    WW II and, 215, 233-38, 246-47
  Rumania and, 136
    WW II, 227, 239, 240-41, 244-45, 247-48
  Slovakia, 227, 232, 245, 250-51
  USSR, 155, 214
    invasion of, 242-43, 244, 261, 264, 292
    occupation by, 256, 272-74, 292-94
    pact with, 235, 238, 264
    postwar activity, 293-94
  West Germany (FRG), creation of, 292-94
  WW I: Central Powers and, 142, 146, 149-155, 159
    and defeat, 155, 159
    postwar conferences, 174, 177-78, 184
  WW II, 218, 219
    Allies and, 292
    Anschluss of, 218, 227, 229-30
    defeat in, 247, 250-255, 256
    peace conferences of, 256-57, 266
    Tripartite pact, 239, 241, 242
  Yugoslavia and, 218, 227, 242, 245, 253-54
  See also Bohemia *and* Prussia
Glasnost, definition, 368
  See also Gorbachev, reforms of
Golden Bull of 1356, 38
Golden Bull of 1222, 32
Gorbachev, reforms of, 368-69, 371, 373, 375, 376-77
  acceptance of, 378, 381-82, 383, 384
  consequences of, 395, 396, 397
  resistance to, 377, 380, 385, 386, 387, 388
Great Britain, 81
  Balkans and, 131-35, 142-43
  Chamberlain plan, 230-31
  Congress of Berlin, 134-35
  East Europe and, 209, 214-15, 283, 397
  France and *Entente Cordiale*, 148
  Germany and, 188, 230, 231, 235
  London, treaty of, 175
  Ottoman question, 103, 104, 131-35, 145

Poland and, 87, 234-35
  Curzon line, 264-66
  Russia/USSR, 148, 215, 264
  Suez crisis, 325, 397
  Teheran Conference, 265
  WW I, 150, *See* Triple Entente
  Yalta conference and, 257, 264-66
  Yugoslavia, 242, 253
Great invasions (2nd-10th centuries), 17-24
Great Powers, 209, 214, 220-21
Greece, Ancient, 15, 16
Greece, 15, 16, 17, 22
  Aegean coast, 179
  Albania and, 197, 255, 377
  Balkan Wars, 144-46
  Bulgar minority, 223
  Declaration of Corfu, 153
  Empire at Nicea, 34, 45
  Greeks in Bulgaria, 34, 61
  Macedonia, 142, 145
  Orthodox Church, 29, 56, 62
  Ottoman domination, 45, 75, 81
  revolt for independence, 82, 83, 103, 131
  Serbs and Romans, 46
  Treaty of Bucharest, 145
  Triple Entente, 153
  WW II, 217, 241, 242, 243, 254
Greek Orthodox Church, 5, 60-62, 66, 87, 103, 183
  in Albania, 197, 399
  birth of, 55
  in Yugoslavia, 184, 301, 402
  See also Uniate church
Guest Workers, 350
Gypsies, 3, 4, 182, 183

Habsburg Dynasty, 216, 394
  Austrian empire and, 76, 81, 88
  consolidation of power, 58, 62-64, 68
  collapse of, 155, 160m
  Congress of Vienna, 79
  Holy Roman empire and, 49, 50, 51, 52, 53, 57
  in Hungary, 65-67
Hanseatic league, 31
Hellenes, 15
Helsinki accords, 345, 388
Hetaerie, Society of, 83

Hohenzollern Dynasty, 106, 136, 155
Holy Alliance (1815), 81, 86
Holy Roman Empire, 35, 45, 54, 57, 58
  Bohemia and, 27, 29-30, 53, 57
  center of, 37-39, 41
  Counter-Reform in, 52, 62-64
  end of in 1806, 81
  founding under Otti I, 27
  Hungary and, 30, 49, 53, 57, 62, 65-68
  Hussites in, 41-43, 50
  Ottoman Turks against, 49, 53, 57, 58, 65-66, 68
  Reformation and, 49, 50, 51, 52
  Thirty years war, 62-64, 65
  See also Habsburg dynasty
Hospodars, definition of, 83
Human rights, 380, 383, 384, 388
Hundred Years War, 36, 38
Hungarian Language, 2, 91, 124-25
Hungarian Revolution of 1956, intro, 319-325, 366, 397
Hungarian Soviet Republic, 169-71, 186, 187, 194, 195, 196, 214
Hungarian War of Independence (1848), 100-02
Hungaro-Croat Compromise (1868), 112, 124, 125
Hungary, 16
  Anjous dynasty in, 37m, 39-40
  anti-Semitism in, 4, 195, 196, 249-50, 255-56
  Arrow-Cross party, 187, 196, 227, 250, 255-56, 284
  Austrian empire, 65, 66-67, 75, 78, 81, 90-91
  Ausgleich, 110-12
  unrest in, 96, 96-98
  revolution of 1848, 98-100, 100-02
  Bohemia and, 30, 39, 43, 44, 62, 63
  bolshevism in, 163, 169-71, 173, 195, 238
  bourgeois revolution (1918), 163, 169
  christianity in, 27, 28, 31
  Communist party, 170, 195-96, 284
    postwar, 262, 284-85
    take-over of, 286-88
  Congress of Vienna, 81, 107
  Croatia and, 16, 30, 31, 39
    compromise with, 112, 124, 125
  war with, 97-98, 99
  Czechoslovakia, invasion of, 229, 231-32, 233
  Danubian federation, 215, 256, 398
  Dual Monarchy, during, 108-26
  early peoples, 18, 19, 20, 21, 22-23, 24, 27
  economics of, 208-11, 215, 274, 286
  ethnic minorities in, 78, 89, 91
    anti-Magyar agitation, 97-100, 101, 102, 112
    in Dual Monarchy, 116-19, 124-26, 163-64, 270
  France, influence of, 47, 76, 77, 78
  Franco-Hungarian treaty, 216
  Germany in WW II, 218, 226, 229-33, 238-39, 244
    occupation by, 249-50
    war with, 284
  Habsburgs and 57, 62, 65-68, 194
  Horthy dictatorship, 194-96, 229, 249-50, 255, 284, 285
  independent Kingdom, 31-32, 33m, 35, 43-45
  Italy: influence of, 39-40, 44-45
    WW II and, 217, 218, 231, 239
  Little Entente against, 218-19
  Magyar minority in other countries, 212
    in Czechoslovakia, 3, 192, 224, 225, 231-32
    deportations of, 269m, 270
    in Rumania, 3, 91, 201, 221, 222, 223, 239-40
    in Slovakia, 342, 395
    in USSR, 3, 372
    in Yugoslavia, 3, 184, 205, 225, 254, 372, 374, 378
  nationalism in, 77, 90-91, 96-100
  Ottoman Turks, 43, 47
    invasions of, 48-50, 52, 53
    war with, 65, 66
  Poland, WW II ally, 233-36, 238-39
  Reformation in, 42-43, 44
    Counter, 51, 65
  Ruthenia, annexation of, 181, 232-33
  Serbia and, 47, 48, 101
  Soviet Republic of, 169-71, 186, 187, 194-96, 214
  Tartar invasions, 34-35

430

Hungary, *continued*
  Transylvania: independence, 49-50
    conflict over with Rumania, 182,
      203, 239, 267
    Treaty of Trianon, 3, 179, 182, 195,
      216, 231, 239, 267
    USSR, WW II and, 244, 250, 255-56,
      267, 285
    Vienna Arbitrations, 228m, 231-32,
      239, 240
    Yugoslavia, WW II and, 239, 242-43,
      254
  WW I, 162-64, 179, 182, 183
  WW II, 218, 229-33, 238-39, 245,
    249-50, 284
    peace treaties of, 229, 239, 266
    See also Austria-Hungary
      and Transylvania
Hungary, People's Republic of, 401
  Church, relations with, 306-07, 330
  collectives in, 307, 312, 370
  COMECON, 329, 384
  Communist party, takeover of, 284-88
  Czechoslovakia, Prague Spring, 336,
    338, 339, 342
  dam agreement, 371, 384
  debt, foreign, 370, 383, 384
  destalinization, 312-13, 319, 329
  dissident groups in, 345-46, 383, 388
  human rights in, 345-46, 382-83, 388
  Petofi Circle, 312, 319-20
  political prisoners, 304, 312, 329, 382
  provisory government (1944), 284-85
  purges in, 285, 302-04
  reforms: of Kadar, 326, 329-30, 342
    of Gorbachev, 382
  Revolution, intro, 319-25, 366
  Rumania, conflict over minority in, 3,
    372-74, 395
  state police, 285-86, 320-21
  tourism, 329, 344, 383
  Warsaw Pact, 276m, 315, 232, 239, 342
  USSR: dependence on, 285, 371
    allied to, 262, 382
    Hungarians in, 372
    military in, 267, 272-73, 284, 296,
      321, 323
    political involvement, 284, 285, 286
Huns, 18, 19, 21, 22
Hussite Wars (1420-1436), 42

Hussites (United Brotherhood), 41-44, 50,
  62, 182
  See also Utraquistes

Illyrian, 15, 21
Illyrism, 90, 97, 125-26
IMF (International Monetary Fund), 389
IMRO (Interior Macedonian
  Revolutionary Organization), 142-43,
  199, 200, 207
Income Tax Law, 369, 383
Indo-European, 2, 15-16
Industrialization, 128, 208, 212
  development of, 10, 137, 211, 380
  inefficiency of, 369, 384
  low level of, 187
  policy of, 308, 309
Inflation, postwar, 344
  in Hungary, 286, 383
  in Poland, 352, 370, 391
  in Yugoslavia, 342, 350, 377
Irredentism, 136, 137, 373
Iron Curtain, intro, 276m
Iron Guard (Guardists), 187, 204,
  239, 241
Islam (Muslim), 5, 51, 61, 402
  among Albanians, 59, 197, 348, 399
  Ottoman Turks and, 44, 53, 58
  in Rumania, 183
  in Yugoslavia, 184, 351, 402
Istria, 110, 268
  France and, 78, 79
  to Italy in Treaty of London, 175
Israel, emigration to, 4, 333, 334
Italy
  Albania, 145, 152, 168, 175, 377
    annexation of, 197, 198, 243
    liberation of, 247, 254-55
    protector of, 216-17
  Austria-Hungary, 115, 117, 118
  Austrian Empire, under, 96, 97, 100,
    109, 114, 115
  Bohemia, 37, 38
  Bulgaria and, in WW II, 217
  Communist party, and USSR, 262
  ethnic minorities, 155, 177, 220
  Germany, WW II ally of, 218, 219,
    228, 234-35, 239, 242
  Goths in, 18, 19, 20m, 21
  Hungary, influence on, 39-40, 44-45

431

Italy, *continued*
  Hungary, WW II, 217, 218, 219, 231, 239
  London Conference, 145
  Munich agreements, 188, 230-31
  Pact of Steel, 234
  Poland, 56, 57, 279
  Revolt of Lombardy and Venetia, 96, 97
  Tardieu Plan, 212
  Treaty of London, 152, 168, 175, 178
  Tripartite Pact, 239
  Triple Alliance, 142, 149
  Turks, war with, 144
  United movement of 1859-60, 106, 109
  WW I, 152, 177
    peace settlements, 177, 178, 179
  WW II, defeat in, 242
  Yugoslavia: annexation by, 264, 268
    dispute with, 216, 217, 243, 253
    WW II, 207

Jacobins, 78
Jagiello dynasty, 53-56
Janissaries, 45, 61, 81
Japan: Axis power, 239
  war with Russia, 143
Jesuits, 51-52, 55-56, 62-65
Jewish peoples in eastern Europe, 4, 31, 61, 95, 142, 181, 182, 183, 195, 273, 334
  anti-Semitism, 115, 118, 136-37, 245, 334
  Communist regimes, under, 4, 334
  concentration camps, 244, 246
  emigration to Israel and USA, 4, 334
  extremist groups, 187, 196
    in Rumania, 201, 203-04, 241
    in Hungary, 195-96, 255
  Nazi persecution of, 4, 237, 244, 249-50
  pogroms, 244, 249-50
  refuge for, 4, 40, 249
  Rumania, WW II, 240-41, 244
  Soviet persecution, 237-38

Karageorgevitch Dynasty, 83
Karlovici, Peace of (1699), 66
Katyn Massacre, 246, 251, 265
KGB, 129, 310
Kingdom of the Serbs, Croats and Slovenes
  See Yugoslavia

Kosovo, Albanians in, 3, 184, 222, 243, 270, 347-49, 374-75, 378, 395, 402
  Albania, annexation by, 243, 255
  conflict over, 348-49, 374-75, 378
  Serbia and, 348
  Yugoslavia, underdevelopment in, 328
  See also Albania *and* Yugoslavia
KOR (Polish Worker's Defense Committee), 345, 354, 356, 361, 363
Kosice Program, 256, 269, 288, 290
Kuciuk-Kainardji, Peace of, 60

Labor Migration, Hungary, 209, 210, 212
Latvia, 151m
  Russian Empire and, 75
  USSR and, 152, 235, 238, 268
Latvian language, 1
Land Reform, post-WW I, 210, 211
League of Nations, 169, 178, 210, 212
  national minorities, 220-27
Lenin, policy on nationalities, 372
Liberum Veto in Poland, 69-70, 72, 79
Lithuania, 75, 151m
  German territories, 178, 180
  Poland and, 173, 180
  USSR, 152, 235, 238, 268
Lithuanian language, 1
Little Entente, 215, 216, 219, 231, 234-35, 251m, 264
Lombards, 19, 21
London Conference (1913), 145
London, Polish Government in Exile, 252, 266, 279, 280
London, Treaty of (1915), 152, 153, 168, 175, 178
Lower Messia (Bulgaria), 2, 16, 20, 21, 22, 32, 34
Lutheranism, 5, 50-51, 52, 55, 182, 183
Luxembourg Dynasty, 36-39, 41

Macedonia, 16, 24, 28, 46
  Albania and, 142, 145, 348
  Balkan Wars, 144-46
  Bulgaria, 34, 132, 297
  Communist party of, 206
  Congress of Berlin, 135, 142
  Greece, from, 223, 399
  IMRO, 142-43, 199, 200, 207
  minorities in, 142
  Ottoman Turks, under, 131

Macedonia, *continued*
  Rumania and, 34, 201
  Serbs and, 131, 141-42, 145
  Treaty of Bucharest, 145
  Yugoslavia, in, 200, 207, 217, 254
    Bulgaro-Macedons in, 3, 184, 199, 222, 270, 349-50
    conflict over, 374, 395
    underdevelopment of, 328
    See also Bulgaria *and* Yugoslavia
Madgeburg, Law of, 30
Magyar minorities, *See* Hungary
March Laws (1848), 96, 100
Marseille Assassination, 207, 218, 242
Marshall Plan, 10, 290
Martial law, *See* Poland, People's Republic of
Marxism, 5, 6, 129
  economic failure of, 396
  guarantees of, 369, 384
Marxism-Leninism, 262, 313, 339
Massacre of Chios, 82
Minorities, Treaty on the Protection of (1919), 221-22
Minority groups in Eastern Europe
  See under minorities of each country
Mohacs, Turkish invasion at, 49
Moldavia, *See* Rumania
Molotov-Ribbentrop Pact,
  See Russo-German Pact
Montenegro, 61, 243
  Balkan Wars, 144-46
  Committee in London, 153-54
  Congress of Berlin, 134-35
  Ottoman Turks and, 131, 132
  Russia and, 83, 141, 148
  Serbia and, 83, 133, 139, 144, 148, 152
  Treaty of San Stefano, 135
  WW I, 148, 152
  Yugoslavia and, 165, 183, 208, 254
Moravia, 2, 16, 21, 27, 42, 44, 52
  Austrian Empire in, 110, 116, 178
  Crown of St. Wenceslas, 62-64, 116
  Czechoslovakia and, 181, 188, 225
  German occupation, 233, 245, 250
  Great Kingdom of, 22
  nationalism of, 98
  See also Bohemia, Czechoslovakia

Moscow Accords, 340-41
Munich, Pact of (1938), 231
Muslim, *See* Islam

Nagyvarad, Peace of (1538), 53
Napoleonic Empire, 78, 115
Nationalism, awakening of, 25, 76-79, 128-30, 144, 197
  in Austrian empire, 88-92, 95-102
  of Balkan peoples, 81-84, 144, 197
  in East Bloc, post-WW II, 342
  in Hungary, 77, 90-91, 96-100, 100-02
  interwar period, 161-64, 164-69, 173, 342
  in Ottoman empire, 94-95, 103
  of Poland, 93-94, 128-30
Nationalization of institutions, 308-09
NATO (North Atlantic Treaty Organization), 385, 386
Nazi, 4, 233
  anti-Semitism of, 237, 244, 249-50
  rise of party, 200
Nemanjic Dynasty, 32, 46, 47
Neuilly, Treaty of (1919), 177, 179
Nuclear power plants, 371
Nystadt, Peace Treaty of (1721), 69

October Diploma, 109, 110
October revolution, *See* Bolshevik revolution
Oliva, Peace of (1660), 69
Olomouc, Peace of, 44
Olympic games, Los Angeles, 387
OPEC, 344
Ostrogoths, 18, 19, 20m, 21
Ottoman Empire, 4, 5, 35-36, 52, 58, 65
  Albania, 144, 145
  Balkans, in, 58-62, 81, 131-35, 141
    wars, 144-47
  Baltaliman pact, 95
  Bulgaria and, 46, 47, 60-61, 81, 131, 132-33, 135, 139-41
  Central Powers and, WW I, 150, 159
  Christians under, 103, 104, 142, 146
  Congress of Vienna, 80-82
  Crimean War, 104, 107, 131
  disturbances in, 94-95
  14th-15th centuries, 45-50
  Greek revolt against, 82

433

Ottoman Empire, *continued*
  Holy Roman Empire, against, 49, 53, 57, 58, 65-66, 68
  Macedonia and, 142-43
  Montenegro and, 144-46
  nationalism of subjects, 103
  peace settlements, WW I, 174, 175
  religious tolerance in, 58
  Russo-Turkish Wars, 60, 71, 80, 133-35, 136
  Serbs, 46-47, 61-62, 81, 82, 131
  Slavs in, 52, 58, 65, 75, 78
  Treaty of Paris, 104-105
  Young Turk revolution, 143, 144

Pact of Steel (1939), 234
Pannonia (West Hungary), 16, 17, 18, 19, 20m, 21
Paris Peace Conference (1919), 159, 165, 166, 168, 173-183, 187, 189-90, 193, 202, 209-10, 220
Paris, Treaty of (1856), 104, 105
Partisans, 253-54, 256, 274, 277
Partitions of Poland, 71, 72, 84-88
  Fourth, 233-38
Passarovic, Peace of (1718), 66
Patriarchate of Constantinople, 60
Pax austriaca, 88
Peace treaties, *See under* name of city
Perestroika, 368
  See also Gorbachev, reforms of
Petofi Circle, 312, 319-20
Petrovic-Njegos Dynasty, 61
Pharnariots, 60, 83
Philosophes, 76
Piast dynasty, Poland, 27, 35, 40
Plague (Black Death), 36
Pogrom of Ujvidek (1942), 249
Poland
  Austrian Galicia, 85, 94, 123, 130, 150, 162
  bolshevism in, 171-72
  Catholic church, 43, 55, 56, 57
    persecution of, 87, 108, 128
  Communist party, 186, 194, 252, 262
  Confederation of Bar, 70
  Congress Kingdom, 80, 85-86
  Congress of Vienna, 79-80
  early peoples, 20, 22
  economics, interwar, 208, 209, 210, 211-12

  foreign aggression, 69-70, 71-72
  France (Little Entente), 151m, 215, 219, 234-35, 264
  French revolution and, 76, 77, 78
  Germany and, 166, 167, 168, 172, 177-78, 215
    influence of, 30-31
    relations with, 233, 246-47
    WW II invasion by, 234-37
  Germans, expulsion of, 256, 269m
  Golden Age, 54-57
  Great Poland, 29, 40-41, 77, 84
  independence, 154-55, 166-68, 172-73, 192, 363
  industrialization, 128, 208, 211
  Jagellio dynasty, 53-56
  Jews in, 40, 181, 237-38, 246
  Katyn Massacre, 246, 251, 265
  Kosciuszko's revolt, 71, 77
  land reform, 211, 224
  liberalization under Alexander, 106-07
  Liberum Veto, 69-70, 72, 79
  London government, 252, 266, 279, 280
  minorities, 220-21, 222, 224
  National Council in Paris, 167
  nationalism, 76, 77, 128-30
  partitions: by Austria, Prussia and Russia, 71, 72, 84-88
    fourth partition, 233-38
  Piast family, 27, 35, 40
  Pilsudski dictatorship, 192-94
  Prussian Poland, 69, 70, 71-72, 84-85, 93, 130
  Red & White parties, 86-87, 106-07
  Reformation in, 51, 55, 56
  revolutions:
    (1830-31), 86-88, 94, 106, 107, 128
    (1848), 93-94
  Russian Poland, 79, 85-88, 94, 106-08, 128-29, 150-52, 166, 167
  Russo-Polish Wars, 69
    (1831), 87
    (1863), 108-109
    (1919), 171-73, 186, 215
  Tartar invasions, 34
  Warsaw uprising, 252-53, 256, 266, 273, 279
  Versailles, Treaty of, 177-78, 180-81, 200

434

Poland, *continued*
  WW I: Allies, 151, 154, 167-68, 172
    Central Powers, 150, 154, 166-67
    peace treaties, 168, 173
  WW II: and Allies, 236, 264-65, 266, 279
    Czechoslovakia, 228, 230-33
    Hungary and, 216, 233-34, 235-36
    occupation during, 234-37
    peace treaties, 257, 265-66, 268-69, 279
    resistance, 251-53, 279
  USSR, WW I and, 150, 152
    War of 1919-20, 215
    WW II invasion by, 230, 234, 236-37, 246, 255-56, 268
Polish People's Republic, 2-6, 8-11, 395
  Catholic church in, 4, 317, 344
    activism of, 353, 354-55, 356, 394
    and state, 318, 319, 331, 365, 389-91
  COMECON and, 331, 354, 360, 401
  Communist party, takeover, 10, 11, 279-81
  debt to West, 331, 343-44, 391
  destalinization, 315, 316-19
  dissidents, 356, 360, 390-91
  economics, 10, 401
    inflation, 352, 370, 391
    problems, 331, 342, 353, 354, 391-92
  Geirek era, 353-54, 356
  Gomulka era, 331-32, 353
  KOR (Worker's Defense Committee), 345, 354, 356, 361, 363, 390, 391
  Lenin shipyards, closing, 393
  martial law, 364-66, 388, 389
    suspension of, 390
  Pope, visits by, 355-56, 389, 390
  Popieluszko murder, 390-91
  Prague Spring, 332, 352
  reforms and, 383-84, 391-92
  shortages in, 355, 362, 370, 391
  Solidarity, 263, 345, 357-366, 388, 389, 395
    underground, 390-93
  state police, *ZOMOS*, 363, 389
  strikes:
    (1956), 317, 325-26, 352
    (1970) 326, 344, 352-53, 358
    (1976) 344, 354
    (1980) 344, 356-58
    strikes (1988), 392
  USA, sanctions by, 389, 391
  USSR: allied with, 279, 371
    Poles in, 372
    Red Army in, 272-73
    and Solidarity, 263, 357, 359, 360-61, 364, 365
    surveillance by, 299, 318-19
    Warsaw Pact and, 315, 359, 360, 366, 389, 401
Polish Corridor, 177-78
Polish language, 2, 128
Polish Organic Statute, 87
Political prisoners, 279, 303-05, 312, 315, 329, 333, 345, 356, 382, 391
  See also Soviet Union
Political reform, 382, 383, 386
Pomerania, 40, 54, 70
Posnania, Poles in, 84, 88, 177
  under Prussia, 71, 80, 94
Potsdam Conference (1945), 266
Prague, defenestration of (1618), 63
Prague Spring (1968), 333-41, 343, 352, 366, 397
Pravda (Moscow), 357, 380
Principalities, Danubian Moldavia and Wallachia, *See* Rumania
Protection of Minorities
  Treaties on (1919), 220-26
Protestantism, 5, 182, 183, 400, 401, 402
  Hussites/Utraquistes and, 41, 43, 44, 50
  Lutheranism and, 50-51, 52, 55
  persecution of, 51, 56, 307
  Reformation of, 50-52, 55-57
    in Bohemia, 49, 52, 62-64
Prussia, 27, 31, 55, 67, 177
  Congress of Vienna, 79-81
  division of, post-WW I, 177, 178
  Holy Alliance and, 81
  Kingdom of, 75
  Prussian Poland, 69-72, 84-85, 130
    revolutions of, 93-94, 107
  See also Germany
Przemyslide dnnasty, 25, 27, 29, 30, 31, 35, 36, 40, 41, 42
Purges, 262, 275-76, 278, 282, 285, 301-04

Rapallo, Treaty of (1922), 214

435

Red Army in Eastern Europe, 253, 256, 267, 272-73, 282-83, 284, 292, 296, 311, 341
Reformation, Protestant, 50-52, 55-57
in Bohemia, 49, 50-52, 53, 62-64
Religion, 4-5, 182, 183, 184, 197, 351, 399-402
persecution of, 4, 52, 87, 279, 305-07, 344, 394
revival of, 344-45, 396
tolerance of, 58, 66, 70, 121
Resources, 120, 209
Revolutions of 1848, 93-103, 108
Riga, Treaty of (1921), 173
Roman Catholic Church, 29
in Albania, 197, 399
in Bohemia, 41, 49, 50, 51, 52, 53
state religion, 63, 64, 119
Byzantine Christianity and, 29
Calvinism and, 51, 55
in Communist Poland, 4, 317, 344
activism of, 353, 354-55, 356, 394
church-state relations, 318, 319, 331, 365, 389-92
Counter Reformation of, 51-52, 55-57
Czech church, 44, 182, 289, 335, 400
German clergy, 30, 38, 41
Habsburgs and, 53, 57, 65, 66, 88, 109
Holy Alliance of, 81, 86
Hussites/Utraquistes and, 41-43, 44, 50
Lutheranism and, 50-51, 52, 55
Ottoman Turks and, 53, 57, 58
under, 103, 104, 142, 146
persecution of, 87, 108, 128
Protestant Reformation and, 50-52, 55-57
socialism, under, 4-5, 399-402
church-state relations, 289, 330, 335
persecution of, 4, 279, 305-07, 342, 345, 394
revival of, 345, 351, 396
wealth of, 41
Roman Empire, 16-19, 45
Rome-Berlin Axis, 234
Rumania (Moldavia and Wallachia), 183
Antonescu dictatorship, 240-41, 244, 247, 281, 283
Austria-Hungary, 116-18, 131, 136, 182
autonomy of, 105, 131, 136, 281
Balkan wars, 145, 147m

Bessarabia and Bukovina, 136, 162, 165
ceded to Russia, 239-40, 244, 267
regained in WW I, 178, 182, 200
Byzantium and, 29, 32
Carol II, reign of, 204-05, 239-40
Communist party: formation of, 137, 201, 203
takeover of, 281-84
WW II, 247
Congress of Berlin, 134m, 135, 136, 137
Couza, reign of, 105-06
Crimean War, autonomy after, 104-06, 131
Dobrudja, 145
Bulgars and, 183, 217, 239, 241, 267
early peoples, 18, 20m, 23m
fascism in, 239-41
French influence, 77, 84, 107
Germany and, 218, 227
Hungary and, 48
conflict over Transylvania, 182, 203, 239, 395
invasion of, 170-71
industrialization, 137, 208, 211
interwar period: politics, 200-05
economics, 208, 209, 210-12, 215
irredentism, 136, 137, 373
Iron Guard in, 187, 204, 239, 241
Jews in, 95, 183
anti-Semitism, 115, 136-137, 201, 203-04
during WW II, 240-41, 244
land reforms, 201, 210-11, 224
minorities, 182-83, 187, 201, 222, 224-26
Germans deported, 3, 269m, 270
treaty on, 220-21, 223, 224
nationalism among, 81, 84, 163, 239, 240
nationalism of, 77, 78, 84, 94-95
Ottoman Turks and, 46-47, 48, 59-60, 75, 81, 83-84, 94
peasant revolts, 137
Principalities, 35, 46, 60, 95
name of "Rumania," 105
Russia, 60, 141
occupation by, 80, 83, 84
uprising against, 94, 95, 104

Rumania, *continued*
  Transylvania, Vlachs in, 32, 35, 47
    WW I annexation of, 149, 163-64, 165, 182, 200-01
    WW II, 267, 282
  Treaty of Paris, 104-05
  Treaty of San Stefano, 135, 136
  Treaty of Trianon, 182
  Treaty of Versailles, 200
  USSR, occupation by, 247-48, 255, 267, 272-73, 281
  Vienna arbitrations, 239-40
  Vlachs in Macedonia, 94-95, 142
  WW I: Central powers, and, 149, 152
    divided loyalties, 149, 150, 153
    and Entente, 151m, 152, 153, 155, 173
    peace treaties, 155, 182
  WW II: and Allies, 247-48
    and Germany, 239-41, 244, 247, 248
    in Little Entente, 216, 219, 231
    aftermath of, 267, 274
  See also Transylvania
Rumanian People's Republic, 2, 4, 6, 7
  agriculture, 307, 342, 380-81
  Balkan conference, 377
  Ceaucescu, rule of, 330-31, 379-81
  Church and, 5, 305, 307, 402
  COMECON, 330
  Communist party: takeover of, 281-84
    and USSR, 262, 282-83
  destalinization, 239-40, 314, 330
  dissident movements, 345, 346, 381
  economics, 274, 281, 342, 402
  foreign debt, 370
  Hungary, conflict over minority of, 3, 372-74, 395
  purges in, 282, 303
  reforms, resistance to, 380, 381
  shortages, 370, 371, 379, 381
  USA, relations with, 283, 380
  USSR, dependence on, 371, 380
    Moldavians in, 372
    occupation by, 281, 282, 296
  Warsaw Pact, 276m, 314

Russia, 28, 58, 60, 75, 114
  anti-Semitism in, 115
  Austria-Hungary and, 135, 142-43, 148-49
  Balkans and, 82-84, 104
    involvement in, 131-35, 142-43
    wars of, 144-46
  Bessarabia/Bukovina and, 135, 136, 165, 244
  Bulgaria and, 132-35, 139-41, 142-43
  Congress of Berlin, 134-35
  Congress of Vienna, 79-81
  Crimean War, 103, 104
  Decembrist's conspiracy, 86
  France, alliances with, 114, 148, 149, 150
  Greek independence and, 82
  Holy Alliance, 81, 86
  Moldavian uprisings, 94, 95, 181
  October revolution (1917), 151m
  Poland and, 69-72, 79, 85-88, 94, 106-08, 123, 128-29
  Revolution of 1904-05, 129
  Rumania (Vlachs) and, 60, 80, 83, 84, 94, 95
  russification, 114, 128
  Russo-Polish wars, 69
    (1831) 87
    (1863) 108-09
    (1919) 171-73, 186, 215
  Russo-Turkish Wars, 60, 71
    (1808-12) 80
    (1863) 133, 135-36
  Slavs in Austria-Hungary and, 114
  Treaty of Paris, 104-05
  Treaty of San Stefano, 135
  See also USSR
Russian revolution (1905), 129
Russian revolutions of 1917, *See* Bolshevik revolution
Russo-German Pact (1939), 235-38, 264
Russo-Japanese war, 143
Russo-Polish non-aggression pact (1934), 215, 236
Russo-Polish Wars, *See* Russia
Russo-Turkish Wars, *See* Russia
Ruthenia, 2, 5, 176, 228m
  in Austria, 116, 117m, 118, 122, 123
  in Austrian Poland, 85, 88, 94
  in Czechoslovakia, 176, 181, 188, 192, 228m
    autonomists, 229, 231
    surrrender of to USSR, 268
  Hungary and, 35, 181, 209
  WW II annexation of, 232-33

Ruthenia, *continued*
  national minorities in, 181, 183, 222, 224, 225
  USSR, 268
  Red Army in, 273

Saint Germain, Treaty of (1919), 165, 177, 179, 180, 182
San Stefano, Treaty of (1878), 135, 136
Sanctions against Poland, 389, 391
Sarajevo assassination, 149-50
Scandinavia, 16
Second World War, *See* World War II
Self-determination, 177, 184-85, 220
Seljuk Turks, 45
Serbia, 2, 16, 20, 32, 46
  Albania and, 146, 348
  See also Kosovo
  Austria-Hungary and, 132-33, 135-36, 138-39, 145-46, 141, 143
  liberation from, 155, 164
  Austro-Serb conflict, 148-50
  autonomy, 82, 131
  Balkan Wars and, 144-46
  Black Hand, 146
  Bosnia-Herzegovina, 132-33, 143, 149
  Chetniks and, 253-54, 279
  Congress of Vienna, 80-81
  Hungary, against, 47, 101
  London conference of 1913, 145
  Macedonia, 46, 142-43, 145
  Montenegro, 133, 139, 144, 146, 148, 152, 165
  nationalism, 81
  Obrenovitch/Karageorgevitch, 82-83, 138-39
  Ottomans, 46, 47, 61-62, 81, 82, 131
  postwar gains, 164-65, 183-84
  pre-war status, 137-39
  Russians and, 81-82, 83, 138, 139, 141, 142, 144, 149
  Sarajevo assassination, 149-50
  Treaty of Bucharest, 145-46
  Treaty of San Stefano, 135
  Turks, against, 133, 137, 139, 144-46
  WW I, 148-55
    treaties of, 173
    Triple Entente, and, 148, 152
  WW II, 279
    Germany and, 247, 253, 279

Yugoslavia, 153, 164, 165, 254, 301
  dominating group in, 205-07, 242, 328, 349, 378
  in military, 379
Serbo-Croatian language, 2, 90
Siberia, 285
Sielicka, Statute of, 40
Silesia, 34, 40, 44, 98, 209, 237
  Crown of St. Wenceslas, 62-64
  ethnic composition of, 116
  Poland and, 178, 180, 237, 265, 268, 353
  Polish-German tension in, 233, 234
  See also Poland
Six-Day War of 1967, 333
Skupshtina, 82-83, 218
Slavic language, 1-2
Slavic peoples, 1, 2
  Austria-Hungary, 78, 115-16, 122-26, 162, 163, 164
  early Slavs, 16, 19, 20m, 21, 22, 24, 25, 27, 29
  nationalism of, 88-90
  pan-Slavism, 97, 98, 99, 114, 115
  in Poland, 83, 85, 88
  Tartars and, 35, 45, 46, 47, 77
  Yugoslavism of, 126, 162, 163
  See also Yugoslavia
Slavonia, 31, 32
  in Croatia, 110, 111, 112, 118
Slovakia, 2, 5, 22, 24, 175
  anti-Semitism in, 245, 334
  autonomists, 98, 118-89, 190-91, 229
  Communist party of, 250, 333, 342
  Czechs, conflict with, 189-92, 229, 245, 395
  Germany, WW II, 229, 245, 256
  resistance to, 250-51
  Hungarian kingdom, 116-20, 122, 125
  Hungarians in, 342, 395
  Hungary, Slovaks in, 42, 66, 89, 98, 179
  Munich pact and independence, 231, 232-33
  nationalism in, 89, 125
  as Soviet Republic, 170, 186
  Treaty of Trianon, 181
  USSR, 244, 251
  See also Czechoslovakia, Slovaks in

Slovenia, 175
  Slovenes, 2, 4, 21, 22, 90
  Illyrian Croatia, 115, 119, 122, 123, 126
  in Yugoslavia, 153, 162, 164, 183-84, 207, 254, 375, 378
  WW II, division of, 243
Smalkald League, 52
Society of Tir, 130
Solidarity, *See* Poland, People's Republic of
Soviet Republics: in Hungary, 169-71, 186, 187, 194-96, 214
  in Slovakia, 170, 186
Spain, 18, 49
Spanish Civil War, 218, 333
St. Bartholomew Day Massacre, 55
St. Germain-en-laye, Treaty of, 165, 177, 179, 180, 182
St. Petersburg, Treaty of (1772), 71
Stalin Era, 295-309, 310
Statute of Sielicka (1364), 40
Suez Canal, opening of, 132
Suez Crisis, 325, 397
Sweden and Poland, 69
Szamizdat, 345, 383, 393
Szatmar, Peace of (1711), 66
Szklarska-Poreda Conference, 262, 296

Tardieu Plan, 212
Tartar invasions, 34-35, 54
Teheran Conference (1943), intro, 261, 265
Terrorism, in Yugoslavia, 349, 374
Teutonic Knights, 31, 40, 53, 54, 55
Third Socialist International, 161, 169, 171, 201, 205
Third World, 341, 346
Thirty Years War (1618-48), 62-64, 65
Thrace, 16, 34
Tilsit, Peace of, 77
Tirana Pact (1926), 217
Torun, Peace of, 53
Tourism, 332, 339, 344, 381
  travel in East Bloc, 337
  to the West, 329, 350, 383
Trade, exports, 381
  foreign deficit, 343, 370, 371, 378, 383
Transylvania, 35
  Austrian empire, under, 53, 60, 64, 65-67, 81, 95
  Communist party, 282
  early, 3, 23m, 24
  German minority in, 32, 95
  Hungary, conflict over minority, 3, 372-74, 395
  under, 32, 33m, 35, 39, 43, 44, 49-50
  Golden age, 63, 65, 66, 95, 136
  in Dual Monarchy, 110, 111, 120-21, 125
  WW II annexed by, 239
  independent principality, 49-50, 52-53, 55
  Jews in, 118
  Magyar minority in, 3, 22-24, 91
  massacre of, 101, 182, 221-23, 239-40
  Ottoman Turks, 47, 48, 49
  under, 52-53, 65
  Rakoczi insurrection, 66, 67
  Rumania, 163-64, 165
  annexed by, WW I, 182, 200-01
  WW II, 267, 282
  under, 372-74
  Rumanians (Vlachs) in, 23m, 32, 35, 78, 91
  in Dual Monarchy, 118, 125, 131
  revolution of 1848, 95, 98, 101
  Stalinism in, 330-31
  village destruction policy, 373-74
  See also Rumania *and* Hungary
Treaties, *See under* city of signing
Trianon, Treaty of (1920), 165, 177, 179, 181-82, 195, 216, 229, 231, 267
Tripartite Pact (1940), 239, 241, 242
Triple Alliance (1882), 142, 146, 148-55, 150, 159
  Europe, plans for, 152, 154-55, 174-75
  map, 151m
  Poland and, 166-67
Triple Entente, 142, 148, 150, 151m, 152-55, 159
  Hungary and, 194
  interwar tension, 220-26
  Protection of Minorities, 221-23
  Rumania and, 201
  system in Europe, 233
Turkey, 101, 377
  See also Ottoman Empire
Turoc-Szent-Marton, 163, 189
Twentieth Party Congress, 315-16
2000 Words Manifesto, 337, 339

439

Ukraine, 2, 5, 123, 181, 240, 371
  Soviets and, 152, 172, 237
  Tartars and, 34, 35
Unemployment, 384
  in Yugoslavia, 342, 350, 377
Uniate Church, 56, 66, 78, 85, 87, 98, 108, 116, 118, 183
  abolition of in Rumania, 301, 305
  birth of, 55
Unions, 345, 393
  See also Solidarity
United Brotherhood, 43, 50, 52
  See also Hussites
United Nations, 399, 400, 401, 402
United States of America (USA), 197, 248
  Czechoslovakia and, 154, 166, 176, 189, 290, 296
  Germany, division of, 264-66
  immigration to, 176
  independence of (1776), 76
  Marshall Plan, 290, 296
  most-favored nations, 380, 389
  national minorities and, 220
  peace settlements, WW I, 176-77
  Poland and, 167-68, 265
    sanctions against, 389, 391
  Rumania and, 283, 380
  USSR, WW II ally, 264
    Cold War, 295
    detente, 327, 344, 367, 375
  Wilson's Fourteen Points, 176
  WW I, 153-54, 220
  WW II, 247, 250, 255, 264, 265, 266
    at Yalta, 257, 266, 296, 397
United Soviet Socialist Republics (USSR)
  Albania and, 255, 261-62, 268, 297
    break with, 327-28, 346, 376
  Allies, WW II and, 234, 235, 248, 261, 264
  Baltic republics, invasion of, 238, 268
  Bessarabia/Bukovina, annexation of, 9, 239, 240
  Bolshevik revolution, 151m, 152, 169, 176, 186, 261
  Bulgaria and, 200, 241-42
    ally of, 262, 330, 381
    occupation of, 255, 265, 267
    war with, 244, 248-49
  China, problems with, 328, 331
  Civil War, 198
  COMECON, 299, 327, 341, 371
  Cominform, 262, 296, 297, 299, 310, 316
  Czechoslovakia, 256, 265, 343
    detente, 288, 326-27, 344, 367, 375
    Prague Spring, 334-41
    relations with, 216, 299-30, 261, 271, 387
    Ruthenia from, 268, 273
  Eastern Europe
    aid to Communist takeovers, 255-56, 261-62, 272, 274-75
    as buffer zone, 214, 215, 264
    destalinizattion of, 239-40, 310-20, 327, 332-33
    economic dependence of, 342, 369-71
    occupation of, 255-56, 265, 343, 264-66, 267, 271, 272-73, 282-83, 284-85, 292, 296, 343, 397
    policy towards, 261-63, 295-96, 310, 341, 343, 369, 397
    trade with, 296, 341-42, 371
  East European minorities in, 3, 372
  East Germany, 296, 385, 386, 387
    Berlin uprising, 311-12
  France, 234-35
  Germany and, 155, 214, 215
    Communist party of, 284-86, 293-94
    division of, 264-66
    invasion by, 242-43, 244, 261, 264, 292
    post-war interference in, 293-94
  Great Britain and, 215, 264
  Hungary and, 382
    revolution of 1956, 320-23
    war with, 244-45, 250
  Poland: ally, 215, 236, 279
    borders, 192, 236, 264-66
    Communist party, 194, 318
    invasion of, 230, 234, 235-37
    wars with, 171-173, 186, 192, 215
    WW I, 150, 152
    WW II, 168, 215, 246, 251-53, 299
  prison camps in, 237-38
  reforms of, 367, 368-69, 371, 375, 395-97
  Rumania, 239, 240
    Communist party, 282-83
    relations with, 330-31, 380, 381

440

USSR, *continued*
  Russo-German Pact, 235-38, 261, 264, 268
  Slovak revolt and, 250-51, 256
  Solidarity and, 246, 263, 268, 332, 357, 359-61, 364, 365, 390
  Stalinism, 295, 300-01
    purges of, 301-05
  succession crisis, 367, 368, 375
  Teheran conferences, 261, 265
  territories gained, WW II, 267-68, 271
  Third international, 169
  Treaty of Brest-Litovsk, 152, 168, 172
  Treaty of Rapallo, 214
  Triple Entente in, 148, 150, 151m
  20th Party Congress, 315-16, 327
  USA and, 264-66, 290, 295
  Warsaw Pact and, 315, 325, 326, 342, 343, 359, 367, 369, 397
  World Communism and, 169, 261, 262, 296, 396
  at Yalta, 256-57, 261, 266, 397
  Yugoslavia and, 261, 264
    break with, 262, 295, 297-300, 346
    loyalty, 278, 296-97
    rapprochement, 328-29, 346, 351
  See also Russia
Ustaschians (Ustasha), 206, 207, 254
Utraquism, 42, 43, 44, 50, 51, 63

Vasvar, Treaty of, 65
Versailles, Treaty of (1919), 177-78, 180, 200
Vidovdan Constitution, 205-06
Vienna Arbitrations (1938 and 1940), 239-40
Vienna, Congress of, 75, 79-81, 84, 102
Vienna, Peace of (1809), 78
Village destruction policy, 373-74
Visigoths, 18, 19, 20m, 21
Vojvodina, 243, 254
  Hungarians in, 3, 184, 205, 225, 254, 372, 374, 378, 395
  Serbia, part of, 378
  Yugoslavia, joining, 164, 183

Wallachia, *See* Rumania
Wars of the North, 69

Warsaw Pact (1955), intro, 315, 328, 371
  Hungary, 329
    revolution and, 323, 326
  members of, 276m, 399, 400, 401, 402
    relations between, 342, 371, 373
  Prague, invasion of, 338, 340, 342, 359, 360, 387
  Poland, 359, 360, 366, 389
  Soyuz '81 maneuvers, 359
  USSR, policy of, 325, 326, 343, 397
Warsaw Uprising (1944), 252-53, 256, 266, 273, 279
West Germany, *See* Federal Republic of Germany
Western nations, involvement in East Europe, foreword, intro, 366, 380, 386, 389, 391, 397
Westphallia, Peace of (1648), 64, 65
World Communism and, 169, 261, 262, 296, 396
World War I (1914-18), 148-56
  alliances, 148, 149, 150, 151m, 152
  balance of power, 152, 153, 155
  conflicts leading to, 142, 146, 148-150
  divided loyalties of minorities, 150, 153, 154, 155
  peace conferences, 174-85
  political consequences of, 186, 220, 225, 227, 256
  Russian revolution and, 152, 153
  Sarajevo assassination, 149, 150
  United States and, 153, 154
World War II (1939-45), 10, 227-58
  Anschluss, 218, 227, 229-33
  Anti-Comintern pact, 238
  German-Soviet war, 242-44
  Hungary and, 231, 238
  Pact of Steel, 234
  post-war treaties, 256-57, 261
  Tripartite pact, 239, 241, 242, 266, 394-95
Writers' Congress, 334

Yalta Conference (1945), intro, 256-57, 261, 266, 279, 296, 397
Yugoslavia (Kingdom of Serbs, Croats and Slovenes)
  Albania and, 377
  conflict over Kosovo, 348-49, 374-75, 378

441

Yugoslavia, *continued*
  Albanians in, 3, 222, 243, 270, 347-49, 395
  assassination of Alexander, 207, 218, 242
  Balkan federation, 297, 298
  borders treaties, 165
  Bulgaria: Macedonian issue, 3, 199, 200, 207, 217, 349-50, 395
    WW II and, 243, 248, 267
  Bulgaro-Macedons in, 184, 222, 270, 349
  China and, 328, 347
  Cominform and, 296, 299
  Committee in London, 153, 154, 278
  Communist party, 205, 206, 262
    takeover by, 275, 277-79, 281
  conflict between republics, 205-07, 328, 349-51, 374-75, 377-79
  Croats in, 184, 205-07
    anti-Serb activity, 243, 245, 349
    persecution of, 278-79
  economics: interwar, 208-12
    problems with, 328, 342, 347, 350, 370, 377
  ethnic composition of, 183-84
  formation of state, 153, 162, 163, 183, 205
  Germans in, 3, 165, 184, 205, 222, 269m, 270
  Germany and, entente, 218, 227
    WW II, 239, 242-43, 245

Hungarians in Vojvodina, 3, 184, 205, 224, 254, 372, 374, 378
Hungary and, WW II, 239, 242-43 (1956), 328
illyrism, 90, 97, 125-26
Italy, 207, 216, 243, 253
  annexation of, 264, 268
Little Entente, 216, 217, 231
minorities, treaties on protection of, 220-26
Partisans, 253-54, 255-56, 274, 277
political repression, 278, 328-29, 351
and reforms, 377-78
religions, 4-5, 184, 279, 351
  detente, 329, 347
Rumania, 3, 184
  WW II, 243, 267
Serbs in, 165, 183-84
  domination by, 205-07, 242, 328, 349, 378
Slovenes, in, 165, 183-84, 205, 207, 254
Tito, void after, 349, 350, 351
USSR: break from 261, 262, 295, 297-300, 346
  loyalty to, 262, 296-97
  rapprochement with, 313, 328-29, 346, 351
  and WW II, 242, 253-54, 255
Vidovdan constitution, 205-06

Zelena Hora Union, 44